GIVE ME LIBERTY!

AN AMERICAN HISTORY

Fifth Edition

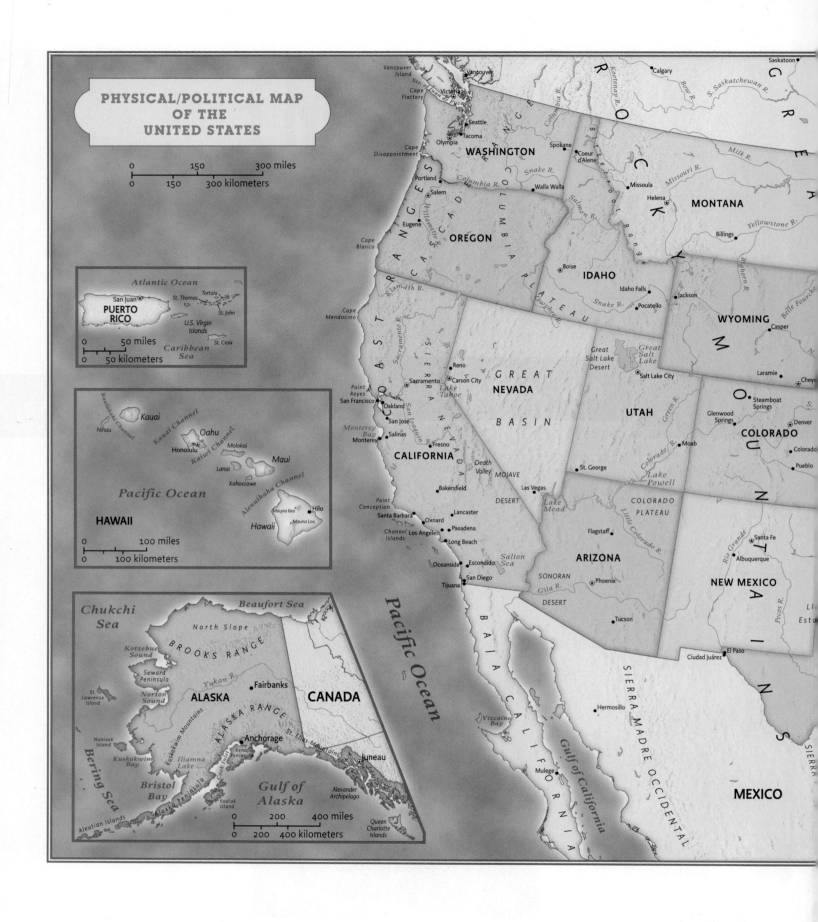

GIVE ME LIBERTY!

AN AMERICAN HISTORY

★

Fifth Edition

Volume 2: From 1865

ERIC FONER

W · W · NORTON & COMPANY
NEW YORK · LONDON

For my mother, Liza Foner (1909–2005), an accomplished artist who lived through most of the twentieth century and into the twenty-first

W. W. Norton & Company has been independent since its founding in 1923, when William Warder Norton and Mary D. Herter Norton first published lectures delivered at the People's Institute, the adult education division of New York City's Cooper Union. The firm soon expanded its program beyond the Institute, publishing books by celebrated academics from America and abroad. By midcentury, the two major pillars of Norton's publishing program—trade books and college texts—were firmly established. In the 1950s, the Norton family transferred control of the company to its employees, and today—with a staff of four hundred and a comparable number of trade, college, and professional titles published each year—W. W. Norton & Company stands as the largest and oldest publishing house owned wholly by its employees.

Editor: Steve Forman
Associate Editor: Scott Sugarman
Project Editor: Jennifer Barnhardt
Editorial Assistants: Travis Carr, Kelly Rafey
Managing Editor, College: Marian Johnson
Managing Editor, College Digital Media: Kim Yi
Production Manager: Sean Mintus
Media Editor: Laura Wilk
Media Project Editor: Rachel Mayer
Media Associate Editor: Michelle Smith
Media Assistant Editor: Chris Hillyer
Marketing Manager, History: Sarah England Bartley
Associate Design Director: Hope Miller Goodell
Designer: Chin-Yee Lai
Photo Editor: Stephanie Romeo
Permissions Manager: Megan Schindel
Permissions Specialist: Bethany Salminen
Composition: Jouve
Illustrations: Mapping Specialists, Ltd.
Manufacturing: Transcontinental

Permission to use copyrighted material is included on page A-83.

The Library of Congress has cataloged the Full Edition as follows:

Names: Foner, Eric, 1943- author.
Title: Give me liberty!: an American history / Eric Foner.
Description: Fifth edition. | New York: W. W. Norton & Company, 2016 | Includes bibliographical references and index.
Identifiers: LCCN 2016018497 | ISBN 9780393283167 (hardcover)
Subjects: LCSH: United States—History. | United States—Politics and government. | Democracy—United States—History. | Liberty—History.
Classification: LCC E178 .F66 2016 | DDC 973—dc23 LC record available at https://lccn.loc.gov/2016018497

ISBN this edition: 978-0-393-28313-6

W. W. Norton & Company, Inc., 500 Fifth Avenue, New York, NY 10110-0017
wwnorton.com
W. W. Norton & Company Ltd., 15 Carlisle Street, London W1D 3BS

2 3 4 5 6 7 8 9 0

ABOUT THE AUTHOR

ERIC FONER is DeWitt Clinton Professor of History at Columbia University, where he earned his B.A. and Ph.D. In his teaching and scholarship, he focuses on the Civil War and Reconstruction, slavery, and nineteenth-century America. Professor Foner's publications include *Free Soil, Free Labor, Free Men: The Ideology of the Republican Party before the Civil War*; *Tom Paine and Revolutionary America*; *Nothing but Freedom: Emancipation and Its Legacy*; *Reconstruction: America's Unfinished Revolution, 1863–1877*; *The Story of American Freedom*; and *Forever Free: The Story of Emancipation and Reconstruction*. His history of Reconstruction won the *Los Angeles Times* Book Award for History, the Bancroft Prize, and the Parkman Prize. He has served as president of the Organization of American Historians and the American Historical Association. In 2006 he received the Presidential Award for Outstanding Teaching from Columbia University. His most recent books are *The Fiery Trial: Abraham Lincoln and American Slavery*, winner of the Bancroft and Lincoln Prizes and the Pulitzer Prize for History, and *Gateway to Freedom: The Hidden History of the Underground Railroad*, winner of the New York Historical Society Book Prize.

CONTENTS

PART 4: TOWARD A GLOBAL PRESENCE, 1870–1920

19. SAFE FOR DEMOCRACY: THE UNITED STATES AND WORLD WAR I, 1916–1920 ... 718

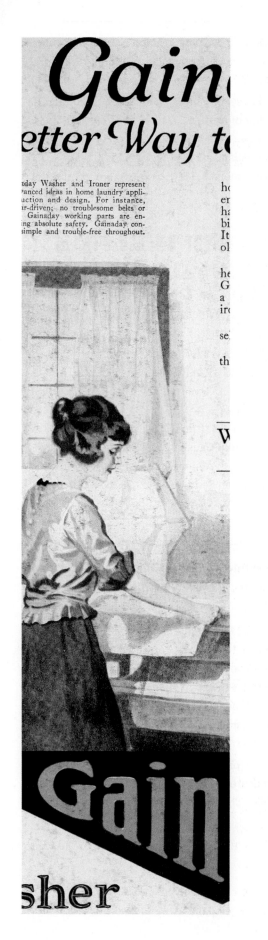

23. THE UNITED STATES AND THE COLD WAR, 1945–1953 ... 890

PART 6: WHAT KIND OF NATION? 1953–2015

24. AN AFFLUENT SOCIETY, 1953–1960 ... 928

MAPS

TABLES AND FIGURES

PREFACE

Give Me Liberty! An American History is a survey of American history from the earliest days of European exploration and conquest of the New World to the first decades of the twenty-first century. It offers students a clear, concise narrative whose central theme is the changing contours of American freedom.

I am extremely gratified by the response to the first four editions of *Give Me Liberty!*, which have been used in survey courses at many hundreds of two- and four-year colleges and universities throughout the country. The comments I have received from instructors and students encourage me to think that *Give Me Liberty!* has worked well in their classrooms. Their comments have also included many valuable suggestions for revisions, which I greatly appreciate. These have ranged from corrections of typographical and factual errors to thoughts about subjects that needed more extensive treatment. In making revisions for this Fifth Edition, I have tried to take these suggestions into account. I have also incorporated the findings and insights of new scholarship that has appeared since the original edition was written.

The most significant changes in this Fifth Edition reflect my desire to integrate the history of the American West and especially the regions known as borderlands more fully into the narrative. In recent years these aspects of American history have been thriving areas of research and scholarship. Of course earlier editions of *Give Me Liberty!* have discussed these subjects, but in this edition their treatment has been deepened

and expanded. I have also added notable works in these areas to many chapter bibliographies and lists of websites.

The definition of the West has changed enormously in the course of American history. In the colonial period, the area beyond the Appalachians—present-day Kentucky, Tennessee, and western Pennsylvania and New York—constituted the West. In the first half of the nineteenth century, the term referred to Ohio, Michigan, Alabama, and Mississippi. After the Civil War, the West came to mean the area beyond the Mississippi River. Today, it is sometimes used to refer mainly to the Pacific coast. But whatever its geographic locale, the West has been as much an idea as a place—an area beyond the frontier of settlement that promised newcomers new kinds of freedom, sometimes at the expense of the freedom of others, such as native inhabitants and migrant laborers. In this edition we follow Americans as they constructed their Wests, and debated the kinds of freedom they would enjoy there.

Borderlands is a more complex idea that has influenced much recent historical scholarship. Borders are lines dividing one country, region, or state from another. Crossing them often means becoming subject to different laws and customs, and enjoying different degrees of freedom. Borderlands are regions that exist on both sides of borders. They are fluid areas where people of different cultural and social backgrounds converge. At various points in American history, shifting borders have opened new opportunities and closed off others in the borderlands. Families living for decades or centuries in a region have suddenly found themselves divided by a newly created border but still living in a borderland that transcends the new division. This happened to Mexicans in modern-day California, Arizona, and New Mexico, for example, in 1848, when the treaty ending the Mexican-American War transferred the land that would become those states from Mexico to the United States.

Borderlands exist within the United States as well as at the boundaries with other countries. For example, in the period before the Civil War, the region straddling the Ohio River contained cultural commonalities that in some ways overrode the division there between free and slave states. The borderlands idea also challenges simple accounts of national development in which empires and colonies pave the way for territorial expansion and a future transcontinental nation. It enables us, for example, to move beyond the categories of conquest and subjugation in understanding how Native Americans and Europeans interacted over the early centuries of contact. This approach also provides a way of understanding how the people of Mexico and the United States interact today in the borderland region of the American Southwest, where many families have members on both sides of the boundary between the two countries.

Small changes relating to these themes may be found throughout the book. The major additions seeking to illuminate the history of the West and of borderlands are as follows:

Chapter 1 now introduces the idea of borderlands with a discussion of the areas where European empires and Indian groups interacted and where authority was fluid and fragile. Chapter 4 contains expanded treatment of the part of the Spanish empire now comprising the borderlands United States (Arizona, California, New Mexico, Texas, and Florida) and how Spain endeavored, with limited success, to consolidate its authority in these regions. In Chapter 6, a new subsection, "The American Revolution as a Borderlands Conflict," examines the impact on both Americans and Canadians of the creation, because of American independence, of a new national boundary separating what once had been two parts of the British empire. Chapter 8 continues this theme with a discussion of the borderlands aspects of the War of 1812. Chapter 9 discusses how a common culture came into being along the Ohio River in the early nineteenth century despite the existence of slavery on one side and free labor on the other. Chapter 13 expands the treatment of Texan independence from Mexico by discussing its impact on both Anglo and Mexican residents of this borderland region. Chapter 14 contains a new examination of the Civil War in the American West.

In Chapter 16, I have expanded the section on the industrial west with new discussions of logging and mining, and added a new subsection on the dissemination of a mythical image of the Wild West in the late nineteenth century. Chapter 17 contains an expanded discussion of Chinese immigrants in the West and the battle over exclusion and citizenship, a debate that centered on what kind of population should be allowed to inhabit the West and enjoy the opportunities the region offered. Chapter 18 examines Progressivism, countering conventional narratives that emphasize the origins of Progressive political reforms in eastern cities by relating how many, from woman suffrage to the initiative, referendum, and recall, emerged in Oregon, California, and other western states. Chapter 20 expands the treatment of western agriculture in the 1920s by highlighting the acceleration of agricultural mechanization in the region and the agricultural depression that preceded the general economic collapse of 1929 and after. In Chapter 22 we see the new employment opportunities for Mexican-American women in the war production factories that opened in the West. In Chapter 26, there is a new subsection on conservatism in the West and the Sagebrush Rebellion of the 1970s and 1980s. Chapter 27 returns to the borderlands theme by discussing the consequences of the creation, in the 1990s, of a free trade zone connecting the two sides of the Mexican-American border. And Chapters 27 and 28 now include expanded discussions of the southwestern borderland as a site of an acrimonious battle over immigration—legal and undocumented—involving the federal and state governments, private vigilantes, and continuing waves of people trying to cross into the United States. The contested borderland now extends many miles into the United States north of the boundary between the two nations, and southward well into Mexico and even Central America.

I have also added a number of new selections to Voices of Freedom, the paired excerpts from primary documents in each chapter. Some of the new documents reflect the stronger emphasis on the West and borderlands; others seek to sharpen the juxtaposition of divergent concepts of freedom at particular moments in American history. And this edition contains many new images—paintings, broadsides, photographs, and others—related to these themes.

Americans have always had a divided attitude toward history. On the one hand, they tend to be remarkably future-oriented, dismissing events of even the recent past as "ancient history" and sometimes seeing history as a burden to be overcome, a prison from which to escape. On the other hand, like many other peoples, Americans have always looked to history for a sense of personal or group identity and of national cohesiveness. This is why so many Americans devote time and energy to tracing their family trees and why they visit historical museums and National Park Service historical sites in ever-increasing numbers. My hope is that this book will convince readers with all degrees of interest that history does matter to them.

The novelist and essayist James Baldwin once observed that history "does not refer merely, or even principally, to the past. On the contrary, the great force of history comes from the fact that we carry it within us, . . . [that] history is literally present in all that we do." As Baldwin recognized, the force of history is evident in our own world. Especially in a political democracy like the United States, whose government is designed to rest on the consent of informed citizens, knowledge of the past is essential—not only for those of us whose profession is the teaching and writing of history, but for everyone. History, to be sure, does not offer simple lessons or immediate answers to current questions. Knowing the history of immigration to the United States, and all of the tensions, turmoil, and aspirations associated with it, for example, does not tell us what current immigration policy ought to be. But without that knowledge, we have no way of understanding which approaches have worked and which have not—essential information for the formulation of future public policy.

History, it has been said, is what the present chooses to remember about the past. Rather than a fixed collection of facts, or a group of interpretations that cannot be challenged, our understanding of history is constantly changing. There is nothing unusual in the fact that each generation rewrites history to meet its own needs, or that scholars disagree among themselves on basic questions like the causes of the Civil War or the reasons for the Great Depression. Precisely because each generation asks different questions of the past, each generation formulates different answers. The past thirty years have witnessed a remarkable expansion of the scope of historical study. The experiences of groups neglected by earlier scholars, including women, African-Americans, working people, and others, have received unprecedented attention from historians. New subfields—social history, cultural history, and family history among them—have taken their place alongside traditional political and diplomatic history.

Give Me Liberty! draws on this voluminous historical literature to present an up-to-date and inclusive account of the American past, paying due attention to the experience of diverse groups of Americans while in no way neglecting the events and processes Americans have experienced in common. It devotes serious attention to political, social, cultural, and economic history, and to their interconnections. The narrative brings together major events and prominent leaders with the many groups of ordinary people who make up American society. *Give Me Liberty!* has a rich cast of characters, from Thomas Jefferson to campaigners for woman suffrage, from Franklin D. Roosevelt to former slaves seeking to breathe meaning into emancipation during and after the Civil War.

Aimed at an audience of undergraduate students with little or no detailed knowledge of American history, *Give Me Liberty!* guides readers through the complexities of the subject without overwhelming them with excessive detail. The unifying theme of freedom that runs through the text gives shape to the narrative and integrates the numerous strands that make up the American experience. This approach builds on that of my earlier book, *The Story of American Freedom* (1998), although *Give Me Liberty!* places events and personalities in the foreground and is more geared to the structure of the introductory survey course.

Freedom, and the battles to define its meaning, have long been central to my own scholarship and undergraduate teaching, which focuses on the nineteenth century and especially the era of the Civil War and Reconstruction (1850–1877). This was a time when the future of slavery tore the nation apart and emancipation produced a national debate over what rights the former slaves, and all Americans, should enjoy as free citizens. I have found that attention to clashing definitions of freedom and the struggles of different groups to achieve freedom as they understood it offers a way of making sense of the bitter battles and vast transformations of that pivotal era. I believe that the same is true for American history as a whole.

No idea is more fundamental to Americans' sense of themselves as individuals and as a nation than freedom. The central term in our political language, freedom—or liberty, with which it is almost always used interchangeably—is deeply embedded in the record of our history and the language of everyday life. The Declaration of Independence lists liberty among mankind's inalienable rights; the Constitution announces its purpose as securing liberty's blessings. The United States fought the Civil War to bring about a new birth of freedom, World War II for the Four Freedoms, and the Cold War to defend the Free World. Americans' love of liberty has been represented by liberty poles, liberty caps, and statues of liberty, and acted out by burning stamps and burning draft cards, by running away from slavery, and by demonstrating for the right to vote. "Every man in the street, white, black, red, or yellow," wrote the educator and statesman Ralph Bunche in 1940, "knows that this is 'the land of the free' . . . 'the cradle of liberty.'"

The very universality of the idea of freedom, however, can be misleading. Freedom is not a fixed, timeless category with a single unchanging definition. Indeed, the history of the United States is, in part, a story of debates, disagreements, and struggles over freedom. Crises like the American Revolution, the Civil War, and the Cold War have permanently transformed the idea of freedom. So too have demands by various groups of Americans to enjoy greater freedom. The meaning of freedom has been constructed not only in congressional debates and political treatises, but on plantations and picket lines, in parlors and even bedrooms.

Over the course of our history, American freedom has been both a reality and a mythic ideal—a living truth for millions of Americans, a cruel mockery for others. For some, freedom has been what some scholars call a "habit of the heart," an ideal so taken for granted that it is lived out but rarely analyzed. For others, freedom is not a birthright but a distant goal that has inspired great sacrifice.

Give Me Liberty! draws attention to three dimensions of freedom that have been critical in American history: (1) the *meanings* of freedom; (2) the *social conditions* that make freedom possible; and (3) the *boundaries* of freedom that determine who is entitled to enjoy freedom and who is not. All have changed over time.

In the era of the American Revolution, for example, freedom was primarily a set of rights enjoyed in public activity—the right of a community to be governed by laws to which its representatives had consented and of individuals to engage in religious worship without governmental interference. In the nineteenth century, freedom came to be closely identified with each person's opportunity to develop to the fullest his or her innate talents. In the twentieth, the "ability to choose," in both public and private life, became perhaps the dominant understanding of freedom. This development was encouraged by the explosive growth of the consumer marketplace (a development that receives considerable attention in *Give Me Liberty!*), which offered Americans an unprecedented array of goods with which to satisfy their needs and desires. During the 1960s, a crucial chapter in the history of American freedom, the idea of personal freedom was extended into virtually every realm, from attire and "lifestyle" to rela-

tions between the sexes. Thus, over time, more and more areas of life have been drawn into Americans' debates about the meaning of freedom.

A second important dimension of freedom focuses on the social conditions necessary to allow freedom to flourish. What kinds of economic institutions and relationships best encourage individual freedom? In the colonial era and for more than a century after independence, the answer centered on economic autonomy, enshrined in the glorification of the independent small producer—the farmer, skilled craftsman, or shopkeeper—who did not have to depend on another person for his livelihood. As the industrial economy matured, new conceptions of economic freedom came to the fore: "liberty of contract" in the Gilded Age, "industrial freedom" (a say in corporate decision-making) in the Progressive era, economic security during the New Deal, and, more recently, the ability to enjoy mass consumption within a market economy.

The boundaries of freedom, the third dimension of this theme, have inspired some of the most intense struggles in American history. Although founded on the premise that liberty is an entitlement of all humanity, the United States for much of its history deprived many of its own people of freedom. Non-whites have rarely enjoyed the same access to freedom as white Americans. The belief in equal opportunity as the birthright of all Americans has coexisted with persistent efforts to limit freedom by race, gender, and class and in other ways.

Less obvious, perhaps, is the fact that one person's freedom has frequently been linked to another's servitude. In the colonial era and nineteenth century, expanding freedom for many Americans rested on the lack of freedom—slavery, indentured servitude, the subordinate position of women—for others. By the same token, it has been through battles at the boundaries—the efforts of racial minorities, women, and others to secure greater freedom—that the meaning and experience of freedom have been deepened and the concept extended into new realms.

Time and again in American history, freedom has been transformed by the demands of excluded groups for inclusion. The idea of freedom as a universal birthright owes much both to abolitionists who sought to extend the blessings of liberty to blacks and to immigrant groups who insisted on full recognition as American citizens. The principle of equal protection of the law without regard to race, which became a central element of American freedom, arose from the antislavery struggle and the Civil War and was reinvigorated by the civil rights revolution of the 1960s, which called itself the "freedom movement." The battle for the right of free speech by labor radicals and birth-control advocates in the first part of the twentieth century helped to make civil liberties an essential element of freedom for all Americans.

Although concentrating on events within the United States, *Give Me Liberty!* also situates American history in the context of developments in other parts of the world. Many of the forces that shaped American history, including the international migration of peoples, the development of slavery, the spread of democracy, and the expansion of capitalism, were worldwide processes not confined to the United States. Today, American ideas, culture, and economic and military power exert unprecedented influence throughout the world. But beginning with the earliest days of settlement, when European empires competed to colonize North America and enrich themselves from its trade, American history cannot be understood in isolation from its global setting.

Freedom is the oldest of clichés and the most modern of aspirations. At various times in our history, it has served as the rallying cry of the powerless and as a justification of the status quo. Freedom helps to bind our culture together and exposes the contradictions between what America claims to be and what it sometimes has been. American history is not a narrative of continual progress toward greater and greater freedom. As the abolitionist Thomas Wentworth Higginson noted after the Civil War, "revolutions may go backward." Though freedom can be achieved, it may also be taken away. This happened, for example, when the equal rights granted to former slaves immediately after the Civil War were essentially nullified during the era of segregation. As was said in the eighteenth century, the price of freedom is eternal vigilance.

In the early twenty-first century, freedom continues to play a central role in American political and social life and thought. It is invoked by individuals and groups of all kinds, from critics of economic globalization to those who seek to secure American freedom at home and export it abroad. I hope that *Give Me Liberty!* will offer beginning students a clear account of the course of American history, and of its central theme, freedom, which today remains as varied, contentious, and ever-changing as America itself.

ACKNOWLEDGMENTS

All works of history are, to a considerable extent, collaborative books, in that every writer builds on the research and writing of previous scholars. This is especially true of a textbook that covers the entire American experience, over more than five centuries. My greatest debt is to the innumerable historians on whose work I have drawn in preparing this volume. The Suggested Reading list at the end of each chapter offers only a brief introduction to the vast body of historical scholarship that has influenced and informed this book. More specifically, however, I wish to thank the following scholars, who generously read portions of this work and offered valuable comments, criticisms, and suggestions:

Joel Benson, Northwest Missouri State University
Lori Bramson, Clark College
Tonia Compton, Columbia College
Adam Costanzo, Texas A&M University
Carl Creasman Jr., Valencia College
Blake Ellis, Lone Star College–CyFair
Carla Falkner, Northeast Mississippi Community College
Van Forsyth, Clark College
Aram Goudsouzian, University of Memphis
Michael Harkins, Harper College
Sandra Harvey, Lone Star College–CyFair
Robert Hines, Palo Alto College
Traci Hodgson, Chemeketa Community College
Tamora Hoskisson, Salt Lake Community College
William Jackson, Salt Lake Community College
Alfred H. Jones, State College of Florida
David Kiracofe, Tidewater Community College

Brad Lookingbill, Columbia College
Jennifer Macias, Salt Lake Community College
Thomas Massey, Cape Fear Community College
Derek Maxfield, Genesee Community College
Marianne McKnight, Salt Lake Community College
Jonson Miller, Drexel University
Ted Moore, Salt Lake Community College
Robert Pierce, Foothills College
Ernst Pinjing, Minot State University
Harvey N. Plaunt, El Paso Community College
Steve Porter, University of Cincinnati
John Putman, San Diego State University
R. Lynn Rainard, Tidewater Community College
Nicole Ribianszky, Georgia Gwinnett College
Nancy Marie Robertson, Indiana University—Purdue University Indianapolis
John Shaw, Portland Community College
Danielle Swiontek, Santa Barbara Community College
Richard Trimble, Ocean County College
Alan Vangroll, Central Texas College
Eddie Weller, San Jacinto College
Andrew Wiese, San Diego State University
Matthew Zembo, Hudson Valley Community College

I am particularly grateful to my colleagues in the Columbia University Department of History: Pablo Piccato, for his advice on Latin American history; Evan Haefeli and Ellen Baker, who read and made many suggestions for improvements in their areas of expertise (colonial America and the history of the West, respectively); and Sarah Phillips, who offered advice on treating the history of the environment.

I am also deeply indebted to the graduate students at Columbia University's Department of History who helped with this project. For this edition, Michael "Mookie" Kidackel offered invaluable assistance in gathering material related to borderlands and Western history. For previous editions, Theresa Ventura assisted in locating material for new sections placing American history in a global context, April Holm did the same for new coverage of the history of American religion and debates over religious freedom, James Delbourgo conducted research for the chapters on the colonial era, and Beverly Gage did the same for the twentieth century. In addition, Daniel Freund provided all-around research assistance. Victoria Cain did a superb job of locating images. I also want to thank my colleagues Elizabeth Blackmar and Alan Brinkley for offering advice and encouragement throughout the writing of this book. I am also grateful to students who, while using the textbook, pointed out to me errors or omissions that I have corrected in this edition: Jordan Farr, Chris Jendry, Rafi Metz, Samuel Phillips-Cooper, Richard Sereyko, and David Whittle.

Many thanks to Joshua Brown, director of the American Social History Project, whose website, History Matters, lists innumerable online resources for the study of American history. Thanks also to the instructors who helped build our robust digital resource and ancillary package. The new InQuizitive for History was developed by Tonia M. Compton (Columbia College), Matt Zembo (Hudson Valley Community College), Jodie Steeley (Merced Community College District), Bill Polasky (Stillman Valley High School), and Ken Adler (Spring Valley High School). Our new History Skills Tutorials were created by Geri Hastings. The Coursepack was thoroughly updated by Beth Hunter (University of Alabama at Birmingham). Allison Faber (Texas A&M University) and Ben Williams (Texas A&M University) revised the Lecture PowerPoint slides. And our Test Bank and Instructor's Manual was revised to include new questions authored by Robert O'Brien (Lone Star College–CyFair) and Tamora M. Hoskisson (Salt Lake Community College).

At W. W. Norton & Company, Steve Forman was an ideal editor—patient, encouraging, and always ready to offer sage advice. I would also like to thank Steve's editorial assistants, Travis Carr and Kelly Rafey, and associate editor, Scott Sugarman, for their indispensable and always cheerful help on all aspects of the project; Ellen Lohman and Bob Byrne for their careful copyediting and proofreading work; Stephanie Romeo and Fay Torresyap for their resourceful attention to the illustrations program; Hope Miller Goodell and Chin-Yee Lai for their refinements of the book design; Leah Clark, Tiani Kennedy, and Debra Morton-Hoyt for splendid work on the covers for the Fifth Edition; Jennifer Barnhardt for keeping the many threads of the project aligned and then tying them together; Sean Mintus for his efficiency and care in book production; Laura Wilk for orchestrating the rich media package that accompanies the textbook; Sarah England Bartley, Steve Dunn, and Mike Wright for their alert reads of the U.S. survey market and their hard work in helping establish *Give Me Liberty!* within it; and Drake McFeely, Roby Harrington, and Julia Reidhead for maintaining Norton as an independent, employee-owned publisher dedicated to excellence in its work.

Many students may have heard stories of how publishing companies alter the language and content of textbooks in an attempt to maximize sales and avoid alienating any potential reader. In this case, I can honestly say that W. W. Norton allowed me a free hand in writing the book and, apart from the usual editorial corrections, did not try to influence its content at all. For this I thank them, while I accept full responsibility for the interpretations presented and for any errors the book may contain. Since no book of this length can be entirely free of mistakes, I welcome readers to send me corrections at ef17@columbia.edu.

My greatest debt, as always, is to my family—my wife, Lynn Garafola, for her good-natured support while I was preoccupied by a project that consumed more than its fair share of my time and energy, and my daughter, Daria, who while a ninth and tenth grader read every chapter as it was written and offered invaluable suggestions about improving the book's clarity, logic, and grammar.

Eric Foner
New York City
July 2016

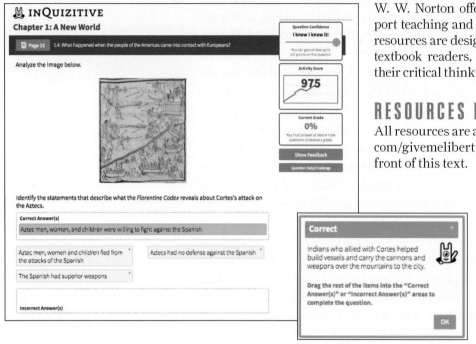

W. W. Norton offers a robust digital package to support teaching and learning with *Give Me Liberty!* These resources are designed to make students more effective textbook readers, while at the same time developing their critical thinking and history skills.

RESOURCES FOR STUDENTS

All resources are available through digital.wwnorton.com/givemeliberty5v2 with the access card at the front of this text.

NORTON INQUIZITIVE FOR HISTORY

Norton InQuizitive for history is an adaptive quizzing tool that improves students' understanding of the themes and objectives from each chapter, while honing their critical-analysis skills with primary source, image, and map analysis questions. Students receive personalized quiz questions with detailed, guiding feedback on the topics in which they need the most help, while the engaging, gamelike elements motivate them as they learn.

HISTORY SKILLS TUTORIALS

The History Skills Tutorials feature three modules—Images, Documents, and Maps—to support students' development of the key skills needed for the history course. These tutorials feature videos of Eric Foner modeling the analysis process, followed by interactive questions that will challenge students to apply what they have learned.

STUDENT SITE

The free and easy-to-use Student Site offers additional resources for students to use outside of class. Resources include interactive iMaps from each chapter, author videos, and a comprehensive Online Reader with a collection of historical longer works, primary sources, novellas, and biographies.

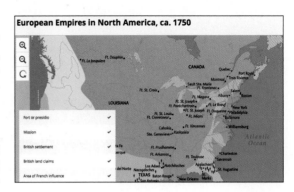

EBOOK

Free and included with new copies of the text, the **Norton Ebook Reader** provides an enhanced reading experience that works on all computers and mobile devices. Features include intuitive highlighting, note-taking, and bookmarking as well as pop-up definitions and enlargeable maps and art. Direct links to InQuizitive also appear in each chapter. Instructors can focus student reading by sharing notes with their classes, including embedded images and video. Reports on student and class-wide access and time on task allow instructors to monitor student reading and engagement.

RESOURCES FOR INSTRUCTORS

All resources are available through www.wwnorton.com/instructors.

NORTON COURSEPACKS

Easily add high-quality digital media to your online, hybrid, or lecture course—all at no cost to students. Norton's Coursepacks work within your existing Learning Management System and are ready to use and easy to customize. The coursepack offers a diverse collection of assignable and assessable resources: **Primary Source Exercises, Guided Reading Exercises, Review Quizzes, U.S. History Tours powered by Google Earth, Flashcards, Map Exercises**, and all of the resources from the **Student Site.**

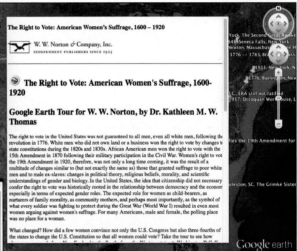

NORTON AMERICAN HISTORY DIGITAL ARCHIVE

The Digital Archive offers roughly 2,000 additional primary source images, audio, and video files spanning American history that can be used in assignments and lecture presentations.

TEST BANK

The Test Bank is authored by Robert O'Brien, Lone Star College–CyFair, and Tamora M. Hoskisson, Salt Lake Community College, and contains more than 4,000 multiple-choice, true/false, short-answer, and essay questions.

INSTRUCTOR'S MANUAL

The Instructor's Manual contains detailed Chapter Summaries, Chapter Outlines, Suggested Discussion Questions, and Supplemental Web, Visual, and Print Resources.

LECTURE AND ART POWERPOINT SLIDES

The Lecture PowerPoint sets authored by Allison Faber, Texas A&M University, and Ben Williams, Texas A&M University, combine chapter review, art, and maps.

GIVE ME LIBERTY!

AN AMERICAN HISTORY

Fifth Edition

CHAPTER 15

"WHAT IS FREEDOM?": RECONSTRUCTION

★

1865–1877

On the evening of January 12, 1865, less than a month after Union forces captured Savannah, Georgia, twenty leaders of the city's black community gathered for a discussion with General William T. Sherman and Secretary of War Edwin M. Stanton. Mostly Baptist and Methodist ministers, the group included several men who within a few years would assume prominent positions during the era of Reconstruction that followed the Civil War. Ulysses S. Houston, pastor of the city's Third African Baptist Church, and James Porter, an episcopal religious leader who had operated a secret school for black children before the war, in a few years would win election to the Georgia legislature. James D. Lynch, who had been born free in Baltimore and educated in New Hampshire, went on to serve as secretary of state of Mississippi.

The conversation revealed that the black leaders brought out of slavery a clear definition of freedom. Asked what he understood by slavery, Garrison Frazier, a Baptist minister chosen as the group's spokesman, responded that it meant one person's "receiving by irresistible power the work of another man, and not by his consent." Freedom he defined as "placing us where we could reap the fruit of our own labor, and take care of ourselves." The way to accomplish this was "to have land, and turn it and till it by our own labor." Frazier insisted that blacks possessed "sufficient intelligence" to maintain themselves in freedom and enjoy the equal protection of the laws.

Sherman's meeting with the black leaders foreshadowed some of the radical changes that would take place during the era known as Reconstruction (meaning, literally, the rebuilding of the shattered nation). In the years following the Civil War, former slaves and their white allies, North and South, would seek to redefine the meaning and boundaries of American freedom. Previously an entitlement of whites, freedom would be expanded to include black Americans. The laws and Constitution would be rewritten to guarantee African-Americans, for the first time in the nation's history, recognition as citizens and equality before the law. Black men would be granted the right to vote, ushering in a period of interracial democracy throughout the South. Black schools, churches, and other institutions would flourish, laying the foundation for the modern African-American community. Many of the advances of Reconstruction would prove temporary, swept away during a campaign of violence in the South and the North's retreat from the ideal of equality. But Reconstruction laid the foundation for future struggles to extend freedom to all Americans.

All this, however, lay in the future in January 1865. Four days after the meeting, Sherman responded to the black delegation by issuing Special Field Order 15. This set aside the Sea Islands and a large area along the South Carolina and Georgia coasts for the settlement of black families on forty-acre plots of land. He also offered them broken-down mules that the army could no longer use. In Sherman's order lay the origins of the phrase "forty acres and a mule," that would reverberate across the South in the next few years. By June, some 40,000 freed slaves had been settled on "Sherman land." Among the emancipated slaves, Sherman's order raised hopes that the end of slavery would be accompanied by the economic independence that they, like other Americans, believed essential to genuine freedom.

FOCUS QUESTIONS

What visions of freedom did the former slaves and slaveholders pursue in the postwar South? –p. 552

What were the sources, goals, and competing visions for Reconstruction? –p. 564

What were the social and political effects of Radical Reconstruction in the South? –p. 574

What were the main factors, in both the North and South, for the abandonment of Reconstruction? –p. 579

The Shackle Broken—by the Genius of Freedom. This 1874 lithograph depicts Robert B. Elliott, a black congressman from South Carolina, delivering a celebrated speech supporting the bill that became the Civil Rights Act of 1875.

THE MEANING OF FREEDOM

With the end of the Civil War, declared an Illinois congressman in 1865, the United States was a "new nation," for the first time "wholly free." The destruction of slavery, however, made the definition of freedom the central question on the nation's agenda. "What is freedom?" asked Congressman James A. Garfield in 1865. "Is it the bare privilege of not being chained? If this is all, then freedom is a bitter mockery, a cruel delusion." Did freedom mean simply the absence of slavery, or did it imply other rights for the former slaves, and if so, which ones: equal civil rights, the vote, ownership of property? During Reconstruction, freedom became a terrain of conflict, its substance open to different, often contradictory interpretations. Out of the conflict over the meaning of freedom arose new kinds of relations between black and white southerners, and a new definition of the rights of all Americans.

Blacks and the Meaning of Freedom

African-Americans' understanding of freedom was shaped by their experiences as slaves and their observation of the free society around them. To begin with, freedom meant escaping the numerous injustices of slavery—punishment by the lash, the separation of families, denial of access to education, the sexual exploitation of black women by their owners—and sharing in the rights and opportunities of American citizens. "If I cannot do like a white man," Henry Adams, an emancipated slave in Louisiana, told his former master in 1865, "I am not free."

Blacks relished the opportunity to demonstrate their liberation from the regulations, significant and trivial, associated with slavery. They openly held mass meetings and religious services free of white supervision, and they acquired dogs, guns, and liquor, all barred to them under slavery. No longer required to obtain a pass from their owners to travel, former slaves throughout the South left the plantations in search of better jobs, family members, or simply a taste of personal liberty. Many moved to southern towns and cities, where, it seemed, "freedom was free-er."

Families in Freedom

With slavery dead, institutions that had existed before the war, like the black family, free blacks' churches and schools, and the secret slave church, were strengthened, expanded, and freed from white supervision. The family was central to the postemancipation black community. Former slaves made remarkable efforts to locate loved ones from whom they had been separated under slavery. One northern reporter in 1865 encountered a freedman who had walked more than 600 miles from Georgia to North Carolina, searching for the wife and children from whom he had been sold away before the war. Meanwhile, widows of black soldiers successfully claimed survivors' pensions, forcing the federal government to acknowledge the validity of prewar relationships that slavery had attempted to deny.

But while Reconstruction witnessed the stabilization of family life, freedom subtly altered relationships within the family. Emancipation increased the power of black men and brought to many black families the nineteenth-century notion that men and women should inhabit separate "spheres." Immediately after the Civil War, planters complained that freedwomen had "withdrawn" from field labor and work as house servants. Many black women preferred to devote more time to their families than had been possible under slavery, and men considered it a badge of honor to see their wives remain at home. Eventually, the dire poverty of the black community would compel a far higher proportion of black women than white women to go to work for wages.

Church and School

At the same time, blacks abandoned white-controlled religious institutions to create churches of their own. On the eve of the Civil War, 42,000 black Methodists worshiped in biracial South Carolina churches; by the end of Reconstruction, only 600 remained. The rise of the independent black church, with Methodists and Baptists commanding the largest followings, redrew the religious map of the South. As the major institution independent of white control, the church played a central role in the black community. A place of worship, it also housed schools, social events, and political gatherings. Black ministers came to play a major role in politics. Some 250 held public office during Reconstruction.

Another striking example of the freedpeople's quest for individual and community improvement was their desire for education. Education, declared a Mississippi freedman, was "the next best thing to liberty." The thirst for learning sprang from many sources—a desire to read the Bible, the need to prepare for the economic marketplace, and the opportunity, which arose in 1867, to take part in politics. Blacks of all ages flocked to the schools established by northern missionary societies, the Freedmen's Bureau, and groups of ex-slaves themselves. Northern journalist Sidney Andrews, who toured the South in 1865, was impressed by how much education also took place outside of the classroom: "I had occasion very frequently to notice that porters in stores and laboring men in warehouses, and cart drivers on the streets, had spelling books with them, and were studying them during the time they were not occupied with their work." Reconstruction also witnessed the creation of the nation's first black colleges, including Fisk University in Tennessee, Hampton Institute in Virginia, and Howard University in the nation's capital.

Political Freedom

In a society that had made political participation a core element of freedom, the right to vote inevitably became central to the former slaves' desire for empowerment and equality. As Frederick Douglass put it soon after the South's surrender in 1865, "Slavery is not abolished until the black man has the ballot." In a "monarchial government," Douglass explained, no "special" disgrace applied to those denied the right to vote. But in a democracy, "where universal suffrage is the rule," excluding

Family Record, a lithograph marketed to former slaves after the Civil War, is an idealized portrait of a middle-class black family, with scenes of slavery and freedom.

Mother and Daughter Reading, Mt. Meigs, Alabama, an 1890 photograph by Rudolph Eickemeyer. During Reconstruction and for years thereafter, former slaves exhibited a deep desire for education, and learning took place outside of school as well as within.

Five Generations of a Black Family, an 1862 photograph that suggests the power of family ties among emancipated slaves

any group meant branding them with "the stigma of inferiority." As soon as the Civil War ended, and in some parts of the South even earlier, free blacks and emancipated slaves claimed a place in the public sphere. They came together in conventions, parades, and petition drives to demand the right to vote and, on occasion, to organize their own "freedom ballots."

Anything less than full citizenship, black spokesmen insisted, would betray the nation's democratic promise and the war's meaning. Speakers at black conventions reminded the nation of Crispus Attucks, who fell at the Boston Massacre, and of black soldiers' contribution to the War of 1812 and during "the bloody struggle through which we have just passed." To demonstrate their patriotism, blacks throughout the South organized Fourth of July celebrations. For years after the Civil War, white southerners would "shut themselves within doors" on Independence Day, as a white resident of Charleston recorded in her diary, while former slaves commemorated the holiday themselves.

Land, Labor, and Freedom

Former slaves' ideas of freedom, like those of rural people throughout the world, were directly related to landownership. Only land, wrote Merrimon Howard, a freedman from Mississippi, would enable "the poor class to enjoy the sweet boon of freedom." On the land they would develop independent communities free of white control. Many former slaves insisted that through their unpaid labor, they had acquired a right to the land. "The property which they hold," declared an Alabama black convention, "was nearly all earned by the sweat of *our* brows." In some parts of the South, blacks in 1865 seized property, insisting that it belonged

Landownership

The First African Church, Richmond, as depicted in *Harper's Weekly*, June 27, 1874. The establishment of independent black churches was an enduring accomplishment of Reconstruction.

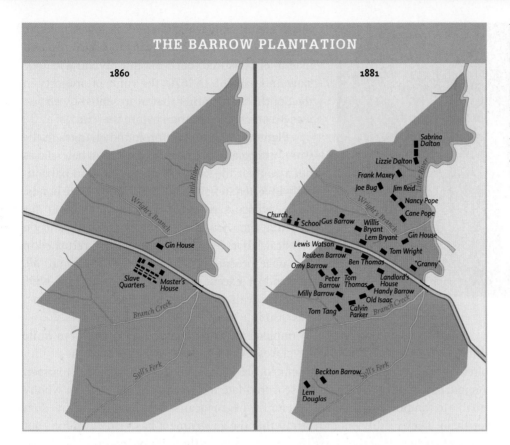

THE BARROW PLANTATION

1860

1881

Two maps of the Barrow plantation illustrate the effects of emancipation on rural life in the South. In 1860, slaves lived in communal quarters near the owner's house. Twenty-one years later, former slaves working as sharecroppers lived scattered across the plantation and had their own church and school.

to them. On one Tennessee plantation, former slaves claimed to be "joint heirs" to the estate and, the owner complained, took up residence "in the rooms of my house."

In its individual elements and much of its language, former slaves' definition of freedom resembled that of white Americans—self-ownership, family stability, religious liberty, political participation, and economic autonomy. But these elements combined to form a vision very much their own. For whites, freedom, no matter how defined, was a given, a birthright to be defended. For African-Americans, it was an open-ended process, a transformation of every aspect of their lives and of the society and culture that had sustained slavery in the first place. Although the freedpeople failed to achieve full freedom as they understood it, their definition did much to shape national debate during the turbulent era of Reconstruction.

Freedom's meaning to former slaves

Masters without Slaves

Most white southerners reacted to military defeat and emancipation with dismay, not only because of the widespread devastation but also because they must now submit to northern demands. "The demoralization is complete," wrote a Georgia girl. "We are whipped, there is no doubt about it." The appalling loss of life, a disaster without parallel in the American experience, affected all classes of southerners. Nearly 260,000 men died for the Confederacy—more than one-fifth of the

Confederate deaths

Winslow Homer's 1876 painting *A Visit from the Old Mistress* depicts an imaginary meeting between a southern white woman and her former slaves. Their stance and gaze suggest the tensions arising from the birth of a new social order. Homer places his subjects on an equal footing, yet maintains a space of separation between them. He exhibited the painting to acclaim at the Paris Universal Exposition in 1878.

South's adult male white population. The wholesale destruction of work animals, farm buildings, and machinery ensured that economic revival would be slow and painful. In 1870, the value of property in the South, not counting that represented by slaves, was 30 percent lower than before the war.

Planter families faced profound changes in the war's aftermath. Many lost not only their slaves but also their life savings, which they had patriotically invested in now-worthless Confederate bonds. Some, whose slaves departed the plantation, for the first time found themselves compelled to do physical labor. General Braxton Bragg returned to his "once prosperous" Alabama home to find "*all, all* was lost, except my debts.*" Bragg and his wife, a woman "raised in affluence," lived for a time in a slave cabin.

Southern planters sought to implement an understanding of freedom quite different from that of the former slaves. As they struggled to accept the reality of emancipation, most planters defined black freedom in the narrowest manner. As journalist Sidney Andrews discovered late in 1865, "The whites seem wholly unable to comprehend that freedom for the negro means the same thing as freedom for them. They readily enough admit that the government has made him free, but appear to believe that they have the right to exercise the same old control." Southern leaders sought to revive the antebellum definition of freedom as if nothing had changed. Freedom still meant hierarchy and mastery; it was a privilege not a right, a carefully defined legal status rather than an open-ended entitlement. Certainly, it implied neither economic autonomy nor civil and political equality. "A man may be free and yet not independent," Mississippi planter Samuel Agnew observed in his diary in 1865. A Kentucky newspaper summed up the stance of much of the white South: the former slave was "*free*, but free only to labor."

The Free Labor Vision

Along with former slaves and former masters, the victorious Republican North tried to implement its own vision of freedom. Central to its definition was the antebellum principle of free labor, now further strengthened as a definition of the good society by the Union's triumph. In the free labor vision of a reconstructed South, emancipated blacks, enjoying the same opportunities for advancement as northern workers, would labor more productively than they had as slaves. At the same time, northern capital and migrants would energize the economy. The South would eventually come to resemble the "free society" of the North, complete with public schools, small towns, and independent farmers. Unified on the basis of free labor, proclaimed Carl Schurz, a refugee from the failed German revolution of 1848 who rose to become a leader of the Republican Party, America would become "a republic, greater, more populous, freer, more prosperous, and more powerful" than any in history.

> *Free labor and the good society*

With planters seeking to establish a labor system as close to slavery as possible, and former slaves demanding economic autonomy and access to land, a long period of conflict over the organization and control of labor followed on plantations throughout the South. It fell to **the Freedmen's Bureau**, an agency established by Congress in March 1865, to attempt to establish a working free labor system.

The Freedmen's Bureau

Under the direction of O. O. Howard, a graduate of Bowdoin College in Maine and a veteran of the Civil War, the Bureau took on responsibilities that can only be described as daunting. The Bureau was an experiment in government social policy that seems to belong more comfortably to the New Deal of the 1930s or the Great Society of the 1960s (see Chapters 21 and 25, respectively) than to nineteenth-century America. Bureau agents were supposed to establish schools, provide aid to the poor and aged, settle disputes between whites and blacks and among the freedpeople, and secure for former slaves and white Unionists equal treatment before the courts. "It is not . . . in your power to fulfill one-tenth of the expectations of those who framed the Bureau," General William T. Sherman wrote to Howard. "I fear you have Hercules' task."

The Bureau lasted from 1865 to 1870. Even at its peak, there were fewer than 1,000 agents in the entire South. Nonetheless, the Bureau's achievements in some areas, notably education and health care, were striking. While the Bureau did not establish schools itself, it coordinated and helped to finance the activities of

The Great Labor Question from a Southern Point of View, a cartoon by the artist Winslow Homer, published in *Harper's Weekly*, July 29, 1865. Homer satirizes the attitudes of many white southerners. While blacks labor in the fields, an idle planter warns a former slave, "My boy, we've toiled and taken care of you long enough—now you've got to work!"

The Freedmen's Bureau, an engraving from *Harper's Weekly*, July 25, 1868, depicts the Bureau agent as a promoter of racial peace in the violent postwar South.

Winslow Homer's 1876 painting *The Cotton Pickers*, one of a series of studies of rural life in Virginia, portrays two black women as dignified figures, without a trace of the stereotyping so common in the era's representations of former slaves. The expressions on their faces are ambiguous, perhaps conveying disappointment that eleven years after the end of slavery they are still at work in the fields.

northern societies committed to black education. By 1869, nearly 3,000 schools, serving more than 150,000 pupils in the South, reported to the Bureau. Bureau agents also assumed control of hospitals established by the army during the war, and expanded the system into new communities. They provided medical care and drugs to both black and white southerners. In economic relations, however, the Bureau's activities proved far more problematic.

The Failure of Land Reform

The idea of free labor, wrote one Bureau agent, was "the noblest principle on earth." All that was required to harmonize race relations in the South was fair wages, good working conditions, and the opportunity to improve the laborer's situation in life. But blacks wanted land of their own, not jobs on plantations. One provision of the law establishing the Bureau gave it the authority to divide abandoned and confiscated land into forty-acre plots for rental and eventual sale to the former slaves.

A nursemaid and her charge, from a daguerreotype around 1865.

In the summer of 1865, however, President Andrew Johnson, who had succeeded Lincoln, ordered nearly all land in federal hands returned to its former owners. A series of confrontations followed, notably in South Carolina and Georgia, where the army forcibly evicted blacks who had settled on "Sherman land." When O. O. Howard, head of the Freedmen's Bureau, traveled to the Sea Islands to inform blacks of the new policy, he was greeted with disbelief and protest. A committee of former slaves drew up petitions to Howard and President Johnson. "We want Homesteads," they declared, "we were promised Homesteads by the government." Land, the freedmen insisted, was essential to the meaning of freedom. Without it, they declared, "we have not bettered our condition" from the days of slavery—"you will see, this is not the condition of really free men."

Because no land distribution took place, the vast majority of rural freedpeople remained poor and without property during Reconstruction. They had no alternative but to work on white-owned plantations, often for their former owners. Far from

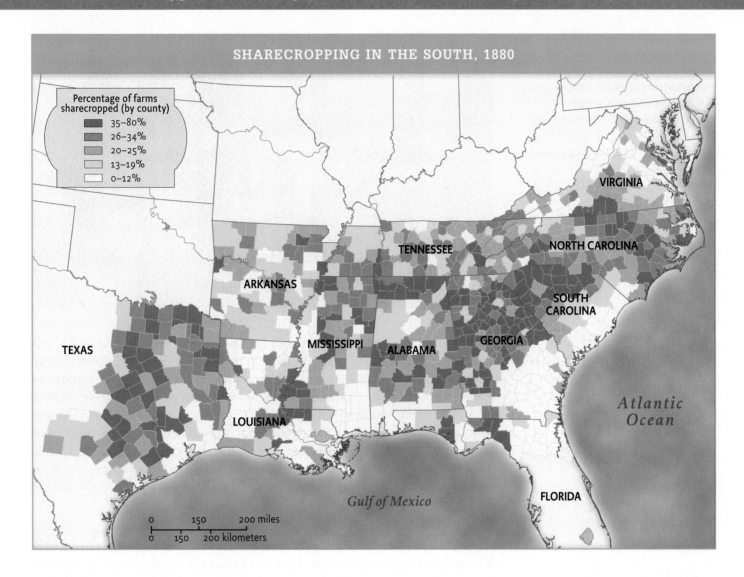

SHARECROPPING IN THE SOUTH, 1880

Percentage of farms sharecropped (by county)
- 35–80%
- 26–34%
- 20–25%
- 13–19%
- 0–12%

being able to rise in the social scale through hard work, black men were largely confined to farm work, unskilled labor, and service jobs, and black women to positions in private homes as cooks and maids. Their wages remained too low to allow for any accumulation. By the turn of the century, a significant number of southern African-Americans had managed to acquire small parcels of land. But the failure of land reform produced a deep sense of betrayal that survived among the former slaves and their descendants long after the end of Reconstruction. "No sir," Mary Gaffney, an elderly ex-slave, recalled in the 1930s, "we were not given a thing but freedom."

By 1880, sharecropping had become the dominant form of agricultural labor in large parts of the South. The system involved both white and black farmers.

Toward a New South

Out of the conflict on the plantations, new systems of labor emerged in the different regions of the South. The task system, under which workers were assigned daily tasks, completion of which ended their responsibilities for that day, survived in the rice kingdom of South Carolina and Georgia. Closely supervised wage labor predominated on the sugar plantations of southern Louisiana. Sharecropping came to dominate the Cotton Belt and much of the Tobacco Belt of Virginia and North Carolina.

Labor systems

THE MEANING OF FREEDOM | 559

The cotton depot at Guthrie, Texas. Bales of cotton have been loaded onto trains for shipment. After the Civil War, more and more white farmers began growing cotton to support their families, permanently altering their formerly self-sufficient way of life.

Sharecropping initially arose as a compromise between blacks' desire for land and planters' demand for labor discipline. The system allowed each black family to rent a part of a plantation, with the crop divided between worker and owner at the end of the year. Sharecropping guaranteed the planters a stable resident labor force. Former slaves preferred it to gang labor because it offered them the prospect of working without day-to-day white supervision. But as the years went on, sharecropping became more and more oppressive. Sharecroppers' economic opportunities were severely limited by a world market in which the price of farm products suffered a prolonged decline.

The rise of sharecropping

The White Farmer

The plight of the small farmer was not confined to blacks in the postwar South. Wartime devastation set in motion a train of events that permanently altered the independent way of life of white yeomen, leading to what they considered a loss of freedom. Before the war, most small farmers had concentrated on raising food for their families and grew little cotton. With much of their property destroyed, many yeomen saw their economic condition worsened by successive crop failures after the war. To obtain supplies from merchants, farmers were forced to take up the growing of cotton and pledge a part of the crop as collateral (property the creditor can seize if a debt is not paid). This system became known as the **crop lien**. Since interest rates were extremely high and the price of cotton fell steadily, many farmers found themselves still in debt after marketing their portion of the crop at year's end. They had no choice but to continue to plant cotton to obtain new loans. By the mid-1870s, white farmers, who cultivated only 10 percent of the South's cotton crop in 1860, were growing 40 percent, and many who had owned their land had fallen into dependency as sharecroppers, who now rented land owned by others.

The crop-lien system

Both black and white farmers found themselves caught in the sharecropping and crop-lien systems. A far higher percentage of black than white farmers in the South rented land rather than owned it. But every census from 1880 to 1940 counted more white than black sharecroppers. The workings of sharecropping and the crop-lien system are illustrated by the case of Matt Brown, a Mississippi farmer who borrowed money each year from a local merchant. He began 1892 with a debt of $226 held over from the previous year. By 1893, although he produced cotton worth $171, Brown's debt had increased to $402, because he had borrowed $33 for food, $29 for clothing, $173 for supplies, and $112 for other items. Brown never succeeded in getting out of debt. He died in 1905; the last entry under his name in the merchant's account book is a coffin.

The burden of debt

The Urban South

Even as the rural South stagnated economically, southern cities experienced remarkable growth after the Civil War. As railroads penetrated the interior, they enabled merchants in market centers like Atlanta to trade directly with the North, bypassing coastal cities that had traditionally monopolized southern commerce. A new urban middle class of merchants, railroad promoters, and bankers reaped the benefits of the spread of cotton production in the postwar South.

Thus, Reconstruction brought about profound changes in the lives of southerners, black and white, rich and poor. In place of the prewar world of master, slave, and self-sufficient yeoman, the postwar South was peopled by new social classes—landowning employers, black and white sharecroppers, cotton-producing white farmers, wage-earning black laborers, and urban entrepreneurs. Each of these groups turned to Reconstruction politics in an attempt to shape to its own advantage the aftermath of emancipation.

Postwar southern society

Aftermath of Slavery

The United States, of course, was not the only society to confront the problem of the transition from slavery to freedom. Indeed, many parallels exist between the debates during Reconstruction and struggles that followed slavery in other parts of the Western Hemisphere over the same issues of land, control of labor, and political power. In every case, former planters (or, in Haiti, where the planter class had been destroyed, the government itself) tried to encourage or require former slaves to go back to work on plantations to grow the same crops as under slavery. Planters elsewhere held the same stereotypical views of black laborers as were voiced by their counterparts in the United States—former slaves were supposedly lazy, were lacking in ambition, and thought that freedom meant an absence of labor.

Emancipation in the Western Hemisphere

For their part, former slaves throughout the hemisphere tried to carve out as much independence as possible, both in their daily lives and in their labor. They attempted to reconstruct family life by withdrawing women and children from field labor (in the West Indies, women turned to marketing their families' crops to earn income). Wherever possible, former slaves acquired land of their own and devoted more time to growing food for their families than to growing crops for the international market. In many places, the plantations either fell to pieces, as in Haiti, or continued operating with a new labor force composed of indentured servants from India and China, as in Jamaica, Trinidad, and British Guiana. Southern planters in the United States brought in a few Chinese laborers in an attempt to replace freedmen, but since the federal government opposed such efforts, the Chinese remained only a tiny proportion of the southern workforce.

VOICES OF FREEDOM

From PETITION OF COMMITTEE IN BEHALF OF THE FREEDMEN TO ANDREW JOHNSON (1865)

In the summer of 1865, President Andrew Johnson ordered land that had been distributed to freed slaves in South Carolina and Georgia returned to its former owners. A committee of freedmen drafted a petition asking for the right to obtain land. Johnson did not, however, change his policy.

We the freedmen of Edisto Island, South Carolina, have learned from you through Major General O. O. Howard . . . with deep sorrow and painful hearts of the possibility of [the] government restoring these lands to the former owners. We are well aware of the many perplexing and trying questions that burden your mind, and therefore pray to god (the preserver of all, and who has through our late and beloved President [Lincoln's] proclamation and the war made us a free people) that he may guide you in making your decisions and give you that wisdom that cometh from above to settle these great and important questions for the best interests of the country and the colored race.

Here is where secession was born and nurtured. Here is where we have toiled nearly all our lives as slaves and treated like dumb driven cattle.

This is our home, we have made these lands what they were, we are the only true and loyal people that were found in possession of these lands. We have been always ready to strike for liberty and humanity, yea to fight if need be to preserve this glorious Union. Shall not we who are freedmen and have always been true to this Union have the same rights as are enjoyed by others? . . . Are not our rights as a free people and good citizens of these United States to be considered before those who were found in rebellion against this good and just government? . . .

[Are] we who have been abused and oppressed for many long years not to be allowed the privilege of purchasing land but be subject to the will of these large land owners? God forbid. Land monopoly is injurious to the advancement of the course of freedom, and if government does not make some provision by which we as freedmen can obtain a homestead, we have not bettered our condition. . . .

We look to you . . . for protection and equal rights with the privilege of purchasing a homestead—a homestead right here in the heart of South Carolina.

From A SHARECROPPING CONTRACT (1866)

Few former slaves were able to acquire land in the post–Civil War South. Most ended up as sharecroppers, working on white-owned land for a share of the crop at the end of the growing season. This contract, typical of thousands of others, originated in Tennessee. The laborers signed with an X, as they were illiterate.

Thomas J. Ross agrees to employ the Freedmen to plant and raise a crop on his Rosstown Plantation. . . . On the following Rules, Regulations and Remunerations.

The said Ross agrees to furnish the land to cultivate, and a sufficient number of mules & horses and feed them to make and house said crop and all necessary farming utensils to carry on the same and to give unto said Freedmen whose names appear below one half of all the cotton, corn and wheat that is raised on said place for the year 1866 after all the necessary expenses are deducted out that accrues on said crop. Outside of the Freedmen's labor in harvesting, carrying to market and selling the same the said Freedmen . . . covenant and agrees to and with said Thomas J. Ross that for and in consideration of one half of the crop before mentioned that they will plant, cultivate, and raise under the management control and Superintendence of said Ross, in good faith, a cotton, corn and oat crop under his management for the year 1866. And we the said Freedmen agrees to furnish ourselves & families in provisions, clothing, medicine and medical bills and all, and every kind of other expenses that we may incur on said plantation for the year 1866 free of charge to said Ross. Should the said Ross furnish us any of the above supplies or any other kind of expenses, during said year, [we] are to settle and pay him out of the net proceeds of our part of the crop the retail price of the county at time of sale or any price we may agree upon—The said Ross shall keep a regular book account, against each and every one or the head of every family to be adjusted and settled at the end of the year.

We furthermore bind ourselves to and with said Ross that we will do good work and labor ten hours a day on an average, winter and summer. . . . We further agree that we will lose all lost time, or pay at the rate of one dollar per day, rainy days excepted. In sickness and women lying in childbed are to lose the time and account for it to the other hands out of his or her part of the crop. . . .

We furthermore bind ourselves that we will obey the orders of said Ross in all things in carrying out and managing said crop for said year and be docked for disobedience. All is responsible for all farming utensils that is on hand or may be placed in care of said Freedmen for the year 1866 to said Ross and are also responsible to said Ross if we carelessly, maliciously maltreat any of his stock for said year to said Ross for damages to be assessed out of our wages.

Samuel (X) Johnson, Thomas (X) Richard, Tinny (X) Fitch, Jessie (X) Simmons, Sophe (X) Pruden, Henry (X) Pruden, Frances (X) Pruden, Elijah (X) Smith

---

QUESTIONS

1. *Why do the black petitioners believe that owning land is essential to the enjoyment of freedom?*

2. *In what ways does the contract limit the freedom of the laborers?*

3. *What do these documents suggest about competing definitions of black freedom in the aftermath of slavery?*

Emancipation and the right to vote

But if struggles over land and labor united its postemancipation experience with that of other societies, in one respect the United States was unique. Only in the United States were former slaves, within two years of the end of slavery, granted the right to vote and, thus, given a major share of political power. Few anticipated this development when the Civil War ended. It came about as the result of one of the greatest political crises of American history—the battle between President Andrew Johnson and Congress over Reconstruction. The struggle resulted in profound changes in the nature of citizenship, the structure of constitutional authority, and the meaning of American freedom.

THE MAKING OF RADICAL RECONSTRUCTION

Andrew Johnson

To Lincoln's successor, Andrew Johnson, fell the task of overseeing the restoration of the Union. Born in poverty in North Carolina, as a youth Johnson worked as a tailor's apprentice. After moving to Tennessee, he achieved success through politics. Beginning as an alderman (a town official), he rose to serve in the state legislature, the U.S. Congress, and for two terms as governor of Tennessee. Johnson identified himself as the champion of his state's "honest yeomen" and a foe of large planters, whom he described as a "bloated, corrupted aristocracy." A strong

Background and outlook

defender of the Union, he became the only senator from a seceding state to remain at his post in Washington, D.C., when the Civil War began in 1861. When northern forces occupied Tennessee, Abraham Lincoln named him military governor. In 1864, Republicans nominated him to run for vice president as a symbol of the party's hope of extending its organization into the South.

In personality and outlook, Johnson proved unsuited for the responsibilities he shouldered after Lincoln's death. A lonely, stubborn man, he was intolerant of criticism and unable to compromise. He lacked Lincoln's political skills and keen sense of public opinion. A fervent believer in states' rights, Johnson insisted that since secession was illegal, the southern states had never actually left the Union or surrendered the right to govern their own affairs. Moreover, while Johnson had supported emancipation once Lincoln made it a goal of the war effort, he held deeply racist views. African-Americans, Johnson believed, had no role to play in Reconstruction.

The Failure of Presidential Reconstruction

A little over a month after Lee's surrender at Appomattox, and with Congress out of session until December, Johnson in May 1865 outlined his plan for reuniting the nation. He issued a series of proclamations that began the period of Presidential Reconstruction (1865–1867). Johnson offered a pardon (which restored political and property rights, except for slaves) to nearly all white southerners who took an oath of allegiance to the Union. He excluded Confederate leaders and wealthy planters whose prewar property had been valued at more than $20,000. This exemption suggested at first that Johnson planned a more punitive Reconstruction than Lincoln had intended. Most of those exempted, however, soon received individual pardons from the president. Johnson also appointed provisional governors and ordered them to call state conventions, elected by whites alone, that would establish loyal governments in the South. Apart from the requirement that they abolish slavery, repudiate secession, and refuse to pay the Confederate debt—all unavoidable consequences of southern defeat—he granted the new governments a free hand in managing local affairs.

Johnson's program

At first, most northerners believed Johnson's policy deserved a chance to succeed. The conduct of the southern governments elected under his program, however, turned most of the Republican North against the president. By and large, white voters returned prominent Confederates and members of the old elite to power. Reports of violence directed against former slaves and northern visitors in the South further alarmed Republicans.

The Black Codes

But what aroused the most opposition to Johnson's Reconstruction policy were the **Black Codes**, laws passed by the new southern governments that attempted to regulate the lives of the former slaves. These laws granted blacks certain rights, such as legalized marriage, ownership of property, and limited access to the courts. But they denied them the rights to testify against whites, to serve on juries or in state militias, or to vote. And in response to planters' demands that the freedpeople be required to work on the plantations, the Black Codes declared that those who failed to sign yearly labor contracts could be arrested and hired out to white landowners. Some states limited the occupations open to blacks and barred them from acquiring land, and others provided that judges could assign black children to work for their former owners without the consent of the parents. "We are not permitted to own the land whereon to build a schoolhouse or a church," complained a black convention in Mississippi. "Where is justice? Where is freedom?"

Regulating the former slaves

Selling a Freedman to Pay His Fine at Monticello, Florida, an engraving from *Frank Leslie's Illustrated Newspaper*, January 19, 1867. Under the Black Codes enacted by southern legislatures immediately after the Civil War, blacks convicted of "vagrancy"—often because they refused to sign contracts to work on plantations—were fined and, if unable to pay, auctioned off to work for the person who paid the fine.

Thaddeus Stevens, leader of the Radical Republicans in the House of Representatives during Reconstruction.

Clearly, the death of slavery did not automatically mean the birth of freedom. But the Black Codes so completely violated free labor principles that they called forth a vigorous response from the Republican North. Wars—especially civil wars—often generate hostility and bitterness. But few groups of rebels in history have been treated more leniently than the defeated Confederates. A handful of southern leaders were arrested but most were quickly released. Only one was executed—Henry Wirz, the commander of Andersonville prison, where thousands of Union prisoners of war had died. Most of the Union army was swiftly demobilized. What motivated the North's turn against Johnson's policies was not a desire to "punish" the white South, but the inability of the South's political leaders to accept the reality of emancipation. "We must see to it," announced Republican senator William Stewart of Nevada, "that the man made free by the Constitution of the United States is a freeman indeed."

The Radical Republicans

When Congress assembled in December 1865, Johnson announced that with loyal governments functioning in all the southern states, the nation had been reunited. In response, Radical Republicans, who had grown increasingly disenchanted with Johnson during the summer and fall, called for the dissolution of these governments and the establishment of new ones with "rebels" excluded from power and black men guaranteed the right to vote. Radicals tended to represent constituencies in New England and the "burned-over" districts of the rural North that had been home to religious revivalism, abolitionism, and other reform movements. Although they differed on many issues, Radicals shared the conviction that Union victory created a golden opportunity to institutionalize the principle of equal rights for all, regardless of race.

The Radicals fully embraced the expanded powers of the federal government born during the Civil War. Traditions of federalism and states' rights, they insisted, must not obstruct a sweeping national effort to protect the rights of all Americans.

The most prominent Radicals in Congress were Charles Sumner, a senator from Massachusetts, and Thaddeus Stevens, a lawyer and iron manufacturer who represented Pennsylvania in the House of Representatives. Before the Civil War, both had been outspoken foes of slavery and defenders of black rights. Early in the Civil War, both had urged Lincoln to free and arm the slaves, and both in 1865 favored black suffrage in the South. "The same national authority," declared Sumner, "that destroyed slavery must see that this other pretension [racial inequality] is not permitted to survive."

> *Thaddeus Stevens*

Thaddeus Stevens's most cherished aim was to confiscate the land of disloyal planters and divide it among former slaves and northern migrants to the South. "The whole fabric of southern society," he declared, "*must* be changed. Without this, this Government can never be, as it has never been, a true republic." But his plan to make "small independent landholders" of the former slaves proved too radical even for many of his Radical colleagues. Congress, to be sure, had already offered free land to settlers in the West in the Homestead Act of 1862. But this land had been in the possession of the federal government, not private individuals (although originally, of course, it had belonged to Indians). Most congressmen believed too deeply in the sanctity of property rights to be willing to take land from one group of owners and distribute it to others. Stevens's proposal failed to pass.

The Origins of Civil Rights

With the South unrepresented, Republicans enjoyed an overwhelming majority in Congress. But the party was internally divided. Most Republicans were moderates, not Radicals. Moderates believed that Johnson's plan was flawed, but they desired to work with the president to modify it. They feared that neither northern nor southern whites would accept black suffrage. Moderates and Radicals joined in refusing to seat the southerners recently elected to Congress, but moderates broke with the Radicals by leaving the Johnson governments in place.

Early in 1866, Senator Lyman Trumbull of Illinois proposed two bills, reflecting the moderates' belief that Johnson's policy required modification. The first extended the life of the Freedmen's Bureau, which had originally been established for only one year. The second, the **Civil Rights Bill of 1866**, was described by one congressman as "one of the most important bills ever presented to the House for its action." It defined all persons born in the United States as citizens and spelled out rights they were to enjoy without regard to race. Equality before the law was central to the measure—no longer could states enact laws like the Black Codes discriminating between white and black citizens. So were free labor values. According to the law, no state could deprive any citizen of the right to make contracts, bring lawsuits, or enjoy equal protection of one's person and property. These, said Trumbull, were the "fundamental rights belonging to every man as a free man." The bill made no mention of the right to vote for blacks. In constitutional terms, the Civil Rights Bill represented the first attempt to give concrete meaning to the Thirteenth Amendment, which had abolished slavery, to define in law the essence of freedom.

To the surprise of Congress, Johnson vetoed both bills. Both, he said, would centralize power in the national government and deprive the states of the authority to regulate their own affairs. Moreover, he argued, blacks did not deserve the rights of citizenship. By acting to secure their rights, Congress was discriminating

President Andrew Johnson, in an 1868 lithograph by Currier and Ives. Because of Johnson's stubborn opposition to the congressional Reconstruction policy, one disgruntled citizen drew a crown on his head with the words, "I am King."

A Democratic Party broadside from the election of 1866 in Pennsylvania uses racist imagery to argue that government assistance aids lazy former slaves at the expense of hardworking whites.

Black suffrage

Significance of the Fourteenth Amendment

"against the white race." The vetoes made a breach between the president and nearly the entire Republican Party inevitable. Congress failed by a single vote to muster the two-thirds majority necessary to override the veto of the Freedmen's Bureau Bill (although later in 1866, it did extend the Bureau's life to 1870). But in April 1866, the Civil Rights Bill became the first major law in American history to be passed over a presidential veto.

The Fourteenth Amendment

Congress now proceeded to adopt its own plan of Reconstruction. In June, it approved and sent to the states for ratification the **Fourteenth Amendment**, which placed in the Constitution the principle of citizenship for all persons born in the United States, and which empowered the federal government to protect the rights of all Americans. The amendment prohibited the states from abridging the "privileges or immunities" of citizens or denying any person of the "equal protection of the laws." This broad language opened the door for future Congresses and the federal courts to breathe meaning into the guarantee of legal equality.

In a compromise between the radical and moderate positions on black suffrage, the amendment did not grant blacks the right to vote. But it did provide that if a state denied the vote to any group of men, that state's representation in Congress would be reduced. (This provision did not apply when states barred women from voting.) The abolition of slavery threatened to increase southern political power, since now all blacks, not merely three-fifths as in the case of slaves, would be counted in determining a state's representation in Congress. The Fourteenth Amendment offered the leaders of the white South a choice—allow black men to vote and keep their state's full representation in the House of Representatives, or limit the vote to whites and sacrifice part of their political power.

The Fourteenth Amendment produced an intense division between the parties. Not a single Democrat in Congress voted in its favor, and only 4 of 175 Republicans were opposed. Radicals, to be sure, expressed their disappointment that the amendment did not guarantee black suffrage. (It was far from perfect, Stevens told the House, but he intended to vote for it, "because I live among men and not among angels.") Nonetheless, by writing into the Constitution the principle that equality before the law regardless of race is a fundamental right of all American citizens, the amendment made the most important change in that document since the adoption of the Bill of Rights.

The Reconstruction Act

The Fourteenth Amendment became the central issue of the political campaign of 1866. Johnson embarked on a speaking tour of the North, called by journalists the "swing around the circle," to urge voters to elect members of Congress committed to his own Reconstruction program. Denouncing his critics, the president made wild accusations that the Radicals were plotting to assassinate him. His behavior further undermined public support for his policies, as did riots that broke out in Memphis and New Orleans, in which white policemen and citizens killed dozens of blacks.

In the northern congressional elections that fall, Republicans opposed to Johnson's policies won a sweeping victory. Nonetheless, at the president's urging, every southern state but Tennessee refused to ratify the Fourteenth Amendment. The intransigence of Johnson and the bulk of the white South pushed moderate Republicans toward the Radicals. In March 1867, over Johnson's veto, Congress adopted the **Reconstruction Act**, which temporarily divided the South into five military districts and called for the creation of new state governments, with black men given the right to vote. Thus began the period of Radical Reconstruction, which lasted until 1877.

A variety of motives combined to produce Radical Reconstruction—demands by former slaves for the right to vote, the Radicals' commitment to the idea of equality, widespread disgust with Johnson's policies, the desire to fortify the Republican Party in the South, and the determination to keep ex-Confederates from office. But the conflict between President Johnson and Congress did not end with the passage of the Reconstruction Act.

A Republican campaign poster from 1868 depicts Ulysses S. Grant and his running mate Henry Wilson not as a celebrated general and U.S. senator but as ordinary workingmen, embodiments of the dignity of free labor.

Impeachment and the Election of Grant

In March 1867, Congress adopted the **Tenure of Office Act**, barring the president from removing certain officeholders, including cabinet members, without the consent of the Senate. Johnson considered this an unconstitutional restriction on his authority. In February 1868, he removed Secretary of War Edwin M. Stanton, an ally of the Radicals. The House of Representatives responded by approving articles of **impeachment**—that is, it presented charges against Johnson to the Senate, which had to decide whether to remove him from office.

That spring, for the first time in American history, a president was placed on trial before the Senate for "high crimes and misdemeanors." By this point, virtually all Republicans considered Johnson a failure as president. But some moderates disliked Benjamin F. Wade, a Radical who, as temporary president of the Senate, would become president if Johnson were removed. Others feared that conviction would damage the constitutional separation of powers between Congress and the executive. Johnson's lawyers assured moderate Republicans that, if acquitted, he would stop interfering with Reconstruction policy. The final tally was 35–19 to convict Johnson, one vote short of the two-thirds necessary to remove him. Seven Republicans had joined the Democrats in voting to acquit the president.

Johnson's acquittal

A few days after the vote, Republicans nominated Ulysses S. Grant, the Union's most prominent military hero, as their candidate for president. Grant's Democratic opponent was Horatio Seymour, the former governor of New York. Reconstruction became the central issue of the bitterly fought 1868 campaign. Republicans identified their opponents with secession and treason, a tactic known as "waving the bloody shirt." Democrats denounced Reconstruction as unconstitutional and

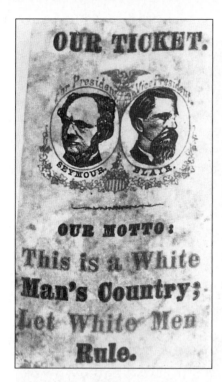

A Democratic ribbon from the election of 1868, with Horatio Seymour and Francis P. Blair Jr., the party's candidates for president and vice president. The ribbon illustrates the explicit appeals to racism that marked the campaign.

THE PRESIDENTIAL ELECTION OF 1868

Non-voting territory

Party	Candidate	Electoral Vote (Share)	Popular Vote (Share)
Republican	Grant	214 (73%)	3,012,833 (53%)
Southern Democrat	Seymour	80 (27%)	2,703,249 (47%)
Not voting due to Reconstruction			
State legislature cast the electoral votes for Grant			

condemned black suffrage as a violation of America's political traditions. They appealed openly to racism. Seymour's running mate, Francis P. Blair Jr., charged Republicans with placing the South under the rule of "a semi-barbarous race" who longed to "subject the white women to their unbridled lust."

The Fifteenth Amendment

Grant won the election of 1868, although by a margin—300,000 of 6 million votes cast—that many Republicans found uncomfortably slim. The result led Congress to adopt the era's third and final amendment to the Constitution. In February 1869, it approved the **Fifteenth Amendment**, which prohibited the federal and state governments from denying any citizen the right to vote because of race. Bitterly opposed by the Democratic Party, it was ratified in 1870.

Although the Fifteenth Amendment opened the door to suffrage restrictions not explicitly based on race—literacy tests, property qualifications, and poll taxes—and did not extend the right to vote to women, it marked the culmination of four decades of abolitionist agitation. As late as 1868, even after Congress had enfranchised black men in the South, only eight northern states allowed African-American men to vote. With the Fifteenth Amendment, the American Anti-Slavery Society disbanded, its work, its members believed, now complete. "Nothing in all history," exclaimed veteran abolitionist William Lloyd Garrison, equaled "this wonderful, quiet, sudden transformation of four millions of human beings from . . . the auction-block to the ballot-box."

The "Great Constitutional Revolution"

The laws and amendments of Reconstruction reflected the intersection of two products of the Civil War era—a newly empowered national state and the idea of a national citizenry enjoying equality before the law. What Republican leader Carl Schurz called the "great Constitutional revolution" of Reconstruction transformed the federal system and with it, the language of freedom so central to American political culture.

Before the Civil War, American citizenship had been closely linked to race. The first Congress, in 1790, had limited to whites the right to become a naturalized citizen when immigrating from abroad. No black person, free or slave, the Supreme Court had declared in the *Dred Scott* decision of 1857, could be a citizen of the United States. The laws and amendments of Reconstruction repudiated the idea that citizenship was an entitlement of whites alone. The principle of equality before the law, moreover, did not apply only to the South. The Reconstruction amendments voided many northern laws discriminating on the basis of race. And, as one congressman noted, the amendments expanded the liberty of whites as well as blacks, including "the millions of people of foreign birth who will flock to our shores."

The new amendments also transformed the relationship between the federal government and the states. The Bill of Rights had linked civil liberties to the autonomy of the states.

UNCLE SAM'S THANKSGIVING DINNER.

Uncle Sam's Thanksgiving Dinner, an engraving by Thomas Nast from *Harper's Weekly*, November 20, 1868, shortly after the election of Ulysses S. Grant, graphically illustrates how the boundaries of freedom had expanded during Reconstruction. The guests include, among others, African-Americans, Asian-Americans, and Native Americans, men and women, all enjoying a harmonious feast. The table's centerpiece contains the slogan, "universal suffrage."

Its language—"Congress shall make no law"—reflected the belief that concentrated national power posed the greatest threat to freedom. The authors of the Reconstruction amendments assumed that rights required national power to enforce them. Rather than a threat to liberty, the federal government, in Charles Sumner's words, had become "the custodian of freedom."

The Reconstruction amendments transformed the Constitution from a document primarily concerned with federal-state relations and the rights of property into a vehicle through which members of vulnerable minorities could stake a claim to freedom and seek protection against misconduct by all levels of government. In the twentieth century, many of the Supreme Court's most important decisions expanding the rights of American citizens were based on the Fourteenth Amendment, perhaps most notably the 1954 *Brown* ruling that outlawed school segregation (see Chapter 24).

Boundaries of Freedom

Reconstruction redrew the boundaries of American freedom. Lines of exclusion that limited the privileges of citizenship to white men had long been central to the practice of American democracy. Only in an unparalleled crisis could they have been replaced, even temporarily, by the vision of a republic of equals embracing black Americans as well as white. That the United States was a "white man's government" had been a widespread belief before the Civil War. It is not difficult to understand why Andrew Johnson, in one of his veto messages, claimed that federal protection of blacks' civil rights violated "all our experience as a people."

Race and rights

Another illustration of the new spirit of racial inclusiveness was the Burlingame Treaty, negotiated by Anson Burlingame, an antislavery congressman from Massachusetts before being named American envoy to China. Other treaties with China had been one-sided, securing trading and political advantages for European

The Burlingame Treaty

powers. The Burlingame Treaty reaffirmed China's national sovereignty, and provided reciprocal protection for religious freedom and against discrimination for citizens of each country emigrating or visiting the other. When Burlingame died, Mark Twain wrote a eulogy that praised him for "outgrow[ing] the narrow citizenship of a state [to] become a citizen of the world."

Reconstruction Republicans' belief in universal rights had its limits. In his remarkable "Composite Nation" speech of 1869, Frederick Douglass condemned prejudice against immigrants from China. America's destiny, he declared, was to transcend race by serving as an asylum for people "gathered here from all corners of the globe by a common aspiration for national liberty." A year later, Charles Sumner moved to strike the word "white" from naturalization requirements. Senators from the western states objected. At their insistence, the naturalization law was amended to make Africans eligible to obtain citizenship when migrating from abroad. But Asians remained ineligible. The racial boundaries of nationality had been redrawn, but not eliminated. The juxtaposition of the amended naturalization law and the Fourteenth Amendment created a significant division in the Asian-American community. Well into the twentieth century, Asian immigrants could not become citizens, but their native-born children automatically did.

Amendment of naturalization law

The Rights of Women

"The contest with the South that destroyed slavery," wrote the Philadelphia lawyer Sidney George Fisher in his diary, "has caused an immense increase in the popular passion for liberty and equality." But advocates of women's rights encountered the limits of the Reconstruction commitment to equality. Women activists saw Reconstruction as the moment to claim their own emancipation. No less than blacks, proclaimed Elizabeth Cady Stanton, women had arrived at a "transition period, from slavery to freedom." The rewriting of the Constitution, declared suffrage leader Olympia Brown, offered the opportunity to sever the blessings of freedom from sex as well as race and to "bury the black man and the woman in the citizen."

Women activists

The destruction of slavery led feminists to search for ways to make the promise of free labor real for women. Every issue of the new women's rights journal, *The Agitator*, edited by Mary Livermore, who had led fund-raising efforts for aid to Union soldiers during the war, carried stories complaining of the limited job opportunities and unequal pay for females who entered the labor market. Other feminists debated how to achieve "liberty for married women." Demands for liberalizing divorce laws (which generally required evidence of adultery, desertion, or extreme abuse to terminate a marriage) and for recognizing "woman's control over her own body" (including protection against domestic violence and access to what later generations would call birth control) moved to the center of many feminists' concerns. "Our rotten marriage institution," one Ohio woman wrote, "is the main obstacle in the way of woman's freedom."

Feminists and Radicals

In one place, women's political rights did expand during Reconstruction—not, however, in a bastion of radicalism such as Massachusetts, but in the Wyoming territory. This had less to do with the era's egalitarian impulse than with the desire to attract female emigrants to an area where men outnumbered women five to one. In 1869, Wyoming's diminutive legislature (it consisted of fewer than twenty men) extended the right to vote to women, and the bill was then signed by the governor, a federal appointee. Wyoming entered the Union in 1890, becoming the first state since New Jersey in the late eighteenth century to allow women to vote.

In general, however, talk of woman suffrage and redesigning marriage found few sympathetic male listeners. Even Radical Republicans insisted that Reconstruction was the "Negro's hour" (the hour, that is, of the black male). The Fourteenth Amendment for the first time introduced the word "male" into the Constitution, in its clause penalizing a state for denying any group of men the right to vote. The Fifteenth Amendment outlawed discrimination in voting based on race but not gender. These measures produced a bitter split both between feminists and Radical Republicans, and within feminist circles.

A Delegation of Advocates of Woman Suffrage Addressing the House Judiciary Committee, an engraving from *Frank Leslie's Illustrated Newspaper*, February 4, 1871. The group includes Elizabeth Cady Stanton, seated just to the right of the speaker, and Susan B. Anthony, at the table on the extreme right.

Some leaders, like Stanton and Susan B. Anthony, opposed the Fifteenth Amendment because it did nothing to enfranchise women. They denounced their former abolitionist allies and moved to sever the women's rights movement from its earlier moorings in the antislavery tradition. On occasion, they appealed to racial and ethnic prejudices, arguing that native-born white women deserved the vote more than nonwhites and immigrants. "Patrick and Sambo and Hans and Yung Tung, who do not know the difference between a monarchy and a republic," declared Stanton, had no right to be "making laws for [feminist leader] Lucretia Mott." But other abolitionist-feminists, like Abby Kelley and Lucy Stone, insisted that despite their limitations, the Reconstruction amendments represented steps in the direction of truly universal suffrage and should be supported. The result was a split in the movement and the creation in 1869 of two hostile women's rights organizations—the National Woman Suffrage Association, led by Stanton, and the American Woman Suffrage Association, with Lucy Stone as president. They would not reunite until 1890.

Thus, even as it rejected the racial definition of freedom that had emerged in the first half of the nineteenth century, Reconstruction left the gender boundary largely intact. When women tried to use the rewritten legal code and Constitution to claim equal rights, they found the courts unreceptive. Myra Bradwell invoked the idea of free labor in challenging an Illinois statute limiting the practice of law to men, but the Supreme Court in 1873 rebuffed her claim. Free labor principles, the justices declared, did not apply to women, since "the law of the Creator" had assigned them to "the domestic sphere."

The gender boundary intact

Despite their limitations, the Fourteenth and Fifteenth Amendments and the Reconstruction Act of 1867 marked a radical departure in American history.

America's great departure

"We have cut loose from the whole dead past," wrote Timothy Howe, a Republican senator from Wisconsin, "and have cast our anchor out a hundred years" into the future. The Reconstruction Act of 1867 inaugurated America's first real experiment in interracial democracy.

RADICAL RECONSTRUCTION IN THE SOUTH

"The Tocsin of Freedom"

Political action by African-Americans

Among the former slaves, the passage of the Reconstruction Act inspired an outburst of political organization. At mass political meetings—community gatherings attended by men, women, and children—African-Americans staked their claim to equal citizenship. Blacks, declared an Alabama meeting, deserved "exactly the same rights, privileges and immunities as are enjoyed by white men. We ask for nothing more and will be content with nothing less."

These gatherings inspired direct action to remedy long-standing grievances. Hundreds took part in sit-ins that integrated horse-drawn public streetcars in cities across the South. Plantation workers organized strikes for higher wages. Speakers, male and female, fanned out across the South. Frances Ellen Watkins Harper, a black veteran of the abolitionist movement, embarked on a two-year tour, lecturing on "Literacy, Land, and Liberation." James D. Lynch, a member of the group that met with General Sherman in 1865, organized Republican meetings. He became known, in the words of a white contemporary, as "a great orator, fluid and graceful," who "stirred the emotions" of his listeners "as no other man could do."

The Union League

Determined to exercise their new rights as citizens, thousands joined the Union League, an organization closely linked to the Republican Party, and the vast majority of eligible African-Americans registered to vote. James K. Green,

Electioneering at the South, an engraving from *Harper's Weekly*, July 25, 1868, depicts a speaker at a political meeting in the rural South. Women as well as men took part in these grassroots gatherings.

a former slave in Hale County, Alabama, and a League organizer, went on to serve eight years in the Alabama legislature. In the 1880s, Green looked back on his political career. Before the war, he declared, "I was entirely ignorant; I knew nothing more than to obey my master; and there were thousands of us in the same attitude. . . . But the tocsin [warning bell] of freedom sounded and knocked at the door and we walked out like free men and shouldered the responsibilities."

By 1870, all the former Confederate states had been readmitted to the Union, and in a region where the Republican Party had not existed before the war, nearly all were under Republican control. Their new state constitutions, drafted in 1868 and 1869 by the first public bodies in American history with substantial black representation, marked a considerable improvement over those they replaced. The constitutions greatly expanded public responsibilities. They established the region's first state-funded systems of free public education, and they created new penitentiaries, orphan asylums, and homes for the insane. The constitutions guaranteed equality of civil and political rights and abolished practices of the antebellum era such as whipping as a punishment for crime, property qualifications for officeholding, and imprisonment for debt. A few states initially barred former Confederates from voting, but this policy was quickly abandoned by the new state governments.

From the Plantation to the Senate, an 1883 lithograph celebrating African-American progress during Reconstruction. Among the black leaders pictured at the top are Reconstruction congressmen Benjamin S. Turner, Josiah T. Walls, and Joseph H. Rainey; Hiram Revels of Mississippi, the first African-American senator; religious leader Richard Allen; and abolitionists Frederick Douglass and William Wells Brown. At the center emancipated slaves work in the cotton fields, and below children attend school and a black family stands outside its home.

The Black Officeholder

Throughout Reconstruction, black voters provided the bulk of the Republican Party's support. But African-Americans did not control Reconstruction politics, as their opponents frequently charged. The highest offices remained almost entirely in white hands, and only in South Carolina, where blacks made up 60 percent of the population, did they form a majority of the legislature. Nonetheless, the fact that some 2,000 African-Americans occupied public offices during Reconstruction represented a fundamental shift of power in the South and a radical departure in American government.

African-Americans were represented at every level of government. Fourteen were elected to the national House of Representatives. Two blacks served in the U.S. Senate during Reconstruction, both representing Mississippi. Hiram Revels, who had been born free in North Carolina, was educated in Illinois, and served as a chaplain in the wartime Union army, in 1870 became the first black senator in American history. The second, Blanche K. Bruce, a former slave, was elected in 1875. The next African-American elected to the Senate was Edward W. Brooke of Massachusetts, who served 1967–1978.

Pinckney B. S. Pinchback of Louisiana, the Georgia-born son of a white planter and a free black woman, served briefly during the winter of 1872–1873 as America's first black governor. More than a century would pass before L. Douglas Wilder of Virginia, elected in 1989, became the second. Some 700 blacks sat in state legislatures during Reconstruction, and scores held local offices ranging

The First Vote, an engraving from *Harper's Weekly*, November 16, 1867, depicts the first biracial elections in southern history. The voters represent key sources of the black political leadership that emerged during Reconstruction—the artisan carrying his tools, the well-dressed city person (probably free before the war), and the soldier.

from justice of the peace to sheriff, tax assessor, and policeman. The presence of black officeholders and their white allies made a real difference in southern life, ensuring that blacks accused of crimes would be tried before juries of their peers and enforcing fairness in such aspects of local government as road repair, tax assessment, and poor relief.

In South Carolina and Louisiana, homes of the South's wealthiest and best-educated free black communities, most prominent Reconstruction officeholders had never experienced slavery. In addition, a number of black Reconstruction officials, like Pennsylvania-born Jonathan J. Wright, who served on the South Carolina Supreme Court, had come from the North after the Civil War. The majority, however, were former slaves who had established their leadership in the black community by serving in the Union army, working as ministers, teachers, or skilled craftsmen, or engaging in Union League organizing. Among the most celebrated black officeholders was Robert Smalls, who had worked as a slave on the Charleston docks before the Civil War and who won national fame in 1862 by secretly guiding the *Planter*, a Confederate vessel, out of the harbor and delivering it to Union forces. Smalls became a powerful political leader on the South Carolina Sea Islands and was elected to five terms in Congress.

Carpetbaggers and Scalawags

The new southern governments also brought to power new groups of whites. Many Reconstruction officials were northerners who for one reason or another had made their homes in the South after the war. Their opponents dubbed them **carpetbaggers**, implying that they had packed all their belongings in a suitcase and left their homes in order to reap the spoils of office in the South. Some carpetbaggers were undoubtedly corrupt adventurers. The large majority, however, were former Union soldiers who decided to remain in the South when the war ended, before there was

Black and white members of the Mississippi senate, 1874–1875, shortly before the end of Reconstruction in the state. The woman in the bottom row is a postmistress.

any prospect of going into politics. Others were investors in land and railroads who saw in the postwar South an opportunity to combine personal economic advancement with a role in helping to substitute, as one wrote, "the civilization of freedom for that of slavery." Teachers, Freedmen's Bureau officers, and others who came to the region genuinely hoping to assist the former slaves represented another large group of carpetbaggers.

Most white Republicans had been born in the South. Former Confederates reserved their greatest scorn for these **scalawags**, whom they considered traitors to their race and region. Some southern-born Republicans were men of stature and wealth, like James L. Alcorn, the owner of one of Mississippi's largest plantations and the state's first Republican governor.

Most scalawags, however, were non-slaveholding white farmers from the southern upcountry. Many had been wartime Unionists, and they now cooperated with the Republicans in order to prevent "rebels" from returning to power. Others hoped Reconstruction governments would help them recover from wartime economic losses by suspending the collection of debts and enacting laws protecting small property holders from losing their homes to creditors. In states like North Carolina, Tennessee, and Arkansas, Republicans initially commanded a significant minority of the white vote. Even in the Deep South, the small white Republican vote was important, because the population remained almost evenly divided between blacks (almost all of whom voted for the party of Lincoln) and whites (overwhelmingly Democratic).

A portrait of Hiram Revels, the first black U.S. senator, by Theodore Kaufmann, a German-born artist who emigrated to the United States in 1855. Lithograph copies sold widely in the North during Reconstruction. Frederick Douglass, commenting on the dignified image, noted that African-Americans "so often see ourselves described and painted as monkeys, that we think it a great piece of fortune to find an exception to this general rule."

Southern Republicans in Power

In view of the daunting challenges they faced, the remarkable thing is not that Reconstruction governments in many respects failed, but how much they did accomplish. Perhaps their greatest achievement lay in establishing the South's first state-supported public schools. The new educational systems served both black and white children, although generally in schools segregated by race. Only in New Orleans were the public schools integrated during Reconstruction, and only in South Carolina did the state university admit black students (elsewhere, separate colleges were established). By the 1870s, in a region whose prewar leaders had made it illegal for slaves to learn and had done little to provide education for poorer whites, more than half the children, black and white, were attending public schools. The new governments also pioneered civil rights legislation. Their laws made it illegal for railroads, hotels, and other institutions to discriminate on the basis of race. Enforcement varied considerably from locality to locality, but Reconstruction established for the first time at the state level a standard of equal citizenship and a recognition of blacks' right to a share of public services.

> *State-supported public schools*

Republican governments also took steps to strengthen the position of rural laborers and promote the South's economic recovery. They passed laws to ensure that agricultural laborers and sharecroppers had the first claim on harvested crops, rather than merchants to whom the landowner owed money. South Carolina created a state Land Commission, which by 1876 had settled 14,000 black families and a few poor whites on their own farms.

> *Plans for economic recovery*

The Quest for Prosperity

Rather than land distribution, however, the Reconstruction governments pinned their hopes for southern economic growth and opportunity for African-Americans and poor whites alike on regional economic development. Railroad construction, they believed, was the key to transforming the South into a society of booming factories, bustling towns, and diversified agriculture. "A free and living republic," declared a Tennessee Republican, would "spring up in the track of the railroad." Every state during Reconstruction helped to finance railroad construction, and through tax reductions and other incentives tried to attract northern manufacturers to invest in the region. The program had mixed results. Economic development in general remained weak. With abundant opportunities existing in the West, few northern investors ventured to the Reconstruction South.

To their supporters, the governments of Radical Reconstruction presented a complex pattern of disappointment and accomplishment. A revitalized southern economy failed to materialize, and most African-Americans remained locked in poverty. On the other hand, biracial democratic government, a thing unknown in American history, for the first time functioned effectively in many parts of the South. Public facilities were rebuilt and expanded, school systems established, and legal codes purged of racism. The conservative elite that had dominated southern government from colonial times to 1867 found itself excluded from political power, while poor whites, newcomers from the North, and former slaves cast ballots, sat on juries, and enacted and administered laws. "We have gone through one of the most remarkable changes in our relations to each other," declared a white South Carolina lawyer in 1871, "that has been known, perhaps, in the history of the world." It is a measure of how far change had progressed that the reaction against Reconstruction proved so extreme.

Emancipation, an 1865 lithograph, is unusual because along with the familiar images of Lincoln and emancipated slaves, it also portrays a poor white family, suggesting that all Americans will benefit from the end of slavery and Reconstruction.

A group of black students and their teacher in a picture taken by an amateur photographer, probably a Union army veteran, while touring Civil War battlefields.

THE OVERTHROW OF RECONSTRUCTION

Reconstruction's Opponents

The South's traditional leaders—planters, merchants, and Democratic politicians—bitterly opposed the new governments. They denounced them as corrupt, inefficient, and examples of "black supremacy." "Intelligence, virtue, and patriotism" in public life, declared a protest by prominent southern Democrats, had given way to "ignorance, stupidity, and vice." Corruption did exist during Reconstruction, but it was confined to no race, region, or party. The rapid growth of state budgets and the benefits to be gained from public aid led in some states to a scramble for influence that produced bribery, insider dealing, and a get-rich-quick atmosphere. Southern frauds, however, were dwarfed by those practiced in these years by the Whiskey Ring, which involved high officials of the Grant administration, and by New York's Tweed Ring, controlled by the Democrats, whose thefts ran into the tens of millions of dollars. (These are discussed in the next chapter.) The rising taxes needed to pay for schools and other new public facilities and to assist railroad development were another cause of opposition to Reconstruction. Many poor whites who had initially supported the Republican Party turned against it when it became clear that their economic situation was not improving.

> *Sources of opposition*

The most basic reason for opposition to Reconstruction, however, was that most white southerners could not accept the idea of former slaves voting, holding office, and enjoying equality before the law. In order to restore white supremacy in southern public life and to ensure planters a disciplined, reliable labor force, they believed, Reconstruction must be overthrown. Opponents launched a campaign of violence in an effort to end Republican rule. Their actions posed a fundamental challenge both for Reconstruction governments in the South and for policymakers in Washington, D.C.

> *Campaign of violence*

"A Reign of Terror"

The Civil War ended in 1865, but violence remained widespread in large parts of the postwar South. In the early years of Reconstruction, violence was mostly

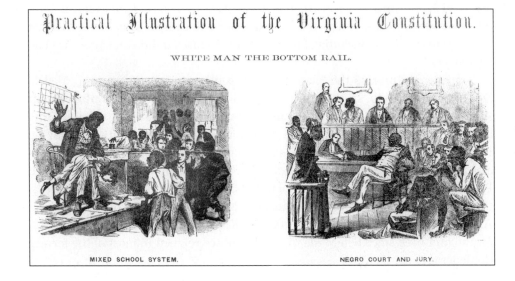

Practical Illustration of the Virginia Constitution.

WHITE MAN THE BOTTOM RAIL.

MIXED SCHOOL SYSTEM. NEGRO COURT AND JURY.

A cartoon from around 1870 illustrates a key theme of the racist opposition to Reconstruction—that blacks had forced themselves upon whites and gained domination over them. A black schoolteacher inflicts punishment on a white student in an integrated classroom, and a racially mixed jury judges a white defendant.

A Prospective Scene in the City of Oaks, a cartoon in the September 1, 1868, issue of the *Independent Monitor*, a Democratic newspaper published in Tuscaloosa, Alabama. The cartoon sent a warning to the Reverend A. S. Lakin, who had moved from Ohio to become president of the University of Alabama, and Dr. N. B. Cloud, a southern-born Republican serving as Alabama's superintendent of public education. The Ku Klux Klan forced both men from their positions. While most of the Klan's victims were black, the two men pictured here are white.

Colfax

The Enforcement Acts

local and unorganized. Blacks were assaulted and murdered for refusing to give way to whites on city sidewalks, using "insolent" language, challenging end-of-year contract settlements, and attempting to buy land. The violence that greeted the advent of Republican governments after 1867, however, was far more pervasive and more directly motivated by politics. In wide areas of the South, secret societies sprang up with the aim of preventing blacks from voting and destroying the organization of the Republican Party by assassinating local leaders and public officials.

The most notorious such organization was the **Ku Klux Klan**, which in effect served as a military arm of the Democratic Party in the South. From its founding in 1866 in Tennessee, the Klan was a terrorist organization. It quickly spread into nearly every southern state. Led by planters, merchants, and Democratic politicians, men who liked to style themselves the South's "respectable citizens," the Klan committed some of the most brutal criminal acts in American history. In many counties, it launched what one victim called a "reign of terror" against Republican leaders, black and white.

The Klan's victims included white Republicans, among them wartime Unionists and local officeholders, teachers, and party organizers. William Luke, an Irish-born teacher in a black school, was lynched in 1870. But African-Americans—local political leaders, those who managed to acquire land, and others who in one way or another defied the norms of white supremacy—bore the brunt of the violence. In York County, South Carolina, where nearly the entire white male population joined the Klan (and women participated by sewing the robes and hoods Klansmen wore as disguises), the organization committed eleven murders and hundreds of whippings.

On occasion, violence escalated from assaults on individuals to mass terrorism and even local insurrections. In Meridian, Mississippi, in 1871, some thirty blacks were murdered in cold blood, along with a white Republican judge. The bloodiest act of violence during Reconstruction took place in Colfax, Louisiana, in 1873, where armed whites assaulted the town with a small cannon. Hundreds of former slaves were murdered, including fifty members of a black militia unit after they had surrendered.

Unable to suppress the Klan, the new southern governments appealed to Washington for help. In 1870 and 1871, Congress adopted three **Enforcement Acts**, outlawing terrorist societies and allowing the president to use the army against them. These laws continued the expansion of national authority during Reconstruction. They defined crimes that aimed to deprive citizens of their civil and political rights as federal offenses rather than violations of state law. In 1871, President Grant dispatched federal marshals, backed up by troops in some areas, to arrest hundreds of accused Klansmen. Many Klan leaders fled the South. After a series of well-publicized trials, the Klan went out of existence. In 1872, for the first time since before the Civil War, peace reigned in most of the former Confederacy.

The Liberal Republicans

Despite the Grant administration's effective response to Klan terrorism, the North's commitment to Reconstruction waned during the 1870s. Many Radicals, including Thaddeus Stevens, who died in 1868, had passed from the scene. Within the Republican Party, their place was taken by politicians less committed to the ideal of equal rights for blacks. Northerners increasingly felt that the South should be able to solve its own problems without constant interference from Washington. The federal government had freed the slaves, made them citizens, and given them the right to vote. Now, blacks should rely on their own resources, not demand further assistance.

In 1872, an influential group of Republicans, alienated by corruption within the Grant administration and believing that the growth of federal power during and after the war needed to be curtailed, formed their own party. They included Republican founders like Lyman Trumbull and prominent editors and journalists such as E. L. Godkin of *The Nation*. Calling themselves Liberal Republicans, they nominated Horace Greeley, editor of the *New York Tribune*, for president.

The Liberals' alienation from the Grant administration initially had little to do with Reconstruction. They claimed that corrupt politicians had come to power in the North by manipulating the votes of immigrants and workingmen, while men of talent and education like themselves had been pushed aside. Democratic criticisms of Reconstruction, however, found a receptive audience among the Liberals. As in the North, they became convinced, the "best men" of the South had been excluded from power while "ignorant" voters controlled politics, producing corruption and misgovernment. Power in the South should be returned to the region's "natural leaders." During the campaign of 1872, Greeley repeatedly called on Americans to "clasp hands across the bloody chasm" by putting the Civil War and Reconstruction behind them.

A Tennessee member of the Ku Klux Klan, photographed in his hooded disguise around 1870.

The Old Plantation Home, a lithograph from 1872 produced by the prominent firm of Currier and Ives in New York City, illustrates how a nostalgic image of slavery as a time of carefree happiness for African-Americans was being promoted even as Reconstruction took place.

Changes in graphic artist Thomas Nast's depiction of blacks in *Harper's Weekly* mirrored the evolution of Republican sentiment in the North. *And Not This Man?*, August 5, 1865, shows the black soldier as an upstanding citizen deserving of the vote. *Colored Rule in a Reconstructed (?) State*, March 14, 1874, suggests that Reconstruction legislatures had become travesties of democratic government.

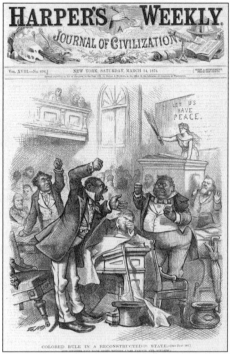

A bankbook issued by the Freedman's Savings and Trust Company, a private corporation established by Congress to promote thrift among the former slaves. Black individuals, families, church groups, and civic organizations deposited nearly $2 million in branches scattered across the South. The bank failed in 1874 because of mismanagement, and thousands of depositors lost their savings.

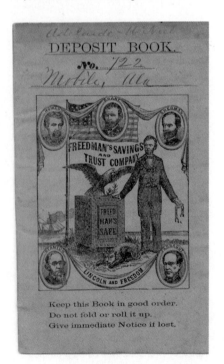

Greeley had spent most of his career, first as a Whig and then as a Republican, denouncing the Democratic Party. But with the Republican split presenting an opportunity to repair their political fortunes, Democratic leaders endorsed Greeley as their candidate. Many rank-and-file Democrats, unable to bring themselves to vote for Greeley, stayed at home on election day. As a result, Greeley suffered a devastating defeat by Grant, whose margin of more than 700,000 popular votes was the largest in a nineteenth-century presidential contest. But Greeley's campaign placed on the northern agenda the one issue on which the Liberal reformers and the Democrats could agree—a new policy toward the South.

The North's Retreat

The Liberal attack on Reconstruction, which continued after 1872, contributed to a resurgence of racism in the North. Journalist James S. Pike, a leading Greeley supporter, in 1874 published *The Prostrate State*, an influential account of a visit to South Carolina. The book depicted a state engulfed by political corruption, drained by governmental extravagance, and under the control of "a mass of black barbarism." The South's problems, Pike insisted, arose from "Negro government." The solution was to restore leading whites to political power. Newspapers that had long supported Reconstruction now began to condemn black participation in southern government. They expressed their views visually as well. Engravings depicting the former slaves as heroic Civil War veterans, upstanding citizens, or victims of violence were increasingly replaced by caricatures presenting them as little more than unbridled animals. Resurgent racism offered a convenient explanation for the alleged "failure" of Reconstruction.

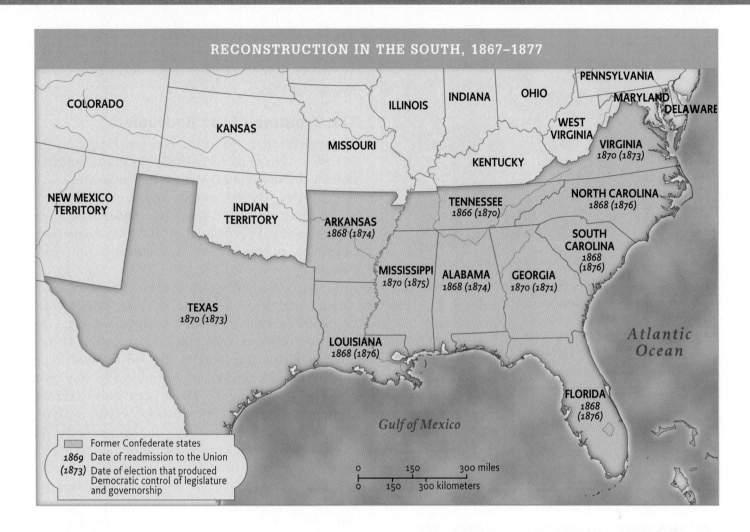

RECONSTRUCTION IN THE SOUTH, 1867–1877

Legend:
Former Confederate states
1869 Date of readmission to the Union
(1873) Date of election that produced Democratic control of legislature and governorship

Other factors also weakened northern support for Reconstruction. In 1873, the country plunged into a severe economic depression. Distracted by economic problems, Republicans were in no mood to devote further attention to the South. The depression dealt the South a severe blow and further weakened the prospect that Republicans could revitalize the region's economy. Democrats made substantial gains throughout the nation in the elections of 1874. For the first time since the Civil War, their party took control of the House of Representatives. Before the new Congress met, the old one enacted a final piece of Reconstruction legislation, the **Civil Rights Act of 1875**. This outlawed racial discrimination in places of public accommodation like hotels and theaters. But it was clear that the northern public was retreating from Reconstruction.

Politics and the economy

The Supreme Court whittled away at the guarantees of black rights Congress had adopted. In the *Slaughterhouse Cases* (1873), white butchers excluded from a state-sponsored monopoly in Louisiana went to court, claiming that their right to equality before the law guaranteed by the Fourteenth Amendment had been violated. The justices rejected their claim, ruling that the amendment had not altered traditional federalism. Most of the rights of citizens, it declared, remained under state

Court rulings on rights

Of Course He Wants to Vote the Democratic Ticket, a cartoon from *Harper's Weekly*, October 21, 1876, comments on the campaign of terror launched by South Carolina Democrats in an attempt to carry the election of 1876.

control. Three years later, in *United States v. Cruikshank*, the Court gutted the Enforcement Acts by throwing out the convictions of some of those responsible for the Colfax Massacre of 1873.

The Triumph of the Redeemers

By the mid-1870s, Reconstruction was clearly on the defensive. Democrats had already regained control of states with substantial white voting majorities such as Tennessee, North Carolina, and Texas. The victorious Democrats called themselves **Redeemers**, since they claimed to have "redeemed" the white South from corruption, misgovernment, and northern and black control.

In those states where Reconstruction governments survived, violence again erupted. This time, the Grant administration showed no desire to intervene. In contrast to the Klan's activities—conducted at night by disguised men—the violence of 1875 and 1876 took place in broad daylight, as if to underscore Democrats' conviction that they had nothing to fear from Washington. In Mississippi, in 1875, white rifle clubs drilled in public and openly assaulted and murdered Republicans. When Governor Adelbert Ames, a Maine-born Union general, frantically appealed to the federal government for assistance, President Grant responded that the northern public was "tired out" by southern problems. On election day, armed Democrats destroyed ballot boxes and drove former slaves from the polls. The result was a Democratic landslide and the end of Reconstruction in Mississippi. "A revolution has taken place," wrote Ames, "and a race are disfranchised—they are to be returned to . . . an era of second slavery."

Similar events took place in South Carolina in 1876. Democrats nominated for governor former Confederate general Wade Hampton. Hampton promised to respect the rights of all citizens of the state, but his supporters, inspired by Democratic tactics in Mississippi, launched a wave of intimidation. Democrats intended to carry the election, one planter told a black official, "if we have to wade in blood knee-deep."

The Disputed Election and Bargain of 1877

Events in South Carolina directly affected the outcome of the presidential campaign of 1876. To succeed Grant, the Republicans nominated Governor Rutherford B. Hayes of Ohio. Democrats chose as his opponent New York's governor, Samuel J. Tilden. By this time, only South Carolina, Florida, and Louisiana remained under Republican control. The election turned out to be so close that whoever captured these states—which both parties claimed to have carried—would become the next president.

Unable to resolve the impasse on its own, Congress in January 1877 appointed a fifteen-member Electoral Commission, composed of senators, representatives, and Supreme Court

THE PRESIDENTIAL ELECTION OF 1876

| | Non-voting territory |

Party	Candidate	Electoral Vote (Share)	Popular Vote (Share)
Republican	Hayes	185 (50%)	4,036,298 (48%)
Democrat	Tilden	184 (50%)	4,300,590 (51%)
Greenback	Cooper	0 (0%)	93,895 (1%)
Disputed (assigned to Hayes by electoral commission)			

justices. Republicans enjoyed an 8–7 majority on the commission, and to no one's surprise, the members decided by that margin that Hayes had carried the disputed southern states and had been elected president. Even as the commission deliberated, however, behind-the-scenes negotiations took place between leaders of the two parties. Hayes's representatives agreed to recognize Democratic control of the entire South and to avoid further intervention in local affairs. They also pledged that Hayes would place a southerner in the cabinet position of postmaster general and that he would work for federal aid to the Texas and Pacific railroad, a transcontinental line projected to follow a southern route. For their part, Democrats promised not to dispute Hayes's right to office and to respect the civil and political rights of blacks.

Thus was concluded the **Bargain of 1877**. Not all of its parts were fulfilled. But Hayes became president, and he did appoint David M. Key of Tennessee as postmaster general. Hayes quickly ordered federal troops to stop guarding the state houses in Louisiana and South Carolina, allowing Democratic claimants to become governor. (Contrary to legend, Hayes did not remove the last soldiers from the South—he simply ordered them to return to their barracks.) But the Texas and Pacific never did get its land grant. Of far more significance, the triumphant southern Democrats failed to live up to their pledge to recognize blacks as equal citizens.

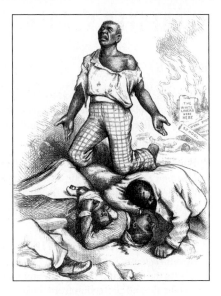

Is This a Republican Form of Government?, a cartoon by Thomas Nast in *Harper's Weekly*, September 2, 1876, illustrates his conviction that the overthrow of Reconstruction meant that the United States was not prepared to live up to its democratic ideals or protect the rights of black citizens threatened by violence.

The End of Reconstruction

As a historical process—the nation's adjustment to the destruction of slavery—Reconstruction continued well after 1877. Blacks continued to vote and, in some states, hold office into the 1890s. But as a distinct era of national history—when Republicans controlled much of the South, blacks exercised significant political power, and the federal government accepted the responsibility for protecting the fundamental rights of all American citizens—Reconstruction had come to an end. Despite its limitations, Reconstruction was a remarkable chapter in the story of American freedom. Nearly a century would pass before the nation again tried to bring equal rights to the descendants of slaves. The civil rights era of the 1950s and 1960s would sometimes be called the Second Reconstruction.

Even while it lasted, however, Reconstruction revealed some of the tensions inherent in nineteenth-century discussions of freedom. The policy of granting black men the vote while denying them the benefits of land ownership strengthened the idea that the free citizen could be a poor, dependent laborer. Reconstruction placed on the national agenda a problem that would dominate political discussion for the next half-century—how, in a modern society, to define the economic essence of freedom.

SUGGESTED READING

BOOKS

- Bottoms, D. Michael. *An Aristocracy of Color: Race and Reconstruction in California and the West*, 1850–1890 (2013). A study of changing race relations, and definitions of race, in the western states.

- Butchart, Ronald E. *Schooling the Freed People: Teaching, Learning, and the Struggle for Black Freedom* (2010). Relates the efforts of black and white teachers to educate the former slaves and some of the conflicts that arose over the purposes of such education.

- Downs, Gregory. *Declarations of Dependence: The Long Reconstruction of Popular Politics in the South, 1861–1908* (2011). Traces the changing ways black and white southerners sought aid and protection from the government during and after the Civil War and Reconstruction.

- Downs, James. *Sick from Freedom: The Deadly Consequences of Emancipation* (2012). How disease shaped the experience of freedom and how the Freedmen's Bureau and other agencies sought to cope with widespread illness among former slaves.

- DuBois, Ellen C. *Feminism and Suffrage: The Emergence of an Independent Women's Movement in America, 1848–1869* (1978). Explores how the split over the exclusion of women from the Fourteenth and Fifteenth Amendments gave rise to a movement for woman suffrage no longer tied to the abolitionist tradition.

- Edwards, Laura. *Gendered Strife and Confusion: The Political Culture of Reconstruction* (1997). Considers how issues relating to gender relations affected the course of southern Reconstruction.

- Fields, Barbara J. *Slavery and Freedom on the Middle Ground: Maryland during the Nineteenth Century* (1985). A study of slavery and emancipation in a key border state.

- Foner, Eric. *Nothing but Freedom: Emancipation and Its Legacy* (1983). Includes a comparison of the emancipation experience in different parts of the Western Hemisphere.

- Foner, Eric. *Reconstruction: America's Unfinished Revolution, 1863–1877* (1988). A comprehensive account of the Reconstruction era.

- Hahn, Steven. *A Nation under Our Feet: Black Political Struggles in the Rural South from Slavery to the Great Migration* (2003). A detailed study of black political activism, stressing nationalist consciousness and emigration movements.

- Hyman, Harold M. *A More Perfect Union: The Impact of the Civil War and Reconstruction on the Constitution* (1973). Analyzes how the laws and constitutional amendments of Reconstruction changed the Constitution and the rights of all Americans.

- Jung, Moon-Ho. *Coolies and Cane: Race, Labor, and Sugar in the Age of Emancipation* (2006). Tells the story of Chinese laborers brought to work in the sugar fields after the end of slavery.

- Litwack, Leon F. *Been in the Storm So Long: The Aftermath of Slavery* (1979). A detailed look at the immediate aftermath of the end of slavery and the variety of black and white responses to emancipation.

- Rable, George C. *But There Was No Peace: The Role of Violence in the Politics of Reconstruction* (1984). The only full-scale study of violence in the Reconstruction South.

- Richardson, Heather C. *West from Appomattox* (2007). An account that fully integrates the West into the history of the Reconstruction era.

- Rodrigue, John C. *Reconstruction in the Cane Fields: From Slavery to Free Labor in Louisiana's Sugar Parishes, 1862–1880* (2001). A study of how an often-neglected part of the South experienced the aftermath of slavery.

- Summers, Mark W. *Railroads, Reconstruction, and the Gospel of Prosperity: Aid under the Radical Republicans, 1865–1877* (1984). A detailed look at southern governments' efforts to promote economic development, and the political corruption that sometimes accompanied it.

WEBSITES

- After Slavery: Race, Labor, and Politics in the Post-Emancipation Carolinas: www.afterslavery.com

- America's Reconstruction: People and Politics after the Civil War: www.digitalhistory.uh.edu/exhibits/reconstruction/index.html

- The Andrew Johnson Impeachment Trial: www.law.umkc.edu/faculty/projects/ftrials/impeach/impeachmt.htm

- Freedmen and Southern Society Project: www.history.umd.edu/Freedmen/

- Freedmen's Bureau Online: http://www.freedmensbureau.com/

CHAPTER REVIEW AND ONLINE RESOURCES

REVIEW QUESTIONS

1. In 1865, former Confederate general Robert Richardson remarked that "the emancipated slaves own nothing, because nothing but freedom has been given to them." Explain whether this would be an accurate assessment of Reconstruction twelve years later.

2. The women's movement split into two separate national organizations in part because the Fifteenth Amendment did not give women the vote. Explain why the two groups split.

3. How did black families, churches, schools, and other institutions contribute to the development of African-American culture and political activism in this period?

4. Why did ownership of land and control of labor become major points of contention between former slaves and whites in the South?

5. By what methods did southern whites seek to limit African-American civil rights and liberties? How did the federal government respond?

6. How did the failure of land reform and continued poverty lead to new forms of servitude for both blacks and whites?

7. What caused the confrontation between President Johnson and Congress over Reconstruction policies?

8. What national issues and attitudes combined to bring an end to Reconstruction by 1877?

9. By 1877, how did the condition of former slaves in the United States compare with that of freedpeople around the globe?

KEY TERMS

the Freedmen's Bureau (p. 557)
sharecropping (p. 560)
crop lien (p. 560)
Black Codes (p. 565)
Civil Rights Bill of 1866 (p. 567)
Fourteenth Amendment (p. 568)
Reconstruction Act (p. 569)
Tenure of Office Act (p. 569)
impeachment (p. 569)
Fifteenth Amendment (p. 570)
carpetbaggers (p. 576)
scalawags (p. 577)
Ku Klux Klan (p. 580)
Enforcement Acts (p. 580)
Civil Rights Act of 1875 (p. 583)
Redeemers (p. 584)
Bargain of 1877 (p. 585)

Go to 🐇 INQUIZITIVE

To see what you know—and learn what you've missed—with personalized feedback along the way.

Visit the *Give Me Liberty!* Student Site for primary source documents and images, interactive maps, author videos featuring Eric Foner, and more.

PART 4

TOWARD A GLOBAL PRESENCE, 1870-1920

Between the era of Reconstruction and the end of World War I, the United States underwent a profound social and economic revolution that affected all aspects of Americans' lives. By 1900, the country had emerged as the world's major industrial power and, thanks to the Spanish-American War of 1898, the possessor of a small overseas empire. Giant new corporations now dominated the economy. Immigrants arrived from abroad in unprecedented numbers, providing labor for the expanding economy and fueling the growth of the nation's cities. In 1920, residents of cities for the first time outnumbered those living in rural areas.

In the first two decades of the twentieth century, the United States became a major participant in world affairs. It repeatedly sent troops to direct the affairs of Caribbean and Central American countries. During World War I, President Woodrow Wilson not only dispatched American soldiers, for the first time, to fight in Europe but also called for continuous American involvement in the creation of a peaceful, economically interconnected world order.

These changes increased the economic opportunities of many Americans. The middle class of clerks, managers, and other white-collar workers expanded significantly. Economic growth drew large numbers of women into the workforce. Millions of new immigrants entered the country. When the outbreak of World War I cut off immigration from Europe, hundreds of thousands of blacks moved from southern farms to jobs in northern cities, gaining access to the industrial economy and changing the country's racial configuration.

What is sometimes called "the second industrial revolution" also led to an era of persistent and often violent labor conflict. To many Americans, social life seemed increasingly polarized between those at the top, who reaped most of the benefits of economic expansion, and workers struggling to make ends meet. In the early twentieth century, increasing numbers of Americans concluded that only the reform of politics and increased government intervention in economic life could curb the power of the new corporations, ensure safe working conditions, and provide economic security for ordinary men and women.

Throughout these years, divergent views of the country's course of development, and the proper role of government in shaping it, found expression in

debates over American freedom. Many Americans held to a traditional understanding of freedom as the absence of external restraints on free individuals operating in a competitive marketplace. In this view, known as "liberty of contract," any government interference with economic relationships represented an infringement on property rights and, therefore, on freedom.

Others turned to collective action, economic and political, to try to reverse what they considered a decline of traditional freedoms. Workers flocked into unions that promised not only higher wages but also "industrial freedom"—a share in basic economic decision making. During the 1890s, millions of farmers joined the Populist movement in an attempt to reverse their declining economic prospects. In the Progressive era of the early twentieth century, reformers sought to expand economic and political freedom by increasing workers' rights, weakening the power of city bosses, and using the power of the state and national governments to regulate corporate behavior. To Progressives, freedom was a positive idea, the effective power to achieve personal and social goals. At the same time, the expansion of the consumer economy and the new freedoms for women offered by city life encouraged the growth of an idea of personal freedom based on individual fulfillment, including self-determination in the most intimate areas of life.

HELLO! THIS IS LIBERTY SPEAKING—BILLIONS OF DOLLARS ARE NEEDED AND NEEDED NOW

Even as definitions of freedom expanded, the number of Americans who enjoyed genuine freedom contracted. In the 1890s and the early twentieth century, the political leaders of the white South imposed on the region's African-Americans a comprehensive system of second-class citizenship that rested on racial segregation, denial of the right to vote, lack of economic opportunities, and the ever-present threat of violence. Many native-born Americans considered immigrants, especially the large numbers arriving from southern and eastern Europe, as unfit for American citizenship. They sought to restrict their numbers and to force those already here to "Americanize" themselves by abandoning traditional cultures for mainstream values.

The country's emergence as a world power intensified these debates over freedom. To its supporters, the new American empire represented a continuation of the country's traditional self-image of promoting liberty and democracy throughout the world. Yet critics of the acquisition of foreign colonies questioned whether an empire could still be considered a democracy. This question gained new urgency during World War I. On the one hand, the war ushered in the final success of the long struggle for woman suffrage, the greatest expansion of democracy in American history. On the other, the federal government and private patriotic organizations embarked on the most extensive campaign in American history to stifle criticism of administration policies and the economic status quo. By 1920, the United States was the world's foremost economic and military power. But the role it would play in world affairs in the future, and the fate of freedom at home, remained unresolved.

CHAPTER 16

AMERICA'S GILDED AGE

★

1870–1890

An immense crowd gathered in New York Harbor on October 28, 1886, for the dedication of *Liberty Enlightening the World*, a fitting symbol for a nation now wholly free. The idea for the statue originated in 1865 with Édouard de Laboulaye, a French educator and the author of several books on the United States, as a response to the assassination of Abraham Lincoln. The statue, de Laboulaye hoped, would celebrate both the historic friendship between France and the United States and the triumph, through the Union's victory in the Civil War, of American freedom. Measuring more than 150 feet from torch to toe and standing atop a huge pedestal, the edifice was the tallest man-made structure in the Western Hemisphere. It exceeded in height, newspapers noted with pride, the Colossus of Rhodes, a wonder of the ancient world.

In time, the Statue of Liberty, as it came to be called, would become Americans' most revered national icon. For over a century it has stood as a symbol of freedom. The statue has offered welcome to millions of immigrants—the "huddled masses yearning to breathe free" celebrated in a poem by Emma Lazarus inscribed on its base in 1903. In the years since its dedication, the statue's familiar image has been reproduced by folk artists in every conceivable medium and has been used by advertisers to promote everything from cigarettes and lawn mowers to war bonds. As its use by Chinese students demanding democracy in the Tiananmen Square protests of 1989 showed, it has become a powerful international symbol as well.

The year of the statue's dedication, 1886, also witnessed the "great upheaval," a wave of strikes and labor protests that touched every part of the nation. The 600 dignitaries (598 of them men) who gathered on what is now called Liberty Island for the dedication hoped the Statue of Liberty would inspire renewed devotion to the nation's political and economic system. But for all its grandeur, the statue could not conceal the deep social divisions and fears about the future of American freedom that accompanied the country's emergence as the world's leading industrial power. Nor did the celebrations address the crucial questions that moved to the center stage of American public life during the 1870s and 1880s and remained there for decades to come: What are the social conditions that make freedom possible, and what role should the national government play in defining and protecting the liberty of its citizens?

THE SECOND INDUSTRIAL REVOLUTION

Between the end of the Civil War and the early twentieth century, the United States underwent one of the most rapid and profound economic revolutions any country has ever experienced. There were numerous causes for this explosive economic growth. The country enjoyed abundant natural resources, a growing supply of labor, an expanding market for manufactured goods, and the availability of capital for investment. In addition, the federal government actively promoted industrial and agricultural development. It enacted high tariffs that protected American

FOCUS QUESTIONS

What factors combined to make the United States a mature industrial society after the Civil War? *–p. 591*

How was the West transformed economically and socially in this period? *–p. 602*

Was the Gilded Age political system effective in meeting its goals? *–p. 619*

How did the economic development of the Gilded Age affect American freedom? *–p. 624*

How did reformers of the period approach the problems of an industrial society? *–p. 628*

Across the Continent, a lithograph from 1868 by the British-born artist Frances F. Palmer, celebrates post–Civil War westward expansion as the spread of civilization—represented by the railroad, telegraph, school, church, and wagon trains—into a wilderness that appears totally uninhabited except for two Indians in the far distance and a herd of buffalo.

industry from foreign competition, granted land to railroad companies to encourage construction, and used the army to remove Indians from western lands desired by farmers and mining companies.

The Industrial Economy

The rapid expansion of factory production, mining, and railroad construction in all parts of the country except the South signaled the transition from Lincoln's America—a world centered on the small farm and artisan workshop—to a mature industrial society. Americans of the late nineteenth century marveled at the triumph of the new economy. "One can hardly believe," wrote the philosopher John Dewey, "there has been a revolution in history so rapid, so extensive, so complete."

By 1913, the United States produced one-third of the world's industrial output—more than the total of Great Britain, France, and Germany combined. Half of all industrial workers now labored in plants with more than 250 employees. On the eve of the Civil War, the first industrial revolution, centered on the textile industry, had transformed New England into a center of manufacturing. But otherwise, the United States was still primarily an agricultural nation. By 1880, for the first time, the Census Bureau found a majority of the workforce engaged in non-farming jobs. The traditional dream of economic independence seemed obsolete. By 1890, two-thirds of Americans worked for wages, rather than owning a farm, business, or craft shop. Drawn to factories by the promise of employment, a new working class emerged in these years. Between 1870 and 1920, almost 11 million Americans moved from farm to city, and another 25 million immigrants arrived from overseas.

Most manufacturing now took place in industrial cities. New York, with its new skyscrapers and hundreds of thousands of workers in all sorts of manufacturing establishments, symbolized dynamic urban growth. After merging with Brooklyn

TABLE 16.1 Indicators of Economic Change, 1870–1920

	1870	1900	1920
Farms (millions)	2.7	5.7	6.4
Land in farms (million acres)	408	841	956
Wheat grown (million bushels)	254	599	843
Employment (millions)	14	28.5	44.5
In manufacturing (millions)	2.5	5.9	11.2
Percentage in workforce[a]			
Agricultural	52	38	27
Industry[b]	29	31	44
Trade, service, administration[c]	20	31	27
Railroad track (thousands of miles)	53	258	407
Steel produced (thousands of tons)	0.8	11.2	46
GNP (billions of dollars)	7.4	18.7	91.5
Per capita (in 1920 dollars)	371	707	920
Life expectancy at birth (years)	42	47	54

[a] Percentages are rounded and do not total 100.
[b] Includes manufacturing, transportation, mining, and construction.
[c] Includes trade, finance, and public administration.

Forging the Shaft, a painting from the 1870s by the American artist John Ferguson Weir, depicts workers in a steel factory making a propeller shaft for an ocean liner. Weir illustrates both the dramatic power of the factory at a time when the United States was overtaking European countries in manufacturing, and the fact that industrial production still required hard physical labor.

in 1898, its population exceeded 3.4 million. The city financed industrialization and westward expansion, its banks and stock exchange funneling capital to railroads, mines, and factories. But the heartland of the second industrial revolution was the region around the Great Lakes, with its factories producing iron and steel, machinery, chemicals, and packaged foods. Pittsburgh had become the world's center of iron and steel manufacturing. Chicago, by 1900 the nation's second-largest city, with 1.7 million inhabitants, was home to factories producing steel and farm machinery and giant stockyards where cattle were processed into meat products for shipment east in refrigerated rail cars. Smaller industrial cities also proliferated, often concentrating on a single industry—cast-iron stoves in Troy, New York, furniture in Grand Rapids, Michigan.

> *The Great Lakes region*

Railroads and the National Market

The railroad made possible what is sometimes called the "second industrial revolution." Spurred by private investment and massive grants of land and money by federal, state, and local governments, the number of miles of railroad track in the United States tripled between 1860 and 1880 and tripled again by 1920, opening vast new areas to commercial farming and creating a truly national market for manufactured goods. In 1886, the railroads adopted a standard national gauge (the distance separating the two rails), making it possible for the first time for trains of one company to travel on any other company's track. By the 1890s, five transcontinental lines transported the products of western mines, farms, ranches, and forests to eastern markets and carried manufactured goods to the West. The railroads reorganized time itself. In 1883, the major companies divided the nation into the four time zones still in use today.

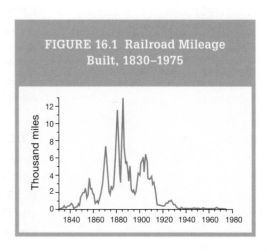

FIGURE 16.1 Railroad Mileage Built, 1830–1975

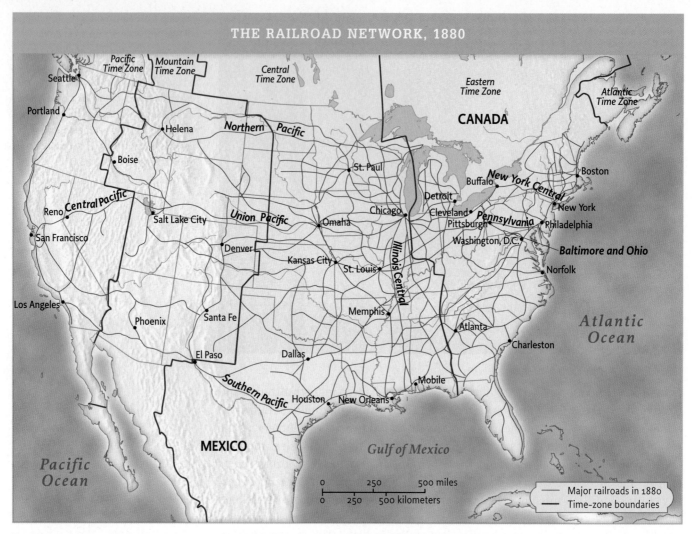

THE RAILROAD NETWORK, 1880

By 1880, the transnational rail network made possible the creation of a truly national market for goods.

Economic integration

The growing population formed an ever-expanding market for the mass production, mass distribution, and mass marketing of goods, essential elements of a modern industrial economy. The spread of national brands like Ivory soap and Quaker Oats symbolized the continuing integration of the economy. So did the growth of national chains, most prominently the Atlantic and Pacific Tea Company, better known as A & P grocery stores. Based in Chicago, the national mail-order firms Montgomery Ward and Sears, Roebuck & Co. sold clothing, jewelry, farm equipment, and numerous other goods to rural families throughout the country.

The Spirit of Innovation

A remarkable series of technological innovations spurred rapid communication and economic growth. The opening of the Atlantic cable in 1866 made it possible to send electronic telegraph messages instantaneously between the United States and Europe. During the 1870s and 1880s, the telephone, typewriter, and handheld camera came into use.

Scientific breakthroughs poured forth from research laboratories in Menlo Park and West Orange, New Jersey, created by the era's greatest inventor, Thomas A. Edison. During the course of his life, Edison helped to establish entirely new industries that transformed private life, public entertainment, and economic activity, including the phonograph, lightbulb, motion picture, and a system for generating and distributing electric power. He opened the first electric generating station in Manhattan in 1882 to provide power to streetcars, factories, and private homes, and he established, among other companies, the forerunner of General Electric to market electrical equipment. The spread of electricity was essential to industrial and urban growth, providing a more reliable and flexible source of power than water or steam. However, it was not Edison but another inventor, Nikola Tesla, an ethnic Serb born in modern-day Croatia who emigrated to the United States at the age of twenty-eight, who developed an electric motor using the system of alternating current that overcame many of the challenges of using electricity for commercial and industrial purposes.

The Greatest Department Store on Earth, a cartoon from *Puck*, November 29, 1899, depicts Uncle Sam selling goods, mostly manufactured products, to the nations of the world. The search for markets overseas would be a recurring theme of twentieth-century American foreign policy.

Competition and Consolidation

Economic growth was dramatic but highly volatile. The combination of a market flooded with goods and the federal monetary policies (discussed later) that removed money from the national economy led to a relentless fall in prices. The

Thomas Edison's laboratory at Menlo Park, New Jersey, and some of the employees of the great inventor.

world economy suffered prolonged downturns in the 1870s and 1890s. Indeed, before the 1930s, the years from 1873 to 1897 were known throughout the world as the Great Depression.

Businesses engaged in ruthless competition. Railroads and other companies tried various means of bringing order to the chaotic marketplace. They formed "pools" that divided up markets between supposedly competing firms and fixed prices. They established **trusts**—legal devices whereby the affairs of several rival companies were managed by a single director. Such efforts to coordinate the economic activities of independent companies generally proved short-lived, disintegrating as individual firms continued their intense pursuit of profits.

> *Pools and trusts*

To avoid cutthroat competition, more and more corporations battled to control entire industries. Many companies fell by the wayside or were gobbled up by others. The process of economic concentration culminated between 1897 and 1904, when some 4,000 firms vanished into larger corporations that served national markets and exercised an unprecedented degree of control over the marketplace. By the time the wave of mergers had been completed, giant corporations like U.S. Steel (created by financier J. P. Morgan in 1901 by combining eight large steel companies into the first billion-dollar economic enterprise), Standard Oil, and International Harvester (a manufacturer of agricultural machinery) dominated major parts of the economy.

> *Corporations*

The Rise of Andrew Carnegie

In an era without personal or corporate income taxes, some business leaders accumulated enormous fortunes and economic power. Under the aggressive leadership of Thomas A. Scott, the Pennsylvania Railroad—for a time the nation's largest corporation—forged an economic empire that stretched across the continent and included coal mines and oceangoing steamships. With an army of professional managers to oversee its far-flung activities, the railroad pioneered modern techniques of business organization.

Another industrial giant was Andrew Carnegie, who emigrated with his family from his native Scotland at the age of thirteen and as a teenager worked in a Pennsylvania textile factory. During the depression that began in 1873, Carnegie set out to establish a steel company that incorporated **vertical integration**—that is, one that controlled every phase of the business from raw materials to transportation, manufacturing, and distribution. By the 1890s, he dominated the steel industry and had accumulated a fortune worth hundreds of millions of dollars. Carnegie's complex of steel factories at Homestead, Pennsylvania, were the most technologically advanced in the world.

The Progress of the Century, a lithograph from 1876, celebrates four of the major technological innovations of the century since American independence: the steamboat, locomotive, steam press, and telegraph.

Carnegie's father, an immigrant Scottish weaver who had taken part in popular efforts to open the British political system to working-class participation, had instilled in his son a commitment to democracy and social equality. From his mother, Carnegie learned that life was a ceaseless struggle in which one must strive to get ahead or sink beneath the waves. His life reflected the tension between these elements of his upbringing. Believing that the rich had a moral obligation to promote the advancement of society, Carnegie denounced the "worship of money" and distributed much of his wealth to various philanthropies, especially the creation of public libraries in towns throughout the country. But he ran his companies with a dictatorial hand. His factories operated nonstop, with two twelve-hour shifts every day of the year except the Fourth of July.

The Electricity Building at the Chicago World's Fair of 1893, painted by Childe Hassam. The electric lighting at the fair astonished visitors and illustrated how electricity was changing the visual landscape.

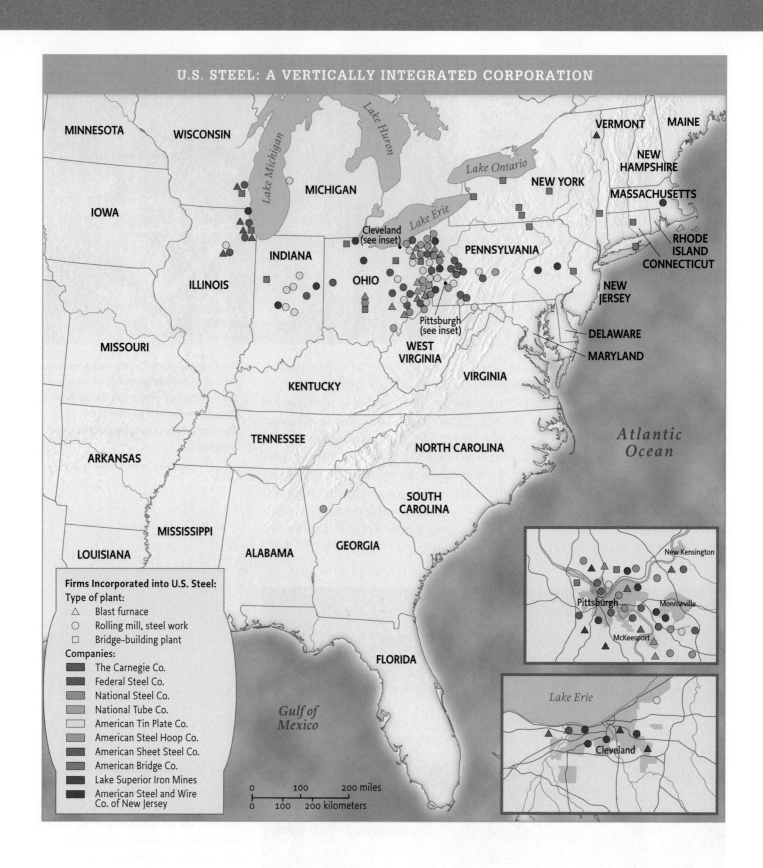

U.S. STEEL: A VERTICALLY INTEGRATED CORPORATION

MINNESOTA

WISCONSIN

Lake Michigan

Lake Huron

MICHIGAN

IOWA

Lake Ontario

Lake Erie

NEW YORK

VERMONT   MAINE

NEW
HAMPSHIRE

MASSACHUSETTS

Cleveland
(see inset)

INDIANA

ILLINOIS

OHIO

PENNSYLVANIA

RHODE
ISLAND
CONNECTICUT

NEW
JERSEY

Pittsburgh
(see inset)

DELAWARE

MARYLAND

MISSOURI

WEST
VIRGINIA

VIRGINIA

KENTUCKY

TENNESSEE

NORTH CAROLINA

ARKANSAS

Atlantic
Ocean

MISSISSIPPI

SOUTH
CAROLINA

LOUISIANA

ALABAMA

GEORGIA

Firms Incorporated into U.S. Steel:
Type of plant:
△ Blast furnace
○ Rolling mill, steel work
□ Bridge-building plant
Companies:
The Carnegie Co.
Federal Steel Co.
National Steel Co.
National Tube Co.
American Tin Plate Co.
American Steel Hoop Co.
American Sheet Steel Co.
American Bridge Co.
Lake Superior Iron Mines
American Steel and Wire
Co. of New Jersey

Gulf of
Mexico

FLORIDA

0   100   200 miles
0   100   200 kilometers

New Kensington

Pittsburgh

Monroeville

McKeesport

Lake Erie

Cleveland

Next!, a cartoon from the magazine *Puck*, September 7, 1904, depicts the Standard Oil Company as an octopus with tentacles wrapped around the copper, steel, and shipping industries, as well as a state house and Congress. One tentacle reaches for the White House.

The Triumph of John D. Rockefeller

If any single name became a byword for enormous wealth, it was John D. Rockefeller, who began his working career as a clerk for a Cleveland merchant and rose to dominate the oil industry. He drove out rival firms through cutthroat competition, arranging secret deals with railroad companies, and fixing prices and production quotas. Rockefeller began with **horizontal expansion**—buying out competing oil refineries. But like Carnegie, he soon established a vertically integrated monopoly, which controlled the drilling, refining, storage, and distribution of oil. By the 1880s, his Standard Oil Company controlled 90 percent of the nation's oil industry. Like Carnegie, Rockefeller gave much of his fortune away, establishing foundations to promote education and medical research. And like Carnegie, he bitterly fought his employees' efforts to organize unions.

Standard Oil

These and other industrial leaders inspired among ordinary Americans a combination of awe, admiration, and hostility. Depending on one's point of view, they were "captains of industry," whose energy and vision pushed the economy forward, or "**robber barons**," who wielded power without any accountability in an unregulated marketplace. Most rose from modest backgrounds and seemed examples of how inventive genius and business sense enabled Americans to seize opportunities for success. But their dictatorial attitudes, unscrupulous methods, repressive labor policies, and exercise of power without any democratic control led to fears that they were undermining political and economic freedom. Concentrated wealth degraded the political process, declared Henry Demarest Lloyd in *Wealth against Commonwealth* (1894), an exposé of how Rockefeller's Standard Oil Company made a mockery of economic competition and political democracy by manipulating the market and bribing legislators. "Liberty and monopoly," Lloyd concluded, "cannot live together."

Captains of industry or robber barons?

A turn-of-the-century photograph of the Casino Grounds, Newport, Rhode Island, an exclusive country club for rich socialites of the Gilded Age.

"The miner's freedom"

Economic insecurity

Workers' Freedom in an Industrial Age

Remarkable as it was, the country's economic growth distributed its benefits very unevenly. For a minority of workers, the rapidly expanding industrial system created new forms of freedom. In some industries, skilled workers commanded high wages and exercised considerable control over the production process. A worker's economic independence now rested on technical skill rather than ownership of one's own shop and tools as in earlier times. What was known as "the miner's freedom" consisted of elaborate work rules that left skilled underground workers free of managerial supervision on the job. Through their union, skilled iron- and steelworkers fixed output quotas and controlled the training of apprentices in the technique of iron rolling. These workers often knew more about the details of production than their employers did.

Such "freedom," however, applied only to a tiny portion of the industrial labor force and had little bearing on the lives of the growing army of semiskilled workers who tended machines in the new factories. For most workers, economic insecurity remained a basic fact of life. During the depressions of the 1870s and 1890s, millions of workers lost their jobs or were forced to accept reductions of pay. The "tramp" became a familiar figure on the social landscape as thousands of men took to the roads in search of work. Many industrial workers labored sixty-hour weeks with no pensions, compensation for injuries, or protections against unemployment. Although American workers received higher wages than their counterparts in Europe, they also experienced more dangerous working conditions. Between 1880 and 1900, an average of 35,000 workers perished each year in factory and mine accidents, the highest rate in the industrial world.

Much of the working class remained desperately poor and to survive needed income from all family members. In 1888, the *Chicago Times* published a series of articles by reporter Nell Cusack under the title "City Slave Girls," exposing wretched conditions among the growing number of women working for wages in the city's homes, factories, and sweatshops. The articles unleashed a flood of letters to the editor from women workers. One woman singled out domestic service—still the largest employment category for women—as "a slave's life," with "long hours, late and early, seven days in the week, bossed and ordered about as before the war."

Sunshine and Shadow: Increasing Wealth and Poverty

At the other end of the economic spectrum, the era witnessed an unprecedented accumulation of wealth. Class divisions became more and more visible. In frontier days, all classes in San Francisco, for example, lived near the waterfront. In the late nineteenth century, upper-class families built mansions on Nob Hill and Van Ness Avenue (known as "millionaire's row"). In eastern cities as well, the rich increasingly resided in their own exclusive neighborhoods and vacationed among members of their own class at exclusive resorts like Newport, Rhode Island. The growing urban middle class of professionals, office workers, and small businessmen moved to new urban and suburban neighborhoods linked to central business districts by streetcars and commuter railways. "Passion for money," wrote the novelist Edith Wharton in *The House of Mirth* (1905), dominated society. Wharton's book traced the difficulties of Lily Bart, a young woman of modest means pressured by her mother and New York high society to "barter" her beauty for marriage to a rich husband in a world where "to be poor . . . amounted to disgrace."

Baxter Street Court, 1890, one of numerous photographs by Jacob Riis depicting living conditions in New York City's slums.

By 1890, the richest 1 percent of Americans received the same total income as the bottom half of the population and owned more property than the remaining 99 percent. Many of the wealthiest Americans consciously pursued an aristocratic lifestyle, building palatial homes, attending exclusive social clubs, schools, and colleges, holding fancy-dress balls, and marrying into each other's families. In 1899, the economist and social historian Thorstein Veblen published *The Theory of the Leisure Class*, a devastating critique of an upper-class culture focused on "conspicuous consumption"—that is, spending money not on needed or even desired goods, but simply to demonstrate the possession of wealth. One of the era's most widely publicized spectacles was an elaborate costume ball organized in 1897 by Mrs. Bradley Martin, the daughter of a New York railroad financier. The theme was the royal court of prerevolutionary France. The Waldorf-Astoria Hotel was decorated to look like the palace of Versailles, the guests wore the dress of the French nobility, and the hostess bedecked herself with the actual jewels of Queen Marie Antoinette.

The top 1 percent

Not that far from the Waldorf, much of the working class lived in desperate conditions. Matthew Smith's 1868 best-seller *Sunshine and Shadow in New York* opened with an engraving that contrasted department store magnate Alexander T. Stewart's two-million-dollar mansion with housing in the city's slums. Two

The opening image in Matthew Smith's book, *Sunshine and Shadow in New York* (1868), contrasts the living conditions of the city's rich and poor.

The Turner thesis

Opportunity and hardship in the West

decades later, Jacob Riis, in *How the Other Half Lives* (1890), offered a shocking account of living conditions among the urban poor, complete with photographs of apartments in dark, airless, overcrowded tenement houses.

THE TRANSFORMATION OF THE WEST

Nowhere did capitalism penetrate more rapidly or dramatically than in the trans-Mississippi West, whose "vast, trackless spaces," as the poet Walt Whitman called them, were now absorbed into the expanding economy. At the close of the Civil War, the frontier of continuous white settlement did not extend very far beyond the Mississippi River. To the west lay millions of acres of fertile and mineral-rich land roamed by giant herds of buffalo whose meat and hides provided food, clothing, and shelter for a population of more than 250,000 Indians.

In 1893, the historian Frederick Jackson Turner gave a celebrated lecture, "The Significance of the Frontier in American History," in which he argued that on the western frontier the distinctive qualities of American culture were forged: individual freedom, political democracy, and economic mobility. The West, he added, acted as a "safety valve," drawing off those dissatisfied with their situation in the East and therefore counteracting the threat of social unrest. Turner's was one of the most influential interpretations of American history ever developed. But his lecture summarized attitudes toward the West that had been widely shared among Americans long before 1893. Ever since the beginning of colonial settlement in British North America, the West—a region whose definition shifted as the population expanded—had been seen as a place of opportunity for those seeking to improve their condition in life.

Many Americans did indeed experience the westward movement in the way Turner described it. From farmers moving into Ohio, Indiana, and Illinois in the decades after the American Revolution to prospectors who struck it rich in the California gold rush of the mid-nineteenth century, millions of Americans and immigrants from abroad found in the westward movement a path to economic opportunity. But Turner seemed to portray the West as an empty space before the coming of white settlers. In fact, of course, it was already inhabited by Native Americans, whose dispossession was essential to the opening of land for settlement by others. Moreover, the West was hardly a uniform paradise of small, independent farmers. Landlords, railroads, and mining companies in the West also utilized Mexican migrant and indentured labor, Chinese working on long-term contracts, and, until the end of the Civil War, African-American slaves.

A Diverse Region

The West, of course, was hardly a single area. West of the Mississippi River lay a variety of regions, all marked by remarkable physical beauty—the Great Plains, the Rocky Mountains, the desert of the Southwest, the Sierra Nevada, and the valleys and coastline of California and the Pacific Northwest. It would take many decades before individual settlers and corporate business enterprises penetrated all these areas. But the process was far advanced by the end of the nineteenth century.

The political and economic incorporation of the American West was part of a global process. In many parts of the world, indigenous inhabitants—the Mapuche in Chile, the Zulu in South Africa, Aboriginal peoples in Australia, American Indians—were pushed aside (often after fierce resistance) as centralizing governments brought large interior regions under their control. In the United States, the incorporation of the West required the active intervention of the federal government, which acquired Indian land by war and treaty, administered land sales, regulated territorial politics, and distributed land and money to farmers, railroads, and mining companies. Western states used land donated by the federal government, in accordance with the Morrill Land-Grant Act passed during the Civil War, to establish public universities. And, of course, the abolition of slavery by the Thirteenth Amendment decided the long contest over whether the West would be a society based on free or slave labor.

Newly created western territories such as Arizona, Idaho, Montana, and the Dakotas remained under federal control far longer than had been the pattern in the East. Eastern territories had taken an average of thirteen years to achieve statehood; it took New Mexico sixty-two years to do so, Arizona forty-nine, and Utah forty-six. Many easterners were wary of granting statehood to the territories until white and non-Mormon settlers counterbalanced the large Latino and Mormon populations.

In the twentieth century, the construction of federally financed irrigation systems and dams would open large areas to commercial farming. Ironically, the West would become known (not least to its own inhabitants) as a place of rugged individualism and sturdy independence. But without active governmental assistance, the region could never have been settled and developed.

Having been granted millions of acres of land by the federal and state governments, railroads sought to encourage emigration to the West so they could sell real estate to settlers. This is a post–Civil War advertisement by a Texas railroad.

The family of David Hilton on their Nebraska homestead in 1887. The Hiltons insisted on being photographed with their organ, away from the modest sod house in which they lived, to represent their aspiration for prosperity.

An engraving from the early 1880s of a California farm adjacent to the Southern Pacific Railroad. Having been granted vast tracts of land by the federal government, the railroad encouraged settlement along its lines.

RES. & RANCH OF H. P. GRAY, EAST OF LEMORE, TULARE CO. CAL.

Farming on the Middle Border

Even as sporadic Indian wars raged, settlers poured into the West. Territorial and state governments eager for population, and railroad companies anxious to sell land they had acquired from the government, flooded European countries and eastern cities with promotional literature promising easy access to land. More land came into cultivation in the thirty years after the Civil War than in the previous two and a half centuries of American history. Hundreds of thousands of families acquired farms under the Homestead Act, and even more purchased land from speculators and from railroad companies that had been granted immense tracts of public land by the federal government. A new agricultural empire producing wheat and corn for national and international markets arose on the Middle Border (Minnesota, the Dakotas, Nebraska, and Kansas), whose population rose from 300,000 in 1860 to 5 million in 1900. The farmers were a diverse group, including native-born easterners, blacks escaping the post-Reconstruction South, and immigrants from Canada, Germany, Scandinavia, and Great Britain. Although ethnic diversity is generally associated with eastern cities, in the late nineteenth century the most multicultural state in the Union was North Dakota.

The new agricultural empire of the West

Despite the promises of promotional pamphlets, farming on the Great Plains was not an easy task. Difficulties came in many forms—from the poisonous rattlesnakes that lived in the tall prairie grass to the blizzards and droughts that periodically afflicted the region. Much of the burden fell on women. Farm families generally invested in the kinds of labor-saving machinery that would bring in cash, not machines that would ease women's burdens in the household (like the back-breaking task of doing laundry). While husbands and sons tended to devote their labor to cash crops, farm wives cared for animals, grew crops for food, and cooked and cleaned. A farm woman in Arizona described her morning chores in her diary:

Farm women

"Get up, turn out my chickens, draw a pail of water . . . make a fire, put potatoes to cook, brush and sweep half inch of dust off floor, feed three litters of chickens, then mix biscuits, get breakfast, milk, besides work in the house, and this morning had to go half mile after calves." On far-flung homesteads, many miles from schools, medical care, and sources of entertainment, farm families suffered from loneliness and isolation—a problem especially severe for women when their husbands left, sometimes for weeks at a time, to market their crops.

Bonanza Farms

John Wesley Powell, the explorer and geologist who surveyed the Middle Border in the 1870s, warned that because of the region's arid land and limited rainfall, development there required large-scale irrigation projects. The model of family farming envisioned by the Homestead Act of 1862 could not apply: no single family could do all the work required on irrigated farms—only cooperative, communal farming could succeed, Powell maintained.

An arid land

Despite the emergence of a few **bonanza farms** that covered thousands of acres and employed large numbers of agricultural wage workers, family farms still dominated the trans-Mississippi West. Even small farmers, however, became increasingly oriented to national and international markets, specializing in the production of single crops for sale in faraway places. At the same time, railroads brought factory-made goods to rural people, replacing items previously produced in farmers' homes. Farm families became more and more dependent on loans to purchase land, machinery, and industrial products, and more and more vulnerable to the ups and downs of prices for agricultural goods in the world market. Agriculture reflected how the international economy was becoming more integrated. The combination of economic depressions and expanding agricultural production in places like Argentina, Australia, and the American West pushed prices of farm products steadily downward. From Italy and Ireland to China, India, and the American South, small farmers throughout the world suffered severe difficulties

Agriculture and the international economy

California Harvest Scene—Dr. Glenn's Farm in Colusa County, an engraving from 1876, illustrates the large scale of operations and heavy investment in machinery common on western "bonanza" farms.

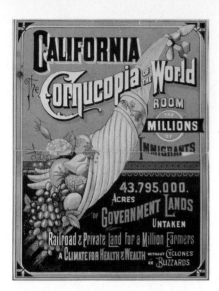

In the late 1800s, California tried to attract immigrants by advertising its pleasant climate and the availability of land, although large-scale corporate farms were coming to dominate the state's agriculture.

The cattle kingdom

Western industries

in the last quarter of the nineteenth century. Many joined the migration to cities within their countries or the increasing international migration of labor.

The future of western farming ultimately lay with giant agricultural enterprises relying heavily on irrigation, chemicals, and machinery—investments far beyond the means of family farmers. A preview of the agricultural future was already evident in California, where, as far back as Spanish and Mexican days, landownership had been concentrated in large units. In the late nineteenth century, California's giant fruit and vegetable farms, owned by corporations like the Southern Pacific Railroad, were tilled not by agricultural laborers who could expect to acquire land of their own, but by migrant laborers from China, the Philippines, Japan, and Mexico, who tramped from place to place following the ripening crops.

In the 1870s, California's "wheat barons," who owned ranches of 30,000 or more acres, shipped their grain from San Francisco all the way to Great Britain, while large-scale growers in the new "Orange Empire" of the southern part of the state sent fruit east by rail, packaged in crates bedecked with images of an Edenic landscape filled with lush orchards.

The Cowboy and the Corporate West

The two decades following the Civil War also witnessed the golden age of the cattle kingdom. The Kansas Pacific Railroad's stations at Abilene, Dodge City, and Wichita, Kansas, became destinations for the fabled drives of millions of cattle from Texas. A collection of white, Mexican, and black men who conducted the cattle drives, the cowboys became symbols of a life of freedom on the open range. Their exploits would later serve as the theme of many a Hollywood movie, and their clothing inspired fashions that remain popular today. But there was nothing romantic about the life of the cowboys, most of whom were low-paid wage workers. (Texas cowboys even went on strike for higher pay in 1883.) The days of the long-distance cattle drive ended in the mid-1880s, as farmers enclosed more and more of the open range with barbed-wire fences, making it difficult to graze cattle on the grasslands of the Great Plains, and two terrible winters destroyed millions of cattle. When the industry recuperated, it was reorganized in large, enclosed ranches close to rail connections.

The West was more than a farming empire. By 1890, a higher percentage of its population lived in cities than was the case in other regions. The economic focus of California's economy remained San Francisco, a major manufacturing center and one of the world's great trading ports. The explosive growth of southern California began in the 1880s, first with tourism, heavily promoted by railroad companies, followed by the discovery of oil in Los Angeles in 1892. Large corporate enterprises appeared throughout the West. The lumber industry, dominated by small-scale producers in 1860, came under the control of corporations that acquired large tracts of forest and employed armies of loggers. Lumbermen had cut trees in the Far West's vast forests since the days of Spanish and Mexican rule. Now, with rising demand for wood for buildings in urban centers and with new railroads making it possible to send timber quickly to the East, production expanded rapidly. Sawmills sprang up near rail lines, and lumber companies acquired thousands of acres of timber land. Loggers who had migrated from the East and Midwest and were used to cutting pine trees had to develop new techniques for felling the far larger giant

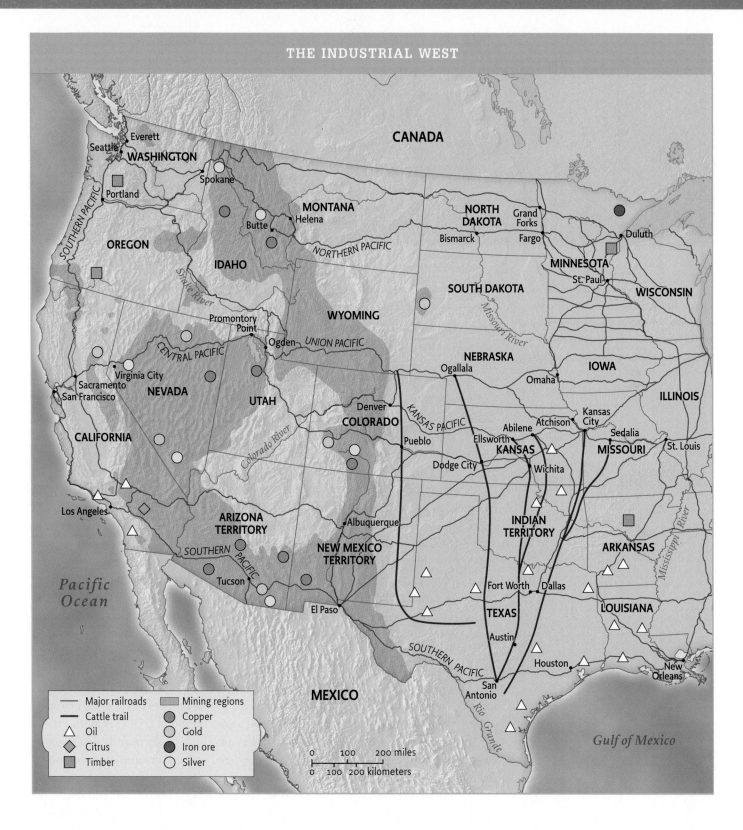

THE INDUSTRIAL WEST

CANADA

WASHINGTON
Everett
Seattle
Spokane
Portland

OREGON

MONTANA
Butte
Helena

IDAHO

Snake River

NORTHERN PACIFIC

NORTH DAKOTA
Grand Forks
Bismarck
Fargo

MINNESOTA
St. Paul
Duluth

WISCONSIN

SOUTH DAKOTA

Missouri River

WYOMING

Promontory Point
Ogden
UNION PACIFIC

CENTRAL PACIFIC

Virginia City
Sacramento
San Francisco

NEVADA

UTAH

NEBRASKA
Ogallala
Omaha

IOWA

ILLINOIS

Colorado River

Denver
COLORADO

KANSAS PACIFIC

Pueblo
Dodge City

KANSAS
Abilene
Ellsworth
Wichita

Atchison
Kansas City
Sedalia
St. Louis

MISSOURI

CALIFORNIA

Los Angeles

ARIZONA TERRITORY

Tucson

SOUTHERN PACIFIC

Albuquerque

NEW MEXICO TERRITORY

El Paso

INDIAN TERRITORY

ARKANSAS

Mississippi River

Fort Worth
Dallas

TEXAS

Austin

Houston

LOUISIANA

New Orleans

Pacific Ocean

MEXICO

San Antonio

Rio Grande

SOUTHERN PACIFIC

Gulf of Mexico

Legend	
— Major railroads	▢ Mining regions
▬ Cattle trail	● Copper
△ Oil	○ Gold
◇ Citrus	● Iron ore
▢ Timber	○ Silver

0   100   200 miles
0   100   200 kilometers

A photograph of Denver, Colorado, in the early 1890s. Although generally thought of as a region of rural pioneers, the West, like the East, experienced rapid urbanization.

Mining in the West

New Mexico

redwoods of northern California. Once they did, coastal forests were decimated, with the high-quality wood being used to construct many of the buildings in San Francisco and other communities. In the early twentieth century, the desire to save the remaining redwoods would become one inspiration for the conservation movement.

Western mining, from Michigan iron ore and copper to gold and silver in California, Nevada, and Colorado, fell under the sway of companies that mobilized eastern and European investment to introduce advanced technology. Gold and silver rushes took place in the Dakotas in 1876, Idaho in 1883, Colorado in the 1890s, and Alaska at the end of the century. Railroad hubs like Albuquerque, Denver, El Paso, and Tucson flourished as gateways to the new mineral regions. But as in California after 1848, the independent prospector working a surface mine with his pick and shovel quickly gave way to deep-shaft corporate mining employing wage workers. As with other western industries, the coming of the railroad greatly expanded the possibilities for mining, making it possible to ship minerals from previously inaccessible places. Moreover, professionally trained engineers from the East and Europe introduced new scientific techniques of mining and smelting ore. For example, the town of Leadville, Colorado, which did not exist before the mid-1870s, became one of the world's great centers of lead production after August R. Meyer, a European mining engineer, analyzed the precise content of silver and lead in the area's minerals. The economic crosscurrents at work in post–Civil War mining were illustrated at Butte, Montana. In the 1880s, absentee owners from San Francisco poured millions of dollars into what they thought was a silver mine, only to learn that they had acquired one of the world's richest deposits of copper. A new town, Anaconda, quickly arose, with a population of 2,000 miners, smelters, engineers, and others, from a wide variety of ethnic backgrounds. In the early twentieth century, the company would be acquired by bankers and other investors from the East.

A similar process occurred in New Mexico, where traditional life based on sheep farming on land owned in common by Mexican villagers had continued more or less unchanged after the United States acquired the area in the Mexican War. The existence of these Spanish and Mexican communal landholdings may have influenced John Wesley Powell's recommendations concerning communal farming. Railroads reached the area in the 1870s, bringing with them eastern mining companies and commercial ranchers and farmers. Because courts only recognized Mexican-era land titles to individual plots of land, communal landholdings were increasingly made available for sale to newcomers. By 1880, three-quarters of New Mexico's sheep belonged to just twenty families. Unable to continue as sheep raisers, more and more Hispanic residents went to work for the new mines and railroads.

A family festival in San Juan, a town in southern California, around 1880. Long after the area was annexed to the United States, the Spanish-speaking residents continued their traditional religious and cultural practices.

The Chinese Presence

Chinese immigration, which had begun at the time of the California gold rush, continued in the postwar years. Before the Civil War, nearly all Chinese newcomers had been unattached men, brought in by labor contractors to work in western gold fields, railroad construction, and factories. In the early 1870s, entire Chinese families began to immigrate. By 1880, 105,000 persons of Chinese descent lived in the United States. Three-quarters lived in California, where Chinese made up over half of the state's farm workers. But Chinese immigrants were present throughout the West and in all sorts of jobs. After the completion of the transcontinental railroad in 1869, many worked in construction on other railroad lines that sprang up throughout the region. Chinese could be found in mines in Idaho, Colorado, and Nevada, as domestic workers in urban households, and in factories producing cigars, clothing, and shoes in western cities. They built levees, drained agricultural fields, and worked on fishing boats. Many men had wives and children in China, and like members of other immigrant groups, they kept in touch by sending letters and money to their families at home and reading magazines aimed at emigrants that reported on local events in China. As will be related in the next chapter, their growing presence sparked an outpouring of anti-Chinese sentiment, leading to laws excluding virtually all Chinese from entering the country.

Conflict on the Mormon Frontier

The Mormons had moved to the Great Salt Lake Valley in the 1840s, hoping to practice their religion free of the persecution that they had encountered in the East. They envisioned their community in Utah as the foundation of a great empire they called Deseret. Given the widespread unpopularity of Mormon polygamy and the close connection of church and state in Mormon theology, conflict with both the federal government and the growing numbers of non-Mormons moving west became inevitable. In 1857, after receiving reports that the work of federal judges in Utah was being obstructed by the territorial governor, the Mormon leader Brigham Young, President James Buchanan removed Young and appointed a non-Mormon to replace him. Young refused to comply, and federal troops entered the Salt Lake Valley, where they remained until the beginning of the Civil War. During this time of tension, a group of Mormons attacked a wagon train of non-Mormon settlers traveling through Utah and intending to settle in California. What came to be

Deseret

Mountain Meadows Massacre

called the Mountain Meadows Massacre resulted in the death of all the adults and older children in the wagon train—over 100 persons. Only a handful of young children survived. Nearly twenty years later, one leader of the assault was convicted of murder and executed.

A ban on polygamy

After the Civil War, Mormon leaders sought to avoid further antagonizing the federal government. In the 1880s, Utah banned the practice of polygamy, a prohibition written into the state constitution as a requirement before Utah gained admission as a state in 1896.

The Subjugation of the Plains Indians

The new West and the Plains Indians

The transcontinental railroad, a symbol of the reunited nation, brought tens of thousands of newcomers to the West and stimulated the expansion of farming, mining, and other enterprises. The incorporation of the West into the national economy spelled the doom of the Plains Indians and their world. Their lives had already undergone profound transformations. In the eighteenth century, the spread of horses, originally introduced by the Spanish, led to a wholesale shift from farming and hunting on foot to mounted hunting of buffalo. New Indian groups migrated to the Great Plains to take advantage of the horse, coalescing into the great tribes of the nineteenth century—the Cheyenne, Comanche, Crow, Kiowa, and Sioux. Persistent warfare took place between the more established tribes and newcomers, including Indians removed from the East, who sought access to their hunting grounds.

Most migrants on the Oregon and California Trails before the Civil War encountered little hostility from Indians, often trading with them for food and supplies. But as settlers encroached on Indian lands, bloody conflict between the army and Plains tribes began in the 1850s and continued for decades.

In 1869, President Ulysses S. Grant announced a new "peace policy" in the West, but warfare soon resumed. Drawing on methods used to defeat the Confederacy,

Albert Bierstadt's 1863 painting, *The Rocky Mountains, Lander's Peak*, depicts Indians as an integral part of the majestic landscape of the West.

This pencil-and-crayon drawing by a Cheyenne Indian from the 1880s depicts a Native American fighting two black members of the U.S. military. After the Civil War, black soldiers, whose presence was resented by many whites, in the North as well as the South, were reassigned to the West.

Hunters shooting buffalo as the Kansas Pacific Railroad cuts across the West, 1870s.

Civil War generals like Philip H. Sheridan set out to destroy the foundations of the Indian economy—villages, horses, and especially the buffalo. Hunting by mounted Indians had already reduced the buffalo population—estimated at 30 million in 1800—but it was army campaigns and the depredations of hunters seeking buffalo hides that rendered the vast herds all but extinct. By 1886, an expedition from the Smithsonian Institution in Washington had difficulty finding twenty-five "good specimens." "A cold wind blew across the prairie when the last buffalo fell," said the Sioux leader Sitting Bull, "a death-wind for my people."

The buffalo

"Let Me Be a Free Man"

The army's relentless attacks broke the power of one tribe after another. In 1877, troops commanded by former Freedmen's Bureau commissioner O. O. Howard pursued the Nez Percé Indians on a 1,700-mile chase across the Far West. The Nez Percé (whose name was given them by Lewis and Clark in 1805 and means "pierced

The Nez Percé

VOICES OF FREEDOM

From SPEECH OF CHIEF JOSEPH OF THE NEZ PERCÉ INDIANS, IN WASHINGTON, D.C. (1879)

Chief Joseph, leader of the Nez Percé Indians, led his people on a 1,700-mile trek through the Far West in 1877 in an unsuccessful effort to escape to Canada. Two years later, he addressed an audience in Washington, D.C., that included President Rutherford B. Hayes, appealing for the freedom and equal rights enshrined in the law after the Civil War.

I have heard talk and talk, but nothing is done. Good words do not last long unless they amount to something. Words do not pay for my dead people. They do not pay for my country, now overrun by white men. . . . Good words will not get my people a home where they can live in peace and take care of themselves. I am tired of talk that comes to nothing. It makes my heart sick when I remember all the . . . broken promises. . . .

If the white man wants to live in peace with the Indian he can live in peace. There need be no trouble. Treat all men alike. Give them the same law. Give them all an even chance to live and grow. All men were made by the same Great Spirit Chief. They are all brothers. The earth is the mother of all people, and all people should have equal rights upon it. You might as well expect the rivers to run backward as that any man who was born a free man should be contented when penned up and denied liberty to go where he pleases. . . .

When I think of our condition my heart is heavy. I see men of my race treated as outlaws and driven from country to country, or shot down like animals. I know that my race must change. We cannot hold our own with the white men as we are. We only ask an even chance to live as other men live. . . .

Let me be a free man—free to travel, free to stop, free to work, free to trade where I choose, free to choose my own teachers, free to follow the religion of my fathers, free to think and talk and act for myself—and I will obey every law, or submit to the penalty.

From LETTER BY SAUM SONG BO, AMERICAN MISSIONARY (OCTOBER 1885)

During the 1880s, Chinese-Americans were subjected to discrimination in every phase of their lives. In 1882, Congress temporarily barred further immigration from China. In 1885, when funds were being raised to build a pedestal for the Statue of Liberty, Saum Song Bo, a Chinese-American writer, contrasted the celebration of liberty with the treatment of the Chinese.

A paper was presented to me yesterday for inspection, and I found it to be specially drawn up for subscription among my countrymen toward the Pedestal Fund of the . . . Statue of Liberty. . . . But the word liberty makes me think of the fact that this country is the land of liberty for men of all nations except the Chinese. I consider it as an insult to us Chinese to call on us to contribute toward building in this land a pedestal for a statue of Liberty. That statue represents Liberty holding a torch which lights the passage of those of all nations who come into this country. But are the Chinese allowed to come? As for the Chinese who are here, are they allowed to enjoy liberty as men of all other nationalities enjoy it? Are they allowed to go about everywhere free from the insults, abuses, assaults, wrongs, and injuries from which men of other nationalities are free? . . .

And this statue of Liberty is a gift from another people who do not love liberty for the Chinese. [To] the Annamese and Tonquinese Chinese [colonial subjects of the French empire in Indochina], . . . liberty is as dear as to the French. What right have the French to deprive them of their liberty?

Whether this statute against the Chinese or the statue to Liberty will be the most lasting monument to tell future ages of the liberty and greatness of this country, will be known only to future generations.

QUESTIONS

1. *What are Chief Joseph's complaints about the treatment of his people?*

2. *Why does Saum Song Bo believe that the Chinese do not enjoy liberty in the United States?*

3. *What are the similarities and differences in the definition of freedom in the two documents?*

Chief Joseph of the Nez Percé, in a photograph possibly taken in Washington, D.C., in 1879, when he was part of an Indian delegation to the nation's capital.

The Comanche Empire

The end of the treaty system

nose" in French) were seeking to escape to Canada after fights with settlers who had encroached on tribal lands in Oregon and Idaho. After four months, Howard forced the Indians to surrender, and they were removed to Oklahoma.

Two years later, the Nez Percé leader, Chief Joseph, delivered a speech in Washington to a distinguished audience that included President Rutherford B. Hayes. Condemning the policy of confining Indians to reservations, Joseph adopted the language of freedom and equal rights before the law so powerfully reinforced by the Civil War and Reconstruction. "Treat all men alike," he pleaded. "Give them the same law. . . . Let me be a free man—free to travel, free to stop, free to work, free to trade where I choose, free to . . . think and talk and act for myself." The government eventually transported the surviving Nez Percé to another reservation in Washington Territory. Until his death in 1904, Joseph would unsuccessfully petition successive presidents for his people's right to return to their beloved Oregon homeland.

Indians occasionally managed to inflict costly delay and even defeat on army units. The most famous Indian victory took place in June 1876 at the **Battle of the Little Bighorn**, when General George A. Custer and his entire command of 250 men perished. The Sioux and Cheyenne warriors, led by Sitting Bull and Crazy Horse, were defending tribal land in the Black Hills of the Dakota Territory. Reserved for them in an 1868 treaty "for as long as the grass shall grow," their lands had been invaded by whites after the discovery of gold. Eventually the Sioux were worn down, partly because of the decimation of the buffalo, and relinquished their claim to the Black Hills. In the Southwest, Cochise, Geronimo, and other leaders of the Apache, who had been relocated by the government a number of times, led bands that crossed and recrossed the border with Mexico, evading the army and occasionally killing civilians. They would not surrender until the mid-1880s.

Another casualty was the Comanche empire, centered in modern-day New Mexico and Colorado. Beginning in the mid-eighteenth century, the Comanche dominated much of the Great Plains and Southwest. The Comanche subordinated local Indian groups to their power, imposed a toll on trade routes like the Santa Fe Trail, and dealt for a time as an equal with the Spanish, French, and American governments. Their power was not finally broken until the 1870s.

Remaking Indian Life

"The life my people want is a life of freedom," Sitting Bull declared. The Indian idea of freedom, however, which centered on preserving their cultural and political autonomy and control of ancestral lands, conflicted with the interests and values of most white Americans. Nearly all officials believed that the federal government should persuade or force the Plains Indians to surrender most of their land and to exchange their religion, communal property, nomadic way of life, and gender relations for Christian worship, private ownership, and small farming on reservations with men tilling the fields and women working in the home.

In 1871, Congress eliminated the treaty system that dated back to the revolutionary era, by which the federal government negotiated agreements with Indians as if they were independent nations. This step was supported by railroad companies that found tribal sovereignty an obstacle to construction and by Republicans who believed that it contradicted the national unity born of the Civil War. The federal government pressed forward with its assault on Indian culture. The Bureau of Indian Affairs established boarding schools where Indian children, removed from the "negative" influences of their parents and tribes, were dressed in non-Indian clothes, given new names, and educated in white ways.

The Dawes Act

The crucial step in attacking "tribalism" came in 1887 with the passage of the **Dawes Act**, named for Senator Henry L. Dawes of Massachusetts, chair of the Senate's Indian Affairs Committee. The Act broke up the land of nearly all tribes into small parcels to be distributed to Indian families, with the remainder auctioned off to white purchasers. Indians who accepted the farms and "adopted the habits of civilized life" would become full-fledged American citizens. The policy proved to be a disaster, leading to the loss of much tribal land and the erosion of Indian cultural traditions. Whites, however, benefited enormously. When the government made 2 million acres of Indian land available in Oklahoma, 50,000 white settlers poured into the territory to claim farms on the single day of April 22, 1889. Further land rushes followed in the 1890s. In the half century after the passage of the Dawes Act, Indians lost 86 million of the 138 million acres of land in their possession in 1887. Overall, according to one estimate, between 1776 and today, via the "right of discovery," treaties, executive orders, court decisions, and outright theft, the United States has acquired over 1.5 billion acres of land from Native Americans, an area twenty-five times as large as Great Britain.

Between Two Worlds, a drawing produced in the 1870s by the Kiowa warrior Wohaw when he was a prisoner in Fort Marion, Florida. Wohaw depicts himself being torn between his traditional way of life, represented by the buffalo, and the culture whites were trying to force him to accept, symbolized by the steer and tiny farmhouse. Wohaw later returned to the West and served in the U.S. Army.

Indian Citizenship

Many laws and treaties in the nineteenth century offered Indians the right to become American citizens if they left the tribal setting and assimilated into American society. But tribal identity was the one thing nearly every Indian wished to maintain, and very few took advantage of these offers. Thus, few Indians were recognized as American citizens. Western courts ruled that the rights guaranteed by the Fourteenth and Fifteenth Amendments did not apply to them, and in *Elk v. Wilkins* (1884) the U.S. Supreme Court agreed, even though John Elk had left his tribe in Oklahoma and lived among white settlers in Nebraska. The Court questioned whether any Indian had achieved the degree of "civilization" required of American citizens.

> Elk v. Wilkins

By 1900, roughly 53,000 Indians had become American citizens by accepting land allotments under the Dawes Act. The following year, Congress granted citizenship to 100,000 residents of Indian Territory (in present-day Oklahoma). The remainder would have to wait until 1919 (for those who fought in World War I) and 1924, when Congress made all Indians American citizens.

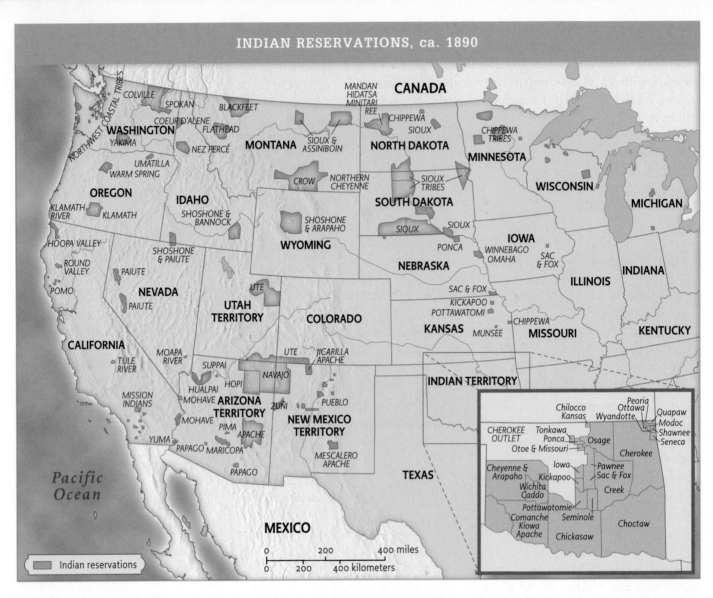

INDIAN RESERVATIONS, ca. 1890

By 1890, the vast majority of the remaining Indian population had been removed to reservations scattered across the western states.

The Ghost Dance and Wounded Knee

A religious movement

Some Indians sought solace in the **Ghost Dance**, a religious revitalization campaign reminiscent of the pan-Indian movements led by earlier prophets like Neolin and Tenskwatawa (discussed in Chapters 4 and 8). Its leaders foretold a day when whites would disappear, the buffalo would return, and Indians could once again practice their ancestral customs "free from misery, death, and disease." Large numbers of Indians gathered for days of singing, dancing, and religious observances. Fearing a general uprising, the government sent troops to the reservations. On December 29, 1890, soldiers opened fire on Ghost Dancers encamped near Wounded Knee Creek in South Dakota, killing between 150 and 200 Indians, mostly women and children.

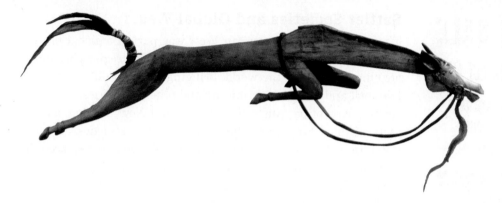

One of the masterpieces of Native American art, this three-foot-long wood sculpture carved by a Lakota Sioux artist around 1870 honors a dead or wounded horse. It has a horsehair mane and tail and leather reins and bridle, and there are holes representing bullet wounds on the torso and red paint representing blood. The horse may be leaping from life to death.

The **Wounded Knee massacre** was widely applauded in the press. An Army Court of Inquiry essentially exonerated the troops and their commander, and twenty soldiers were later awarded the Medal of Honor, a recognition of exceptional heroism in battle, for their actions at Wounded Knee. Like federal efforts to exert control over the Mormons in Utah, the suppression of the Ghost Dance revealed the limits on Americans' efforts to seek in the West the freedom to practice nonmainstream religions.

The Wounded Knee massacre marked the end of four centuries of armed conflict between the continent's native population and European settlers and their descendants. By 1900, the Indian population had fallen to 250,000, the lowest point in American history. A children's book about Indians published around this time stated flatly, "The Indian pictured in these pages no longer exists." Yet despite everything, Indians survived, and in the twentieth century their numbers once again would begin to grow.

Responses to Wounded Knee

Boys from the Lakota tribe on their arrival (*left*) and during their stay at Carlisle, a boarding school that aimed to "civilize" Indians, by J. N. Choate, a local photographer.

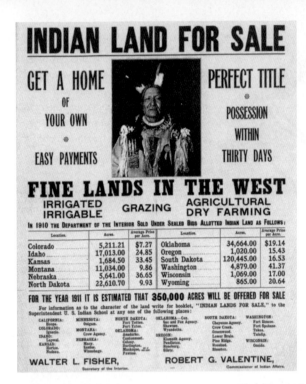

INDIAN LAND FOR SALE

GET A HOME
OF
YOUR OWN
*
EASY PAYMENTS

PERFECT TITLE
*
POSSESSION
WITHIN
THIRTY DAYS

FINE LANDS IN THE WEST
IRRIGATED
IRRIGABLE   GRAZING   AGRICULTURAL
DRY FARMING

WALTER L. FISHER,
Secretary of the Interior.

ROBERT G. VALENTINE,
Commissioner of Indian Affairs.

A 1911 poster advertising the federal government's sale of land formerly possessed by Indians. Under the Dawes Act of 1887, Indian families were allotted individual farms and the remaining land on reservations, so-called surplus land, was made available to whites.

Settler Societies and Global Wests

The conquest of the American West was part of a global process whereby settlers moved boldly into the interior of regions in temperate climates around the world, bringing their familiar crops and livestock and establishing mining and other industries. Countries such as Argentina, Australia, Canada, and New Zealand, as well as the United States, are often called "settler societies," because immigrants from overseas quickly outnumbered and displaced the original inhabitants—unlike in India and most parts of colonial Africa, where fewer Europeans ventured and those who did relied on the labor of the indigenous inhabitants.

In the late nineteenth century, even as the population of the American West grew dramatically, Canada marked the completion of its first transcontinental railroad, although the more severe climate limited the number of western settlers to a much smaller population than in the American West (and as a result, the displacement of Indians did not produce as much conflict and bloodshed). In many settler societies, native peoples were subjected to cultural reconstruction similar to policies in the United States. In Australia, the government gathered the Aboriginal populations—their numbers devastated by disease—in "reserves" reminiscent of American Indian reservations. Australia went further than the United States in the forced assimilation of surviving Aboriginal peoples. The government removed large numbers of children from their families to be adopted by whites—a policy only abandoned in the 1970s and for which the prime minister formally apologized in 2008 in a national moment of reconciliation called Sorry Day.

The ghost dance, performed by a group of Sioux Indians, as depicted by the artist Frederic Remington in *Harper's Weekly*, December 6, 1890.

Myth, Reality, and the Wild West

The West has long played many roles in Americans' national self-consciousness. It has been imagined as a place of individual freedom and unbridled opportunity for those dissatisfied with their lives in the East and as a future empire that would dominate the continent and the world. Even as farms, mines, and cities spread over the landscape in the post–Civil War years, a new image of the West began to circulate—the Wild West, a lawless place ruled by cowboys and Indians (two groups by this time vastly outnumbered by other westerners), and marked by gunfights, cattle drives, and stagecoach robberies.

An advertisement for Buffalo Bill's Wild West Show, which brought an image of the West as a violent yet romantic place of gunfights, Indian rituals, and buffalo hunts to audiences in the East and Europe.

This image of a violent yet romantic frontier world would later become a staple of Hollywood movies. In the late nineteenth century, it was disseminated in vaudeville shows that achieved immense popularity. Although not the first, William "Buffalo Bill" Cody was the most important popularizer of this idea of the West. A former hunter and scout for the U.S. Army, Cody developed an elaborate theatrical presentation that toured for decades across the United States and Europe. Buffalo Bill's Wild West Show included reenactments of battles with Indians (including Custer's Last Stand), buffalo hunts, Indian rituals, and feats by the sharpshooter Annie Oakley. Along with Cody, other persons who had actually participated in these events appeared in the show, including the Indian warrior Sitting Bull and a group of Sioux fighters. The image of the Wild West also circulated in cheap popular books known as dime novels and sensational journalistic accounts.

Theater audiences and readers found fantasies of adventure in observing western violence from a safe distance and marveled at the skills of horseback riding, roping, and shooting on display. They imagined the West as a timeless place immune to the corruptions of civilization, which offered a striking contrast to the increasingly sedentary lives of men in eastern cities. Indeed, despite the inclusion of Oakley, this West of the imagination was emphatically a male preserve. The real West—for example, the struggles of farm families—played no role in this depiction. Nor did pervasive labor conflict in mining centers, or the role of the federal government and eastern capital in the region's development. The West's multiracial, multiethnic population also disappeared, although different groups added their own elements to the mythical west. Mexican-Americans, for example, made a folk hero of Gregorio Cortez, a Texas outlaw renowned for his ability to outwit pursuers. The West Coast also had no place in the picture—the imagined West seemed to stop at the Rocky Mountains.

> *Fantasies of the West*

POLITICS IN A GILDED AGE

The era from 1870 to 1890 is the only period of American history commonly known by a derogatory name—**the Gilded Age**, after the title of an 1873 novel by Mark Twain and Charles Dudley Warner. "Gilded" means covered with a layer of gold, but it also suggests that the glittering surface masks a core of little real value and is therefore deceptive. Twain and Warner were referring not only to the remarkable expansion of the economy in this period but also to the corruption caused by corporate dominance of politics and to the oppressive treatment of those left behind in the scramble for wealth. "Get rich, dishonestly if we can, honestly if we must," was the era's slogan, according to *The Gilded Age*.

The Corruption of Politics

As they had earlier in the nineteenth century, Americans during the Gilded Age saw their nation as an island of political democracy in a world still dominated by undemocratic governments. In Europe, only France and Switzerland enjoyed universal male suffrage. Even in Britain, which prided itself on its tradition of political liberty, most of the working class could not vote until the passage of the Reform Act of 1884.

Corporations' influence

Nonetheless, the power of the new corporations, seemingly immune to democratic control, raised disturbing questions for the American understanding of political freedom as popular self-government. Political corruption was rife. "The galleries and lobbies of every legislature," observed an Illinois Republican leader, "are thronged with men seeking to procure an advantage" for one corporation or another. In Pennsylvania's legislature, the "third house" of railroad lobbyists was said to enjoy as much influence as the elected chambers. In the West, many lawmakers held stock or directorships in lumber companies and railroads that received public aid.

New York's Tweed Ring

Urban politics fell under the sway of corrupt political machines like New York's Tweed Ring, which plundered the city of tens of millions of dollars. "Boss" William M. Tweed's organization reached into every neighborhood. He forged close ties with railroad men and labor unions, and he won support from the city's immigrant poor by fashioning a kind of private welfare system that provided food, fuel, and jobs in hard times. A combination of political reformers and businessmen tired of paying tribute to the ring ousted Tweed in the early 1870s, although he remained popular among the city's poor, who considered him an urban Robin Hood.

The Bosses of the Senate, a cartoon from *Puck*, January 23, 1889, shows well-fed monopolists towering over the obedient senators. Above them, a sign rewrites the closing words of Lincoln's Gettysburg Address: "This is a Senate of the Monopolists, by the Monopolists, and for the Monopolists."

At the national level, many lawmakers supported bills aiding companies in which they had invested money or from which they received stock or salaries. The most notorious example of corruption came to light during Grant's presidency. This was Crédit Mobilier, a corporation formed by an inner ring of Union Pacific Railroad stockholders to oversee the line's government-assisted construction. Essentially, it enabled the participants to sign contracts with themselves, at an exorbitant profit, to build the new line. The arrangement was protected by the distribution of stock to influential politicians, including Speaker of the House Schuyler Colfax, who was elected vice president in 1868. In another example of corruption, the Whiskey Ring of the Grant administration united Republican officials, tax collectors, and whiskey manufacturers in a massive scheme that defrauded the federal government of millions of tax dollars.

> *The Crédit Mobilier scandal*

The Politics of Dead Center

In national elections, party politics bore the powerful imprint of the Civil War. Republicans controlled the industrial North and Midwest and the agrarian West and were particularly strong among members of revivalist churches, Protestant immigrants, and blacks. Organizations of Union veterans formed a bulwark of Republican support. Every Republican candidate for president from 1868 to 1900 except James G. Blaine had fought in the Union army. (In the 1880 campaign, all four candidates—Republican James A. Garfield, Democrat Winfield Scott Hancock, Prohibitionist Neal Dow, and James B. Weaver of the Greenback-Labor Party, discussed later—had been Union generals during the war.) By 1893, a lavish system of pensions for Union soldiers and their widows and children consumed more than 40 percent of the federal budget. Democrats, after 1877, dominated the South and did well among Catholic voters, especially Irish-Americans, in the nation's cities.

> *Political stalemate*

The parties were closely divided. In three of the five presidential elections between 1876 and 1892, the margin separating the major candidates was less than 1 percent of the popular vote. Twice, in 1876 and 1888, the candidate with an electoral-college majority trailed in the popular vote. The congressional elections of 1874, when Democrats won control of the House of Representatives, ushered in two decades of political stalemate. A succession of one-term presidencies followed: Rutherford B. Hayes (elected in 1876), James A. Garfield (succeeded, after his assassination in 1881, by Chester A. Arthur), Grover Cleveland in 1884, Benjamin Harrison in 1888, and Cleveland, elected for the second time, in 1892. Only for brief periods did the same party control the White House and both houses of Congress. More than once, Congress found itself paralyzed as important bills shuttled back and forth between the House and Senate, and special sessions to complete legislation became necessary. Gilded Age presidents made little effort to mobilize public opinion or exert executive leadership. Their staffs were quite small. Grover Cleveland himself answered the White House doorbell.

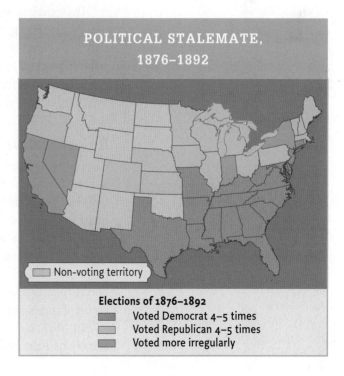

POLITICAL STALEMATE, 1876–1892

Non-voting territory

Elections of 1876–1892

Voted Democrat 4–5 times
Voted Republican 4–5 times
Voted more irregularly

In some ways, American democracy in the Gilded Age seemed remarkably healthy. Elections were closely contested, party loyalty was intense, and 80 percent or more of eligible voters turned out to cast ballots. It was an era of massive party rallies and spellbinding political oratory. James G. Blaine was among the members of Congress tainted by the Crédit Mobilier scandal, but Robert G. Ingersoll's speech before the Republican national convention of 1876 nearly secured Blaine's nomination for president by depicting him as a "plumed knight" who had raised his "shining lance" against the country's enemies.

Party activism

Government and the Economy

The nation's political structure, however, proved ill equipped to deal with the problems created by the economy's rapid growth. Despite its expanded scope and powers arising from the Civil War, the federal government remained remarkably small by modern standards. Activities from education to medical care, business regulation, civil and criminal prosecutions, and many others were almost entirely under the control of local and state governments or private institutions. The federal workforce in 1880 numbered 100,000 (today, it exceeds 2.5 million).

A small federal goverment

Nationally, both parties came under the control of powerful political managers with close ties to business interests. Republicans strongly supported a high tariff to protect American industry, and throughout the 1870s they pursued a fiscal policy based on reducing federal spending, repaying much of the national debt, and withdrawing greenbacks—the paper money issued by the Union during the Civil War—from circulation. Democrats opposed the high tariff, but the party's national leadership remained closely linked to New York bankers and financiers and resisted demands from debt-ridden agricultural areas for an increase in the money supply. In 1879, for the first time since the war, the United States returned to the **gold standard**—that is, paper currency became exchangeable for gold at a fixed rate.

A high tariff

By reducing competition from foreign manufactured goods and leaving the banks, not the government, in control of issuing money, Republican economic policies strongly favored the interests of eastern industrialists and bankers. These policies worked to the disadvantage of southern and western farmers, who had to pay a premium for manufactured goods while the prices they received for their produce steadily declined.

Reform Legislation

Gilded Age national politics did not entirely lack accomplishments. Inspired in part by President Garfield's assassination by a disappointed office seeker, the **Civil Service Act of 1883** created a merit system for federal employees, with appointment via competitive examinations rather than political influence. Although it applied at first to only 10 percent of government workers, the act marked the first step in establishing a professional civil service and removing officeholding from the hands of political machines. (However, since funds raised from political appointees had helped to finance the political parties, civil service reform had the unintended result of increasing politicians' dependence on donations from business interests.)

Establishing a professional Civil Service

In 1887, in response to public outcries against railroad practices, Congress established the **Interstate Commerce Commission** (ICC) to ensure that the rates railroads charged farmers and merchants to transport their goods were "reasonable" and did not offer more favorable treatment to some shippers. The ICC was the first federal agency intended to regulate economic activity, but since it lacked the power to establish rates on its own—it could only sue companies in court—it had little impact on railroad practices. Three years later, Congress passed the **Sherman Antitrust Act**, which banned all combinations and practices that restrained free trade. The measure posed a significant threat to corporate efforts to dominate sectors of the economy. But the courts primarily used it as a way to suppress labor unions. Nonetheless, these laws helped to establish the precedent that the national government could regulate the economy to promote the public good.

Political Conflict in the States

The nation had to weather the effects of drastic economic change and periodic economic crises without leadership from Washington. At the state and local levels, however, the Gilded Age was an era of political ferment and conflict over the proper uses of governmental authority. In the immediate aftermath of the Civil War, state governments in the North, like those in the Reconstruction South, greatly expanded their responsibility for public health, welfare, and education, and cities invested heavily in public works such as park construction and improved water and gas services. Those who suffered from economic change called on the activist state created by the war to redress their own grievances.

Third parties enjoyed significant if short-lived success in local elections. The Greenback-Labor Party proposed that the federal government stop taking "greenback" money out of circulation. This, it argued, would make more funds available for investment and give the government, not private bankers, control of the money supply. It also condemned the use of militias and private police against strikes. In the late 1870s, the party controlled local government in a number of industrial and mining communities and contributed to the election of twenty-one members of Congress independent of the two major parties.

The policies of railroad companies produced a growing chorus of protest, especially in the West. Farmers and local merchants complained of excessively high freight rates, discrimination in favor of large producers and shippers, and high fees charged by railroad-controlled grain warehouses. Critics of the railroads came together in the Patrons of Husbandry, or Grange, which moved to establish cooperatives for storing and marketing farm output in the hope of forcing the carriers "to take our produce at a fair price." Founded in 1867, the Grange claimed more than 700,000 members by the mid-1870s. Its members called on state governments to establish fair freight rates and warehouse charges. In several states, the Grange

This political cartoon from the 1884 presidential campaign depicts Republican nominee James G. Blaine as a champion of a high tariff that would protect American workers from cheap foreign labor. Blaine's attire is a reference to the nominating speech at the Republican convention by Robert G. Ingersoll, who referred to the candidate as a "plumed knight."

A Republican campaign poster for Benjamin Harrison in the election of 1888 emphasizes the party's policy of protection, or a high tariff on imported manufactured goods, as benefiting industry, labor, and farmers.

succeeded in having commissions established to investigate—and, in some cases, regulate—railroad practices.

At the same time, the labor movement, revitalized during the Civil War, demanded laws establishing eight hours as a legal day's work. Seven northern legislatures passed such laws, but since most lacked strong means of enforcement they remained dead letters. But the efforts of farmers and workers to use the power of the state to counteract the inequalities of the Gilded Age inspired a far-reaching debate on the relationship between political and economic freedom in an industrial society.

FREEDOM IN THE GILDED AGE

The Social Problem

As the United States matured into an industrial economy, Americans struggled to make sense of the new social order. Debates over political economy engaged the attention of millions, reaching far beyond the tiny academic world into the public sphere inhabited by self-educated workingmen and farmers, reformers of all kinds, newspaper editors, and politicians. This broad public discussion produced thousands of books, pamphlets, and articles on such technical issues as land taxation and currency reform, as well as widespread debate over the social and ethical implications of economic change.

Many Americans sensed that something had gone wrong in the nation's social development. Talk of "better classes," "respectable classes," and "dangerous classes" dominated public discussion, and bitter labor strife seemed to have become the rule. During the Gilded Age, Congress and a number of states established investigating committees to inquire into the relations between labor and capital. Their hearings produced powerful evidence of distrust between employees and employers. In 1881, the Massachusetts Bureau of Labor Statistics reported that virtually every worker it interviewed in Fall River, the nation's largest center of textile production, complained of overwork, poor housing, and tyrannical employers.

Freedom, Inequality, and Democracy

The appearance of what Massachusetts cotton manufacturer Edward Atkinson called "a permanent factory population" living on the edge of poverty alongside a growing class of millionaires posed a sharp challenge to traditional definitions of freedom. "The great curse of the Old World—the division of society into classes," declared *The Nation*, had come to America. It became increasingly difficult to view wage labor as a temporary resting place on the road to economic independence.

The concentration of wealth

Given the vast expansion of the nation's productive capacity, many Americans viewed the concentration of wealth as inevitable, natural, and justified by progress. By the turn of the century, advanced economics taught that wages were determined by the iron law of supply and demand and that wealth rightly flowed not to those who worked the hardest but to men with business skills and access to money. The close link between freedom and equality, forged in the Revolution and reinforced during the Civil War, appeared increasingly out of date. The task of social science, wrote iron manufacturer Abram Hewitt, was to devise ways of making "men who are equal in liberty" content with the "inequality in . . . distribution" inevitable in modern society.

Freedom and equality disconnected

Among the first to take up this challenge were the self-styled "liberal" reformers. (Their beliefs were quite different from those called liberals in modern America, who advocate that an activist government try to address social needs.) This group of editors and professionals broke with the Republican Party in 1872 and helped to bring about a change in northern opinion regarding Reconstruction. But their program was not confined to the South. Gilded Age liberals feared that with lower-class groups seeking to use government to advance their own interests, democracy was becoming a threat to individual liberty and the rights of property. Some urged a return to the long-abandoned principle that voting should be limited to property owners. During the 1830s, Alexis de Tocqueville had reported that opponents of democracy "hide their heads." By the 1870s, wrote one observer, "expressions of doubt and distrust in regard to universal suffrage are heard constantly . . . [at] the top of our society."

Gilded Age reform

Social Darwinism in America

The idea of the natural superiority of some groups to others, which before the Civil War had been invoked to justify slavery in an otherwise free society, now reemerged in the vocabulary of modern science to explain the success and failure of individuals and social classes. In 1859, the British scientist Charles Darwin published *On the Origin of Species*. One of the most influential works of science ever

Darwin

The Ironworkers' Noontime, painted in 1880–1881 by Thomas Anshutz, an artist born in West Virginia, whose family owned iron factories. Unlike artists who depicted factories and workers earlier in the century, Anshutz does not try to reconcile nature and industry (there are no reminders of the natural environment). Nor does he emphasize the dignity of labor. The workers seem dwarfed by the factory, and some seem exhausted.

to appear, it expounded the theory of evolution whereby plant and animal species best suited to their environment took the place of those less able to adapt.

In a highly oversimplified form, language borrowed from Darwin or developed by his followers, such as "natural selection," "the struggle for existence," and "the survival of the fittest," entered public discussion of social problems in the Gilded Age. According to what came to be called **Social Darwinism**, evolution was as natural a process in human society as in nature, and government must not interfere. Especially misguided, in this view, were efforts to uplift those at the bottom of the social order, such as laws regulating conditions of work or public assistance to the poor. The giant industrial corporation, Social Darwinists believed, had emerged because it was better adapted to its environment than earlier forms of enterprise. To restrict its operations by legislation would reduce society to a more primitive level.

Evolution applied to society

Even the depressions of the 1870s and 1890s did not shake the widespread view that the poor were essentially responsible for their own fate. Charity workers and local governments spent much time and energy distinguishing the "deserving" poor (those, like widows and orphans, destitute through no fault of their own) from the "undeserving," a far larger number. Failure to advance in society was widely thought to indicate a lack of character, an absence of self-reliance and determination in the face of adversity. As late as 1900, half the nation's largest cities offered virtually no public relief, except to persons living in poorhouses. To improve their lot, according to the philosophy of Social Darwinism, workers should practice personal economy, keep out of debt, and educate their children in the principles of the marketplace, not look to the government for aid.

William Graham Sumner

The era's most influential Social Darwinist was Yale professor William Graham Sumner. For Sumner, freedom meant "the security given to each man" that he can acquire, enjoy, and dispose of property "exclusively as he chooses," without interference from other persons or from government. Freedom thus defined required frank acceptance of inequality. Society faced two and only two alternatives: "liberty, inequality, survival of the fittest; not-liberty, equality, survival of the unfittest." In 1883, Sumner published *What Social Classes Owe to Each Other*. His answer, essentially, was nothing: "In a free state," no one was entitled to claim "help from, and cannot be charged to [offer] help to, another." Government, Sumner believed, existed only to protect "the property of men and the honor of women," not to upset social arrangements decreed by nature.

Liberty of Contract

The growing influence of Social Darwinism helped to popularize an idea that would be embraced by the business and professional classes in the last quarter of the nineteenth century—a "negative" definition of freedom as limited government and an unrestrained free market. Central to this social vision was the idea of contract. "The laws of contract," wrote one reformer, "are the foundation of civilization." Labor contracts reconciled freedom and authority in the workplace. So long as labor relations were governed by contracts freely arrived at by independent individuals, neither the government nor unions had a right to interfere with working conditions, and Americans had no grounds to complain of a loss of freedom.

The free market

Demands by workers that the government enforce an eight-hour day, provide relief to the unemployed, or in other ways intervene in the economy struck liberals as an example of how the misuse of political power posed a threat to liberty. "The right of each man to labor as much or as little as he chooses, and to enjoy his own earnings, is the very foundation stone of . . . freedom," wrote Chicago newspaper editor Horace White. The principle of free labor, which originated as a celebration of the independent small producer in a society of broad equality and social harmony, was transformed into a defense of the unrestrained operations of the capitalist marketplace.

The principle of free labor

The Courts and Freedom

In elevating liberty of contract from one element of freedom to its very essence, the courts played a significant role. The Fourteenth Amendment had empowered the federal government to overturn state laws that violated citizens' rights. By the 1880s, **liberty of contract**, not equality before the law for former slaves, came to be defined as the amendment's true meaning. State and federal courts regularly struck down state laws regulating economic enterprise as an interference with the right of the free laborer to choose his employment and working conditions, and of the entrepreneur to utilize his property as he saw fit. For decades, the courts viewed state regulation of business—especially laws establishing maximum hours of work and safe working conditions—as an insult to free labor.

At first, the Supreme Court was willing to accept laws regulating enterprises that represented a significant "public interest." In *Munn v. Illinois*, an 1877 decision, it upheld the constitutionality of an Illinois law that established a state board empowered to eliminate railroad rate discrimination and set maximum charges. Nine years later, however, in *Wabash v. Illinois*, the Court essentially reversed itself, ruling that only the federal government, not the states, could regulate railroads engaged in interstate commerce, as all important lines were. The decision led directly to the passage of the Interstate Commerce Act of 1887. But on virtually every occasion when cases brought by the ICC against railroads made their way to the Supreme Court, the company emerged victorious.

Rulings on the railroads

The courts generally sided with business enterprises that complained of a loss of economic freedom. In 1885, the New York Court of Appeals invalidated a state law that prohibited the manufacture of cigars in tenement dwellings on the grounds that such legislation deprived the worker of the "liberty" to work "where he will." Although women still lacked political rights, they were increasingly understood to possess the same economic "liberty," defined in this way, as men. On the grounds that it violated women's freedom, the Illinois Supreme Court in 1895 declared unconstitutional a state law that outlawed the production of garments in sweatshops and established a forty-eight-hour workweek for women and children. In the same year, in *United States v. E. C. Knight Co.*, the U.S. Supreme Court ruled that the Sherman Antitrust Act of 1890, which barred combinations in restraint of trade, could not be used to break up a sugar refining monopoly, since the Constitution empowered Congress to regulate commerce, but not manufacturing. Their unwillingness to allow regulation of the economy, however, did not prevent the courts from acting to impede labor organization. The Sherman Act, intended to

Women and work

E. C. Knight

Capital and Labor, a cotton textile from around 1870, illustrates the free labor ideal, with an employer and employee shaking hands and laborers enjoying dignity at work and a "happy home" in this detail. One image and its caption ("The Two Powers in Accord") illustrates the idea of a harmony of interests between worker and employer, a key tenet of free-labor thought. Others stress the dignity of the workingman, based partly on his skill and partly on his ability to provide a comfortable home for his family. The portrait of American industry here stands in stark contrast to the widespread labor strife of the Gilded Age.

prevent business mergers that stifled competition, was used by judges primarily to issue injunctions prohibiting strikes on the grounds that they illegally interfered with the freedom of trade.

In a 1905 case that became almost as notorious as *Dred Scott* and gave the name "Lochnerism" to the entire body of liberty of contract decisions, the Supreme Court in *Lochner v. New York* voided a state law establishing ten hours per day or sixty per week as the maximum hours of work for bakers. The law, wrote Associate Justice Rufus Peckham for the 5-4 majority, "interfered with the right of contract between employer and employee" and therefore infringed upon individual freedom. By this time, the Court was invoking "liberty" in ways that could easily seem absurd. In one case, it overturned as a violation of "personal liberty" a Kansas law prohibiting "yellow-dog" contracts, which made nonmembership in a union a condition of employment. In another, it struck down state laws requiring payment of coal miners in money rather than paper usable only at company-owned stores. Workers, observed mine union leader John P. Mitchell, could not but feel that "they are being guaranteed the liberties they do not want and denied the liberty that is of real value to them."

> Lochner v. New York

LABOR AND THE REPUBLIC

"The Overwhelming Labor Question"

As Mitchell's remark suggests, public debate in the late nineteenth century more than at almost any other moment in American history divided along class lines. The shift from the slavery controversy to what one politician called "the overwhelming labor question" was dramatically illustrated in 1877, the year of both the end of Reconstruction and the first national labor walkout—the **Great Railroad Strike**. When workers protesting a pay cut paralyzed rail traffic in much of the country, militia units tried to force them back to work. After troops fired on

The Strike, an 1886 painting by the German-born artist Robert Koehler, who had grown up in a working-class family in Milwaukee. Koehler depicts a confrontation between a factory owner, dressed in a silk top hat, and angry workers. A woman and her children, presumably members of a striker's family, watch from the side while another woman, at the center, appears to plead for restraint. The threat of violence hangs in the air, and a striker in the lower right-hand corner reaches for a stone. The painting was inspired by events in Pittsburgh during the Great Railroad Strike of 1877.

strikers in Pittsburgh, killing twenty people, workers responded by burning the city's railroad yards, destroying millions of dollars in property. General strikes paralyzed Chicago and St. Louis. The strike revealed both a strong sense of solidarity among workers and the close ties between the Republican Party and the new class of industrialists. President Rutherford B. Hayes, who a few months earlier had ordered federal troops in the South to end their involvement in local politics, ordered the army into the North. The workers, the president wrote in his diary, were "put down by force."

"The days are over," declared the *New York Times*, "in which this country could rejoice in its freedom from the elements of social strife which have long abounded in the old countries." In the aftermath of 1877, the federal government constructed armories in major cities to ensure that troops would be on hand in the event of further labor difficulties. Henceforth, national power would be used not to protect beleaguered former slaves, but to guarantee the rights of property.

Ruins of the Pittsburgh Round House, a photograph in the July 1895 issue of *Scribner's Magazine*, shows the widespread destruction of property during the Great Railroad Strike of July 1877.

The Knights of Labor and the "Conditions Essential to Liberty"

The 1880s witnessed a new wave of labor organizing. At its center stood the **Knights of Labor**. The Knights were the first group to try to organize unskilled workers as well as skilled, women alongside men, and blacks as well as whites (although even the Knights excluded the despised Asian immigrants on the West Coast). The group reached a peak membership of nearly 800,000 in 1886 (making it the largest labor organization of the nineteenth century) and involved millions of workers in strikes, boycotts, political action, and educational and social activities.

Labor reformers of the Gilded Age put forward a wide array of programs, from the eight-hour day to public employment in hard times, currency reform, anarchism, socialism, and the creation of a vaguely defined "cooperative commonwealth." All

these ideas arose from the conviction that the social conditions of the 1880s needed drastic change. Americans, declared Terence V. Powderly, head of the Knights of Labor, were not "the free people that we imagine we are."

The labor movement launched a sustained assault on the understanding of freedom grounded in Social Darwinism and liberty of contract. Because of unrestrained economic growth and political corruption, the Knights charged, ordinary Americans had lost control of their economic livelihoods and their own government. Reaching back across the divide of the Civil War, labor defined employers as a new "slave power." Concentrated capital, warned George E. McNeill, a shoemaker and factory worker who became one of the movement's most eloquent writers, was now "a greater power than that of the state." "Extremes of wealth and poverty," he warned, threatened the very existence of democratic government. The remedy was to "engraft republican principles into our industrial system" by guaranteeing a basic set of economic rights for all Americans.

Critique of concentrated capital

Labor raised the question whether meaningful freedom could exist in a situation of extreme economic inequality. On July 4, 1886, the Federated Trades of the Pacific Coast rewrote the Declaration of Independence. Workers, the new Declaration claimed, had been subjected not to oppressive government but to "the unjust domination of a special class." It went on to list among mankind's inalienable rights, "Life and the means of living, Liberty and the conditions essential to liberty."

Middle-Class Reformers

Dissatisfaction with social conditions in the Gilded Age extended well beyond aggrieved workers. Supreme Court justice John Marshall Harlan in the late 1880s spoke of a "deep feeling of unease," a widespread fear that the country "was in real danger of another kind of slavery that would result from the aggregation of capital in the hands of a few individuals." Alarmed by fear of class warfare and the growing power of concentrated capital, social thinkers offered numerous plans for change. In the last quarter of the century, more than 150 utopian or cataclysmic novels appeared, predicting that social conflict would end either in a new, harmonious social order or in total catastrophe. One popular novel of the era, *Caesar's Column* (1891) by Ignatius Donnelly, ended with civilized society destroyed in a savage civil war between labor and capital.

Of the many books proposing more optimistic remedies for the unequal distribution of wealth, the most popular were *Progress and Poverty* (1879) by Henry George, *The Cooperative Commonwealth* (1884) by Laurence Gronlund, and Edward Bellamy's *Looking Backward* (1888). All three were among the century's greatest best-sellers, their extraordinary success testifying to what George called "a widespread consciousness . . . that there is something *radically* wrong in the present social organization." All three writers, though in very different ways, sought to reclaim an imagined golden age of social harmony and American freedom.

An engraving from *Frank Leslie's Illustrated Newspaper*, October 16, 1886, shows black delegate Frank J. Farrell introducing Terence V. Powderly, leader of the Knights of Labor, at the labor organization's national convention in Richmond, Virginia. The Knights were among the few nineteenth-century labor groups to recruit black members.

Progress and Poverty

Although it had no direct impact on government policy, *Progress and Poverty* probably commanded more public attention than any book on economics in American

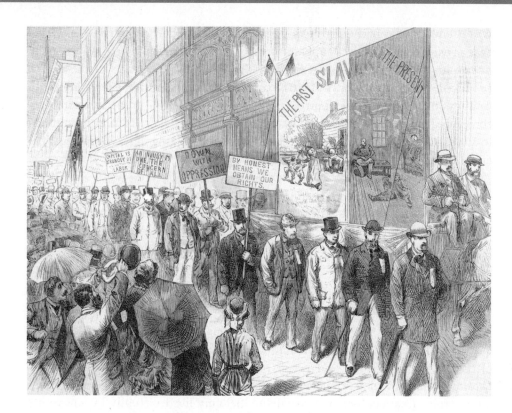

The Great Labor Parade of September 1, from Frank Leslie's Illustrated Newspaper, September 13, 1884. A placard illustrates how the labor movement identified Gilded Age employers with the Slave Power of the pre–Civil War era.

history. An antislavery newspaper editor in California in the 1850s and 1860s, Henry George had witnessed firsthand the rapid monopolization of land in the state. His book began with a famous statement of "the problem" suggested by its title—the growth of "squalor and misery" alongside material progress. His solution was the **single tax**, which would replace other taxes with a levy on increases in the value of real estate. The single tax would be so high that it would prevent speculation in both urban and rural land. No one knows how many of Henry George's readers actually believed in this way of solving the nation's ills. But millions responded to his clear explanation of economic relationships and his stirring account of how the "social distress" long thought to be confined to the Old World had made its appearance in the New.

The "single tax"

Freedom lay at the heart of George's analysis. The "proper name" for the political movement spawned by his book, he once wrote, was "freedom men," who would "do for the question of industrial slavery" what the Republican Party had done for the slavery of blacks. George rejected the traditional equation of liberty with ownership of land (since the single tax in effect made land the "common property" of the entire society). In other ways, however, his definition of freedom was thoroughly in keeping with mainstream thought. Despite calling for a single massive public intervention in the economy, George saw government as a "repressive power," whose functions in the "co-operative society" of the future would be limited to enhancing the quality of life—building "public baths, museums, libraries, gardens," and the like.

"Freedom men"

The Cooperative Commonwealth

Quite different in outlook was *The Cooperative Commonwealth*, the first book to popularize socialist ideas for an American audience. Its author, Laurence Gronlund, was a lawyer who had emigrated from Denmark in 1867. Socialism—the belief that private control of economic enterprises should be replaced by government ownership in order to ensure a fairer distribution of the benefits of the wealth produced—became a major political force in western Europe in the late nineteenth century. In the United States, however, where access to private property was widely considered essential to individual freedom, socialist beliefs were largely confined to immigrants, whose writings, frequently in foreign languages, attracted little attention.

Gronlund began the process of socialism's Americanization. While Karl Marx, the nineteenth century's most influential socialist theorist, had predicted that socialism would come into being via a working-class revolution, Gronlund portrayed it as the end result of a process of peaceful evolution, not violent upheaval. He thus made socialism seem more acceptable to middle-class Americans who desired an end to class conflict and the restoration of social harmony.

Bellamy's Utopia

Not until the early twentieth century would socialism become a significant presence in American public life. As Gronlund himself noted, the most important result of *The Cooperative Commonwealth* was to prepare an audience for Edward Bellamy's *Looking Backward*, which promoted socialist ideas while "ignoring that name" (Bellamy wrote of nationalism, not socialism). Bellamy lived virtually his entire life in the small industrial city of Chicopee Falls, Massachusetts. In *Looking Backward*, his main character falls asleep in the late nineteenth century only to awaken in the year 2000, in a world where cooperation has replaced class strife, "excessive individualism," and cutthroat competition. Inequality has been banished and with it the idea of liberty as a condition to be achieved through individual striving free of governmental restraint. Freedom, Bellamy insisted, was a social condition, resting on interdependence, not autonomy.

From today's vantage point, Bellamy's utopia—with citizens obligated to labor for years in an Industrial Army controlled by a single Great Trust—seems a chilling social blueprint. Yet the book inspired the creation of hundreds of nationalist clubs devoted to bringing into existence the world of 2000 and left a profound mark on a generation of reformers and intellectuals. Bellamy held out the hope of retaining the material abundance made possible by industrial capitalism while eliminating inequality. In proposing that the state guarantee economic security to all, Bellamy offered a far-reaching expansion of the idea of freedom.

Protestants and Moral Reform

Mainstream Protestants played a major role in seeking to stamp out sin during the Gilded Age. What one historian calls a "Christian lobby" promoted political solutions to what it saw as the moral problems raised by labor conflict and the growth of cities, and threats to religious faith by Darwinism and other scientific advances.

Unlike the pre–Civil War period, when "moral suasion" was the preferred approach of many reformers, powerful national organizations like the Woman's Christian Temperance Union, National Reform Association, and Reform Bureau now campaigned for federal legislation that would "Christianize the government"

Edward Bellamy, author of the utopian novel *Looking Backward*.

by outlawing sinful behavior. Among the proposed targets were the consumption of alcohol, gambling, prostitution, polygamy, and birth control. Most of these groups spoke less about improving society than stamping out the sins of individuals. In a striking departure from the prewar situation, southerners joined in the campaign for federal regulation of individual behavior, something whites in the region had previously strongly opposed, fearing it could lead to action against slavery. The key role played by the white South in the campaign for moral legislation helped earn the region a reputation as the Bible Belt—a place where political action revolved around religious principles. Although efforts to enact a national law requiring businesses to close on Sunday failed, the Christian lobby's efforts in the 1880s and 1890s set the stage for later legislation such as the Mann Act of 1910, banning the transportation of women across state lines for immoral purposes (an effort to suppress prostitution), and Prohibition.

The Bible Belt

A Social Gospel

Most of the era's Protestant preachers concentrated on attacking individual sins like drinking and Sabbath-breaking and saw nothing immoral about the pursuit of riches. But the outlines of what came to be called the Social Gospel were taking shape in the writings of Walter Rauschenbusch, a Baptist minister in New York City, Washington Gladden, a Congregational clergyman in Columbus, Ohio, and others. They insisted that freedom and spiritual self-development required an equalization of wealth and power and that unbridled competition mocked the Christian ideal of brotherhood.

Rauschenbusch and Gladden

The **Social Gospel** movement originated as an effort to reform Protestant churches by expanding their appeal in poor urban neighborhoods and making them more attentive to the era's social ills. The movement's adherents established missions and relief programs in urban areas that attempted to alleviate poverty, combat child labor, and encourage the construction of better working-class housing. They worked with the Knights of Labor and other groups demanding health and safety laws. Some suggested that a more cooperative organization of the economy should replace competitive capitalism. Within American Catholicism, as well, a group of priests and bishops emerged who attempted to alter the church's traditional hostility to movements for social reform and its isolation from contemporary currents of social thought. With most of its parishioners working men and women, they argued, the church should lend its support to the labor movement. These developments suggested the existence of widespread dissatisfaction with the "liberty of contract" understanding of freedom.

The Haymarket Affair

The year of the dedication of the Statue of Liberty, 1886, also witnessed an unprecedented upsurge in labor activity. Inspired by a successful strike by western railroad unions against lines controlled by the powerful financier Jay Gould, workers flooded into the Knights of Labor. Its membership, only 100,000 in 1885, rose more than sevenfold in the following year. On May 1, 1886, some 350,000 workers in cities across the country demonstrated for an eight-hour day. Having originated in the United States, May 1, or May Day as it came to be called, soon became an annual

The first May Day

date of parades, picnics, and protests, celebrated around the world by organized labor.

The most dramatic events of 1886 took place in Chicago, a city with a large and vibrant labor movement that brought together native-born and immigrant workers, whose outlooks ranged from immigrant socialism and anarchism to American traditions of equality and anti-monopoly. In 1885, the iron moulders union—one of the most powerful organizations of skilled industrial workers in the country—had organized a strike against a wage reduction at the great McCormick plant that produced agricultural machinery. The company brought in strikebreakers and private police, who battled in the streets with the strikers. Fearing chaos, the mayor and prominent business leaders persuaded the company to settle on the union's terms. But in February 1886, after the company installed new machinery that reduced its dependence on the iron moulders' traditional skills, it announced that henceforth the factory would operate on a nonunion basis. The result was a bitter, prolonged strike.

This time, Chicago's city government sided with the company. On May 3, 1886, four strikers were killed by police when they attempted to prevent strikebreakers from entering the factory. The next day, a rally was held in Haymarket Square to protest the killings. Near the end of the speeches, someone—whose identity has never been determined—threw a bomb into the crowd, killing a policeman. The panicked police opened fire, shooting several bystanders and a number of their own force. Soon after, police raided the offices of labor and radical groups and arrested their leaders. Employers took the opportunity presented by the **Haymarket Affair** to paint the labor movement as a dangerous and un-American force, prone to violence and controlled by foreign-born radicals. Eight anarchists were charged with plotting and carrying out the bombing. Even though the evidence against them was extremely weak, a jury convicted the "Haymarket martyrs." Four were hanged, one committed suicide in prison, and the remaining three were imprisoned until John Peter Altgeld, a pro-labor governor of Illinois, commuted their sentences in 1893.

Seven of the eight men accused of plotting the Haymarket bombing were foreign-born—six Germans and an English immigrant. The last was Albert Parsons, a native of Alabama who had served in the Confederate army in the Civil War and edited a Republican newspaper in Texas during Reconstruction. Fearing violence because of his political views and the fact that his wife, Lucy Parsons, was black, Albert Parsons moved to Chicago during the 1870s. Having survived the Ku Klux Klan in Reconstruction Texas, Parsons perished on the Illinois gallows for a crime that he, like the other "Haymarket martyrs," did not commit.

Labor and Politics

The Haymarket affair took place amid an outburst of independent labor political activity. One study has identified more than

---

Strikes in Chicago

In a political cartoon from *Frank Leslie's Weekly*, November 13, 1886, Uncle Sam congratulates a workingman for the defeat of Henry George's candidacy for mayor of New York City on the United Labor Party ticket. A disappointed anarchist fulminates in the background. Local labor parties did win many local victories in 1886.

UNCLE SAM (TO LABOR PARTY REPRESENTATIVE)—"You did splendidly, my boy, for a first attempt; but, for your own good and that of the country, get rid of that dangerous companion of yours as soon as possible."

100 local political tickets associated with the Knights of Labor between 1886 and 1888, from Anniston, Alabama, to Whitewater, Wisconsin. Their major aim was to end the use of public and private police forces and court injunctions against strikes and labor organizations. At least sixty achieved some kind of electoral success. In Kansas City, a coalition of black and Irish-American workers and middle-class voters elected Tom Hanna as mayor. He proceeded to side with unions rather than employers in industrial disputes.

The most celebrated labor campaign took place in New York City, where in 1886, somewhat to his own surprise, Henry George found himself thrust into the role of labor's candidate for mayor. George's aim in running was to bring attention to the single tax on land. The labor leaders who organized the United Labor Party had more immediate goals in mind, especially stopping the courts from barring strikes and jailing unionists for conspiracy. George ran a spirited campaign, speaking at factories, immigrant associations, and labor parades and rallies. A few days after the dedication of the Statue of Liberty, New Yorkers flocked to the polls to elect their mayor. Nearly 70,000 voted for George, who finished second, eclipsing the total of the Republican candidate, Theodore Roosevelt, and coming close to defeating Democrat Abram Hewitt.

In a political system that within living memory had witnessed the disappearance of the Whig Party, the rise and fall of the Know-Nothings, and the emergence of the Republicans, the events of 1886 suggested that labor might be on the verge of establishing itself as a permanent political force. In fact, that year marked the high point of the Knights of Labor. Facing increasing employer hostility and linked by employers and the press to the violence and radicalism associated with the Haymarket events, the Knights soon declined. The major parties, moreover, proved remarkably resourceful in appealing to labor voters.

Thus, America's Gilded Age witnessed deep and sometimes violent divisions over the definition of freedom in a rapidly industrializing society. The battle between upholders of Social Darwinism and laissez-faire, who saw freedom as the right of individuals to pursue their economic interests without outside restraint, and those who believed in collective efforts to create "industrial freedom" for ordinary Americans, would continue for many decades. In the early twentieth century, reformers would turn to new ways of addressing the social conditions of freedom and new means of increasing ordinary Americans' political and economic liberty. But before this, in the 1890s, the nation would face its gravest crisis since the Civil War, and the boundaries of freedom would once again be redrawn.

In this pro-labor cartoon from 1888, a workingman rescues liberty from the stranglehold of monopolies and the pro-business major parties.

SUGGESTED READING

BOOKS

- Bensel, Richard F. *The Political Economy of American Industrialization, 1877–1900* (2000). A study of the policies and political divisions that contributed to and resulted from the second industrial revolution.

- Blackhawk, Ned. *Violence Over the Land: Indians and Empires in the Early American West* (2006). A history of the long conflict between Native Americans and the federal government for control of the trans-Mississippi West.

- Deutsch, Sarah. *No Separate Refuge: Culture, Class, and Gender on the Anglo-Hispanic Frontier in the American Southwest, 1880–1940* (1987). A careful analysis of the changing experience of people of Hispanic origin in the Southwest during these years.

- Fink, Leon. *Workingmen's Democracy: The Knights of Labor and American Politics* (1983). Examines the rise of the Knights of Labor and their forays into local politics in the mid-1880s.

- Foster, Gaines. *Moral Reconstruction: Christian Lobbyists and the Federal Legislation of Morality, 1865–1920* (2002). Traces the rise of efforts to use the federal government to promote Protestant notions of moral behavior.

- Freeberg, Ernest. *The Age of Edison: Electric Light and the Invention of Modern America* (2013). Explores the numerous ways electricity altered Americans' lives.

- Hamalainen, Pekka. *The Comanche Empire* (2008). The rise and fall of Comanche domination over much of the southwestern United States.

- Hofstadter, Richard. *Social Darwinism in American Thought* (1944). A classic study of a major tendency in American thought during the Gilded Age.

- Jeffrey, Julie R. *Frontier Women: "Civilizing" the West? 1840–1880* (rev. ed., 1998). A study, based on letters and diaries, of the experience of women on the western frontier.

- Kasson, Joy S. *Buffalo Bill's Wild West: Celebrity, Memory, and Popular History* (2000). An account of the popular theatrical production that helped to fix an image of the Wild West in the American imagination.

- Morgan, H. Wayne. *From Hayes to McKinley: National Party Politics, 1877–1896* (1969). The standard narrative of national politics during these years.

- Shannon, Fred A. *The Farmer's Last Frontier: Agriculture 1860–1897* (1945). Remains an excellent introduction to the experience of farmers in the last four decades of the nineteenth century.

- Sproat, John G. *"The Best Men": Liberal Reformers in the Gilded Age* (1968). Traces the origins, outlook, and political impact of reformers dissatisfied with the corruption of national politics.

- Thomas, John L. *Alternative Americas: Henry George, Edward Bellamy, Henry Demarest Lloyd and the Adversary Tradition* (1983). A thorough exposition of the thought of three critics of Gilded Age society.

- Trachtenberg, Alan. *The Incorporation of America: Culture and Society in the Gilded Age* (1982). An influential survey of how economic change affected American life during the Gilded Age.

- White, Richard. *Railroaded: The Transcontinentals and the Making of Modern America* (2011). A careful study of the building of the transcontinental railroad and how it epitomized the political corruption and financial mismanagement so widespread in the Gilded Age.

WEBSITES

- First-hand Accounts of California 1849–1900: http://memory.loc.gov/ammem/cbhtml/cbhome.html

- Indian Peoples of the Northern Great Plains: http://arc.lib.montana.edu/indian-great-plains

- The Dramas of Haymarket: www.chicagohistory.org/dramas/overview/over.htm

CHAPTER REVIEW AND ONLINE RESOURCES

REVIEW QUESTIONS

1. The American economy thrived because of federal involvement, not the lack of it. How did the federal government actively promote industrial and agricultural development in this period?

2. Why were railroads so important to America's second industrial revolution? What events demonstrate their influence on society and politics as well as the economy?

3. Why did organized efforts of farmers, workers, and local reformers largely fail to achieve substantive change in the Gilded Age?

4. Describe the involvement of American family farmers in the global economy after 1870 and its effects on their independence.

5. According to *The Gilded Age* by Mark Twain and Charles Dudley Warner, the era's slogan was "Get rich, dishonestly if we can, honestly if we must." Explain how this was true of the politics of the era.

6. How did American political leaders seek to remake Indians and change the ways they lived?

7. Explain how social thinkers misapplied Charles Darwin's ideas to justify massive disparities in wealth and power and to deny government a role in equalizing opportunity.

8. How did social reformers such as Edward Bellamy, Henry George, and advocates of the social gospel conceive of liberty and freedom differently than the proponents of the liberty of contract ideal and laissez faire?

9. In what ways did the West provide a "safety valve" for the problems in the industrial East? In what ways did it reveal some of the same problems?

KEY TERMS

trusts (p. 596)

vertical integration (p. 597)

horizontal expansion (p. 599)

robber barons (p. 599)

bonanza farms (p. 605)

Battle of the Little Bighorn (p. 614)

Dawes Act (p. 615)

Ghost Dance (p. 616)

Wounded Knee massacre (p. 617)

the Gilded Age (p. 619)

gold standard (p. 622)

Civil Service Act of 1883 (p. 622)

Interstate Commerce Commission (p. 622)

Sherman Antitrust Act (p. 623)

Social Darwinism (p. 626)

liberty of contract (p. 627)

Great Railroad Strike (p. 628)

Knights of Labor (p. 629)

single tax (p. 631)

Social Gospel (p. 633)

Haymarket Affair (p. 634)

Go to 🐰 INQUIZITIVE

To see what you know—and learn what you've missed—with personalized feedback along the way.

Visit the *Give Me Liberty!* Student Site for primary source documents and images, interactive maps, author videos featuring Eric Foner, and more.

CHAPTER 17

FREEDOM'S BOUNDARIES, AT HOME AND ABROAD

★

1890–1900

One of the most popular songs of 1892 bore the title "Father Was Killed by a Pinkerton Man." It was inspired by an incident during a bitter strike at Andrew Carnegie's steelworks at Homestead, Pennsylvania, the nineteenth century's most widely publicized confrontation between labor and capital. The strike pitted one of the nation's leading industrial corporations against a powerful union, the Amalgamated Association, which represented the skilled iron- and steelworkers among the complex's 3,800 employees.

Homestead's twelve steel mills were the most profitable and technologically advanced in the world. The union contract gave the Amalgamated Association a considerable say in their operation, including the right to approve the hiring of new workers and to regulate the pace of work. To Carnegie and Henry Clay Frick, his partner and chairman of the Carnegie Steel Company, the union's power increasingly seemed an intolerable infringement on management's rights. In 1892, they decided to operate the plant on a nonunion basis. Frick surrounded the factory with a fence topped by barbed wire, constructed barracks to house strikebreakers, and fired the entire workforce. Henceforth, only workers who agreed not to join the union could work at Homestead. In response, the workers, including the unskilled laborers not included in the Amalgamated Association, blockaded the steelworks and mobilized support from the local community. The battle memorialized in song took place on July 6, 1892, when armed strikers confronted 300 private policemen from the Pinkerton Detective Agency. Seven workers and three Pinkerton agents were killed, and the Pinkertons were forced to retreat. Four days later, the governor of Pennsylvania dispatched 8,000 militiamen to open the complex on management's terms. The strikers held out until November, but the union's defeat was now inevitable. In the end, the Amalgamated Association was destroyed.

The Carnegie corporation's tactics and the workers' solidarity won the strikers widespread national sympathy. "Ten thousand Carnegie libraries," declared the *St. Louis Post-Dispatch*, "would not compensate the country for the evils resulting from Homestead." The strike became an international cause célèbre as well. British newspapers pointed out that their country restricted the use of private police forces far more severely than the United States. Britons, they claimed, understood economic liberty better than Americans.

Homestead demonstrated that neither a powerful union nor public opinion could influence the conduct of the largest corporations. The writer Hamlin Garland, who visited Homestead two years after the strike, found the workforce sullen and bitter. He described a town "as squalid and unlovely as could be imagined," with dingy houses over which hung dense clouds of black smoke. It was "American," he wrote, "only in the sense in which [it] represents the American idea of business."

In fact, two American ideas of freedom collided at Homestead—the employers' definition, based on the idea that property rights, unrestrained by union rules or public regulation, sustained the public good, and the workers' conception, which stressed economic security and independence from what they considered the "tyranny" of employers. The strife at Homestead also reflected

FOCUS QUESTIONS

What were the origins and the significance of Populism? –p. 640

How did the liberties of blacks after 1877 give way to legal segregation across the South? –p. 648

In what ways did the boundaries of American freedom grow narrower in this period? –p. 656

How did the United States emerge as an imperial power in the 1890s? –p. 663

Painted in 1899 by the American artist Francis Davis Millet soon after his return from Asia, where he served as a newspaper correspondent during the Spanish-American War, *The Expansionist* depicts a well-dressed couple in a parlor filled with maps of the world and goods and mementos from Asia. In the wake of the emergence of the United States as the ruler of an overseas empire, it suggests that manifest destiny involves not just territorial expansion but acquiring the spoils of travel and war.

broader battles over American freedom during the 1890s. Like the Homestead workers, many Americans came to believe that they were being denied economic independence and democratic self-government, long central to the popular understanding of freedom.

During the 1890s, millions of farmers joined the Populist movement in an attempt to reverse their declining economic prospects and to rescue the government from what they saw as control by powerful corporate interests. The 1890s witnessed the imposition of a new racial system in the South that locked African-Americans into the status of second-class citizenship, denying them many of the freedoms white Americans took for granted. Increasing immigration produced heated debates over whether the country should reconsider its traditional self-definition as a refuge for foreigners seeking greater freedom on American shores. At the end of the 1890s, in the Spanish-American War, the United States for the first time acquired overseas possessions and found itself ruling over subject peoples from Puerto Rico to the Philippines. Was the democratic republic, many Americans wondered, becoming an empire like those of Europe? Rarely has the country experienced at one time so many debates over both the meaning of freedom and freedom's boundaries.

THE POPULIST CHALLENGE

The Farmers' Revolt

Even as labor unrest crested, a different kind of uprising was ripening in the South and the trans-Mississippi West, a response to falling agricultural prices and growing economic dependency in rural areas. Like industrial workers, small farmers faced increasing economic insecurity. In the South, the sharecropping system, discussed in Chapter 15, locked millions of tenant farmers, white and black, into perpetual poverty. The interruption of cotton exports during the Civil War had led to the rapid expansion of production in India, Egypt, and Brazil. The glut of cotton on the world market led to declining prices (from 11 cents a pound in 1881 to 4.6 cents in 1894), throwing millions of small farmers deep into debt and threatening them with the loss of their land. In the West, farmers who had mortgaged their property to purchase seed, fertilizer, and equipment faced the prospect of losing their farms when unable to repay their bank loans. Farmers increasingly believed that their plight derived from the high freight rates charged by railroad companies, excessive interest rates for loans from merchants and bankers, and the fiscal policies of the federal government (discussed in the previous chapter) that reduced the supply of money and helped to push down farm prices.

Through the Farmers' Alliance, the largest citizens' movement of the nineteenth century, farmers sought to remedy their condition. Founded in Texas in the late 1870s, the Alliance spread to forty-three states by 1890. The farmers' alternatives, said J. D. Fields, a Texas Alliance leader, were "success and freedom, or failure and servitude." At first, the Alliance remained aloof from politics, attempting to improve rural conditions by the cooperative financing and marketing of crops.

Alliance "exchanges" would loan money to farmers and sell their produce. But it soon became clear that farmers on their own could not finance this plan, and banks refused to extend loans to the exchanges. The Alliance therefore proposed that the federal government establish warehouses where farmers could store their crops until they were sold. Using the crops as collateral, the government would then issue loans to farmers at low interest rates, thereby ending their dependence on bankers and merchants. Since it would have to be enacted by Congress, the "subtreasury plan," as this proposal was called, led the Alliance into politics.

The People's Party

In the early 1890s, the Alliance evolved into the People's Party (or **Populists**), the era's greatest political insurgency. The party did not just appeal to farmers. It sought to speak for all the "producing classes" and achieved some of its greatest successes in states like Colorado and Idaho, where it won the support of miners and industrial workers. But its major base lay in the cotton and wheat belts of the South and West.

Building on the Farmers' Alliance network of local institutions, the Populists embarked on a remarkable effort of community organization and education. To spread their message they published numerous pamphlets on political and economic questions, established more than 1,000 local newspapers, and sent traveling speakers throughout rural America. Wearing "a huge black sombrero and a black Prince Albert coat," Texas Populist orator "Cyclone" Davis traveled the

Andrew Carnegie's ironworks at Homestead, Pennsylvania.

A group of Kansas Populists, perhaps on their way to a political gathering, in a photograph from the 1890s.

NATIONAL WATCHMAN ECONOMIC SERIES.
VOL. 1.   JULY 1, 1892.   NO. 1.

NOT A REVOLT;
IT IS A REVOLUTION.

HON. THOMAS E. WATSON,
MEMBER OF CONGRESS FROM GEORGIA.

PUBLISHED BY
NATIONAL WATCHMAN PUBLISHING COMPANY,
WASHINGTON, D. C.

Tom Watson, the Georgia Populist leader, on the cover of the party's "campaign book" for 1892.

In an 1891 cartoon from a Texas Populist newspaper, northern and southern Civil War veterans clasp hands across the "bloody chasm" (a phrase first used by the New York editor Horace Greeley during his campaign for president in 1872). Beneath each figure is an explanation of why voting alignments have previously been based on sectionalism—the North fears "rebel" rule, the white South "Negro supremacy."

THE BLUE AND THE GRAY.
"LET US CLASP HANDS ACROSS THE BLOODY CHASM."—Horace Greeley anticipated the inevitable. The Farmers' Alliance takes up his burden twenty years after he laid it down.

Great Plains accompanied by the writings of Thomas Jefferson, which he quoted to demonstrate the evils of banks and large corporations. At great gatherings on the western plains, similar in some ways to religious revival meetings, and in small-town southern country stores, one observer wrote, "people commenced to think who had never thought before, and people talked who had seldom spoken. . . . Little by little they commenced to theorize upon their condition."

Here was the last great political expression of the nineteenth-century vision of America as a commonwealth of small producers whose freedom rested on the ownership of productive property and respect for the dignity of labor. "Day by day," declared the *People's Party Paper* of Georgia in 1893, "the power of the individual sinks. Day by day the power of the classes, or the corporations, rises. . . . In all essential respects, the republic of our fathers is dead."

But although the Populists used the familiar language of nineteenth-century radicalism, they were hardly a backward-looking movement. They embraced the modern technologies that made large-scale cooperative enterprise possible—the railroad, the telegraph, and the national market—while looking to the federal government to regulate them in the public interest. They promoted agricultural education and believed farmers should adopt modern scientific methods of cultivation. They believed the federal government could move beyond partisan conflict to operate in a businesslike manner to promote the public good—a vision soon to be associated with the Progressive movement and, many years later, politicians like Jimmy Carter and Barack Obama.

The Populist Platform

The Populist platform of 1892, adopted at the party's Omaha convention, remains a classic document of American reform (see the Appendix for the full text). Written by Ignatius Donnelly, a Minnesota editor and former Radical Republican congressman during Reconstruction, it spoke of a nation "brought to the verge of moral, political, and material ruin" by political corruption and economic inequality. "The fruits of the toil of millions," the platform declared, "are boldly stolen to build up colossal fortunes . . . while their possessors despise the republic and endanger liberty." The platform put forth a long list of proposals to restore democracy and economic opportunity, many of which would be adopted during the next half-century: the direct election of U.S. senators, government control of the currency, a graduated income tax, a system of low-cost public financing to enable farmers to market their crops, and recognition of the right of workers to form labor unions. In addition, Populists called for public ownership of the railroads to guarantee farmers inexpensive access to markets for their crops. A generation would pass before a major party offered so sweeping a plan for political action to create the social conditions of freedom.

The Populist Coalition

In some southern states, the Populists made remarkable efforts to unite black and white small farmers on a common political and economic program. The obstacles to such an alliance were immense—not merely the heritage of racism and the political legacy of the Civil War, but the fact that many white Populists were landowning farmers while most blacks were tenants and agricultural laborers. Unwelcome in the southern branches of the Farmers' Alliance, black farmers formed their own organization, the Colored Farmers' Alliance. In 1891, it tried to organize a strike of cotton pickers on plantations in South Carolina, Arkansas, and Texas. The action was violently suppressed by local authorities and landowners, some of them sympathetic to the white Alliance but unwilling to pay higher wages to their own laborers.

> *Colored Farmers' Alliance*

In general, southern white Populists' racial attitudes did not differ significantly from those of their non-Populist neighbors. Nonetheless, recognizing the need for allies to break the Democratic Party's stranglehold on power in the South, some white Populists insisted that black and white farmers shared common grievances and could unite for common goals. Tom Watson, Georgia's leading Populist, worked the hardest to forge a black-white alliance. "You are kept apart," he told interracial audiences, "that you may be separately fleeced of your earnings.... This race antagonism perpetuates a monetary system which beggars both." While many blacks refused to abandon the party of Lincoln, others were attracted by the Populist appeal. In 1894, a coalition of white Populists and black Republicans won control of North Carolina, bringing to the state a "second Reconstruction" complete

> *Blacks and Populism*

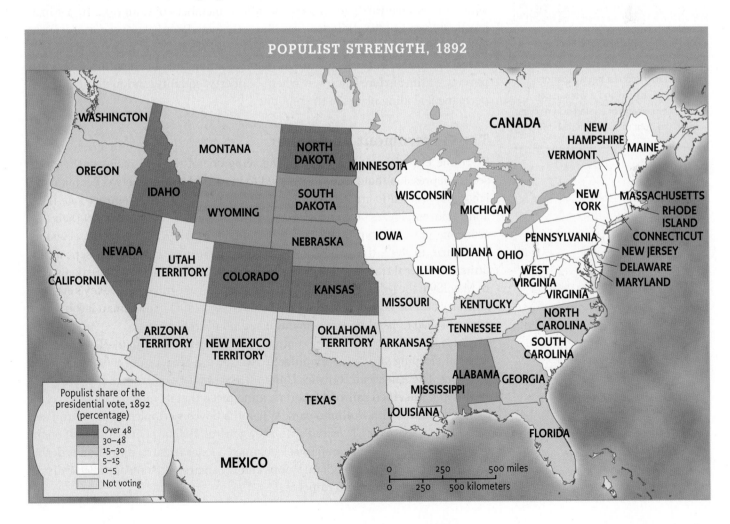

POPULIST STRENGTH, 1892

Populist share of the presidential vote, 1892 (percentage)

- Over 48
- 30–48
- 15–30
- 5–15
- 0–5
- Not voting

INDEPENDENCE DAY—COLORADO.

Most Populists in the West supported woman suffrage. In this cartoon published in a Colorado Populist newspaper on July 4, 1894, a man and a woman celebrate the passage of a referendum giving women the right to vote in that state.

with increased spending on public education and a revival of black officeholding. In most of the South, however, Democrats fended off the Populist challenge by resorting to the tactics they had used to retain power since the 1870s—mobilizing whites with warnings about "Negro supremacy," intimidating black voters, and stuffing ballot boxes on election day.

The Populist movement also engaged the energies of thousands of reform-minded women from farm and labor backgrounds. Some, like Mary Elizabeth Lease, a former homesteader and one of the first female lawyers in Kansas, became prominent organizers, campaigners, and strategists. Lease was famous for her speeches urging farmers to "raise less corn and more hell" (although she apparently never actually uttered those exact words, which would have been considered inappropriate for a woman in public). "We fought England for our liberty," Lease declared, "and put chains on four million blacks. We wiped out slavery and . . . began a system of white wage slavery worse than the first." During the 1890s, referendums in Colorado and Idaho approved extending the vote to women, while in Kansas and California the proposal went down in defeat. Populists in all these states endorsed women's suffrage.

Populist presidential candidate James Weaver received more than 1 million votes in 1892. The party carried five western states, with twenty-two electoral votes, and elected three governors and fifteen members of Congress. In his inaugural address in 1893, Lorenzo Lewelling, the new Populist governor of Kansas, anticipated a phrase made famous seventy years later by Martin Luther King Jr.: "I have a dream. . . . In the beautiful vision of a coming time I behold the abolition of poverty. A time is foreshadowed when . . . liberty, equality, and justice shall have permanent abiding places in the republic."

The Government and Labor

Were the Populists on the verge of replacing one of the two major parties? The severe depression that began in 1893 led to increased conflict between capital and labor and seemed to create an opportunity for expanding the Populist vote. Time and again, employers brought state or federal authority to bear to protect their own economic power or put down threats to public order. Even before the economic downturn, in 1892, the governor of Idaho declared martial law and sent militia units and federal troops into the mining region of Coeur d'Alene to break a strike. In May 1894, the federal government deployed soldiers to disperse **Coxey's Army**—a band of several hundred unemployed men led by Ohio businessman Jacob Coxey, who marched to Washington demanding economic relief.

The Pullman Strike

Also in 1894, workers in the company-owned town of Pullman, Illinois, where railroad sleeping cars were manufactured, called a strike to protest a reduction in wages. The American Railway Union, whose 150,000 members included both skilled and unskilled railroad laborers, announced that its members would refuse to handle trains with Pullman cars. When the boycott crippled national rail service, President Grover Cleveland's attorney general, Richard Olney (himself on the board of several railroad companies), obtained a federal court injunction ordering the strikers back to work. Federal troops and U.S. marshals soon occupied railroad centers like Chicago and Sacramento.

The strike collapsed when the union's leaders, including its charismatic president, Eugene V. Debs, were jailed for contempt of court for violating the judicial order. In the case of *In re Debs*, the Supreme Court unanimously confirmed the sentences and approved the use of injunctions against striking labor unions. On his release from prison in November 1895, more than 100,000 persons greeted Debs at a Chicago railroad depot.

Populism and Labor

In 1894, Populists made determined efforts to appeal to industrial workers. Populist senators supported the demand of Coxey's Army for federal unemployment relief, and Governor Davis Waite of Colorado, who had edited a labor newspaper before his election, sent the militia to protect striking miners against company police. In the state and congressional elections of that year, as the economic depression deepened, voters by the millions abandoned the Democratic Party of President Cleveland.

In rural areas, the Populist vote increased in 1894. But urban workers did not rally to the Populists, whose core issues—the subtreasury plan and lower mortgage interest rates—had little meaning for them and whose demand for higher prices for farm goods would raise the cost of food and reduce the value of workers' wages. Moreover, the revivalist atmosphere of many Populist gatherings and the biblical cadences of Populist speeches were alien to the largely immigrant and Catholic

Coxey's Army on the march in 1894.

Federal troops pose atop a railroad engine after being sent to Chicago to help suppress the Pullman Strike of 1894.

Labor votes

industrial working class. Urban working-class voters in 1894 instead shifted en masse to the Republicans, who claimed that raising tariff rates (which Democrats had recently reduced) would restore prosperity by protecting manufacturers and industrial workers from the competition of imported goods and cheap foreign labor. In one of the most decisive shifts in congressional power in American history, the Republicans gained 117 seats in the House of Representatives.

Bryan and Free Silver

"Cross of gold" speech

In 1896, Democrats and Populists joined to support William Jennings Bryan for the presidency. A thirty-six-year-old congressman from Nebraska, Bryan won the Democratic nomination after delivering to the national convention an electrifying speech that crystallized the farmers' pride and grievances. "Burn down your cities and leave our farms," Bryan proclaimed, "and your cities will spring up again as if by magic; but destroy our farms and grass will grow in the streets of every city in the country." Bryan called for the "free coinage" of silver—the unrestricted minting of silver money. In language ringing with biblical imagery, Bryan condemned the gold standard: "You shall not press down upon the brow of labor this crown of thorns. You shall not crucify mankind upon a cross of gold."

At various points in the nineteenth century, from debates over "hard" versus "soft" money in the Jacksonian era to the greenback movement after the Civil War, the "money question" had played a central role in American politics. Bryan's demand for "free silver" was the latest expression of the view that increasing the amount of currency in circulation would raise the prices farmers received for their crops and make it easier to pay off their debts. His nomination wrested control of the Democratic Party from long-dominant leaders like President Grover Cleveland, who were closely tied to eastern businessmen.

A cartoon from the magazine *Judge*, September 14, 1896, condemns William Jennings Bryan and his "cross of gold" speech for defiling the symbols of Christianity. Bryan tramples on the Bible while holding his golden cross; a vandalized church is visible in the background.

There was more to Bryan's appeal, however, than simply free silver. A devoutly religious man, he was strongly influenced by the Social Gospel movement (discussed in the previous chapter) and tried to apply the teachings of Jesus Christ to uplifting the "little people" of the United States. He championed a vision of the government helping ordinary Americans that anticipated provisions of the New Deal of the 1930s, including a progressive income tax, banking regulation, and the right of workers to form unions.

Many Populists were initially cool to Bryan's campaign. Their party had been defrauded time and again by Democrats in the South. Veteran Populists feared that their broad program was in danger of being reduced to "free silver." But realizing that they could not secure victory alone, the party's leaders endorsed Bryan's candidacy. Bryan broke with tradition and embarked on a nationwide speaking tour, seeking to rally farmers and workers to his cause.

The Campaign of 1896

Republicans met the silverite challenge head on, insisting that gold was the only "honest" currency. Abandoning the gold standard, they insisted, would destroy business confidence and prevent recovery from the depression by making creditors unwilling to extend loans, since they could not be certain of the value of the money in which they would be repaid. The party nominated for president Ohio governor

William McKinley, who as a congressman in 1890 had shepherded to passage the strongly protectionist McKinley Tariff.

The election of 1896 is sometimes called the first modern presidential campaign because of the amount of money spent by the Republicans and the efficiency of their national organization. Eastern bankers and industrialists, thoroughly alarmed by Bryan's call for monetary inflation and his fiery speeches denouncing corporate arrogance, poured millions of dollars into Republican coffers. (McKinley's campaign raised some $10 million; Bryan's around $300,000.) While McKinley remained at his Ohio home, where he addressed crowds of supporters from his front porch, his political manager Mark Hanna created a powerful national machine that flooded the country with pamphlets, posters, and campaign buttons.

The results revealed a nation as divided along regional lines as in 1860. Bryan carried the South and West and received 6.5 million votes. McKinley swept the more populous industrial states of the Northeast and Midwest, attracting 7.1 million. The Republican candidate's electoral margin was even greater: 271 to 176. The era's bitter labor strife did not carry over into the electoral arena; indeed, party politics seemed to mute class conflict rather than to reinforce it. Industrial America, from financiers and managers to workers, now voted solidly Republican, a loyalty reinforced when prosperity returned after 1897.

According to some later critics, the popular children's classic *The Wonderful Wizard of Oz*, published by L. Frank Baum in 1900, offered a commentary on the election of 1896 and its aftermath. In this interpretation, the Emerald City (where everything is colored green, for money) represents Washington, D.C., and the Wizard of Oz, who remains invisible in his palace and rules by illusion, is President McKinley. The only way to get to the city is via a Yellow Brick Road (the color of gold). The Wicked Witches of the East and West represent oppressive industrialists and mine owners. In the much-beloved film version made in the 1930s, Dorothy, the all-American girl from the heartland state of Kansas, wears ruby slippers. But in the book her shoes are silver, supposedly representing the money preferred by ordinary people.

Whatever Baum's symbolism, one thing was clear. McKinley's victory shattered the political stalemate that had persisted since 1876 and created one of the most enduring political majorities in American history. During McKinley's presidency, Republicans placed their stamp on economic policy by passing the Dingley Tariff of 1897, raising rates to the highest level in history, and the Gold Standard Act

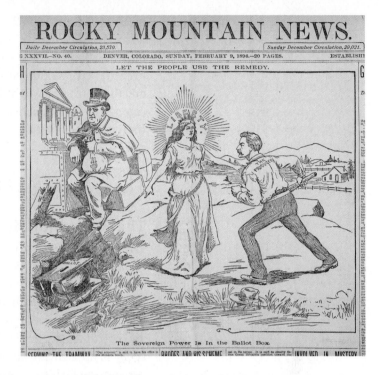

In another Populist cartoon from a Colorado newspaper, the figure of Liberty directs a member of the producing classes to use the ballot box to combat the "money power."

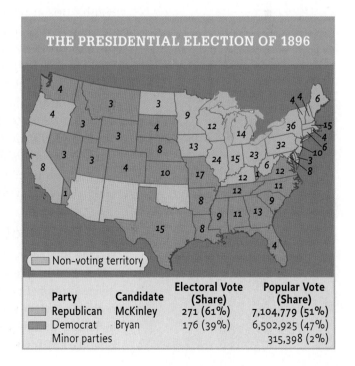

THE PRESIDENTIAL ELECTION OF 1896

Non-voting territory

Party	Candidate	Electoral Vote (Share)	Popular Vote (Share)
Republican	McKinley	271 (61%)	7,104,779 (51%)
Democrat	Bryan	176 (39%)	6,502,925 (47%)
Minor parties			315,398 (2%)

of 1900. Not until 1932, in the midst of another economic depression, would the Democrats become the nation's majority party. The election of 1896 also proved to be the last presidential election with extremely high voter turnout (in some states, over 90 percent of those eligible). From then on, with the South solidly Democratic and the North overwhelmingly Republican, few states witnessed vigorous two-party campaigns. Voter participation began a downhill trend, although it rose again from the mid-1930s through the 1960s. Today, only around half the electorate casts ballots.

THE SEGREGATED SOUTH

The Redeemers in Power

The failure of Populism in the South opened the door for the full imposition of a new racial order. The coalition of merchants, planters, and business entrepreneurs who dominated the region's politics after 1877, who called themselves Redeemers, had moved to undo as much as possible of Reconstruction. State budgets were slashed, taxes, especially on landed property, reduced, and public facilities like hospitals and asylums closed. Hardest hit were the new public school systems. Louisiana spent so little on education that it became the only state in the Union in which the percentage of whites unable to read and write actually increased between 1880 and 1900. Black schools, however, suffered the most, as the gap between expenditures for black and white pupils widened steadily. "What I want here is Negroes who can make cotton," declared one planter, "and they don't need education to help them make cotton."

Undoing Reconstruction

New laws authorized the arrest of virtually any person without employment and greatly increased the penalties for petty crimes. "They send [a man] to the penitentiary if he steals a chicken," complained a former slave in North Carolina. As the South's prison population rose, the renting out of convicts became a profitable business. Every southern state placed at least a portion of its convicted criminals, the majority of them blacks imprisoned for minor offenses, in the hands of private businessmen. Railroads, mines, and lumber companies competed for this new form of cheap, involuntary labor. Conditions in labor camps were often barbaric, with disease rife and the death rates high. "One dies, get another" was the motto of the system's architects. The Knights of Labor made convict labor a major issue in the South. In 1892, miners in Tennessee burned the stockade where convict workers were housed and shipped them out of the region. Tennessee abolished the convict lease system three years later but replaced it with a state-owned coal mine using prison labor that reaped handsome profits for decades.

A group of Florida convict laborers. Southern states notoriously used convicts for public labor, or leased them out to work in dire conditions for private employers.

The Failure of the New South Dream

During the 1880s, Atlanta editor Henry Grady tirelessly promoted the promise of a **New South**, an era of prosperity based on industrial expansion and agricultural diversification. In fact, while planters, merchants, and industrialists prospered, the region as a whole sank deeper and deeper into poverty. Some industry did develop, including mining in the Appalachians, textile production in the Carolinas and Georgia, and furniture and cigarette manufacturing in certain southern cities. The new upcountry cotton factories offered jobs to entire families of poor whites from the surrounding countryside. But since the main attractions for investors were the South's low wages and taxes and the availability of convict labor, these enterprises made little contribution to regional economic development. With the exception of Birmingham, Alabama, which by 1900 had developed into an important center for the manufacture of iron and steel, southern cities were mainly export centers for cotton, tobacco, and rice, with little industry or skilled labor. Overall, the region remained dependent on the North for capital and manufactured goods. In 1900, southern per capita income amounted to only 60 percent of the national average. As late as the 1930s, President Franklin D. Roosevelt would declare the South the nation's "number one" economic problem.

Coal miners, in a photograph by Lewis Hine. Mining was one occupation in which blacks and whites often worked side by side.

Black Life in the South

As the most disadvantaged rural southerners, black farmers suffered the most from the region's condition. In the Upper South, economic development offered some opportunities—mines, iron furnaces, and tobacco factories employed black laborers, and a good number of black farmers managed to acquire land. In the rice kingdom of coastal South Carolina and Georgia, planters found themselves unable to acquire the capital necessary to repair irrigation systems and machinery destroyed by the war. By the turn of the century, most of the great plantations had fallen to pieces, and many blacks acquired land and took up self-sufficient farming. In most of the Deep South, however, African-Americans owned a smaller percentage of the land in 1900 than they had at the end of Reconstruction.

In southern cities, the network of institutions created after the Civil War—schools and colleges, churches, businesses, women's clubs, and the like—served as the foundation for increasingly diverse black urban communities. They supported the growth of a black middle class, mostly professionals like teachers and physicians, or businessmen like undertakers and shopkeepers serving the needs of black customers. But the labor market was rigidly divided along racial lines. Black men were excluded from

The growth of a black middle class

Taken by an unknown photographer around the turn of the twentieth century, this picture is entitled "a southern baptism." With the elimination of black voting, the church assumed even more importance in black life.

An 1878 poster seeking recruits for the Kansas Exodus.

A photograph of townspeople in Nicodemus, a community established by members of the 1879–1880 "Exodus" of southern African-Americans to Kansas.

supervisory positions in factories and workshops and white-collar jobs such as clerks in offices. A higher percentage of black women than white worked for wages, but mainly as domestic servants. They could not find employment among the growing numbers of secretaries, typists, and department store clerks.

The Kansas Exodus

Overall, one historian has written, the New South was "a miserable landscape dotted only by a few rich enclaves that cast little or no light upon the poverty surrounding them." Trapped at the bottom of a stagnant economy, some blacks sought a way out through emigration from the South. In 1879 and 1880, an estimated 40,000 to 60,000 African-Americans migrated to Kansas, seeking political equality, freedom from violence, access to education, and economic opportunity. The name participants gave to this migration—the Exodus, derived from the biblical account of the Jews escaping slavery in Egypt—indicated that its roots lay in deep longings for the substance of freedom. Those promoting the **Kansas Exodus**, including former fugitive slave Benjamin "Pap" Singleton, the organizer of a real estate company, distributed flyers and lithographs picturing Kansas as an idyllic land of rural plenty. Lacking the capital to take up farming, however, most black migrants ended up as unskilled laborers in towns and cities. But few chose to return to the South. In the words of one minister active in the movement, "We had rather suffer and be free."

Despite deteriorating prospects in the South, most African-Americans had little alternative but to stay in the region. The real expansion of job opportunities was taking place in northern cities. But most northern employers refused to offer jobs to blacks in the expanding industrial economy, preferring to hire white migrants from rural areas and immigrants from Europe. Not until the outbreak of World War I in Europe in 1914 cut off immigration did northern employers open industrial jobs to blacks, setting in motion the Great Migration discussed in Chapter 19. Until then, the vast majority of African-Americans remained in the South.

The Decline of Black Politics

Neither black voting nor black officeholding came to an abrupt end in 1877. Blacks continued to cast ballots in large numbers, although Democrats solidified their control of state and local affairs by redrawing district lines and substituting appointive for elective officials in counties with black majorities. A few blacks even served in Congress in the 1880s and 1890s. Nonetheless, political opportunities became more and more restricted. Not until the 1990s would the number of black legislators in the South approach the level seen during Reconstruction.

For black men of talent and ambition, other avenues—business, the law, the church—increasingly seemed to offer greater opportunities for personal advancement and community service than politics. The banner of political leadership passed to black women activists. The National Association of Colored Women, founded in 1896, brought together local and regional women's clubs to press for both women's rights and racial uplift. Most female activists emerged from the small urban black middle class and preached the necessity of "respectable" behavior as part and parcel of the struggle for equal rights. They aided poor families, offered lessons in home life and childrearing, and battled gambling and drinking in black communities. Some poor blacks resented middle-class efforts to instruct them in proper behavior. But by insisting on the right of black women to be considered as "respectable" as their white counterparts, the women reformers challenged the racial ideology that consigned all blacks to the status of degraded second-class citizens.

Black women reformers

For nearly a generation after the end of Reconstruction, despite fraud and violence, black southerners continued to cast ballots. In some states, the Republican Party remained competitive. In Virginia, a coalition of mostly black Republicans and anti-Redeemer Democrats formed an alliance known as the Readjuster movement (the name derived from their plan to scale back, or "readjust," the state debt). They governed the state between 1879 and 1883. Tennessee and Arkansas also witnessed the formation of biracial political coalitions that challenged Democratic Party rule. Despite the limits of the Populists' interracial alliance, the threat of a biracial political insurgency frightened the ruling Democrats and contributed greatly to the disenfranchisement movement.

Biracial politics

The Elimination of Black Voting

Between 1890 and 1906, every southern state enacted laws or constitutional provisions meant to eliminate the black vote. Since the Fifteenth Amendment prohibited the use of race as a qualification for the suffrage, how were such measures even possible? Southern legislatures drafted laws that on paper appeared color-blind, but that were actually designed to end black voting. The most popular devices were the poll tax (a fee that each citizen had to pay in order to retain the right to vote), literacy tests, and the requirement that a prospective voter demonstrate to election officials an "understanding" of the state constitution. Six southern states also adopted a **grandfather clause**, exempting from the new requirements descendants of persons eligible to vote before the Civil War (when only whites, of course, could cast ballots in the South). The racial intent of the grandfather clause was so clear that the Supreme Court in 1915 invalidated such laws for violating the Fifteenth Amendment. The other methods of limiting black voting, however, remained on the books.

Poll tax

Grandfather clause

Some white leaders presented **disenfranchisement** as a "good government" measure—a means of purifying politics by ending the fraud, violence, and manipulation of voting returns regularly used against Republicans and Populists. But ultimately, as a Charleston newspaper declared, the aim was to make clear that the white South "does not desire or intend ever to include black men among its citizens." Although election officials often allowed whites who did not meet the new qualifications to register, numerous poor and illiterate whites also lost the right to vote, a result welcomed by many planters and urban reformers. Louisiana, for example, reduced the number of blacks registered to vote from 130,000 in 1894 to 1,342 a decade later. But 80,000 white voters also lost the right. Disenfranchisement led directly to the rise of a generation of southern "demagogues," who mobilized white voters by extreme appeals to racism. Tom Watson, who as noted above had tried to forge an interracial Populist coalition in the 1890s, reemerged early in the twentieth century as a power in Georgia public life through vicious speeches whipping up prejudice against blacks, Jews, and Catholics.

As late as 1940, only 3 percent of adult black southerners were registered to vote. The elimination of black and many white voters, which reversed the nineteenth-century trend toward more inclusive suffrage, could not have been accomplished without the acquiescence of the North. In 1891, the Senate defeated a proposal for federal protection of black voting rights in the South. Apart from the grandfather clause, the Supreme Court gave its approval to disenfranchisement laws. According to the Fourteenth Amendment, any state that deprived male citizens of the franchise was supposed to lose part of its representation in Congress. But like much of the Constitution, this provision was consistently violated so far as African-Americans were concerned. As a result, southern congressmen wielded far greater power on the national scene than their tiny electorates warranted. As for blacks, for decades thereafter, they would regard "the loss of suffrage as being the loss of freedom."

The Law of Segregation

Along with disenfranchisement, the 1890s saw the widespread imposition of segregation in the South. Laws and local customs requiring the separation of the races had numerous precedents. They had existed in many parts of the pre–Civil War North. Southern schools and many other institutions had been segregated during Reconstruction. In the 1880s, however, southern race relations remained unsettled. Some railroads, theaters, and hotels admitted blacks and whites on an equal basis while others separated them by race or excluded blacks altogether.

In 1883, in the *Civil Rights Cases*, the Supreme Court invalidated the Civil Rights Act of 1875, which had outlawed racial discrimination by hotels, theaters, railroads, and other public facilities. The Fourteenth Amendment, the Court insisted, prohibited unequal treatment by state authorities, not private businesses. In 1896, in the landmark decision in **Plessy v. Ferguson**, the Court gave its approval to state laws requiring separate facilities for blacks and whites. The case arose in Louisiana, where the legislature had required railroad companies to maintain a separate car or section for black passengers. A Citizens Committee of black residents of New Orleans came together to challenge the law. To create a test case, Homer Plessy, a light-skinned African-American, refused a conductor's order to move to the "colored only" part of his railroad car and was arrested.

To argue the case before the Supreme Court, the Citizens Committee hired Albion W. Tourgée, who as a judge in North Carolina during Reconstruction had waged a courageous battle against the Ku Klux Klan. "Citizenship is national and knows no color," he insisted, and racial segregation violated the Fourteenth Amendment's guarantee of equal protection before the law. But in a 7-1 decision, the Court upheld the Louisiana law, arguing that segregated facilities did not discriminate so long as they were "**separate but equal**." The lone dissenter, John Marshall Harlan, reprimanded the majority with an oft-quoted comment: "Our constitution

be exercised tomorrow against other classes and other people?" Brewer proved to be an accurate prophet. In 1904, the Court cited *Fong Yue Ting* in upholding a law barring anarchists from entering the United States, demonstrating how restrictions on the rights of one group can become a precedent for infringing on the rights of others.

Exclusion profoundly shaped the experience of Chinese-Americans, long stigmatizing them as incapable of assimilation and justifying their isolation from mainstream society. Congress for the first time also barred groups of whites from entering the country, beginning in 1875 with prostitutes and convicted felons, and in 1882 adding "lunatics" and those likely to become a "public charge." "Are we still a [place of refuge] for the oppressed of all nations?" wondered James B. Weaver, the Populist candidate for president in 1892.

The Emergence of Booker T. Washington

The social movements that had helped to expand the nineteenth-century boundaries of freedom now redefined their objectives so that they might be realized within the new economic and intellectual framework. Prominent black leaders, for example, took to emphasizing economic self-help and individual advancement into the middle class as an alternative to political agitation.

Booker T. Washington, advocate of industrial education and economic self-help.

Symbolizing the change was the juxtaposition, in 1895, of the death of Frederick Douglass with Booker T. Washington's widely praised speech, titled the "**Atlanta Compromise**," at the Atlanta Cotton Exposition that urged blacks to adjust to segregation and abandon agitation for civil and political rights. Born a slave in 1856, Washington had studied as a young man at Hampton Institute, Virginia. He adopted the outlook of Hampton's founder, General Samuel Armstrong, who emphasized that obtaining farms or skilled jobs was far more important to African-Americans emerging from slavery than the rights of citizenship. Washington put this view into practice when he became head of Tuskegee Institute in Alabama, a center for vocational education (education focused on training for a job rather than broad learning).

Tuskegee Institute

In his Atlanta speech, Washington repudiated the abolitionist tradition that stressed ceaseless agitation for full equality. He urged blacks not to try to combat segregation: "In all the things that are purely social we can be as separate as the fingers, yet one as the hand in all things essential to mutual progress." Washington advised his people to seek the assistance of white employers who, in a land racked by labor turmoil, would prefer a docile, dependable black labor force to unionized whites. Washington's ascendancy rested in large part on his success in channeling aid from wealthy northern whites to Tuskegee and to black politicians and newspapers who backed his program. But his support in the black community also arose from a widespread sense that in the world of the late nineteenth century, frontal assaults on white power were impossible and that blacks should concentrate on building up their segregated communities.

Washington's Atlanta speech

The Rise of the AFL

Within the labor movement, the demise of the Knights of Labor and the ascendancy of the **American Federation of Labor** (AFL) during the 1890s reflected a similar shift away from a broadly reformist past to more limited goals. As the Homestead

VOICES OF FREEDOM

From BOOKER T. WASHINGTON, ADDRESS AT THE ATLANTA COTTON EXPOSITION (1895)

In 1895, the year of the death of Frederick Douglass, Booker T. Washington delivered a speech at an exposition in Atlanta advocating a new strategy for racial progress. Blacks, he declared, should remain in the South, turn away from agitation for civil and political rights, adjust to segregation, and seek, with white cooperation, to improve their economic condition.

A ship lost at sea for many days suddenly sighted a friendly vessel. From the mast of the unfortunate vessel was seen a signal, "Water, water; we die of thirst!" The answer from the friendly vessel at once came back, "Cast down your bucket where you are." . . . The captain of the distressed vessel, at last heeding the injunction, cast down his bucket, and it came up full of fresh, sparkling water from the mouth of the Amazon River. To those of my race who depend on bettering their condition in a foreign land or who underestimate the importance of cultivating friendly relations with the Southern white man, who is their next door neighbor, I would say: "Cast down your bucket where you are"—cast it down in making friends in every manly way of the people of all races by whom we are surrounded.

Cast it down in agriculture, mechanics, in commerce, in domestic service, and in the professions. . . . Our greatest danger is that in the great leap from slavery to freedom we may overlook the fact that the masses of us are to live by the productions of our hands, and fail to keep in mind that we shall prosper in proportion as we learn to dignify and glorify common labour, and put brains and skill into the common occupations of life. . . . No race can prosper till it learns that there is as much dignity in tilling a field as in writing a poem. . . . Nor should we permit our grievances to overshadow our opportunities.

To those of the white race who look to the incoming of those of foreign birth and strange tongue and habits for the prosperity of the South, were I permitted I would repeat what I say to my own race, "Cast down your bucket where you are." Cast it down among the eight millions of Negroes. . . . In all things that are purely social we can be as separate as the fingers, yet one as the hand in all things essential to mutual progress. . . .

The wisest among my race understand that the agitation of questions of social equality is the extremest folly, and that progress in the enjoyment of all the privileges that will come to us must be the result of severe and constant struggle rather than of artificial forcing. No race that has anything to contribute to the markets of the world is long in any degree ostracized.

From W. E. B. DU BOIS, "OF MR. BOOKER T. WASHINGTON AND OTHERS" (1903)

The most powerful critique of Washington's program came from the pen of the black educator and activist W. E. B. Du Bois. In *The Souls of Black Folk*, a collection of essays on the state of American race relations, he sought to revive the tradition of agitation for basic civil, political, and educational rights.

————————

Easily the most striking thing in the history of the American Negro since 1876 is the ascendancy of Mr. Booker T. Washington. . . . The time is come when one may speak in all sincerity and utter courtesy of the mistakes and shortcomings of Mr. Washington's career, as well as of his triumphs. . . .

This is an age of unusual economic development, and Mr. Washington's programme naturally takes an economic cast, becoming a gospel of Work and Money to such an extent as apparently almost completely to overshadow the higher aims of life. . . . The reaction from the sentiment of wartime has given impetus to race prejudice against Negroes, and Mr. Washington withdraws many of the high demands of Negroes as men and American citizens. In other periods of intensified prejudice all the Negro's tendency to self assertion has been called forth; at this period a policy of submission is advocated. In the history of nearly all other races and peoples the doctrine preached at such crises has been that manly self respect is worth more than lands and houses, and that a people who voluntarily surrender such respect, or cease striving for it, are not worth civilizing. Mr. Washington distinctly asks that black people give up, at least for the present, three things,—First, political power, Second, insistence on civil rights, Third, higher education of Negro youth,—and concentrate all their energies on industrial education, the accumulation of wealth, and the conciliation of the South. . . . The question then comes: Is it possible, and probable, that nine millions of men can make effective progress in economic lines if they are deprived of political rights, made a servile caste, and allowed only the most meagre chance for developing their exceptional men? If history and reason give any distinct answer to these questions, it is an emphatic No. . . . [Blacks are] bound to ask of this nation three things. 1. The right to vote. 2. Civic equality. 3. The education of youth according to ability. . . .

Negroes must insist continually, in season and out of season, that voting is necessary to modern manhood, that color discrimination is barbarism, and that black boys need education as well as white boys. . . . By every civilized and peaceful method we must strive for the rights which the world accords to men.

QUESTIONS

1. *What does Washington believe are the main routes to black advancement?*

2. *Why does Du Bois think that Washington's outlook reflects major elements of social thought in the 1890s?*

3. *How do the two men differ in their understanding of what is required for blacks to enjoy genuine freedom?*

Samuel Gompers

and Pullman strikes demonstrated, direct confrontations with the large corporations were likely to prove suicidal. Unions, declared Samuel Gompers, the AFL's founder and longtime president, should not seek economic independence, pursue the Knights' utopian dream of creating a "cooperative commonwealth," or form independent parties with the aim of achieving power in government. Rather, the labor movement should devote itself to negotiating with employers for higher wages and better working conditions for its members. Like Washington, Gompers spoke the language of the era's business culture. Indeed, the AFL policies he pioneered were known as "business unionism." Gompers embraced the idea of "freedom of contract," shrewdly turning it into an argument against interference by judges with workers' right to organize unions.

During the 1890s, union membership rebounded from its decline in the late 1880s. But at the same time, the labor movement became less and less inclusive. Abandoning the Knights' ideal of labor solidarity, the AFL restricted membership to skilled workers—a small minority of the labor force—effectively excluding the vast majority of unskilled workers and, therefore, nearly all blacks, women, and new European immigrants. AFL membership centered on sectors of the economy like printing and building construction that were dominated by small competitive businesses. AFL unions had little presence in basic industries like steel and rubber, or in the large-scale factories that now dominated the economy.

Skilled workers

The Women's Era

Changes in the women's movement reflected the same combination of expanding activities and narrowing boundaries. The 1890s launched what would later be called the "women's era"—three decades during which women, although still denied the vote, enjoyed larger opportunities than in the past for economic independence and played a greater and greater role in public life. By now, nearly every state had adopted laws giving married women control over their own wages and property and the right to sign separate contracts and make separate wills. Nearly 5 million women worked for wages in 1900. Although most were young, unmarried, and concentrated in traditional jobs such as domestic service and the garment industry, a generation of college-educated women was beginning to take its place in better-paying clerical and professional positions.

Through a network of women's clubs, temperance associations, and social reform organizations, women exerted a growing influence on public affairs. Founded in 1874, the Woman's Christian Temperance Union (WCTU) grew to become the era's largest female organization, with a membership by

"A Woman's Liquor Raid," an illustration in the *National Police Gazette* in 1879, depicts a group of temperance crusaders destroying liquor containers in a Frederickstown, Ohio, saloon.

1890 of 150,000. Under the banner of Home Protection, it moved from demanding the prohibition of alcoholic beverages (blamed for leading men to squander their wages on drink and treat their wives abusively) to a comprehensive program of economic and political reform, including the right to vote. Women, insisted Frances Willard, the group's president, must abandon the idea that "weakness" and dependence were their nature and join assertively in movements to change society. "A wider freedom is coming to the women of America," she declared in an 1895 speech to male and female strikers in a Massachusetts shoe factory. "Too long has it been held that woman has no right to enter these movements. So much for the movements. Politics is the place for woman."

At the same time, the center of gravity of feminism shifted toward an outlook more in keeping with prevailing racial and ethnic norms. The earlier "feminism of equal rights," which claimed the ballot as part of a larger transformation of women's status, was never fully repudiated. The movement continued to argue for women's equality in employment, education, and politics. But with increasing frequency, the native-born, middle-class women who dominated the suffrage movement claimed the vote as educated members of a "superior race."

A new generation of suffrage leaders suggested that educational and other voting qualifications did not conflict with the movement's aims, so long as they applied equally to men and women. Immigrants and former slaves had been enfranchised with "ill-advised haste," declared Carrie Chapman Catt, president of the National American Woman Suffrage Association (created in 1890 to reunite the rival suffrage organizations formed after the Civil War). Indeed, Catt suggested, extending the vote to native-born white women would help to counteract the growing power of the "ignorant foreign vote" in the North and the dangerous potential for a second Reconstruction in the South. Elitism within the movement was reinforced when many advocates of suffrage blamed the "slum vote" for the defeat of a women's suffrage referendum in California. In 1895, the same year that Booker T. Washington delivered his Atlanta address, the National American Woman Suffrage Association held its annual convention in that segregated city. Eight years later, the association met in New Orleans, where the delegates sang "Dixie" and listened to speeches by former Confederate officers that denounced blacks as barbarians. Like other American institutions, the organized movement for women's suffrage had made its peace with nativism and racism.

A drawing for the 1896 meeting of the National American Woman Suffrage Association depicts Elizabeth Cady Stanton (with the Woman's Bible, which she wrote, on her lap) and Susan B. Anthony seated on either side of George Washington. They, in turn, are flanked by Utah and Wyoming, which as territories had been the first parts of the United States to give women the right to vote. Although the image might lead viewers to assume that Stanton and Anthony had joined Washington in heaven, they were both still alive in 1896.

Woman suffrage movement

BECOMING A WORLD POWER

The New Imperialism

In the last years of the 1890s, the narrowed definition of nationhood was projected abroad, as the United States took its place as an imperial power on the international stage. In world history, the last quarter of the nineteenth century is known as the age of imperialism, when rival European empires carved up large parts of the world among themselves. For most of this period, the United States remained a second-rate power. In 1880, the head of the Ottoman empire decided to close three foreign embassies to reduce expenses. He chose those in Sweden, Belgium, and the United States. In that year, the American navy was smaller than Denmark's or Chile's. When European powers met at the Berlin Congress of 1884–1885 to divide most of Africa among themselves, the United States attended because of its relationship with Liberia but did not sign the final agreement.

The global context for imperialism

Throughout the nineteenth century, large empires dominated much of the globe. After 1870, a "new imperialism" arose, dominated by European powers and Japan. Belgium, Great Britain, and France consolidated their hold on colonies in Africa, and newly unified Germany acquired colonies there as well. The British and Russians sought to increase their influence in Central Asia, and all the European powers struggled to dominate parts of China. By the early twentieth century, most of Asia, Africa, the Middle East, and the Pacific had been divided among these empires. The justification for this expansion of imperial power was that it would bring modern "civilization" to the supposedly backward peoples of the non-European world. The natives, according to their colonial occupiers, would be instructed in Western values, labor practices, and the Christian religion. Eventually, they would be accorded the right of self-government, although no one could be sure how long this would take. In the meantime, "empire" was another word for "exploitation."

American Expansionism

Territorial expansion, of course, had been a feature of American life from well before independence. But the 1890s marked a major turning point in America's relationship with the rest of the world. Americans were increasingly aware of themselves as an emerging world power. "We are a great imperial Republic destined to exercise a controlling influence upon the actions of mankind and to affect the future of the world," proclaimed Henry Watterson, an influential newspaper editor.

"A great imperial Republic"

Until the 1890s, American expansion had taken place on the North American continent. Ever since the Monroe Doctrine (see Chapter 10), to be sure, many Americans had considered the Western Hemisphere an American sphere of influence. There was persistent talk of acquiring Cuba, and President Grant had sought to annex the Dominican Republic, only to see the Senate reject the idea. The last territorial acquisition before the 1890s had been Alaska, purchased from Russia by Secretary of State William H. Seward in 1867, to much derision from those who could not see the purpose of American ownership of "Seward's icebox." Seward, however, was mostly interested in the Aleutian Islands, a part of Alaska that stretched much of the way to Asia (see the map on p. 670) and that, he believed, could be the site of coaling stations for merchant ships plying the Pacific.

Expanding trade

Most Americans who looked overseas were interested in expanded trade, not territorial possessions. The country's agricultural and industrial production could no longer be entirely absorbed at home. By 1890, companies like Singer Sewing Machines and John D. Rockefeller's Standard Oil Company aggressively marketed their products abroad. Especially during economic downturns, business leaders insisted on the necessity of greater access to foreign customers. Middle-class

American women, moreover, were becoming more and more desirous of clothing and food from abroad, and their demand for consumer goods such as "Oriental" fashions and exotic spices for cooking spurred the economic penetration of the Far East.

The Lure of Empire

One group of Americans who spread the nation's influence overseas were religious missionaries, thousands of whom ventured abroad in the late nineteenth century to spread Christianity, prepare the world for the second coming of Christ, and uplift the poor. Inspired by Dwight Moody, a Methodist evangelist, the Student Volunteer Movement for Foreign Missions sent more than 8,000 missionaries to "bring light to heathen worlds" across the globe. Missionary work offered employment to those with few opportunities at home, including blacks and women, who made up a majority of the total.

Missionaries

A small group of late-nineteenth-century thinkers actively promoted American expansionism, warning that the country must not allow itself to be shut out of the scramble for empire. In *Our Country* (1885), Josiah Strong, a prominent Congregationalist clergyman, sought to update the idea of manifest destiny. Having demonstrated their special aptitude for liberty and self-government on the North American continent, Strong announced, Anglo-Saxons should now spread their institutions and values to "inferior races" throughout the world. The economy would benefit, he insisted, since one means of civilizing "savages" was to turn them into consumers of American goods.

Josiah Strong

Naval officer Alfred T. Mahan, in *The Influence of Sea Power upon History* (1890), argued that no nation could prosper without a large fleet of ships engaged in international trade, protected by a powerful navy operating from overseas bases. Mahan published his book in the same year that the census bureau announced that there was no longer a clear line separating settled from unsettled land. Thus, the frontier no longer existed. "Americans," wrote Mahan, "must now begin to look outward." His arguments influenced the outlook of James G. Blaine, who served as secretary of state during Benjamin Harrison's presidency (1889–1893). Blaine urged the president to try to acquire Hawaii, Puerto Rico, and Cuba as strategic naval bases.

A cartoon in *Puck*, December 1, 1897, imagines the annexation of Hawaii by the United States as a shotgun wedding. The minister, President McKinley, reads from a book entitled *Annexation Policy*. The Hawaiian bride appears to be looking for a way to escape. Most Hawaiians did not support annexation.

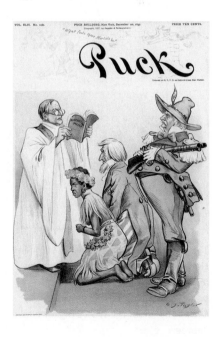

Although independent, Hawaii was already closely tied to the United States through treaties that exempted imports of its sugar from tariff duties and provided for the establishment of an American naval base at Pearl Harbor. Hawaii's economy was dominated by American-owned sugar plantations that employed a workforce of native islanders and Chinese, Japanese, and Filipino laborers under long-term contracts. Early in 1893, a group of American planters organized a rebellion that overthrew the Hawaii government of Queen Liliuokalani. On the eve of leaving office, Harrison submitted a treaty of annexation to the Senate. After determining that a majority of Hawaiians did not favor the treaty, Harrison's successor, Grover Cleveland, withdrew it. In July 1898, in the midst of the Spanish-American War, the United States finally annexed the Hawaiian Islands. In 1993, the U.S. Congress passed, and President Bill Clinton signed, a resolution expressing regret to native Hawaiians for "the overthrow of the Kingdom of Hawaii . . . with the participation of agents and citizens of the United States."

The depression that began in 1893 heightened the belief that a more aggressive foreign policy was necessary to stimulate American exports. In the face of social conflict and the new immigration, government and private organizations promoted a unifying patriotism. These were the years when rituals like the Pledge of Allegiance and the practice of standing for the playing of "The Star-Spangled Banner" came into existence. Americans had long honored the Stars and Stripes, but the "cult of the flag," including an official Flag Day, dates to the 1890s. New, mass-circulation newspapers also promoted nationalistic sentiments. By the late 1890s, papers like William Randolph Hearst's *New York Journal* and Joseph Pulitzer's *New York World*—dubbed the "**yellow press**" by their critics after the color in which Hearst printed a popular comic strip—were selling a million copies each day by mixing sensational accounts of crime and political corruption with aggressive appeals to patriotic sentiments.

The "yellow press"

The "Splendid Little War"

All these factors contributed to America's emergence as a world power in the Spanish-American War of 1898. But the immediate origins of the war lay not at home but in the long Cuban struggle for independence from Spain. Ten years of guerrilla war had followed a Cuban revolt in 1868. The movement for independence resumed in 1895. As reports circulated of widespread suffering caused by the Spanish policy of rounding up civilians and moving them into detention camps, the Cuban struggle won growing support in the United States.

Cuba

Demands for intervention escalated after February 15, 1898, when an explosion—probably accidental, a later investigation concluded—destroyed the American battleship **U.S.S. *Maine*** in Havana Harbor, with the loss of nearly 270

The U.S.S. Maine

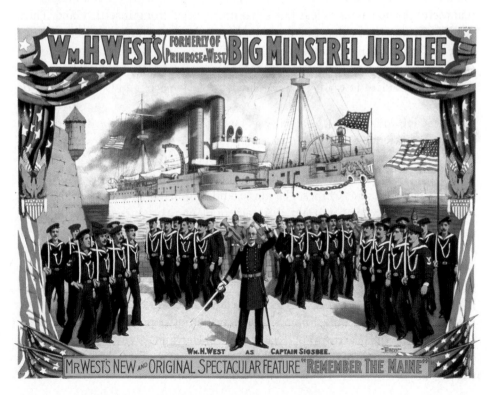

The destruction of the battleship *Maine* in Havana Harbor (later found to have been an accident) provided the occasion for patriotic pageants like "Remember the *Maine*," by William H. West's Big Minstrel Jubilee.

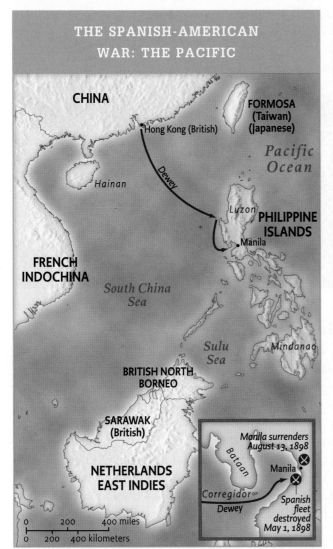

THE SPANISH-AMERICAN
WAR: THE PACIFIC

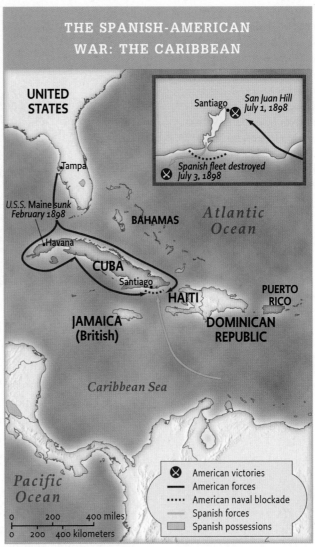

THE SPANISH-AMERICAN
WAR: THE CARIBBEAN

lives. The yellow press blamed Spain and insisted on retribution. After Spain rejected an American demand for a cease-fire on the island and eventual Cuban independence, President McKinley in April asked Congress for a declaration of war. The purpose, declared Senator Henry Teller of Colorado, was to aid Cuban patriots in their struggle for "liberty and freedom." To underscore the government's humanitarian intentions, Congress adopted the Teller Amendment, stating that the United States had no intention of annexing or dominating the island.

Secretary of State John Hay called the Spanish-American conflict a "splendid little war." It lasted only four months and resulted in fewer than 400 American combat deaths. Having shown little interest in imperial expansion before 1898, McKinley now embraced the idea. The war's most decisive engagement, in fact, took place not in Cuba but at Manila Bay, a strategic harbor in the Philippine Islands in the distant Pacific Ocean. Here, on May 1, the American navy under Admiral George Dewey defeated a Spanish fleet. Soon afterward, soldiers went ashore, becoming the first American army units to engage in combat outside the Western Hemisphere. July witnessed another naval victory off Santiago, Cuba, and the landing of American troops on Cuba and Puerto Rico.

In both the Pacific and the Caribbean, the United States achieved swift victories over Spain in the Spanish-American War.

The Spanish-American War

Charge of the Rough Riders at San Juan Hill, a painting by Frederic Remington, depicts the celebrated unit, commanded by Theodore Roosevelt, in action in Cuba during the Spanish-American War of 1898. Roosevelt, on horseback, leads the troops. Remington had been sent to the island the previous year by publisher William Randolph Hearst to provide pictures of Spanish atrocities during the Cuban war for independence in the hope of boosting the *New York Journal*'s circulation.

Roosevelt at San Juan Hill

The "Rough Riders"

The most highly publicized land battle of the war took place in Cuba. This was the charge up San Juan Hill, outside Santiago, by Theodore Roosevelt's Rough Riders. An ardent expansionist, Roosevelt had long believed that a war would reinvigorate the nation's unity and sense of manhood, which had suffered, he felt, during the 1890s. A few months shy of his fortieth birthday when war broke out, Roosevelt resigned his post as assistant secretary of the navy to raise a volunteer cavalry unit, which rushed to Cuba to participate in the fighting. Roosevelt envisioned his unit as a cross section of American society and enrolled athletes from Ivy League colleges, western cowboys, representatives of various immigrant groups, and even some American Indians. But with the army still segregated, he excluded blacks from his regiment. Ironically, when the Rough Riders reached the top of San Juan Hill, they found that black units had preceded them—a fact Roosevelt omitted in his reports of the battle, which were widely reproduced in the popular press. His exploits made Roosevelt a national hero. He was elected governor of New York that fall and in 1900 became McKinley's vice president.

An American Empire

American possessions

With the backing of the yellow press, the war quickly escalated from a crusade to aid the suffering Cubans to an imperial venture that ended with the United States in possession of a small overseas empire. McKinley became convinced that the United States could neither return the Philippines to Spain nor grant them independence, for which he believed the inhabitants unprepared. In an interview with a group of Methodist ministers, the president spoke of receiving a divine revelation that Americans had a duty to "uplift and civilize" the Filipino people and to train them for self-government. In the treaty with Spain that ended the war, the United States acquired the Philippines, Puerto Rico, and the Pacific island of Guam. As for Cuba, before recognizing its independence, McKinley forced the island's new government

Platt Amendment

to approve the **Platt Amendment** to the new Cuban constitution (drafted by Sena-

Hacienda La Fortuna, a sugar plantation, as depicted by the Puerto Rican artist Francisco Oller in 1885. From left to right the buildings are a warehouse, plantation home, and modern steam-powered sugar mill. The acquisition of the island by the United States in the Spanish-American War strengthened the hold of "sugar barons" on the Puerto Rican economy.

tor Orville H. Platt of Connecticut), which authorized the United States to intervene militarily whenever it saw fit. The United States also acquired a permanent lease on naval stations in Cuba, including what is now the facility at Guantánamo Bay.

The Platt Amendment passed the Cuban Congress by a single vote. Cuban patriots were terribly disappointed. José Martí had fomented revolution in Cuba from exile in the United States and then traveled to the island to take part in the uprising, only to be killed in a battle with Spanish soldiers in 1895. "To change masters is not to be free," Martí had written. And the memory of the betrayal of 1898 would help to inspire another Cuban revolution half a century later.

American interest in its new possessions had more to do with trade than gaining wealth from natural resources or large-scale American settlement. Puerto Rico and Cuba were gateways to Latin America, strategic outposts from which American naval and commercial power could be projected throughout the hemisphere. The Philippines, Guam, and Hawaii lay astride shipping routes to the markets of Japan and China. In 1899, soon after the end of the Spanish-American War, Secretary of State John Hay announced the **Open Door Policy**, demanding that European powers that had recently divided China into commercial spheres of influence grant equal access to American exports. The Open Door referred to the free movement of goods and money, not people. Even as the United States banned the immigration of Chinese into this country, it insisted on access to the markets and investment opportunities of Asia.

Trade

Open Door Policy

The Philippine War

Many Cubans, Filipinos, and Puerto Ricans had welcomed American intervention as a way of breaking Spain's long hold on these colonies. Large planters looked forward to greater access to American markets, and local elites hoped that the American presence would fend off radical changes proposed by rebellious nationalist movements. Nationalists and labor leaders admired America's democratic ideals and believed that American participation in the destruction of Spanish rule would lead to social reform and political self-government.

American intervention

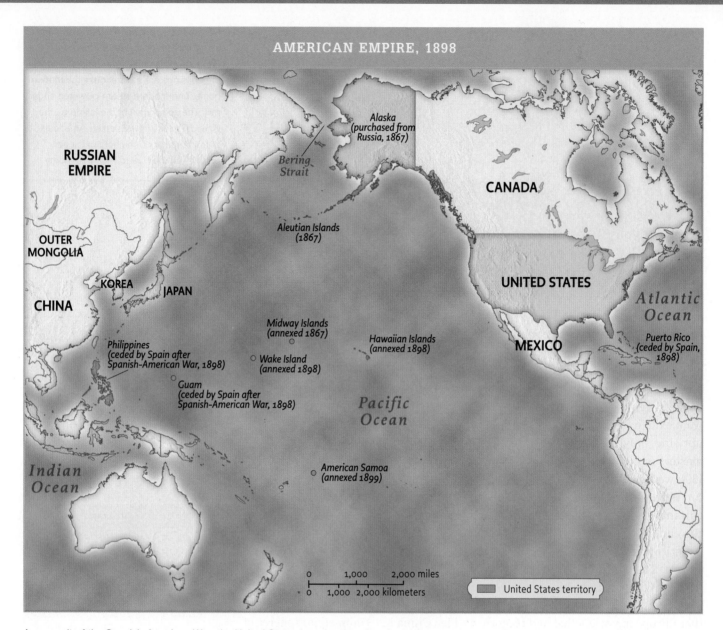

AMERICAN EMPIRE, 1898

Alaska (purchased from Russia, 1867)

Bering Strait

RUSSIAN EMPIRE

CANADA

OUTER MONGOLIA

Aleutian Islands (1867)

KOREA

JAPAN

CHINA

UNITED STATES

Atlantic Ocean

Midway Islands (annexed 1867)

Hawaiian Islands (annexed 1898)

MEXICO

Puerto Rico (ceded by Spain, 1898)

Philippines (ceded by Spain after Spanish-American War, 1898)

Wake Island (annexed 1898)

Guam (ceded by Spain after Spanish-American War, 1898)

Pacific Ocean

Indian Ocean

American Samoa (annexed 1899)

0   1,000   2,000 miles
0 1,000 2,000 kilometers

United States territory

As a result of the Spanish-American War, the United States became the ruler of a far-flung overseas empire.

Filipino movement

But the American determination to exercise continued control, direct or indirect, led to a rapid change in local opinion, nowhere more so than in the Philippines. Filipinos had been fighting a war against Spain since 1896. After Dewey's victory at Manila Bay, their leader, Emilio Aguinaldo, established a provisional government with a constitution modeled on that of the United States. But once McKinley decided to retain possession of the islands, the Filipino movement turned against the United States. The result was a second war, far longer (it lasted from 1899 to 1903) and bloodier (it cost the lives of more than 100,000 Filipinos and 4,200 Americans) than the Spanish-American conflict. Today, the **Philippine War** is perhaps the least remembered of all American wars. At the time, however, it was closely followed and widely debated in the United States. Both sides committed atrocities. Insurgents killed Filipinos who cooperated with the Americans. The U.S. Army burned villages and moved the inhabitants into camps where thousands perished of disease, and launched a widespread campaign of torture, including the infamous "water cure" or simulated drowning, later revived in the Iraq and Afghanistan wars of the 21st century and known as waterboarding. Press reports of these practices tarnished the nation's self-image as liberators. "We do not intend to free the people of the Philippines," complained Mark Twain. "We have gone there to conquer."

> *Campaign of torture*

The McKinley administration justified its policies on the grounds that its aim was to "uplift and civilize and Christianize" the Filipinos (although most residents of the islands were already Roman Catholics). William Howard Taft, who became governor-general of the Philippines in 1901, believed it might take a century to raise Filipinos to the condition where they could appreciate "what Anglo-Saxon liberty is."

Once in control of the Philippines, the colonial administration took seriously the idea of modernizing the islands. It expanded railroads and harbors, brought in American schoolteachers and public health officials, and sought to modernize agriculture (although efforts to persuade local farmers to substitute corn for rice ran afoul of the Filipino climate and cultural traditions). The United States, said President McKinley, had an obligation to its "little brown brothers." Yet in all the new possessions, American policies tended to serve the interests of land-based local elites—native-born landowners in the Philippines, American sugar planters in Hawaii and Puerto Rico—and such policies bequeathed enduring poverty to the

> *Modernizing the Philippines*

A BIGGER JOB THAN HE THOUGHT FOR.
UNCLE SAM—Behave, You Fool! Durn Me, If I Ain't Most Sorry I Undertook to Rescue You.

In this cartoon comment on the American effort to suppress the movement for Philippine independence, Uncle Sam tries to subdue a knife-wielding insurgent.

Simulated drowning or the "water cure," later known as waterboarding, was widely employed by American soldiers to elicit information from captured enemy combatants during the Philippine War. Over a century later, its use during the "war on terror" would arouse worldwide criticism.

William Howard Taft, the rotund American governor-general of the Philippines, astride a local water buffalo.

majority of the rural population. Under American rule, Puerto Rico, previously an island of diversified small farmers, became a low-wage plantation economy controlled by absentee corporations. By the 1920s, its residents were among the poorest in the entire Caribbean.

Citizens or Subjects?

American rule also brought with it American racial attitudes. In an 1899 poem, the British writer Rudyard Kipling urged the United States to take up the "white man's burden" of imperialism. American proponents of empire agreed that the domination of non-white peoples by whites formed part of the progress of civilization. Among the soldiers sent to the Philippines to fight Aguinaldo were a number of black regiments. Their letters from the front suggested that American atrocities arose from white troops applying to the Filipino population the same "treatment for colored peoples" practiced at home.

America's triumphant entry into the ranks of imperial powers sparked an intense debate over the relationship among political democracy, race, and American citizenship. The American system of government had no provision for permanent colonies. The right of every people to self-government was one of the main principles of the Declaration of Independence. The idea of an "empire of liberty" assumed that new territories would eventually be admitted as equal states and their residents would be American citizens. In the aftermath of the Spanish-American War, however, nationalism, democracy, and American freedom emerged more closely identified than ever with notions of Anglo-Saxon superiority.

Leaders of both parties, while determined to retain the new overseas possessions, feared that people of what one congressman called "an alien race and foreign tongue" could not be incorporated into the Union. The Foraker Act of 1900 declared Puerto Rico an "insular territory," different from previous territories in the West. Its 1 million inhabitants were defined as citizens of Puerto Rico, not the United States, and denied a future path to statehood. Filipinos occupied a similar status. In a series of cases decided between 1901 and 1904 and known collectively as the **Insular Cases**, the Supreme Court held that the Constitution did not fully apply to the territories recently acquired by the United States—a significant limitation of the scope of American freedom. Congress, the Court declared, must recognize the "fundamental" personal rights of residents of the Philippines and Puerto Rico. But otherwise it could govern them as it saw fit for an indefinite period of time. Thus, two principles central to American freedom since the War of Independence—no taxation without representation, and government based on the consent of the governed—were abandoned when it came to the nation's new possessions.

In the twentieth century, the territories acquired in 1898 would follow different paths. Hawaii, which had a sizable population of

American missionaries and planters, became a traditional territory. Its population, except for Asian immigrant laborers, became American citizens, and it was admitted as a state in 1959. After nearly a half-century of American rule, the Philippines achieved independence in 1946. Until 1950, the U.S. Navy administered Guam, which remains today an "unincorporated" territory. As for Puerto Rico, it is sometimes called "the world's oldest colony," because ever since the Spanish conquered the island in 1493 it has lacked full self-government. Congress extended American citizenship to Puerto Ricans in 1917. Puerto Rico today remains in a kind of political limbo, poised on the brink of statehood or independence. The island has the status of a commonwealth.

Some of the 1,200 Filipinos exhibited at the 1904 Louisiana Purchase Exposition in St. Louis. The federal government displayed the Filipinos in a "native" setting in order to win public support for the annexation of the Philippines.

It elects its own government but lacks a voice in Congress (and in the election of the U.S. president), and key issues such as defense and environmental policy are controlled by the United States.

Whatever the end result, the Spanish-American War established a precedent for American intervention in the affairs of other countries, especially those in the Western Hemisphere. In the twentieth century, the United States would intervene in Latin America to change local governments, either by direct military action or via support for military coups, no fewer than forty times.

Drawing the Global Color Line

Just as American ideas about liberty and self-government had circulated around the world in the Age of Revolution, American racial attitudes had a global impact in the age of empire. The turn of the twentieth century was a time of worldwide concern about immigration, race relations, and the "white man's burden," all of which inspired a global sense of fraternity among "Anglo-Saxon" nations. Chinese exclusion in the United States strongly influenced anti-Chinese laws adopted in Canada.

> *"White man's burden"*

One "lesson" these countries learned from the United States was that the "failure" of Reconstruction demonstrated the impossibility of multiracial democracy. The extremely hostile account of Reconstruction by the British writer James Bryce in his widely read book *The American Commonwealth* (published in London in 1888) circulated around the world. Bryce called African-Americans "children of nature" and insisted that giving them the right to vote had been a terrible mistake, which had produced all kinds of corruption and misgovernment. His book was frequently cited by the founders of the Australian Commonwealth (1901) to justify their "white Australia" policy, which barred the further immigration of Asians. The Union of South Africa, inaugurated in 1911, saw its own policy of racial separation—later known as apartheid—as following in the footsteps of segregation in the United States. Even American proposals that did not become law, such as the literacy test for immigrants vetoed by President Cleveland, influenced measures adopted overseas. The United States, too, learned from other countries. The Gentleman's Agreement that limited Japanese immigration early in the twentieth century (see Chapter 19) followed a similar arrangement between Japan and Canada.

> *Multiracial democracy*

The first step towards lightening

The White Man's Burden

is through teaching the virtues of cleanliness.

Pears' Soap

An advertisement employs the idea of a White Man's Burden (borrowed from a poem by Rudyard Kipling) as a way of promoting the virtues of Pears' Soap. Accompanying text claims that Pears' is "the ideal toilet soap" for "the cultured of all nations," and an agent of civilization in "the dark corners of the earth."

This propaganda photograph from 1898 depicts the Spanish-American War as a source of national reconciliation in the United States (with Confederate and Union soldiers shaking hands) and of freedom for Cuba (personified by a girl whose arm holds a broken chain).

"Republic or Empire?"

The emergence of the United States as an imperial power sparked intense debate. Opponents formed the **Anti-Imperialist League**. It united writers and social reformers who believed American energies should be directed at home, businessmen fearful of the cost of maintaining overseas outposts, and racists who did not wish to bring non-white populations into the United States. Among its prominent members were E. L. Godkin, the editor of *The Nation*, the novelist William Dean Howells, and the labor leader George E. McNeill. The league held meetings throughout the country and published pamphlets called Liberty Tracts, warning that empire was incompatible with democracy. America's historic mission, the league declared, was to "help the world by an example of successful self-government," not to conquer other peoples. A "republic of free men," anti-imperialists proclaimed, should assist the people of Puerto Rico and the Philippines in their own "struggles for liberty," rather than subjecting them to colonial rule.

In 1900, Democrats again nominated William Jennings Bryan to run against McKinley. The Democratic platform opposed the Philippine War for placing the United States in the "un-American" position of "crushing with military force" another people's desire for "liberty and self-government." George S. Boutwell, president of the Anti-Imperialist League, declared that the most pressing question in the election was the nation's future character—"republic or empire?"

But without any sense of contradiction, proponents of an imperial foreign policy also adopted the language of freedom. Anti-imperialists were the real "infidels to the gospel of liberty," claimed Senator Albert Beveridge of Indiana, because America ventured abroad not for material gain or national power, but to bring "a new day of freedom" to the peoples of the world. America's was a "benevolent" imperialism, rooted in a national mission to uplift backward cultures and spread liberty across the globe. Beveridge did not, however, neglect more practical considerations. American trade, he insisted, "henceforth must be with Asia. The Pacific is our ocean. . . . Where shall we turn for consumers of our surplus? Geography answers the question. China is our natural customer." And the Philippines held the key to "the commercial situation of the entire East." Riding the wave of patriotic sentiment inspired by the war, and with the economy having recovered from the depression of 1893–1897, McKinley in 1900 repeated his 1896 triumph.

At the dawn of the twentieth century, the United States seemed poised to take its place among the world's great powers. Writers at home and overseas confidently predicted that American influence would soon span the globe. In his 1902 book *The New Empire*, Brooks Adams, a grandson of John Quincy Adams, predicted that because of its economic power, the United States would soon "outweigh any single empire, if not all empires combined." Years would pass before this prediction was fulfilled. But in 1900, many features that would mark American life for much of the twentieth century were already apparent. The United States led the world in industrial production. The merger movement of 1897–1904 (discussed in the previous chapter) left broad sections of the economy under the control of giant corporations. The political system had stabilized. The white North and South had achieved reconciliation, while rigid lines of racial exclusion—the segregation of blacks, Chinese exclusion, Indian reservations—limited the boundaries of freedom and citizenship.

The Two Great Missioners of Civilization, an 1898 cartoon from the magazine *Judge*, celebrates imperialism by showing the United States and Great Britain striding through the sugar fields dispensing civilization to benighted natives, followed closely by the railroad, another agent of progress.

Yet the questions central to nineteenth-century debates over freedom—the relationship between political and economic liberty, the role of government in creating the conditions of freedom, and the definition of those entitled to enjoy the rights of citizens—had not been permanently answered. Nor had the dilemma of how to reconcile America's role as an empire with traditional ideas of freedom been resolved. These were the challenges bequeathed by the nineteenth century to the first generation of the twentieth.

SUGGESTED READING

BOOKS

- Aleinikoff, Alexander. *Semblances of Sovereignty: The Constitution, the State, and American Citizenship* (2002). Includes a careful discussion of the citizenship status of American minorities and residents of overseas possessions.

- Blight, David. *Race and Reunion: The Civil War in American Memory* (2001). Examines how a memory of the Civil War that downplayed the issue of slavery played a part in sectional reconciliation and the rise of segregation.

- Blum, Edward. *Reforging the White Republic: Race, Religion, and American Nationalism, 1865–1898* (2005). Explores the development of a shared religious culture that united north-ern and southern Protestants in support of white supremacy and overseas expansion.

- Factor, Robert L. *The Black Response to America: Men, Ideals, and Organization from Frederick Douglass to the NAACP* (1970). Discusses black social and political thought, including that of Booker T. Washington and his critics.

- Goodwyn, Lawrence. *The Populist Moment: A Short History of the Agrarian Revolt in America* (1978). A sympathetic account of the rise and fall of Populism.

- Higginbotham, Evelyn. *Righteous Discontent: The Women's Movement in the Black Baptist Church, 1880–1920* (1993).

Explains how black women developed ways of exerting their influence in public life even as black men were losing the right to vote.

- Hoganson, Kristin L. *Consumers' Imperium: The Global Production of American Domesticity, 1865–1920* (2007). Shows how the consumer desires of middle-class women helped to spur the consolidation of an American empire.

- Hsu, Madeline. *Dreaming of Gold, Dreaming of Home: Transnationalism and Migration between the United States and South China, 1882–1934* (2000). Examines the enduring connections between Chinese immigrants in the United States and their home communities.

- Krause, Paul. *The Battle for Homestead, 1880–1892: Politics, Culture, and Steel* (1992). An account of the era's most celebrated conflict between capital and labor.

- LaFeber, Walter. *The New Empire: An Interpretation of American Expansion, 1860–1898* (1963). A classic examination of the forces that led the United States to acquire an overseas empire.

- Lake, Marilyn, and Henry Reynolds. *Drawing the Global Color Line* (2008). Traces the global transmission of ideas about white supremacy in the late nineteenth century.

- Linn, Brian M. *The Philippine War, 1899–1902* (2000). A detailed history of America's "forgotten war."

- McClain, Charles J. *In Search of Equality: The Chinese Struggle against Discrimination in Nineteenth-Century America* (1994). Explores how Chinese-Americans worked to combat the discrimination to which they were subjected and to assert their rights.

- McMillen, Neil R. *Dark Journey: Black Mississippians in the Age of Jim Crow* (1989). A powerful account of black life in the segregation era and the boundaries within which it operated.

- Perez, Louis A. *The War of 1898: The United States and Cuba in History and Historiography* (1998). Presents the Cuban side of the Spanish-American War, including a detailed discussion of the Cuban movement for independence and how American intervention affected it.

- Postel, Charles. *The Populist Vision* (2007). A history of the Populist movement that stresses how it anticipated many public policies of the twentieth century.

- Sanders, Elizabeth. *Roots of Reform: Farmers, Workers, and the American State, 1877–1917* (1999). Emphasizes the role of farmers' movements in putting forth many of the proposals associated with political reform in the late nineteenth and early twentieth centuries.

- Woodward, C. Vann. *Origins of the New South, 1877–1913* (1951). A classic treatment of the New South, emphasizing how its rulers failed to meet the needs of most southerners, white as well as black.

WEBSITES

- 1896: The Presidential Campaign: http://projects.vassar.edu/1896/1896home.html

- The Chinese in California, 1850–1920: http://bancroft.berkeley.edu/collections/chineseinca

- The Rise and Fall of Jim Crow: www.pbs.org/wnet/jimcrow

- The World of 1898: The Spanish-American War: www.loc.gov/rr/hispanic/1898

CHAPTER REVIEW AND ONLINE RESOURCES

REVIEW QUESTIONS

1. What economic and political issues gave rise to the Populist Party, and what changes did the party advocate?

2. How did employers use state and federal forces to protect their own economic interests, and what were the results?

3. Compare and contrast the goals, strategies, and membership of the American Federation of Labor and the Knights of Labor (you may want to refer back to Chapter 16).

4. Who were the Redeemers, and how did they change society and politics in the New South?

5. Explain how changes in the politics, economics, social factors, and spread of violence affected the situation of blacks in the New South.

6. How did religion and the idea of the Lost Cause give support to a new understanding of the Civil War?

7. What ideas and interests motivated the United States to create an empire in the late nineteenth century?

8. Compare the arguments for and against U.S. imperialism. Be sure to consider the views of Josiah Strong and Emilio Aguinaldo.

9. What rights did Chinese immigrants and Chinese Americans gain in these years, and what limitations did they experience? How did their experiences set the stage for other restrictions on immigration?

KEY TERMS

Populists (p. 641)

Coxey's Army (p. 644)

New South (p. 648)

Kansas Exodus (p. 650)

grandfather clause (p. 651)

disenfranchisement (p. 651)

Plessy v. Ferguson (p. 652)

"separate but equal" (p. 652)

lynching (p. 654)

Lost Cause (p. 655)

new immigrants (p. 656)

Immigration Restriction League (p. 657)

Chinese Exclusion Act (p. 657)

Atlanta Compromise (p. 659)

American Federation of Labor (p. 659)

yellow press (p. 666)

U.S.S. *Maine* (p. 666)

Platt Amendment (p. 668)

Open Door Policy (p. 669)

Philippine War (p. 670)

Insular Cases (p. 672)

Anti-Imperialist League (p. 674)

Go to 🐰 INQUIZITIVE

To see what you know—and learn what you've missed—with personalized feedback along the way.

Visit the *Give Me Liberty!* **Student Site** for primary source documents and images, interactive maps, author videos featuring Eric Foner, and more.

CHAPTER 18

THE PROGRESSIVE ERA

★

1900–1916

It was late afternoon on March 25, 1911, when fire broke out at the Triangle Shirtwaist Company. The factory occupied the top three floors of a ten-story building in the Greenwich Village neighborhood of New York City. Here some 500 workers, mostly young Jewish and Italian immigrant women, toiled at sewing machines producing ladies' blouses, some earning as little as three dollars per week. Those who tried to escape the blaze discovered that the doors to the stairwell had been locked—the owners' way, it was later charged, of discouraging theft and unauthorized bathroom breaks. The fire department rushed to the scene with high-pressure hoses. But their ladders reached only to the sixth floor. As the fire raged, onlookers watched in horror as girls leapt from the upper stories. By the time the blaze had been put out, 46 bodies lay on the street and 100 more were found inside the building.

The Triangle Shirtwaist Company was typical of manufacturing in the nation's largest city, a beehive of industrial production in small, crowded factories. New York was home to 30,000 manufacturing establishments with more than 600,000 employees—more industrial workers than in the entire state of Massachusetts. Triangle had already played a key role in the era's labor history. When 200 of its workers tried to join the International Ladies' Garment Workers Union (ILGWU), the owners responded by firing them. This incident helped to spark a general walkout of female garment workers in 1909—the Uprising of the 20,000. Among the strikers' demands was better safety in clothing factories. The impoverished immigrants forged an alliance with middle- and upper-class female supporters, including members of the Women's Trade Union League, which had been founded in 1903 to help bring women workers into unions. Alva Belmont, the ex-wife of railroad magnate William Vanderbilt, contributed several of her cars to a parade in support of the striking workers. By the time the walkout ended early in 1911, the ILGWU had won union contracts with more than 300 firms. But the Triangle Shirtwaist Company was not among them.

The Triangle fire was not the worst fire disaster in American history (seven years earlier, over 1,000 people had died in a blaze on the *General Slocum* excursion boat in New York Harbor). But it had an unrivaled impact on public consciousness. More than twenty years later, Franklin D. Roosevelt would refer to it in a press conference as an example of why the government needed to regulate industry. In its wake, efforts to organize the city's workers accelerated, and the state legislature passed new factory inspection laws and fire safety codes.

Triangle focused attention on the social divisions that plagued American society during the first two decades of the twentieth century, a period known as the Progressive era. These were years when economic expansion produced millions of new jobs and brought an unprecedented array of goods within reach of American consumers. Cities expanded rapidly—by 1920, for the first time, more Americans lived in towns and cities than in rural areas. Yet severe inequality remained the most visible feature of the urban landscape, and persistent labor strife raised anew the question of government's role in combating it. The fire and its aftermath also highlighted how traditional gender roles were changing as women took on new responsibilities in the workplace and in the making of public policy.

FOCUS QUESTIONS

Why was the city such a central element in Progressive America? –*p. 680*

How did the labor and women's movements challenge the nineteenth-century meanings of American freedom? –*p. 690*

In what ways did Progressivism include both democratic and anti-democratic impulses? –*p. 700*

How did the Progressive presidents foster the rise of the nation-state? –*p. 709*

Sixth Avenue and Thirtieth Street, a 1907 painting by John Sloan, depicts a busy street in New York City in an area known as the Tenderloin, with an elevated railroad overhead. Sloan was one of a group of painters called the Ashcan School because of their focus on everyday city life. Here, he emphasizes the vitality of the city and the mingling of people of different social classes on its streets. Billboards and shop windows entice passers-by, while two fashionably dressed women observe a disoriented, possibly intoxicated, poor woman carrying a can of beer. Sloan later wrote, "This canvas has surely caught the atmosphere of the Tenderloin: drab, shabby, happy, sad, and human." Art © 2013 Delaware Art Museum/Artists Rights Society (ARS), New York.

The word "Progressive" came into common use around 1910 as a way of describing a broad, loosely defined political movement of individuals and groups who hoped to bring about significant change in American social and political life. Progressives included forward-looking businessmen who realized that workers must be accorded a voice in economic decision making, and labor activists bent on empowering industrial workers. Other major contributors to **Progressivism** were members of female reform organizations who hoped to protect women and children from exploitation, social scientists who believed that academic research would help to solve social problems, and members of an anxious middle class who feared that their status was threatened by the rise of big business.

Everywhere in early-twentieth-century America the signs of economic and political consolidation were apparent—in the power of a small directorate of Wall Street bankers and corporate executives, the manipulation of democracy by corrupt political machines, and the rise of new systems of managerial control in workplaces. In these circumstances, wrote Benjamin P. DeWitt, in his 1915 book *The Progressive Movement*, "the individual could not hope to compete. . . . Slowly, Americans realized that they were not free."

As this and the following chapter will discuss, Progressive reformers responded to the perception of declining freedom in varied, contradictory ways. The era saw the expansion of political and economic freedom through the reinvigoration of the movement for woman suffrage, the use of political power to expand workers' rights, and efforts to improve democratic government by weakening the power of city bosses and giving ordinary citizens more influence on legislation. It witnessed the flowering of understandings of freedom based on individual fulfillment and personal self-determination—the ability to participate fully in the ever-expanding consumer marketplace and, especially for women, to enjoy economic and sexual freedoms long considered the province of men. At the same time, many Progressives supported efforts to limit the full enjoyment of freedom to those deemed fit to exercise it properly. The new system of white supremacy born in the 1890s became fully consolidated in the South. Growing numbers of native-born Americans demanded that immigrants abandon their traditional cultures and become fully "Americanized." And efforts were made at the local and national levels to place political decision making in the hands of experts who did not have to answer to the electorate. The idea of freedom remained as contested as ever in Progressive America.

AN URBAN AGE AND A CONSUMER SOCIETY

Farms and Cities

The Progressive era was a period of explosive economic growth, fueled by increasing industrial production, a rapid rise in population, and the continued expansion of the consumer marketplace. In the first decade of the twentieth century, the economy's total output rose by about 85 percent. For the last time in American history, farms and cities grew together. As farm prices recovered from their low point during the depression of the 1890s, American agriculture entered what would later be remembered as its "golden age." The expansion of urban areas stimulated demand for farm goods. Farm families poured into the western Great Plains. More than 1 million claims for free government land were filed under the Homestead Act of 1862—more than in the previous forty years combined. Between 1900 and 1910, the combined population of Texas and Oklahoma rose by nearly 2 million people, and Kansas, Nebraska, and the Dakotas added 800,000. Irrigation transformed the Imperial Valley of California and parts of Arizona into major areas of commercial farming.

But it was the city that became the focus of Progressive politics and of a new mass-consumer society. The United States counted twenty-one cities whose population exceeded 100,000 in 1910, the largest of them New York, with 4.7 million residents. The twenty-three square miles of Manhattan Island were home to over 2 million people, more than lived in thirty-three of the states. Fully a quarter of them inhabited the Lower East Side, an immigrant neighborhood more densely populated than Bombay or Calcutta in India.

The stark urban inequalities of the 1890s continued into the Progressive era. Immigrant families in New York's downtown tenements often had no electricity or indoor toilets. Three miles to the north stood the mansions of Fifth Avenue's Millionaire's Row. According to one estimate, J. P. Morgan's financial firm directly or indirectly controlled 40 percent of all financial and industrial capital in the United States. Alongside such wealth, reported the Commission on Industrial Relations, established by Congress in 1912, more than one-third of the country's mining and manufacturing workers lived in "actual poverty."

A colored photograph from around 1900 shows the teeming street life of Mulberry Street, on New York City's densely populated Lower East Side. The massive immigration of the early twentieth century transformed the life of urban centers throughout the country and helped to spark the Progressive movement.

The mansion of Cornelius Vanderbilt II on New York City's Fifth Avenue, in a 1920 photograph. Designed in the style of a French château, it took up the entire block. Today, the Bergdorf Goodman department store occupies the site.

City of Ambition, 1910, by the photographer Alfred Stieglitz, captures the stark beauty of New York City's new skyscrapers. Photograph © 2013 Georgia O'Keeffe Museum/Artists Rights Society (ARS), New York.

A photograph by Lewis Hine, who used his camera to chronicle the plight of child laborers shown here: a young spinner in a Vermont cotton factory.

The city captured the imagination of artists, writers, and reformers. The glories of the American landscape had been the focal point of nineteenth-century painters (exemplified by the Hudson River school, which produced canvases celebrating the wonders of nature). The city and its daily life now became their preoccupation. Painters like George W. Bellows and John Sloan and photographers such as Alfred Stieglitz and Edward Steichen captured the electric lights, crowded bars and theaters, and soaring skyscrapers of the urban landscape. With its youthful, exuberant energies, the city seemed an expression of modernity itself.

The Muckrakers

Others saw the city as a place where corporate greed undermined traditional American values. At a time when more than 2 million children under the age of fifteen worked for wages, Lewis Hine photographed child laborers to draw attention to persistent social inequality. A new generation of journalists writing for mass-circulation national magazines exposed the ills of industrial and urban life. *The Shame of the Cities* by Lincoln Steffens (published as a series in *McClure's Magazine* in 1901–1902 and in book form in 1904) showed how party bosses and business leaders profited from political corruption. *McClure's* also hired Ida Tarbell to expose the arrogance and economic machinations of John D. Rockefeller's Standard Oil Company. Published in two volumes in 1904, her *History of the Standard Oil Company* was the most substantial product of what Theodore Roosevelt disparaged as **muckraking**—the use of journalistic skills to expose the underside of American life.

Major novelists of the era took a similar unsparing approach to social ills. Theodore Dreiser's *Sister Carrie* (1900) traced a young woman's moral corruption in Chicago's harsh urban environment. Perhaps the era's most influential novel was Upton Sinclair's *The Jungle* (1906), whose description of unsanitary slaughterhouses and the sale of rotten meat stirred public outrage and led directly to the passage of the Pure Food and Drug Act and the Meat Inspection Act of 1906.

Immigration as a Global Process

If one thing characterized early-twentieth-century cities, it was their immigrant character. The "new immigration" from southern and eastern Europe (discussed in Chapter 17) had begun around 1890 but reached its peak during the Progressive era. Between 1901 and the outbreak of World War I in Europe in 1914, some 13 million immigrants came to the United States, the majority from Italy, Russia, and the Austro-Hungarian empire. In fact, Progressive-era immigration formed part of a larger process of worldwide migration set in motion by industrial expansion and the decline of traditional agriculture. Poles emigrated not only to Pittsburgh and Chicago but to work in German factories and Scottish mines. Italians sought jobs in Belgium, France, and Argentina as well as the United States. As many as 750,000 Chinese migrated to other countries each year.

During the years from 1840 to 1914 (when immigration to the United States would be virtually cut off, first by the outbreak of World War I and then by legislation), perhaps 40 million persons emigrated to the United States and another 20 million to other parts of the Western Hemisphere, including Canada,

Argentina, Brazil, and the Caribbean. This population flow formed one part of a massive shifting of peoples throughout the world.

Numerous causes inspired this uprooting of population. Rural southern and eastern Europe and large parts of Asia were regions marked by widespread poverty and illiteracy, burdensome taxation, and declining economies. Political turmoil at home, like the revolution that engulfed Mexico after 1911, also inspired emigration. Not all of these immigrants could be classified as "free laborers," however. Large numbers of Chinese, Mexican, and Italian migrants, including many who came to the United States, were bound to long-term labor contracts. These contracts were signed with labor agents, who then provided the workers to American employers. But all the areas attracting immigrants were frontiers of one kind or another—agricultural, mining, or industrial—with expanding job opportunities.

Most European immigrants to the United States entered through **Ellis Island**. Located in New York Harbor, this became in 1892 the nation's main facility for processing immigrants. Millions of Americans today trace their ancestry to an immigrant who passed through Ellis Island. The less fortunate, who failed a medical examination or were judged to be anarchists, prostitutes, or in other ways undesirable, were sent home.

At the same time, an influx of Asian and Mexican newcomers was taking place in the West. After the exclusion of immigrants from China in the late nineteenth century, a small number of Japanese arrived, primarily to work as agricultural laborers in California's fruit and vegetable fields and on Hawaii's sugar plantations. By 1910, the population of Japanese origin had grown to 72,000. Between 1910 and 1940, Angel Island in San Francisco Bay—the "Ellis Island of the West"—served as the main entry point for immigrants from Asia.

Far larger was Mexican immigration. Between 1900 and 1930, some 1 million Mexicans (more than 10 percent of that country's population) entered the United States—a number exceeded by only a few European countries. Mexicans generally entered through El Paso, Texas, the main southern gateway into the United States. Many ended up in the San Gabriel Valley of California, where citrus growers searching for cheap labor had earlier experimented with Native American, South Asian, Chinese, and Filipino migrant workers.

By 1910, one-seventh of the American population was foreign-born, the highest percentage in the country's history. More than 40 percent of New York City's population had been born abroad. In Chicago and smaller industrial cities like Providence, Milwaukee, and San Francisco, the figure exceeded 30 percent. Although many newcomers moved west

		NUMBER OF CITIES
YEAR	**URBAN POPULATION (PERCENTAGE)**	**WITH 100,000+ POPULATION**
1880	20%	12
1890	28	15
1900	38	18
1910	50	21
1920	68	26

TABLE 18.1 Rise of the City, 1880–1920

An illustration in the 1912 publication *The New Immigration* depicts the various "types" entering the United States.

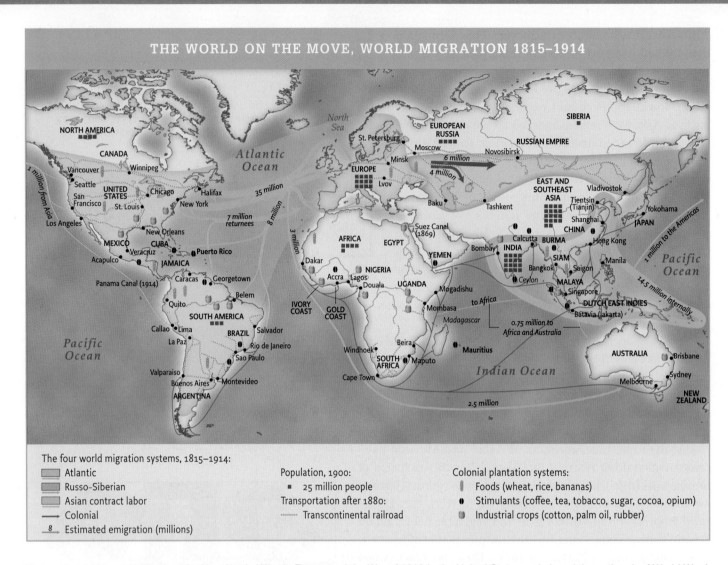

THE WORLD ON THE MOVE, WORLD MIGRATION 1815–1914

The four world migration systems, 1815–1914:

- ▭ Atlantic
- ▭ Russo-Siberian
- ▭ Asian contract labor
- → Colonial
- _8_→ Estimated emigration (millions)

Population, 1900:
- ▪ 25 million people

Transportation after 1880:
- ‒‒‒‒‒ Transcontinental railroad

Colonial plantation systems:
- ▮ Foods (wheat, rice, bananas)
- ◑ Stimulants (coffee, tea, tobacco, sugar, cocoa, opium)
- ▮ Industrial crops (cotton, palm oil, rubber)

The century between 1815, when the Napoleonic Wars in Europe and the War of 1812 in the United States ended, and the outbreak of World War I in 1914, witnessed a series of massive shifts in the world's population. The 35 million people who crossed the Atlantic to North America formed the largest migration stream, but millions of migrants also moved to South America, eastern Russia, and various parts of Asia.

to take part in the expansion of farming, most clustered in industrial centers. By 1910, nearly three-fifths of the workers in the twenty leading manufacturing and mining industries were foreign-born.

The Immigrant Quest for Freedom

A land of freedom

Like their nineteenth-century predecessors, the new immigrants arrived imagining the United States as a land of freedom, where all persons enjoyed equality before the law, could worship as they pleased, enjoyed economic opportunity, and had been emancipated from the oppressive social hierarchies of their homelands. "America is a free country," one Polish immigrant wrote home. "You don't have to be a serf to anyone." Agents sent abroad by the American government to investigate the reasons for large-scale immigration reported that the main impetus was a desire to share in the "freedom and prosperity enjoyed by the people of the United States." Freedom, they added, was largely an economic ambition—a desire to escape from "hopeless poverty" and achieve a standard of living impossible at home. While some of the new immigrants, especially Jews fleeing religious persecution in the Russian empire, thought of themselves as permanent emigrants, the majority initially planned to earn enough money to return home and purchase land. Groups like Mexicans and Italians included many "birds of passage," who remained only temporarily in the United States. In 1908, a year of economic downturn in the United States, more Italians left the country than entered.

An immigrant from Mexico, arriving around 1912 in a cart drawn by a donkey.

The new immigrants clustered in close-knit "ethnic" neighborhoods with their own shops, theaters, and community organizations, and often continued to speak their native tongues. As early as 1900, more than 1,000 foreign-language newspapers were published in the United States. Churches were pillars of these immigrant communities. In New York's East Harlem, even anti-clerical Italian immigrants, who resented the close alliance in Italy between the Catholic Church and the oppressive state, participated eagerly in the annual festival of the Madonna of Mt. Carmel. After Italian-Americans scattered to the suburbs, they continued to return each year to reenact the festival.

"Ethnic" neighborhoods

Although most immigrants earned more than was possible in the impoverished regions from which they came, they endured low wages, long hours, and dangerous working conditions. In the mines and factories of Pennsylvania and the Midwest, eastern European immigrants performed low-wage unskilled labor, while native-born workers dominated skilled and supervisory jobs. The vast majority of Mexican immigrants became poorly paid agricultural, mine, and railroad laborers, with little prospect of upward economic mobility. "My people are not in America," remarked one Slavic priest, "they are under it."

Consumer Freedom

Cities, however, were also the birthplace of a mass-consumption society that added new meaning to American freedom. There was, of course, nothing unusual in the idea that the promise of American life lay, in part, in the enjoyment by the masses of citizens of goods available in other countries only to the well-to-do. Not until the Progressive era, however, did the advent of large downtown department stores, chain stores in urban neighborhoods, and retail mail-order houses for farmers and small-town residents make available to consumers throughout the country the vast array of goods now pouring from the nation's factories. By 1910, Americans could purchase, among many other items, electric sewing machines, washing machines, vacuum cleaners, and record players. Low wages, the unequal distribution of income, and the South's persistent poverty limited the consumer economy, which would not fully come into its own until after World War II. But it was in Progressive

TABLE 18.2 Immigrants and Their Children as Percentage of Population, Ten Major Cities, 1920	
CITY	**PERCENTAGE**
New York City	76%
Cleveland	72
Boston	72
Chicago	71
Detroit	65
San Francisco	64
Minneapolis	63
Pittsburgh	59
Seattle	55
Los Angeles	45

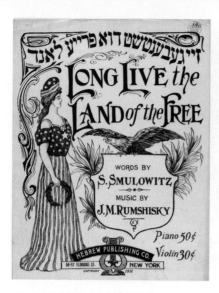

A piece of sheet music, published in 1911 and directed at Jewish immigrants, celebrates the United States as the Land of the Free.

Women at work in a shoe factory, 1908.

America that the promise of mass consumption became the foundation for a new understanding of freedom as access to the cornucopia of goods made available by modern capitalism.

Leisure activities also took on the characteristics of mass consumption. Amusement parks, dance halls, and theaters attracted large crowds of city dwellers. The most popular form of mass entertainment at the turn of the century was vaudeville, a live theatrical entertainment consisting of numerous short acts typically including song and dance, comedy, acrobats, magicians, and trained animals. In the 1890s, brief motion pictures were already being introduced into vaudeville shows. As the movies became longer and involved more sophisticated plot narratives, separate theaters developed. By 1910, 25 million Americans per week, mostly working-class urban residents, were attending "nickelodeons"—motion-picture theaters whose five-cent admission charge was far lower than at vaudeville shows.

The Working Woman

The new visibility of women in urban public places—at work, as shoppers, and in places of entertainment like cinemas and dance halls—indicated that traditional gender roles were changing dramatically in Progressive America. As the Triangle fire revealed, more and more women were working for wages. Black women still worked primarily as domestics or in southern cotton fields. Immigrant women were largely confined to low-paying factory employment. But for native-born white women, the kinds of jobs available expanded enormously. By 1920, around 25 percent of employed women were office workers or telephone operators, and only 15 percent worked in domestic service, the largest female job category of the nineteenth century. Female work was no longer confined to young, unmarried white women and adult black women. In 1920, of 8 million women working for wages, one-quarter were married and living with their husbands.

The working woman—immigrant and native, working-class and professional— became a symbol of female emancipation. Women faced special limitations on their economic freedom, including wage discrimination and exclusion from many jobs. Yet almost in spite of themselves, union leader Abraham Bisno remarked, young immigrant working women developed a sense of independence: "They acquired the *right to a personality*," something alien to the highly patriarchal family structures

	TABLE 18.3 Percentage of Women 14 Years and Older in the Labor Force, 1900–1930		
YEAR	ALL WOMEN	MARRIED WOMEN	WOMEN AS % OF LABOR FORCE
1900	20.4%	5.6%	18%
1910	25.2	10.7	24
1920	23.3	9.0	24
1930	24.3	11.7	25

Age, at the center of political discussion during the Progressive era. Lack of "industrial freedom" was widely believed to lie at the root of the much-discussed "labor problem." Since in an industrial age the prospect of managing one's own business seemed increasingly remote, many Progressives believed that the key to increasing industrial freedom lay in empowering workers to participate in economic decision making via strong unions. Louis D. Brandeis, an active ally of the labor movement whom President Woodrow Wilson appointed to the Supreme Court in 1916, maintained that unions embodied an essential principle of freedom—the right of people to govern themselves. The contradiction between "political liberty" and "industrial slavery," Brandeis insisted, was America's foremost social problem. Workers deserved a voice not only in establishing wages and working conditions but also in making such managerial decisions as the relocation of factories, layoffs, and the distribution of profits.

> *Louis D. Brandeis*

The Socialist Presence

Economic freedom was also a rallying cry of American socialism, which reached its greatest influence during the Progressive era. Founded in 1901, the **Socialist Party** brought together surviving late-nineteenth-century radicals such as Populists and followers of Edward Bellamy, with a portion of the labor movement. The party called for immediate reforms such as free college education, legislation to improve the condition of laborers, and, as an ultimate goal, democratic control over the economy through public ownership of railroads and factories. It was the task of socialism, said western labor leader John O'Neill, to "gather together the shards of liberty"—the fragments of the American heritage of freedom—scattered by a government controlled by capitalist millionaires.

> *American socialism*

By 1912, the Socialist Party claimed 150,000 dues-paying members, published hundreds of newspapers, enjoyed substantial support in the American Federation of Labor, and had elected scores of local officials. Socialism flourished in diverse communities throughout the country. On the Lower East Side of New York City, it arose from the economic exploitation of immigrant workers and Judaism's tradition of social reform. Here, a vibrant socialist culture developed, complete with Yiddish-language newspapers and theaters, as well as large public meetings and street demonstrations. In 1914, the district elected socialist Meyer London to Congress. Another center of socialist strength was Milwaukee, where Victor Berger, a German-born teacher and newspaper editor, mobilized local AFL unions into a potent political force that elected Emil Seidel mayor in 1910. Seidel's administration provided aid to the unemployed, forced the police to recognize the rights of strikers, and won the respect of middle-class residents for its honesty and freedom from machine domination. Socialism also made inroads among tenant farmers in old Populist areas like Oklahoma, and in the mining regions of Idaho and Montana.

Roller skaters with socialist leaflets during a New York City strike in 1916. A "scab" is a worker who crosses the picket line during a strike.

The Gospel of Debs

No one was more important in spreading the socialist gospel or linking it to ideals of equality, self-government, and freedom than Eugene V. Debs, the railroad union leader who, as noted in the previous chapter, had been jailed during the Pullman Strike of 1894. For two decades, Debs criss-crossed the country preaching that

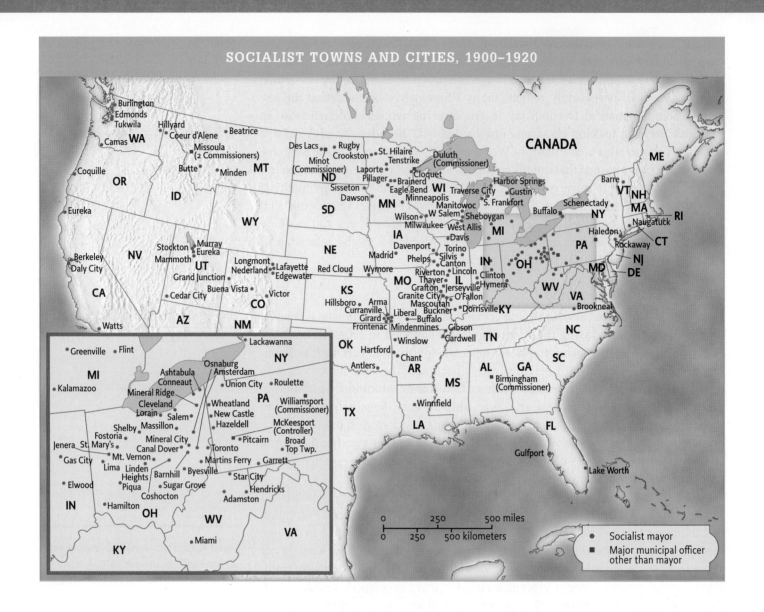

SOCIALIST TOWNS AND CITIES, 1900–1920

Although the Socialist Party never won more than 6 percent of the vote nationally, it gained control of numerous small and medium-sized cities between 1900 and 1920.

control of the economy by a democratic government held out the hope of uniting "political equality and economic freedom." As a champion of the downtrodden, Debs managed to bridge the cultural divide between New York's Jewish immigrants, prairie socialists of the West, and native-born intellectuals attracted to the socialist ideal. "While there is a lower class," proclaimed Debs, "I am in it. . . . While there is a soul in prison, I am not free."

Throughout the Atlantic world of the early twentieth century, socialism was a rising presence. Debs would receive more than 900,000 votes for president (6 percent of the total) in 1912. In that year, the socialist *Appeal to Reason*, published in Girard, Kansas, with a circulation of 700,000, was the largest weekly newspaper in the country, and socialist Max Hayes polled one-third of the vote when he challenged Samuel Gompers for the presidency of the AFL. In western Europe, socialism experienced even more pronounced growth. In the last elections before the outbreak of World War I in 1914, socialists in France, Germany, and Scandinavia won between one-sixth and one-third of the vote. "Socialism is coming," declared the *Appeal to Reason*. "It is coming like a prairie fire and nothing can stop it."

AFL and IWW

Socialism was only one example of widespread discontent in Progressive America. The labor strife of the Gilded Age continued into the early twentieth century. Having survived the depression of the 1890s, the American Federation of Labor saw its membership triple to 1.6 million between 1900 and 1904. At the same time, it sought to forge closer ties with forward-looking corporate leaders willing to deal with unions as a way to stabilize employee relations. AFL president Gompers joined with George Perkins of the J. P. Morgan financial empire and Mark Hanna, who had engineered McKinley's election in 1896, in the National Civic Federation, which accepted the right of **collective bargaining** for "responsible" unions. It helped to settle hundreds of industrial disputes and encouraged improvements in factory safety and the establishment of pension plans for long-term workers. Most employers nonetheless continued to view unions as an intolerable interference with their authority, and resisted them stubbornly.

One Big Union, the emblem of the Industrial Workers of the World.

The AFL mainly represented the most privileged American workers—skilled industrial and craft laborers, nearly all of them white, male, and native-born. In 1905, a group of unionists who rejected the AFL's exclusionary policies formed the **Industrial Workers of the World** (IWW). Part trade union, part advocate of a workers' revolution that would seize the means of production and abolish the state, the IWW made solidarity its guiding principle, extending "a fraternal hand to every wage-worker, no matter what his religion, fatherland, or trade." The organization sought to mobilize those excluded from the AFL—the immigrant factory-labor force, migrant timber and agricultural workers, women, blacks, and even the despised Chinese on the West Coast. The IWW's most prominent leader was William "Big Bill" Haywood, who had worked in western mines as a youth. Dubbed by critics "the most dangerous man in America," Haywood became a national figure in 1906 when he was kidnapped and spirited off to Idaho, accused of instigating the murder of a former anti-union governor. Defended by labor lawyer Clarence Darrow, Haywood was found not guilty.

> *"Big Bill" Haywood*

The New Immigrants on Strike

The Uprising of the 20,000 in New York's garment industry, mentioned earlier, was one of a series of mass strikes among immigrant workers that placed labor's demand for the right to bargain collectively at the forefront of the reform agenda. These strikes demonstrated that while ethnic divisions among workers impeded labor solidarity, ethnic cohesiveness could also be a basis of unity, so long as strikes were organized on a democratic basis. IWW organizers printed leaflets, posters, and banners in multiple languages and insisted that each nationality enjoy representation on the committee coordinating a walkout. It drew on the sense of solidarity within immigrant communities to persuade local religious leaders, shopkeepers, and officeholders to support the strikes.

> *The right to collective bargaining*

The labor conflict that had the greatest impact on public consciousness took place in Lawrence, Massachusetts. The city's huge woolen mills employed

VOICES OF FREEDOM

From CHARLOTTE PERKINS GILMAN, *WOMEN AND ECONOMICS* (1898)

***Women and Economics*, by the prolific feminist social critic and novelist Charlotte Perkins Gilman, influenced the new generation of women aspiring to greater independence. It insisted that how people earned a living shaped their entire lives, and that therefore women must free themselves from the home to achieve genuine freedom.**

It is not motherhood that keeps the housewife on her feet from dawn till dark; it is house service, not child service. Women work longer and harder than most men. . . . A truer spirit is the increasing desire of young girls to be independent, to have a career of their own, at least for a while, and the growing objection of countless wives to the pitiful asking for money, to the beggary of their position. More and more do fathers give their daughters, and husbands their wives, a definite allowance,—a separate bank account,—something . . . all their own.

The spirit of personal independence in the women of today is sure proof that a change has come. . . . The radical change in the economic position of women is advancing upon us. . . . The growing individualization of democratic life brings inevitable change to our daughters as well as to our sons. . . . One of its most noticeable features is the demand in women not only for their own money, but for their own work for the sake of personal expression. Few girls today fail to manifest some signs of this desire for individual expression. . . .

Economic independence for women necessarily involves a change in the home and family relation. But, if that change is for the advantage of individual and race, we need not fear it. It does not involve a change in the marriage relation except in withdrawing the element of economic dependence, nor in the relation of mother to child save to improve it. But it does involve the exercise of human faculty in women, in social service and exchange rather than in domestic service solely. . . . [Today], when our still developing social needs call for an ever-increasing . . . freedom, the woman in marrying becomes the house-servant, or at least the housekeeper, of the man. . . . When women stand free as economic agents, they will [achieve a] much better fulfilment of their duties as wives and mothers and [contribute] to the vast improvement in health and happiness of the human race.

From JOHN MITCHELL, "THE WORKINGMAN'S CONCEPTION OF INDUSTRIAL LIBERTY" (1910)

During the Progressive era, the idea of "industrial liberty" moved to the center of political discussion. Progressive reformers and labor leaders like John Mitchell, head of the United Mine Workers, condemned the prevailing idea of liberty of contract in favor of a broader definition of economic freedom.

While the Declaration of Independence established civil and political liberty, it did not, as you all know, establish industrial liberty. . . . Liberty means more than the right to choose the field of one's employment. He is not a free man whose family must buy food today with the money that is earned tomorrow. He is not really free who is forced to work unduly long hours and for wages so low that he can not provide the necessities of life for himself and his family; who must live in a crowded tenement and see his children go to work in the mills, the mines, and the factories before their bodies are developed and their minds trained. To have freedom a man must be free from the harrowing fear of hunger and want; he must be in such a position that by the exercise of reasonable frugality he can provide his family with all of the necessities and the reasonable comforts of life. He must be able to educate his children and to provide against sickness, accident, and old age. . . .

A number of years ago the legislatures of several coal producing States enacted laws requiring employers to pay the wages of their workmen in lawful money of the United States and to cease the practice of paying wages in merchandise. From time immemorial it had been the custom of coal companies to conduct general supply stores, and the workingmen were required, as a condition of employment, to accept products in lieu of money in return for services rendered. This system was a great hardship to the workmen. . . . The question of the constitutionality of this legislation was carried into the courts and by the highest tribunal it was declared to be an invasion of the workman's liberty to deny him the right to accept merchandise in lieu of money as payment of his wages. . . . [This is] typical of hundreds of instances in which laws that have been enacted for the protection of the workingmen have been declared by the courts to be unconstitutional, on the grounds that they invaded the liberty of the working people. . . . Is it not natural that the workingmen should feel that they are being guaranteed the liberties they do not want and denied the liberty that is of real value to them? May they not exclaim, with Madame Roland [of the French Revolution], "O Liberty! Liberty! How many crimes are committed in thy name!"

QUESTIONS

1. *What does Gilman see as the main obstacles to freedom for women?*

2. *What does Mitchell believe will be necessary to establish "industrial liberty"?*

3. *How do the authors differ in their view of the relationship of the family to individual freedom?*

Striking New York City garment workers carrying signs in multiple languages, 1913.

The New York shirtwaist strike of 1909 inspired workers in other cities. Here women in Rochester, New York, boldly hold aloft a strike banner.

32,000 men, women, and children representing twenty-five nationalities. They worked six days per week and earned an average of sixteen cents per hour. When the state legislature in January 1912 enacted a fifty-four-hour limit to the workweek, employers reduced the weekly take-home pay of those who had been laboring longer hours. Workers spontaneously went on strike, and called on the IWW for assistance.

In February, Haywood and a group of women strikers devised the idea of sending strikers' children out of the city for the duration of the walkout. Socialist families in New York City agreed to take them in. The sight of the children, many of whom appeared pale and half-starved, marching up Fifth Avenue from the train station led to a wave of sympathy for the strikers. "I have worked in the slums of New York," wrote one observer, "but I have never found children who were so uniformly ill-nourished, ill-fed, and ill-clothed." A few days later, city officials ordered that no more youngsters could leave Lawrence. When a group of mothers and children gathered at the railroad station in defiance of the order, club-wielding police drove them away, producing outraged headlines around the world. The governor of Massachusetts soon intervened, and the strike was settled on the workers' terms. A banner carried by the Lawrence strikers gave a new slogan to the labor movement: "We want bread and roses, too"—a declaration that workers sought not only higher wages but the opportunity to enjoy the finer things of life.

Another highly publicized labor uprising took place in New Orleans, where a 1907 strike of 10,000 black and white dockworkers prevented employers' efforts to eliminate their unions and reduce their wages. This was a remarkable expression of interracial solidarity at a time when segregation had become the norm throughout the South. Other strikes proved less successful. A six-month walkout of 25,000 silk workers in Paterson, New Jersey, in 1913 failed despite publicity generated by the Paterson pageant, in which the strikers reenacted highlights of their struggle before a sympathetic audience at New York's Madison Square Garden.

A strike against the Rockefeller-owned Colorado Fuel and Iron Company was also unsuccessful. Mostly recent immigrants from Europe and Mexico, the strikers demanded recognition of the United Mine Workers of America, wage increases, an eight-hour workday, and the right to shop and live in places not owned by the company. When the walkout began, in September 1913, the mine owners evicted 11,000 strikers and their families from company housing. They moved into tent colonies, which armed militia units soon surrounded. On April 20, 1914, the militia attacked the largest tent city, at Ludlow, and burned it to the ground, killing an estimated twenty to thirty men, women, and children. Seven months after the Ludlow Massacre, the strike was called off.

Labor and Civil Liberties

The fiery organizer Mary "Mother" Jones, who at the age of eighty-three had been jailed after addressing the Colorado strikers, later told a New York audience that the union "had only the Constitution; the other side had the bayonets." Yet the struggle of workers for the right to strike and of labor radicals against restraints on open-air speaking made free speech a significant public issue in the early twentieth century. By and large, the courts rejected their claims. But these battles laid the foundation for the rise of civil liberties as a central component of freedom in twentieth-century America.

State courts in the Progressive era regularly issued injunctions prohibiting strikers from speaking, picketing, or distributing literature during labor disputes. Like the abolitionists before them, the labor movement, in the name of freedom, demanded the right to assemble, organize, and spread their views. The investigations of the Commission on Industrial Relations revealed the absence of free speech in many factory communities, with labor organizers prohibited from speaking freely under threat of either violence from private police or suppression by local authorities. "I don't think we live in a free country or enjoy civil liberties," Clarence Darrow told the commission.

The IWW's battle for civil liberties breathed new meaning into the idea of freedom of expression. Lacking union halls, its organizers relied on songs, street theater, impromptu organizing meetings, and street corner gatherings to spread their message and attract support. In response to IWW activities, officials in Los Angeles, Spokane, Denver, and more than a dozen other cities limited or prohibited outdoor meetings. To arouse popular support, the IWW filled the jails with members who defied local law by speaking in public. Sometimes, prisoners were brutally treated, as in Spokane, where three died and hundreds were hospitalized after being jailed for violating a local law requiring prior approval of the content of public speeches. In nearly all the free-speech fights, however, the IWW eventually forced local officials to give way. "Whether they agree or disagree with its methods or aims," wrote one journalist, "all lovers of liberty everywhere owe a debt to this organization for . . . [keeping] alight the fires of freedom."

The New Feminism

During the Progressive era, the word "feminism" first entered the political vocabulary. Inspired by the writings of Charlotte Perkins Gilman, the Feminist Alliance, a small organization of New York professional women, developed plans to build apartment houses with communal kitchens, cafeterias, and daycare centers, to free women from the constraints of the home. However, because they were unable to obtain a mortgage, the buildings were never constructed. In 1914, a mass

> *Free speech and the right to strike*

A 1900 cartoon from *Puck*, *Divorce the Lesser Evil*. On the left, a quarreling husband and wife are chained to an "unhappy marriage." Justice is about to sever the marriage with her sword, while a minister tries to prevent her. Divorce laws had been liberalized after the Civil War; by the 1890s the United States had the highest divorce rate in the Western world. In the caption, the Church declares divorce an "awful immorality," to which Justice replies, "Divorce is rather an aid to morality."

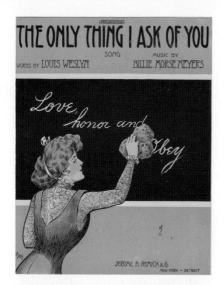

A sheet music cover, with a modern woman erasing the word "obey" from marriage vows.

Isadora Duncan brought a new freedom to an old art form.

meeting at New York's Cooper Union debated the question "What is Feminism?" The meeting was sponsored by Heterodoxy, a women's club located in Greenwich Village that brought together female professionals, academics, and reformers. Feminism, said one speaker, meant woman's emancipation "both as a human being and a sex-being." **New feminism**'s forthright attack on traditional rules of sexual behavior added a new dimension to the idea of personal freedom.

Heterodoxy was part of a new radical "bohemia" (a social circle of artists, writers, and others who reject conventional rules and practices). Its definition of feminism merged issues like the vote and greater economic opportunities with open discussion of sexuality. In New York's Greenwich Village and counterparts in Chicago, San Francisco, and other cities, a "lyrical left" came into being in the prewar years. Its members formed discussion clubs, attended experimental theaters, and published magazines. They confidently expected to preside over the emancipation of the human spirit from the prejudices of the nineteenth century.

One symbol of the new era was Isadora Duncan, who brought from California a new, expressive dance based on the free movement of a body liberated from the constraints of traditional technique and costume. "I beheld the dance I had always dreamed of," wrote the novelist Edith Wharton on seeing a Duncan performance, "satisfying every sense as a flower does, or a phrase of Mozart's." Another sign of artistic revolution was the Armory Show of 1913, an exhibition that exposed New Yorkers to new cubist paintings from Europe by artists previously unknown in the United States, like Pablo Picasso.

The lyrical left made freedom the key to its vision of society. At the famed salon in heiress Mabel Dodge's New York living room, a remarkable array of talented radicals gathered to discuss with equal passion labor unrest, modern trends in the arts, and sexual liberation. "What [women] are really after," explained Crystal Eastman, is "*freedom*." A graduate of New York University Law School, Eastman had taken a leading role both in the suffrage movement and in investigating industrial accidents. But her definition of freedom went beyond the vote, beyond "industrial democracy," to encompass emotional and sexual self-determination.

The Rise of Personal Freedom

During the Progressive era, as journalist William M. Reedy jested, it struck "sex o'clock" in America. The founder of psychiatry, Sigmund Freud, lectured at Clark University in Worcester, Massachusetts, in 1909, and discovered that his writings on infantile sexuality, repression, and the irrational sources of human behavior were widely known "even in prudish America." Issues of intimate personal relations previously confined to private discussion blazed forth in popular magazines and public debates.

For the generation of women who adopted the word "feminism" to express their demand for greater liberty, free sexual expression and reproductive choice emerged as critical definitions of women's emancipation. Greenwich Village became a center of sexual experimentation. The aura of tolerance attracted many homosexuals to the area, and although organized demands for gay rights lay far in the future, the gay community became an important element of the Village's lifestyle. But new sexual attitudes spread far beyond bohemia; they flourished among the young, unmarried, self-supporting women who made sexual freedom a hallmark of their oft-proclaimed personal independence.

The Birth-Control Movement

The growing presence of women in the labor market reinforced demands for access to birth control, an issue that gave political expression to changing sexual behavior. In the nineteenth century, the right to "control one's body" generally meant the ability to refuse sexual advances, including those of a woman's husband. Now, it suggested the ability to enjoy an active sexual life without necessarily bearing children. Emma Goldman, who had emigrated to the United States from Lithuania at the age of sixteen, toured the country lecturing on subjects from anarchism to the need for more enlightened attitudes toward homosexuality. She regularly included the right to birth control in her speeches and distributed pamphlets with detailed information about various contraceptive devices. "I demand freedom for both sexes," she proclaimed, "freedom of action, freedom in love and freedom in motherhood." Goldman constantly ran afoul of the law. By one count, she was arrested more than forty times for dangerous or "obscene" statements or simply to keep her from speaking.

By forthrightly challenging the laws banning contraceptive information and devices, Margaret Sanger, one of eleven children of an Irish-American working-class family, placed the **birth control movement** at the heart of the new feminism. In 1911, she began a column on sex education, "What Every Girl Should Know," for *The Call*, a New York socialist newspaper. Postal officials barred one issue, containing a column on venereal disease, from the mails. The next issue of *The Call* included a blank page with the headline: "What Every Girl Should Know—Nothing; by order of the U. S. Post Office."

By 1914, the intrepid Sanger was openly advertising birth-control devices in her own journal, *The Woman Rebel*. "No woman can call herself free," she proclaimed, "who does not own and control her own body [and] can choose consciously whether she will or will not be a mother." In 1916, Sanger opened a clinic in a working-class neighborhood of Brooklyn and began distributing contraceptive devices to poor Jewish and Italian women, an action for which she was sentenced to a month in prison. Few Progressives rallied to her defense. But for a time, the birth-control issue became a crossroads where the paths of labor radicals, cultural modernists, and feminists intersected. The IWW and Socialist Party distributed Sanger's writings. Like the IWW free-speech fights and Goldman's persistent battle for the right to lecture, Sanger's travail was part of a rich history of dissent in the Progressive era that helped to focus enlightened opinion on the ways local authorities and national obscenity legislation set rigid limits to Americans' freedom of expression. Slowly, laws banning birth control began to change. But since access was determined by individual states, even when some liberalized their laws, birth control remained unavailable in many others.

Native American Progressivism

Many groups participated in the Progressive impulse. Founded in 1911, the **Society of American Indians** was a reform organization typical of the era. It brought together Indian intellectuals to promote discussion of the plight of Native

The much-beloved and much-feared Emma Goldman, speaking in favor of birth control to an almost entirely male crowd in New York City in 1916, with a poster advertising a series of her lectures, illustrating the remarkable variety of topics on which she spoke.

Mothers with baby carriages wait outside Margaret Sanger's birth-control clinic in Brownsville, Brooklyn, 1916.

Americans in the hope that public exposure would be the first step toward remedying injustice. Because many of the society's leaders had been educated at government-sponsored boarding schools, the society united Indians of many tribal backgrounds. It created a pan-Indian public space independent of white control.

Many of these Indian intellectuals were not unsympathetic to the basic goals of federal Indian policy, including the transformation of communal landholdings on reservations into family farms. But Carlos Montezuma, a founder of the Society of American Indians, became an outspoken critic. Born in Arizona, he had been captured as a child by members of a neighboring tribe and sold to a traveling photographer, who brought him to Chicago. There Montezuma attended school and eventually obtained a medical degree.

In 1916, Montezuma established a newsletter, *Wassaja* (meaning "signaling"), that condemned federal paternalism toward the Indians and called for the abolition of the Bureau of Indian Affairs. Convinced that outsiders exerted too much power over life on the reservations, he insisted that self-determination was the only way for Indians to escape poverty and marginalization: "We must free ourselves. . . . We must be independent." But he also demanded that Indians be granted full citizenship and all the constitutional rights of other Americans. Montezuma's writings had little influence at the time on government policy, but Indian activists would later rediscover him as a forerunner of Indian radicalism.

THE POLITICS OF PROGRESSIVISM

Effective Freedom

Worldwide progressivism

Progressivism was an international movement. In the early twentieth century, cities throughout the world experienced similar social strains arising from rapid industrialization and urban growth. In 1850, London and Paris were the only cities whose population exceeded 1 million. By 1900, there were twelve—New York, Chicago, and Philadelphia in the United States, and others in Europe, Latin America, and Asia. Facing similar social problems, reformers across the globe exchanged ideas and envisioned new social policies. Sun Yat-Sen, the Chinese leader, was influenced by the writings of Henry George and Edward Bellamy.

European social legislation

As governments in Britain, France, and Germany instituted old age pensions, minimum wage laws, unemployment insurance, and the regulation of workplace safety, American reformers came to believe they had much to learn from the Old World. The term "social legislation," meaning governmental action to address urban problems and the insecurities of working-class life, originated in Germany but soon entered the political vocabulary of the United States.

Progressives believed that the modern era required a fundamental rethinking of the functions of political authority, whether the aim was to combat the power of the giant corporations, protect consumers, civilize the marketplace, or guarantee industrial freedom at the workplace. Drawing on the reform programs of the Gilded Age and the example of European legislation, Progressives sought to reinvigorate the idea of an activist, socially conscious government. Even in South Carolina, with its strong tradition of belief in local autonomy, Governor Richard I. Manning urged his constituents to modify their view of government as "a threat to individual liberty," to see it instead as "a means for solving the ills of the body politic."

Progressives could reject the traditional assumption that powerful government posed a threat to freedom, because their understanding of freedom was itself in flux. "Effective freedom," wrote the philosopher John Dewey, was a positive, not a negative, concept—the "power to do specific things." As such, it depended on "the *distribution* of powers that exists at a given time." Thus, freedom inevitably became a political question.

A photograph from 1910 depicts needy constituents of New York political boss Timothy "Big Tim" Sullivan receiving free pairs of shoes. Each year, Sullivan distributed two thousand pairs on his mother's birthday. Such largesse endeared political bosses to many voters, to the annoyance of municipal reformers.

State and Local Reforms

Throughout the Western world, social legislation proliferated in the early twentieth century. In the United States, with a political structure more decentralized than in European countries, state and local governments enacted most of the era's reform measures. In cities, Progressives worked to reform the structure of government to reduce the power of political bosses, establish public control of "natural monopolies" like gas and water works, and improve public transportation. They raised property taxes in order to spend more money on schools, parks, and other public facilities.

Gilded Age mayors Hazen Pingree and Samuel "Golden Rule" Jones pioneered urban Progressivism. A former factory worker who became a successful shoe manufacturer, Pingree served as mayor of Detroit from 1889 to 1897. He battled the business interests that had dominated city government, forcing gas and telephone companies to lower their rates, and established a municipal power plant. Jones had instituted an eight-hour day and paid vacations at his factory that produced oil drilling equipment. As mayor of Toledo, Ohio, from 1897 to 1905, he founded night schools and free kindergartens, built new parks, and supported the right of workers to unionize. Since state legislatures defined the powers of city government, urban Progressives often carried their campaigns to the state level. Pingree became governor of Michigan in 1896, in which post he continued his battle against railroads and other corporate interests.

Urban Progressivism

Progressivism in the West

Although often associated with eastern cities, Progressivism was also a major presence in the West. Former Populists and those who believed in the moral power of the frontier gravitated to Progressive programs to regulate the railroads and other

Children at play at the Hudson-Bank Gymnasium, built in 1898 in a New York immigrant neighborhood by the Outdoor Recreation League, one of many Progressive-era groups that sought to improve life in urban centers.

large corporations, and to the idea that direct democracy could revitalize corrupt politics. Important Progressive leaders worked for reform in western states and municipalities, including Hiram Johnson of California and Robert La Follette of Wisconsin.

Oregon stood at the forefront of Progressive reform. The leading figure in that state was William U'Ren, a lawyer who had entered politics as a supporter of Henry George's single-tax program. U'Ren concluded that without changes to the political system, entrenched interests would always be able to block reforms such as George's. He was the founder of the Oregon System, which included such measures as the initiative and referendum (also known as direct legislature, which enabled voters to propose and vote on laws), direct primaries to choose candidates for office (an effort to weaken the power of political bosses), and the recall (by which officials could be removed from office by popular vote). Using the initiative, Progressives won the vote for women in the state. The Oregon system, studied and emulated in many other states, came into being via an alliance of the urban middle class with reform-minded farmers and workers. But fault lines appeared when labor-oriented Progressives tried to use the initiative and referendum to increase taxes on the well-to-do and require the state to provide jobs for the unemployed. Both measures failed. Moreover, the initiative system quickly became out of control. In the 1912 election, voters in Portland were asked to evaluate forty measures seeking to become law. Nonetheless, between 1910 and 1912, Oregon's West Coast neighbors, Washington and California, also adopted the initiative and referendum and approved woman suffrage.

In California, where a Republican machine closely tied to the Southern Pacific Railroad had dominated politics for decades, Progressives took power under Governor Hiram Johnson, who held office from 1911 to 1917. As public prosecutor, Johnson had secured the conviction for bribery of San Francisco political boss Abraham Ruef. Having promised to "kick the Southern Pacific [Railroad] out of politics," he secured passage of the Public Utilities Act, one of the country's strongest railroad-regulation measures, as well as laws banning child labor and limiting the working hours of women.

Public Utilities Act

The most influential Progressive administration at the state level was that of Robert M. La Follette, who made Wisconsin a "laboratory for democracy." After serving as a Republican member of Congress, La Follette became convinced that an alliance of railroad and lumber companies controlled state politics. Elected governor in 1900, he instituted a series of measures known as the Wisconsin Idea, including nominations of candidates for office through primary elections rather than by political bosses, the taxation of corporate wealth, and state regulation

Wisconsin Idea

of railroads and public utilities. Other measures created a statewide system of insurance against illness, death, and accident, barred the sale to private companies of land, mineral rights, and other natural resources owned by the state, required safety devices on various forms of machinery, and prohibited child labor. To staff his administration, he drew on nonpartisan faculty members from the University of Wisconsin. Wisconsin offered the most striking merger of the social and political impulses that went under the name of Progressivism.

Progressive Democracy

"We are far from free," wrote Randolph Bourne in 1913, "but the new spirit of democracy is the angel that will free us." Progressives hoped to reinvigorate democracy by restoring political power to the citizenry and civic harmony to a divided society. Alarmed by the upsurge in violent class conflict and the unrestricted power of corporations, they believed that political reforms could help to create a unified "people" devoted to greater democracy and social reconciliation. Yet increasing the responsibilities of government made it all the more important to identify who was entitled to political participation and who was not.

Promoting civic harmony

The Progressive era saw a host of changes implemented in the political process, many seemingly contradictory in purpose. The electorate was simultaneously expanded and contracted, empowered and removed from direct influence on many functions of government. Democracy was enhanced by the **Seventeenth Amendment**—which provided that U.S. senators be chosen by popular vote rather than by state legislatures—by widespread adoption of the popular election of judges, and by the use of primary elections among party members to select candidates for office. The era culminated with a constitutional amendment enfranchising women—the largest expansion of democracy in American history.

But the Progressive era also witnessed numerous restrictions on democratic participation, most strikingly the disenfranchisement of blacks in the South, a process, as noted in Chapter 17, supported by many white southern Progressives as a way of ending election fraud. To make city government more honest and efficient, many localities replaced elected mayors with appointed nonpartisan commissions or city managers—a change that insulated officials from machine domination but also from popular control. New literacy tests and residency and registration requirements, common in northern as well as southern states, limited the right to vote among the poor. Taken as a whole, the electoral changes of the Progressive era represented a significant reversal of the idea that voting was an inherent right of American citizenship. In the eyes of many Progressives, the "fitness" of voters, not their absolute numbers, defined a functioning democracy.

Restricting democratic participation

Government by Expert

"He didn't believe in democracy; he believed simply in government." The writer H. L. Mencken's quip about Theodore Roosevelt came uncomfortably close to the mark for many Progressive advocates of an empowered state. Most Progressive thinkers were highly uncomfortable with the real world of politics, which seemed to revolve around the pursuit of narrow class, ethnic, and regional interests. Robert M. La Follette's reliance on college professors to staff important posts in his

Professors in government

Children in the courtyard at Hull House, the settlement house established in Chicago by Jane Addams.

administration reflected a larger Progressive faith in expertise. The government could best exercise intelligent control over society through a democracy run by impartial experts who were in many respects unaccountable to the citizenry.

This impulse toward order, efficiency, and centralized management—all in the name of social justice—was an important theme of Progressive reform. The title of Walter Lippmann's influential 1914 work of social commentary, *Drift and Mastery*, posed the stark alternatives facing the nation. "Drift" meant continuing to operate according to the outmoded belief in individual autonomy. "Mastery" required applying scientific inquiry to modern social problems. The new generation of educated professionals, Lippmann believed, could be trusted more fully than ordinary citizens to solve America's deep social problems. Political freedom was less a matter of direct participation in government than of qualified persons devising the best public policies.

Jane Addams and Hull House

But alongside this elitist politics, Progressivism also included a more democratic vision of the activist state. As much as any other group, organized women reformers spoke for the more democratic side of Progressivism. Still barred from voting and holding office in most states, women nonetheless became central to the political history of the Progressive era. Women challenged the barriers that excluded them from formal political participation and developed a democratic, grassroots vision of Progressive government. In so doing, they placed on the political agenda new understandings of female freedom. The immediate catalyst was a growing awareness among women reformers of the plight of poor immigrant communities and the emergence of the condition of women and child laborers as a major focus of public concern.

> *Jane Addams*

The era's most prominent female reformer was Jane Addams, who had been born in 1860, the daughter of an Illinois businessman. After graduating from college, Addams, who never married, resented the prevailing expectation that a woman's life should be governed by what she called the "family claim"—the obligation to devote herself to parents, husband, and children. In 1889, she founded Hull House in Chicago, a **settlement house** devoted to improving the lives of the immigrant poor. Hull House was modeled on Toynbee Hall, which Addams had visited after its establishment in a working-class neighborhood of London in 1884. Unlike previous reformers, who had aided the poor from afar, settlement-house workers moved into poor neighborhoods. They built kindergartens and playgrounds for children, established employment bureaus and health clinics, and showed female victims of domestic abuse how to gain legal protection. By 1910, more than 400 settlement houses had been established in cities throughout the country.

"Spearheads for Reform"

> *The "new woman"*

Addams was typical of the Progressive era's "new woman." By 1900, there were more than 80,000 college-educated women in the United States. Many found a calling in providing social services, nursing, and education to poor families in the growing cities. The efforts of middle-class women to uplift the poor, and of laboring women to uplift themselves, helped to shift the center of gravity of politics toward activist government. Women like Addams discovered that even well-organized social work was not enough to alleviate the problems of inadequate housing, income, and health. Government action was essential. Hull House instigated an array of reforms in Chicago, soon adopted elsewhere, including stronger building and sanitation codes, shorter working hours and safer labor conditions, and the right of labor to organize.

Female activism spread throughout the country. Ironically, the exclusion of blacks from jobs in southern textile mills strengthened the region's movement against child labor. Reformers portrayed child labor as a menace to white supremacy, depriving white children of educations they would need as adult members of the dominant race. These reformers devoted little attention to the condition of black children. Women's groups in Alabama were instrumental in the passage of a 1903 state law restricting child labor. By 1915, every southern state had followed suit. But with textile mill owners determined to employ children and many poor families dependent on their earnings, these laws were enforced only sporadically.

Visiting nurse on a New York City rooftop, 1908. Efforts to uplift the immigrant poor offered new opportunities for professional employment to many women during the Progressive era.

The settlement houses have been called "spearheads for reform." They produced prominent Progressive figures like Julia Lathrop, the first woman to head a federal agency (the Children's Bureau, established in 1912 to investigate the conditions of mothers and children and advocate their interests). Florence Kelley, the daughter of Civil War–era Radical Republican congressman William D. Kelley and a veteran of Hull House, went on to mobilize women's power as consumers as a force for social change. In the Gilded Age, the writer Helen Campbell had brilliantly exposed the contradiction of a market economy in which fashionable women wore clothing produced by poor women in wretched sweatshops. "Emancipation on the one side," she pointedly observed, "has meant no corresponding emancipation for the other." A generation later, under Kelley's leadership, the National Consumers' League became the nation's leading advocate of laws governing the working conditions of women and children. Freedom of choice in the marketplace, Kelley insisted, enabled socially conscious consumers to "unite with wage earners" by refusing to purchase goods produced under exploitative conditions.

Mayor Mary W. Howard (center) and the town council of Kanab, Utah. They served from 1912 to 1914, the first all-female municipal government in American history.

The Campaign for Woman Suffrage

After 1900, the campaign for woman suffrage moved beyond the mostly elite membership of the 1890s to engage a broad coalition ranging from middle-class members of women's clubs to unionists, socialists, and settlement-house workers. For the first time, it became a mass movement. Membership in the

National American Woman Suffrage Association grew from 13,000 in 1893 to more than 2 million by 1917. The group campaigned throughout the country for the right to vote and began to enjoy some success. By 1900, more than half the states allowed women to vote in local elections dealing with school issues, and Wyoming, Colorado, Idaho, and Utah had adopted full woman suffrage. The West also led the way in women holding public office. The first women to become mayors of major cities, governors, and members of Congress hailed from the West—Mayor Bertha Landes in Seattle (1926–1928), Congresswoman Jeanette Rankin of Montana (elected 1916 and 1940), and, in the 1920s, governors Miriam "Ma" Ferguson of Texas and Nellie Tayloe Ross of Wyoming.

Suffrage in the West

Cynics charged that Wyoming legislators used suffrage to attract more female migrants to their predominantly male state, while Utah hoped to enhance the political power of husbands in polygamous marriages banned by law but still practiced by some Mormons. In Colorado and Idaho, however, the success of referendums in the 1890s reflected the power of the Populist Party, a strong supporter of votes for women. Between 1910 and 1914, seven more western states enfranchised women. In 1913, Illinois became the first state east of the Mississippi River to allow women to vote in presidential elections.

Spirit of militancy

These campaigns, which brought women aggressively into the public sphere, were conducted with a new spirit of militancy. They also made effective use of the techniques of advertising, publicity, and mass entertainment characteristic of modern consumer society. California's successful 1911 campaign utilized automobile parades, numerous billboards and electric signs, and countless suffrage buttons and badges. Nonetheless, state campaigns were difficult, expensive, and usually unsuccessful. The movement increasingly focused its attention on securing a national constitutional amendment giving women the right to vote.

A woman suffrage parade in Minneapolis/ St. Paul, Minnesota in 1914. The marchers wear traditional costumes of Scandinavian countries and carry the flags of Norway and Sweden.

Maternalist Reform

Ironically, the desire to exalt women's role within the home did much to inspire the rein-vigoration of the suffrage movement. Many of the era's experiments in public policy arose from the conviction that the state had an obligation to protect women and children. Female reformers helped to launch a mass movement for direct government action to improve the living standards of poor mothers and children. Laws providing for mothers' pensions (state aid to mothers of young children who lacked male support) spread rapidly after 1910. The pensions tended to be less than generous, and local eligibility requirements opened the door to unequal treatment (white widows benefited the most, single mothers were widely discriminated against, and black women were almost entirely excluded). **Maternalist reforms** like mothers' pensions rested on the assumption that the government should encourage women's capacity for bearing and raising children and enable them to be economically independent at the same time. Both feminists and believers in conventional domestic roles supported such measures. The former hoped that these laws would subvert women's dependence on men, the latter that they would strengthen traditional families and the mother-child bond.

Louisine Havemeyer, one of New York City's wealthiest women, was a strong advocate of woman suffrage. Here, in a 1915 photograph, she passes the Torch of Liberty to a group of New Jersey women.

Other Progressive legislation recognized that large numbers of women did in fact work outside the home, but defined them as a dependent group (like children) in need of state protection in ways male workers were not. In 1908, in the landmark case of ***Muller v. Oregon***, Louis D. Brandeis filed a brief citing scientific and sociological studies to demonstrate that because women had less strength and endurance than men, long hours of labor were dangerous for women, while their unique ability to bear children gave the government a legitimate interest in their working conditions. Persuaded by Brandeis's argument, the Supreme Court unanimously upheld the constitutionality of an Oregon law setting maximum working hours for women.

Women and Muller v. Oregon

Thus, three years after the notorious *Lochner* decision invalidating a New York law limiting the working hours of male bakers (discussed in Chapter 16), the Court created the first large breach in "liberty of contract" doctrine. But the cost was high: at the very time that women in unprecedented numbers were entering the labor market and earning college degrees, Brandeis's brief and the Court's opinion solidified the view of women workers as weak, dependent, and incapable of enjoying the same economic rights as men. By 1917, thirty states had enacted laws limiting the hours of labor of female workers. Many women derived great benefit from these laws; others saw them as an infringement on their freedom.

"Liberty of contract"

While the maternalist agenda built gender inequality into the early foundations of the welfare state, the very use of government to regulate working conditions called into question basic assumptions concerning liberty of contract. Although not

According to this cartoon, giving women the right to vote will clean up political corruption and misgovernment.

all reformers were willing to take the step, it was easy to extend the idea of protecting women and children to demand that government better the living and working conditions of men as well, by insuring them against the impact of unemployment, old age, ill health, and disability. Brandeis himself insisted that government should concern itself with the health, income, and future prospects of all its citizens.

The Idea of Economic Citizenship

Brandeis envisioned a different welfare state from that of the maternalist reformers, one rooted less in the idea of healthy motherhood than in the notion of universal economic entitlements, including the right to a decent income and protection against unemployment and work-related accidents. For him, the right to assistance derived from citizenship itself, not some special service to the nation (as in the case of mothers) or upstanding character (which had long differentiated the "deserving" from the "undeserving" poor).

> Right to assistance

This vision, too, enjoyed considerable support in the Progressive era. By 1913, twenty-two states had enacted workmen's compensation laws to benefit workers, male or female, injured on the job. This legislation was the first wedge that opened the way for broader programs of social insurance. To avoid the stigma of depending on governmental assistance, contributions from workers' own wages funded these programs in part, thus distinguishing them from charity dispensed by local authorities to the poor. But state minimum wage laws and most laws regulating working hours applied only to women. Women and children may have needed protection, but interference with the freedom of contract of adult male workers was still widely seen as degrading. The establishment of a standard of living and working conditions beneath which no American, male or female, should be allowed to fall would await the coming of the New Deal.

> Workmen's compensation laws

THE PROGRESSIVE PRESIDENTS

Despite the ferment of Progressivism on the city and state levels, the most striking political development of the early twentieth century was the rise of the national state. The process of nationalization was occurring throughout American life. National corporations dominated the economy; national organizations like the American Medical Association came into being to raise the incomes and respect of professions. The process was even reflected in the consolidation of local baseball teams into the American and National Leagues and the advent in 1903 of the World Series. Only energetic national government, Progressives believed, could create the social conditions of freedom.

Despite creative experiments in social policy at the city and state levels, the tradition of localism seemed to most Progressives an impediment to a renewed sense of national purpose. Poverty, economic insecurity, and lack of industrial democracy were national problems that demanded national solutions. The democratic national state, wrote *New Republic* editor Herbert Croly, offered an alternative to control of Americans' lives by narrow interests that manipulated politics or by the all-powerful corporations. Croly proposed a new synthesis of American political traditions. To achieve the "Jeffersonian ends" of democratic self-determination and individual freedom, he insisted, the country needed to employ the "Hamiltonian means" of government intervention in the economy. Each in his own way, the Progressive presidents—Theodore Roosevelt, William Howard Taft, and Woodrow Wilson—tried to address this challenge.

> **Nationalization**

Theodore Roosevelt

In September 1901, the anarchist Leon Czolgosz assassinated William McKinley while the president visited the Pan-American Exposition in Buffalo, New York. At the age of forty-two, Vice President Theodore Roosevelt became the youngest man ever to hold the office of president. Roosevelt was an impetuous, energetic individual with a penchant for what he called the "strenuous life" of manly adventure. In many ways, he became the model for the twentieth-century president, an official actively and continuously engaged in domestic and foreign affairs. (The foreign policies of the Progressive presidents will be discussed in the next chapter.) Roosevelt regarded the president as "the steward of the public welfare." He moved aggressively to set the political agenda.

Roosevelt's program, which he called the Square Deal, attempted to confront the problems caused by economic consolidation by distinguishing between "good" and "bad" corporations. The former, among which he included U.S. Steel, served the public interest. The latter were run by greedy financiers interested only in profit, and had no right to exist.

Soon after assuming office, Roosevelt shocked the corporate world by announcing his intention to prosecute under the Sherman Antitrust Act the Northern Securities Company. Created by financier J. P. Morgan, this "holding company" owned the stock and directed the affairs of three major western railroads. It monopolized transportation between the Great Lakes and the Pacific. Morgan was outraged.

President Theodore Roosevelt addressing a crowd in 1902.

Putting the Screws on Him, a 1904 cartoon, depicts President Theodore Roosevelt squeezing ill-gotten gains out of the trusts.

The Old Faithful geyser, the most famous site in Yellowstone, the nation's first national park, in a photograph from the 1880s.

"Wall Street is paralyzed," quipped one newspaper, "at the thought that a President of the United States should sink to enforce the law." In 1904, the Supreme Court ordered Northern Securities dissolved, a major victory for the antitrust movement.

Roosevelt and Economic Regulation

Roosevelt also believed that the president should be an honest broker in labor disputes, rather than automatically siding with employers as his predecessors had usually done. When a strike paralyzed the West Virginia and Pennsylvania coalfields in 1902, he summoned union and management leaders to the White House. By threatening a federal takeover of the mines, he persuaded the owners to allow the dispute to be settled by a commission he himself would appoint.

Reelected in 1904, Roosevelt pushed for more direct federal regulation of the economy. Appealing to the public for support, he condemned the misuse of the "vast power conferred by vast wealth." He proposed to strengthen the Interstate Commerce Commission, which the Supreme Court had essentially limited to collecting economic statistics. By this time, journalistic exposés, labor unrest, and the agitation of Progressive reformers had created significant public support for Roosevelt's regulatory program. In 1906, Congress passed the Hepburn Act, giving the ICC the power to examine railroads' business records and to set reasonable rates, a significant step in the development of federal intervention in the corporate economy. That year, as has been noted, also saw the passage of the **Pure Food and Drug Act**, which established a federal agency to police the quality and labeling of food and drugs, and the Meat Inspection Act. Many businessmen supported these measures, recognizing that they would benefit from greater public confidence in the quality and safety of their products. But even they were alarmed by Roosevelt's calls for federal inheritance and income taxes and the regulation of all interstate businesses.

John Muir and the Spirituality of Nature

If the United States lagged behind Europe in many areas of social policy, it led the way in the conservation of natural resources. The first national park, Yellowstone in Wyoming, was created by Congress in 1872, partly to preserve an area of remarkable natural beauty and partly at the urging of the Northern Pacific Railroad, which was anxious to promote western tourism. In the 1890s, the Scottish-born naturalist John Muir organized the Sierra Club to help preserve forests from uncontrolled logging by timber companies.

Muir's love of nature stemmed from deep religious feelings. Nearly blinded in an accident in an Indianapolis machine shop where he worked in his twenties, he found in the restoration of his sight an inspiration to appreciate God's creation. He called forests "God's first temples." In nature, he believed, men could experience directly the presence of God. Muir's outlook blended evangelical Protestantism with a romantic view of nature inspired by the Transcendentalists of the pre–Civil War era—like Henry David Thoreau, he lamented the intrusions of civilization on the natural environment. But unlike the Transcendentalists, Muir developed a broad following. As more and more Americans lived in cities, they came to see nature less as something to conquer and more as a place for recreation and personal growth.

The Conservation Movement

In the 1890s, Congress authorized the president to withdraw "forest reserves" from economic development, a restriction on economic freedom in the name of a greater social good. But it was under Theodore Roosevelt that the **conservation movement** became a concerted federal policy. A dedicated outdoorsman who built a ranch in North Dakota in the 1880s, Roosevelt moved to preserve parts of the natural environment from economic exploitation.

Relying for advice on Gifford Pinchot, the head of the U.S. Forest Service, he ordered that millions of acres be set aside as wildlife preserves and encouraged Congress to create new national parks. The creation of parks like Yellowstone, Yosemite, and Glacier required the removal of Indians who hunted and fished there as well as the reintroduction of animals that had previously disappeared. City dwellers who visited the national parks did not realize that these were to a considerable extent artificially created and managed environments, not primordial nature.

In some ways, conservation was a typical Progressive reform. Manned by experts, the government could stand above political and economic battles, serving the public good while preventing "special interests" from causing irreparable damage to the environment. The aim was less to end the economic utilization of natural resources than to develop responsible, scientific plans for their use. Pinchot halted timber companies' reckless assault on the nation's forests. But unlike Muir, he believed that development and conservation could go hand in hand and that logging, mining, and grazing on public lands should be controlled, not eliminated. Conservation also reflected the Progressive thrust toward efficiency and control—in this case, control of nature itself.

In the view of Progressive conservationists, the West's scarcest resource—water—cried out for regulation. Governments at all levels moved to control the power of western rivers, building dams and irrigation projects to regularize their flow, prevent waste, and provide water for large-scale agriculture and urban development. With such projects came political conflict, as cities like Los Angeles and San Francisco battled with rural areas for access to water. After secretly buying up large tracts of land in the Owens Valley east of the city, for example, the city of Los Angeles constructed a major aqueduct between 1908 and 1913, over the vigorous objections of the valley's residents. By the 1920s, so much water had been diverted to the city that the once thriving farming and ranching businesses of Owens Valley could no longer operate.

Theodore Roosevelt (center) posing with a group in a grove of giant sequoia trees in California in 1903. He called on Americans to protect these "monuments of beauty."

Water in the West

Taft in Office

Having served nearly eight years as president, Roosevelt did not run again in 1908. His chosen successor was William Howard Taft, a federal judge from Ohio who had served as governor of the Philippines after the Spanish-American War. Taft defeated William Jennings Bryan, making his third unsuccessful race for the White House. Taft's inaugural address expressed the Progressive view of the state: "The scope of a modern government . . . has been widened far beyond the principles laid down by the old 'laissez-faire' school of political writers."

Although temperamentally more conservative than Roosevelt, Taft pursued antitrust policy even more aggressively. He persuaded the Supreme Court in 1911

Antitrust policy

to declare John D. Rockefeller's Standard Oil Company (one of Roosevelt's "good" trusts) in violation of the Sherman Antitrust Act and to order its breakup into separate marketing, producing, and refining companies. The government also won a case against American Tobacco, which the Court ordered to end pricing policies that were driving smaller firms out of business. In these decisions, the justices announced a new standard for judging large corporations—the "rule of reason"—which in effect implemented Roosevelt's old distinction between good and bad trusts. Big businesses were not, in and of themselves, antitrust violators, unless they engaged in policies that stifled competition.

The "rule of reason"

Taft supported the **Sixteenth Amendment** to the Constitution, which authorized Congress to enact a graduated income tax (one whose rate of taxation is higher for wealthier citizens). It was ratified shortly before he left office. A 2 percent tax on incomes over $4,000 had been included in a tariff enacted in 1894 but had been quickly declared unconstitutional by the Supreme Court as a "communistic threat to property." The movement to resurrect the income tax united southern and western farmers who wished to reduce government dependence on revenue from the tariff, which they believed discriminated against nonindustrial states, and Progressives who believed that taxation should be based on the ability to pay. A key step in the modernization of the federal government, the income tax provided a reliable and flexible source of revenue for a national state whose powers, responsibilities, and expenditures were growing rapidly.

Graduated income tax

Despite these accomplishments, Taft seemed to gravitate toward the more conservative wing of the Republican Party. Only a few months after taking office, he signed the Payne-Aldrich Tariff, which reduced rates on imported goods but not nearly as much as reformers wished. Taft's rift with Progressives grew deeper when Richard A. Ballinger, the secretary of the interior, concluded that Roosevelt had exceeded his authority in placing land in forest reserves. Ballinger decided to return some of this land to the public domain, where mining and lumber companies would have access to it. Gifford Pinchot accused Ballinger of colluding with business interests and repudiating the environmental goals of the Roosevelt administration. When Taft fired Pinchot in 1910, the breach with party Progressives became irreparable. In 1912, Roosevelt challenged Taft for the Republican nomination. Defeated, Roosevelt launched an independent campaign as the head of the new **Progressive Party**.

Ballinger and Pinchot

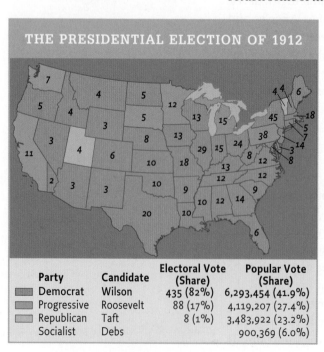

THE PRESIDENTIAL ELECTION OF 1912

Party	Candidate	Electoral Vote (Share)	Popular Vote (Share)
Democrat	Wilson	435 (82%)	6,293,454 (41.9%)
Progressive	Roosevelt	88 (17%)	4,119,207 (27.4%)
Republican	Taft	8 (1%)	3,483,922 (23.2%)
Socialist	Debs		900,369 (6.0%)

The Election of 1912

All the crosscurrents of Progressive-era thinking about what *McClure's Magazine* called "the problem of the relation of the State and the corporation" came together in the presidential campaign of 1912. The four-way contest between Taft, Roosevelt, Democrat Woodrow Wilson, and Socialist Eugene V. Debs became a national debate on the relationship between political and economic freedom in the age of big business. At one end of the political spectrum stood Taft, who stressed that economic individualism could remain the foundation of the social order so long as government and private entrepreneurs cooperated in addressing social ills. At the other end was Debs. Relatively few Americans supported the Socialist Party's goal of abolishing the "capitalistic system" altogether, but its immediate demands—including public ownership of the railroads and banking system, government aid to the unemployed, and laws establishing shorter working hours and a minimum wage—summarized forward-looking Progressive thought.

But it was the battle between Wilson and Roosevelt over the role of the federal government in securing economic freedom that galvanized public attention in 1912. The two represented competing strands of Progressivism. Both believed government action necessary to preserve individual freedom, but they differed over the dangers of increasing the government's power and the inevitability of economic concentration. Though representing a party thoroughly steeped in states' rights and laissez-faire ideology, Wilson was deeply imbued with Progressive ideas. "Freedom today," he declared, "is something more than being let alone. The program of a government of freedom must in these days be positive, not negative merely." As governor of New Jersey, Wilson had presided over the implementation of a system of workmen's compensation and state regulation of utilities and railroads.

Eugene V. Debs, the Socialist Party candidate, speaking in Chicago during the 1912 presidential campaign.

New Freedom and New Nationalism

Strongly influenced by Louis D. Brandeis, with whom he consulted frequently during the campaign, Wilson insisted that democracy must be reinvigorated by restoring market competition and freeing government from domination by big business. Wilson feared big government as much as he feared the power of the corporations. The **New Freedom**, as he called his program, envisioned the federal government strengthening antitrust laws, protecting the right of workers to unionize, and actively encouraging small businesses—creating, in other words, the conditions for the renewal of economic competition without increasing government regulation of the economy. Wilson warned that corporations were as likely to corrupt government as to be managed by it, a forecast that proved remarkably accurate.

Wilson's New Freedom

To Roosevelt's supporters, Wilson seemed a relic of a bygone era; his program, they argued, served the needs of small businessmen but ignored the inevitability of economic concentration and the interests of professionals, consumers, and labor. Wilson and Brandeis spoke of the "curse of bigness." What the nation actually needed, Walter Lippmann countered, was frank acceptance of the benefits of bigness, coupled with the intervention of government to counteract its abuses. Lippmann was expressing the core of the **New Nationalism**, Roosevelt's program of 1912. Only the "controlling and directing power of the government," Roosevelt insisted, could restore "the liberty of the oppressed." He called for heavy taxes on personal and corporate fortunes and federal regulation of industries, including railroads, mining, and oil.

Roosevelt's New Nationalism

The Progressive Party platform offered numerous proposals to promote social justice. Drafted by a group of settlement-house activists, labor reformers, and social scientists, the platform laid out a blueprint for a modern, democratic welfare

Progressive Party Platform

state, complete with woman suffrage, federal supervision of corporate enterprise, national labor and health legislation for women and children, an eight-hour day and "living wage" for all workers, and a national system of social insurance covering unemployment, medical care, and old age. Described by Roosevelt as the "most important document" since the end of the Civil War, the platform brought together many of the streams of thought and political experiences that flowed into Progressivism. Roosevelt's campaign helped to give freedom a modern social and economic content and established an agenda that would define political liberalism for much of the twentieth century.

Wilson's First Term

The Republican split ensured a sweeping victory for Wilson, who won about 42 percent of the popular vote, although Roosevelt humiliated Taft by winning about 27 percent to the president's 23 percent. In office, Wilson proved himself a strong executive leader. He established an office at the Capitol so that he could confer regularly with members of Congress about pending legislation, and he was the first president to hold regular press conferences in order to influence public opinion directly and continuously. He delivered messages personally to Congress rather than sending them in written form, as had all his predecessors since John Adams.

Wilson's initiatives

With Democrats in control of Congress, Wilson moved aggressively to implement his version of Progressivism. The first significant measure of his presidency was the Underwood Tariff, which substantially reduced duties on imports and, to make up for lost revenue, imposed a graduated income tax on the richest 5 percent of Americans. There followed the Clayton Act of 1914, which exempted labor unions from antitrust laws and barred courts from issuing injunctions curtailing the right to strike. In 1916 came the Keating-Owen Act outlawing child labor in the manufacture of goods sold in interstate commerce (the Supreme Court would later declare it unconstitutional), the Adamson Act establishing an eight-hour workday on the nation's railroads, and the Warehouse Act, reminiscent of the Populist subtreasury plan, which extended credit to farmers when they stored their crops in federally licensed warehouses.

The Expanding Role of Government

Some of Wilson's policies seemed more in tune with Roosevelt's New Nationalism than the New Freedom of 1912. He abandoned the idea of aggressive trust-busting in favor of greater government supervision of the economy. Wilson presided over the creation of two powerful new public agencies. In 1913, Congress created the

The Federal Reserve System

Federal Reserve System, consisting of twelve regional banks. They were overseen by a central board appointed by the president and empowered to handle the issuance of currency, aid banks in danger of failing, and influence interest rates so as to promote economic growth. The law was a delayed response to the Panic of 1907, when the failure of several financial companies threatened a general collapse of the banking system. With the federal government lacking a modern central bank, it had been left to J. P. Morgan to assemble the funds to prop up threatened financial institutions. Morgan's actions highlighted the fact that in the absence of federal regulation of banking, power over finance rested entirely in private hands.

A second expansion of national power occurred in 1914, when Congress established the **Federal Trade Commission** (FTC) to investigate and prohibit "unfair" business activities such as price-fixing and monopolistic practices. Both the Federal Reserve and FTC were welcomed by many business leaders as a means of restoring order to the economic marketplace and warding off more radical measures for curbing corporate power. But they reflected the remarkable expansion of the federal role in the economy during the Progressive era.

By 1916, the social ferment and political mobilizations of the Progressive era had given birth to a new American state. With new laws, administrative agencies, and independent commissions, government at the local, state, and national levels had assumed the authority to protect and advance "industrial freedom." Government had established rules for labor relations, business behavior, and financial policy, protected citizens from market abuses, and acted as a broker among the groups whose conflicts threatened to destroy social harmony. But a storm was already engulfing Europe that would test the Progressive faith in empowered government as the protector of American freedom.

> *The Federal Trade Commission*

SUGGESTED READING

BOOKS

- Bodnar, John. *The Transplanted: A History of Immigrants in Urban America* (1985). A comprehensive account of American immigration.

- Cott, Nancy F. *The Grounding of Modern Feminism* (1987). A careful study of feminist ideas in the Progressive era.

- Dawley, Alan. *Struggles for Justice: Social Responsibility and the Liberal State* (1991). Examines the varieties of Progressive reform and various efforts to use the power of government for social betterment.

- Diner, Steven. *A Very Different Age: Americans of the Progressive Era* (1998). A survey of the main trends of the Progressive period.

- Glickman, Lawrence B. *A Living Wage: Workers and the Making of American Consumer Society* (1997). Traces the origins and development of the idea that workers are entitled to a "living wage."

- Hofstadter, Richard. *The Age of Reform: From Bryan to F.D.R.* (1955). A classic account of the ideas of reformers from Populism to the New Deal.

- Johnston, Robert D. *The Radical Middle Class: Populist Democracy and the Question of Capitalism in Progressive Era*

Portland (2003). Analyzes how Progressivism operated in one important city.

- Lears, Jackson. *Rebirth of a Nation: The Making of Modern America, 1877–1920* (2009). A comprehensive history of the Gilded Age and Progressive era, stressing the extent of social and cultural change.

- Montgomery, David. *The Fall of the House of Labor: The Workplace, the State, and American Labor Activism, 1865–1925* (1987). An account of the labor battles of the era and the gradual decline of labor's power, especially at the workplace.

- Orsi, Robert A. *The Madonna of 115th Street: Faith and Community in Italian Harlem, 1880–1950* (1985). An influential study of a single immigrant community and the role of religion in binding it together.

- Peiss, Kathy. *Cheap Amusements: Working Women and Leisure in Turn-of-the-Century New York* (1986). Explores the rise of mass entertainment and how it affected women's lives in Progressive America.

- Recchiuti, John L. *Civic Engagement: Social Science and Progressive-Era Reform in New York City* (2006). Examines the influence of a group of reform-minded scholars on the politics of the Progressive era.

- Rodgers, Daniel T. *Atlantic Crossings: Social Politics in a Progressive Age* (1998). A comprehensive study of the flow of Progressive ideas and policies back and forth across the Atlantic.

- Stansell, Christine. *American Moderns: Bohemian New York and the Creation of a New Century* (2000). A colorful account of the Greenwich Village radicals who expanded the idea of personal freedom in the Progressive era.

- Stromquist, Shelton. *Re-Inventing "The People": The Progressive Movement, the Class Problem, and the Origins of Modern Liberalism* (2006). Discusses how the desire to re-create social harmony in an age of labor conflict shaped Progressivism.

- Tichi, Cecelia. *Civic Passions: Seven Who Launched Progressive America* (2009). An exploration of the careers of some of the most prominent leaders of Progressive reform.

WEBSITES

- Evolution of the Conservation Movement, 1860–1920: http://lcweb2.loc.gov/ammem/amrvhtml/conshome.html

- Immigration to the United States, 1789–1930: http://ocp.hul.harvard.edu/immigration/

- Triangle Shirtwaist Factory Fire: www.ilr.cornell.edu/trianglefire/

- Urban Experience in Chicago: Hull House and Its Neighborhoods: http://hullhouse.uic.edu/hull/urbanexp

- Votes for Women: http://memory.loc.gov/ammem/naw/nawshome.html

CHAPTER REVIEW AND ONLINE RESOURCES

REVIEW QUESTIONS

1. Identify the main groups and ideas that drove the Progressive movement.

2. Explain how immigration to the United States in this period was part of a global movement of peoples.

3. Describe how Fordism transformed American industrial and consumer society.

4. Socialism was a rising force across the globe in the early twentieth century. How successful was the movement in the United States?

5. Explain why the Industrial Workers of the World (IWW) grew so rapidly and aroused so much opposition.

6. How did immigrants adjust to life in America? What institutions or activities became important to their adjustment, and why?

7. What did Progressive-era feminists want to change in society, and how did their actions help to spearhead broader reforms?

8. How did ideas of women's roles, shared by maternalist reformers, lead to an expansion of activism by and rights for women?

9. How did each Progressive-era president view the role of the federal government?

10. Pick a Progressive-era reform (a movement, specific legislation, and organization) and describe how it shows how Progressives could work for both the expansion of democracy and restrictions on it.

KEY TERMS

Progressivism (p. 680)

muckraking (p. 682)

Ellis Island (p. 683)

Fordism (p. 688)

"American standard of living" (p. 689)

scientific management (p. 690)

Socialist Party (p. 691)

collective bargaining (p. 693)

Industrial Workers of the World (p. 693)

new feminism (p. 698)

birth control movement (p. 699)

Society of American Indians (p. 699)

Seventeenth Amendment (p. 703)

settlement house (p. 704)

maternalist reforms (p. 707)

Muller v. Oregon (p. 707)

Pure Food and Drug Act (p. 710)

conservation movement (p. 711)

Sixteenth Amendment (p. 712)

Progressive Party (p. 712)

New Freedom (p. 713)

New Nationalism (p. 713)

Federal Trade Commission (p. 715)

Go to INQUIZITIVE

To see what you know—and learn what you've missed—with personalized feedback along the way.

Visit the *Give Me Liberty!* Student Site for primary source documents and images, interactive maps, author videos featuring Eric Foner, and more.

CHAPTER 19

SAFE FOR DEMOCRACY: THE UNITED STATES AND WORLD WAR I

★

1916–1920

In 1902, W. T. Stead published a short volume with the arresting title *The Americanization of the World; or, the Trend of the Twentieth Century*. Stead was an English editor whose sensational writings included an exposé of London prostitution, *Maiden Tribute of Modern Babylon*. He would meet his death in 1912 as a passenger on the *Titanic*, the ocean liner that foundered after striking an iceberg in the North Atlantic. Impressed by Americans' "exuberant energies," Stead predicted that the United States would soon emerge as "the greatest of world-powers." But what was most striking about his work was that Stead located the source of American power less in the realm of military might or territorial acquisition than in the country's single-minded commitment to the "pursuit of wealth" and the relentless international spread of American culture—art, music, journalism, even ideas about religion and gender relations. He foresaw a future in which the United States promoted its interests and values through an unending involvement in the affairs of other nations. Stead proved to be an accurate prophet.

The Spanish-American War had established the United States as an international empire. Despite the conquest of the Philippines and Puerto Rico, however, the country's overseas holdings remained tiny compared to those of Britain, France, and Germany. And no more were added, except for a strip of land surrounding the Panama Canal, acquired in 1903, and the Virgin Islands, purchased from Denmark in 1917. In 1900, Great Britain ruled over more than 300 million people in possessions scattered across the globe, and France had nearly 50 million subjects in Asia and Africa. Compared with these, the American presence in the world seemed very small. As Stead suggested, America's empire differed significantly from those of European countries—it was economic, cultural, and intellectual, rather than territorial.

The world economy at the dawn of the twentieth century was already highly globalized. An ever-increasing stream of goods, investments, and people flowed from country to country. Although Britain still dominated world banking and the British pound remained the major currency of international trade, the United States had become the leading industrial power. By 1914, it produced more than one-third of the world's manufactured goods. Already, Europeans complained of an "American invasion" of steel, oil, agricultural equipment, and consumer goods. Spearheads of American culture like movies and popular music were not far behind.

Europeans were fascinated by American ingenuity and mass production techniques. Many feared American products and culture would overwhelm their own. "What are the chief new features of London life?" one British writer asked in 1901. "They are the telephone, the portable camera, the phonograph, the electric street car, the automobile, the typewriter. . . . In every one of these the American maker is supreme." Meanwhile, hundreds of thousands of Americans traveled abroad each year in the early twentieth century. And American racial and ethnic groups became heavily engaged in overseas politics. Through fraternal, religious, and political organizations based in their ethnic and racial communities, Irish-Americans supported Irish independence, American Jews protested the treatment of their co-religionists in Russia, and black Americans hoped to uplift Africa. American influence was growing throughout the world.

FOCUS QUESTIONS

In what ways did the Progressive presidents promote the expansion of American power overseas? *–p. 720*

How did the United States get involved in World War I? *–p. 725*

How did the United States mobilize resources and public opinion for the war effort? *–p. 730*

How did the war affect race relations in the United States? *–p. 737*

Why was 1919 such a watershed year for the United States and the world? *–p. 749*

The American painter John Singer Sargent was commissioned by the British government to create a painting depicting World War I and sent to the front lines in France. The result, *Gassed*, completed in 1919 after the war's end, was doubtless not what the authorities had in mind. Revolted by the carnage he had witnessed, Sargent painted a line of soldiers, their eyes bandaged because of exposure to mustard gas, being led off by a medic to receive treatment. More wounded men lie in the foreground. Sargent was one of many artists and intellectuals who concluded that the war had been a ghastly mistake.

America's burgeoning connections with the outside world led to increasing military and political involvement. In the two decades after 1900, many of the basic principles that would guide American foreign policy for the rest of the century were formulated. The "open door"—the free flow of trade, investment, information, and culture—emerged as a key principle of American foreign relations. "Since the manufacturer insists on having the world as a market," wrote Woodrow Wilson, "the flag of his nation must follow him and the doors of nations which are closed against him must be battered down."

Americans in the twentieth century often discussed foreign policy in the language of freedom. At least in rhetoric, the United States ventured abroad—including intervening militarily in the affairs of other nations—not to pursue strategic goals or to make the world safe for American economic interests, but to promote liberty and democracy. A supreme faith in America's historic destiny and in the righteousness of its ideals enabled the country's leaders to think of the United States simultaneously as an emerging great power and as the worldwide embodiment of freedom.

More than any other individual, Woodrow Wilson articulated this vision of America's relationship to the rest of the world. His foreign policy, called by historians **liberal internationalism**, rested on the conviction that economic and political progress went hand in hand. Thus, greater worldwide freedom would follow inevitably from increased American investment and trade abroad. Frequently during the twentieth century, this conviction would serve as a mask for American power and self-interest. It would also inspire sincere efforts to bring freedom to other peoples. In either case, liberal internationalism represented a shift from the nineteenth-century tradition of promoting freedom primarily by example, to active intervention to remake the world in the American image.

American involvement in World War I provided the first great test of Wilson's belief that American power could "make the world safe for democracy." Most Progressives embraced the country's participation in the war, believing that the United States could help to spread Progressive values throughout the world. The government quickly came to view critics of American involvement not simply as citizens with a different set of opinions, but as enemies of the very ideas of democracy and freedom. As a result, the war produced one of the most sweeping repressions of the right to dissent in all of American history. Rather than bringing Progressivism to other peoples, the war destroyed it at home.

AN ERA OF INTERVENTION

Just as they expanded the powers of the federal government in domestic affairs, the Progressive presidents were not reluctant to project American power outside the country's borders. At first, they confined their interventions to the Western Hemisphere, whose affairs the United States had claimed a special right to oversee ever since the Monroe Doctrine of 1823. Between 1901 and 1920, U.S. marines landed in Caribbean countries more than twenty times. Usually, they were dispatched to create a welcoming economic environment for American companies that wanted stable access to raw materials like bananas and sugar, and for bankers nervous that their loans to local governments might not be repaid.

"I Took the Canal Zone"

Just as he distinguished between good and bad trusts, Theodore Roosevelt divided the world into "civilized" and "uncivilized" nations. The former, he believed, had an obligation to establish order in an unruly world. Roosevelt became far more active in international diplomacy than most of his predecessors, helping, for example, to negotiate a settlement of the Russo-Japanese War of 1905, a feat for which he was awarded the Nobel Peace Prize. Closer to home, his policies were more aggressive. "I have always been fond of the West African proverb," he wrote, "'Speak softly and carry a big stick.'" And although he declared that the United States "has not the slightest desire for territorial aggrandizement at the expense of its southern neighbors," Roosevelt pursued a policy of intervention in Central America.

In his first major action in the region, Roosevelt engineered the separation of Panama from Colombia in order to facilitate the construction of a canal linking the Atlantic and Pacific Oceans. The idea of a canal across the fifty-one-mile-wide Isthmus of Panama had a long history. In 1879–1881, the French engineer Ferdinand de Lesseps attempted to construct such a waterway but failed because of inadequate funding and the toll exacted on his workers by yellow fever and malaria. Roosevelt had long been a proponent of American naval development. He was convinced that a canal would facilitate the movement of naval and commercial vessels between the two oceans. In 1903, when Colombia, of which Panama was a part, refused to cede land for the project, Roosevelt helped to set in motion an uprising by conspirators led by Philippe Bunau-Varilla, a representative of the Panama Canal Company. An American gunboat prevented the Colombian army from suppressing the rebellion.

Upon establishing Panama's independence, Bunau-Varilla signed a treaty giving the United States both the right to construct and operate a canal and sovereignty over the **Panama Canal Zone**, a ten-mile-wide strip of land through which the route would run. A remarkable feat of engineering, the canal was the largest construction project in American history to that date. Like the building of the transcontinental railroad in the 1860s and much construction work today, it involved the widespread use of immigrant labor. Most of the 60,000 workers came from the Caribbean islands of Barbados and Jamaica, but others hailed from Europe, Asia, and the United States. In keeping with American segregation policies, the best jobs were reserved for white Americans, who lived in their own communities complete with schools, churches, and libraries. The project also required a massive effort to eradicate the mosquitoes that carried the tropical diseases responsible, in part, for the failure of earlier efforts. When completed in 1914, the canal reduced the sea voyage between the East and West Coasts of the United States by 8,000 miles.

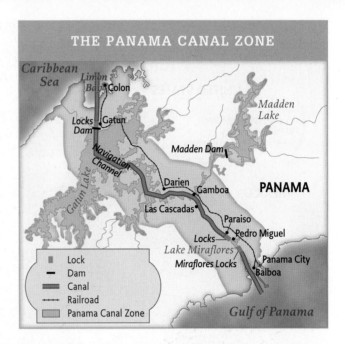

Constructed in the first years of the twentieth century, after Theodore Roosevelt helped engineer Panama's independence from Colombia, the Panama Canal drastically reduced the time it took for commercial and naval vessels to sail from the Atlantic to the Pacific Ocean.

The Panama Canal

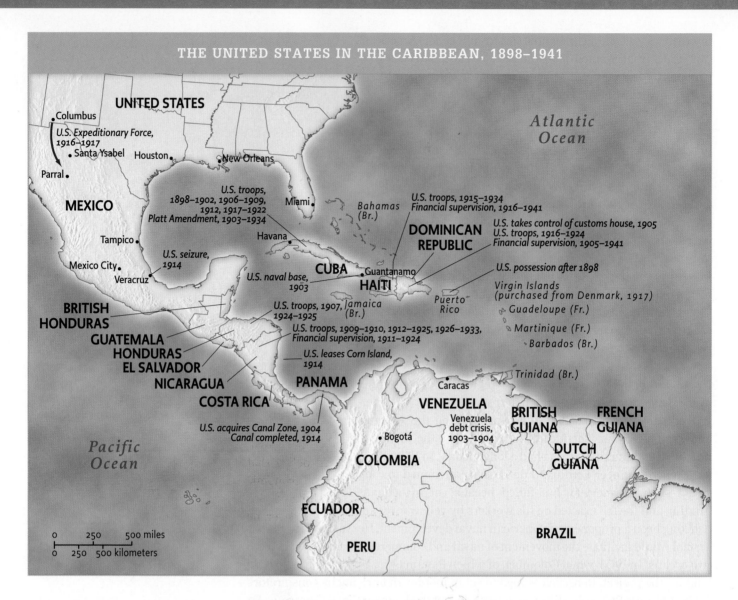

THE UNITED STATES IN THE CARIBBEAN, 1898–1941

Between 1898 and 1941, the United States intervened militarily numerous times in Caribbean countries, generally to protect the economic interests of American banks and investors.

"I took the Canal Zone," Roosevelt exulted. But the manner in which the canal had been initiated, and the continued American rule over the Canal Zone, would long remain a source of tension. In 1977, as a symbol of a new, noninterventionist U.S. attitude toward Latin America, President Jimmy Carter negotiated treaties that led to turning over the canal's operation and control of the Canal Zone to Panama in the year 2000 (see Chapter 26).

The Roosevelt Corollary

An international police power

Roosevelt's actions in Panama anticipated the full-fledged implementation of a principle that came to be called the **Roosevelt Corollary** to the Monroe Doctrine. This held that the United States had the right to exercise "an international police power" in the Western Hemisphere—a significant expansion of Monroe's pledge to defend the hemisphere against European intervention. Early in Roosevelt's administration, British, Italian, and German naval forces blockaded Venezuela to ensure the payment of debts to European bankers. Roosevelt persuaded them to withdraw, but the incident convinced him that financial instability in the New World would invite intervention from the Old. In 1904, Roosevelt ordered American forces to seize the customs houses of the Dominican Republic to ensure payment of that country's debts to European and American investors. He soon arranged an "executive agreement" giving a group of American banks control over Dominican finances. In 1906, he dispatched troops to Cuba to oversee a disputed election; they remained in the country until 1909. Roosevelt also encouraged investment by American corporations like the United Fruit Company, whose huge banana planta-tions soon dominated the economies of Honduras and Costa Rica.

> *The U.S. in Latin America*

Roosevelt's successor, William Howard Taft, landed marines in Nicaragua to protect a government friendly to American economic interests. In general, however, Taft emphasized economic investment and loans from American banks, rather than direct military intervention, as the best way to spread American influence. As a result, his foreign policy became known as **Dollar Diplomacy**. In Honduras, Nicaragua, the Dominican Republic, and even Liberia—the West African nation established in 1816 as a home for freed American slaves—Taft pressed for more efficient revenue collection, stable government, and access to land and labor by American companies.

Moral Imperialism

The son of a Presbyterian minister, Woodrow Wilson brought to the presidency a missionary zeal and a sense of his own and the nation's moral righteousness. He appointed as secretary of state William Jennings Bryan, a strong anti-imperialist. Wilson repudiated Dollar Diplomacy and promised a new foreign policy that would respect Latin America's independence and free it from foreign economic domination. But Wilson could not abandon the conviction that the United States had a responsibility to teach other peoples the lessons of democracy. Moreover, he

> *Responsibility to spread democracy*

The World's Constable, a cartoon commenting on Theodore Roosevelt's "new diplomacy," *in Judge*, January 14, 1905, portrays Roosevelt as an impartial policeman, holding in one hand the threat of force and in the other the promise of the peaceful settlement of disputes. Roose-velt stands between the "undisciplined" non-white peoples of the world and the imperialist powers of Europe and Japan.

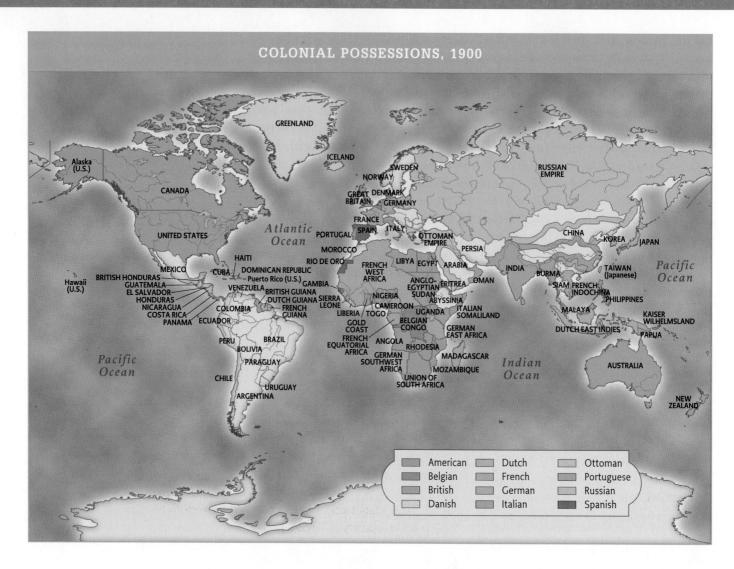

COLONIAL POSSESSIONS, 1900

American
Belgian
British
Danish
Dutch
French
German
Italian
Ottoman
Portuguese
Russian
Spanish

believed, the export of American manufactured goods and investments went hand in hand with the spread of democratic ideals. To Wilson, expanding American economic influence served a higher purpose than mere profit. Americans, he told a group of businessmen in 1916, were "meant to carry liberty and justice" throughout the world. "Go out and sell goods," he urged them, "that will make the world more comfortable and happy, and convert them to the principles of America."

Wilson's **moral imperialism** produced more military interventions in Latin America than the foreign policy of any president before or since. In 1915, he sent marines to occupy Haiti after the government refused to allow American banks to oversee its financial dealings. In 1916, he established a military government in the Dominican Republic, with the United States controlling the country's customs collections and paying its debts. American soldiers remained in the Dominican Republic until 1924 and in Haiti until 1934. They built roads and schools, but did little or nothing to promote democracy. Wilson's foreign policy underscored a paradox of modern American history: the presidents who spoke the most about freedom were likely to intervene most frequently in the affairs of other countries.

Wilson's interventions

Wilson and Mexico

Wilson's major preoccupation in Latin America was Mexico, where in 1911 a revolution led by Francisco Madero overthrew the government of dictator Porfirio Díaz. Two years later, without Wilson's knowledge but with the backing of the U.S. ambassador and of American companies that controlled Mexico's oil and mining industries, military commander Victoriano Huerta assassinated Madero and seized power.

Wilson was appalled. The United States, he announced, would not extend recognition to a "government of butchers." He would "teach" Latin Americans, he added, "to elect good men." When civil war broke out in Mexico, Wilson ordered American troops to land at Vera Cruz to prevent the arrival of weapons meant for Huerta's forces. But to Wilson's surprise, Mexicans greeted the marines as invaders rather than liberators. Vera Cruz, after all, was where the forces of the conquistador Hernán Cortés had landed in the sixteenth century and those of Winfield Scott during the Mexican War. More than 100 Mexicans and 19 Americans died in the fighting that followed.

Huerta resigned in 1914 and fled the country. Meanwhile, various Mexican factions turned on one another. A peasant uprising in the southern part of the country, led by Emiliano Zapata, demanded land reform. The Wilson administration offered support to Venustiano Carranza, a leader more devoted to economic modernization. In 1916, the war spilled over into the United States when several hundred men loyal to Francisco "Pancho" Villa, the leader of another peasant force, raided Columbus, New Mexico, a few miles north of the border, leading to the death of seventeen Americans. With Carranza's approval, Wilson ordered 10,000 troops under the command of General John J. Pershing on an expedition into Mexico that unsuccessfully sought to arrest Villa. Chaos in Mexico continued—within the next few years, Zapata, Carranza, and Villa all fell victim to assassination. Mexico was a warning that it might be more difficult than Wilson assumed to use American might to reorder the internal affairs of other nations, or to apply moral certainty to foreign policy.

> *Vera Cruz*

> *Pancho Villa*

A 1915 postcard portrays two soldiers—one American, one Mexican—at the border between the two countries shortly before Woodrow Wilson ordered American troops into Mexico. The photograph is intended to show a difference in discipline between the two.

AMERICA AND THE GREAT WAR

In June 1914, a Serbian nationalist assassinated Archduke Franz Ferdinand, heir to the throne of the Austro-Hungarian empire, in Sarajevo. (Today, Sarajevo is the capital of Bosnia and Herzegovina.) This deed set in motion a chain of events that plunged Europe into the most devastating war the world had ever seen. In the years before 1914, European nations had engaged in a scramble to obtain colonial possessions overseas and had constructed a shifting series of alliances seeking military domination within Europe. In the aftermath of the assassination, Austria-Hungary, the major power in eastern Europe, declared war on Serbia. Within a little more than a month, because of the European powers' interlocking military alliances, Britain, France, Russia, and Japan (the Allies) found themselves at war with the Central Powers—Germany, Austria-Hungary, and the Ottoman empire, whose holdings included modern-day Turkey and much of the Middle East.

German forces quickly overran Belgium and part of northern France. The war then settled into a prolonged stalemate, with bloody, indecisive battles succeeding one another. New military technologies—submarines, airplanes, machine guns, tanks, and poison gas—produced unprecedented slaughter. In one five-month battle at Verdun, in 1916, 600,000 French and German soldiers perished—nearly as many deaths as in the entire American Civil War. By the time the war ended, an estimated 10 million soldiers, and uncounted millions of civilians, had perished.

The Great War, or World War I as it came to be called, dealt a severe blow to the optimism and self-confidence of Western civilization. For decades, philosophers, reformers, and politicians had hailed the triumph of reason and human progress. Despite increasingly bitter rivalries between European powers, especially Germany and Britain, as they competed for political and military dominance at home and carved up Asia and Africa into rival empires, mankind seemed to have moved beyond the time when disputes were settled by war. The conflict was also a shock to European socialist and labor movements. Of the two great ideologies that had arisen in the nineteenth century, nationalism and socialism, the former proved more powerful. Karl Marx had called on the "workers of the world" to unite against their oppressors. Instead, they marched off to kill each other.

Neutrality and Preparedness

As war engulfed Europe, Americans found themselves sharply divided. British-Americans sided with their nation of origin, as did many other Americans who associated Great Britain with liberty and democracy and Germany with repressive government. On the other hand, German-Americans identified with Germany. Irish-Americans bitterly opposed any aid to the British, a sentiment reinforced in 1916 when authorities in London suppressed the Easter Rebellion, an uprising demanding Irish independence, and executed several of its leaders. Immigrants from the Russian empire, especially Jews, had no desire to see the United States aid the czar's regime. Indeed, the presence of Russia, the world's largest despotic state, as an ally of Britain and France made it difficult to see the war as a clear-cut battle between democracy and autocracy. Many feminists, pacifists, and social reformers, moreover, had become convinced that peace was essential to further efforts to enhance social justice at home. They lobbied vigorously against American involvement. So did large numbers of religious leaders, who viewed war as a barbaric throwback to a less Christian era.

When war broke out in 1914, President Wilson proclaimed American neutrality. But as in the years preceding the War of 1812, naval warfare in Europe reverberated in the United States. Britain declared a naval blockade of Germany and began to stop American merchant vessels. Germany launched submarine warfare against ships entering and leaving British ports. In May 1915, a German submarine sank the British liner *Lusitania* (which was carrying a large cache of arms) off the coast of Ireland, causing the death of 1,198 passengers, including 124 Americans. Wilson composed a note of protest so strong that Bryan resigned as secretary of state, fearing that the president was laying the foundation for military intervention. Bryan had advocated warning Americans not to travel

Americans divided

Wilbur Wright, who with his brother Orville made the first powered flight in 1903, circling the Statue of Liberty six years later. World War I would reveal the military uses for this new technology.

on the ships of belligerents, but Wilson felt this would represent a retreat from the principle of freedom of the seas.

The sinking of the *Lusitania* outraged American public opinion and strengthened the hand of those who believed that the United States must prepare for possible entry into the war. These included longtime advocates of a stronger military establishment, like Theodore Roosevelt, and businessmen with close economic ties to Britain, the country's leading trading partner and the recipient of more than $2 billion in wartime loans from American banks. Wilson himself had strong pro-British sympathies and viewed Germany as "the natural foe of liberty." By the end of 1915, he had embarked on a policy of "preparedness"—a crash program to expand the American army and navy.

Preparedness

The Road to War

In May 1916, Germany announced the suspension of submarine warfare against noncombatants. Wilson's preparedness program seemed to have succeeded in securing the right of Americans to travel freely on the high seas without committing American forces to the conflict. "He kept us out of war" became the slogan of his campaign for reelection. With the Republican Party reunited after its split in 1912, the election proved to be one of the closest in American history. Wilson defeated Republican candidate Charles Evans Hughes by only twenty-three electoral votes and about 600,000 popular votes out of more than 18 million cast. Partly because he seemed to promise not to send American soldiers to Europe, Wilson carried ten of the twelve states that had adopted woman suffrage. Without the votes of women, Wilson would not have been reelected.

Wilson's reelection

On January 22, 1917, Wilson called for a "peace without victory" in Europe and outlined his vision for a world order including freedom of the seas, restrictions on armaments, and self-determination for nations great and small. Almost immediately, however, Germany announced its intention to resume submarine warfare against ships sailing to or from the British Isles, and several American

"Peace without victory"

World War I was the first war in which soldiers moved to the battlefront in motorized trucks. This photograph is from 1918.

In the spring of 1918, they helped to repulse a German advance near Paris and by July were participating in a major Allied counteroffensive. In September, in the Meuse-Argonne campaign, American soldiers under the command of General John J. Pershing, fresh from his campaigns in Mexico, helped to push back the German army. With 1.2 million American soldiers taking part and well over 100,000 dead and wounded, Meuse-Argonne, which lasted a month and a half, was the main American engagement of the war and one of the most significant and deadliest battles in American history. It formed part of a massive Allied offensive involving British, French, and Belgian soldiers and those from overseas European possessions. With his forces in full retreat, the German kaiser abdicated on November 9. Two days later, Germany sued for peace. More than 100,000 Americans had died, a substantial number, but they were only 1 percent of the 10 million soldiers killed in the Great War.

THE WAR AT HOME

The Progressives' War

Looking back on American participation in the European conflict, Randolph Bourne summed up one of its lessons: "War is the health of the state." Bourne saw the expansion of government power as a danger, but it struck most Progressives as a golden opportunity. To them, the war offered the possibility of reforming American society along scientific lines, instilling a sense of national unity and self-sacrifice, and expanding social justice. That American power could now disseminate Progressive values around the globe heightened the war's appeal.

Almost without exception, Progressive intellectuals and reformers, joined by prominent labor leaders and native-born socialists, rallied to Wilson's support. The roster included intellectuals like John Dewey, journalists such as Walter Lippmann and Herbert Croly, AFL head Samuel Gompers, socialist writers like Upton Sinclair, and prominent reformers including Florence Kelley and Charlotte Perkins Gilman. In *The New Republic*, Dewey urged Progressives to recognize the "social possibilities of war." The crisis, he wrote, offered the prospect of attacking the "immense inequality of power" within the United States, thus laying the foundation for Americans to enjoy "effective freedom."

War as an opportunity

The Wartime State

An expanding state

Like the Civil War, World War I created, albeit temporarily, a national state with unprecedented powers and a sharply increased presence in Americans' everyday lives. Under the **Selective Service Act** of May 1917, 24 million men were required to register with the draft, and the army soon swelled from 120,000 to 5 million men. The war seemed to bring into being the New Nationalist state Theodore Roosevelt and so many Progressives had desired. New federal agencies moved to regulate industry, transportation, labor relations, and agriculture. Headed by Wall Street financier Bernard Baruch, the **War Industries Board** presided over all elements of war production from the distribution of raw materials to the prices of manufactured goods. To spur efficiency, it established standardized specifications for everything from automobile tires to shoe colors (three were permitted—black, brown, and white). The Railroad Administration took control of the nation's transportation system, and the Fuel Agency rationed coal and oil. The Food Administration instructed farmers on modern methods of cultivation and promoted the more efficient preparation of meals. Its director, Herbert Hoover, mobilized the shipment of American food to the war-devastated Allies, popularizing the slogan "Food will win the war."

These agencies generally saw themselves as partners of business as much as regulators. They guaranteed government suppliers a high rate of profit and encouraged cooperation among former business rivals by suspending antitrust laws. At the same time, however, the War Labor Board, which included representatives of government, industry, and the American Federation of Labor, pressed for the establishment of a minimum wage, eight-hour workday, and the right to form unions. During the war, wages rose substantially, working conditions in many industries improved, and union membership doubled. To finance the war, corporate and individual income taxes rose enormously. By 1918, the wealthiest Americans were paying 60 percent of their income in taxes. Tens of millions of Americans answered the call to demonstrate their patriotism by purchasing Liberty bonds. Once peace arrived, the wartime state quickly withered away. But for a time, the federal government seemed well on its way to fulfilling the Progressive vision of promoting economic rationalization, industrial justice, and a sense of common national purpose.

The Propaganda War

During the Civil War, it had been left to private agencies—Union Leagues, the Loyal Publication Society, and others—to mobilize prowar public opinion. But the Wilson administration decided that patriotism was too important to leave to the private sector. Many Americans were skeptical about whether democratic America should enter a struggle between rival empires. Some vehemently opposed American participation, notably the Industrial Workers of the World (IWW) and the bulk of the Socialist Party, which in 1917 condemned the declaration of war as "a crime against the people of the United States" and called on "the workers of all countries" to refuse to fight. As the major national organization to oppose Wilson's policy, the Socialist Party became a rallying point for antiwar sentiment. In mayoral elections across the country in the fall of 1917, the Socialist vote averaged 20 percent, far above the party's previous total.

In April 1917, the Wilson administration created the Committee on Public Information (CPI) to explain to Americans and the world, as its director, George Creel, put it, "the cause that compelled America to take arms in defense of its liberties and free institutions." Enlisting academics, journalists, artists, and advertising men, the CPI flooded the country with prowar propaganda, using every available

All combatants issued propaganda posters. The American poster uses an image of the Statue of Liberty to sell war bonds. The German one, satirically entitled *We Are Barbarians*, refutes the charge of barbarism hurled at Germans by the Allies. It relates that Germany outstrips England and France in Nobel Prizes, provision for the elderly, book publication, education, and literacy.

Douglas Fairbanks, one of the era's most celebrated movie stars, addressing a 1918 rally urging people to buy Liberty bonds.

Wartime propaganda

medium from pamphlets (of which it issued 75 million) to posters, newspaper advertisements, and motion pictures. It trained and dispatched across the country 75,000 Four-Minute Men, who delivered brief standardized talks (sometimes in Italian, Yiddish, and other immigrant languages) to audiences in movie theaters, schools, and other public venues.

Never before had an agency of the federal government attempted the "conscious and intelligent manipulation of the organized habits and opinions of the masses," in the words of young Edward Bernays, a member of Creel's staff who would later create the modern profession of public relations. The CPI's activities proved, one adman wrote, that it was possible to "sway the ideas of whole populations, change their habits of life, create belief, practically universal in any policy or idea." In the 1920s, advertisers would use what they had learned to sell goods. But the CPI also set a precedent for governmental efforts to shape public opinion in later international conflicts, from World War II to the Cold War and Iraq.

"The Great Cause of Freedom"

The CPI couched its appeal in the Progressive language of social cooperation and expanded democracy. Abroad, this meant a peace based on the principle of national self-determination. At home, it meant improving "industrial democracy." A Progressive journalist, Creel believed the war would accelerate the movement toward solving the "age-old problems of poverty, inequality, oppression, and unhappiness." He took to heart a warning from historian Carl Becker that a simple contrast between German tyranny and American democracy would not seem plausible to the average worker: "You talk to him of our ideals of liberty and he thinks of the shameless exploitation of labor and of the ridiculous gulf between wealth and poverty." CPI pamphlets foresaw a postwar society complete with a "universal eight-hour day" and a living wage for all.

While "democracy" served as the key term of wartime mobilization, "freedom" also took on new significance. The war, a CPI advertisement proclaimed, was being fought in "the great cause of freedom." Thousands of persons, often draftees, were enlisted to pose in giant human tableaus representing symbols of liberty. One living representation of the Liberty Bell at Fort Dix, New Jersey, included 25,000 people. The most common visual image in wartime propaganda was the Statue of Liberty, employed especially to rally support among immigrants. "You came here seeking Freedom," stated a caption on one Statue of Liberty poster. "You must now help preserve it." Buying Liberty bonds became a demonstration of patriotism. Wilson's speeches cast the United States as a land of liberty fighting alongside a "concert of free people" to secure self-determination for the oppressed peoples of the world. The idea of freedom, it seems, requires an antithesis, and the CPI found one in the German kaiser and, more generally, the German nation and people. Government propaganda whipped up hatred of the wartime foe by portraying it as a nation of barbaric Huns.

The Coming of Woman Suffrage

The enlistment of "democracy" and "freedom" as ideological war weapons inevitably inspired demands for their expansion at home. In 1916, Wilson had cautiously endorsed votes for women. America's entry into the war threatened to tear

Women during World War I: two women hauling ice—a job confined to men before the war—and woman suffrage demonstrators in front of the White House.

the suffrage movement apart, since many advocates had been associated with opposition to American involvement. Indeed, among those who voted against the declaration of war was the first woman member of Congress, the staunch pacifist Jeannette Rankin of Montana. "I want to stand by my country, but I cannot vote for war," she said. Although defeated in her reelection bid in 1918, Rankin would return to Congress in 1940. She became the only member to oppose the declaration of war against Japan in 1941, which ended her political career. In 1968, at the age of eighty-five, Rankin took part in a giant march on Washington to protest the war in Vietnam.

As during the Civil War, however, most leaders of woman suffrage organizations enthusiastically enlisted in the effort. Women sold war bonds, organized patriotic rallies, and went to work in war production jobs. Some 22,000 served as clerical workers and nurses with American forces in Europe. Many believed wartime service would earn them equal rights at home.

At the same time, a new generation of college-educated activists, organized in the National Woman's Party, pressed for the right to vote with militant tactics many older suffrage advocates found scandalous. The party's leader, Alice Paul, had studied in England between 1907 and 1910 when the British suffrage movement adopted a strategy that included arrests, imprisonments, and vigorous denunciations of a male-dominated political system. How could the country fight for democracy abroad, Paul asked, while denying it to women at home? She compared Wilson to the kaiser, and a group of her followers chained themselves to the White House fence, resulting in a seven-month prison sentence. When they began a hunger strike, the prisoners were force-fed.

> *Alice Paul*

The combination of women's patriotic service and widespread outrage over the mistreatment of Paul and her fellow prisoners pushed the administration toward full-fledged support for woman suffrage. "We have made partners of the women in this war," Wilson proclaimed. "Shall we admit them only to a partnership of suffering and sacrifice and toil and not to a partnership of privilege and right?" In 1920, the long struggle ended with the ratification of the Nineteenth Amendment barring states from using sex as a qualification for the suffrage. The United States became the twenty-seventh country to allow women to vote.

> *The Nineteenth Amendment*

A 1915 cartoon showing the western states where women had won the right to vote. Women in the East reach out to a western woman carrying a torch of liberty.

THE AWAKENING

A 1916 cartoon from the publication of the Woman's Christian Temperance Union shows petitions for Prohibition flooding into Congress.

ON TO WASHINGTON!
STORM THE CAPITOL WITH PETITIONS FOR NATIONAL CONSTITUTIONAL

Prohibition

The war gave a powerful impulse to other campaigns that had engaged the energies of many women in the Progressive era. Ironically, efforts to stamp out prostitution and protect soldiers from venereal disease led the government to distribute birth-control information and devices—the very action for which Margaret Sanger had recently been jailed, as noted in the previous chapter.

Prohibition, a movement inherited from the nineteenth century that had gained new strength and militancy in Progressive America, finally achieved national success during the war. Numerous impulses flowed into the renewed campaign to ban intoxicating liquor. Employers hoped it would create a more disciplined labor force. Urban reformers believed that it would promote a more orderly city environment and undermine urban political machines that used saloons as places to organize. Women reformers hoped Prohibition would protect wives and children from husbands who engaged in domestic violence when drunk or who squandered their wages at saloons. Many native-born Protestants saw Prohibition as a way of imposing "American" values on immigrants.

Like the suffrage movement, Prohibitionists first concentrated on state campaigns. By 1915, they had won victories in eighteen southern and midwestern states where the immigrant population was small and Protestant denominations like Baptists and Methodists strongly opposed drinking. But like the suffrage movement, Prohibitionists came to see national legislation as their best strategy. The war gave them added ammunition. Many prominent breweries were owned by German-Americans, making beer seem unpatriotic. The Food Administration insisted that grain must be used to

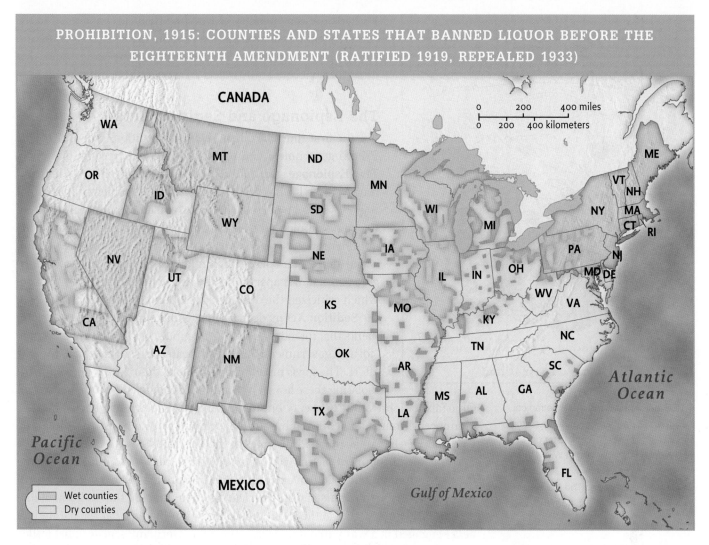

PROHIBITION, 1915: COUNTIES AND STATES THAT BANNED LIQUOR BEFORE THE EIGHTEENTH AMENDMENT (RATIFIED 1919, REPEALED 1933)

produce food, not distilled into beer and liquor. In December 1917, Congress passed the **Eighteenth Amendment**, prohibiting the manufacture and sale of intoxicating liquor. It was ratified by the states in 1919 and went into effect at the beginning of 1920.

Liberty in Wartime

World War I raised questions already glimpsed during the Civil War that would trouble the nation again during the McCarthy era and in the aftermath of the terrorist attacks of 2001: What is the balance between security and freedom? Does the Constitution protect citizens' rights during wartime? Should dissent be equated with lack of patriotism? The conflict demonstrated that during a war, traditional civil liberties are likely to come under severe pressure.

In 1917, Randolph Bourne ridiculed Progressives who believed they could mold the war according to their own "liberal purposes." The conflict, he predicted, would empower not reformers but the "least democratic forces in American life." The accuracy of Bourne's prediction soon become apparent. Despite the administration's idealistic language of democracy and freedom, the war inaugurated the most intense repression of civil liberties the nation has ever known.

In the early years of the twentieth century, many states and localities in the South and West banned the manufacture and sale of alcoholic beverages. ("Wet" counties allowed alcoholic beverages, "dry" counties banned them.) Prohibition became national with the adoption of the Eighteenth Amendment in 1919.

Security and freedom

ORGIE MANIACLE

ALL FOR HONOR

ALL FOR DEMOCRACY

ALL FOR WORLD PEACE

ALL FOR JESUS

EDITOR   CAPITALIST   POLITICIAN   MINISTER

Having Their Fling

A 1917 antiwar cartoon from the radical magazine *The Masses* depicts an editor, capitalist, politician, and minister celebrating American involvement in World War I and hoping to benefit from it. President Woodrow Wilson barred *The Masses* and other antiwar publications from the mails.

Perhaps the very nobility of wartime rhetoric contributed to the massive suppression of dissent. For in the eyes of Wilson and many of his supporters, America's goals were so virtuous that disagreement could only reflect treason to the country's values.

The Espionage and Sedition Acts

For the first time since the Alien and Sedition Acts of 1798, the federal government enacted laws to restrict freedom of speech. The **Espionage Act** of 1917 prohibited not only spying and interfering with the draft but also "false statements" that might impede military success. The postmaster general barred from the mails numerous newspapers and magazines critical of the administration. The victims ranged from virtually the entire socialist press and many foreign-language publications to *The Jeffersonian*, a newspaper owned by ex-Populist leader Tom Watson, which criticized the draft as a violation of states' rights. In 1918, the **Sedition Act** made it a crime to make spoken or printed statements that intended to cast "contempt, scorn, or disrepute" on the "form of government," or that advocated interference with the war effort. The government charged more than 2,000 persons with violating these laws. Over half were convicted. A court sentenced Ohio farmer John White to twenty-one months in prison for saying that the murder of innocent women and children by German soldiers was no worse than what the United States had done in the Philippines in the war of 1899–1903.

The most prominent victim was Eugene V. Debs, convicted in 1918 under the Espionage Act for delivering an antiwar speech. Before his sentencing, Debs gave the court a lesson in the history of American freedom, tracing the tradition of dissent from Thomas Paine to the abolitionists, and pointing out that the nation had never engaged in a war without internal opposition. Germany sent socialist leader Karl Liebknecht to prison for four years for opposing the war; in the United States, Debs's sentence was ten years. After the war's end, Wilson rejected the advice of his attorney general that he commute Debs's sentence. Debs ran for president while still in prison in 1920 and received 900,000 votes. It was left to Wilson's successor, Warren G. Harding, to release Debs from prison in 1921.

Coercive Patriotism

Even more extreme repression took place at the hands of state governments and private groups. Americans had long displayed the flag (and used it in advertisements for everything from tobacco products to variety shows). But during World War I, attitudes toward the American flag became a test of patriotism. Persons suspected of disloyalty were forced to kiss the flag in public; those who made statements critical of the flag could be imprisoned. During the war, thirty-three states outlawed the possession or display of red or black flags (symbols, respectively, of communism and anarchism), and twenty-three outlawed a newly created offense, "criminal syndicalism," the advocacy of unlawful acts to accomplish political change or "a change in industrial ownership."

"Criminal syndicalism"

"Who is the real patriot?" Emma Goldman asked while on trial for conspiring to violate the Selective Service Act. She answered, those who "love America with open eyes," who were not blind to "the wrongs committed in the name of patriotism." But from the federal government to local authorities and private groups, patriotism came to be equated with support for the government, the war, and the American economic system, while antiwar sentiment, labor radicalism, and sympathy for the Russian Revolution became "un-American." Local authorities formally investigated residents who failed to subscribe to Liberty Loans. Throughout the country, schools revised their course offerings to ensure their patriotism and required teachers to sign loyalty oaths.

The 250,000 members of the newly formed American Protective League (APL) helped the Justice Department identify radicals and critics of the war by spying on their neighbors and carrying out "slacker raids" in which thousands of men were stopped on the streets of major cities and required to produce draft registration cards. Many private groups seized upon the atmosphere of repression as a weapon against domestic opponents. Employers cooperated with the government in crushing the Industrial Workers of the World (IWW), a move long demanded by business interests. In July 1917, vigilantes in Bisbee, Arizona, rounded up some 1,200 striking copper miners and their sympathizers, herded them into railroad boxcars, and transported them into the desert, where they were abandoned. Few ever returned to Bisbee. In August, a crowd in Butte, Montana, lynched IWW leader Frank Little. The following month, operating under one of the broadest warrants in American history, federal agents swooped down on IWW offices throughout the country, arresting hundreds of leaders and seizing files and publications.

The war experience, commented Walter Lippmann, demonstrated "that the traditional liberties of speech and opinion rest on no solid foundation." Yet while some Progressives protested individual excesses, most failed to speak out against the broad suppression of freedom of expression. Civil liberties, by and large, had never been a major concern of Progressives, who had always viewed the national state as the embodiment of democratic purpose and insisted that freedom flowed from participating in the life of society, not standing in opposition. Strong believers in the use of national power to improve social conditions, Progressives found themselves ill prepared to develop a defense of minority rights against majority or governmental tyranny. From the AFL to *New Republic* intellectuals, moreover, supporters of the war saw the elimination of socialists and alien radicals as a necessary prelude to the integration of labor and immigrants into an ordered society, an outcome they hoped would emerge from the war.

WHO IS AN AMERICAN?

In many respects, Progressivism was a precursor to major developments of the twentieth century—the New Deal, the Great Society, the socially active state. But in accepting the idea of "race" as a permanent, defining characteristic of individuals and social groups, Progressives bore more resemblance to nineteenth-century thinkers than to later twentieth-century liberals, with whom they are sometimes compared.

A poster demands that citizens prove they are "100% American" by purchasing war bonds.

Florine Stettheimer's *New York/Liberty*, painted in 1918, depicts the Statue of Liberty, warships, and airplanes in an exuberant tribute to New York City and to the idea of freedom in the wake of World War I.

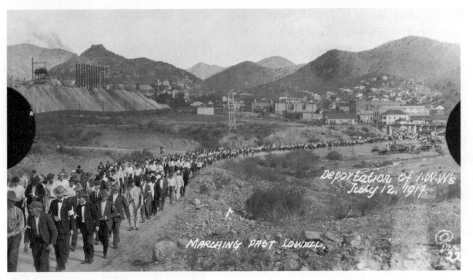

Deportation of I.W.Ws
July 12, 1917.

MARCHING PAST LOWELL.

A long line of striking miners being led out of Bisbee, Arizona, in July 1917. Some 1,200 members of the Industrial Workers of the World were transported into the desert by armed vigilantes and abandoned there.

Eugenics

The melting pot

The "Race Problem"

Even before American participation in World War I, what contemporaries called the "race problem"—the tensions that arose from the country's increasing ethnic diversity—had become a major subject of public concern. "Race" referred to far more than black-white relations. The *Dictionary of Races of Peoples*, published in 1911 by the U.S. Immigration Commission, listed no fewer than forty-five immigrant "races," each supposedly with its own inborn characteristics. They ranged from Anglo-Saxons at the top down to Hebrews, Northern Italians, and, lowest of all, Southern Italians—supposedly violent, undisciplined, and incapable of assimilation.

Popular best-sellers like *The Passing of the Great Race*, published in 1916 by Madison Grant, president of the New York Zoological Society, warned that the influx of new immigrants and the low birthrate of native white women threatened the foundations of American civilization. The new science of eugenics, which studied the alleged mental characteristics of different races, gave anti-immigrant sentiment an air of professional expertise. If democracy could not flourish in the face of vast inequalities of economic power, neither, most Progressives believed, could it survive in a nation permanently divided along racial and ethnic lines.

Americanization and Pluralism

Somehow, the very nationalization of politics and economic life served to heighten awareness of ethnic and racial difference and spurred demands for "Americanization"—the creation of a more homogeneous national culture. A 1908 play by the Jewish immigrant writer Israel Zangwill, *The Melting Pot*, gave a popular name to the process by which newcomers were supposed to merge their identity into existing American nationality. Public and private groups of all kinds—including educators, employers, labor leaders, social reformers, and public officials—took up the task of Americanizing new immigrants. The Ford Motor Company's famed sociological department entered the homes of immigrant workers to evaluate their clothing, furniture, and food preferences and enrolled them in English-language courses. Ford fired those who failed to adapt to American standards after a reasonable period of time. Americanization programs often targeted women as the bearers and transmitters of culture. In Los Angeles, teachers and religious missionaries worked to teach English to Mexican-American women so that they could then assimilate American values. Fearful that adult newcomers remained too stuck in their Old World ways, public schools paid great attention to Americanizing immigrants' children. The challenge facing schools, wrote one educator, was "to

An Americanization Celebration. A photograph of a Catholic assembly on National Slavic Day, September 3, 1914, illustrates how immigrants strove to demonstrate their patriotism. Children wear Old World dress, but most of the adults are in American clothing or nurses' uniforms.

implant in their children, so far as can be done, the Anglo-Saxon conception of righteousness, law and order, and popular government."

A minority of Progressives questioned Americanization efforts and insisted on respect for immigrant subcultures. At Hull House, teachers offered English-language instruction but also encouraged immigrants to value their European heritage. Probably the most penetrating critique issued from the pen of Randolph Bourne, whose 1916 essay "Trans-National America" exposed the fundamental flaw in the Americanization model. "There is no distinctive American culture," Bourne pointed out. Interaction between individuals and groups had produced the nation's music, poetry, and other cultural expressions. Bourne envisioned a democratic, cosmopolitan society in which immigrants and natives alike submerged their group identities in a new "trans-national" culture.

Randolph Bourne

A 1919 Americanization pageant in Milwaukee, in which immigrants encounter Abraham Lincoln and the Statue of Liberty.

With President Wilson declaring that some Americans "born under foreign flags" were guilty of "disloyalty . . . and must be absolutely crushed," the federal and state governments demanded that immigrants demonstrate their unwavering devotion to the United States. The Committee on Public Information renamed the Fourth of July, 1918, Loyalty Day and asked ethnic groups to participate in patriotic pageants. New York City's celebration included a procession of 75,000 persons with dozens of floats and presentations linking immigrants with the war effort and highlighting their contributions to American society. Leaders of ethnic groups that had suffered discrimination saw the war as an opportunity to gain greater rights. Prominent Jewish leaders promoted enlistment and

The Wanderer finds Liberty in America

VOICES OF FREEDOM

From WOODROW WILSON, WAR MESSAGE TO CONGRESS (1917)

More than any other individual in the early twentieth century, President Woodrow Wilson articulated a new vision of America's relationship to the rest of the world. In his message to a special session of Congress on April 2, 1917, Wilson asked for a declaration of war. In his most celebrated sentence, Wilson declared, "The world must be made safe for democracy."

Let us be very clear, and make very clear to all the world what our motives and our objects are.... Our object ... is to vindicate the principles of peace and justice in the life of the world as against selfish and autocratic power and to set up amongst the really free and self-governed peoples of the world such a concert of purpose and of action as will henceforth ensure the observance of those principles.... The menace to peace and freedom lies in the existence of autocratic governments backed by organized force which is controlled wholly by their will, not by the will of their people.

A steadfast concert for peace can never be maintained except by a partnership of democratic nations. No autocratic government could be trusted to keep faith within it or observe its covenants.... Only free peoples can hold their purpose and their honour steady to a common end and prefer the interests of mankind to any narrow interest of their own....

We are now about to accept gage of battle with this natural foe to liberty and shall, if necessary, spend the whole force of the nation to check and nullify its pretensions and its power. We are glad, now that we see the facts with no veil of false pretense about them, to fight thus for the ultimate peace of the world and for the liberation of its peoples, the German peoples included: for the rights of nations great and small and the privilege of men everywhere to choose their way of life and of obedience. The world must be made safe for democracy. Its peace must be planted upon the tested foundations of political liberty. We have no selfish ends to serve. We desire no conquest, no dominion.... If there should be disloyalty, it will be dealt with with a firm hand of stern repression....

It is a fearful thing to lead this great peaceful people into war, into the most terrible and disastrous of all wars, civilization itself seeming to be in the balance. But the right is more precious than peace, and we shall fight for the things which we have always carried nearest our hearts—for democracy, ... for the rights and liberties of small nations, for a universal dominion of right by such a concert of free peoples as shall bring peace and safety to all nations and make the world itself at last free.

From EUGENE V. DEBS, SPEECH TO THE JURY BEFORE SENTENCING UNDER THE ESPIONAGE ACT (1918)

Socialist leader Eugene V. Debs was arrested for delivering an antiwar speech and convicted of violating the Espionage Act. In his speech to the jury, he defended the right of dissent in wartime.

Gentlemen, you have heard the report of my speech at Canton [Ohio] on June 16, and I submit that there is not a word in that speech to warrant the charges set out in the indictment. . . . In what I had to say there my purpose was to have the people understand something about the social system in which we live and to prepare them to change this system by perfectly peaceable and orderly means into what I, as a Socialist, conceive to be a real democracy. . . . I have never advocated violence in any form. I have always believed in education, in intelligence, in enlightenment; and I have always made my appeal to the reason and to the conscience of the people.

In every age there have been a few heroic souls who have been in advance of their time, who have been misunderstood, maligned, persecuted, sometimes put to death. . . . Washington, Jefferson, Franklin, Paine, and their compeers were the rebels of their day. . . . But they had the moral courage to be true to their convictions. . . .

William Lloyd Garrison, Wendell Phillips, Elizabeth Cady Stanton . . . and other leaders of the abolition movement who were regarded as public enemies and treated accordingly, were true to their faith and stood their ground. . . . You are now teaching your children to revere their memories, while all of their detractors are in oblivion. . . .

The war of 1812 was opposed and condemned by some of the most influential citizens; the Mexican War was vehemently opposed and bitterly denounced, even after the war had been declared and was in progress, by Abraham Lincoln, Charles Sumner, Daniel Webster. . . . They were not indicted; they were not charged with treason. . . .

Isn't it strange that we Socialists stand almost alone today in upholding and defending the Constitution of the United States? The revolutionary fathers . . . understood that free speech, a free press and the right of free assemblage by the people were fundamental principles in democratic government. . . . I believe in the right of free speech, in war as well as in peace.

QUESTIONS

1. *What does Wilson think is the greatest threat to freedom in the world?*

2. *Why does Debs relate the history of wartime dissent in the United States?*

3. *Does anything in Wilson's speech offer a harbinger of the extreme repression of free speech that occurred during World War I?*

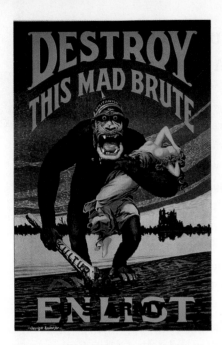

A vivid example of the anti-German propaganda produced by the federal government to encourage prowar sentiment during World War I.

Restricting German language

Intelligence tests

expressions of loyalty. The Chinese-American press insisted that even those born abroad and barred from citizenship should register for the draft, to "bring honor to the people of our race."

The Anti-German Crusade

German-Americans bore the brunt of forced Americanization. The first wave of German immigrants had arrived before the Civil War. By 1914, German-Americans numbered nearly 9 million, including immigrants and persons of German parentage. They had created thriving ethnic institutions including clubs, sports associations, schools, and theaters. On the eve of the war, many Americans admired German traditions in literature, music, and philosophy, and one-quarter of all the high school students in the country studied the German language. But after American entry into the war, the use of German and expressions of German culture became a target of prowar organizations. In Iowa, Governor William L. Harding issued a proclamation requiring that all oral communication in schools, public places, and over the telephone be conducted in English. Freedom of speech, he declared, did not include "the right to use a language other than the language of the country."

By 1919, the vast majority of the states had enacted laws restricting the teaching of foreign languages. Popular words of German origin were changed: "hamburger" became "liberty sandwich," and "sauerkraut" "liberty cabbage." Many communities banned the playing of German music. The government jailed Karl Muck, the director of the Boston Symphony and a Swiss citizen, as an enemy alien after he insisted on including the works of German composers like Beethoven in his concerts. The war dealt a crushing blow to German-American culture. By 1920, the number of German-language newspapers had been reduced to 276 (one-third the number twenty years earlier), and only 1 percent of high school pupils still studied German. The Census of 1920 reported a 25 percent drop in the number of Americans admitting to having been born in Germany.

Toward Immigration Restriction

Even as Americanization programs sought to assimilate immigrants into American society, the war strengthened the conviction that certain kinds of undesirable persons ought to be excluded altogether. The new immigrants, one advocate of restriction declared, appreciated the values of democracy and freedom far less than "the Anglo-Saxon," as evidenced by their attraction to "extreme political doctrines" like anarchism and socialism. Stanford University psychologist Lewis Terman introduced the term "IQ" (intelligence quotient) in 1916, claiming that this single number could measure an individual's mental capacity. Intelligence tests administered to recruits by the army seemed to confirm scientifically that blacks and the new immigrants stood far below native white Protestants on the IQ scale, further spurring demands for immigration restriction.

In 1917, over Wilson's veto, Congress required that immigrants be literate in English or another language. The war accelerated other efforts to upgrade the American population. Some were inspired by the idea of improving the human race by discouraging reproduction among less "desirable" persons. Indiana in 1907 had passed a law authorizing doctors to sterilize insane and "feeble-minded" inmates in mental institutions so that they would not pass their "defective" genes on to children. Numerous other states now followed suit. In *Buck v. Bell* (1927), the Supreme Court upheld the constitutionality of these laws. Justice Oliver Wendell Holmes's opinion included the famous statement, "Three generations of imbeciles are enough." By the time the practice ended in the 1960s, some 63,000 persons had been involuntarily sterilized.

A 1919 cartoon, *Close the Gate,* warns that unrestricted immigration allows dangerous radicals to enter the United States.

Groups Apart: Mexicans, Puerto Ricans, and Asian-Americans

No matter how coercive, Americanization programs assumed that European immigrants and especially their children could eventually adjust to the conditions of American life, embrace American ideals, and become productive citizens enjoying the full blessings of American freedom. This assumption did not apply to non-white immigrants or to blacks. Although the melting-pot idea envisioned that newcomers from Europe would leave their ethnic enclaves and join the American mainstream, non-whites confronted ever-present boundaries of exclusion.

The war led to further growth of the Southwest's Mexican population. Wartime demand for labor from the area's mine owners and large farmers led the government to exempt Mexicans temporarily from the literacy test enacted in 1917. Mexicans were legally classified as white, and many Progressive reformers viewed the growing Mexican population as candidates for Americanization. Teachers and religious missionaries sought to instruct them in English, convert them to Protestantism, and in other ways promote their assimilation into the mainstream culture. Yet public officials in the Southwest treated them as a group apart. Segregation, by law and custom, was common in schools, hospitals, theaters, and other institutions in states with significant Mexican populations. By 1920, nearly all Mexican children in California and the Southwest were educated in their own schools or classrooms. Phoenix, Arizona, established separate public schools for Indians, Mexicans, blacks, and whites. Although in far smaller numbers than blacks, Mexican-Americans also suffered lynchings—over 200 between 1880 and 1930. Discrimination led to the formation of La Grán Liga Mexicanista de Beneficencia y Protección, which aimed to improve the conditions of Mexicans in the United States and "to strike back at the hatred of some bad sons of Uncle Sam who believe themselves better than the Mexicans."

Mexicans in the Southwest

Puerto Ricans also occupied an ambiguous position within American society. On the eve of American entry into World War I, Congress terminated the status "citizen of Puerto Rico" and conferred American citizenship on residents of the island. The aim was to dampen support for Puerto Rican independence and to strengthen the American hold on a strategic outpost in the Caribbean. The change did not grant islanders the right to vote for president, or representation in Congress. Puerto Rican men, nonetheless, were subject to the draft and fought overseas. José

Puerto Rico

de Diego, the Speaker of the House of the island's legislature, wrote the president in 1917 asking that Puerto Rico be granted the democracy the United States was fighting for in Europe.

Even more restrictive were policies toward Asian-Americans. In 1906, the San Francisco school board ordered all Asian students confined to a single public school. When the Japanese government protested, president Theodore Roosevelt persuaded the city to rescind the order. He then negotiated the Gentlemen's Agreement of 1907 whereby Japan agreed to end migration to the United States except for the wives and children of men already in the country. In 1913, California barred all aliens incapable of becoming naturalized citizens (that is, all Asians) from owning or leasing land.

The Color Line

By far the largest non-white group, African-Americans were excluded from nearly every Progressive definition of freedom described in Chapter 18. After their disenfranchisement in the South, few could participate in American democracy. Barred from joining most unions and from skilled employment, black workers had little access to "industrial freedom." A majority of adult black women worked outside the home, but for wages that offered no hope of independence. Predominantly domestic and agricultural workers, they remained unaffected by the era's laws regulating the hours and conditions of female labor. Nor could blacks, the majority desperately poor, participate fully in the emerging consumer economy, either as employees in the new department stores (except as janitors and cleaning women) or as purchasers of the consumer goods now flooding the marketplace.

Progressive intellectuals, social scientists, labor reformers, and suffrage advocates displayed a remarkable indifference to the black condition. Israel Zangwill did not include blacks in the melting-pot idea popularized by his Broadway play. Walter Weyl waited until the last fifteen pages of *The New Democracy* to introduce the "race problem." His comment, quoted in the previous chapter, that the chief obstacles to freedom were economic, not political, revealed little appreciation of how the denial of voting rights underpinned the comprehensive system of inequality to which southern blacks were subjected.

Most settlement-house reformers accepted segregation as natural and equitable, assuming there should be white settlements for white neighborhoods and black settlements for black. White leaders of the woman suffrage movement said little about black disenfranchisement. In the South, members of upper-class white women's clubs sometimes raised funds for black schools and community centers. But suffrage leaders insisted that the vote was a racial entitlement, a "badge and synonym of freedom," in the words of Rebecca Felton of Georgia, that should not be denied to "free-born white women." During Reconstruction, women had been denied constitutional recognition because it was "the Negro's hour." Now, World War I's "woman's hour" excluded blacks. The amendment that achieved woman suffrage left the states free to limit voting by poll taxes and literacy tests. Living in the South, the vast majority of the country's black women still could not vote.

The Gentlemen's Agreement

Exclusion of blacks

A poster advertising the 1915 film *The Birth of a Nation*, which had its premiere at Woodrow Wilson's White House. The movie glorified the Ku Klux Klan and depicted blacks during Reconstruction as unworthy of participation in government and a danger to white womanhood.

Roosevelt, Wilson, and Race

The Progressive presidents shared prevailing attitudes concerning blacks. Theodore Roosevelt shocked white opinion by inviting Booker T. Washington to dine with him in the White House and by appointing a number of blacks to federal offices. But in 1906, when a small group of black soldiers shot off their guns in Brownsville, Texas, killing one resident, and none of their fellows would name them, Roosevelt ordered the dishonorable discharge of three black companies—156 men in all, including six winners of the Congressional Medal of Honor. Roosevelt's ingrained belief in Anglo-Saxon racial destiny (he called Indians "savages" and blacks "wholly unfit for the suffrage") did nothing to lessen Progressive intellectuals' enthusiasm for his New Nationalism. Even Jane Addams, one of the few Progressives to take a strong interest in black rights and a founder of the National Association for the Advancement of Colored People (NAACP), went along when the Progressive Party convention of 1912 rejected a civil rights plank in its platform and barred black delegates from the South.

Woodrow Wilson, a native of Virginia, could speak without irony of the South's "genuine representative government" and its exalted "standards of liberty." His administration imposed racial segregation in federal departments in Washington, D.C., and dismissed numerous black federal employees. Wilson allowed D. W. Griffith's film *Birth of a Nation*, which glorified the Ku Klux Klan as the defender of white civilization during Reconstruction, to have its premiere at the White House in 1915. "Have you a 'new freedom' for white Americans and a new slavery for your African-American fellow citizens?" William Monroe Trotter, the militant black editor of the *Boston Guardian* and founder of the all-black National Equal Rights League, asked the president.

Blacks subject to disenfranchisement and segregation were understandably skeptical of the nation's claim to embody freedom and fully appreciated the ways the symbols of liberty could coexist with brutal racial violence. In one of hundreds of lynchings during the Progressive era, a white mob in Springfield, Missouri, in 1906 falsely accused three black men of rape, hanged them from an electric light pole, and burned their bodies in a public orgy of violence. Atop the pole stood a replica of the Statue of Liberty.

W. E. B. Du Bois and the Revival of Black Protest

Black leaders struggled to find a strategy to rekindle the national commitment to equality that had flickered brightly, if briefly, during Reconstruction. No one thought more deeply, or over so long a period, about the black condition and the challenge it posed to American democracy than the scholar and activist W. E. B. Du Bois. Born in Great Barrington, Massachusetts, in 1868, and educated at Fisk and Harvard universities, Du Bois lived to his ninety-fifth year. The unifying theme of his career was Du Bois's effort to reconcile the contradiction between what he called "American freedom for whites and the continuing subjection of Negroes." His book *The Souls of Black Folk* (1903) issued a clarion call for blacks dissatisfied with the accommodationist policies of Booker T. Washington to press for equal rights. Du Bois believed that educated African-Americans like himself—the "talented tenth"

A cartoon from the *St. Louis Post-Dispatch*, April 17, 1906, commenting on the lynching of three black men in Springfield, Missouri. The shadow cast by the Statue of Liberty forms a gallows on the ground.

The "talented tenth"

W. E. B. Du Bois, founder of the NAACP and editor of its magazine, *The Crisis,* in his New York office.

Bailey v. Alabama

Rallying to the war

of the black community—must use their education and training to challenge inequality.

In some ways, Du Bois was a typical Progressive who believed that investigation, exposure, and education would lead to solutions for social problems. As a professor at Atlanta University, he projected a grandiose plan for decades of scholarly study of black life in order to make the country aware of racism and point the way toward its elimination. But he also understood the necessity of political action.

In 1905, Du Bois gathered a group of black leaders at Niagara Falls (meeting on the Canadian side since no American hotel would provide accommodations) and organized the Niagara movement, which sought to reinvigorate the abolitionist tradition. "We claim for ourselves," Du Bois wrote in the group's manifesto, "every single right that belongs to a freeborn American, political, civil, and social; and until we get these rights we will never cease to protest and assail the ears of America." The Declaration of Principles adopted at Niagara Falls called for restoring to blacks the right to vote, an end to racial segregation, and complete equality in economic and educational opportunity. These would remain the cornerstones of the black struggle for racial justice for decades to come. Four years later, Du Bois joined with a group of mostly white reformers, shocked by a lynching in Springfield, Illinois (Lincoln's adult home), to create the **National Association for the Advancement of Colored People**. The NAACP, as it was known, launched a long struggle for the enforcement of the Fourteenth and Fifteenth Amendments.

The NAACP's legal strategy won a few victories. In *Bailey v. Alabama* (1911), the Supreme Court overturned southern "peonage" laws that made it a crime for sharecroppers to break their labor contracts. Six years later, it ruled unconstitutional a Louisville zoning regulation excluding blacks from living in certain parts of the city (primarily because it interfered with whites' right to sell their property as they saw fit). Overall, however, the Progressive era witnessed virtually no progress toward racial justice.

Closing Ranks

Among black Americans, the wartime language of freedom inspired hopes for a radical change in the country's racial system. With the notable exception of William Monroe Trotter, most black leaders saw American participation in the war as an opportunity to make real the promise of freedom. To Trotter, much-publicized German atrocities were no worse than American lynchings; rather than making the world safe for democracy, the government should worry about "making the South safe for the Negroes." Yet the black press rallied to the war. Du Bois himself, in widely reprinted editorials, called on African-Americans to enlist in the army to help "make our own America a real land of the free."

Black participation in the Civil War had helped to secure the destruction of slavery and the achievement of citizenship. But during World War I, closing ranks did not bring significant gains. The navy barred blacks entirely, and the segregated army confined most of the 400,000 blacks who served in the war to supply units rather than combat. Wilson feared, as he noted in his diary, that the overseas experience would "go to their heads." And the U.S. Army campaigned strenuously to persuade the French not to treat black soldiers as equals—not to eat or socialize with them, or even shake their hands. Contact with African colonial soldiers fighting alongside the British and French did widen the horizons of black American soldiers. But while colonial troops marched in the victory parade in Paris, the Wilson administration did not allow black Americans to participate.

One of a series of paintings by the black artist Jacob Lawrence called *The Migration Series*, inspired by the massive movement of African-Americans to the North during and after World War I. For each, Lawrence composed a brief title, in this case, "In the North the Negro had better educational facilities."

The Great Migration and the "Promised Land"

Nonetheless, the war unleashed social changes that altered the contours of American race relations. The combination of increased wartime production and a drastic falloff in immigration from Europe once war broke out opened thousands of industrial jobs to black laborers for the first time, inspiring a large-scale migration from South to North. On the eve of World War I, 90 percent of the African-American population still lived in the South. Most northern cities had tiny black populations, and domestic and service work still predominated among both black men and black women in the North. But between 1910 and 1920, half a million blacks left the South. The black population of Chicago more than doubled, New York City's rose 66 percent, and smaller industrial cities like Akron, Buffalo, and Trenton showed similar gains.

Many motives sustained the **Great Migration**—higher wages in northern factories than were available in the South (even if blacks remained confined to menial and unskilled positions), opportunities for educating their children, escape from the threat of lynching, and the prospect of exercising the right to vote. Migrants spoke of a Second Emancipation, of "crossing over Jordan," and of leaving the realm of pharaoh for the Promised Land. One group from Mississippi stopped to sing, "I am bound for the land of Canaan," after their train crossed the Ohio River into the North.

The black migrants, mostly young men and women, carried with them "a new vision of opportunity, of social and economic freedom," as Alain Locke explained in the preface to his influential book *The New Negro* (1925). Yet the migrants encountered vast disappointments—severely restricted employment opportunities, exclusion from unions, rigid housing segregation, and outbreaks of violence that made it clear

CITY	BLACK POPULATION, 1910	BLACK POPULATION, 1920	PERCENT INCREASE
New York	91,709	152,467	66.3%
Philadelphia	84,459	134,229	58.9
Chicago	44,103	109,458	148.2
St. Louis	43,960	69,854	58.9
Detroit	5,741	40,838	611.3
Pittsburgh	25,623	37,725	47.2
Cleveland	8,448	34,451	307.8

TABLE 19.1 The Great Migration

that no region of the country was free from racial hostility. More white southerners than blacks moved north during the war, often with similar economic aspirations. But the new black presence, coupled with demands for change inspired by the war, created a racial tinderbox that needed only an incident to trigger an explosion.

Racial Violence, North and South

Violence in East St. Louis and Chicago

Dozens of blacks were killed during a 1917 riot in East St. Louis, Illinois, where employers had recruited black workers in an attempt to weaken unions (most of which excluded blacks from membership). In 1919, more than 250 persons died in riots in the urban North. Most notable was the violence in Chicago, touched off by the drowning by white bathers of a black teenager who accidentally crossed the unofficial dividing line between black and white beaches on Lake Michigan. The riot that followed raged for five days and involved pitched battles between the races throughout the city. By the time the National Guard restored order, 38 persons had been killed and more than 500 injured.

Violence was not confined to the North. In the year after the war ended, seventy-six persons were lynched in the South, including several returning black veterans wearing their uniforms. In Phillips County, Arkansas, attacks on striking black sharecroppers by armed white vigilantes left as many as 200 persons dead and required the intervention of the army to restore order. The worst race riot in American history occurred in Tulsa, Oklahoma, in 1921, when more than 300 blacks were killed and over 10,000 left homeless after a white mob, including police and National Guardsmen, burned an all-black section of the city to the ground. The **Tulsa riot** erupted after a group of black veterans tried to prevent the lynching of a youth who had accidentally tripped and fallen on a white female elevator operator, causing rumors of rape to sweep the city.

Tulsa riot

The Rise of Garveyism

World War I kindled a new spirit of militancy. The East St. Louis riot of 1917 inspired a widely publicized Silent Protest Parade on New York's Fifth Avenue in which

Buildings in Tulsa, Oklahoma, burn during the city's riot of June 1921. An estimated 300 people died when white mobs destroyed the city's black neighborhood in the worst outbreak of racial violence in American history.

10,000 blacks silently carried placards reading, "Mr. President, Why Not Make America Safe for Democracy?" In the new densely populated black ghettos of the North, widespread support emerged for the Universal Negro Improvement Association, a movement for African independence and black self-reliance launched by **Marcus Garvey**, a recent immigrant from Jamaica. Freedom for Garveyites meant national self-determination. Blacks, they insisted, should enjoy the same internationally recognized identity enjoyed by other peoples in the aftermath of the war. "Everywhere we hear the cry of freedom," Garvey proclaimed in 1921. "We desire a freedom that will lift us to the common standard of all men, . . . freedom that will give us a chance and opportunity to rise to the fullest of our ambition and that we cannot get in countries where other men rule and dominate." Du Bois and other established black leaders viewed Garvey as little more than a demagogue. They applauded when the government deported him after a conviction for mail fraud. But the massive following his movement achieved testified to the sense of betrayal that had been kindled in black communities during and after the war.

Marcus Garvey, leader of the largest black movement of the World War I era.

1919

A Worldwide Upsurge

The combination of militant hopes for social change and disappointment with the war's outcome was evident far beyond the black community. In the Union of Soviet Socialist Republics (or Soviet Union), as Russia had been renamed after the revolution, Lenin's government had nationalized landholdings, banks, and factories and proclaimed the socialist dream of a workers' government. The Russian Revolution and the democratic aspirations unleashed by World War I sent tremors of hope and fear throughout the world. Like 1848 and, in the future, 1968, 1919 was a year of worldwide social and political upheaval. Inspired by Lenin's call for revolution, communist-led governments came to power in Bavaria (a part of Germany) and Hungary. General strikes demanding the fulfillment of wartime promises of "industrial democracy" took place in Belfast, Glasgow, and Winnipeg. In Spain, anarchist peasants began seizing land. Crowds in India challenged British rule, and nationalist movements in other colonies demanded independence. "We are living and shall live all our lives in a revolutionary world," wrote Walter Lippmann.

Global uprisings

The worldwide revolutionary upsurge produced a countervailing mobilization by opponents of radical change. Even as they fought the Germans, the Allies viewed the Soviet government as a dire threat and attempted to overturn it. In the summer of 1918, Allied expeditionary forces—British, French, Japanese, and Americans—landed in Russia to aid Lenin's opponents in the civil war that had engulfed the country. The last of them did not leave until 1920.

Wilson's policies toward the Soviet Union revealed the contradictions within the liberal internationalist vision. On the one hand, in keeping with the principles of the Fourteen Points and its goal of a worldwide economic open door, Wilson hoped to foster trade with the new government. On the other, fear of communism as a source of international instability and a threat to private property inspired military intervention in Russia. The Allies did not invite the Soviet Union to the

The Soviet Union

Versailles peace conference, and Wilson refused to extend diplomatic recognition to Lenin's government. The Soviet regime survived, but in the rest of the world the tide of change receded. By the fall, the mass strikes had been suppressed and conservative governments had been installed in central Europe. Anticommunism would remain a pillar of twentieth-century American foreign policy.

Upheaval in America

In the United States, 1919 also brought unprecedented turmoil. It seemed all the more disorienting for occurring in the midst of a worldwide flu epidemic that killed over 20 million persons, including nearly 700,000 Americans. Racial violence, as noted above, was widespread. In June, bombs exploded at the homes of prominent Americans, including the attorney general, A. Mitchell Palmer, who escaped uninjured. Among aggrieved American workers, wartime language linking patriotism with democracy and freedom inspired hopes that an era of social justice and economic empowerment was at hand. In 1917, Wilson had told the AFL, "While we are fighting for freedom, we must see to it among other things that labor is free." Labor took him seriously—more seriously, it seems, than Wilson intended. The government, as one machinist put it, had "proclaimed to the World that the freedom and democracy we are fighting for shall be practiced in the industries of America."

By the war's end, many Americans believed that the country stood on the verge of what Herbert Hoover called "a new industrial order." Sidney Hillman, leader of the garment workers' union, was one of those caught up in the utopian dreams inspired by the war and reinforced by the Russian Revolution. "One can hear the footsteps of the Deliverer," he wrote. "Labor will rule and the World will be free." In 1919, more than 4 million workers engaged in strikes—the greatest wave of labor unrest in American history. There were walkouts, among many others, by textile workers, telephone operators, and Broadway actors. Throughout the country, workers appropriated the imagery and rhetoric of the war, parading in army uniforms with Liberty buttons, denouncing their employers as "kaisers," and demanding "freedom in the workplace." They were met by an unprecedented mobilization of employers, government, and private patriotic organizations.

The strike wave began in January 1919 in Seattle, where a walkout of shipyard workers mushroomed into a general strike that for once united AFL unions and the IWW. For five days, a committee of labor leaders oversaw city services, until federal troops arrived to end the strike. In September, Boston policemen struck for higher wages and shorter working hours. Declaring "there is no right to strike against the public safety," Massachusetts governor Calvin Coolidge called out the National Guard to patrol the city and fired the entire police force. In the nation's coalfields, a company manager observed, wartime propaganda had raised unrealistic expectations among workers, who took the promise of "an actual emancipation" too "literally." When the war ended, miners demanded an end to company absolutism. Their strike was ended by a court injunction obtained by Attorney General Palmer.

The Great Steel Strike

The wartime rhetoric of economic democracy and freedom helped to inspire the era's greatest labor uprising, the 1919 steel strike. Centered in Chicago, it united some 365,000 mostly immigrant workers in demands for union recognition, higher wages, and an eight-hour workday. Before 1917, the steel mills were little autocracies where managers arbitrarily established wages and working conditions and suppressed all efforts at union organizing. During the war, workers flooded into the Amalgamated Association, the union that had been nearly destroyed by its defeat at Homestead a generation earlier. By the end of 1918, they had won an eight-hour day. Employers' anti-union activities resumed following the armistice that ended the fighting. "For why this war?" asked one Polish immigrant steelworker at a union meeting. "For why we buy Liberty bonds? For the mills? No, for freedom and America—for everybody. No more [work like a] horse and wagon. For eight-hour day."

In response to the strike, steel magnates launched a concerted counterattack. Employers appealed to anti-immigrant sentiment among native-born workers, many of whom returned to work, and conducted a propaganda campaign that associated the strikers with the IWW, communism, and disloyalty. "Americanism vs. Alienism" was the issue of the strike, declared the *New York Tribune*. With middle-class opinion having turned against the labor movement and the police in Pittsburgh assaulting workers on the streets, the strike collapsed in early 1920.

The Red Scare

Many Progressives hoped to see the wartime apparatus of economic planning continue after 1918. The Wilson administration, however, quickly dismantled the agencies that had established controls over industrial production and the labor market, although during the 1930s they would serve as models for some policies of Franklin D. Roosevelt's New Deal. Wartime repression of dissent, however, continued. It reached its peak with the **Red Scare of 1919–1920**, a short-lived but intense period of political intolerance inspired by the postwar strike wave and the social tensions and fears generated by the Russian Revolution.

Convinced that episodes like the steel strike were part of a worldwide communist conspiracy, Attorney General A. Mitchell Palmer in November 1919 and January 1920 dispatched federal agents to raid the offices of radical and labor organizations throughout the country. They carried search warrants so broad that they reminded those with a sense of history of the writs of assistance against which James Otis had eloquently protested as being destructive of liberty in 1761. The Palmer Raids were overseen by the twenty-four-year-old director of the Radical Division of the Justice Department, J. Edgar Hoover. More than 5,000 persons were arrested, most of them without warrants, and held for months without charge. The government deported hundreds of immigrant radicals, including Emma Goldman. Hoover also began compiling files on thousands of Americans suspected of holding radical political ideas, a practice he would later continue as head of the Federal Bureau of Investigation.

The abuse of civil liberties in early 1920 was so severe that Palmer came under heavy criticism from Congress and much of the press. Secretary of Labor Louis Post began releasing imprisoned immigrants, and the Red Scare collapsed. Even the explosion of a bomb outside the New York Stock Exchange in September 1920, which killed forty persons, failed to rekindle it. (The perpetrators of this terrorist

An advertisement placed by a steel company in a Pittsburgh newspaper announces, in several languages, that the steel strike of 1919 "has failed." The use of the figure of Uncle Sam illustrates how the companies clothed their anti-union stance in the language of patriotism.

Local police with literature seized from a Communist Party office in Cambridge, Massachusetts, November 1919.

Part of the crowd that greeted President Woodrow Wilson in November 1918 when he traveled to Paris to take part in the peace conference. An electric sign proclaims "Long Live Wilson."

Versailles peace conference

explosion, the worst on American soil until the Oklahoma City bombing of 1995, were never identified.) The reaction to the Palmer Raids planted the seeds for a new appreciation of the importance of civil liberties that would begin to flourish during the 1920s. But in their immediate impact, the events of 1919 and 1920 dealt a devastating setback to radical and labor organizations of all kinds and kindled an intense identification of patriotic Americanism with support for the political and economic status quo. The IWW had been effectively destroyed, and many moderate unions lay in disarray. The Socialist Party crumbled under the weight of governmental repression (the New York legislature expelled five Socialist members, and Congress denied Victor Berger the seat to which he had been elected from Wisconsin) and internal differences over the Russian Revolution.

Wilson at Versailles

The beating back of demands for fundamental social change was a severe rebuke to the hopes with which so many Progressives had enlisted in the war effort. Wilson's inability to achieve a just peace based on the Fourteen Points compounded the sense of failure. Late in 1918, the president traveled to France to attend the Versailles peace conference. Greeted by ecstatic Paris crowds, he declared that American soldiers had come to Europe "as crusaders, not merely to win a war, but to win a cause . . . to lead the world on the way of liberty." But he proved a less adept negotiator than his British and French counterparts, David Lloyd George and Georges Clemenceau.

Although the Fourteen Points had called for "open covenants openly arrived at," the negotiations were conducted in secret. The resulting **Versailles Treaty** did accomplish some of Wilson's goals. It established the **League of Nations**, the body central to his vision of a new international order. It applied the principle of self-determination to eastern Europe and redrew the map of that region. From the ruins of the Austro-Hungarian empire and parts of Germany and czarist Russia, new European nations emerged from the war—Finland, Poland, Czechoslovakia, Austria, Hungary, Latvia, Lithuania, Estonia, and Yugoslavia. Some enjoyed ethno-linguistic unity, while others comprised unstable combinations of diverse nationalities.

Despite Wilson's pledge of a peace without territorial acquisitions or vengeance, the Versailles Treaty was a harsh document that all but guaranteed future conflict in Europe. Clemenceau won for France the right to occupy the Saar Basin and Rhineland—iron- and coal-rich parts of Germany. The treaty placed strict limits on the size of Germany's future army and navy. Lloyd George persuaded Wilson to agree to a clause declaring Germany morally responsible for the war and setting astronomical reparations payments (they were variously estimated at between $33 billion and $56 billion), which crippled the German economy.

German reparations

The Wilsonian Moment

To many people around the world, the Great War destroyed European claims that theirs was a higher civilization, which gave them the right to rule over more barbaric peoples. In this sense, it helped to heighten the international prestige of the United States, a latecomer to the war. Like the ideals of the American Revolution, the Wilsonian rhetoric of self-determination reverberated across the globe, especially among colonial peoples seeking independence. In fact, they took Wilson's rhetoric more seriously than he did. Despite his belief in self-determination, he believed that colonial peoples required a long period of tutelage before they were ready for independence.

Spread of Wilsonian ideals

Nonetheless, Wilsonian ideals quickly spread around the globe—not simply the idea that government must rest on the consent of the governed, but also Wilson's stress on the "equality of nations," large and small, and that international disputes should be settled by peaceful means rather than armed conflict. These stood in sharp contrast to the imperial ideas and practices of Europe. In Eastern Europe, whose people sought to carve new, independent nations from the ruins of the Austro-Hungarian and Ottoman empires, many considered Wilson a "popular saint." The leading Arabic newspaper, *Al-Ahram*, published in Egypt, then under British rule, gave extensive coverage to Wilson's speech asking Congress to declare war in the name of democracy, and to the Fourteen Points, and translated the Declaration of Independence into Arabic for its readers. In Beijing, students demanding that China free itself of foreign domination gathered at the American embassy shouting, "Long live Wilson." Japan proposed to include in the charter of the new League of Nations a clause recognizing the equality of all people, regardless of race. Hundreds of letters, petitions, and declarations addressed to President Wilson made their way to the Paris headquarters of the American delegation to the peace conference. Few reached the president, as his private secretary, Gilbert Close, carefully screened his mail.

Self-determination

Outside of Europe, however, the idea of "self-determination" was stillborn. When the peace conference opened, Secretary of State Robert Lansing warned that the phrase was "loaded with dynamite" and would "raise hopes which can never be realized." Wilson's language, he feared, had put "dangerous" ideas "into the minds of certain races" and would inspire "impossible demands, and cause trouble in many lands." As Lansing anticipated, advocates of colonial independence descended on Paris to lobby the peace negotiators. Arabs demanded that a unified independent state be carved from the old Ottoman empire in the Middle East. Nguyen That Thanh, a young Vietnamese patriot working in Paris, pressed his people's claim for greater rights within the French empire. Citing the Declaration of Independence, he appealed unsuccessfully to Wilson to help bring an end to French rule in Vietnam. W. E. B. Du Bois organized a Pan-African Congress in Paris that put forward the idea of a self-governing nation to be carved out of

EUROPE IN 1914

Allies
Central Powers
Neutral nations

World War I and the Versailles Treaty redrew the map of Europe and the Middle East. The Austro-Hungarian and Ottoman empires ceased to exist, and Germany and Russia were reduced in size. A group of new states emerged in eastern Europe, embodying the principle of self-determination, one of Woodrow Wilson's Fourteen Points.

British and French empires

Germany's African colonies. Koreans, Indians, Irish, and others also pressed claims for self-determination.

The British and French, however, had no intention of applying this principle to their own empires. They rebuffed the pleas of colonial peoples for self-rule. During the war, the British had encouraged Arab nationalism as a weapon against the Ottoman empire and had also pledged to create a homeland in Palestine for the persecuted Jews of Europe. In fact, the victors of World War I divided Ottoman territory into a series of new territories, including Syria, Lebanon, Iraq, and Palestine, controlled by the victorious Allies under League of Nations "mandates." South Africa, Australia, and Japan acquired former German colonies in Africa and Asia. Nor did Ireland achieve its independence at Versailles. Only at the end of 1921 did Britain finally agree to the creation of the Irish Free State, while continuing to rule the northeastern corner of the island. As for the Japanese proposal to establish

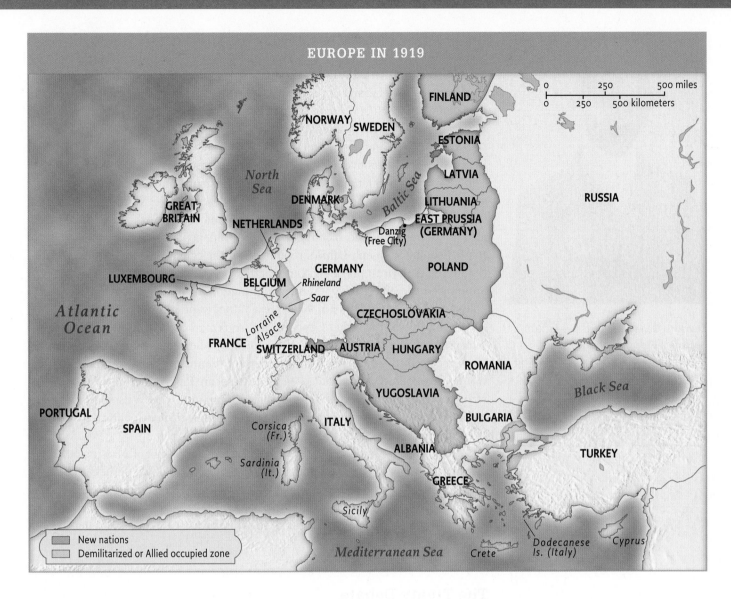

EUROPE IN 1919

North Sea

Atlantic Ocean

Baltic Sea

FINLAND

NORWAY SWEDEN

ESTONIA

LATVIA

LITHUANIA

DENMARK

EAST PRUSSIA (GERMANY)

Danzig (Free City)

RUSSIA

GREAT BRITAIN

NETHERLANDS

GERMANY

POLAND

LUXEMBOURG

BELGIUM

Rhineland

Saar

Lorraine

Alsace

FRANCE

SWITZERLAND

CZECHOSLOVAKIA

AUSTRIA HUNGARY

ROMANIA

YUGOSLAVIA

Black Sea

PORTUGAL

SPAIN

Corsica (Fr.)

ITALY

Sardinia (It.)

BULGARIA

ALBANIA

TURKEY

GREECE

Sicily

Dodecanese Is. (Italy)

Cyprus

Mediterranean Sea *Crete*

■ New nations
■ Demilitarized or Allied occupied zone

0 250 500 miles
0 250 500 kilometers

the principle of racial equality, Wilson, with the support of Great Britain and Australia, engineered its defeat.

The Seeds of Wars to Come

Du Bois, as noted above, hoped that black participation in the war effort would promote racial justice at home and self-government for colonies abroad. "We return," he wrote in *The Crisis* in May 1919, "we return from fighting, we return fighting. Make way for Democracy!" But the war's aftermath both in the United States and overseas left him bitterly disappointed. Du Bois concluded that Wilson had "never at any single moment meant to include in his democracy" black Americans or the colonial peoples of the world. "Most men today," he complained, "cannot conceive of a freedom that does not involve somebody's slavery." In 1903, in *The Souls of Black Folk*, Du Bois had made the memorable prediction that "the problem of the twentieth century is the problem of the color-line." He now forecast a "fight for freedom"

The disappointing aftermath of the war

Mahatma Gandhi, pictured here in 1919, became the leader of the nonviolent movement for independence for India. He was among those disappointed by the failure of the Versailles peace conference to apply the principle of self-determination to the colonial world.

that would pit "black and brown and yellow men" throughout the world against racism and imperialism.

Disappointment at the failure to apply the Fourteen Points to the non-European world created a pervasive cynicism about Western use of the language of freedom and democracy. Wilson's apparent willingness to accede to the demands of the imperial powers helped to spark a series of popular protest movements across the Middle East and Asia, and the rise of a new anti-Western nationalism. It inspired the May 4 movement in China, a mass protest against the decision at the Versailles peace conference to award certain German concessions (parts of China governed by foreign powers) to Japan. Some leaders, like Nguyen That Thanh, who took the name Ho Chi Minh, turned to communism, in whose name he would lead Vietnam's long and bloody struggle for independence. With the collapse of the Wilsonian moment, Lenin's reputation in the colonial world began to eclipse that of the American president. But whether communist or not, these movements announced the emergence of anticolonial nationalism as a major force in world affairs, which it would remain for the rest of the twentieth century.

"Your liberalness," one Egyptian leader remarked, speaking of Britain and America, "is only for yourselves." Yet ironically, when colonial peoples demanded to be recognized as independent members of the international community, they would invoke both the heritage of the American Revolution—the first colonial struggle that produced an independent nation—and the Wilsonian language whereby the self-governing nation-state is the most legitimate political institution, and all nations deserve equal respect.

As Du Bois recognized, World War I sowed the seeds not of a lasting peace but of wars to come. German resentment over the peace terms would help to fuel the rise of Adolf Hitler and the coming of World War II. In the breakup of Czechoslovakia and Yugoslavia, violence over the status of Northern Ireland, and seemingly unending conflicts in the Middle East, the world was still haunted by the ghost of Versailles.

The Treaty Debate

Fear of international involvement

One final disappointment awaited Wilson on his return from Europe. He viewed the new League of Nations as the war's finest legacy. But many Americans feared that membership in the League would commit the United States to an open-ended involvement in the affairs of other countries. Wilson asserted that the United States could not save the world without being continually involved with it. His opponents, led by Senator Henry Cabot Lodge of Massachusetts, argued that the League threatened to deprive the country of its freedom of action.

A considerable majority of senators would have accepted the treaty with "reservations" ensuring that the obligation to assist League members against attack did not supersede the power of Congress to declare war. As governor of New Jersey and as president, Wilson had proved himself to be a skilled politician capable of compromising with opponents. In this case, however, convinced that the treaty reflected "the hand of God," Wilson refused to negotiate with congressional leaders.

In October 1919, in the midst of the League debate, Wilson suffered a serious stroke. Although the extent of his illness was kept secret, he remained incapacitated for the rest of his presidency. In effect, his wife, Edith, headed the government for the next seventeen months. In November 1919 and again in March 1920, the Senate rejected the Versailles Treaty.

American involvement in World War I lasted barely nineteen months, but it cast a long shadow over the following decade—and, indeed, the rest of the century. In its immediate aftermath, the country retreated from international involvements. But in the long run, Wilson's combination of idealism and power politics had an enduring impact. His appeals to democracy, open markets, and a special American mission to instruct the world in freedom, coupled with a willingness to intervene abroad militarily to promote American interests and values, would create the model for twentieth-century American international relations.

On its own terms, the war to make the world safe for democracy failed. Even great powers cannot always bend the world to their purposes. The war brought neither stability nor democracy to most of the world, and it undermined freedom in the United States. It also led to the eclipse of Progressivism. Republican candidate Warren G. Harding, who had no connection with the party's Progressive wing, swept to victory in the presidential election of 1920. Harding's campaign centered on a "return to normalcy" and a repudiation of what he called "Wilsonism." He received 60 percent of the popular vote. Begun with idealistic goals and grand hopes for social change, American involvement in the Great War laid the foundation for one of the most conservative decades in the nation's history.

Interrupting the Ceremony, a 1918 cartoon from the *Chicago Tribune*, depicts Senate opponents of the Versailles Treaty arriving just in time to prevent the United States from becoming permanently ensnared in "foreign entanglements" through the League of Nations.

SUGGESTED READING

BOOKS

- Bederman, Gail. *Manliness and Civilization: A Cultural History of Race and Gender in the United States, 1880–1917* (1995). Explores how ideas concerning civilization and gender affected American foreign policy.

- Capozzola, Christopher. *Uncle Sam Wants You: World War I and the Making of the Modern American Citizen* (2008). A careful study of public and private efforts to enforce patriotic ideas and actions during World War I.

- Dawley, Alan. *Changing the World: American Progressives in War and Revolution* (2003). Presents the war as a fulfillment and betrayal of the Progressive impulse.

- Gilmore, Glenda E. *Gender and Jim Crow: Women and the Politics of White Supremacy in North Carolina, 1896–1920* (1996). A careful study of how black and white women negotiated the boundaries of segregation in a southern state.

- Green, Elna C. *Southern Strategies: Southern Women and the Woman Suffrage Question* (1997). Describes how southern women campaigned for the vote without challenging the subordinate status of African-Americans.

- Greene, Julie. *The Canal Builders: Making American Empire at the Panama Canal* (2009). Tells the story of the construction of the Panama Canal and the tens of thousands of workers who did the work.

Grossman, James R. *Land of Hope: Chicago, Black Southerners, and the Great Migration* (1989). An in-depth study of the migration of blacks to one American city.

Healy, David. *Drive to Hegemony: The United States in the Caribbean, 1898–1917* (1988). Examines American foreign policy in the Caribbean from McKinley to Wilson.

Jensen, Kimberly. *Mobilizing Minerva: American Women in the First World War* (2008). Examines the participation of women in the war effort and its impact on gender relations.

Kennedy, David M. *Over Here: The First World War and American Society* (1980). A comprehensive account of how the war affected domestic life in the United States.

Manela, Erez. *The Wilsonian Moment* (2007). Details how the Wilsonian ideal of self-determination was received around the world, with results Wilson did not anticipate.

Meier, August. *Negro Thought in America, 1880–1915* (1966). A pioneering study of the ideas of black leaders, including W. E. B. Du Bois.

Mitchell, David J. *1919: Red Mirage* (1970). A global account of the upheavals of 1919.

Preston, William, Jr. *Aliens and Dissenters: Federal Suppression of Radicals, 1903–1933* (1963). An influential study of the federal government's efforts to suppress dissenting ideas, especially during and immediately after World War I.

Renda, Mary A. *Taking Haiti: Military Occupation and the Culture of U.S. Imperialism, 1915–1940* (2001). Examines the causes and consequences of the American occupation of Haiti.

Stein, Judith. *The World of Marcus Garvey: Race and Class in Modern Society* (1986). Places the Garvey movement in an Atlantic perspective linking Africa, the United States, and the West Indies.

Sullivan, Patricia. *Lift Every Voice: The NAACP and the Making of the Civil Rights Movement* (2009). A sweeping history of the country's preeminent civil rights organization, from its founding to the 1950s.

Tuttle, William. *Race Riot: Chicago in the Red Summer of 1919* (1970). A vivid account of the most violent racial upheaval of the era.

WEBSITES

Red Scare: http://newman.baruch.cuny.edu/digital/redscare/

The Bisbee Deportation of 1917: www.library.arizona.edu/exhibits/bisbee/

The U.S.A. and Latin America: www.casahistoria.net/uslatam.htm

CHAPTER REVIEW AND ONLINE RESOURCES

REVIEW QUESTIONS

1. Explain the role of the United States in the global economy by 1920.

2. What were the assumptions underlying the Roosevelt Corollary? How did the doctrine affect U.S. relations with European nations and those in the Western hemisphere?

3. What did President Wilson mean by "moral imperialism," and what measures were taken to apply this to Latin America?

4. How did the ratification of both the Eighteenth and Nineteenth Amendments suggest both the restrictive and democratizing nature of Progressivism?

5. Why did Progressives see in the expansion of governmental powers in wartime an opportunity to reform American society?

6. What were the goals and methods of the Committee on Public Information during World War I?

7. What are governmental and private examples of coercive patriotism during the war? What were the effects of those efforts?

8. What were the major causes—both real and imaginary—of the Red Scare?

9. How did World War I and its aftermath provide African-Americans with opportunities?

10. Identify the goals of those pressing for global change in 1919, and of those who opposed them.

KEY TERMS

liberal internationalism (p. 720)

Panama Canal Zone (p. 721)

Roosevelt Corollary (p. 722)

Dollar Diplomacy (p. 723)

moral imperialism (p. 724)

Lusitania (p. 726)

Zimmermann Telegram (p. 728)

Fourteen Points (p. 728)

Selective Service Act (p. 731)

War Industries Board (p. 731)

Eighteenth Amendment (p. 735)

Espionage Act (p. 736)

Sedition Act (p. 736)

National Association for the Advancement of Colored People (p. 746)

Great Migration (p. 747)

Tulsa riot (p. 748)

Marcus Garvey (p. 749)

Red Scare of 1919–1920 (p. 751)

Versailles Treaty (p. 752)

League of Nations (p. 752)

Go to 🐇 INQUIZITIVE

To see what you know—and learn what you've missed—with personalized feedback along the way.

Visit the *Give Me Liberty!* Student Site for primary source documents and images, interactive maps, author videos featuring Eric Foner, and more.

PART 5

DEPRESSION AND WARS, 1920-1953

For the United States and the world at large, the decades between the end of World War I and the middle of the twentieth century marked one of the most painful eras in modern history. These years witnessed the Great Depression (1929–1939), World War II (1939–1945), and the advent of a Cold War that pitted the United States and the Soviet Union, former wartime allies, against each other in a global contest for power. These epochal events produced the deaths of tens of millions of people and wreaked economic havoc on hundreds of millions of others. By the end of this period, the United States and the world lived with the anxiety caused by the constant threat of nuclear war.

After World War I, the United States withdrew from active involvement in international affairs and enjoyed a decade of economic prosperity. During the 1920s, conservatism dominated the political arena. The labor movement suffered setback after setback, the government turned its back on many of the reforms of the Progressive era, and organized feminism faded from the public sphere. A nineteenth-century understanding of freedom based on liberty of contract in an unregulated marketplace gained a new lease on life during the administrations of Warren G. Harding and Calvin Coolidge.

If political dissent faded during the 1920s, cultural differences seemed stronger than ever. In the name of personal freedom, many Americans embraced a new culture, centered in the nation's cities, based on consumption and enjoyment of new mass forms of leisure and entertainment, including radio and motion pictures. Other Americans, living in rural areas of the South and West where traditional religion still held sway, saw the new urban culture as a threat to long-established moral values. During the 1920s, debates over immigration, Prohibition, the teaching of Darwin's theory of evolution in public schools, and the behavior of young, sexually liberated women in the nation's cities reflected the tension between older and newer cultures, each with its own definition of freedom.

The heady days of the 1920s came to an abrupt end with the stock market crash of 1929, which ushered in the Great Depression, the greatest economic crisis in American history. President Franklin D. Roosevelt presided over a profound political and social transformation in government, society, and the understandings of freedom. During his presidency, the federal government undertook unprecedented initiatives in an attempt to stimulate economic recovery and expand Americans' economic liberties. The government determined what farmers could plant, required employers to deal with unions, insured bank deposits, regulated the stock market, loaned money to home owners, and provided payments to a majority of the elderly and unemployed. It transformed the physical environment through hydroelectric dams, reforestation projects, and rural electrification. The New Deal helped to inspire, and was powerfully influenced by, a popular upsurge that redefined the idea of freedom to include a public guarantee of economic security for ordinary citizens.

AMERICANS
will **always** fight for liberty

Even as the United States struggled with the economic crisis, events abroad drew the country into the largest war in human history. The rise of powerful dictatorships bent on military expansion—Germany in Europe and Japan in Asia—led inexorably to World War II. Most Americans hoped to remain aloof from the crisis. When the Japanese attacked the American naval base at Pearl Harbor, Hawaii, on December 7, 1941, the United States entered the war. World War II expanded even further the size and power of the national government. War production finally ended the Depression and drew millions of Americans from rural areas into the army or to industrial centers in the North and West. The Four Freedoms—Roosevelt's statement of Allied war aims—became the wartime rallying cry. Unlike during World War I, the federal government promoted group equality as central to American freedom—although the internment of more than 100,000 Japanese-Americans revealed the limits of racial tolerance. The war also placed on the national agenda, for the first time since Reconstruction, the contradiction between the nation's rhetoric of freedom and the condition of its black population. It inspired an upsurge of black militancy, expressed in the slogan "double-V"—victory over enemies overseas, and over racial inequality at home.

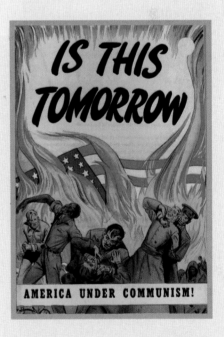

IS THIS TOMORROW

AMERICA UNDER COMMUNISM!

No retreat into isolationism followed World War II. However, the wartime alliance among the United States, Britain, and the Soviet Union soon shattered, replaced by the worldwide contest known as the Cold War. By the 1950s, through a series of global anticommunist alliances, the United States had taken on a permanent military presence throughout the world. As in previous wars, freedom both helped to mobilize public support for the Cold War and was subtly changed in the process. The defense of freedom—increasingly equated with "free enterprise"—became the rationale for the doctrine of "containment," or global opposition to the spread of communism. The Cold War also inspired an anticommunist crusade within the United States. In the late 1940s and early 1950s, thousands of Americans accused of holding "subversive" beliefs lost their jobs, and an atmosphere of political conformity dominated public life. The battle to defend the "free world" abroad produced severe infringements on freedom at home.

In popular memory, the decade that followed World War I is recalled as the Jazz Age or the Roaring Twenties. With its flappers (young, sexually liberated women), speakeasies (nightclubs that sold liquor in violation of Prohibition), and a soaring stock market fueled by easy credit and a get-rich-quick outlook, it was a time of revolt against moral rules inherited from the nineteenth century. Observers from Europe, where class divisions were starkly visible in work, politics, and social relations, marveled at the uniformity of American life. Factories poured out standardized consumer goods, their sale promoted by national advertising campaigns. Conservatism dominated a political system from which radical alternatives seemed to have been purged. Radio and the movies spread mass culture throughout the nation. Americans seemed to dress alike, think alike, go to the same movies, and admire the same larger-than-life national celebrities.

Many Americans, however, did not welcome the new secular, commercial culture. They resented and feared the ethnic and racial diversity of America's cities and what they considered the lax moral standards of urban life. The 1920s was a decade of profound social tensions—between rural and urban Americans, traditional and "modern" Christianity, participants in the burgeoning consumer culture and those who did not fully share in the new prosperity.

THE BUSINESS OF AMERICA

A Decade of Prosperity

"The chief business of the American people," said Calvin Coolidge, who became president after Warren G. Harding's sudden death from a heart attack in 1923, "is business." Rarely in American history had economic growth seemed more dramatic, cooperation between business and government so close, and business values so widely shared. After a sharp postwar recession that lasted into 1922, the 1920s was a decade of prosperity. Productivity and economic output rose dramatically as new industries—chemicals, aviation, electronics—flourished and older ones like food processing and the manufacture of household appliances adopted Henry Ford's moving assembly line.

The automobile was the backbone of economic growth. The most celebrated American factories now turned out cars, not textiles and steel as in the nineteenth century. Annual automobile production tripled during the 1920s, from 1.5 to 4.8 million. General Motors, which learned the secret of marketing numerous individual models and stylish designs, surpassed Ford with its cheap, standardized Model T (replaced in 1927 by the Model A). By 1929, half of all American families owned a car (a figure not reached in England until 1980). The automobile industry stimulated the expansion of steel, rubber, and oil production, road construction, and other sectors of the economy. It promoted tourism and the growth of suburbs (already, some commuters were driving to work) and helped to reduce rural isolation.

During the 1920s, American multinational corporations extended their sway throughout the world. With Europe still recovering from the Great War, American investment overseas far exceeded that of other countries. The dollar replaced the

A 1927 photograph shows Nicola Sacco and Bartolomeo Vanzetti outside the courthouse in Dedham, Massachusetts, surrounded by security agents and onlookers. They are about to enter the courthouse, where the judge will pronounce their death sentences.

British pound as the most important currency of international trade. American companies produced 85 percent of the world's cars and 40 percent of its manufactured goods. General Electric and International Telephone and Telegraph bought up companies in other countries. International Business Machines (IBM) was the world's leader in office supplies. American oil companies built new refineries overseas. American companies took control of raw materials abroad, from rubber in Liberia to oil in Venezuela.

Growth of American corporations

One unsuccessful example of the global spread of American corporations was Fordlandia, an effort by the auto manufacturer Henry Ford to create a town in the heart of Brazil's Amazon rain forest. Ford hoped to secure a steady supply of rubber for car tires. But as in the United States, where he had compelled immigrant workers to adopt American dress and diet, he wanted to bring local inhabitants up to what he considered the proper standard of life (this meant, for example, forbidding his workers from using alcohol and tobacco and trying to get them to stop eating traditional Brazilian foods). Eventually, the climate and local insects destroyed the rubber trees that Ford's engineers, lacking experience in tropical agriculture, had planted much too close together, while the workers rebelled against the long hours of labor and regimentation of the community.

Ford's River Rouge auto plant at Dearborn, Michigan, was the world's largest factory complex in the 1920s. It included not only assembly areas but its own steel mill.

A New Society

During the 1920s, consumer goods of all kinds proliferated, marketed by salesmen and advertisers who promoted them as ways of satisfying Americans' psychological desires and everyday needs. Frequently purchased on credit through new installment buying plans, they rapidly altered daily life. Telephones made

FIGURE 20.1 Household
Appliances, 1900–1930

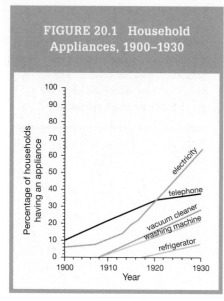

Celebrity culture

Standard of living

Economic imbalance

communication easier. Vacuum cleaners, washing machines, and refrigerators transformed work in the home and reduced the demand for domestic servants. Boosted by Prohibition and an aggressive advertising campaign that, according to the company's sales director, made it "impossible for the consumer to *escape*" the product, Coca-Cola became a symbol of American life.

Americans spent more and more of their income on leisure activities like vacations, movies, and sporting events. By 1929, weekly movie attendance had reached 80 million, double the figure of 1922. Hollywood films now dominated the world movie market. Movies had been produced early in the century in several American cities, but shortly before World War I filmmakers gravitated to Hollywood, a district of Los Angeles, attracted by the open space, year-round sunshine for outdoor filming, and varied scenery. In 1910, two French companies, Pathé and Gaumont, had been the world's leading film producers. By 1925, American releases outnumbered French by eight to one. In the 1920s, both companies abandoned film production for the more profitable business of distributing American films in Europe.

Radios and phonographs brought mass entertainment into Americans' living rooms. The number of radios in Americans' homes rose from 190,000 in 1923 to just under 5 million in 1929. These developments helped to create and spread a new celebrity culture, in which recording, film, and sports stars moved to the top of the list of American heroes. During the 1920s, more than 100 million records were sold each year. RCA Victor sold so many recordings of the great opera tenor Enrico Caruso that he is sometimes called the first modern celebrity. He was soon joined by the film actor Charlie Chaplin, baseball player Babe Ruth, and boxer Jack Dempsey. Ordinary Americans followed every detail of their lives. Perhaps the decade's greatest celebrity, in terms of intensive press coverage, was the aviator Charles Lindbergh, who in 1927 made the first solo nonstop flight across the Atlantic.

André Siegfried, a Frenchman who visited the United States four times, commented in 1928 that a "new society" had come into being, in which Americans considered their "standard of living" a "sacred acquisition, which they will defend at any price." In this new "mass civilization," widespread acceptance of going into debt to purchase consumer goods had replaced the values of thrift and self-denial, central to nineteenth-century notions of upstanding character. Work, once seen as a source of pride in craft skill, now came to be valued as a path to individual fulfillment through consumption and entertainment.

The Limits of Prosperity

"Big business in America," remarked the journalist Lincoln Steffens, "is producing what the socialists held up as their goal—food, shelter, and clothing for all." But signs of future trouble could be seen beneath the prosperity of the 1920s. The fruits of increased production were very unequally distributed. Real wages for industrial workers (wages adjusted to take account of inflation) rose by one-quarter between 1922 and 1929, but corporate profits rose at more than twice that rate. The process of economic concentration continued unabated. A handful of firms dominated numerous sectors of the economy. In 1929, 1 percent of the nation's banks controlled half of its financial resources. Most of the small auto companies that had existed earlier in the century had fallen by the wayside. General Motors, Ford, and Chrysler now controlled four-fifths of the industry.

At the beginning of 1929, the share of national income of the wealthiest 5 percent of American families exceeded that of the bottom 60 percent. A majority of families had no savings, and an estimated 40 percent of the population remained in poverty, unable to participate in the flourishing consumer economy. Improved productivity meant that goods could be produced with fewer workers. During the 1920s, more Americans worked in the professions, retailing, finance, and education, but the number of manufacturing workers declined by 5 percent, the first such drop in the nation's history. Parts of New England were already experiencing the chronic unemployment caused by deindustrialization. Many of the region's textile companies failed in the face of low-wage competition from southern factories, or shifted production to take advantage of the South's cheap labor. Most advertisers directed their messages at businessmen and the middle class. At the end of the decade, 75 percent of American households still did not own a washing machine, and 60 percent had no radio.

The Farmers' Plight

Nor did farmers share in the decade's prosperity. The "golden age" of American farming had reached its peak during World War I, when the need to feed war-torn Europe and government efforts to maintain high farm prices had raised farmers' incomes and promoted the purchase of more land on credit. Thanks to mechanization and the increased use of fertilizer and insecticides, agricultural production continued to rise even when government subsidies ended and world demand stagnated. As a result, farm incomes declined steadily and banks foreclosed tens of thousands of farms whose owners were unable to meet mortgage payments.

For the first time in the nation's history, the number of farms and farmers declined during the 1920s. For example, half the farmers in Montana lost their land to foreclosure between 1921 and 1925. Extractive industries, like mining and

The spread of the telephone network hastened the nation's integration and opened further job opportunities for women. Lewis Hine photographed this telephone operator in the 1920s.

Depression in rural America

Farmers, like this family of potato growers in rural Minnesota, did not share in the prosperity of the 1920s.

Kansas agricultural workers breaking new ground with disk plows, which eased the task of readying the sod of the Great Plains for planting and encouraged the emergence of larger farms. Simon Fishman, a Jewish farmer known as the "wheat king," in jacket and tie, is on the first tractor.

Factory farms

America's image

Public relations

lumber, also suffered as their products faced a glut on the world market. During the decade, some 3 million persons migrated out of rural areas. Many headed for southern California, whose rapidly growing economy needed new labor. The population of Los Angeles, the West's leading industrial center, a producer of oil, automobiles, aircraft, and, of course, Hollywood movies, rose from 575,000 to 2.2 million during the decade, largely because of an influx of displaced farmers from the Midwest. Well before the 1930s, rural America was in an economic depression.

The 1920s, however, was not simply a period of decline on the farm but of significant technological change. The mechanization of agriculture had been taking place since the mid-nineteenth century, especially in the West, but it now accelerated dramatically. New inventions came into widespread use on the Great Plains, especially the steam tractor and the disk plow, which killed weeds, chopped up the sod, and left the surface layer much easier to plant. Mechanization encouraged an increase in the scale of agriculture. From farms growing wheat to California orange groves, the western states became home to modern "factory farms," employing large numbers of migrant laborers. Massive irrigation projects completed in the previous decades made the Far West much more suitable for farming. Farm output boomed in previously arid parts of California, Arizona, New Mexico, and Texas. With immigration from Asia barred and blacks unwanted, agribusinesses recruited workers from across the southern border, and immigrants from Mexico came to make up the vast majority of the West's low-wage farm migrants. On the Great Plains, extensive plowing while ignoring environmental risks set the stage for the Dust Bowl of the 1930s.

The Image of Business

Hollywood films spread images of "the American way of life" across the globe. America, wrote the historian Charles Beard, was "boring its way" into the world's consciousness. In high wages, efficient factories, and the mass production of consumer goods, Americans seemed to have discovered the secret of permanent prosperity. Businessmen like Henry Ford and engineers like Herbert Hoover were cultural heroes. Photographers such as Lewis Hine and Margaret Bourke-White and painters like Charles Sheeler celebrated the beauty of machines and factories. *The Man Nobody Knows*, a 1925 best-seller by advertising executive Bruce Barton, portrayed Jesus Christ as "the greatest advertiser of his day, . . . a virile go-getting he-man of business," who "picked twelve men from the bottom ranks and forged a great organization."

After the Ludlow Massacre of 1914, discussed in Chapter 18, John D. Rockefeller himself hired a public relations firm to repair his tarnished image. Now, persuaded by the success of World War I's Committee on Public Information, numerous firms established public relations departments to justify corporate practices to the public and counteract its long-standing distrust of big business.

They succeeded in changing popular attitudes toward Wall Street. Congressional hearings of 1912–1914 headed by Louisiana congressman Arsène Pujo had laid bare the manipulation of stock prices by a Wall Street "money trust." The Pujo investigation had reinforced the widespread view of the stock market as a place where insiders fleeced small investors—as, indeed, they frequently did. But in the 1920s, as the steadily rising price of stocks made front-page news, the market attracted more investors. Many assumed that stock values would rise forever. By 1928, an estimated 1.5 million Americans owned stock—still a small minority of the country's 28 million families, but far more than in the past.

Stock market

The Decline of Labor

With the defeat of the labor upsurge of 1919 and the dismantling of the wartime regulatory state, business appropriated the rhetoric of Americanism and "industrial freedom" as weapons against labor unions. Some corporations during the 1920s implemented a new style of management. They provided their employees with private pensions and medical insurance plans, job security, and greater workplace safety. They established sports programs to occupy their employees' leisure time. They spoke of "welfare capitalism," a more socially conscious kind of business leadership, and trumpeted the fact that they now paid more attention to the "human factor" in employment.

Welfare capitalism

At the same time, however, employers in the 1920s embraced the American Plan, at whose core stood the open shop—a workplace free of both government regulation and unions, except, in some cases, "company unions" created and controlled by management. Collective bargaining, declared one group of employers,

River Rouge Plant, by the artist Charles Sheeler, exemplifies the "machine-age aesthetic" of the 1920s. Sheeler found artistic beauty in Henry Ford's giant automobile assembly factory. The plant employed 75,000 workers, but none are visible in the painting; what interests Sheeler is machinery, not man.

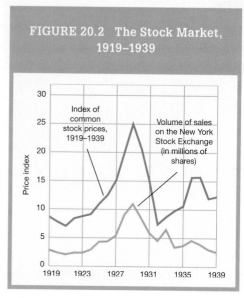

FIGURE 20.2 The Stock Market, 1919–1939

Index of common stock prices, 1919–1939

Volume of sales on the New York Stock Exchange (in millions of shares)

This graph illustrates the rapid rise and dramatic collapse of stock prices and the number of shares traded during the 1920s and early 1930s.

Reconceiving feminism

Debate over the ERA

represented "an infringement of personal liberty and a menace to the institutions of a free people." Prosperity, they insisted, depended on giving business complete freedom of action. This message was reinforced in a propaganda campaign that linked unionism and socialism as examples of the sinister influence of foreigners on American life. Even the most forward-looking companies continued to employ strikebreakers, private detectives, and the blacklisting of union organizers to prevent or defeat strikes.

During the 1920s, organized labor lost more than 2 million members, and unions agreed to demand after demand by employers in an effort to stave off complete elimination. In cities like Minneapolis, New Orleans, and Seattle, once centers of thriving labor movements, unions all but disappeared. Uprisings by the most downtrodden workers did occur sporadically throughout the decade. Southern textile mills witnessed desperate strikes by workers who charged employers with "making slaves out of the men and women" who labored there. Facing the combined opposition of business, local politicians, and the courts, as well as the threat of violence, such strikes were doomed to defeat.

The Equal Rights Amendment

The idealistic goals of World War I, wrote the young Protestant minister Reinhold Niebuhr, seemingly had been abandoned: "We are rapidly becoming the most conservative nation on earth." Like the labor movement, feminists struggled to adapt to the new political situation. The achievement of suffrage in 1920 eliminated the bond of unity between various activists, each "struggling for her own conception of freedom," in the words of labor reformer Juliet Stuart Poyntz. Black feminists insisted that the movement must now demand enforcement of the Fifteenth Amendment in the South, but they won little support from white counterparts. A few prominent feminists, including Elizabeth Cady Stanton's daughter Harriot Stanton Blatch, joined the rapidly diminishing Socialist Party, convinced that women should support an independent electoral force that promoted governmental protection of vulnerable workers.

The long-standing division between two competing conceptions of woman's freedom—one based on motherhood, the other on individual autonomy and the right to work—now crystallized in the debate over an **Equal Rights Amendment** (ERA) to the Constitution promoted by Alice Paul and the National Woman's Party. This amendment proposed to eliminate all legal distinctions "on account of sex." In Paul's opinion, the ERA followed logically from winning the right to vote. Having gained political equality, she insisted, women no longer required special legal protection—they needed equal access to employment, education, and all the other opportunities of citizens. To supporters of mothers' pensions and laws limiting women's hours of labor, which the ERA would sweep away, the proposal represented a giant step backward. Apart from the National Woman's Party, every major female organization, from the League of Women Voters to the Women's Trade Union League, opposed the ERA.

In the end, none of these groups achieved success in the 1920s. The ERA campaign failed, as did a proposed constitutional amendment giving Congress the power to prohibit child labor, which farm groups and business organizations opposed. In 1929, Congress repealed the Sheppard-Towner Act of 1921, a major achievement of the maternalist reformers that had provided federal assistance to programs for infant and child health.

Women's Freedom

If political feminism faded, the prewar feminist demand for personal freedom survived in the vast consumer marketplace and in the actual behavior of the decade's much-publicized liberated young women. Female liberation resurfaced as a lifestyle, the stuff of advertising and mass entertainment, stripped of any connection to political or economic radicalism. No longer one element in a broader program of social reform, sexual freedom now meant individual autonomy or personal rebellion. With her bobbed hair, short skirts, public smoking and drinking, and unapologetic use of birth-control methods such as the diaphragm, the young, single **flapper** epitomized the change in standards of sexual behavior, at least in large cities. She frequented dance halls and music clubs where white people now performed "wild" dances like the Charleston that had long been popular in black communities. She attended sexually charged Hollywood films featuring stars like Clara Bow, the provocative "'It' Girl," and Rudolph Valentino, the original on-screen "Latin Lover." When Valentino died of a sudden illness in 1926, crowds of grieving women tried to storm the funeral home.

What had been scandalous a generation earlier—women's self-conscious pursuit of personal pleasure—became a device to market goods from automobiles to cigarettes. In 1904, a woman had been arrested for smoking in public in New

Tipsy, a 1930 painting by the Japanese artist Kobayakawa Kiyoshi, illustrates the global appeal of the "new woman" of the 1920s. The subject, a *moga* ("modern girl" in Japanese), sits alone in a nightclub wearing Western clothing, makeup, and hairstyle, accompanied by a cigarette and a martini. The title of the work suggests that Kiyoshi does not entirely approve of her behavior, but he presents her as self-confident and alluring. Japanese police took a dim view of "modern" women, arresting those who applied makeup in public.

Many American authorities were no more welcoming to "new women." The superintendent of public buildings and grounds in Washington, D.C., decreed that women's bathing suits must fall no higher than six inches above the knee. Here, in 1922, he enforces his edict.

(*Left*) Advertisers marketed cigarettes to women as symbols of female independence. The August 27, 1925 cover of *Life* magazine shows a young man and a young woman dressed identically at the beach in revealing bathing suits (by 1920s standards), both enjoying cigarettes. (*Right*) An ad for a washing machine promises to liberate women from the "slavery" of everyday laundering at home.

York City. Two decades later, Edward Bernays, the "father" of modern public relations, masterminded a campaign to persuade women to smoke, dubbing cigarettes women's "torches of freedom." The new freedom, however, was available only during one phase of a woman's life. Once she married, what Jane Addams had called the "family claim" still ruled. And marriage, according to one advertisement, remained "the one pursuit that stands foremost in the mind of every girl and woman." Having found a husband, women were expected to seek freedom within the confines of the home, finding "liberation," according to the advertisements, in the use of new labor-saving appliances.

BUSINESS AND GOVERNMENT

The Retreat from Progressivism

In 1924, a social scientist remarked that the United States had just passed through "one of the most critical ten-year periods" in its history. Among the changes was the disintegration of Progressivism as a political movement and body of thought. The government's success in whipping up mass hysteria during the war seemed to undermine the very foundation of democratic thought—the idea of the rational, self-directed citizen. Followers of Sigmund Freud emphasized the unconscious, instinctual motivations of human behavior; scientists pointed to wartime IQ tests allegedly demonstrating that many Americans were mentally unfit for self-government. "The great bulk of people are stupid," declared one advertising executive, explaining why advertisements played on the emotions rather than providing actual information.

During the 1920s, Walter Lippmann published two of the most penetrating indictments of democracy ever written, *Public Opinion* and *The Phantom Public*, which repudiated the Progressive hope of applying "intelligence" to social problems in a mass democracy. Instead of acting out of careful consideration of the issues or even individual self-interest, Lippmann claimed, the American voter was ill-informed and prone to fits of enthusiasm. Not only were modern problems beyond the understanding of ordinary men and women (a sentiment that had earlier led Lippmann to favor administration by experts), but the independent citizen was nothing but a myth. Like advertising copywriters and journalists, he continued, the government had perfected the art of creating and manipulating public opinion—a process Lippmann called the "manufacture of consent."

In 1929, the sociologists Robert and Helen Lynd published *Middletown*, a classic study of life in Muncie, Indiana, a typical community in the American heartland. The Lynds found that new leisure activities and a new emphasis on consumption had replaced politics as the focus of public concern. Elections were no longer "lively centers" of public attention as in the nineteenth century, and voter participation had fallen dramatically. National statistics bore out their point; the turnout of eligible voters, over 80 percent in 1896, dropped to less than 50 percent in 1924. Many factors helped to explain this decline, including the consolidation of one-party politics in the South, the long period of Republican dominance in national elections, and the enfranchisement of women, who for many years voted in lower numbers than men. But the shift from public to private concerns also played a part. "The American citizen's first importance to his country," declared a Muncie newspaper, "is no longer that of a citizen but that of a consumer."

The Republican Era

Government policies reflected the pro-business ethos of the 1920s. Recalling the era's prosperity, one stockbroker later remarked, "God, J. P. Morgan and the Republican Party were going to keep everything going forever." Business lobbyists dominated national conventions of the Republican Party. They called on the federal government to lower taxes on personal incomes and business profits, maintain high tariffs, and support employers' continuing campaign against unions. The administrations of Warren G. Harding and Calvin Coolidge obliged. "Never before, here or anywhere else," declared the *Wall Street Journal*, "has a government been so completely fused with business." The two presidents appointed so many pro-business members of the Federal Reserve Board, the Federal Trade Commission, and other Progressive-era agencies that, complained Nebraska senator George W. Norris, they in effect repealed the regulatory system. The Harding administration did support Secretary of Commerce Herbert Hoover's successful effort to persuade the steel industry to reduce the workday from twelve to eight hours. But it resumed the practice of obtaining court injunctions to suppress strikes, as in a 1922 walkout of 250,000 railroad workers protesting a wage cut.

The policies of President Calvin Coolidge were music to the ears of big business, according to one 1920s cartoonist, who entitled this image "Yes Sir, He's My Baby," after a popular song.

"This decision affirms your constitutional right to starve." A 1923 cartoon criticizes the Supreme Court decision declaring unconstitutional a Washington, D.C., law establishing a minimum wage for women. Justice George Sutherland, appointed to the Court the previous year by President Warren G. Harding, wrote the majority decision.

A conservative Supreme Court

Under William Howard Taft, appointed chief justice in 1921, the Supreme Court remained strongly conservative. A resurgence of laissez-faire jurisprudence eclipsed the Progressive ideal of a socially active national state. The Court struck down a federal law that barred goods produced by child labor from interstate commerce. It even repudiated *Muller v. Oregon* (see Chapter 18) in a 1923 decision (*Adkins v. Children's Hospital*) overturning a minimum wage law for women in Washington, D.C. Now that women enjoyed the vote, the justices declared, they were entitled to the same workplace freedom as men. "This," lamented Florence Kelley, "is a new Dred Scott decision," which, in the name of liberty of contract, "fills those words with the bitterest and most cruel mockery."

Corruption in Government

Warren G. Harding took office as president in 1921 promising a "return to normalcy" after an era of Progressive reform and world war. Reflecting the prevailing get-rich-quick ethos, his administration quickly became one of the most corrupt in American history. A likeable, somewhat ineffectual individual—he called himself "a man of limited talents from a small town"—Harding seemed to have little regard for either governmental issues or the dignity of the presidency. Prohibition did not cause him to curb his appetite for liquor. He continued a previous illicit affair with a young Ohio woman, Nan Britton. The relationship did not become known until 1927, when Britton published *The President's Daughter*, about their child to whom Harding had left nothing in his will.

Although his cabinet included men of integrity and talent, like Secretary of State Charles Evans Hughes and Secretary of Commerce Herbert Hoover, Harding also surrounded himself with cronies who used their offices for private gain. Attorney General Harry Daugherty accepted payments not to prosecute accused criminals. The head of the Veterans' Bureau, Charles Forbes, received kickbacks from the sale of government supplies. The most notorious scandal involved Secretary of the Interior Albert Fall, who accepted nearly $500,000 from private businessmen to whom he leased government oil reserves at **Teapot Dome**, Wyoming. Fall became the first cabinet member in history to be convicted of a felony.

Progressive Optimism, a satirical comment on Robert La Follette's campaign for president in 1924 as the candidate of the Progressive Party, has a disheveled westerner (labeled Wisconsin, La Follette's state) tied to a stake in the desert while a goat dressed as a cowboy and labeled "Third Party" heads off to bring the party's message to the "uneducated East."

The Election of 1924

Harding's successor, Calvin Coolidge, who as governor of Massachusetts had won national fame for using state troops against striking Boston policemen in 1919, was a dour man of few words. But in contrast to his predecessor he seemed to exemplify Yankee honesty. The scandals subsided, but otherwise Coolidge continued his predecessor's policies. He twice vetoed the **McNary-Haugen bill**, the top legislative priority of congressmen from farm states. This bill sought to have the government purchase agricultural products for sale overseas in order to raise farm prices. Coolidge denounced it as an unwarranted interference with the free market. In 1924, Coolidge was reelected in a landslide, defeating John W. Davis, a Wall Street lawyer nominated on the 103rd ballot by a badly divided Democratic convention. (This was when the comedian Will Rogers made the quip,

A 1924 cartoon commenting on the scandals of the Harding administration. The White House, Capitol, and Washington Monument have been sold to the highest bidder.

often repeated in future years, "I am a member of no organized political party; I am a Democrat.")

One-sixth of the electorate in 1924 voted for Robert La Follette, running as the candidate of a new Progressive Party, which called for greater taxation of wealth, the conservation of natural resources, public ownership of the railroads, farm relief, and the end of child labor. Although such ideas had been proposed many times before World War I, Coolidge described the platform as a blueprint for a "communistic and socialistic" America. Despite endorsements from veteran Progressives like Jane Addams and John Dewey and the American Federation of Labor, La Follette could raise no more than $250,000 for his campaign. He carried only his native Wisconsin. But his candidacy demonstrated the survival of some currents of dissent in a highly conservative decade.

Economic Diplomacy

Foreign affairs also reflected the close working relationship between business and government. "Any student of modern diplomacy," declared Huntington Wilson, a State Department official, "knows that in these days of competition, capital, trade, agriculture, labor and statecraft all go hand in hand if a country is to profit." The 1920s marked a retreat from Wilson's goal of internationalism in favor of unilateral American actions mainly designed to increase exports and investment opportunities overseas. Indeed, what is sometimes called the "isolationism" of the 1920s represented a reaction against the disappointing results of Wilson's military and diplomatic pursuit of freedom and democracy abroad. The United States did play

Isolationism

VOICES OF FREEDOM

From LUCIAN W. PARRISH, SPEECH IN CONGRESS ON IMMIGRATION (1921)

In the immediate aftermath of World War I, fears of foreign radicalism sparked by labor upheavals, and the increased concern with Americanizing immigrants, greatly strengthened demands to curtail immigration. During a debate in the House of Representatives in April 1921, Lucian W. Parrish, a Democrat from Texas, laid out the case for immigration restriction.

We should stop immigration entirely until such a time as we can amend our immigration laws and so write them that hereafter no one shall be admitted except he be in full sympathy with our Constitution and laws, willing to declare himself obedient to our flag, and willing to release himself from any obligations he may owe to the flag of the country from which he came.

It is time that we act now, because within a few short years the damage will have been done. The endless tide of immigration will have filled our country with a foreign and unsympathetic element. Those who are out of sympathy with our Constitution and the spirit of our Government will be here in large numbers, and the true spirit of Americanism left us by our fathers will gradually become poisoned by this uncertain element.

The time once was when we welcomed to our shores the oppressed and downtrodden people from all the world, but they came to us because of oppression at home and with the sincere purpose of making true and loyal American citizens, and in truth and in fact they did adapt themselves to our ways of thinking and contributed in a substantial sense to the progress and development that our civilization has made. But that time has passed now; new and strange conditions have arisen in the countries over there; new and strange doctrines are being taught. The governments of the Orient are being overturned and destroyed, and anarchy and bolshevism are threatening the very foundation of many of them and no one can foretell what the future will bring to many of those countries of the Old World now struggling with these problems.

Our country is a self-sustaining country. It has taught the principles of real democracy to all the nations of the earth; its flag has been the synonym of progress, prosperity, and the preservation of the rights of the individual, and there can be nothing so dangerous as for us to allow the undesirable foreign element to poison our civilization and thereby threaten the safety of the institutions that our forefathers have established for us. . . .

We must hold this country true to the American thought and the American ideals.

From MAJORITY OPINION, JUSTICE JAMES C. MCREYNOLDS, IN *MEYER V. NEBRASKA* (1923)

A landmark in the development of civil liberties, the Supreme Court's decision in *Meyer v. Nebraska* **rebuked the coercive Americanization impulse of World War I, overturning a Nebraska law that required all school instruction to take place in English.**

The problem for our determination is whether the statute [prohibiting instruction in a language other than English] as construed and applied unreasonably infringes the liberty guaranteed ... by the Fourteenth Amendment. ...

The American people have always regarded education and acquisition of knowledge as matters of supreme importance which should be diligently promoted. ... The calling always has been regarded as useful and honorable, essential, indeed, to the public welfare. Mere knowledge of the German language cannot reasonably be regarded as harmful. Heretofore it has been commonly looked upon as helpful and desirable. [Meyer] taught this language in school as part of his occupation. His right to teach and the right of parents to engage him so to instruct their children, we think, are within the liberty of the Amendment.

It is said the purpose of the legislation was to promote civil development by inhibiting training and education of the immature in foreign tongues and ideals before they could learn English and acquire American ideals. ... It is also affirmed that the foreign born population is very large, that certain communities commonly use foreign words, follow foreign leaders, move in a foreign atmosphere, and that the children are therefore hindered from becoming citizens of the most useful type and the public safety is impaired.

That the State may do much, go very far, indeed, in order to improve the quality of its citizens, physically, mentally, and morally, is clear; but the individual has certain fundamental rights which must be respected. The protection of the Constitution extends to all, to those who speak other languages as well as to those born with English on the tongue. Perhaps it would be highly advantageous if all had ready understanding of our ordinary speech, but this cannot be coerced by methods which conflict with the Constitution. ... No emergency has arisen which rendered knowledge by a child of some language other than English so clearly harmful as to justify its inhibition with the consequent infringement of rights long freely enjoyed.

QUESTIONS

1. *Why does Parrish consider continued immigration dangerous?*

2. *How does the decision in* Meyer v. Nebraska *expand the definition of liberty protected by the Fourteenth Amendment?*

3. *How do the two excerpts reflect deep divisions over the nature of American society during the 1920s?*

A German cartoon inspired by President Calvin Coolidge's dispatch of American troops to Nicaragua. While Coolidge insisted that the United States acted in the interest of preserving international order, residents of other countries often saw the United States as a grasping imperial power.

Intervention in Nicaragua and its consequences

host to the Washington Naval Arms Conference of 1922 that negotiated reductions in the navies of Britain, France, Japan, Italy, and the United States. But the country remained outside the League of Nations. Even as American diplomats continued to press for access to markets overseas, the Fordney-McCumber Tariff of 1922 raised taxes on imported goods to their highest levels in history, a repudiation of Wilson's principle of promoting free trade.

Much foreign policy was conducted through private economic relationships rather than governmental action. The United States emerged from World War I as both the world's foremost center of manufacturing and the major financial power, thanks to British and French debts for American loans that had funded their war efforts. During the 1920s, New York bankers, sometimes acting on their own and sometimes with the cooperation of the Harding and Coolidge administrations, solidified their international position by extending loans to European and Latin American governments. They advanced billions of dollars to Germany to enable the country to meet its World War I reparations payments. American industrial firms, especially in auto, agricultural machinery, and electrical equipment manufacturing, established plants overseas to supply the world market and take advantage of inexpensive labor. American investors gained control over raw materials such as copper in Chile and oil in Venezuela. In 1928, in the so-called Red Line Agreement, British, French, and American oil companies divided oil-producing regions in the Middle East and Latin America among themselves.

As before World War I, the government dispatched soldiers when a change in government in the Caribbean threatened American economic interests. Having been stationed in Nicaragua since 1912, American marines withdrew in 1925. But the troops soon returned in an effort to suppress a nationalist revolt headed by General Augusto César Sandino. Having created a National Guard headed by General Anastasio Somoza, the marines finally departed in 1933. A year later, Somoza assassinated Sandino and seized power. For the next forty-five years, he and his family ruled and plundered Nicaragua. Somoza's son was overthrown in 1979 by a popular movement calling itself the Sandinistas (see Chapter 26).

THE BIRTH OF CIVIL LIBERTIES

Among the casualties of World War I and the 1920s was Progressivism's faith that an active federal government embodied the national purpose and enhanced the enjoyment of freedom. Wartime and postwar repression, Prohibition, and the pro-business policies of the 1920s all illustrated, in the eyes of many Progressives, how public power could go grievously wrong.

This lesson opened the door to a new appreciation of civil liberties—rights an individual may assert even against democratic majorities—as essential elements of American freedom. Building on prewar struggles for freedom of expression by labor unions, socialists, and birth-control advocates, some reformers now developed a greater appreciation of the necessity of vibrant, unrestricted political debate. In the name of a "new freedom for the individual," the 1920s saw the birth of a coherent concept of civil liberties and the beginnings of significant legal protection for freedom of speech against the government.

The "Free Mob"

Wartime repression continued into the 1920s. Under the heading "Sweet Land of Liberty," *The Nation* magazine in 1923 detailed recent examples of the degradation of American freedom—lynchings in Alabama, Arkansas, and Florida; the beating by Columbia University students of an undergraduate who had written a letter defending freedom of speech and the press; the arrest of a union leader in New Jersey and 400 members of the IWW in California; a refusal to allow a socialist to speak in Pennsylvania. Throughout the 1920s, artistic works with sexual themes were subjected to rigorous censorship. The Postal Service removed from the mails books it deemed obscene. The Customs Service barred works by the sixteenth-century French satirist Rabelais, the modern novelist James Joyce, and many others from entering the country. A local crusade against indecency made the phrase "Banned in Boston" a term of ridicule among upholders of artistic freedom. Boston's Watch and Ward Committee excluded sixty-five books from the city's bookstores, including works by the novelists Upton Sinclair, Theodore Dreiser, and Ernest Hemingway.

Hollywood producers feared that publicity over actress Mary Pickford's divorce, actor Wallace Reid's death from a drug overdose, and a murder trial involving actor Fatty Arbuckle would reinforce the belief that movies promoted immorality. In 1930, the film industry adopted the Hays code, a sporadically enforced set of guidelines that prohibited movies from depicting nudity, long kisses, and adultery, and barred scripts that portrayed clergymen in a negative light or criminals sympathetically. Filmmakers hoped that self-censorship would prevent censorship by local governments, a not uncommon occurrence since the courts deemed movies a business subject to regulation, not a form of expression. Not until 1951, in a case involving *The Miracle*, a film many Catholics found offensive, would the Supreme Court declare movies an artistic form protected by the First Amendment.

Even as Europeans turned in increasing numbers to American popular culture and consumer goods, some came to view the country as a repressive cultural wasteland. Americans, commented the British novelist D. H. Lawrence, who lived for a time in the United States, prided themselves on being the "land of the free," but "the free mob" had destroyed the right to dissent. "I have never been in any country," he wrote, "where the individual has such an abject fear of his fellow countrymen." Disillusionment with the conservatism of American politics and the materialism of the culture inspired some American artists and writers to emigrate to Paris. The Lost Generation of cultural exiles included novelists and poets like Ernest Hemingway, Gertrude Stein, and F. Scott Fitzgerald. Europe, they felt, valued art and culture, and appreciated unrestrained freedom of expression (and, of course, allowed individuals to drink legally).

A "Clear and Present Danger"

During World War I, the Unitarian minister John Haynes Holmes later recalled, "there suddenly came to the fore in our nation's life the new issue of civil liberties."

Augusto Sandino, who led a rebellion against the U.S. military occupation of Nicaragua in the late 1920s. He was assassinated in 1934 by General Anastasio Somoza, who became a dictator and established a family dynasty that ruled Nicaragua until overthrown in 1979 by a popular movement known as the Sandinistas.

The Lost Generation

The American Civil Liberties Union

Schenck v. United States

The arrest of antiwar dissenters under the Espionage and Sedition Acts inspired the formation in 1917 of the Civil Liberties Bureau, which in 1920 became the **American Civil Liberties Union** (ACLU). For the rest of the century, the ACLU would take part in most of the landmark cases that helped to bring about a "rights revolution." Its efforts helped to give meaning to traditional civil liberties like freedom of speech and invented new ones, like the right to privacy. When it began, however, the ACLU was a small, beleaguered organization. A coalition of pacifists, Progressives shocked by wartime repression, and lawyers outraged at what they considered violations of Americans' legal rights, it saw its own pamphlets defending free speech barred from the mails by postal inspectors.

Prior to World War I, the Supreme Court had done almost nothing to protect the rights of unpopular minorities. Now, it was forced to address the question of the permissible limits on political and economic dissent. In its initial decisions, it dealt the concept of civil liberties a series of devastating blows. In 1919, the Court upheld the constitutionality of the Espionage Act and the conviction of Charles T. Schenck, a socialist who had distributed antidraft leaflets through the mails. Speaking for the Court, Justice Oliver Wendell Holmes declared that the First Amendment did not prevent Congress from prohibiting speech that presented a "clear and present danger" of inspiring illegal actions. Free speech, he observed, "would not protect a man in falsely shouting fire in a theater and causing a panic."

For the next half-century, Holmes's doctrine would remain the basic test in First Amendment cases. Since the Court usually allowed public officials to decide what speech was in fact "dangerous," it hardly provided a stable basis for the defense of free expression in times of crisis. A week after *Schenck v. United States*, the Court unanimously upheld the conviction of Eugene V. Debs for a speech condemning the war. It also affirmed the wartime jailing of the editor of a German-language newspaper whose editorials had questioned the draft's constitutionality.

The defendants in *U.S. v. Abrams*, on the day of their deportation to Russia in 1921. Jacob Abrams is on the right. They were convicted under the Espionage Act of 1918 for impeding the war effort by distributing pamphlets critical of the American intervention in Russia after the Russian revolution.

The Court and Civil Liberties

Also in 1919, the Court upheld the conviction of Jacob Abrams and five other men for distributing pamphlets critical of American intervention in Russia after the Russian revolution. This time, however, Holmes and Louis Brandeis dissented, marking the emergence of a court minority committed to a broader defense of free speech. Six years after *Abrams*, the two again dissented when the majority upheld the conviction of Benjamin Gitlow, a communist whose *Left-wing Manifesto* calling for revolution led to his conviction under a New York law prohibiting "criminal anarchy." "The only meaning of free speech," Holmes now declared, was that advocates of every set of beliefs, even "proletarian dictatorship," should have the right to convert the public to their views in the great "marketplace of ideas" (an apt metaphor for a consumer society). In approving Gitlow's conviction, the Court majority observed that the Fourteenth Amendment obligated the states to refrain from unreasonable restraints on freedom of speech and the press. The comment marked a major step in the long process by which the Bill of Rights was transformed from an ineffective statement of principle into a significant protection of Americans' freedoms.

The tide of civil-liberties decision making slowly began to turn. By the end of the 1920s, the Supreme Court had voided a Kansas law that made it a crime to advocate unlawful acts to change the political or economic system, and one from Minnesota authorizing censorship of the press. The new regard for free speech went beyond political expression. In 1930, the Court threw out the conviction of Mary Ware Dennett for sending a sex-education pamphlet, *The Sex Side of Life*, through the mails. Three years later, a federal court overturned the Customs Service's ban on James Joyce's novel *Ulysses*, a turning point in the battle against the censorship of works of literature.

Overturning censorship

Meanwhile, Brandeis was crafting an intellectual defense of civil liberties on grounds somewhat different from Holmes's model of a competitive market in ideas. In 1927, the Court upheld the conviction of the prominent California socialist and women's rights activist Anita Whitney for attending a convention of the Communist Labor Party where speakers advocated violent revolution. Brandeis voted with the majority on technical grounds. But he issued a powerful defense of freedom of speech as essential to active citizenship in a democracy: "Those who won our independence believed . . . that freedom to think as you will and to speak as you think are indispensable to the discovery and spread of political truth. . . . The greatest menace to freedom is an inert people." A month after the decision, the governor of California pardoned Whitney, terming freedom of speech the "indispensable birthright of every free American." The intrepid Mrs. Whitney was soon back in court for violating a California law making it a crime to display a red flag. In 1931, the Supreme Court overturned the law as "repugnant to the guaranty of liberty contained in the Fourteenth Amendment." A judicial defense of civil liberties was slowly being born.

A broader defense of free speech

A 1923 lithograph by George Bellows captures the dynamic style of the most prominent evangelical preacher of the 1920s, Billy Sunday.

THE CULTURE WARS

The Fundamentalist Revolt

Although many Americans embraced modern urban culture with its religious and ethnic pluralism, mass entertainment, and liberated sexual rules, others found it alarming. Many evangelical Protestants felt threatened by the decline of traditional values and the increased visibility of Catholicism and Judaism because of immigration. They also resented the growing presence within mainstream Protestant denominations of "modernists" who sought to integrate science and religion and adapt Christianity to the new secular culture. "The day is past," declared Harry Emerson Fosdick, pastor of New York's First Presbyterian Church and a prominent modernist, "when you can ask thoughtful men to hold religion in one compartment of their minds and their modern world view in another."

Convinced that the literal truth of the Bible formed the basis of Christian belief, fundamentalists launched a campaign to rid Protestant denominations of modernism and to combat the new individual freedoms that seemed to contradict traditional morality. Their most flamboyant apostle was Billy Sunday, a talented professional baseball player who became a revivalist preacher. Between 1900 and 1930, Sunday drew huge crowds with a highly theatrical preaching style and a message denouncing sins ranging from Darwinism to alcohol. He was said to have preached to 100 million people during his lifetime—more than any other individual in history.

Much of the press portrayed **fundamentalism** as a movement of backwoods bigots. In fact, it was a national phenomenon. Even in New York City, the center of the new modern culture, Fosdick was removed from his ministry in 1924 (whereupon John D. Rockefeller Jr. built the interdenominational Riverside Church for him). Fundamentalism remained an important strain of 1920s culture and politics.

> Billy Sunday

Federal agents with confiscated liquor in Colorado in 1920, shortly after the advent of Prohibition.

Prohibition, which fundamentalists strongly supported, succeeded in reducing the consumption of alcohol as well as public drunkenness and drink-related diseases. Often portrayed (especially in Hollywood movies) as a glamorous episode of gangland battles and drinkers easily outwitting the police, Prohibition in fact was effectively enforced, albeit selectively. While wealthy Americans continued to enjoy access to liquor, many poor, black, and immigrant communities suffered large-scale arrests and jailings, often accompanied by police violence. Later deemed an unmitigated failure, enforcement of Prohibition in fact led to the building of new federal prisons and laid the foundation for powerful national action against crime and immorality, a precursor to the more recent federal war on drugs.

Prohibition, however, remained a deeply divisive issue. The greatest expansion of national

authority since Reconstruction, it raised major questions of local rights, individual freedom, and the wisdom of attempting to impose religious and moral values on the entire society through legislation. It divided the Democratic Party into "wet" and "dry" wings, leading to bitter battles at the party's 1924 and 1928 national conventions. Too many Americans deemed Prohibition a violation of individual freedom for the flow of illegal liquor to stop. In urban areas, Prohibition led to large profits for the owners of illegal speakeasies and the "bootleggers" who supplied them. It produced widespread corruption as police and public officials accepted bribes to turn a blind eye to violations of the law. These developments reinforced fundamentalists' identification of urban life and modern notions of freedom with immorality and a decline of Christian liberty.

With the coming of Prohibition, the U.S. borders with Canada and Mexico divided "wet" and "dry" nations. (Left) A scene on the Canadian side of the border with the state of Washington. One hundred feet into Canada, billboards welcome Americans to a country where it is still legal to consume alcohol. (Right) American automobiles are parked in front of bars in the border city of Tijuana, Mexico.

The Scopes Trial

In 1925, a trial in Tennessee threw into sharp relief the division between traditional values and modern, secular culture. John Scopes, a teacher in a Tennessee public school, was arrested for violating a state law that prohibited the teaching of Charles Darwin's theory of evolution. His trial became a national sensation. The proceedings were even carried live on national radio.

The **Scopes trial** reflected the enduring tension between two American definitions of freedom. Fundamentalist Christians, strongest in rural areas of the South and West, clung to the traditional idea of "moral" liberty—voluntary adherence to time-honored religious beliefs. The theory that man had evolved over millions of years from ancestors like apes contradicted the biblical account of creation. Those who upheld the Tennessee law identified evolutionists with feminists, socialists, and religious modernists, all of whom, they claimed, substituted human judgment for the word of God. To Scopes's defenders, including the American Civil Liberties Union, which had persuaded him to violate the law in order to test its constitutionality, freedom meant above all the right to independent thought and individual self-expression. To them, the Tennessee law offered a lesson in the dangers of religious intolerance and the merger of church and state.

Evolution debate

Because of extreme heat, some sessions of the Scopes trial were held outdoors, in front of the courthouse in Dayton, Tennessee. A photographer snapped this picture of the trial's climactic moment, when Clarence Darrow (standing at the center) questioned William Jennings Bryan (seated) about interpretation of the Bible.

The renowned labor lawyer Clarence Darrow defended Scopes. The trial's highlight came when Darrow called William Jennings Bryan to the stand as an "expert witness" on the Bible. Viewing the trial as a "duel to the death" between science and Christianity, he accepted Darrow's challenge. But Bryan revealed an almost complete ignorance of modern science and proved unable to respond effectively to Darrow's sarcastic questioning. Does the serpent really crawl on its belly as punishment for having tempted Eve in the Garden of Evil? When Bryan answered "yes," Darrow inquired how it got around before being cursed—on its tail? Asked whether God had actually created the world in six days, Bryan replied that these should be understood as ages, "not six days of twenty-four hours"—thus opening the door to the very nonliteral interpretation of the Bible fundamentalists rejected.

Fundamentalism

The jury found Scopes guilty, although the Tennessee Supreme Court later overturned the decision on a technicality. Shortly after the trial ended, Bryan died and the movement for anti-evolution laws disintegrated. Fundamentalists retreated for many years from battles over public education, preferring to build their own schools and colleges where teaching could be done as they saw fit and preachers were trained to spread their interpretation of Christianity. The battle would be rejoined, however, toward the end of the twentieth century, when fundamentalism reemerged as an important force in politics. To this day, the teaching of the theory of evolution in public schools arouses intense debate in parts of the United States.

The Second Klan

Few features of urban life seemed more alien to rural and small-town native-born Protestants than their immigrant populations and cultures. The wartime obsession with "100 percent Americanism" continued into the 1920s, a decade of citizenship education programs in public schools, legally sanctioned visits to

"100 percent Americanism"

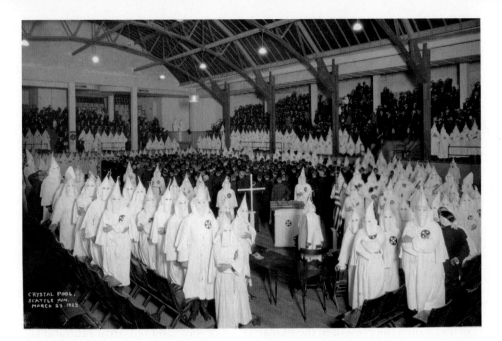

A Ku Klux Klan gathering in Seattle, Washington, in 1923. The unrobed members of the audience are covering their faces to avoid identification. Unlike the Klan of the Reconstruction era, the second Ku Klux Klan was more powerful in the North and West than in the South.

immigrants' homes to investigate their household arrangements, and vigorous efforts by employers to instill appreciation for "American values." Only "an agile and determined immigrant," commented the *Chicago Tribune,* could "hope to escape Americanization by at least one of the many processes now being prepared for his special benefit." In 1922, Oregon became the only state ever to require all students to attend public schools—a measure aimed, said the state's attorney general, at abolishing parochial education and preventing "bolshevists, syndicalists and communists" from organizing their own schools.

Perhaps the most menacing expression of the idea that enjoyment of American freedom should be limited on religious and ethnic grounds was the resurgence of the Ku Klux Klan. The Klan had been reborn in Atlanta in 1915 after the lynching of Leo Frank, a Jewish factory manager accused of killing a teenage girl. By the mid-1920s, it claimed more than 3 million members, nearly all white, native-born Protestants, many of whom held respected positions in their communities. Unlike the Klan of Reconstruction, the organization now sank deep roots in parts of the North and West. It became the largest private organization in Indiana, and for a time controlled the state Republican Party. It was partly responsible for the Oregon law banning private schools. In southern California, its large marches and auto parades made the Klan a visible presence. The new Klan attacked a far broader array of targets than during Reconstruction. American civilization, it insisted, was endangered not only by blacks but by immigrants (especially Jews and Catholics) and all the forces (feminism, unions, immorality, even, on occasion, the giant corporations) that endangered "individual liberty."

Klan in the North and West

Closing the Golden Door

The Klan's influence faded after 1925, when its leader in Indiana was convicted of assaulting a young woman. But the Klan's attacks on modern secular culture and

Defining and denying citizenship

political radicalism and its demand that control of the nation be returned to "citizens of the old stock" reflected sentiments widely shared in the 1920s. The decade witnessed a flurry of legislation that offered a new answer to the venerable question "Who is an American?" In 1924, Congress declared all Native Americans born in the United States to be American citizens, although many western states continued to deny the vote to those living on reservations.

Far more sweeping was a fundamental change in immigration policy. Immigration restriction had a long history. The Naturalization Act of 1790 had barred blacks and Asians from naturalization, with the ban lifted for the former in 1870. Beginning in 1875, various classes of immigrants had been excluded, among them prostitutes, the mentally retarded, and those with contagious diseases. Nonetheless, prior to World War I virtually all the white persons who wished to pass

Immigration restriction

through the "golden door" into the United States and become citizens were able to do so. During the 1920s, however, the pressure for wholesale immigration restriction became irresistible. One index of the changing political climate was that large employers dropped their traditional opposition. Fears of immigrant radicalism now outweighed the desire for cheap unskilled labor, especially since mechanization had halted the growth of the industrial labor force and the Great Migration of World War I had accustomed industrialists to employing African-Americans.

TABLE 20.1 Selected Annual Immigration Quotas under the 1924 Immigration Act

COUNTRY	QUOTA	IMMIGRANTS IN 1914
Northern and Western Europe:		
Great Britain and Northern Ireland	65,721	48,729 (Great Britain only)
Germany	25,957	35,734
Ireland	17,853	24,688 (includes Northern Ireland)
Scandinavia (Sweden, Norway, Denmark, Finland)	7,241	29,391
Southern and Eastern Europe:		
Poland	6,524	(Not an independent state; included in Germany, Russia, and Austria-Hungary)
Italy	5,802	283,738
Russia	2,784	255,660
Other:		
Africa (total of various colonies and countries)	1,000	1,539
Western Hemisphere	No quota limit	122,695
Asia (China, India, Japan, Korea)	0	11,652

In 1921, a temporary measure restricted immigration from Europe to 357,000 per year (one-third of the annual average before the war). Three years later, Congress permanently limited European immigration to 150,000 per year, distributed according to a series of national quotas that severely restricted the numbers from southern and eastern Europe. The Johnson-Reed, or Immigration, Act aimed to ensure that descendants of the old immigrants forever outnumbered the children of the new. However, to satisfy the demands of large farmers in California who relied heavily on seasonal Mexican labor, the 1924 law established no limits on immigration from the Western Hemisphere.

The 1924 law also barred the entry of all those ineligible for naturalized citizenship—that is, the entire population of Asia, even though Japan had fought on the American side in World War I. The only Asians still able to enter the United States were residents of the Philippines, who were deemed to be "American nationals" (although not citizens) because the islands had been U.S. territory since the Spanish-American War. Largely to bar further Philippine immigration, Congress in 1934 established a timetable for the islands' independence, which was finally achieved in 1946. The 1934 law established an immigration quota of fifty Filipinos a year to the mainland United States, but allowed their continued entry into the Hawaiian Islands to work as plantation laborers.

The law of 1924 established, in effect, for the first time a new category—the **illegal alien**. With it came a new enforcement mechanism, the Border Patrol, charged with policing the land boundaries of the United States and empowered to arrest and deport persons who entered the country in violation of the new nationality quotas or other restrictions. Later associated almost exclusively with Latinos, "illegal aliens" at first referred mainly to southern and eastern Europeans who tried to sneak across the border from Mexico or Canada.

The Only Way to Handle It, a cartoon endorsing immigration restriction.

The "illegal alien"

The immigration law of 1924 established the Border Patrol to stop those barred from entry from sneaking into the United States from Mexico. At first, the patrol was a modest operation. Here, two officers police the California-Mexico border.

Race and the Law

The new immigration law reflected the heightened emphasis on "race" as a determinant of public policy. By the early 1920s, political leaders of both North and South agreed upon the relegation of blacks to second-class citizenship. In a speech in Alabama in 1921, President Harding unconsciously echoed W. E. B. Du Bois by affirming that the "problem" of race was a global one, not confined to the South. Unlike Du Bois, he believed the South showed the way to the problem's solution. "It would be helpful," he added, "to have that word 'equality' eliminated from this consideration." Clearly, the Republican Party of the Civil War era was dead.

But "race policy" meant far more than black-white relations. "America must be kept American," declared President Coolidge in his annual message to Congress in 1923. His secretary of labor, James J. Davis, commented that immigration policy, once

based on the need for labor and the notion of the United States as an asylum of liberty, must now rest on a biological definition of the ideal population. Although enacted by a highly conservative Congress strongly influenced by nativism, the 1924 immigration law also reflected the Progressive desire to improve the "quality" of democratic citizenship and to employ scientific methods to set public policy. It revealed how these aims were overlaid with pseudo-scientific assumptions about the superiority and inferiority of particular "races."

The seemingly "scientific" calculation of the new quotas—based on the "national origins" of the American population dating back to 1790—involved a highly speculative analysis of past census returns, with the results altered to increase allowable immigration by politically influential groups like Irish-Americans. Non-whites (one-fifth of the population in 1790) were excluded altogether when calculating quotas—otherwise, Africa would have received a far higher quota than the tiny number allotted to it. But then, the entire concept of race as a basis for public policy lacked any rational foundation. The Supreme Court admitted as much in 1923 when it rejected the claim of Bhagat Singh Thind, an Indian-born World War I veteran, who asserted that as a "pure Aryan," he was actually white and could therefore become an American citizen. "White," the Court declared, was not a scientific concept at all, but part of "common speech, to be interpreted with the understanding of the common man" (a forthright statement of what later scholars would call the "social construction" of race).

Pluralism and Liberty

During the 1920s, some Americans challenged the idea that southern and eastern Europeans were unfit to become citizens, or could only do so by abandoning their traditions in favor of Anglo-Saxon ways. Horace Kallen, himself of German-Jewish origin, in 1924 coined the phrase "cultural pluralism" to describe a society that gloried in ethnic diversity rather than attempting to suppress it. Toleration of difference was part of the "American Idea," Kallen wrote. Anthropologists like Franz Boas, Alfred Kroeber, and Ruth Benedict insisted that no scientific basis existed for theories of racial superiority or for the notion that societies and races could be ranked on a fixed scale running from "primitive" to "civilized."

These writings, however, had little immediate impact on public policy. In the 1920s, the most potent defense of a pluralist vision of American society came from the new immigrants themselves. Every major city still contained ethnic enclaves with their own civic institutions, theaters, churches, and foreign-language newspapers. Their sense of separate identity had been heightened by the emergence of independent nation-states in eastern Europe after the war. It would be wrong, to be sure, to view ethnic communities as united in opposition to Americanization. In a society increasingly knit together by mass culture and a consumer economy, few could escape the pull of assimilation. The department store, dance hall, and motion picture theater were as much agents of Americanization as the school and workplace. From the perspective of many immigrant women, moreover, assimilation often seemed not so much the loss of an inherited culture as a loosening of patriarchal bonds and an expansion of freedom. But most immigrants resented the coercive aspects of Americanization programs, so often based on the idea of the superiority of Protestant mainstream culture.

The Zion Lutheran Church in Nebraska where Robert Meyer was arrested for teaching a Bible lesson in German, in violation of state law. The case led to the landmark Supreme Court decision of *Meyer v. Nebraska*, an important rebuke to World War I xenophobia.

Promoting Tolerance

In the face of immigration restriction, Prohibition, a revived Ku Klux Klan, and widespread anti-Semitism and anti-Catholicism, immigrant groups asserted the validity of cultural diversity and identified toleration of difference—religious, cultural, and individual—as the essence of American freedom. In effect, they reinvented themselves as "ethnic" Americans, claiming an equal share in the nation's life but, in addition, the right to remain in many respects culturally distinct. The Roman Catholic Church urged immigrants to learn English and embrace "American principles," but it continued to maintain separate schools and other institutions. In 1924, the Catholic Holy Name Society brought 10,000 marchers to Washington to challenge the Klan and to affirm Catholics' loyalty to the nation. Throughout the country, organizations like the Anti-Defamation League of B'nai B'rith (founded in 1916 to combat anti-Semitism) and the National Catholic Welfare Council lobbied, in the name of "personal liberty," for laws prohibiting discrimination against immigrants by employers, colleges, and government agencies. The Americanization movement, declared a Polish newspaper in Chicago, had "not the smallest particle of the true American spirit, the spirit of freedom, the brightest virtue of which is the broadest possible tolerance."

> *Ethnic Americans*

The efforts of immigrant communities to resist coerced Americanization and of the Catholic Church to defend its school system broadened the definition of liberty for all Americans. In landmark decisions, the Supreme Court struck down Oregon's law, mentioned earlier, requiring all students to attend public schools and Nebraska's prohibiting teaching in a language other than English—one of the anti-German measures of World War I. "The protection of the Constitution," the decision in *Meyer v. Nebraska* (1923) declared, "extends to all, to those who speak other languages as well as to those born with English on the tongue," a startling rebuke to enforced Americanization. The decision expanded the freedom of all immigrant groups. In its aftermath, federal courts overturned various Hawaii laws imposing special taxes and regulations on private Japanese-language schools. In these cases, the Court also interpreted the Fourteenth Amendment's guarantee of equal liberty to include the right to "marry, establish a home and bring up children" and to practice religion as one chose, "without interference from the state." The

> *Freedom broadened*

A foundation for pluralism

decisions gave pluralism a constitutional foundation and paved the way for the Court's elaboration, two generations later, of a constitutional right to privacy.

The Emergence of Harlem

The 1920s also witnessed an upsurge of self-consciousness among black Americans, especially in the North's urban ghettos. With European immigration all but halted, the Great Migration of World War I continued apace. Nearly 1 million blacks left the South during the 1920s, and the black population of New York, Chicago, and other urban centers more than doubled. New York's Harlem gained an international reputation as the "capital" of black America, a mecca for migrants from the South and immigrants from the West Indies, 150,000 of whom entered the United States between 1900 and 1930. Unlike the southern newcomers, most of whom had been agricultural workers, the West Indians included a large number of well-educated professional and white-collar workers. Their encounter with American racism appalled them. "I had heard of prejudice in America," wrote the poet and novelist Claude McKay, who emigrated from Jamaica in 1912, "but never dreamed of it being so intensely bitter."

The capital of black America

The 1920s became famous for "slumming," as groups of whites visited Harlem's dance halls, jazz clubs, and speakeasies in search of exotic adventure. The Harlem of the white imagination was a place of primitive passions, free from the puritanical restraints of mainstream American culture. The real Harlem was a community of widespread poverty, its residents confined to low-wage jobs and, because housing discrimination barred them from other neighborhoods, forced to pay exorbitant

"Slumming"

A black family arriving in Chicago in 1922, as part of the Great Migration from the rural South.

rents. Most Harlem businesses were owned by whites; even the famed Cotton Club excluded black customers and employed only light-skinned dancers in its renowned chorus line. Few blacks, North or South, shared in the prosperity of the 1920s.

The Harlem Renaissance

But Harlem also contained a vibrant black cultural community that established links with New York's artistic mainstream. Poets and novelists like Countee Cullen, Langston Hughes, and Claude McKay were befriended and sponsored by white intellectuals and published by white presses. Broadway for the first time presented black actors in serious dramatic roles, as well as shows like *Dixie to Broadway* and *Blackbirds* that featured great entertainers including the singers Florence Mills and Ethel Waters and the tap dancer Bill Robinson. At the same time, the theater flourished in Harlem, freeing black writers and actors from the constraints imposed by white producers.

The term "**New Negro**," associated in politics with pan-Africanism and the militancy of the Garvey movement, in art meant the rejection of established stereotypes and a search for black values to put in their place. This quest led the writers of what came to be called the **Harlem Renaissance** to the roots of the black experience—Africa, the rural South's folk traditions, and the life of the urban ghetto. Claude McKay made the major character of his novel *Home to Harlem* (1928) a free spirit who wandered from one scene of exotic life to another in search of a beautiful girl he had known. W. E. B. Du Bois feared that a novel like McKay's, with its graphic sex and violence, actually reinforced white prejudices about black life. Harlem Renaissance writings, however, also contained a strong element of protest. This mood was exemplified by McKay's poem "If We Must Die," a response to the race riots of 1919. The poem affirmed that blacks would no longer allow themselves to be murdered defenselessly by whites:

> If we must die, let it not be like hogs
> Hunted and penned in an inglorious spot,

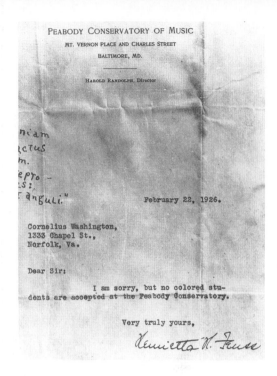

Racism severely limited the opportunities open to black Americans. Here, the internationally renowned Peabody Conservatory of Music informs a black applicant that he cannot pursue his musical education there.

Segregated institutions sprang up to serve the expanding black communities created by the Great Migration. Here, black residents of the nation's capital enjoy an outing at Suburban Gardens, a black-owned amusement park.

While round us bark the mad and hungry dogs,
Making their mock at our accursed lot. . . .
Like men we'll face the murderous, cowardly pack,
Pressed to the wall, dying, but fighting back!

Winston Churchill would invoke McKay's words to inspire the British public during World War II.

Ossian Sweet

The celebrated case of Ossian Sweet, a black physician who moved into a previously all-white Detroit neighborhood in 1925, reflected the new spirit of assertiveness among many African-Americans. When a white mob attacked his home, someone (probably Sweet's brother) fired into the crowd, killing a man. Indicted for murder along with his two brothers, Sweet was defended by Clarence Darrow, fresh from his participation in the Scopes trial. The jury proved unable to agree on a verdict. A second prosecution, of Sweet's brother, ended in acquittal.

THE GREAT DEPRESSION

The Election of 1928

Few men elected as president have seemed destined for a more successful term in office than Herbert Hoover. Born in Iowa in 1874, the son of a blacksmith and his schoolteacher wife, Hoover accumulated a fortune as a mining engineer working for firms in Asia, Africa, and Europe. During and immediately after World War I, he gained international fame by coordinating overseas food relief. The British economist John Maynard Keynes, a severe critic of the 1919 Versailles Treaty, called Hoover "the only man" to emerge from the peace conference "with an enhanced reputation." He "had never known failure," wrote the novelist Sherwood Anderson. Hoover seemed to exemplify what was widely called the "new era" of American capitalism. In 1922, while serving as secretary of commerce, he published *American Individualism*, which condemned government regulation as an interference with the economic opportunities of ordinary Americans, but also insisted that self-interest should be subordinated to public service. Hoover considered himself a Progressive, although he preferred what he called "associational action," in which private agencies directed regulatory and welfare policies, to government intervention in the economy.

After "silent Cal" Coolidge in 1927 handed a piece of paper to a group of reporters that

A 1928 campaign poster for the Republican ticket of Herbert Hoover and Charles Curtis.

stated, "I do not choose to run for president in 1928," Hoover quickly emerged as his successor. Accepting the Republican nomination, Hoover celebrated the decade's prosperity and promised that poverty would "soon be banished from this earth." His Democratic opponent was Alfred E. Smith, the first Catholic to be nominated by a major party. Born into poverty on New York's Lower East Side, Smith had become a fixture in Tammany Hall politics. Although he had no family connection with the new immigrants from southern and eastern Europe (his grandparents had emigrated from Ireland), Smith became their symbolic spokesman. The Triangle fire of 1911 made him an advocate of Progressive social legislation. He served three terms as governor of New York, securing passage of laws limiting the hours of working women and children and establishing widows' pensions. Smith denounced the Red Scare and called for the repeal of Prohibition. His bid for the Democratic nomination in 1924 had been blocked by delegates beholden to nativists and Klansmen, but he secured the nod four years later.

Given the prevailing prosperity and his own sterling reputation, Hoover's victory was inevitable. Other than on Prohibition, moreover, the Democratic platform did not differ much from the Republican one, leaving little to discuss except the candidates' personalities and religions. Smith's Catholicism became the focus of the race. Many Protestant ministers and religious publications denounced him for his faith. For the first time since Reconstruction, Republicans carried several southern states, reflecting the strength of anti-Catholicism and nativism among religious fundamentalists. "Hoover," wrote one previously Democratic southern newspaper editor, "is sprung from American soil and stock," while Smith represented "the aliens." On the other hand, Smith carried the nation's twelve largest cities and won significant support in economically struggling farm areas. With more than 58 percent of the vote, Hoover was elected by a landslide. But Smith's campaign helped to lay the foundation for the triumphant Democratic coalition of the 1930s, based on urban ethnic voters, farmers, and the South.

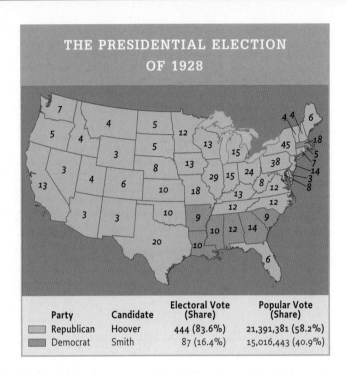

THE PRESIDENTIAL ELECTION OF 1928

Party	Candidate	Electoral Vote (Share)	Popular Vote (Share)
Republican	Hoover	444 (83.6%)	21,391,381 (58.2%)
Democrat	Smith	87 (16.4%)	15,016,443 (40.9%)

Role of religion in the election

President Herbert Hoover (front row, right), at the opening day baseball game in Washington, April 17, 1929.

The Coming of the Depression

On October 21, 1929, President Hoover traveled to Michigan to take part in the Golden Anniversary of the Festival of Light, organized by Henry Ford to commemorate the invention of the lightbulb by Thomas Edison fifty years earlier. Hoover's speech was a tribute to progress, and especially to the businessmen and scientists from whose efforts "we gain constantly in better standards of living, more stability of employment . . . and decreased suffering." Eight days later, on Black Tuesday, the stock market crashed. As panic selling set in, more than $10 billion in market value (equivalent to more than ten times that amount in today's money) vanished in five hours. Soon, the United States and, indeed, the entire world found themselves in the grip of the **Great Depression**, the greatest economic disaster in modern history.

BUY! REPEATED
BUY! PERSISTENT
BUY! ADVICES

The American Institute of Finance *repeatedly* and *persistently* recommends the purchase of *the same* stock. This persistent repetition on the same stock makes it practically impossible for the advice to escape the attention of clients.

The following nine stocks have been definitely recommended for purchase no less than 113 times in a twenty-month period—an average of over five recommendations a month.

Have *YOU* made *REAL PROFITS* in These Stocks?
Did *YOU* BUY

(14 advices in 18 mos.)	Allied Chemical	@	140 up—now 290
(12 advices in 19 mos.)	Air Reduction	@	138 up—now 330
(11 advices in 18 mos.)	American Smelting	@	155 up—now 360
(10 advices in 20 mos.)	Chicago, R. I. & Pacific	@	70 up—now 135
(10 advices in 18 mos.)	Gold Dust Corp.	@	45 up—now 150
(11 advices in 19 mos.)	Inter. Harvester	@	135 up—now 400
(10 advices in 18 mos.)	Jewel Tea	@	58 up—now 170*
(18 advices in 20 mos.)	Mathieson Alkali	@	86 up—now 190
(17 advices in 19 mos.)	Peoples Gas	@	128 up—now 250

* Price includes recent "rights."

Three months before the stock market crash, *The Magazine of Wall Street* was avidly encouraging readers to purchase stocks.

Oct. 29—Dies Irae, a 1929 lithograph by James N. Rosenberg, depicts skyscrapers tottering, stockbrokers jumping from windows, and crowds panicking as the stock market crashes. The title means "Day of Wrath."

The **stock market crash** did not, by itself, cause the Depression. Even before 1929, signs of economic trouble had become evident. Southern California and Florida experienced frenzied real-estate speculation and then spectacular busts, with banks failing, land remaining undeveloped, and mortgages foreclosed. The highly unequal distribution of income and the prolonged depression in farm regions reduced American purchasing power. Sales of new autos and household consumer goods stagnated after 1926. European demand for American goods also declined, partly because industry there had recovered from wartime destruction.

A fall in the bloated stock market, driven ever higher during the 1920s by speculators, was inevitable. But it came with such severity that it destroyed many of the investment companies that had been created to buy and sell stock, wiping out thousands of investors, and it greatly reduced business and consumer confidence. Around 26,000 businesses failed in 1930. Those that survived cut back on further investment and began laying off workers. The global financial system, which was based on the gold standard, was ill equipped to deal with the downturn. Germany defaulted on reparations payments to France and Britain, leading these governments to stop repaying debts to American banks. Throughout the industrial world, banks failed as depositors withdrew money, fearful that they could no longer count on the promise to redeem paper money in gold. Millions of families lost their life savings.

Although stocks recovered somewhat in 1930, they soon resumed their relentless downward slide. Between 1929 and 1932, the price of a share of U.S. Steel fell from $262 to $22, and General Motors from $73 to $8. Four-fifths of the Rockefeller family fortune disappeared. William C. Durant, one of the founders of General Motors, lost all his money and ended up running a bowling alley in Flint, Michigan. In 1932, the economy hit rock bottom. Since 1929, the gross national product (the value of all the goods and services in the country) had fallen by one-third, prices by nearly 40 percent, and more than 11 million Americans—25 percent of the labor force—could not find work. U.S. Steel, which had employed 225,000 full-time workers in 1929, had none at the end of 1932, when it was operating at only 12 percent of capacity. Those who retained their jobs confronted reduced hours and dramatically reduced wages. Every industrial economy suffered, but the United States, which had led the way in prosperity in the 1920s, was hit hardest of all.

Americans and the Depression

The Depression transformed American life. Hundreds of thousands of people took to the road in search of work. Hungry men and women lined the streets of major cities. In Detroit, 4,000 children stood in bread lines each day seeking food. Thousands of families, evicted from their homes, moved into ramshackle shantytowns, dubbed Hoovervilles, that sprang up in parks and on abandoned

land. Cities quickly spent the little money they had available for poor relief. In Chicago, where half the working population was unemployed at the beginning of 1932, Mayor Anton Cermak telephoned people individually, begging them to pay their taxes. "We saw want and despair walking the streets," wrote a Chicago social worker, "and our friends, sensible, thrifty families, reduced to poverty." When the Soviet Union advertised its need for skilled workers, it received more than 100,000 applications from the United States.

The Depression actually reversed the long-standing movement of population from farms to cities. Many Americans left cities to try to grow food for their families. In 1935, 33 million people lived on farms—more than at any previous point in American history. But rural areas, already poor, saw families reduce the number of meals per day and children go barefoot. With the future shrouded in uncertainty, the American suicide rate rose to the highest level in the nation's history, and the birthrate fell to the lowest.

"The American way of life," the confident slogan of the consumer culture, and common sayings like "safe as a bank" took on a hollow ring. The image of big business, carefully cultivated during the 1920s, collapsed as congressional investigations revealed massive irregularities committed by bankers and stockbrokers. Banks had knowingly sold worthless bonds. Prominent Wall Streeters had unloaded their own portfolios while advising small investors to maintain their holdings. Richard Whitney, the president of the New York Stock Exchange, was convicted of stealing from customers, including from a fund to aid widows and orphans. He ended up in jail.

Unemployed men lined up outside a Chicago soup kitchen in 1931. Charitable institutions like this one were overwhelmed by the advent of the Great Depression.

The celebrated photographer Dorothea Lange took this photograph of an unemployed man on a San Francisco breadline in 1933.

Resignation and Protest

Many Americans reacted to the Depression with resignation or blamed themselves for economic misfortune. Others responded with protests that were at first spontaneous and uncoordinated, since unions, socialist organizations, and other groups

Police battling "bonus marchers" in Washington, D.C., July 1932. Soon afterward, President Hoover sent federal troops to evict the marchers.

Nation-wide protests and demonstrations

that might have provided disciplined leadership had been decimated during the 1920s. In the spring of 1932, 20,000 unemployed World War I veterans descended on Washington to demand early payment of a bonus due in 1945, only to be driven away by federal soldiers led by the army's chief of staff, Douglas MacArthur. Throughout the country, the unemployed demonstrated for jobs and public relief. That summer, led by the charismatic Milo Reno, a former Iowa Populist, the National Farmers' Holiday Association protested low prices by temporarily blocking roads in the Midwest to prevent farm goods from getting to market.

Communist Party

Only the minuscule Communist Party seemed able to give a political focus to the anger and despair. "The most fully employed persons I met during the Depression," one labor leader later recalled, "were the Communists." They "brought misery out of hiding," forming unemployed councils, sponsoring marches and demonstrations for public assistance, and protesting the eviction of unemployed families from their homes. The press discussed the idea that the United States was on the verge of a revolution. The insurance firm Lloyd's of London reported an upsurge in American requests for riot insurance. The Hoover administration in 1931 opposed efforts to save money by reducing the size of the army, warning that this would "lessen our means of maintaining domestic peace and order."

Hoover's Response

In the eyes of many Americans, President Hoover's response to the Depression seemed inadequate and uncaring. Leading advisers, including Andrew Mellon, the wealthy secretary of the treasury, told Hoover that economic downturns were a normal part of capitalism, which weeded out unproductive firms and encouraged moral virtue among the less fortunate. Businessmen strongly opposed federal aid to the unemployed, and many publications called for individual "belt-tightening" as the road to recovery. Some initially saw a silver lining in the Depression. Wages had fallen so sharply, reported *Fortune* magazine, that "you can have your garden taken care of in Los Angeles for $1 a week" or hire an "affable Negro to fry your chicken and do your washing for $8 a month in Virginia."

"Belt-tightening"

The federal government had never faced an economic crisis as severe as the Great Depression. Few political leaders understood how important consumer spending had become in the American economy. Most held to the conventional view that government intervention to aid those who had lost their jobs would do little to spur economic recovery and would encourage Americans to rely on government charity to address misfortune. In 1931, Hoover quoted former president Grover Cleveland from four decades earlier: "The Government should not support the people. . . . Federal aid . . . weakens the sturdiness of our national character."

Strongly opposed on principle to direct federal intervention in the economy, Hoover remained committed to "associational action." He put his faith in voluntary steps by business to maintain investment and employment—something few found it possible to do—and efforts by local charity organizations to assist needy neighbors. He called numerous conferences of business and labor leaders and established commissions to encourage firms to cooperate in maintaining prices and wages without governmental dictation. Hoover attempted to restore public confidence, making frequent public statements that "the tide had turned." But these made him increasingly seem out of touch with reality. About the unemployed men who appeared on city streets offering apples at five cents apiece, Hoover would later write, "Many persons left their jobs for the more profitable one of selling apples."

Communist Party headquarters in New York City, 1932. The banners illustrate the variety of activities the party organized in the early 1930s.

The Worsening Economic Outlook

Some administration remedies, like the **Smoot-Hawley Tariff**, which Hoover signed with some reluctance in 1930, made the economic situation worse. Raising the already high taxes on imported goods, it inspired similar increases abroad, further reducing international trade. A tax increase Hoover pushed through Congress in 1932 in an attempt to balance the federal budget further reduced Americans' purchasing power. Other initiatives inspired ridicule. When he approved funds to provide food for livestock, one observer remarked that the president would feed "jackasses but . . . not starving babies."

By 1932, Hoover had to admit that voluntary action had failed to stem the Depression. He signed laws creating the **Reconstruction Finance Corporation**, which loaned money to failing banks, railroads, and other businesses, and the Federal Home Loan Bank System, which offered aid to homeowners threatened with foreclosure. Having vetoed previous bills to create employment through public-works projects like road and bridge construction, he now approved a measure appropriating nearly $2 billion for such initiatives and helping to fund local relief efforts. These were dramatic departures from previous federal economic policy. But further than this, Hoover would not go. He adamantly opposed offering direct relief to the unemployed—it would do them a "disservice," he told Congress.

Government action

A Hooverville—a shantytown created by homeless squatters—outside Seattle, Washington, in 1933.

Assessing freedom in the 1920s

Freedom in the Modern World

In 1927, the New School for Social Research in New York City organized a series of lectures on the theme of Freedom in the Modern World. Founded eight years earlier as a place where "free thought and intellectual integrity" could flourish in the wake of wartime repression, the school's distinguished faculty included the philosopher John Dewey and historian Charles Beard (who had resigned from Columbia University in 1917 to protest the dismissal of antiwar professors). The lectures painted a depressing portrait of American freedom on the eve of the Great Depression. "The idea of freedom," declared economist Walton H. Hamilton, had become "an intellectual instrument for looking backward. . . . Liberty of contract has been made the be-all and end-all of personal freedom; . . . the domain of business has been defended against control from without in the name of freedom." The free exchange of ideas, moreover, had not recovered from the crisis of World War I. The "sacred dogmas of patriotism and Big Business," said the educator Horace Kallen, dominated teaching, the press, and public debate. A definition of freedom reigned supreme that celebrated the unimpeded reign of economic enterprise yet tolerated the surveillance of private life and individual conscience.

An unemployed man and woman selling apples on a city street during the Great Depression.

The prosperity of the 1920s had reinforced this definition of freedom. With the economic crash, compounded by the ineffectiveness of the Hoover administration's response, it would be discredited. By 1932, the seeds had already been planted for a new conception of freedom that combined two different elements in a sometimes uneasy synthesis. One was the Progressive belief in a socially conscious state making what Dewey called "positive and constructive changes" in economic arrangements. The other, which arose in the 1920s, centered on respect for civil liberties and cultural pluralism and declared that realms of life like group identity, personal behavior, and the free expression of ideas lay outside legitimate state concern. These two principles would become the hallmarks of modern liberalism, which during the 1930s would redefine American freedom.

A new conception of freedom

CHAPTER 21

THE NEW DEAL

★

1932–1940

Early in 1941, the unemployed Woody Guthrie, soon to become one of the country's most popular songwriters and folk singers, brought his family to Portland, Oregon. He hoped to star in a film about the great public-works projects under way on the Columbia River. Given a temporary job by the Bonneville Power Authority, the public agency that controlled the Columbia dams, Guthrie produced a song every day for the next month. One, "Roll on, Columbia," became a popular statement of the benefits that resulted when government took the lead in improving the lot of ordinary citizens:

> And on up the river is Grand Coulee Dam,
> The mightiest thing ever built by a man,
> To run the great factories and water the land,
> It's roll on, Columbia, roll on. . . .
> Your power is turning our darkness to dawn.
> So, roll on, Columbia, roll on.©

The Columbia River winds its way on a 1,200-mile course from Canada through Washington and Oregon to the Pacific Ocean. Because of its steep descent from uplands to sea level, it produces an immense amount of energy. Residents of the economically underdeveloped Pacific Northwest had long dreamed of tapping this unused energy for electricity and irrigation. But not until the 1930s did the federal government launch the program of dam construction that transformed the region. The project created thousands of jobs for the unemployed, and the network of dams produced abundant cheap power.

When the Grand Coulee Dam went into operation in 1941, it was the largest man-made structure in world history. It eventually produced more than 40 percent of the nation's hydroelectric power. The dam provided the cheapest electricity in the country for towns that sprang up out of nowhere, farms on what had once been deserts in eastern Washington and Oregon, and factories that would soon be producing aluminum for World War II airplanes. The project also had less appealing consequences. From time immemorial, the Columbia River had been filled with salmon. But the Grand Coulee Dam made no provision for the passage of fish, and the salmon all but vanished. This caused little concern during the Depression but became a source of controversy later in the century as Americans became more attuned to preserving the natural environment.

The Grand Coulee Dam was part of what one scholar has called a "public works revolution" that transformed the American economy and landscape during the 1930s. The Roosevelt administration spent far more money on building roads, dams, airports, bridges, and housing than on any other activity.

Franklin D. Roosevelt believed regional economic development like that in the Northwest would promote economic growth, ease the domestic and working lives of ordinary Americans, and keep control of key natural resources in public rather than private hands. "It promises," one supporter wrote, "a world replete with more freedom and happiness than mankind has ever known."

The Columbia River project reflected broader changes in American life and thought during the **New Deal** of the 1930s. Roosevelt oversaw the transformation

FOCUS QUESTIONS

What were the major policy initiatives of the New Deal in the Hundred Days? *-p. 804*

Who were the main proponents of economic justice in the 1930s, and what measures did they advocate? *-p. 815*

What were the major initiatives of the Second New Deal, and how did they differ from the First New Deal? *-p. 820*

How did the New Deal recast the meaning of American freedom? *-p. 823*

How did New Deal benefits apply to women and minorities? *-p. 829*

How did the Popular Front influence American culture in the 1930s? *-p. 835*

An unusual piece of folk art, this painting by Frank Teacher Jr., a worker in a coal mine near Pittsburgh, celebrates President Franklin D. Roosevelt and his alliance with organized labor—in this case, the United Mine Workers of America—during the New Deal. Teacher died in a mine accident in 1958.

803

of the Democratic Party into a coalition of farmers, industrial workers, the reform-minded urban middle class, liberal intellectuals, northern African-Americans, and, somewhat incongruously, the white supremacist South, united by the belief that the federal government must provide Americans with protection against the dislocations caused by modern capitalism. "Liberalism," traditionally understood as limited government and free-market economics, took on its modern meaning. Thanks to the New Deal, it now referred to active efforts by the national government to modernize and regulate the market economy and to uplift less fortunate members of society.

Freedom, too, underwent a transformation during the 1930s. The Depression had discredited the ideas that social progress rests on the unrestrained pursuit of wealth and that, apart from unfortunates like widows and orphans, most poverty is self-inflicted. The New Deal elevated a public guarantee of economic security to the forefront of American discussions of freedom. The 1930s were a decade of dramatic social upheaval. Social and political activists, most notably a revitalized labor movement, placed new issues on the political agenda. When one writer in 1941 published a survey of democratic thought beginning in the ancient world, he concluded that what distinguished his own time was its awareness of "the social conditions of freedom." Thanks to the New Deal, he wrote, "economic security" had "at last been recognized as a political condition of personal freedom." Regional economic development like that in the Northwest reflected this understanding of freedom. So did other New Deal measures, including the Social Security Act, which offered aid to the unemployed and aged, and the Fair Labor Standards Act, which established a national minimum wage.

Yet while the New Deal significantly expanded the meaning of freedom, it did not erase freedom's boundaries. Its benefits flowed to industrial workers but not tenant farmers, to men far more fully than women, and to white Americans more than blacks, who, in the South, still were deprived of the basic rights of citizenship.

THE FIRST NEW DEAL

FDR and the Election of 1932

It is indeed paradoxical that Franklin D. Roosevelt, who had been raised in privilege on a New York country estate, came to be beloved as the symbolic representative of ordinary citizens. But like Lincoln, with whom he is often compared, Roosevelt's greatness lay in his willingness to throw off the "dogmas of the quiet past" (Lincoln's words) to confront an unprecedented national crisis. FDR, as he liked to be called, was born in 1882, a fifth cousin of Theodore Roosevelt. He graduated from Harvard in 1904 and six years later won election to the New York legislature from Duchess County, site of his family's home at Hyde Park. After serving as undersecretary of the navy during World War I, he ran for vice president on the ill-fated Democratic ticket of 1920 headed by James M. Cox. In 1921, he contracted polio and lost the use of his legs, a fact carefully concealed from the

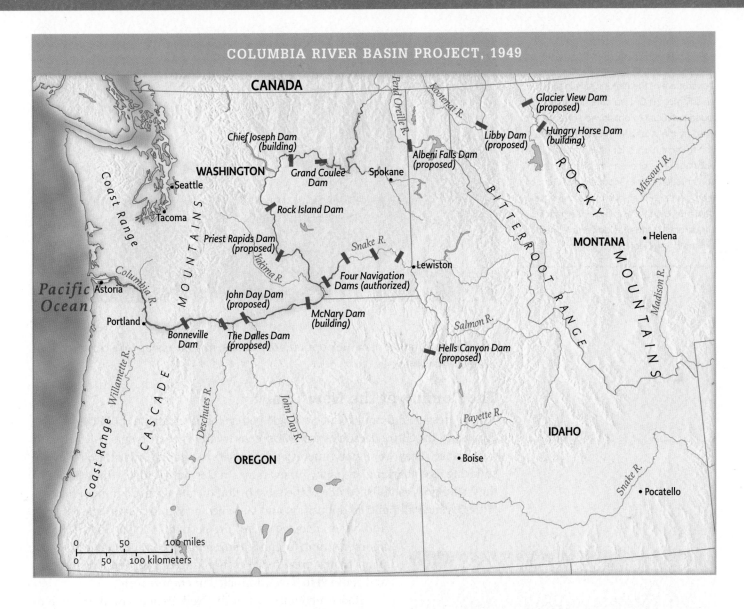

COLUMBIA RIVER BASIN PROJECT, 1949

A 1949 map of the Columbia River project, showing its numerous dams, including the Grand Coulee, the largest man-made structure in the world at the time of its opening in 1941.

public in that pre-television era. Very few Americans realized that the president who projected an image of vigorous leadership during the 1930s and World War II was confined to a wheelchair.

In his speech accepting the Democratic nomination for president in 1932, Roosevelt promised a "new deal" for the American people. But his campaign offered only vague hints of what this might entail. Roosevelt spoke of the government's responsibility to guarantee "every man . . . a right to make a comfortable living." But he also advocated a balanced federal budget and criticized his opponent, President Hoover, for excessive government spending. The biggest difference between the parties during the campaign was the Democrats' call for the repeal of Prohibition, although Roosevelt certainly suggested a greater awareness of the plight of ordinary Americans and a willingness to embark on new ways to address the Great Depression. Battered by the economic crisis, Americans in 1932 were desperate for new leadership, and Roosevelt won a resounding victory.

A "new deal"

This panel depicting the construction of a dam was painted in 1939 by William Gropper as part of a mural for the new Department of the Interior building in Washington, D.C. Like other artists who found it difficult to obtain work, he was hired by the Works Progress Administration to paint murals for government buildings. This one was inspired by the construction of the Grand Coulee Dam on the Columbia River, one of the many New Deal projects that expanded the nation's infrastructure and provided employment to victims of the Depression.

He received 57 percent of the popular vote, and Democrats swept to a commanding majority in Congress.

The Coming of the New Deal

The Depression did not produce a single pattern of international public response. For nearly the entire decade of the 1930s, conservative governments ruled Britain and France. They were more interested in preserving public order than relieving suffering or embarking on policy innovations. In Germany, Adolf Hitler, leader of the Nazi Party, established one of the most brutal dictatorships in human history. Hitler banned all political opposition and launched a reign of terror against Jews and others deemed to be "un-German." In the Soviet Union, another tyrant, Joseph Stalin, embarked on successive five-year plans that at great social cost produced rapid industrialization and claimed to have eliminated unemployment.

Roosevelt conceived of the New Deal as an alternative to socialism on the left, Nazism on the right, and the inaction of upholders of unregulated capitalism. He hoped to reconcile democracy, individual liberty, and economic recovery and development. "You have made yourself," the British economist John Maynard Keynes wrote to FDR, "the trustee for those in every country who seek to mend the evils of our condition by reasoned experiment within the framework of the existing social system." If Roosevelt failed, Keynes added, the only remaining choice would be between "orthodoxy" (that is, doing nothing) and "revolution."

Roosevelt did not enter office with a blueprint for dealing with the Depression. At first, he relied heavily for advice on a group of intellectuals and social workers who took up key positions in his administration. They included Secretary of Labor Frances Perkins, a veteran of Hull House and the New

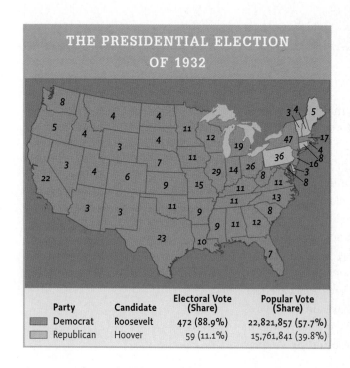

THE PRESIDENTIAL ELECTION OF 1932

Party	Candidate	Electoral Vote (Share)	Popular Vote (Share)
Democrat	Roosevelt	472 (88.9%)	22,821,857 (57.7%)
Republican	Hoover	59 (11.1%)	15,761,841 (39.8%)

York Consumers' League who had been among the eyewitnesses to the Triangle fire of 1911; Harry Hopkins, who had headed emergency relief efforts during Roosevelt's term as governor of New York; Secretary of the Interior Harold Ickes, a veteran of Theodore Roosevelt's Progressive campaign of 1912; and Louis Brandeis, who had advised Woodrow Wilson during the 1912 campaign and now offered political advice to FDR while serving on the Supreme Court.

The presence of these individuals reflected how Roosevelt drew on the reform traditions of the Progressive era. But Progressivism, as noted in Chapter 18, was hardly a unified movement, and Roosevelt's advisers did not speak with one voice. Brandeis believed that large corporations not only wielded excessive power but also had contributed to the Depression by keeping prices artificially high and failing to increase workers' purchasing power. They should be broken up, he insisted, not regulated. But the "brains trust"—a group of academics that included a number of Columbia University professors—saw bigness as inevitable in a modern economy. The competitive marketplace, they argued, was a thing of the past, and large firms needed to be managed and directed by the government, not dismantled. Their view prevailed during what came to be called the First New Deal.

Presidents Herbert Hoover and Franklin D. Roosevelt on their way to the latter's inauguration on March 4, 1933. The two men strongly disliked one another. They barely spoke during the ride and never saw each other again after that day.

The Banking Crisis

"This nation asks for action and action now," Roosevelt announced on taking office on March 4, 1933. The country, wrote the journalist and political commentator Walter Lippmann, "was in such a state of confused desperation that it would have followed almost any leader anywhere he chose to go." FDR spent much of 1933

A "run" on a bank: crowds of people wait outside a New York City bank, hoping to withdraw their money.

The Spirit of the New Deal, a 1933 cartoon in the *Washington Star*, depicts the federal government, through the National Recovery Administration, promoting peace between workers and employers.

trying to reassure the public. In his inaugural address, he declared that "the only thing we have to fear is fear itself." (See the Appendix for the full text.)

Roosevelt confronted a banking system on the verge of collapse. As bank funds invested in the stock market and corporate bonds lost their value and panicked depositors withdrew their savings, bank after bank had closed its doors. By March 1933, banking had been suspended in a majority of the states—that is, people could not gain access to money in their bank accounts. Roosevelt declared a "bank holiday," temporarily halting all bank operations, and called Congress into special session. On March 9, it rushed to pass the **Emergency Banking Act**, which provided funds to shore up threatened institutions.

Further measures soon followed that transformed the American financial system. The Glass-Steagall Act barred commercial banks from becoming involved in the buying and selling of stocks. Until its repeal in the 1990s, the law prevented many of the irresponsible practices that had contributed to the stock market crash. The same law established the Federal Deposit Insurance Corporation (FDIC), a government system that insured the accounts of individual depositors. And Roosevelt took the United States off the gold standard—that is, he severed the link between the country's currency and its gold reserves, thus making possible the issuance of more money in the hope of stimulating business activity. Together, these measures rescued the financial system and greatly increased the government's power over it. About 5,000 banks—one-third of the nation's total—had failed between 1929 and 1933, representing a loss of tens of millions of dollars to depositors. In 1936, not a single bank failed in the United States.

The NRA

The Emergency Banking Act was the first of an unprecedented flurry of legislation during the first three months of Roosevelt's administration, a period known as the **Hundred Days**. Seizing on the sense of crisis and the momentum of his electoral victory, Roosevelt won rapid passage of laws he hoped would promote economic recovery. He persuaded Congress to create a host of new agencies, whose initials soon became part of the language of politics—NRA, AAA, CCC. Never in American history had a president exercised such power in peacetime or so rapidly expanded the role of the federal government in people's lives.

The centerpiece of Roosevelt's plan for combating the Depression, the **National Industrial Recovery Act**, was to a large extent modeled on the government–business partnership established by the War Industries Board of World War I, although in keeping with FDR's nondogmatic approach, it also owed something to Herbert Hoover's efforts to build stronger government–business cooperation. Roosevelt called it "the most important and far-reaching legislation ever enacted by the American Congress." The act established the **National Recovery Administration**

Expanded role of federal government

(NRA), which would work with groups of business leaders to establish industry codes that set standards for output, prices, and working conditions. Thus, "cutthroat" competition (in which companies took losses to drive competitors out of business) would be ended. These industry-wide arrangements would be exempt from antitrust laws.

The NRA reflected how even in its early days, the New Deal reshaped understandings of freedom. In effect, FDR had repudiated the older idea of liberty based on the idea that the best way to encourage economic activity and ensure a fair distribution of wealth was to allow market competition to operate, unrestrained by the government. And to win support from labor, section 7a of the new law recognized the workers' right to organize unions—a departure from the "open shop" policies of the 1920s and a step toward government support for what workers called "industrial freedom."

Right to organize unions

Headed by Hugh S. Johnson, a retired general and businessman, the NRA quickly established codes that set standards for production, prices, and wages in the textile, steel, mining, and auto industries. Johnson launched a publicity campaign to promote the NRA and its symbol, the Blue Eagle, which stores and factories that abided by the codes displayed. But after initial public enthusiasm, the NRA became mired in controversy. Large companies dominated the code-writing process. An inquiry conducted by the labor lawyer Clarence Darrow in 1934 concluded that they used the NRA to drive up prices, limit production, lay off workers, and divide markets among themselves at the expense of smaller competitors. Many anti-union employers ignored section 7a. The government lacked the manpower to police the 750 codes in effect by 1935. The NRA produced neither economic recovery nor peace between employers and workers. It did, however, help to undercut the pervasive sense that the federal government was doing nothing to deal with the economic crisis.

NRA controversy

A Civilian Conservation Corps workforce in Yosemite National Park, 1935.

Government Jobs

Relief

The Hundred Days also brought the government into providing relief to those in need. Roosevelt and most of his advisers shared the widespread fear that direct government payments to the unemployed would undermine individual self-reliance. Indeed, one of the first measures of the Hundred Days had been the Economy Act, which reduced federal spending in an attempt to win the confidence of the business community. But with nearly a quarter of the workforce unemployed, spending on relief was unavoidable. In May 1933, Congress created the Federal Emergency Relief Administration, to make grants to local agencies that aided those impoverished by the Depression. FDR, however, much preferred to create temporary jobs, thereby combating unemployment while improving the nation's infrastructure of roads, bridges, public buildings, and parks.

In March 1933, Congress established the **Civilian Conservation Corps** (CCC), which set unemployed young men to work on projects like forest preservation, flood control, and the improvement of national parks and wildlife preserves. By the time the program ended in 1942, more than 3 million persons had passed through CCC camps, where they received government wages of $30 per month. The CCC made a major contribution to the enhancement of the American environment.

Public-Works Projects

One section of the National Industrial Recovery Act created the **Public Works Administration** (PWA), with an appropriation of $3.3 billion. Directed by Secretary

A map published by the Public Works Administration in 1935 depicts some of the numerous infrastructure projects funded by the New Deal. Among the most famous public-works projects are the Triborough Bridge in New York City, the Overseas Highway in Florida, and the Grand Coulee Dam in Washington. Overall, the New Deal spent $250 billion (in today's money) to construct, among other things, 40,000 public buildings, 72,000 schools, 80,000 bridges, and 8,000 parks.

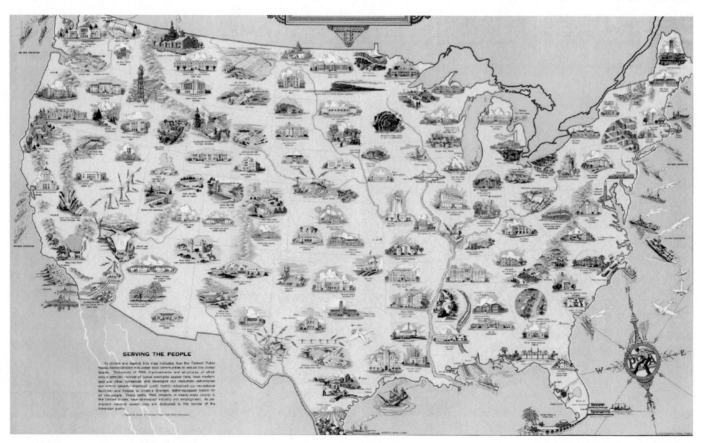

SERVING THE PEOPLE

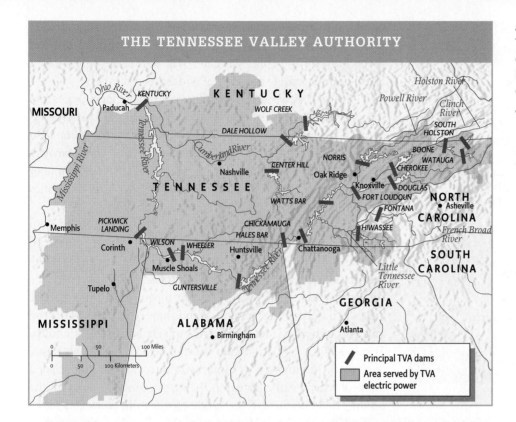

THE TENNESSEE VALLEY AUTHORITY

A map showing the reach of the Tennessee Valley Authority, covering all or parts of seven southeastern states. Numerous reservoirs and power plants dot the landscape.

of the Interior Harold Ickes, it contracted with private construction companies to build roads, schools, hospitals, and other public facilities, including New York City's Triborough Bridge and the Overseas Highway between Miami and Key West, Florida. In November 1933, yet another agency, the Civil Works Administration (CWA), was launched. Unlike the PWA, it directly hired workers for construction projects. By January 1934, it employed more than 4 million persons in the construction of highways, tunnels, courthouses, and airports. But as the cost spiraled upward and complaints multiplied that the New Deal was creating a class of Americans permanently dependent on government jobs, Roosevelt ordered the CWA dissolved.

> *The CWA*

Some New Deal public-works initiatives looked to government-planned economic transformation as much as economic relief. The **Tennessee Valley Authority** (TVA), another product of the Hundred Days, built a series of dams to prevent floods and deforestation along the Tennessee River and to provide cheap electric power for homes and factories in a seven-state region where many families still lived in isolated log cabins. The TVA put the federal government, for the first time, in the business of selling electricity in competition with private companies. It significantly improved the lives of many southerners and offered a preview of the program of regional planning that spurred the economic development of the West.

> *The TVA*

The New Deal and Agriculture

Another policy initiative of the Hundred Days addressed the disastrous plight of American farmers. The **Agricultural Adjustment Act** (AAA) authorized the federal government to set production quotas for major crops and pay farmers to

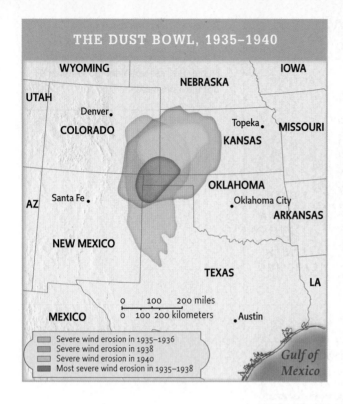

THE DUST BOWL, 1935–1940

WYOMING

NEBRASKA

IOWA

UTAH

Denver

COLORADO

Topeka

MISSOURI

KANSAS

AZ

Santa Fe

OKLAHOMA

Oklahoma City

ARKANSAS

NEW MEXICO

TEXAS

LA

0   100   200 miles
0   100 200 kilometers

MEXICO

Austin

Gulf of Mexico

☐ Severe wind erosion in 1935–1936
☐ Severe wind erosion in 1938
☐ Severe wind erosion in 1940
☐ Most severe wind erosion in 1935–1938

plant less in an attempt to raise farm prices. Many crops already in the field were destroyed. In 1933, the government ordered more than 6 million pigs slaughtered as part of the policy, a step critics found strange at a time of widespread hunger.

The AAA succeeded in significantly raising farm prices and incomes. But not all farmers benefited. Money flowed to property-owning farmers, ignoring the large number who worked on land owned by others. The AAA policy of paying landowning farmers not to grow crops encouraged the eviction of thousands of poor tenants and sharecroppers. Many joined the rural exodus to cities or to the farms of the West Coast.

The onset in 1930 of a period of unusually dry weather in the nation's heartland worsened the Depression's impact on rural America. By mid-decade, the region suffered from the century's most severe drought. Mechanized agriculture in this semiarid region had pulverized the topsoil and killed native grasses that prevented erosion. Winds now blew much of the soil away, creating the **Dust Bowl**, as the affected areas of Oklahoma, Texas, Kansas, and Colorado were called. A local newspaper described the situation in Cimarron County, Oklahoma: "Not a blade of wheat; cattle dying on the range, ninety percent of the poultry dead because of the sand storms, milk cows gone dry."

One storm in 1934 carried dust as far as Washington, D.C. The drought and dust storms displaced more than 1 million farmers. John Steinbeck's novel *The Grapes of Wrath* (1939) and a popular film based on the book captured their plight, tracing a dispossessed family's trek from Oklahoma to California.

The Resettlement Administration

Another New Deal initiative, the Resettlement Administration, established in 1934, sought to relocate rural and urban families suffering from the Depression to communities planned by the federal government. Headed by Columbia University

A giant dust storm engulfs a town in western Kansas on April 14, 1935, known as Black Sunday in the American West.

Sharecroppers evicted from the farms on which they had been working in New Madrid County, Missouri, as a result of government subsidies to farm owners to reduce crop production.

economist Rexford G. Tugwell, one of Roosevelt's advisers, it set up relief camps for migrant workers in California (many of whom had been displaced by the dust storms) and built several new communities, including Greenbelt just outside Washington, D.C.

The New Deal and Housing

Owning one's home had long been a widely shared American ambition. "A man is not a whole and complete man," Walt Whitman had written in the 1850s, "unless he owns a house and the ground it stands on." For many members of the middle class, home ownership had become a mark of respectability. For workers, it offered economic security at a time of low wages, erratic employment, and limited occupational mobility. On the eve of World War I, a considerably higher percentage of immigrant workers than the native-born middle class owned their homes.

The Depression devastated the American housing industry. The construction of new residences all but ceased, and banks and savings and loan associations that had financed home ownership collapsed or, to remain afloat, foreclosed on many homes (a quarter of a million in 1932 alone). In 1931, President Hoover convened a Conference on Home Building and Home Ownership to review the housing crisis. The president called owning a home an American "birthright," the embodiment of the spirit of "enterprise, of independence, and of . . . freedom." Rented apartments, he pointed out, did not inspire "immortal ballads" like *Home, Sweet Home* or *The Little Gray Home in the West*. Papers presented at the conference revealed that millions of Americans lived in overcrowded, unhealthy urban slums or in

As it did in other sectors of the economy, the Great Depression led to a collapse in the construction industry.

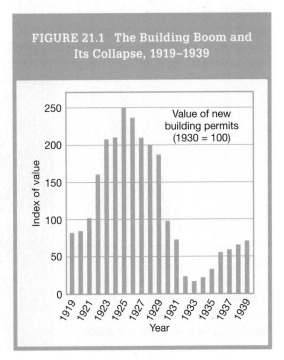

FIGURE 21.1 The Building Boom and Its Collapse, 1919–1939

Value of new building permits (1930 = 100)

A MULE AND A PLOW

RESETTLEMENT ADMINISTRATION
Small Loans Give Farmers a New Start

The artist Bernarda Shahn, wife of the more famous painter Ben Shahn, created this lithograph in the mid-1930s for the Resettlement Administration, a New Deal agency that relocated rural and urban families—especially victims of the Dust Bowl—to planned communities.

ramshackle rural dwellings. Private enterprise alone, it seemed clear, was unlikely to solve the nation's housing crisis.

Hoover's administration established a federally sponsored bank to issue home loans. Not until the New Deal, however, did the government systematically enter the housing market. Roosevelt spoke of "the security of the home" as a fundamental right akin to "the security of livelihood, and the security of social insurance." In 1933 and 1934, his administration moved energetically to protect home owners from foreclosure and to stimulate new construction. The Home Owners Loan Corporation and **Federal Housing Administration** (FHA) insured millions of long-term mortgages issued by private banks. At the same time, the federal government itself built thousands of units of low-rent housing. New Deal housing policy represented a remarkable departure from previous government practice. Thanks to the FHA and, later, the Veterans' Administration, home ownership came within the reach of tens of millions of families. It became cheaper for most Americans to buy single-family homes than to rent apartments.

Other important measures of Roosevelt's first two years in office included the ratification of the Twenty-first Amendment to the Constitution, which repealed Prohibition; the establishment of the Federal Communications Commission to oversee the nation's broadcast airwaves and telephone communications; and the creation of the Securities and Exchange Commission to regulate the stock and bond markets.

Taken together, the First New Deal was a series of experiments, some of which succeeded and some of which did not. They transformed the role of the federal government, constructed numerous public facilities, and provided relief to millions of needy persons. Public employment rescued millions of Americans from the ravages of the Depression. But while the economy improved somewhat, sustained recovery had not been achieved. Some 10 million Americans—more than 20 percent of the workforce—remained unemployed when 1934 came to an end.

Russell Lee's 1939 photograph of a migrant family saying grace before eating by the side of the road near Fort Gibson, Oklahoma, shows how, even in the most difficult circumstances, families struggled to maintain elements of their normal lives.

The Court and the New Deal

In 1935, the Supreme Court, still controlled by conservative Republican judges who held to the nineteenth-century understanding of freedom as liberty of contract, began to invalidate key New Deal laws. First came the NRA, declared unconstitutional in May in a case brought by the Schechter Poultry Company of Brooklyn, which had been charged with violating the code adopted by the chicken industry. In a unanimous decision, the Court declared the NRA unlawful because in its codes and other regulations it delegated legislative powers to the president and attempted to regulate local businesses that did not engage in interstate commerce. In January 1936, the AAA fell in *United States v. Butler*, which declared it an unconstitutional exercise of congressional power over local economic activities. In June, by a 5-4 vote, the justices ruled that New York could not establish a minimum wage for women and children.

Having failed to end the Depression or win judicial approval, the First New Deal ground to a halt. Meanwhile, pressures were mounting outside Washington that propelled the administration toward more radical departures in policy.

THE GRASSROOTS REVOLT

Labor's Great Upheaval

The most striking development of the mid-1930s was the mobilization of millions of workers in mass-production industries that had successfully resisted unionization. "Labor's great upheaval," as this era of unprecedented militancy was called, came as a great surprise. Unlike in the past, however, the federal government now seemed to be on the side of labor, a commitment embodied in the National Industrial Recovery Act and in the Wagner Act (discussed later) of 1935, which granted workers the legal right to form unions. With the severe reduction of European immigration, ethnic differences among workers had diminished in importance. American-born children of the new immigrants now dominated the industrial labor force, and organizers no longer had to distribute materials in numerous languages as the IWW had done. And a cadre of militant labor leaders, many of them socialists and communists with long experience in organization, had survived the repression of the 1920s. They provided leadership to the labor upsurge.

American factories at the outset of the New Deal were miniature dictatorships in which unions were rare, workers could be beaten by supervisors and fired at will, and management determined the length of the workday and speed of the assembly line. In industrial communities scattered across the country, local government firmly supported the companies. "Jesus Christ couldn't speak in Duquesne for the union," declared the mayor of that Pennsylvania steel town. Workers' demands during the 1930s went beyond better wages. They included an end to employers' arbitrary power in the workplace, and basic civil liberties for workers, including the rights to picket, distribute literature, and meet to discuss their grievances. All these goals required union recognition.

Roosevelt's election as president did much to rekindle hope among those who called themselves, in the words of a worker writing to Secretary of Labor Frances

The Illegal Act, a cartoon critical of the Supreme Court's decision declaring the NRA unconstitutional. FDR tells a drowning Uncle Sam, "I'm sorry, but the Supreme Court says I must chuck you back in."

> *Mobilization of workers*

> *Basic civil liberties for workers*

THE SECOND NEW DEAL

In 1935, President Roosevelt sent a message to 100,000 American clergymen asking about economic and social conditions in their communities. The responses indicated that their financially hard-pressed churches could not respond effectively via traditional charity to the massive needs of their congregations.

Spurred by the failure of his initial policies to pull the country out of the Depression and the growing popular clamor for greater economic equality, and buoyed by Democratic gains in the midterm elections of 1934, Roosevelt in 1935 launched the Second New Deal. The first had focused on economic recovery. The emphasis of the second was economic security—a guarantee that Americans would be protected against unemployment and poverty. "Boys," Roosevelt's relief administrator, Harry Hopkins, told his staff, "this is our hour. We've got to get everything we want—a [public] works program, social security, wages and hours, everything—now or never."

Economic security

The idea that lack of consumer demand caused the Depression had been popularized by Huey Long, Francis Townsend, and the CIO. More and more New Dealers concluded that the government should no longer try to plan business recovery but should try to redistribute the national income so as to sustain mass purchasing power in the consumer economy. A series of measures in 1935 attacked head-on the problem of weak demand and economic inequality. Congress levied a highly publicized tax on large fortunes and corporate profits—a direct response to the popularity of Huey Long's Share Our Wealth campaign. It created the Rural Electrification Agency (REA) to bring electric power to homes that lacked it—80 percent of farms were still without electricity in 1934—in part to enable more Americans to purchase household appliances.

The Rural Electrification Agency

The REA proved to be one of the Second New Deal's most successful programs. By 1950, 90 percent of the nation's farms had been wired for electricity, and almost all now possessed radios, electric stoves, refrigerators, and mechanical equipment to milk cows. In addition, the federal government under the Second New Deal tried to promote soil conservation and family farming. This effort resulted from the belief that the country would never achieve prosperity so long as farmers' standard of living lagged well behind that of city dwellers, and that rural poverty resulted mainly from the poor use of natural resources. Thus, farmers received federal assistance in reducing soil loss in their fields. The federal government also purchased significant amounts of marginal and eroded land and converted these areas from farms into national grasslands and parks. It encouraged more environmentally conscious agricultural techniques. These measures (like those of the AAA) mainly benefited landowners, not sharecroppers, tenants, or migrant workers. In the long run, the Second New Deal failed to arrest the trend toward larger farms and fewer farmers.

The WPA and the Wagner Act

In 1934, Roosevelt had severely curtailed federal employment for those in need. Now, he approved the establishment of the **Works Progress Administration** (WPA), which hired some 3 million Americans, in virtually every walk of life, each year until it ended in 1943. Under Harry Hopkins's direction, the WPA changed

A poster by the artist Vera Bock for the Federal Art Project of the Works Progress Administration depicts farmers and laborers joining hands to produce prosperity.

An art exhibit in a New York City alley in 1938. The Works Progress Administration tried to broaden the audience for art by displaying it in unusual venues.

the physical face of the United States. It constructed thousands of public buildings and bridges, more than 500,000 miles of roads, and 600 airports. It built stadiums, swimming pools, and sewage treatment plants. Unlike previous work relief programs, the WPA employed many out-of-work white-collar workers and professionals, even doctors and dentists.

Perhaps the most famous WPA projects were in the arts. The WPA set hundreds of artists to work decorating public buildings with murals. It hired writers to produce local histories and guidebooks to the forty-eight states and to record the recollections of ordinary Americans, including hundreds of former slaves. Its Federal Theater Project put on plays, including an all-black production of *Macbeth* and Sinclair Lewis's drama *It Can't Happen Here*, about fascism coming to the United States. The Federal Music Project established orchestras and choral groups, and the Federal Dance Project sponsored ballet and modern dance programs. Thanks to the WPA, audiences across the country enjoyed their first glimpse of live musical and theatrical performances and their first opportunity to view exhibitions of American art. Also in 1935, Congress created the National Youth Administration to provide relief to American teenagers and young adults.

Funding the arts

Another major initiative of the Second New Deal, the **Wagner Act**, was known at the time as "Labor's Magna Carta" (a reference to an early landmark in the history of freedom). This brought democracy into the American workplace by empowering the National Labor Relations Board to supervise elections in which employees voted on union representation. It also outlawed "unfair labor practices," including the firing and blacklisting of union organizers. The bill's main sponsor, Robert Wagner of New York, told the Senate that the ability of workers to pool their strength through collective bargaining represented the "next step" in "the evolution

National Labor Relations Board

of American freedom." He also promised that unionization and higher wages would aid economic recovery by boosting the purchasing power of ordinary Americans.

The American Welfare State

The Social Security Act

The centerpiece of the Second New Deal was the **Social Security Act** of 1935. It embodied Roosevelt's conviction that the national government had a responsibility to ensure the material well-being of ordinary Americans. It created a system of unemployment insurance, old age pensions, and aid to the disabled, the elderly poor, and families with dependent children.

None of these were original ideas. The Progressive platform of 1912 had called for old age pensions. Assistance to poor families with dependent children descended from the mothers' pensions promoted by maternalist reformers. Many European countries had already adopted national unemployment insurance plans. What was new, however, was that in the name of economic security, the American government would now supervise not simply temporary relief but a permanent system of social insurance.

The Social Security Act launched the American version of the **welfare state**—a term that originated in Britain during World War II to refer to a system of income assistance, health coverage, and social services for all citizens. The act illustrated both the extent and the limits of the changes ushered in by the Second New Deal. The American welfare state marked a radical departure from previous government policies, but compared with similar programs in Europe, it has always been far more decentralized, involved lower levels of public spending, and covered fewer citizens. The original Social Security bill, for example, envisioned a national system of health insurance. But Congress dropped this after ferocious opposition from the American Medical Association, which feared government regulation of doctors' activities and incomes.

A 1935 poster promoting the new Social Security system.

The Social Security System

Some New Dealers desired a program funded by the federal government's general tax revenues, and with a single set of eligibility standards administered by national officials. But Secretary of Labor Frances Perkins, along with powerful members of Congress, wished to keep relief in the hands of state and local authorities and believed that workers should contribute directly to the cost of their own benefits. Roosevelt himself preferred to fund Social Security by taxes on employers and workers, rather than out of general government revenues. He wanted to ensure that Social Security did not add to the federal deficit and believed that paying such taxes gave contributors "a legal, moral, and political right" to collect their old age pensions and unemployment benefits, which no future Congress could rescind.

As a result, Social Security emerged as a hybrid of national and local funding, control, and eligibility standards. Old age pensions were administered nationally but paid for by taxes on employers and employees. Such taxes also funded payments to the unemployed, but this program was highly decentralized, with the states retaining considerable control over the level of benefits. The states paid most of the cost of direct poor relief, under the program called Aid to Dependent Children, and eligibility and the level of payments varied enormously from place to place. As will be discussed later, the combination of local administration and the fact that domestic and agricultural workers were not covered by unemployment and old age benefits meant that Social Security at first excluded large numbers of Americans, especially unmarried women and non-whites.

Nonetheless, Social Security represented a dramatic departure from the traditional functions of government. The Second New Deal transformed the relationship between the federal government and American citizens. Before the 1930s, national political debate often revolved around the question of *whether* the federal government should intervene in the economy. After the New Deal, debate rested on *how* it should intervene. In addition, the government assumed a responsibility, which it has never wholly relinquished, for guaranteeing Americans a living wage and protecting them against economic and personal misfortune. "Laissez-faire is dead," wrote Walter Lippmann, "and the modern state has become responsible for the modern economy [and] the task of insuring . . . the standard of life for its people."

FDR delivering one of his "fireside chats" in 1938. Roosevelt was the first president to make effective use of the radio to promote his policies.

A RECKONING WITH LIBERTY

The Depression made inevitable, in the words of one writer, a "reckoning with liberty." For too many Americans, Roosevelt proclaimed, "life was no longer free; liberty no longer real; men could no longer follow the pursuit of happiness." The 1930s produced an outpouring of books and essays on freedom. The large majority took for granted the need for a new definition. In a volume entitled *Land of the Free* (1938), the poet Archibald MacLeish used photographs of impoverished migrants and sharecroppers to question the reality of freedom in desperate times. "We told ourselves we were free," he wrote. Now, "we wonder if the liberty is done . . . or if there's something different men can mean by Liberty."

Like the Civil War, the New Deal recast the idea of freedom by linking it to the expanding power of the national state. "Our democracy," wrote Father John A. Ryan, a prominent Catholic social critic, "finds itself . . . in a new age where not political freedom but social and industrial freedom is the most insistent cry." Influenced by Ryan, the National Catholic Welfare Conference in 1935 declared that "social justice" required a government guarantee of continuous employment and a "decent livelihood and adequate security" for all Americans.

FDR and the Idea of Freedom

Along with being a superb politician, Roosevelt was a master of political communication. At a time when his political opponents controlled most newspapers, he harnessed radio's power to bring his message directly into American homes. By the mid-1930s, more than two-thirds of American families owned radios. They listened avidly to Roosevelt's radio addresses, known as "fireside chats."

Roosevelt adeptly appealed to traditional values in support of new policies. He gave the term "liberalism" its modern meaning. In the nineteenth century, liberalism had been a shorthand for limited government and free-market economics. Roosevelt consciously chose to employ it to describe a large, active, socially conscious state. He reclaimed the word "freedom" from conservatives and made it

"Fireside chats"

VOICES OF FREEDOM

From FRANKLIN D. ROOSEVELT, "FIRESIDE CHAT" (1934)

President Roosevelt pioneered the use of the new mass medium of radio to speak directly to Americans in their homes. He used his "fireside chats" to mobilize support for New Deal programs, link them with American traditions, and outline his definition of freedom.

To those who say that our expenditures for public works and other means for recovery are a waste that we cannot afford, I answer that no country, however rich, can afford the waste of its human resources. Demoralization caused by vast unemployment is our greatest extravagance. Morally, it is the greatest menace to our social order. Some people try to tell me that we must make up our minds that in the future we shall permanently have millions of unemployed just as other countries have had them for over a decade. What may be necessary for those countries is not my responsibility to determine. But as for this country, I stand or fall by my refusal to accept as a necessary condition of our future a permanent army of unemployed. . . .

In our efforts for recovery we have avoided, on the one hand, the theory that business should and must be taken over into an all-embracing Government. We have avoided, on the other hand, the equally untenable theory that it is an interference with liberty to offer reasonable help when private enterprise is in need of help. The course we have followed fits the American practice of Government, a practice of taking action step by step, of regulating only to meet concrete needs, a practice of courageous recognition of change. I believe with Abraham Lincoln, that "the legitimate object of Government is to do for a community of people whatever they need to have done but cannot do at all or cannot do so well for themselves in their separate and individual capacities."

I am not for a return to that definition of liberty under which for many years a free people were being gradually regimented into the service of the privileged few. I prefer and I am sure you prefer that broader definition of liberty under which we are moving forward to greater freedom, to greater security for the average man than he has ever known before in the history of America.

From JOHN STEINBECK, *THE HARVEST GYPSIES: ON THE ROAD TO THE GRAPES OF WRATH* (1938)

John Steinbeck's popular novel *The Grapes of Wrath* (1939), and the film version that followed shortly thereafter, focused national attention on the plight of homeless migrants displaced from their farms as a result of the Great Depression. Before that book appeared, Steinbeck had published a series of newspaper articles based on eyewitness accounts of the migrants, which became the basis for his novel.

In California, we find a curious attitude toward a group that makes our agriculture successful. The migrants are needed, and they are hated. . . . The migrants are hated for the following reasons, that they are ignorant and dirty people, that they are carriers of disease, that they increase the necessity for police and the tax bill for schooling in a community, and that if they are allowed to organize they can, simply by refusing to work, wipe out the season's crops. . . .

Let us see what kind of people they are, where they come from, and the routes of their wanderings. In the past they have been of several races, encouraged to come and often imported as cheap labor. Chinese in the early period, then Filipinos, Japanese and Mexicans. These were foreigners, and as such they were ostracized and segregated and herded about. . . . But in recent years the foreign migrants have begun to organize, and at this danger they have been deported in great numbers, for there was a new reservoir from which a great quantity of cheap labor could be obtained.

The drought in the middle west has driven the agricultural populations of Oklahoma, Nebraska and parts of Kansas and Texas westward. . . . Thousands of them are crossing the borders in ancient rattling automobiles, destitute and hungry and homeless, ready to accept any pay so that they may eat and feed their children. . . .

The earlier foreign migrants have invariably been drawn from a peon class. This is not the case with the new migrants. They are small farmers who have lost their farms, or farm hands who have lived with the family in the old American way. . . . They have come from the little farm districts where democracy was not only possible but inevitable, where popular government, whether practiced in the Grange, in church organization or in local government, was the responsibility of every man. And they have come into the country where, because of the movement necessary to make a living, they are not allowed any vote whatever, but are rather considered a properly unprivileged class. . . .

As one little boy in a squatter's camp said, "When they need us they call us migrants, and when we've picked their crop, we're bums and we got to get out."

QUESTIONS

1. *What does Roosevelt mean by the difference between the definition of liberty that has existed in the past and his own "broader definition of liberty"?*

2. *According to Steinbeck, how do Depression-era migrant workers differ from those in earlier periods?*

3. *Do the migrant workers described by Steinbeck enjoy liberty as Roosevelt understands it?*

This 1935 cartoon by William Gropper portrays Uncle Sam as Gulliver tied down by Lilliputians in the famous eighteenth-century novel *Gulliver's Travels* by Jonathan Swift. In this case, the bonds are the numerous agencies and laws created by the New Deal, which, Gropper suggests, are inhibiting the country from getting back on its feet during the Great Depression.

Freedom and economic security

Opposition to the New Deal

a rallying cry for the New Deal. In his second fireside chat, Roosevelt juxtaposed his own definition of liberty as "greater security for the average man" to the older notion of liberty of contract, which served the interests of "the privileged few." Henceforth, he would consistently link freedom with economic security and identify entrenched economic inequality as its greatest enemy. "The liberty of a democracy," he declared in 1938, was not safe if citizens could not "sustain an acceptable standard of living."

Even as Roosevelt invoked the word to uphold the New Deal, "liberty"—in the sense of freedom from powerful government—became the fighting slogan of his opponents. Their principal critique of the New Deal was that its "reckless spending" undermined fiscal responsibility and its new government regulations restricted American freedom. When conservative businessmen and politicians in 1934 formed an organization to mobilize opposition to Roosevelt's policies, they called it the American Liberty League. Robert Taft of Ohio, leader of the Republicans in Congress, accused Roosevelt of sacrificing "individual freedom" in a misguided effort to "improve the conditions of the poor."

As the 1930s progressed, opponents of the New Deal invoked the language of liberty with greater and greater passion. The U.S. Chamber of Commerce charged FDR with attempting to "Sovietize" America. Even though his own administration had abandoned laissez-faire in the face of economic disaster, former president Hoover launched strident attacks on his successor for endangering "fundamental American liberties." In *The Challenge to Liberty* (1934),

Hoover called the New Deal "the most stupendous invasion of the whole spirit of liberty" the nation had ever seen.

The Election of 1936

By 1936, with working-class voters providing massive majorities for the Democratic Party and businesses large and small bitterly estranged from the New Deal, politics reflected class divisions more completely than at any other time in American history. Conceptions of freedom divided sharply as well. Americans, wrote George Soule, editor of *The New Republic*, confronted "two opposing systems of concepts about liberty," reflecting "the needs and purposes of two opposing [parts] of the population." One was the idea of "freedom for private enterprise," the other "socialized liberty" based on "an equitably shared abundance."

> *Politics and class divisions*

A fight for the possession of "the ideal of freedom," reported the *New York Times*, emerged as the central issue of the presidential campaign of 1936. The Democratic platform insisted that in a modern economy the government has an obligation to establish a "democracy of opportunity for all the people." In his speech accepting renomination, Roosevelt launched a blistering attack against "economic royalists" who, he charged, sought to establish a new tyranny over the "average man." Economic rights, he went on, were the precondition of liberty—poor men "are not free men." Throughout the campaign, FDR would insist that the threat posed to economic freedom by the "new despotism" of large corporations was the main issue of the election.

> *Economic freedom*

As Roosevelt's opponent, Republicans chose Kansas governor Alfred Landon, a former Theodore Roosevelt Progressive. Landon denounced Social Security and other measures as threats to individual liberty. Opposition to the New Deal planted the seeds for the later flowering of an antigovernment conservatism bent on upholding the free market and dismantling the welfare state. But in 1936 Roosevelt won a landslide reelection, with more than 60 percent of the popular vote. He carried every state except Maine and Vermont. Roosevelt's victory was all the more remarkable in view of the heavy support most of the nation's newspapers and nearly the entire business community gave to the Republicans. His success stemmed from strong backing from organized labor and his ability to unite southern white and northern black voters, Protestant farmers and urban Catholic and Jewish ethnics, industrial workers and middle-class home owners. These groups made up the so-called New Deal coalition, which would dominate American politics for nearly half a century.

Fall In!, a cartoon commenting on Roosevelt's proposal to "pack" the Supreme Court, from the *Richmond Times-Dispatch*, January 8, 1937.

The Court Fight

Roosevelt's second inaugural address was the first to be delivered on January 20. In order to lessen a newly elected president's wait before taking office, the recently ratified Twentieth Amendment had moved inauguration day from March 4. FDR called on the nation to redouble its efforts to aid those "who have too little." The Depression, he admitted, had not been conquered: "I see one-third of a nation ill-housed, ill-clad, and ill-nourished." Emboldened by his electoral triumph, Roosevelt now made what many considered a serious political miscalculation. On the pretense that several members of the Supreme Court were too old to perform

"Court packing" plan

their functions, he proposed that the president be allowed to appoint a new justice for each one who remained on the Court past age seventy (an age that six of the nine had already surpassed). FDR's aim, of course, was to change the balance of power on a Court that, he feared, might well invalidate Social Security, the Wagner Act, and other measures of the Second New Deal.

The plan aroused cries that the president was an aspiring dictator. Congress rejected it. But Roosevelt accomplished his underlying purpose. The Supreme Court, it is sometimes said, follows the election returns. Coming soon after Roosevelt's landslide victory of 1936, the threat of **"Court packing"** inspired an astonishing about-face on the part of key justices. Beginning in March 1937, the Court suddenly revealed a new willingness to support economic regulation by both the federal government and the states. It upheld a minimum wage law of the state of Washington similar to the New York measure it had declared unconstitutional a year earlier. It turned aside challenges to Social Security and the Wagner Act. In subsequent cases, the Court affirmed federal power to regulate wages, hours, child labor, agricultural production, and numerous other aspects of economic life.

The about-face for the Court

Announcing a new judicial philosophy, Chief Justice Charles Evans Hughes pointed out that the words "freedom of contract" did not appear in the Constitution. "Liberty," however, did, and this, Hughes continued, required "the protection of law against the evils which menace the health, safety, morals, and welfare of the people." The Court's new willingness to accept the New Deal marked a permanent change in judicial policy. Having declared dozens of economic laws unconstitutional in the decades leading up to 1937, the justices have rarely done so since.

The End of the Second New Deal

Even as the Court made its peace with Roosevelt's policies, the momentum of the Second New Deal slowed. The landmark United States Housing Act did pass in 1937, initiating the first major national effort to build homes for the poorest Americans. But the Fair Labor Standards bill failed to reach the floor for over a year. When it finally passed in 1938, it banned goods produced by child labor from interstate commerce, set forty cents as the minimum hourly wage, and required overtime pay for hours of work exceeding forty per week. This last major piece of New Deal legislation established the practice of federal regulation of wages and working conditions, another radical departure from pre-Depression policies.

The year 1937 also witnessed a sharp downturn of the economy. With economic conditions improving in 1936, Roosevelt had reduced federal funding for farm subsidies and WPA work relief. The result was disastrous. As government spending fell, so did business investment, industrial production, and the stock market. Unemployment, still 14 percent at the beginning of 1937, rose to nearly 20 percent by year's end.

In 1936, in *The General Theory of Employment, Interest, and Money*, John Maynard Keynes had challenged economists' traditional belief in the sanctity of balanced budgets. Large-scale government spending, he insisted, was necessary to sustain purchasing power and stimulate

The New Deal did not really solve the problem of unemployment, which fell below 10 percent only in 1941, as the United States prepared to enter World War II.

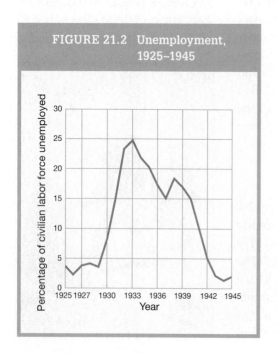

FIGURE 21.2 Unemployment, 1925–1945

economic activity during downturns. Such spending should be enacted even at the cost of a budget deficit (a situation in which the government spends more money than it takes in). By 1938, Roosevelt was ready to follow this prescription, which would later be known as Keynesian economics. In April, he asked Congress for billions more for work relief and farm aid. By the end of the year, the immediate crisis had passed. But the events of 1937–1938 marked a major shift in New Deal philosophy. Rather than economic planning, as in 1933–1934, or economic redistribution, as in 1935–1936, public spending would now be the government's major tool for combating unemployment and stimulating economic growth. The Second New Deal had come to an end.

Keynesian economics

THE LIMITS OF CHANGE

Roosevelt conceived of the Second New Deal, and especially Social Security, as expanding the meaning of freedom by extending assistance to broad groups of needy Americans—the unemployed, elderly, and dependent—as a right of citizenship, not charity or special privilege. But political realities, especially the power of inherited ideas about gender and black disenfranchisement in the South, powerfully affected the drafting of legislation. New Deal programs were justified as ways of bringing economic security to "the people" rather than to specific disadvantaged groups. But different Americans experienced the New Deal in radically different ways.

The New Deal and American Women

The New Deal brought more women into government than ever before in American history. A number of talented women, including Secretary of Labor Frances Perkins, advised the president and shaped public policy. Most prominent of all was Eleanor Roosevelt, FDR's distant cousin whom he had married in 1905. She transformed the role of First Lady, turning a position with no formal responsibilities into a base for political action. She traveled widely, spoke out on public issues, wrote a regular newspaper column that sometimes disagreed openly with her husband's policies, and worked to enlarge the scope of the New Deal in areas like civil rights, labor legislation, and work relief.

But even as the New Deal increased women's visibility in national politics, organized feminism, already in disarray during the 1920s, disappeared as a political force. Indeed, the Depression inspired widespread demands for women to remove themselves from the labor market to make room for unemployed men. Because the Depression hit industrial employment harder than low-wage clerical and service jobs where women predominated, the proportion of the workforce

Eleanor Roosevelt transformed the role of First Lady by taking an active and visible part in public life. Here she visits a West Virginia coal mine in 1933.

made up of women rose. The government tried to reverse this trend. The Economy Act of 1933 prohibited both members of a married couple from holding federal jobs. Until its repeal in 1937, it led to the dismissal of numerous female civil service employees whose husbands worked for the government. Many states and localities prohibited the hiring of women whose husbands earned a "living wage," and employers from banks to public school systems barred married women from jobs. Although the CIO organized female workers, it, too, adhered to the idea that women should be supported by men. "The working wife whose husband is employed," said a vice president of the United Auto Workers, "should be barred from industry."

Most New Deal programs did not exclude women from benefits (although the CCC restricted its camps to men). But the ideal of the male-headed household powerfully shaped social policy. Since paying taxes on one's wages made one eligible for the most generous Social Security programs—old age pensions and unemployment insurance—they left most women uncovered, since they did not work outside the home. The program excluded the 3 million mostly female domestic workers altogether. "Those who need protection most are completely overlooked," the sister of a household worker complained to Secretary of Labor Perkins. "What about the poor domestics, both in private homes and private institutions. What have you done for them? Nothing."

The Southern Veto

Roosevelt made the federal government the symbolic representative of all the people, including racial and ethnic groups generally ignored by previous administrations. Yet the power of the Solid South helped to mold the New Deal welfare state into an entitlement of white Americans. After the South's blacks lost the right to vote around the turn of the century, Democrats enjoyed a political monopoly in the region. Democratic members of Congress were elected again and again. With results predetermined, many whites did not bother to vote (only about 20 percent of eligible southern voters cast ballots in the election of 1920). But this tiny electorate had an enormous impact on national policy. Committee

This photograph from 1933 depicts a march in New York City organized by the Association of Unemployed Single Women. Many men believed that public works jobs and governmental relief should not go to women, who could be supported by their husbands or fathers.

chairmanships in Congress rest on seniority—how many years a member has served in office. Beginning in 1933, when Democrats took control of Congress, southerners assumed the key leadership positions. Despite his personal popularity, Roosevelt felt he could not challenge the power of southern Democrats if he wished legislation to pass. At their insistence, the Social Security law excluded agricultural and domestic workers, the largest categories of black employment.

Roosevelt spoke of Social Security's universality, but the demand for truly comprehensive coverage came from the political left and black organizations. Congressman Ernest Lundeen of Minnesota in 1935 introduced a bill establishing a federally controlled system of old age, unemployment, and health benefits for all wage workers, plus support for female heads of households with dependents. Black organizations like the Urban League and the NAACP supported the Lundeen bill and lobbied strenuously for a system that enabled agricultural and domestic workers to receive unemployment and old age benefits and that established national relief standards. The Social Security Act, however, not Lundeen's proposal, became law. Its limitations, complained the *Pittsburgh Courier*, a black newspaper, reflected the power of "reactionary elements in the South who cannot bear the thought of Negroes getting pensions and compensations" and who feared that the inclusion of black workers would disrupt the region's low-wage, racially divided labor system.

A 1936 photograph shows a black farmer, with his son, repaying a loan from the Farm Security Administration, which sought to improve the conditions of poor landowning farmers and sharecroppers. The client wears what is probably his nicest attire to meet with the government official.

The Stigma of Welfare

Because of the "southern veto," the majority of black workers found themselves confined to the least generous and most vulnerable wing of the new welfare state. The public assistance programs established by Social Security, notably aid to dependent children and to the poor elderly, were open to all Americans who could demonstrate financial need. But they set benefits at extremely low levels and authorized the states to determine eligibility standards, including "moral" behavior as defined by local authorities. As a result, public assistance programs allowed for widespread discrimination in the distribution of benefits. Because recipients did not pay Social Security taxes, they came to bear the humiliating stigma of dependency on government handouts, which would soon come to be known as "welfare."

Welfare discrimination

In 1942, the National Resources Planning Board noted that because of their exclusion from programs "which give aid under relatively favorable conditions," blacks were becoming disproportionately dependent on welfare, a program widely viewed with popular disfavor. The situation, the report concluded, seemed certain to stigmatize blacks as recipients of unearned government assistance, and welfare as a program for minorities, thus dooming it forever to inadequate "standards of aid." Over time, this is precisely what happened, until the federal government abolished its responsibility for welfare in 1996 entirely, during the presidency of Bill Clinton.

During the 1930s, the South remained rigidly segregated. This 1939 photograph by Dorthea Lange depicts a "colored" movie theater in the Mississippi Delta.

and launched his own program of spending on housing, parks, and public works. La Guardia's was one of numerous "little New Deals" that brought ethnic working-class voters to power in communities throughout the industrial heartland.

Thanks to the virtual cutoff of southern and eastern European immigration in 1924, the increasing penetration of movies, chain stores, and mass advertising into ethnic communities, and the common experience of economic crisis, the 1930s witnessed an acceleration of cultural assimilation. But the process had a different content from the corporate-sponsored Americanization plans of the preceding years. For the children of the new immigrants, labor and political activism became agents of a new kind of Americanization. One could participate fully in the broader society without surrendering one's ideals and ethnic identity. "Unionism is Americanism" became a CIO rallying cry. "The Mesabi Range," a Minnesota miner wrote to Secretary of Labor Perkins, complaining of low wages and management hostility to unions in the iron-rich region, "isn't Americanized yet."

The Heyday of American Communism

The left

In the mid-1930s, for the first time in American history, the left—an umbrella term for socialists, communists, labor radicals, and many New Deal liberals—enjoyed a shaping influence on the nation's politics and culture. The CIO and Communist Party became focal points for a broad social and intellectual impulse that helped to redraw the boundaries of American freedom. An obscure, faction-ridden organization when the Depression began, the Communist Party experienced remarkable growth during the 1930s. The party's membership never exceeded 100,000, but several times that number passed through its ranks.

The party's commitment to socialism resonated with a widespread belief that the Depression had demonstrated the bankruptcy of capitalism. But it was not so much the party's ideology as its vitality—its involvement in a mind-boggling array of activities, including demonstrations of the unemployed, struggles for industrial unionism, and a renewed movement for black civil rights—that for a time made it the center of gravity for a broad democratic upsurge. At the height of the **Popular Front**—a period during the mid-1930s when the Communist Party sought to ally itself with socialists and New Dealers in movements for social change, urging reform of the capitalist system rather than revolution—Communists gained an unprecedented respectability. Earl Browder, the party's leader, even appeared on the cover of *Time* magazine. It is one of the era's ironies that an organization with an undemocratic structure and closely tied to Stalin's dictatorial regime in Russia should have contributed to the expansion of freedom in the United States. But the Communist Party helped to imbue New Deal liberalism with a militant spirit and a more pluralistic understanding of Americanism.

The Popular Front

Redefining the People

In theater, film, and dance, the Popular Front vision of American society sank deep roots and survived much longer than the political moment from which it sprang.

A card issued by the Communist Party during the 1936 campaign illustrates the party's attempt at "Americanization" (note the images of the American Revolution and Abraham Lincoln), as well as its emphasis on interracialism. James Ford, an African-American, was the party's vice-presidential candidate.

In this broad left-wing culture, social and economic radicalism, not support for the status quo, defined true Americanism, ethnic and racial diversity was the glory of American society, and the "American way of life" meant unionism and social citizenship, not the unbridled pursuit of wealth. The American "people," viewed by many intellectuals in the 1920s as representing mean-spirited fundamentalism and crass commercialism, were suddenly rediscovered as embodiments of democratic virtue.

The "common man," Roosevelt proclaimed, embodied "the heart and soul of our country." During the 1930s, artists and writers who strove to create socially meaningful works eagerly took up the task of depicting the daily lives of ordinary

History of Southern Illinois, a mural sponsored by the Illinois Federal Art Project, illustrates the widespread fascination during the 1930s with American traditions and the lives of ordinary Americans. On the left, a man strums a guitar, while workers labor on the waterfront.

A Dorothea Lange photograph of a sharecropper and his family outside their modest home.

A scene from the Emancipation episode of Martha Graham's *American Document*, photographed by Barbara Morgan. The dancers are Martha Graham and Erick Hawkins. Photograph © Barbara Morgan, Barbara Morgan Archive.

farmers and city dwellers. Art about the people—such as Dorothea Lange's photographs of migrant workers and sharecroppers—and art created by the people—such as black spirituals—came to be seen as expressions of genuine Americanism. The Federal Music Project dispatched collectors with tape recorders to help preserve American folk music. Films celebrated populist figures who challenged and defeated corrupt businessmen and politicians, as in *Mr. Deeds Goes to Town* (1936) and *Mr. Smith Goes to Washington* (1939). New immigrants, especially Jews and Italians, played a prominent role in producing and directing Hollywood films of the 1930s. Their movies, however, glorified not urban ethnic communities but ordinary small-town middle-class Americans.

Promoting Diversity

"A new conception of America is necessary," wrote the immigrant labor radical Louis Adamic in 1938. Despite bringing ethnic and northern black voters into its political coalition, the Democratic Party said little about ethno-cultural issues, fearful of rekindling the divisive battles of the 1920s. But the Popular Front forthrightly sought to promote the idea that the country's strength lay in diversity, tolerance, and the rejection of ethnic prejudice and class privilege. The CIO avidly promoted the idea of ethnic and racial inclusiveness. It broke decisively with the AFL's tradition of exclusionary unionism. "We are the only Americans who take them into our organization as equals," wrote labor organizer Rose Pesotta, referring to the Mexican-Americans who flocked to the Cannery and Agricultural Workers union.

Popular Front culture presented a heroic but not uncritical picture of the country's past. Martha Graham's modern dance masterpiece *American Document* (1938), an embodiment of Popular Front aesthetics with its emphasis on America's folk traditions and multi-ethnic heritage, centered its account of history on the Declaration of Independence and the Gettysburg Address. Yet Graham did not neglect what her narrator called "things we are ashamed of," including the dispossession of the Indians and the plight of the unemployed. Graham's answer to Hector St. John de Crèvecoeur's old question, "What, then, is the American, this new man?" was that Americans were not only middle-class Anglo-Saxons but also blacks, immigrants, and the working class. Earl Robinson's song "Ballad for Americans," a typical expression of Popular Front culture that celebrated the religious, racial, and ethnic diversity of American society, became a national hit and was performed in 1940 at the Republican national convention.

Challenging the Color Line

It was fitting that "Ballad for Americans" reached the top of the charts in a version performed by the magnificent black singer

Paul Robeson. Popular Front culture moved well beyond New Deal liberalism in condemning racism as incompatible with true Americanism. In the 1930s, groups like the American Jewish Committee and the National Conference of Christians and Jews actively promoted ethnic and religious tolerance, defining pluralism as "the American way." But whether in Harlem or East Los Angeles, the Communist Party was the era's only predominantly white organization to make fighting racism a top priority. "The communists," declared Charles H. Houston, the NAACP's chief lawyer, "made it impossible for any aspirant to Negro leadership to advocate less than full economic, political and social equality."

Communist influence spread even to the South. The Communist-dominated International Labor Defense mobilized popular support for black defendants victimized by a racist criminal justice system. It helped to make the **Scottsboro case** an international cause célèbre. The case revolved around nine young black men arrested for the rape of two white women in Alabama in 1931. Despite the weakness of the evidence against the "Scottsboro boys" and the fact that one of the two accusers recanted, Alabama authorities three times put them on trial and three times won convictions. Landmark Supreme Court decisions overturned the first two verdicts and established legal principles that greatly expanded the definition of civil liberties—that defendants have a constitutional right to effective legal representation, and that states cannot systematically exclude blacks from juries. But the Court allowed the third set of convictions to stand, which led to prison sentences for five of the defendants. In 1937, a defense lawyer worked out a deal whereby Alabama authorities released nearly all the defendants on parole, although the last of the "Scottsboro boys" did not leave prison until thirteen years had passed.

The "Scottsboro boys," flanked by two prison guards, with their lawyer, Samuel Liebowitz.

Despite considerable resistance from white workers determined to preserve their monopoly of skilled positions and access to promotions, the CIO welcomed black members and advocated the passage of antilynching laws and the return of voting rights to southern blacks. The CIO brought large numbers of black industrial workers into the labor movement for the first time and ran extensive educational campaigns to persuade white workers to recognize the interests they shared with their black counterparts. Black workers, many of them traditionally hostile to unions because of their long experience of exclusion, responded with enthusiasm to CIO organizing efforts. The union offered the promise of higher wages, dignity in the workplace, and an end to the arbitrary power of often racist foremen. Ed McRea, a white CIO organizer in Memphis, Tennessee, reported that he had little difficulty persuading black workers of the value of unionization: "You didn't have any trouble explaining this to blacks, with the kinds of oppression and conditions they had. It was a question of freedom."

Unionization of black workers

Labor and Civil Liberties

Another central element of Popular Front public culture was its mobilization for civil liberties, especially the right of labor to organize. The struggle to launch industrial unions encountered sweeping local restrictions on freedom of speech as well as repression by private and public police forces. Nationwide publicity about the wave of violence directed against the Southern Tenant Farmers Union in the

Freedom of speech and assembly

South and the CIO in industrial communities in the North elevated the rights of labor to a central place in discussions of civil liberties. The American Civil Liberties Union, primarily concerned in the 1920s with governmental repression, by 1934 concluded that "the masters of property" posed as great a danger to freedom of speech and assembly as political authorities.

Efforts to organize labor

Beginning in 1936, a Senate subcommittee headed by Robert M. La Follette Jr. exposed the methods employers used to combat unionization, including spies and private police forces. Workers had "no liberties at all," an employee of General Motors wrote to the committee from Saginaw, Michigan. The extensive violence unleashed against strikers in California's cotton and lettuce fields made that state, the committee report concluded, seem more like a "European dictatorship" than part of the United States.

Labor militancy helped to produce an important shift in the understanding of civil liberties. Previously conceived of as individual rights that must be protected against infringement by the government, the concept now expanded to include violations of free speech and assembly by powerful private groups. As a result, just as the federal government emerged as a guarantor of economic security, it also became a protector of freedom of expression.

Civil Liberties Unit

By the eve of World War II, civil liberties had assumed a central place in the New Deal understanding of freedom. In 1939, Attorney General Frank Murphy established a Civil Liberties Unit in the Department of Justice. "For the first time in our history," Murphy wrote the president, "the full weight of the Department will be thrown behind the effort to preserve in this country the blessings of liberty." Meanwhile, the same Supreme Court that in 1937 relinquished its role as a judge of economic legislation moved to expand its authority over civil liberties. The justices insisted that constitutional guarantees of free thought and expression were essential to "nearly every other form of freedom" and therefore deserved special protec-

A May Day parade in New York City in 1935 includes a placard celebrating the Bill of Rights.

tion by the courts. Thus, civil liberties replaced liberty of contract as the judicial foundation of freedom. In 1937, the Court overturned on free speech grounds the conviction of Angelo Herndon, a Communist organizer jailed in Georgia for "inciting insurrection." Three years later, it invalidated an Alabama law that prohibited picketing in labor disputes. Since 1937, the large majority of state and national laws overturned by the courts have been those that infringe on civil liberties, not on the property rights of business.

The new appreciation of free expression was hardly universal. In 1938, the House of Representatives established the **House Un-American Activities Committee** to investigate disloyalty. Its expansive definition of "un-American" included communists, labor radicals, and the left of the Democratic Party, and its hearings led to the dismissal of dozens of federal employees on charges of subversion. Two years later, Congress enacted the Smith Act, which made it a federal crime to "teach, advocate, or encourage" the overthrow of the government. A similar pursuit of radical views took place at the state level. The New York legislature's Rapp-Coudert Committee held sweeping hearings investigating "subversive" influences in New York City's public colleges, resulting in the firing in 1941 of some sixty faculty members charged with communist sympathies.

Pushback against free expression

The End of the New Deal

By then the New Deal, as an era of far-reaching social reform, had already begun to recede. One reason was that more and more southern Democrats were finding themselves at odds with Roosevelt's policies. In 1938, the administration released a "Report on Economic Conditions in the South," along with a letter by the president referring to the region as "the nation's No. 1 economic problem." The document revealed that the South lagged far behind other parts of the country in industrialization and investment in education and public health. Its per capita income stood at half that of the rest of the nation. Also in 1938, a new generation of homegrown radicals—southern New Dealers, black activists, labor leaders, communists, even a few elected officials—founded the Southern Conference for Human Welfare to work for unionization, unemployment relief, and racial justice.

Southern Conference for Human Welfare

Until the late 1930s, prominent southern Democrats had been strong supporters of the New Deal, while at the same time working to shape legislation to allow for the local administration of relief and the exclusion of most black workers. Now, southern business and political leaders feared that continuing federal intervention in their region would encourage unionization and upset race relations. Roosevelt concluded that the enactment of future New Deal measures required a liberalization of the southern Democratic Party. In 1938, he tried to persuade the region's voters to replace conservative congressmen with ones who would support his policies. The South's small electorate dealt him a stinging rebuke. In the North, where the economic downturn, the "Court-packing" plan, and the upsurge of CIO militancy alarmed many middle-class voters, Republicans increased their congressional representation.

Southern leaders and the New Deal

A period of political stalemate followed the congressional election of 1938. For many years, a conservative coalition of southern Democrats and northern Republicans dominated Congress. Further reform initiatives became almost impossible,

Isaac Soyer's painting of dispirited men and women at an employment agency in 1937 illustrates that despite its many accomplishments, the New Deal failed to solve the problem of mass joblessness.

Political stalemate

and Congress moved to abolish existing ones, beginning with the Federal Theater Project, which had alarmed conservatives because of the presence of radicals and homosexuals on its payroll. Congress repealed an earlier tax on corporate profits and rejected a proposed program of national medical insurance. The administration, moreover, increasingly focused its attention on the storm gathering in Europe. Even before December 1941, when the United States entered World War II, "Dr. Win the War," as Roosevelt put it, had replaced "Dr. New Deal."

The New Deal in American History

Given the scope of the economic calamity it tried to counter, the New Deal seems in many ways quite limited. Compared to later European welfare states, Social Security remained restricted in scope and modest in cost. The New Deal failed to address the problem of racial inequality, which in some ways it actually worsened.

Failures and accomplishments of the New Deal

Yet even as the New Deal receded, its substantial accomplishments remained. It greatly expanded the federal government's role in the American economy and made it an independent force in relations between industry and labor. The government influenced what farmers could and could not plant, required employers to deal with unions, insured bank deposits, regulated the stock market, loaned money to home owners, and provided payments to a majority of the elderly and unemployed. It transformed the physical environment through hydroelectric dams, reforestation projects, rural electrification, and the construction of innumerable public facilities. It restored faith in democracy and made the government an institution directly experienced in Americans' daily lives and directly concerned with their welfare. It redrew the map of American politics. It helped to inspire, and was powerfully influenced by, a popular upsurge that recast the idea of freedom to include a public guarantee of economic security for ordinary citizens and that identified economic inequality as the greatest threat to American freedom.

The New Deal certainly improved economic conditions in the United States. But it did not generate sustained prosperity. More than 15 percent of the workforce remained unemployed in 1940. Only the mobilization of the nation's resources to fight World War II would finally end the Great Depression.

SUGGESTED READING

BOOKS

- Blackwelder, Julia Kirk. *Women of the Depression* (1998). Examines how female members of three communities— Anglo, Mexican-American, and black—coped with the Great Depression.

- Brinkley, Alan. *Voices of Protest: Huey Long, Father Coughlin, and the Great Depression* (1982). An account of the political careers of two key figures of the New Deal era and their influence on national events.

- Carpenter, Joel A. *Revive Us Again: The Reawakening of American Fundamentalism* (1999). Shows how evangelicals adapted to the Depression and used mass communications to spread their message.

- Cohen, Lizabeth. *Making a New Deal: Industrial Workers in Chicago, 1919–1939* (1990). Describes how the assimilation of immigrants and their children paved the way for the creation of the New Deal political coalition.

- Denning, Michael. *The Cultural Front: The Laboring of American Culture in the Twentieth Century* (1996). A comprehensive account of the rise of cultural activity associated with the political left and the New Deal.

- Egan, Timothy. *The Worst Hard Time* (2006). A social history of the Dust Bowl during the Depression, including the stories of victims and survivors.

- Katznelson, Ira. *Fear Itself: The New Deal and the Origins of Our Time* (2013). Examines the shaping of New Deal policy and especially the compromises Roosevelt had to make to get measures through a Congress dominated by segregationist members from the South.

- Kessler-Harris, Alice. *In Pursuit of Equity: Men, Women, and the Quest for Economic Citizenship in 20th-Century America* (2001). Explores how assumptions regarding the proper roles of men and women helped to shape New Deal measures such as Social Security.

- Kirby, Jack T. *Rural Worlds Lost: The American South, 1920–1960* (1987). Traces the transformation of the South in these four decades, with emphasis on how the New Deal affected the southern states.

- Leuchtenberg, William E. *Franklin D. Roosevelt and the New Deal, 1932–1940* (1963). Still the standard one-volume account of Roosevelt's first two terms as president.

- Naison, Mark. *Communists in Harlem during the Depression* (1983). Examines the rise and decline of the Communist Party in a center of black life, and its impact on the movement for racial justice.

- Phillips, Sarah T. *The Land, This Nation: Conservation, Rural America, and the New Deal* (2007). Examines New Deal policies regarding agricultural development, rural conservation, and land use, and its attempt to modernize and uplift rural life.

- Sanchez, George. *Becoming Mexican American: Ethnicity, Culture, and Identity in Chicano Los Angeles, 1900–1945* (1995). A careful study of Mexican-Americans in Los Angeles, including their participation in the social unrest of the 1930s and the movement for deporting them during that decade.

- Smith, Jason B. *Building New Deal Liberalism: The Political Economy of Public Works* (2006). Places the great construction projects of the 1930s at the center of New Deal economic policy.

- Sullivan, Patricia. *Days of Hope: Race and Democracy in the New Deal Era* (1996). Analyzes how the New Deal inspired the emergence of a biracial movement for civil rights in the South.

- Williams, Mason B. *City of Ambition: FDR, La Guardia, and the Making of Modern New York* (2014). An illuminating study of the most prominent "little New Deal" and its long-term results.

- Zieger, Robert H. *The CIO, 1935–1955* (1995). A comprehensive history of the Congress of Industrial Organizations, the major labor group to emerge during the New Deal.

WEBSITES

- America from the Great Depression to World War II: http://memory.loc.gov/ammem/fsowhome.html

- FDR Cartoon Archive: www.nisk.k12.ny.us/fdr/FDRcartoons.html

- Flint Sit-Down Strike: www.historicalvoices.org/flint/

- New Deal Network: http://newdeal.feri.org

CHAPTER REVIEW AND ONLINE RESOURCES

REVIEW QUESTIONS

1. Discuss how regional planning such as the Tennessee Valley Authority and the Columbia River project reflected broader changes in American life during the New Deal.

2. What actions did President Roosevelt and Congress take to help the banking system recover as well as to reform how it operated in the long run?

3. How did the actions of the AAA benefit many farmers, injure others, and provoke attacks by conservatives?

4. Explain what labor did in the 1930s to rise from being "slaves of the depression" to secure "economic freedom and industrial democracy" for American workers.

5. How did the emphasis of the Second New Deal differ from the First New Deal?

6. How did the entrenched power of southern white conservatives limit African-Americans' ability to enjoy the full benefits of the New Deal and eliminate racial violence and discrimination? Why did African-Americans still support the Democratic Party?

7. Analyze the effects of the Indian Reorganization Act of 1934 on Native Americans.

8. Explain how New Deal programs contributed to the stigma of blacks as welfare-dependent.

9. How did the New Deal build on traditional ideas about the importance of home ownership to Americans, and how did it change Americans' ability to own their own homes?

10. What were the major characteristics of liberalism by 1939?

KEY TERMS

New Deal (p. 803)

Emergency Banking Act (p. 808)

Hundred Days (p. 808)

National Industrial Recovery Act (p. 808)

National Recovery Administration (p. 808)

Civilian Conservation Corps (p. 810)

Public Works Administration (p. 810)

Tennessee Valley Authority (p. 811)

Agricultural Adjustment Act (p. 811)

Dust Bowl (p. 812)

Federal Housing Administration (p. 814)

Congress of Industrial Organizations (p. 817)

sit-down strike (p. 817)

Share Our Wealth movement (p. 819)

Works Progress Administration (p. 820)

Wagner Act (p. 821)

Social Security Act (p. 822)

welfare state (p. 822)

Court packing (p. 828)

Indian New Deal (p. 832)

Popular Front (p. 836)

Scottsboro case (p. 839)

House Un-American Activities Committee (p. 841)

Go to 🦉 INQUIZITIVE

To see what you know—and learn what you've missed—with personalized feedback along the way.

Visit the *Give Me Liberty!* Student Site for primary source documents and images, interactive maps, author videos featuring Eric Foner, and more.

Fascism

France, and the United States to oppose this action convinced Hitler that the democracies could not muster the will to halt his aggressive plans. Italian leader Benito Mussolini, the founder of fascism, a movement similar to Hitler's Nazism, invaded and conquered Ethiopia. When General Francisco Franco in 1936 led an uprising against the democratically elected government of Spain, Hitler poured in arms, seeing the conflict as a testing ground for new weaponry. In 1939, Franco emerged victorious from a bitter civil war, establishing yet another fascist government in Europe. As part of a campaign to unite all Europeans of German origin in a single empire, Hitler in 1938 annexed Austria and the Sudetenland, an ethnically German part of Czechoslovakia. Shortly thereafter, he gobbled up all of that country.

As the 1930s progressed, Roosevelt became more and more alarmed at Hitler's aggression as well as his accelerating campaign against Germany's Jews, whom the Nazis stripped of citizenship and property and began to deport to concentration camps. In a 1937 speech in Chicago, FDR called for international action to "quarantine" aggressors. But no further steps followed. Roosevelt had little choice but to follow the policy of "appeasement" adopted by Britain and France, who hoped that agreeing to Hitler's demands would prevent war. British prime minister Neville Chamberlain returned from the Munich conference of 1938, which awarded Hitler the Sudetenland, proclaiming that he had guaranteed "peace in our time."

Appeasement

Isolationism

To most Americans, the threat arising from Japanese and German aggression seemed very distant. Moreover, Hitler had more than a few admirers in the United States. Obsessed with the threat of communism, some Americans approved of his expansion of German power as a counterweight to the Soviet Union. Businessmen did not wish to give up profitable overseas markets. Henry Ford did business with Nazi Germany throughout the 1930s. Indeed, Ford plants there employed slave labor provided by the German government. Trade with Japan also continued, including shipments of American trucks and aircraft and considerable amounts of oil. Until 1941, 80 percent of Japan's oil supply came from the United States.

International trade

Many Americans remained convinced that involvement in World War I had been a mistake. Senate hearings in 1934–1935 headed by Gerald P. Nye of North Dakota revealed that international bankers and arms exporters had pressed the Wilson administration to enter that war and had profited handsomely from it. Pacifism spread on college campuses, where tens of thousands of students took part in a "strike for peace" in 1935. Ethnic allegiances reinforced Americans' traditional reluctance to enter foreign conflicts. Many Americans of German and Italian descent celebrated the expansion of national power in their countries of origin, even when they disdained their dictatorial governments. Irish-Americans remained strongly anti-British.

Isolationism—the 1930s version of Americans' long-standing desire to avoid foreign entanglements—dominated Congress. Beginning in 1935, lawmakers passed a series of **Neutrality Acts** that banned travel on belligerents' ships and the sale of arms to countries at war. These policies, Congress hoped, would allow the United States to avoid the conflicts over freedom of the seas that had contributed to involvement in World War I. Despite the fact that the Spanish Civil War pitted a democratic government against an aspiring fascist dictator, the Western democracies, including

The Neutrality Acts

the United States, imposed an embargo on arms shipments to both sides. Some 3,000 Americans volunteered to fight in the Abraham Lincoln Brigade on the side of the Spanish republic. But with Germany supplying the forces of Franco, the decision by democratic countries to abide by the arms embargo contributed substantially to his victory.

War in Europe

In the Munich agreement of 1938, Britain and France had caved in to Hitler's aggression. In 1939, the Soviet Union proposed an international agreement to oppose further German demands for territory. Britain and France, who distrusted Stalin and saw Germany as a bulwark against the spread of communist influence in Europe, refused. Stalin then astonished the world by signing a nonaggression pact with Hitler, his former sworn enemy. On September 1, immediately after the signing of the Nazi–Soviet pact, Germany invaded Poland. This time, Britain and France, who had pledged to protect Poland against aggression, declared war. But Germany appeared unstoppable. Within a year, the Nazi *blitzkrieg* (lightning war) had overrun Poland and much of Scandinavia, Belgium, and the Netherlands. On June 14, 1940, German troops occupied Paris. Hitler now dominated nearly all of Europe, as well as North Africa. In September 1940, Germany, Italy, and Japan created a military alliance known as the Axis.

In a 1940 cartoon, war clouds engulf Europe, while Uncle Sam observes that the Atlantic Ocean no longer seems to shield the United States from involvement.

For one critical year, Britain stood virtually alone in fighting Germany. Winston Churchill, who became prime minister in 1940, vowed to resist a threatened Nazi invasion. In the Battle of Britain of 1940-1941, German planes launched devastating attacks on London and other cities. The Royal Air Force eventually turned back the air assault. But Churchill pointedly called on the "new world, with all its power and might," to step forward to rescue the old.

The Battle of Britain

Toward Intervention

Roosevelt viewed Hitler as a mad gangster whose victories posed a direct threat to the United States. But most Americans remained desperate to remain out of the conflict. "What worries me, especially," FDR wrote to Kansas editor William Allen White, "is that public opinion over here is patting itself on the back every morning and thanking God for the Atlantic Ocean and the Pacific Ocean." After a tumultuous debate, Congress in 1940 agreed to allow the sale of arms to Britain on a "cash and carry" basis—that is, they had to be paid for in cash and transported in British ships. It also approved plans for military rearmament. But with a presidential election looming, Roosevelt was reluctant to go further. Opponents of involvement in Europe organized the America First Committee, with hundreds of thousands of members and a leadership that included such well-known figures as Henry Ford, Father Coughlin, and Charles A. Lindbergh.

The America First Committee

In 1940, breaking with a tradition that dated back to George Washington, Roosevelt announced his candidacy for a third term as president. The international

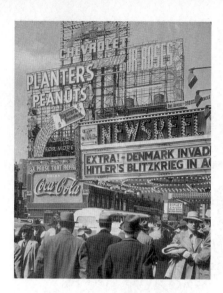

A newsreel theater in New York's Times Square announces Hitler's *blitzkrieg* in Europe in the spring of 1940.

Interventionist movements

situation was too dangerous and domestic recovery too fragile, he insisted, for him to leave office. Republicans chose as his opponent a political amateur, Wall Street businessman and lawyer Wendell Willkie. Differences between the candidates were far more muted than in 1936. Both supported the law, enacted in September 1940, that established the nation's first peacetime draft. Willkie endorsed New Deal social legislation. He captured more votes than Roosevelt's previous opponents, but FDR still emerged with a decisive victory. Soon after his victory, in a fireside chat in December 1940, Roosevelt announced that the United States would become the "great arsenal of democracy," providing Britain and China with military supplies in their fight against Germany and Japan.

During 1941, the United States became more and more closely allied with those fighting Germany and Japan. But with Britain virtually bankrupt, it could no longer pay for supplies. At Roosevelt's urging, Congress passed the **Lend-Lease Act**, which authorized military aid so long as countries promised somehow to return it all after the war. Under the law's provisions, the United States funneled billions of dollars' worth of arms to Britain and China, as well as the Soviet Union, after Hitler renounced his nonaggression pact and invaded that country in June 1941. FDR also froze Japanese assets in the United States, halting virtually all trade between the countries, including the sale of oil vital to Japan.

Those who believed that the United States must intervene to stem the rising tide of fascism tried to awaken a reluctant country to prepare for war. Interventionists popularized slogans that would become central to wartime mobilization. In June 1941, refugees from Germany and the occupied countries of Europe joined with Americans to form the Free World Association, which sought to bring the United States into the war against Hitler. The same year saw the formation of Freedom House. With a prestigious membership that included university presidents, ministers, businessmen, and labor leaders, Freedom House described the war raging in Europe as an ideological struggle between dictatorship and the "free world." In October 1941, it sponsored a "Fight for Freedom" rally at New York's Madison Square Garden, complete with a patriotic variety show entitled "It's Fun to Be Free." The rally ended by demanding an immediate declaration of war against Germany.

Pearl Harbor

December 7, 1941

Until November 1941, the administration's attention focused on Europe. But at the end of that month, intercepted Japanese messages revealed that an assault in the Pacific was imminent. No one, however, knew where it would come. On December 7, 1941, Japanese planes, launched from aircraft carriers, bombed the naval base at Pearl Harbor in Hawaii, the first attack by a foreign power on American soil since the War of 1812. Japan launched the attack in the hope of crippling American naval power in the Pacific. With a free hand in its campaign of conquest in East Asia, Japan would gain access to supplies of oil and other resources it could no longer obtain from the United States. It hoped that destroying the American fleet would establish Japan for years to come as the dominant power in the region.

Pearl Harbor was a complete and devastating surprise. In a few hours, more than 2,000 American servicemen were killed, and 187 aircraft and 18 naval

The battleships *West Virginia* and *Tennessee* in flames during the Japanese attack on Pearl Harbor. Both were repaired and later took part in the Pacific war.

vessels, including 8 battleships, destroyed or damaged. By a stroke of fortune, no aircraft carriers—which would prove decisive in the Pacific war—happened to be docked at Pearl Harbor on December 7.

To this day, conspiracy theories abound suggesting that FDR knew of the attack and did nothing to prevent it so as to bring the United States into the war. No credible evidence supports this charge. Indeed, with the country drawing ever closer to intervention in Europe, Roosevelt hoped to keep the peace in the Pacific. But Secretary of Labor Frances Perkins, who saw the president after the attack, remarked that he seemed calm—"his terrible moral problem had been resolved." Terming December 7 "a date which will live in infamy," Roosevelt asked Congress for a declaration of war against Japan. The combined vote in Congress was 388 in favor and 1 against—pacifist Jeanette Rankin of Montana, who had also voted against American entry into World War I. The next day, Germany declared war on the United States. America had finally joined the largest war in human history.

> *Declaration of war*

The War in the Pacific

World War II has been called a "gross national product war," meaning that its outcome turned on which coalition of combatants could outproduce the other. In retrospect, it appears inevitable that the entry of the United States, with its superior industrial might, would ensure the defeat of the **Axis powers**. But the first few months of American involvement witnessed an unbroken string of military disasters. Having earlier occupied substantial portions of French Indochina (now Vietnam, Laos, and Cambodia), Japan in early 1942 conquered Burma (Myanmar) and Siam (Thailand). Japan also took control of the Dutch East Indies (Indonesia), whose extensive oil fields

> *Military disasters*

Some of the 13,000 American troops forced to surrender to the Japanese on Corregidor Island in the Philippines in May 1942.

Members of the U.S. Marine Corps, Navy, and Coast Guard taking part in an amphibious assault during the "island hopping" campaign in the Pacific theater of World War II.

could replace supplies from the United States. And it occupied Guam, the Philippines, and other Pacific islands. At Bataan, in the Philippines, the Japanese forced 78,000 American and Filipino troops to lay down their arms—the largest surrender in American military history. Thousands perished on the ensuing "death march" to a prisoner-of-war camp, and thousands more died of disease and starvation after they arrived. At the same time, German submarines sank hundreds of Allied merchant and naval vessels during the Battle of the Atlantic.

Soon, however, the tide of battle began to turn. In May 1942, in the Battle of the Coral Sea, the American navy turned back a Japanese fleet intent on attacking Australia. The following month, it inflicted devastating losses on the Japanese navy in the Battle of Midway Island. American codebreakers had managed to decipher the Japanese communications code, so the navy was forewarned about the timing of the assault at Midway and prepared an ambush for the attacking fleet. In the battle, four Japanese aircraft carriers, along with other vessels, were destroyed. Midway was the turning point of the Pacific naval war. The victories there and in the Coral Sea allowed American forces to launch the bloody campaigns that one by one drove the Japanese from fortified islands like Guadalcanal and the Solomons in the western Pacific and brought American troops ever closer to Japan.

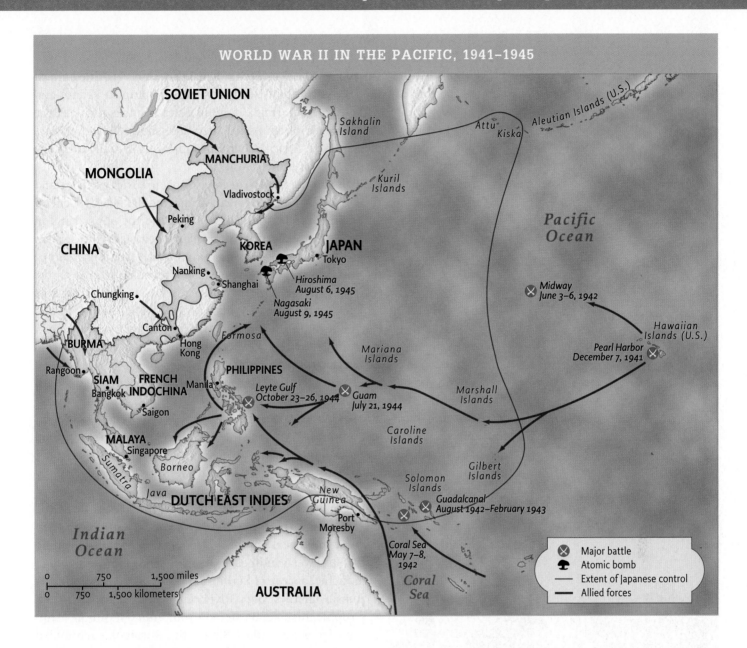

WORLD WAR II IN THE PACIFIC, 1941–1945

The War in Europe

The "Grand Alliance" of World War II in Europe brought together the United States, Great Britain, and the Soviet Union, each led by an iron-willed, larger-than-life figure: Roosevelt, Winston Churchill, and Joseph Stalin. United in their determination to defeat Nazi Germany, they differed not only in terms of the societies they represented but also in their long-range goals. Stalin was set on establishing enough control over eastern Europe that his country would never again be invaded from the west. Churchill hoped to ensure that the British Empire emerged intact from the war. Roosevelt, like Woodrow Wilson before him, hoped to establish a new international order so that world wars would never again take place.

Although the Japanese navy never fully recovered from its defeats at the Coral Sea and Midway in 1942, it took three more years for American forces to near the Japanese homeland.

Facing wars in two hemispheres, Roosevelt had to determine how best to deploy American manpower and resources. Bearing the brunt of the fighting after Hitler invaded the Soviet Union in 1941, Stalin demanded an early Allied attack across the English Channel to confront German forces in occupied France and relieve pressure on his beleaguered army. Churchill's strategy was to attack the "soft underbelly" of Axis power through Allied operations in the Mediterranean, starting with an invasion of North Africa. Churchill's approach prevailed, and the cross-Channel invasion did not come until 1944.

In November 1942, British and American forces invaded North Africa and by May 1943 forced the surrender of the German army commanded by General Erwin Rommel. By the spring of 1943, the Allies also gained the upper hand in the Atlantic, as British and American destroyers and planes devastated the German submarine fleet. But even though Roosevelt was committed to liberating Europe from Nazi control, American troops did not immediately become involved on the European continent. As late as the end of 1944, more American military personnel were deployed in the Pacific than against Germany. In July 1943, American and British forces invaded Sicily, beginning the liberation of Italy. A popular uprising in Rome overthrew the Mussolini government, whereupon Germany occupied most of the country. Fighting there raged throughout 1944.

The major involvement of American troops in Europe did not begin until June 6, 1944. On that date, known as **D-Day**, nearly 200,000 American, British, and Canadian soldiers under the command of General Dwight D. Eisenhower landed in Normandy in northwestern France. More than a million troops followed them ashore in the next few weeks, in the most massive sea–land operation in history. After fierce fighting, German armies retreated eastward. By August, Paris had been liberated.

The crucial fighting in Europe, however, took place on the eastern front, the scene of an epic struggle between Germany and the Soviet Union. More than 3 million German soldiers took part in the 1941 invasion. After sweeping through western Russia, German armies in August 1942 launched a siege of Stalingrad, a city located deep inside Russia on the Volga River. This proved to be a catastrophic mistake. Bolstered by an influx of military supplies from the United States, the Russians surrounded the German troops and forced them to surrender. Some 800,000 Germans and 1.2 million Russians perished in the fighting. The German surrender at Stalingrad in January 1943 marked the turning point of the European war. Combined with a Russian victory at Kursk six months later in the greatest tank battle in history, the campaign in the east devastated Hitler's forces and sent surviving units on a long retreat back toward Germany.

Of 13.6 million German casualties in World War II, 10 million came on the Russian front. They represented only part of the war's vast toll in human lives. Millions of Poles and at least 20 million Russians, probably many more, perished—not only soldiers but civilian victims

Ally victories

German prisoners of war guarded by an American soldier shortly after D-Day in June 1944. By this time, the Germans were drafting very young men into their armies.

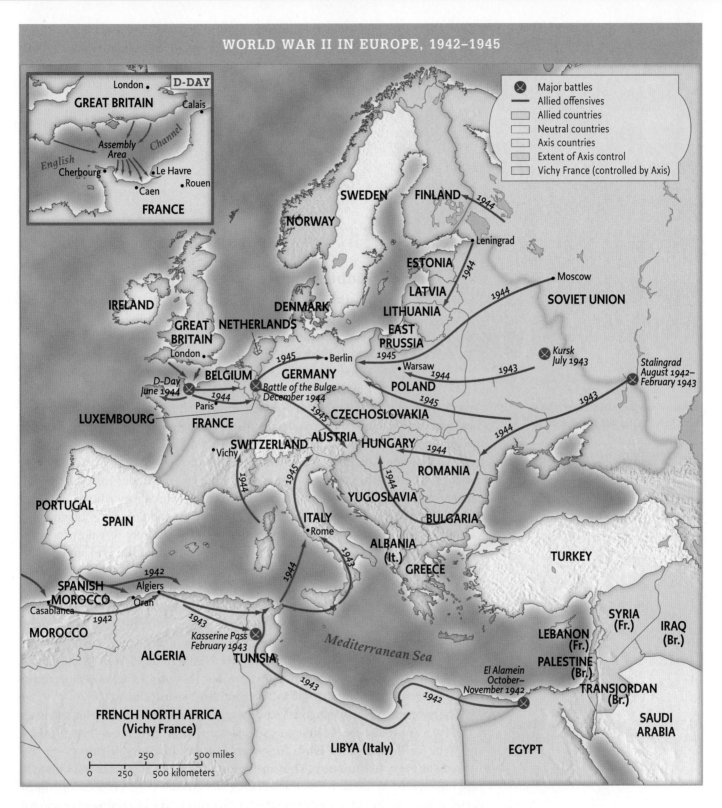

WORLD WAR II IN EUROPE, 1942–1945

D-DAY

GREAT BRITAIN
London
Calais
Assembly Area
English Channel
Cherbourg
Le Havre
Rouen
Caen
FRANCE

Legend:
- Major battles
- Allied offensives
- Allied countries
- Neutral countries
- Axis countries
- Extent of Axis control
- Vichy France (controlled by Axis)

SWEDEN
FINLAND
1944
NORWAY
Leningrad
1944
ESTONIA
Moscow
LATVIA
1944
SOVIET UNION
LITHUANIA
IRELAND
DENMARK
EAST PRUSSIA
Kursk July 1943
NETHERLANDS
GREAT BRITAIN
London
1945
Berlin
1945
Warsaw
1943
Stalingrad August 1942–February 1943
BELGIUM
GERMANY
Battle of the Bulge December 1944
1944
POLAND
1943
D-Day June 1944
1944
Paris
1945
CZECHOSLOVAKIA
1945
1944
LUXEMBOURG
FRANCE
AUSTRIA
SWITZERLAND
Vichy
HUNGARY
1944
1945
ROMANIA
1944
PORTUGAL
YUGOSLAVIA
1944
SPAIN
ITALY
Rome
BULGARIA
1944
ALBANIA (It.)
1943
GREECE
TURKEY
1942
SPANISH MOROCCO
Algiers
Oran
Casablanca
1942
1943
Kasserine Pass February 1943
Mediterranean Sea
SYRIA (Fr.)
IRAQ (Br.)
LEBANON (Fr.)
MOROCCO
ALGERIA
TUNISIA
PALESTINE (Br.)
El Alamein October–November 1942
TRANSJORDAN (Br.)
1943
1942
FRENCH NORTH AFRICA (Vichy France)
SAUDI ARABIA
LIBYA (Italy)
EGYPT

0   250   500 miles
0 250 500 kilometers

Most of the land fighting in Europe during World War II took place on the eastern front between the German and Soviet armies.

Prisoners at a German concentration camp liberated by Allied troops in 1945.

Military diversity

Redirecting the economy

of starvation, disease, and massacres by German soldiers. After his armies had penetrated eastern Europe in 1941, moreover, Hitler embarked on the "final solution"—the mass extermination of "undesirable" peoples—Slavs, gypsies, homosexuals, and, above all, Jews. By 1945, 6 million Jewish men, women, and children had died in Nazi death camps. What came to be called the **Holocaust** was the horrifying culmination of the Nazi belief that Germans constituted a "master race" destined to rule the world.

THE HOME FRONT

Mobilizing for War

By the end of World War II, some 50 million American men had registered for the draft and 10 million had been inducted into the military. The army exemplified how the war united American society in new ways. Military service threw together Americans from every region and walk of life, and almost every racial and ethnic background (African-Americans continued to serve in segregated units). It brought into contact young men who would never have encountered each other in peacetime. Many were the children of immigrants who now emerged from urban ethnic communities to fight alongside Americans from rural regions with very different cultures and outlooks. The federal government ended voluntary enlistment in 1942, relying entirely on the draft for manpower. This ensured that wartime sacrifice was widely shared throughout American society. By contrast, in the decades following the Vietnam War, the armed forces have been composed entirely of volunteers and the military includes very few men and women from middle- and upper-class backgrounds.

World War II also transformed the role of the national government. FDR created federal agencies like the War Production Board, the War Manpower Commission, and the Office of Price Administration to regulate the allocation of labor, control the shipping industry, establish manufacturing quotas, and fix wages, prices, and rents. The number of federal workers rose from 1 million to 4 million, part of a tremendous growth in new jobs that pushed the unemployment rate down from 14 percent in 1940 to 2 percent three years later.

The government built housing for war workers and forced civilian industries to retool for war production. Michigan's auto factories now turned out trucks, tanks, and jeeps for the army. By 1944, American factories produced a ship every day and a plane every five minutes. The gross national product rose from $91 billion to $214 billion during the war, and the federal government's expenditures amounted to twice the combined total of the previous 150 years. The government marketed billions of dollars' worth of war bonds, increased taxes, and began the practice of withholding income tax directly from weekly paychecks. Before the war, only the 4 million wealthiest Americans paid income taxes; by 1945, more than 40 million did so. The government, one historian writes, moved during the war from "class taxation" to "mass taxation."

Business and the War

The relationship between the federal government and big business changed dramatically from the days of the Second New Deal. "If you are going to go to war in a capitalist country," observed Secretary of War Henry Stimson, "you had better let business make money out of the process." As corporate executives flooded into federal agencies concerned with war production, Roosevelt offered incentives to spur production—low-interest loans, tax concessions, and contracts with guaranteed profits. The great bulk of federal spending went to the largest corporations, furthering the long-term trend toward economic concentration. By the end of the war, the 200 biggest industrial companies accounted for almost half of all corporate assets in the United States.

Big business

Americans marveled at the achievements of wartime manufacturing. Thousands of aircraft, 100,000 armored vehicles, and 2.5 million trucks rolled off American assembly lines, and entirely new products like synthetic rubber replaced natural resources now controlled by Japan. Government-sponsored scientific research perfected inventions like radar, jet engines, and early computers that helped to win the war and would have a large impact on postwar life. These accomplishments not only made it possible to win a two-front war but also helped to restore the reputation of business and businessmen, which had reached a low point during the Depression.

Innovation in manufacturing

War-related production essentially ended the Great Depression. In this photograph from 1942, workers wait to be paid at a Maryland shipyard.

Bombers being manufactured at Ford's Willow Run factory, "the greatest single manufacturing plant the world has ever seen," according to the *Washington Post*. During the war, Ford, General Motors, and other automakers produced tanks, armored vehicles, and airplanes for the armed forces rather than cars for consumers.

Federal funds reinvigorated established manufacturing areas and created entirely new industrial centers. World War II saw the West Coast emerge as a focus of military-industrial production. The government invested billions of dollars in the shipyards of Seattle, Portland, and San Francisco and in the steel plants and aircraft factories of southern California. By the war's end, California had received one-tenth of all federal spending, and Los Angeles had become the nation's second largest manufacturing center. Nearly 2 million Americans moved to California for jobs in defense-related industries, and millions more passed through for military training and embarkation to the Pacific war.

In the South, the combination of rural out-migration and government investment in military-related factories and shipyards hastened a shift from agricultural to industrial employment. During the war, southern per capita income rose from 60 percent to 70 percent of the national average. But the South remained very poor when the war ended. Much of its rural population still lived in small wooden shacks with no indoor plumbing. The region had only two cities—Houston and New Orleans—with populations exceeding 500,000. Despite the expansion of war production, the South's economy still relied on agriculture and extractive industries—mining, lumber, oil—or manufacturing linked to farming, like the production of cotton textiles.

Labor in Wartime

Organized labor repeatedly described World War II as a crusade for freedom that would expand economic and political democracy at home and abroad and win for unions a major voice in politics and industrial management. During the war, labor entered a three-sided arrangement with government and business that allowed union membership to soar to unprecedented levels. In order to secure industrial peace and stabilize war production, the federal government forced reluctant employers to recognize unions. In 1944, when Montgomery Ward, the large mail-order company, defied a pro-union order, the army seized its headquarters and physically evicted its president. For their part, union leaders agreed not to strike and conceded employers' right to "managerial prerogatives" and a "fair profit."

Despite the gains produced by labor militancy during the 1930s, unions only became firmly established in many sectors of the economy during World War II. By 1945, union membership stood at nearly 15 million, one-third of the non-farm labor force and the highest proportion in American history. But if labor became a partner in government, it was very much a junior partner. The decline of the New Deal, already evident in the late 1930s, proceeded during the war. Congress continued to be dominated by a conservative alliance of Republicans and southern Democrats. They left intact core New Deal programs like Social Security but eliminated agencies thought to be controlled by leftists, including the Civilian Conservation Corps, National Youth Administration, and Works

TABLE 22.1 Labor Union Membership	

YEAR	NUMBER OF MEMBERS
1933	2,857,000
1934	3,728,000
1935	3,753,000
1936	4,107,000
1937	5,780,000
1938	8,265,000
1939	8,980,000
1940	8,944,000
1941	10,489,000
1942	10,762,000
1943	13,642,000
1944	14,621,000
1945	14,796,000

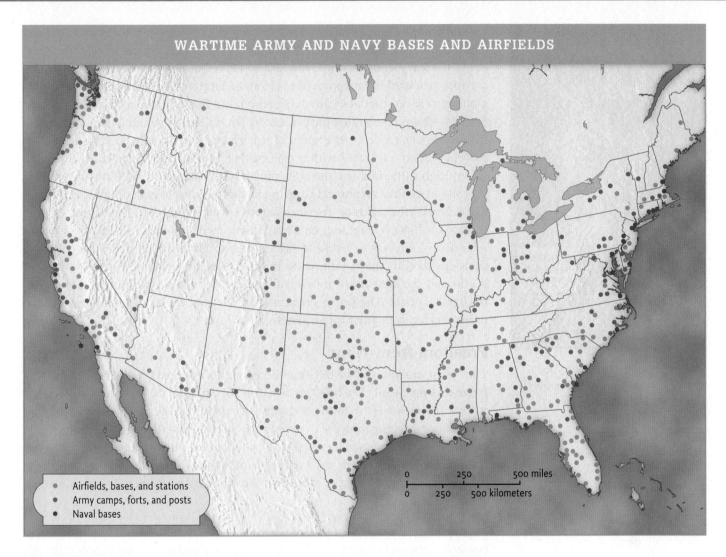

WARTIME ARMY AND NAVY BASES AND AIRFIELDS

- Airfields, bases, and stations
- Army camps, forts, and posts
- Naval bases

Progress Administration. Congress rejected Roosevelt's call for a cap on personal incomes and set taxes on corporate profits at a level far lower than FDR requested. Despite the "no-strike" pledge, 1943 and 1944 witnessed numerous brief walkouts in which workers protested the increasing speed of assembly-line production and the disparity between wages frozen by government order and expanding corporate profits.

As this map indicates, the military and naval facilities built by the federal government during World War II were concentrated in the South and West, sparking the economic development of these regions.

Fighting for the Four Freedoms

Previous conflicts, including the Mexican War and World War I, had deeply divided American society. In contrast, World War II came to be remembered as the Good War, a time of national unity in pursuit of indisputably noble goals. But all wars require the mobilization of patriotic public opinion. By 1940, "To sell *goods*, we must sell *words*" had become a motto of advertisers. Foremost among the words that helped to "sell" World War II was "freedom."

Mobilizing public opinion

In this recruitment poster for the Boy Scouts, a svelte Miss Liberty prominently displays the Bill of Rights, widely celebrated during World War II as the centerpiece of American freedom.

Talk of freedom pervaded wartime America. To Roosevelt, the Four Freedoms expressed deeply held American values worthy of being spread worldwide. Freedom from fear meant not only a longing for peace but also a more general desire for security in a world that appeared to be out of control. Freedom of speech and religion scarcely required detailed explanation. But their prominent place among the Four Freedoms accelerated the process by which First Amendment protections of free expression moved to the center of Americans' definition of liberty. In 1941, the administration celebrated with considerable fanfare the 150th anniversary of the Bill of Rights (the first ten amendments to the Constitution). FDR described their protections against tyrannical government as defining characteristics of American life, central to the rights of "free men and free women." In 1943, the Supreme Court reversed a 1940 ruling and, on First Amendment grounds, upheld the right of Jehovah's Witnesses to refuse to salute the American flag in public schools. The decision stood in sharp contrast to the coercive patriotism of World War I, and it affirmed the sanctity of individual conscience as a bedrock of freedom, even in times of crisis. The justices contrasted the American system of constitutional protection for unpopular minorities with Nazi tyranny.

Freedom from Want

The "most ambiguous" of the Four Freedoms, *Fortune* magazine remarked, was freedom from want. Yet this "great inspiring phrase," as a Pennsylvania steelworker put it in a letter to the president, seemed to strike the deepest chord in a nation just emerging from the Depression. Roosevelt initially meant it to refer to the elimination of barriers to international trade. But he quickly came to link freedom from want to an economic goal more relevant to the average citizen—protecting the future "standard of living of the American worker and farmer" by guaranteeing

Patriotic Fan. This fan, marketed to women during World War II, illustrates how freedom and patriotism were closely linked. At the far left and right, owners are instructed in ways to help win the war and preserve American freedom. The five middle panels suggest some of the era's definitions of freedom: freedom "to listen" (presumably without government censorship); self-government; freedom of assembly; the right to choose one's work; and freedom "to play."

that the Depression would not resume after the war. This, he declared, would bring "real freedom for the common man."

When Norman Rockwell's paintings of the Four Freedoms first appeared in the *Saturday Evening Post*, each was accompanied by a brief essay. Three of these essays, by the celebrated authors Stephen Vincent Benét, Booth Tarkington, and Will Durant, emphasized that the values Rockwell depicted were essentially American and the opposite of those of the Axis powers. For *Freedom from Want*, the editors chose an unknown Filipino poet, Carlos Bulosan, who had emigrated to the United States at the age of sixteen. Bulosan's essay showed how the Four Freedoms could inspire hopes for a better future as well as nostalgia for Rockwell's imagined small-town past. Bulosan wrote of those Americans still outside the social mainstream—migrant workers, cannery laborers, black victims of segregation—for whom freedom meant having enough to eat, sending their children to school, and being able to "share the promise and fruits of American life."

> Saturday Morning Post *essays*

The Office of War Information

The history of the Office of War Information (OWI), created in 1942 to mobilize public opinion, illustrates how the political divisions generated by the New Deal affected efforts to promote the Four Freedoms. The liberal Democrats who dominated the OWI's writing staff sought to make the conflict "a 'people's war' for freedom." The OWI feared that Americans had only a vague understanding of the war's purposes and that the populace seemed more fervently committed to paying back the Japanese for their attack on Pearl Harbor than ridding the world of fascism. They utilized radio, film, the press, and other media to give the conflict an ideological meaning, while seeking to avoid the nationalist hysteria of World War I.

> *Mobilizing public opinion*

Each side in World War II invoked history to rally support for its cause. "Rise of Asia" depicts Japan liberating Asia from "ABCD" imperial oppressors (Americans, British, Chinese, Dutch), while the poster issued by the Office of War Information in the United States links the words of Abraham Lincoln to the struggle against Nazi tyranny.

Wartime mobilization drew on deep-seated American traditions. The portrait of the United States holding aloft the torch of liberty in a world overrun by oppression reached back at least as far as the American Revolution. The description of a world half slave and half free recalled the Great Emancipator. But critics charged that the OWI seemed most interested in promoting the definition of freedom Roosevelt had emphasized during the 1930s. One of its first pamphlets listed as elements of freedom the right to a job at fair pay and to adequate food, clothing, shelter, and medical care. Concerned that the OWI was devoting as much time to promoting New Deal social programs as to the war effort, Congress eliminated most of its funding.

The Fifth Freedom

Privitization of propaganda

After Congress curtailed the OWI, the "selling of America" became overwhelmingly a private affair. Under the watchful eye of the War Advertising Council, private companies joined in the campaign to promote wartime patriotism, while positioning themselves and their brand names for the postwar world. Alongside advertisements urging Americans to purchase war bonds, guard against revealing military secrets, and grow "victory gardens" to allow food to be sent to the army, the war witnessed a burst of messages marketing advertisers' definition of freedom. Without directly criticizing Roosevelt, they repeatedly suggested that he had overlooked a fifth freedom. The National Association of Manufacturers and individual companies bombarded Americans with press releases, radio programs, and advertisements attributing the amazing feats of wartime production to "free enterprise."

Prosperity at home

Americans on the home front enjoyed a prosperity many could scarcely remember. Despite the rationing of scarce consumer items like coffee, meat, and

In this advertisement by the Liberty Motors and Engineering Corporation, published in the February 1944 issue of *Fortune*, Uncle Sam offers the Fifth Freedom—"free enterprise"—to war-devastated Europe. To spread its message, the company offered free enlargements of its ad.

gasoline, consumers found more goods available in 1944 than when the war began. With the memory of the Depression still very much alive, businessmen predicted a postwar world filled with consumer goods, with "freedom of choice" among abundant possibilities assured if only private enterprise were liberated from government controls. One advertisement for Royal typewriters, entitled "What This War Is All About," explained that victory would "hasten the day when you . . . can once more walk into any store in the land and buy anything you want." Certainly, ads suggested, the war did not imply any alteration in American institutions. "I'm fighting for freedom," said a soldier in an ad by the Nash-Kelvinator Corporation. "So don't anybody tell me I'll find America changed."

Women at Work

During the war, the nation engaged in an unprecedented mobilization of "womanpower" to fill industrial jobs vacated by men. OWI publications encouraged women to go to work, Hollywood films glorified the independent woman, and private advertising celebrated the achievements of Rosie the Riveter, the female industrial laborer depicted as muscular and self-reliant in Norman Rockwell's famous magazine cover. With 15 million men in the armed forces, women in 1944 made up more than one-third of the civilian labor force, and 350,000 served in auxiliary military units.

Glorifying the working woman

Even though most women workers still labored in clerical and service jobs, new opportunities suddenly opened in industrial, professional, and government positions previously restricted to men. On the West Coast, one-third of the workers in aircraft manufacturing and shipbuilding were women. For the first time in history,

New opportunities for women

A female lathe operator in a Texas plant that produced transport planes.

This photograph captures the enthusiasm of three "fly girls"—female pilots employed by the air force to deliver cargo and passengers and test military aircraft. Known as WASPs (Women Airforce Service Pilots), they eventually numbered over 1,000 aviators, who trained at an all-female base at Avenger Field in Sweetwater, Texas. They did not take part in combat, but thirty-eight died in service.

married women in their thirties outnumbered the young and single among female workers. Women forced unions like the United Auto Workers to confront issues like equal pay for equal work, maternity leave, and childcare facilities for working mothers. Defense companies sponsored swing bands and dances to boost worker morale and arranged dates between male and female workers. Having enjoyed what one wartime worker called "a taste of freedom"—doing "men's" jobs for men's wages and, sometimes, engaging in sexual activity while unmarried—many women hoped to remain in the labor force once peace returned.

The Pull of Tradition

"We as a nation," proclaimed one magazine article, "must change our basic attitude toward the work of women." But change proved difficult. The government, employers, and unions depicted work as a temporary necessity, not an expansion of women's freedom. Advertisements assured women laboring in factories that they, too, were "fighting for freedom." But their language spoke of sacrifice and military victory, not rights, independence, or self-determination. One union publication even declared, "There should be a law requiring the women who have taken over men's jobs to be laid off after the war." When the war ended, most female war workers, especially those in better-paying industrial employment, did indeed lose their jobs.

Despite the upsurge in the number of working women, the advertisers' "world of tomorrow" rested on a vision of family-centered prosperity. Like Norman Rockwell's Four Freedoms paintings, these wartime discussions of freedom simultaneously looked forward to a day of material abundance and back to a time when the family stood as the bedrock of society. The "American way of life" celebrated during the war centered on the woman with "a husband to meet every night at the door," and a home stocked with household appliances and consumer goods. Advertisements portrayed working women dreaming of their boyfriends in the army and emphasized that with the proper makeup, women could labor in a factory and remain attractive to men. Men in the army seem to have assumed that they would return home to resume traditional family life. In one wartime radio program, a young man described his goal for peacetime: "Havin' a home and some kids, and breathin' fresh air out in the suburbs . . . livin' and workin' decent, like free people."

VISIONS OF POSTWAR FREEDOM

Toward an American Century

The prospect of an affluent future provided a point of unity between New Dealers and conservatives, business and labor. And the promise of prosperity to some extent united two of the most celebrated blueprints for the postwar world. One was *The American Century*, publisher Henry Luce's 1941 effort to mobilize the American people

Luce's The American Century

both for the coming war and for an era of postwar world leadership. Americans, Luce's book insisted, must embrace the role history had thrust upon them as the "dominant power in the world." They must seize the opportunity to share with "all peoples" their "magnificent industrial products" and the "great American ideals," foremost among which stood "love of freedom." After the war, American power and American values would underpin a previously unimaginable prosperity—"the abundant life," Luce called it—produced by "free economic enterprise."

The idea of an American mission to spread democracy and freedom goes back to the Revolution. But traditionally, it had envisioned the country as an example, not an active agent imposing the American model throughout the globe. Luce's essay anticipated important aspects of the postwar world. But its bombastic rhetoric and a title easily interpreted as a call for an American imperialism aroused immediate opposition among liberals and the left. Henry Wallace offered their response in "The Price of Free World Victory," an address delivered in May 1942 to the Free World Association.

> *Imposing the American model*

Wallace, secretary of agriculture during the 1930s and one of the more liberal New Dealers, had replaced Vice President John Nance Garner as Roosevelt's running mate in 1940. In contrast to Luce's American Century, a world of business dominance no less than of American power, Wallace predicted that the war would usher in a "century of the common man." The "march of freedom," said Wallace, would continue in the postwar world. That world, however, would be marked by international cooperation, not any single power's rule. Governments acting to "humanize" capitalism and redistribute economic resources would eliminate hunger, illiteracy, and poverty.

> *Henry Wallace*

Luce and Wallace both spoke the language of freedom. Luce offered a confident vision of worldwide free enterprise, while Wallace anticipated a global New Deal. But they had one thing in common—a new conception of America's role in the world, tied to continued international involvement, the promise of economic abundance, and the idea that the American experience should serve as a model for all other nations. Neither took into account the ideas that other countries might have developed as to how to proceed once the war had ended.

"The Way of Life of Free Men"

Even as Congress moved to dismantle parts of the New Deal, liberal Democrats and their left-wing allies unveiled plans for a postwar economic policy that would allow all Americans to enjoy freedom from want. In 1942 and 1943, the reports of the National Resources Planning Board (NRPB) offered a blueprint for a peacetime economy based on full employment, an expanded welfare state, and a widely shared American standard of living. Economic security and full employment were the board's watchwords. It called for a "new bill of rights" that would include all Americans in an expanded Social Security system and guarantee access to education, health care, adequate housing, and jobs for able-bodied adults. The NRPB's plan for a "full-employment economy" with a "fair distribution of income," said *The Nation*, embodied "the way of life of free men."

The reports continued a shift in liberals' outlook that dated from the late 1930s. Rather than seeking to reform the institutions of capitalism, liberals

Despite the new independence enjoyed by millions of women, propaganda posters during World War II emphasized the male-dominated family as an essential element of American freedom.

would henceforth rely on government spending to secure full employment, social welfare, and mass consumption, while leaving the operation of the economy in private hands. The reports appeared to reflect the views of British economist John Maynard Keynes, who, as noted in the previous chapter, had identified government spending as the best way to promote economic growth, even if it caused budget deficits. The war had, in effect, ended the Depression by implementing a military version of Keynesianism. In calling for massive spending on job creation and public works—urban redevelopment, rural electrification, an overhaul of the transportation system, and the like—the NRPB proposed the continuation of Keynesian spending in peacetime. But this went so far beyond what Congress was willing to support that it eliminated the NRPB's funding.

An Economic Bill of Rights

Mindful that public-opinion polls showed a large majority of Americans favoring a guarantee of employment for those who could not find work, the president in 1944 called for an "Economic Bill of Rights." The original Bill of Rights restricted the power of government in the name of liberty. FDR proposed to expand its power in order to secure full employment, an adequate income, medical care, education, and a decent home for all Americans.

Already ill and preoccupied with the war, Roosevelt spoke only occasionally of the Economic Bill of Rights during the 1944 presidential campaign. The replacement of Vice President Henry Wallace by Harry S. Truman, then a little-known senator from Missouri, suggested that the president did not intend to do battle with Congress over social policy. Congress did not enact the Economic Bill of Rights. But in 1944, it extended to the millions of returning veterans an array of benefits, including unemployment pay, scholarships for further education, low-cost mortgage loans, pensions, and job training. The Servicemen's Readjustment Act, or **GI Bill of Rights**, was one of the most far-reaching pieces of social legislation in American history. Aimed at rewarding members of the armed forces for their service and preventing the widespread unemployment and economic disruption that had followed World War I, it profoundly shaped postwar society. By 1946, more than 1 million veterans were attending college under its provisions, making up half of total college enrollment. Almost 4 million would receive home mortgages, spurring the postwar suburban housing boom.

During 1945, unions, civil rights organizations, and religious groups urged Congress to enact the Full Employment Bill, which tried to do for the entire economy what the GI Bill promised veterans. The measure established a "right to employment" for all Americans and required the

Ben Shahn's poster, *Our Friend*, for the Congress of Industrial Organizations' political action committee, urges workers to vote for FDR during his campaign for a fourth term. Art © Estate of Ben Shahn/ Licensed by VAGA, New York, NY.

federal government to increase its level of spending to create enough jobs in case the economy failed to do so. The target of an intense business lobbying campaign, the bill only passed in 1946 with the word "Full" removed from its title and after its commitment to governmental job creation had been eliminated. But as the war drew to a close, most Americans embraced the idea that the government must continue to play a major role in maintaining employment and a high standard of living.

The Full Employment Bill

The Road to Serfdom

The failure of the Full Employment Bill confirmed the political stalemate that had begun with the elections of 1938. It also revealed the renewed intellectual respectability of fears that economic planning represented a threat to liberty. When the *New Republic* spoke of full employment as the "road to freedom," it subtly acknowledged the impact of *The Road to Serfdom* (1944), a surprise best-seller by Friedrich A. Hayek, a previously obscure Austrian-born economist. Hayek claimed that even the best-intentioned government efforts to direct the economy posed a threat to individual liberty. He offered a simple message—"Planning leads to dictatorship."

Coming at a time when the miracles of war production had reinvigorated belief in the virtues of capitalism, and with the confrontation with Nazism highlighting the danger of merging economic and political power, Hayek offered a new intellectual justification for opponents of active government. In a complex economy, he insisted, no single person or group of experts could possibly possess enough knowledge to direct economic activity intelligently. A free market, he wrote, mobilizes the fragmented and partial knowledge scattered throughout society far more effectively than a planned economy.

Friedrich A. Hayek and laissez-faire economics

Unlike many of his disciples, Hayek was not a doctrinaire advocate of laissez-faire. His book endorsed measures that later conservatives would denounce as forms of socialism—minimum wage and maximum hours laws, antitrust enforcement, and a social safety net guaranteeing all citizens a basic minimum of food, shelter, and clothing. Hayek, moreover, criticized traditional conservatives for fondness for social hierarchy and authoritarian government. "I am not a conservative," he would later write. But by equating fascism, socialism, and the New Deal and by identifying economic planning with a loss of freedom, he helped lay the foundation for the rise of modern conservatism and a revival of laissez-faire economic thought. As the war drew to a close, the stage was set for a renewed battle over the government's proper role in society and the economy, and the social conditions of American freedom.

THE AMERICAN DILEMMA

The unprecedented attention to freedom as the defining characteristic of American life had implications that went far beyond wartime mobilization. World War II reshaped Americans' understanding of themselves as a people. The struggle against Nazi tyranny and its theory of a master race discredited ethnic and racial inequality. Originally promoted by religious and ethnic minorities in the 1920s and the Popular Front in the 1930s, a pluralist vision of American society now became part of official rhetoric. What set the United States apart from

Embracing pluralism

... where every boy can dream of being President. Where free schools, free opportunity, free enterprise, have built the most decent nation on earth. A nation built upon the rights of all men * *This is your America*

... *Keep it Free!*

Another *This Is America* propaganda poster emphasizes the American dream of equal opportunity for all. All the children in the classroom, however, are white.

its wartime foes, the government insisted, was not only dedication to the ideals of the Four Freedoms but also the principle that Americans of all races, religions, and national origins could enjoy those freedoms equally. Racism was the enemy's philosophy; Americanism rested on toleration of diversity and equality for all. By the end of the war, the new immigrant groups had been fully accepted as loyal ethnic Americans, rather than members of distinct and inferior "races." And the contradiction between the principle of equal freedom and the actual status of blacks had come to the forefront of national life.

Patriotic Assimilation

Among other things, World War II created a vast melting pot, especially for European immigrants and their children. Millions of Americans moved out of urban ethnic neighborhoods and isolated rural enclaves into the army and industrial plants where they came into contact with people of very different backgrounds. What one historian has called their "patriotic assimilation" differed sharply from the forced Americanization of World War I. While the Wilson administration had established Anglo-Saxon culture as a national norm, Roosevelt promoted pluralism as the only source of harmony in a diverse society. The American way of life, wrote the novelist Pearl Buck in an OWI pamphlet, rested on brotherhood—the principle that "persons of many lands can live together . . . and if they believe in freedom they can become a united people."

Government and private agencies eagerly promoted equality as the definition of Americanism and a counterpoint to Nazism. Officials rewrote history to establish racial and ethnic tolerance as the American way. To be an American, FDR declared, had always been a "matter of mind and heart," and "never . . . a matter of race or ancestry"—a statement more effective in mobilizing support for the war than in accurately describing the nation's past. Mindful of the intolerance spawned by World War I, the OWI highlighted nearly every group's contributions to American life and celebrated the strength of a people united in respect for diversity. One OWI pamphlet described prejudice as a foreign import rather than a homegrown product and declared bigots more dangerous than spies—they were "fighting for the enemy."

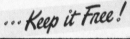

Racism and nativism discredited

Horrified by the uses to which the Nazis put the idea of inborn racial difference, biological and social scientists abandoned belief in a link among race, culture, and intelligence, an idea only recently central to their disciplines. Ruth Benedict's *Races and Racism* (1942) described racism as "a travesty of scientific knowledge." In the same year, Ashley Montagu's *Man's Most Dangerous Myth: The Fallacy of Race* became a best-seller. By the war's end, racism and nativism had been stripped of intellectual respectability, at least outside the South, and were viewed as psychological disorders.

Celebrating diversity

Hollywood, too, did its part, portraying fighting units whose members, representing various regional, ethnic, and religious backgrounds, put aside group loyalties and prejudices for the common cause. *Air Force* featured a bomber crew that included an Anglo-Saxon officer, a Jewish sergeant, and a Polish-American gunner. In the film *Bataan*, the ethnically balanced platoon included a black soldier, even though the real army was racially segregated. The war's most popular motion picture, *This Is the Army*, starring, among others, future president Ronald Reagan, offered a vision of postwar society that celebrated the ethnic diversity of the American people.

Intolerance, of course, hardly disappeared from American life. One correspondent complained to Norman Rockwell that he included too many "foreign-looking" faces in his *Freedom of Worship* painting. Many business and government circles still excluded Jews. Along with the fact that early reports of the Holocaust were too terrible to be believed, anti-Semitism contributed to the government's unwillingness to allow more than a handful of European Jews (21,000 during the course of the war) to find refuge in the United States. Roosevelt himself learned during the war of the extent of Hitler's "final solution" to the Jewish presence in Europe. But he failed to authorize air strikes that might have destroyed German death camps.

Nonetheless, the war made millions of ethnic Americans, especially the children of the new immigrants, feel fully American for the first time. During the war, one New York "ethnic" recalled, "the Italo-Americans stopped being Italo and started becoming Americans." But the event that inspired this comment, the Harlem race riot of 1943, suggested that patriotic assimilation stopped at the color line.

The *Bracero* Program

The war had a far more ambiguous meaning for non-white groups than for whites. On the eve of Pearl Harbor, racial barriers remained deeply entrenched in American life. Southern blacks were still trapped in a rigid system of segregation. Asians could not emigrate to the United States or become naturalized citizens. As noted in the previous chapter, more than 400,000 Mexican-Americans had been "voluntarily" repatriated by local authorities in the Southwest during the Depression. Most American Indians still lived on reservations, in dismal poverty.

The war set in motion changes that would reverberate in the postwar years. Under the **bracero program** agreed to by the Mexican and American governments in 1942 (the name derives from *brazo*, the Spanish word for arm), tens of thousands of contract laborers crossed into the United States to take up jobs as domestic and agricultural workers. Initially designed as a temporary response to the wartime labor shortage, the program lasted until 1964. During the period of the *bracero* program, more than 4.5 million Mexicans entered the United States under government labor contracts (while a slightly larger number were arrested for illegal entry by the Border Patrol). *Braceros* were supposed to receive decent housing and wages. But since they could not become citizens and could be deported at any time, they found it almost impossible to form unions or secure better working conditions.

Although the *bracero* program reinforced the status of immigrants from Mexico as an unskilled labor force, wartime employment opened new opportunities for second-generation Mexican-Americans. Hundreds of thousands of men and women emerged from ethnic neighborhoods, or *barrios*, to work in defense industries and serve in the army (where, unlike blacks, they fought alongside whites). For Mexican-American women in particular, the war afforded new opportunities for public participation and higher incomes. "Rosita the Riveter" took her place alongside "Rosie" in the West Coast's multiethnic war production factories. Government publications and newspaper accounts celebrated their role as patriotic mothers who encouraged their sons to enlist in the army and offered moral support while they were away at war. A new "Chicano" culture—a fusion of Mexican heritage and American experience—was being born. Contact with other groups led many to learn English and sparked a rise in interethnic marriages.

One series of posters issued by the Office of War Information to mobilize support for the war effort emphasized respect for the country's racial and ethnic diversity. This one, directed at Hispanics, suggests that there is no contradiction between pride in ethnic heritage and loyalty to the United States.

AMERICANOS TODOS
★
LUCHAMOS POR LA VICTORIA

★ AMERICANS ALL ★
LET'S FIGHT FOR VICTORY

VOICES OF FREEDOM

From LEAGUE OF UNITED LATIN AMERICAN CITIZENS, "WORLD WAR II AND MEXICAN AMERICANS" (1945)

Founded in 1929, the League of United Latin American Citizens (LULAC) campaigned for equal treatment for Americans of Latino descent and their full integration into American life. Soon after the war ended, an editorial in its publication *LULAC News* condemned continuing discrimination, reflecting how the war sparked a rising demand for equal rights among many minority groups.

"We do not serve Mexicans here." "You will have to get out as no Mexicans are allowed." "Your uniform and service ribbons mean nothing here. We still do not allow Mexicans."

These, and many other stronger-worded ones, are the embarrassing and humiliating retorts given our returning veterans of Latin American descent and their families. They may all be worded differently, and whereas some are toned with hate and loathness while others are toned with sympathy and remorse, still the implication remains that these so-called "Mexicans" are considered unworthy of equality, regardless of birthright or service. . . .

Why this hate, this prejudice, this tendency to discriminate against a people whose only fault seems to be that they are heirs of a culture older than any known "American Culture," to find them-

selves a part of a land and people they have helped to build and to defend, to find themselves a part of a minority group whose acquired passive nature keeps them from boldly demanding those rights and privileges which are rightfully theirs? Can it be the result of difference in race, nationality, language, loyalty, or ability?

There is no difference in race. Latin Americans, or so-called "Mexicans," are Caucasian or white. . . . There is no difference in nationality. These "Mexicans" were born and bred in this country and are just as American as Jones or Smith. . . . Difference in language? No, these "Mexicans" speak English. Accented, perhaps, in some cases, but English all over the United States seems to be accented. . . . Difference in loyalty? How can that be when all revere the same stars and stripes, when they don the same service uniforms for the same principles? Difference in intelligence and ability? Impossible. . . .

This condition is not a case of difference; it is a case of ignorance. . . . An ignorance of the cultural contributions of Americans of Latin American descent to the still young American Culture; . . . an ignorance of a sense of appreciation for a long, profitable, and loyal association with a group of Americans whose voice cries out in desperate supplication: "We have proved ourselves true and loyal Americans . . . now give us social, political, and economic equality."

From CHARLES H. WESLEY, "THE NEGRO HAS ALWAYS WANTED THE FOUR FREEDOMS," IN *WHAT THE NEGRO WANTS* (1944)

In 1944, the University of North Carolina Press published *What the Negro Wants*, a book of essays by fourteen prominent black leaders. Virtually every contributor called for the right to vote in the South, the dismantling of segregation, and access to the "American standard of living." Several essays also linked the black struggle for racial justice with movements against European imperialism in Africa and Asia. When he read the manuscript, W. T. Couch, the director of the press, was stunned. "If this is what the Negro wants," he told the book's editor, "nothing could be clearer than what he needs, and needs most urgently, is to revise his wants." In this excerpt, the historian Charles H. Wesley explains that blacks are denied each of the Four Freedoms, and also illustrates how the war strengthened black internationalism.

[Negroes] have wanted what other citizens of the United States have wanted. They have wanted freedom and opportunity. They have wanted the pursuit of the life vouchsafed to all citizens of the United States by our own liberty documents. They have wanted freedom of speech, [but] they were supposed to be silently acquiescent in all aspects of their life.... They have wanted freedom of religion, for they had been compelled to "steal away to Jesus" ... in order to worship God as they desired.... They have wanted freedom from want.... However, the Negro has remained a marginal worker and the competition with white workers has left him in want in many localities of an economically sufficient nation. They have wanted freedom from fear. They have been cowed, browbeaten or beaten, as they have marched through the years of American life....

The Negro wants democracy to begin at home.... The future of our democratic life is insecure so long as the hatred, disdain and disparagement of Americans of African ancestry exist....

The Negro wants not only to win the war but also to win the peace.... He wants the peace to be free of race and color restrictions, of imperialism and exploitation, and inclusive of the participation of minorities all over the world in their own governments. When it is said that we are fighting for freedom, the Negro asks, "Whose freedom?" Is it the freedom of a peace to exploit, suppress, exclude, debase and restrict colored peoples in India, China, Africa, Malaya in the usual ways? ... Will Great Britain and the United States specifically omit from the Four Freedoms their minorities and subject peoples? The Negro does not want such a peace.

QUESTIONS

1. *What evidence does the editorial offer that Latinos are deserving of equality?*

2. *Why does Wesley believe that black Americans are denied the Four Freedoms?*

3. *What differences and what commonalities exist between these two claims for greater rights in American society?*

Mexican-American Rights

The **zoot suit riots** of 1943, in which club-wielding sailors and policemen attacked Mexican-American youths wearing flamboyant clothing on the streets of Los Angeles, illustrated the limits of wartime tolerance. But the contrast between the war's rhetoric of freedom and pluralism and the reality of continued discrimination inspired a heightened consciousness of civil rights. Mexican-Americans brought complaints of discrimination before the Fair Employment Practices Commission (FEPC) to fight the practice in the Southwest of confining them to the lowest-paid work or paying them lower wages than white workers doing the same jobs.

Perhaps half a million Mexican-American men and women served in the armed forces. And with discrimination against Mexicans an increasing embarrassment in view of Roosevelt's Good Neighbor policy, Texas (the state with the largest population of Mexican descent) in 1943 unanimously passed the oddly-named Caucasian Race—Equal Privileges resolution. It stated that since "all the nations of the North and South American continents" were united in the struggle against Nazism, "all persons of the Caucasian race" were entitled to equal treatment in places of public accommodation. Since Texas law had long defined Mexicans as white, the measure applied to them while not challenging the segregation of blacks. The resolution lacked an enforcement mechanism. Indeed, because of continued discrimination in Texas, the Mexican government for a time prohibited the state from receiving laborers under the *bracero* program.

Caucasian Race–Equal Privileges resolution

Indians during the War

The war also brought many American Indians closer to the mainstream of American life. Some 25,000 served in the army (including the famous Navajo "code-talkers," who transmitted messages in their complex native language, which the Japanese could not decipher). Insisting that the United States lacked the authority to draft Indian men into the army, the Iroquois issued their own declaration of war against the Axis powers. Tens of thousands of Indians left reservations for jobs in war industries. Exposed for the first time to urban life and industrial society, many chose not to return to the reservations after the war ended (indeed, the reservations did not share in wartime prosperity). Some Indian veterans took advantage of the GI Bill to attend college after the war, an opportunity that had been available to very few Indians previously.

Asian-Americans in Wartime

Asian-Americans' war experience was paradoxical. More than 50,000—the children and grandchildren of immigrants from China, Japan, Korea, and the Philippines—fought in the army, mostly in all-Asian units. With China an ally in the Pacific war, Congress in 1943 ended decades of complete exclusion by establishing a nationality quota for Chinese immigrants. The annual limit of 105 hardly suggested a desire for a large-scale influx. But the image of the Chinese as gallant fighters defending their country against Japanese aggression called into question long-standing racial stereotypes. As in the case of Mexican-Americans, large numbers of Chinese-Americans moved out of ethnic ghettos to work alongside whites in jobs on the home front.

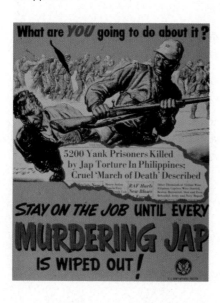

Wartime propaganda in the United States sought to inspire hatred against the Pacific foe. This poster, issued by the U.S. Army, recalls the Bataan death march in the Philippines.

The experience of Japanese-Americans was far different. Many Americans viewed the war against Germany as an ideological struggle. But both sides saw the Pacific war as a race war. Japanese propaganda depicted Americans as a self-indulgent people contaminated by ethnic and racial diversity as opposed to the racially "pure" Japanese. In the United States, long-standing prejudices and the shocking attack on Pearl Harbor combined to produce an unprecedented hatred of Japan. "In all our history," according to one historian, "no foe has been detested as were the Japanese." Government propaganda and war films portrayed the Japanese foe as rats, dogs, gorillas, and snakes—bestial and subhuman. They blamed Japanese aggression on a violent racial or national character, not, as in the case of Germany and Italy, on tyrannical rulers.

About 70 percent of Japanese-Americans in the continental United States lived in California, where they dominated vegetable farming in the Los Angeles area. One-third were first-generation immigrants, or *issei*, but a substantial majority were *nisei*—American-born, and therefore citizens. Many of the latter spoke only English, had never been to Japan, and had tried to assimilate despite prevailing prejudice. But the Japanese-American community could not remain unaffected by the rising tide of hatred. The government bent over backward to include German-Americans and Italian-Americans in the war effort. It ordered the arrest of only a handful of the more than 800,000 German and Italian nationals in the United States when the war began. But it viewed every person of Japanese ethnicity as a potential spy.

Japanese-American Internment

California, as discussed in Chapter 19, had a long history of hostility toward the Japanese. Now, inspired by exaggerated fears of a Japanese invasion of the West Coast and pressured by whites who saw an opportunity to gain possession of Japanese-American property, the military persuaded FDR to issue Executive Order 9066. Promulgated in February 1942, this ordered the relocation of all persons of Japanese descent from the West Coast. That spring and summer, authorities removed more than 110,000 men, women, and children—nearly two-thirds of them American citizens—to camps far from their homes. The order did not apply to persons of Japanese descent living in Hawaii, where they represented nearly 40 percent of the population. Despite Hawaii's vulnerability, its economy could not function without Japanese-American labor. But **Japanese-American internment** provided ammunition for Japan's claim that its aggressions in Asia were intended to defend the rights of non-white peoples against colonial rule and a racist United States.

The internees were subjected to a quasi-military discipline in the camps. Living in former horse stables, makeshift shacks, or barracks behind barbed wire fences, they were awakened for roll call at 6:45 each morning and ate their meals (which rarely included the Japanese cooking to which they were accustomed) in giant mess halls. Armed guards patrolled the camps, and searchlights shone all night. Privacy was difficult to come by, and medical facilities were often nonexistent. Nonetheless, the internees did their best to create an atmosphere of home, decorating their accommodations with pictures, flowers, and curtains, planting

Fumiko Hayashida holds her thirteen-month-old daughter, while waiting for relocation to an internment camp. Both wear baggage tags, as if they were pieces of luggage. This photo, taken by a journalist for the *Seattle Post-Intelligencer*, came to symbolize the entire internment experience. Ms. Hayashida celebrated her 100th birthday in 2011.

Executive Order 9066

Life in internment camps

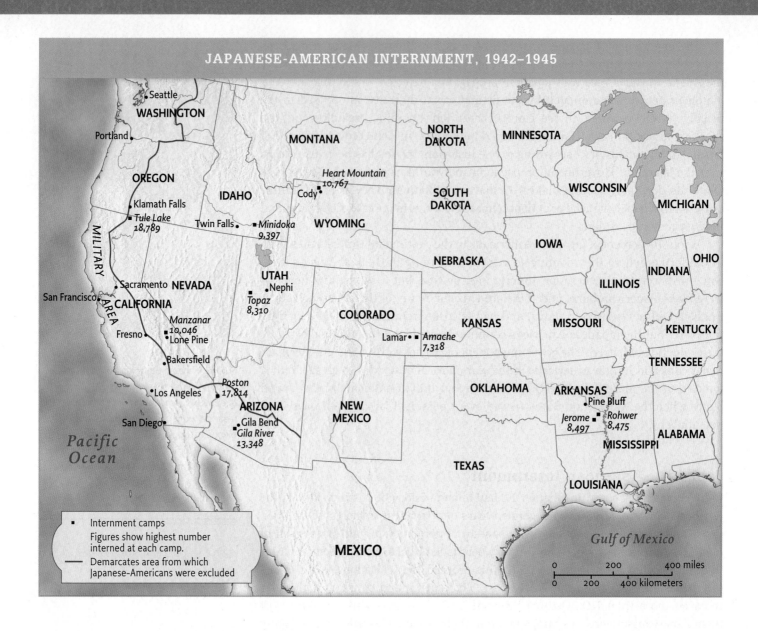

JAPANESE-AMERICAN INTERNMENT, 1942–1945

Legend:

- Internment camps
  Figures show highest number interned at each camp.
- Demarcates area from which Japanese-Americans were excluded

Map labels: Seattle, WASHINGTON, Portland, OREGON, Klamath Falls, Tule Lake 18,789, MILITARY AREA, Sacramento, San Francisco, CALIFORNIA, Fresno, Manzanar 10,046, Lone Pine, Bakersfield, Los Angeles, Poston 17,814, San Diego, Pacific Ocean, IDAHO, Cody, Heart Mountain 10,767, Twin Falls, Minidoka 9,397, WYOMING, NEVADA, UTAH, Nephi, Topaz 8,310, ARIZONA, Gila Bend, Gila River 13,348, NEW MEXICO, MONTANA, NORTH DAKOTA, SOUTH DAKOTA, NEBRASKA, COLORADO, Lamar, Amache 7,318, KANSAS, OKLAHOMA, TEXAS, MEXICO, MINNESOTA, WISCONSIN, IOWA, MISSOURI, ARKANSAS, Pine Bluff, Jerome 8,497, Rohwer 8,475, LOUISIANA, MICHIGAN, ILLINOIS, INDIANA, OHIO, KENTUCKY, TENNESSEE, MISSISSIPPI, ALABAMA, Gulf of Mexico

Scale: 0 200 400 miles / 0 200 400 kilometers

More than 100,000 Japanese-Americans—the majority American citizens—were forcibly moved from their homes to internment camps during World War II.

Courts' non-intervention

vegetable gardens, and setting up activities like sports clubs and art classes for themselves.

Internment revealed how easily war can undermine basic freedoms. There were no court hearings, no due process, and no writs of habeas corpus. One searches the wartime record in vain for public protests among non-Japanese against the gravest violation of civil liberties since the end of slavery. The press supported the policy almost unanimously. In Congress, only Senator Robert Taft of Ohio spoke out against it. Groups publicly committed to fighting discrimination, from the Communist Party to the NAACP and the American Jewish Committee, either defended the policy or remained silent.

The courts refused to intervene. In 1944, in ***Korematsu v. United States***, the Supreme Court denied the appeal of Fred Korematsu, a Japanese-American citizen who had been arrested for refusing to present himself for internment. Speaking for a 6-3 majority, Justice Hugo Black, usually an avid defender of civil liberties, upheld the legality of the internment policy, insisting that an order applying only to persons of Japanese descent was not based on race. The Court has never overturned the *Korematsu* decision. As Justice Robert H. Jackson warned in his dissent, it "lies about like a loaded weapon ready for the hand of any authority that can bring forward a plausible claim" of national security.

The government marketed war bonds to the internees. It established a loyalty oath program, expecting Japanese-Americans to swear allegiance to the government that had imprisoned them and to enlist in the army. Some young men refused, and about 200 were sent to prison for resisting the draft. "Let us out and then maybe I'll think about risking my skin for 'the land of the free,'" one of the resisters remarked. But 20,000 Japanese-Americans joined the armed forces from the camps, along with another 13,000 from Hawaii. Contradictions abounded in the wartime experiences of Japanese-Americans. In 1944, Sono Isato danced the role of an American beauty queen in the musical *On the Town* on Broadway, and her brother fought for the U.S. Army in the Pacific theater, while the government interned their father because he had been born in Japan.

> *Japanese-Americans in the military*

A long campaign for acknowledgment of the injustice done to Japanese-Americans followed the end of the war. In 1988, Congress apologized for internment and provided $20,000 in compensation to each surviving victim. President Bill Clinton subsequently awarded Fred Korematsu the Presidential Medal of Freedom.

> *Apology and restitution*

Blacks and the War

Although the treatment of Japanese-Americans revealed the stubborn hold of racism in American life, the wartime message of freedom portended a major transformation in the status of blacks. "There never has been, there isn't now, and there never will be," Roosevelt declared, "any race of people on the earth fit to serve as masters over their fellow men." Yet Nazi Germany cited American practices as proof of its own race policies. Washington remained a rigidly segregated city, and the Red Cross refused to mix blood from blacks and whites in its blood banks (thereby, critics charged, in effect accepting Nazi race theories). Charles Drew, the black scientist who pioneered the techniques of storing and shipping blood plasma—a development of immense importance to the treatment of wounded soldiers—protested bitterly against this policy, pointing out that it had no scientific basis. In 1940 and 1941, even as Roosevelt called for aid to the free peoples of Europe, thirteen lynchings took place in the United States.

During World War II, Red Cross blood banks separated blood from black and white Americans—one illustration of the persistence of racial segregation. This 1943 poster by the NAACP points out that the concept of "Negro" and "white" blood has no scientific basis.

The war spurred a movement of black population from the rural South to the cities of the North and West that dwarfed the Great Migration of World War I and the 1920s. In the **second Great Migration**, about 700,000 black migrants poured out of the South on what they called "liberty trains," seeking jobs in the industrial heartland. They encountered sometimes violent hostility. In 1943, a fight at a Detroit city park spiraled into a race riot that left thirty-four persons dead, and a "hate strike" of 20,000 workers protested the upgrading of black employees in a plant manufacturing aircraft engines. The war failed to end lynching. Isaac Simmons, a black minister, was murdered in 1944 for refusing to sell his land to a white man who believed it might contain oil. The criminals went unpunished. This took place in Liberty, Mississippi.

Blacks and Military Service

When World War II began, the air force and marines had no black members. The army restricted the number of black enlistees and contained only five black officers, three of them chaplains. The navy accepted blacks only as waiters and cooks.

During the war, more than 1 million blacks served in the armed forces. They did so in segregated units, largely confined to construction, transport, and other noncombat tasks. Many northern black draftees were sent to the South for military training, where they found themselves excluded from movie theaters and servicemen's clubs on military bases and abused when they ventured into local towns. Black soldiers sometimes had to give up their seats on railroad cars to accommodate Nazi prisoners of war. "Nothing so lowers Negro morale," wrote the NAACP's magazine, *The Crisis*, "as the frequent preferential treatment of Axis prisoners of war in contrast with Army policy toward American troops who happen to be Negro."

Segregation in the armed forces

Post-war segregation

When southern black veterans returned home and sought benefits through the GI Bill, they encountered even more evidence of racial discrimination. On the surface, the GI Bill contained no racial differentiation in offering benefits like health care, college tuition assistance, job training, and loans to start a business or purchase a farm. But local authorities who administered its provisions allowed southern black veterans to use its education benefits only at segregated colleges, limited their job training to unskilled work and low-wage service jobs, and restricted loans for farm purchase to white veterans.

Birth of the Civil Rights Movement

In 1942, a public-opinion survey sponsored by the army's Bureau of Intelligence found that the vast majority of white Americans were "unaware that there is any such thing as a 'Negro problem'" and were convinced that blacks were satisfied with their social and economic conditions. They would soon discover their mistake.

The war years witnessed the birth of the modern civil rights movement. Angered by the almost complete exclusion of African-Americans from jobs in the rapidly expanding war industries (of 100,000 aircraft workers in 1940, fewer than 300 were blacks), the black labor leader A. Philip Randolph in July 1941 called for a March on Washington. His demands included access to defense employment, an end to segregation, and a national antilynching law. Randolph, who as founder of the Brotherhood of Sleeping Car Porters had long battled racism among both employers and unions, hurled Roosevelt's rhetoric back at the president. Randolph declared racial discrimination "undemocratic, un-American, and pro-Hitler."

The prospect of thousands of angry blacks descending on Washington, remarked one official, "scared the government half to death." To persuade Randolph to call off the march, Roosevelt issued Executive Order 8802, which banned discrimination in defense jobs and established a Fair Employment Practices Commission (FEPC) to monitor compliance. The black press hailed the order as a new Emancipation Proclamation.

This Is the Enemy, a 1942 poster by Victor Ancona and Karl Koehler, suggests a connection between Nazism abroad and lynching at home.

Essentially an investigative agency, the FEPC lacked enforcement powers. But its very existence marked a significant shift in public policy. Its hearings exposed patterns of racial exclusion so ingrained that firms at first freely admitted that their want ads asked for "colored" applicants for positions as porters and janitors and "white" ones for skilled jobs, and that they allowed black women to work only as laundresses and cooks. The first federal agency since Reconstruction to campaign for equal opportunity for black Americans, the FEPC played an important role in obtaining jobs for black workers in industrial plants and shipyards. In southern California, the aircraft manufacturer Lockheed ran special buses into black neighborhoods to bring workers to its plants. By 1944, more than 1 million blacks, 300,000 of them women, held manufacturing jobs. ("My sister always said that Hitler was the one that got us out of the white folks' kitchen," recalled one black woman.)

FEPC

The Double-V

When the president "said that we should have the Four Freedoms," a black steelworker declared, he meant to include "all races." During the war, NAACP membership grew from 50,000 to nearly 500,000. The Congress of Racial Equality (CORE), founded by an interracial group of pacifists in 1942, held sit-ins in northern cities to integrate restaurants and theaters. After a Firestone tire factory in Memphis fired a black woman for trying to enter a city bus before white passengers had been seated, black workers at the plant went on strike until she was reinstated.

In February 1942, the *Pittsburgh Courier* coined the phrase that came to symbolize black attitudes during the war—the **double-V**. Victory over Germany and Japan, it insisted, must be accompanied by victory over segregation at home. While the Roosevelt administration and the white press saw the war as an expression of American ideals, black newspapers pointed to the gap between those ideals and reality. Side by side with ads for war bonds, *The Crisis* insisted that a segregated army "cannot fight for a free world."

The double-V

Surveying wartime public opinion, a political scientist concluded that "symbols of national solidarity" had very different meanings to white and black Americans. To blacks, freedom from fear meant, among other things, an end to lynching, and freedom from want included doing away with "discrimination in getting jobs." If, in whites' eyes, freedom was a "possession to be defended," he observed, to blacks and other racial minorities it remained a "goal to be achieved." "*Our* fight for freedom," said a returning black veteran of the Pacific war, "begins when we get to San Francisco."

What the Negro Wants

During the war, a broad political coalition centered on the left but reaching well beyond it called for an end to racial inequality in America. The NAACP and American Jewish Congress cooperated closely in advocating laws to ban discrimination in employment and housing. Despite considerable resistance from rank-and-file white workers, CIO unions, especially those with strong left-liberal and communist influence, made significant efforts to organize black workers and win them access to skilled positions. AFL craft unions by and large continued their long tradition of excluding black workers. But during World War II, the CIO was probably more racially integrated than any labor organization since the Knights of Labor in the 1880s.

Labor and race

THE AMERICAN DILEMMA | 879

A sign displayed opposite a Detroit housing project in 1942 symbolizes one aspect of what Gunnar Myrdal called "the American Dilemma"—the persistence of racism in the midst of a worldwide struggle for freedom.

World War II reinvigorated the movement for civil rights. Here African-Americans attempt to register to vote in Atlanta, Georgia.

As blacks demanded an end to segregation, southern politicians took up the cry of protecting white supremacy. The latter also spoke the language of freedom. Defenders of the racial status quo interpreted freedom to mean the right to shape their region's institutions without outside interference. The "war emergency," insisted Governor Frank Dixon of Alabama, "should not be used as a pretext to bring about the abolition of the color line." Even as the war gave birth to the modern civil rights movement, it also planted the seeds for the South's "massive resistance" to desegregation during the 1950s.

In the rest of the country, however, the status of black Americans assumed a place at the forefront of enlightened liberalism. Far more than in the 1930s, federal officials spoke openly of the need for a dramatic change in race relations. American democracy, noted Secretary of War Stimson, had not yet addressed "the persistent legacy of the original crime of slavery." Progress came slowly. But the National War Labor Board banned racial wage differentials. In *Smith v. Allwright* (1944), the Supreme Court outlawed all-white primaries, one of the mechanisms by which southern states deprived blacks of political rights. In the same year, the navy began assigning small numbers of black sailors to previously all-white ships. In the final months of the war, it ended segregation altogether, and the army established a few combat units that included black and white soldiers.

After a world tour in 1942 to rally support for the Allies, Wendell Willkie, Roosevelt's opponent of 1940, published *One World*. It sold 1 million copies, faster than any nonfiction work in American history. Willkie's travels persuaded him that Asia, Africa, and Latin America would play a pivotal role in the postwar era. But the book's great surprise came in Willkie's attack on "our imperialisms at home." Unless the United States addressed the "mocking paradox" of racism, he insisted, its claim to world leadership would lack moral authority. "If we want to talk about freedom," Willkie wrote, "we must mean freedom for everyone inside our frontiers."

An American Dilemma

No event reflected the new concern with the status of black Americans more than the publication in 1944 of *An American Dilemma*, a sprawling account of the country's racial past, present, and future written by the Swedish social scientist Gunnar Myrdal. The book offered an uncompromising portrait of how deeply racism was entrenched in law, politics, economics, and social behavior. But Myrdal combined this sobering analysis with admiration for what he called the American Creed—belief in equality, justice, equal opportunity, and freedom. The war, he argued, had made Americans more aware than ever of the contradiction between this creed and the reality of racial inequality. He concluded that "there is bound to be a redefinition of the Negro's status as a result of this War."

Myrdal's notion of a conflict between American values and American racial policies was hardly new—Frederick Douglass and W. E. B. Du Bois had said much the same thing. But in the context of a worldwide struggle against Nazism and rising black demands for equality at home, his book struck a chord. It identified a serious national problem and seemed to offer an almost painless path to peaceful change, in which the federal government would take the lead in outlawing discrimination. This coupling of an appeal to American principles with federal social engineering established a liberal position on race relations that would survive for many years.

Wartime vision of racial justice

By 1945, support for racial justice had finally taken its place on the liberal-left agenda alongside full employment, civil liberties, and the expansion of the New Deal welfare state. Roosevelt himself rarely spoke out on racial issues. But many liberals insisted that racial discrimination must be confronted head-on through federal antilynching legislation, equal opportunity in the workplace, an end to segregated housing and schools, and the expansion of Social Security programs to cover agricultural and domestic workers. This wartime vision of a racially integrated full employment economy formed a bridge between the New Deal and the Great Society of the 1960s (see Chapter 25).

Black Internationalism

In the nineteenth century, black radicals like David Walker and Martin Delany had sought to link the fate of African-Americans with that of peoples of African descent in other parts of the world, especially the Caribbean and Africa. In the first decades of the twentieth century, this kind of international consciousness was reinvigorated. Garveyism (discussed in Chapter 19) was one example; another was reflected in the five Pan-African Congresses that met between 1919 and 1945. Attended by black intellectuals from the United States, the Caribbean, Europe, and Africa, these gatherings denounced the colonial rule of Africa and sought to establish a sense of unity among all people in the African diaspora (a term used to describe the scattering of a people who share a single national, religious, or racial identity). At the home of George Padmore, a West Indian labor organizer and editor living in London, black American leaders like W. E. B. Du Bois and Paul Robeson came into contact with future leaders of African independence movements such as Jomo Kenyatta (Kenya), Kwame Nkrumah (Ghana), and Nnamdi Azikiwe (Nigeria). "I discovered Africa in London," Robeson remarked.

Pan-African Congresses

Through these gatherings, Du Bois, Robeson, and others developed an outlook that linked the plight of black Americans with that of people of color worldwide. Racism, they came to believe, originated not in irrational hatred but in the slave trade and slavery. In the modern age, it was perpetuated by colonialism. Thus, freeing Africa from colonial rule would encourage greater equality at home.

A global cause

World War II stimulated among African-Americans an even greater awareness of the links between racism in the United States and colonialism abroad. In 1942, the *Pittsburgh Courier*, a major black newspaper, began publishing regular columns on events in India (where the British had imprisoned leaders of the movement for national

Paul Robeson, the black actor, singer, and battler for civil rights, leading Oakland dockworkers in singing the national anthem in 1942. World War II gave a significant boost to the vision, shared by Robeson and others on the left, of an America based on genuine equality.

independence) and China. In the same year, Robeson founded the Council on African Affairs, which tried to place colonial liberation at the top of the black American agenda.

THE END OF THE WAR

As 1945 opened, Allied victory was assured. In December 1944, in a desperate gamble, Hitler launched a surprise counterattack in France that pushed Allied forces back fifty miles, creating a large bulge in their lines. The largest single battle ever fought by the U.S. Army, the Battle of the Bulge produced more than 70,000 American casualties. But by early 1945 the assault had failed.

V-E Day

In March, American troops crossed the Rhine River and entered the industrial heartland of Germany. Hitler took his own life, and shortly afterward Soviet forces occupied Berlin. On May 8, known as **V-E Day** (for victory in Europe), came the formal end to the war against Germany. In the Pacific, American forces moved ever closer to Japan. They reconquered Guam in August 1944 and landed in the Philippines two months later, where they destroyed most of the remainder of the enemy fleet in the naval battle of Leyte Gulf.

"The Most Terrible Weapon"

Truman and the atomic bomb

Franklin D. Roosevelt defeated Republican nominee Thomas E. Dewey, the governor of New York, to win an unprecedented fourth term in 1944. But FDR did not live to see the Allied victory. He succumbed to a stroke on April 12, 1945. To his successor, Harry S. Truman, fell one of the most momentous decisions ever confronted by an American president—whether to use the atomic bomb against Japan. Truman did not know about the bomb until after he became president. Then, Secretary of War Stimson informed him that the United States had secretly developed "the most terrible weapon ever known in human history."

The bomb was a practical realization of the theory of relativity, a rethinking of the laws of physics developed early in the twentieth century by the German scientist Albert Einstein. Energy and matter, Einstein showed, represented two forms of the same phenomenon. According to his famous equation $E = mc^2$, the energy contained in matter equals its mass times the speed of light squared—an enormous amount. By using certain forms of uranium, or the man-made element plutonium, an atomic reaction could be created that transformed part of the mass into energy. This energy could be harnessed to provide a form of controlled power, or it could be unleashed in a tremendous explosion.

Having fled to the United States from Hitler's Germany, Einstein in 1939 warned Roosevelt that Nazi scientists were trying to develop an atomic weapon and urged the president to do likewise. In the following year, FDR authorized what came to be known as the **Manhattan Project**, a top-secret program in which American scientists developed an atomic bomb during World War II. The weapon was tested successfully in the New Mexico desert in July 1945.

> *Manhattan Project*

The Dawn of the Atomic Age

On August 6, 1945, an American plane dropped an atomic bomb that detonated over Hiroshima, Japan—a target chosen because almost alone among major Japanese cities, it had not yet suffered damage. In an instant, nearly every building in the city was destroyed. Of the city's population of 280,000 civilians and 40,000 soldiers,

> *Hiroshima and Nagasaki*

After the dropping of the atomic bomb on Hiroshima, Japan, the federal government restricted the circulation of images of destruction. But soon after the end of the war it dispatched photographers to compile a Strategic Bombing Survey, to assess the bomb's impact. This photograph, which long remained classified, shows the remains of an elementary school.

"Fat Man," the atomic bomb dropped on Nagasaki, Japan, on August 9, 1945.

approximately 70,000 died immediately. Because atomic bombs release deadly radiation, the death toll kept rising in the months that followed. By the end of the year, it reached at least 140,000. Thousands more perished over the next five years. On August 9, the United States exploded a second bomb over Nagasaki, killing 70,000 persons. On the same day, the Soviet Union declared war on Japan and invaded Manchuria. Within a week, Japan surrendered.

Because of the enormous cost in civilian lives—more than twice America's military fatalities in the entire Pacific war—the use of the bomb remains controversial. The Japanese had fought ferociously while being driven from one Pacific island after another. An American invasion of Japan, some advisers warned Truman, might cost as many as 250,000 American lives. No such invasion was planned, however, until the following year, and considerable evidence had accumulated that Japan was nearing surrender. Already some of its officials had communicated a willingness to end the war if Emperor Hirohito could remain on his throne. This fell short of the Allies' demand for "unconditional surrender," but the victors would, in the end, agree to Hirohito's survival. Japan's economy had been crippled and its fleet destroyed, and it would now have to fight the Soviet Union as well as the United States. Some of the scientists who had worked on the bomb urged Truman to demonstrate its power to international observers. But Truman did not hesitate. The bomb was a weapon, he reasoned, and weapons are created to be used.

The Nature of the War

The dropping of the atomic bombs was the logical culmination of the way World War II had been fought. All wars inflict suffering on noncombatants. But never before had civilian populations been so ruthlessly targeted. Military personnel represented 90 percent of those who died in World War I. But of the estimated 50 million persons who perished during World War II (including 400,000 American soldiers), perhaps 20 million were civilians. Germany had killed millions of members of "inferior races." It had repeatedly bombed London and other cities. The Allies carried out even more deadly air assaults on civilian populations. Early in 1945, the firebombing of Dresden killed some 100,000 people, mostly women, children, and elderly men. On March 9, nearly the same number died in an inferno caused by the bombing of Tokyo.

Four years of war propaganda had dehumanized the Japanese in Americans' eyes, and few persons criticized Truman's decision in 1945. But public doubts began to surface, especially after John Hersey published *Hiroshima* (1946), a graphic account of the horrors suffered by the civilian population. General Dwight D. Eisenhower, who thought the use of the bomb unnecessary, later wrote, "I hated to see our country be the first to use such a weapon."

Planning the Postwar World

Even as the war raged, a series of meetings between Allied leaders formulated plans for the postwar world. Churchill, Roosevelt, and Stalin met at Tehran, Iran, in 1943, and at Yalta, in the southern Soviet Union, early in 1945, to hammer out

The war and civilian populations

Public response to bombs

agreements. The final "Big Three" confer-ence took place at Potsdam, near Berlin, in July 1945. It involved Stalin, Truman, and Churchill (replaced midway in the talks by Clement Attlee, who became prime minister when his Labour Party swept the British elections). At the **Potsdam conference**, the Allied leaders established a military admin-istration for Germany and agreed to place top Nazi leaders on trial for war crimes.

Relations among the three Allies were often uneasy, as each maneuvered to maxi-mize its postwar power. Neither Britain nor the United States trusted Stalin. The delay in the Allied invasion of France until 1944, which left the Soviets to do the bulk of the fighting against Germany, angered the Russians. But since Stalin's troops had won the war on the eastern front, it was difficult to resist his demand that eastern Europe become a Soviet sphere of influence (a region whose governments can be counted on to do a great power's bidding).

The Big Three—Stalin, Roosevelt, and Churchill—at their first meeting, in Tehran, Iran, in 1943, where they discussed the opening of a second front against Germany in western Europe.

Yalta and Bretton Woods

At the **Yalta conference**, Roosevelt and Churchill entered only a mild protest against Soviet plans to retain control of the Baltic states (Estonia, Latvia, and Lithuania) and a large part of eastern Poland, in effect restoring Russia's pre–World War I western borders. Stalin agreed to enter the war against Japan later in 1945, to include noncommunists in the pro-Soviet government of Poland, and to allow "free and unfettered elections" there. But he was intent on establishing communism in eastern Europe. He believed, as he put it to Yugoslav communist leader Josip Broz ("Tito"), that in modern war, "whoever occupies a territory also imposes his own social system." Yalta saw the high-water mark of wartime American–Soviet cooperation. But it planted seeds of conflict, since the participants soon disagreed over the fate of eastern Europe.

Disputes over eastern Europe

Tension also existed between Britain and the United States. Churchill rejected American pressure to place India and other British colonies on the road to independence. He concluded private deals with Stalin to divide southern and eastern Europe into British and Soviet spheres of influence.

Britain also resisted, unsuccessfully, American efforts to reshape and domi-nate the postwar economic order. A meeting of representatives of forty-five nations at Bretton Woods, New Hampshire, in July 1944 replaced the British pound with the dollar as the main currency for international transactions. During the 1930s, as noted in the previous chapter, FDR had taken the United States off the gold standard, allowing the government to issue more money in the hope of stimulating business activity. The **Bretton Woods conference** reestablished the link between the dollar and gold. It set the dollar's value at $35 per ounce of gold and gave other currencies a fixed relationship to the dollar. The conference also created

Shaping the postwar economic order

two American-dominated financial institutions. The World Bank would provide money to developing countries and to help rebuild Europe. The International Monetary Fund would work to prevent governments from devaluing their currencies to gain an advantage in international trade, as many had done during the Depression.

Although the details took many years to emerge, Bretton Woods created the framework for the postwar capitalist economic system, based on a freer international flow of goods and investment and a recognition of the United States as the world's financial leader. Determined to avoid a recurrence of the Great Depression, American leaders believed that the removal of barriers to free trade would encourage the growth of the world economy, an emphasis that remains central to American foreign policy to this day.

The United Nations

Early in the war, the Allies also agreed to establish a successor to the League of Nations. In a 1944 conference at Dumbarton Oaks, near Washington, D.C., they developed the structure of the **United Nations** (UN). There would be a General Assembly—essentially a forum for discussion where each member enjoyed an equal voice—and a Security Council responsible for maintaining world peace. Along with ten rotating members, the council would have five permanent ones— Britain, China, France, the Soviet Union, and the United States—each with the power to veto resolutions. In June 1945, representatives of fifty-one countries met in

San Francisco to adopt the UN Charter, which outlawed force or the threat of force as a means of settling international disputes. In July, the U.S. Senate endorsed the charter. In contrast to the bitter dispute over membership in the League of Nations after World War I, only two members of the U.S. Senate voted against joining the UN. At the conclusion of the San Francisco conference that established the United Nations, President Truman urged Americans to recognize that "no matter how great our strength, we must deny ourselves the license to do always as we please. This is the price which each nation will have to pay for world peace. . . . And what a reasonable price that is."

Peace, but Not Harmony

World War II produced a radical redistribution of world power. Japan and Germany, the two dominant military powers in their regions before the war, were utterly defeated. Britain and France, though victorious, were substantially weakened. Only the United States and the Soviet Union were able to project significant influence beyond their national borders.

Overall, however, the United States was clearly the dominant world power. "What Rome was to the ancient world," wrote the journalist Walter Lippmann, "America is to be to the world of tomorrow." But peace did not usher in an era of international harmony. The Soviet occupation of eastern Europe created a division soon to be solidified in the Cold War. The dropping of the atomic bombs left a worldwide legacy of fear.

It remained to be seen how seriously the victorious Allies took their wartime rhetoric of freedom. In August 1941, four months before the United States entered the war, FDR and British prime minister Winston Churchill had met for a conference, on warships anchored off the coast of Newfoundland, and issued the **Atlantic Charter**. The charter promised that "the final destruction of Nazi tyranny" would be followed by open access to markets, the right of "all peoples" to choose their form of government, and a global extension of the New Deal so that people everywhere would enjoy "improved labor standards, economic advancement and social security." It referred specifically to two of Roosevelt's Four Freedoms— freedom from want and freedom from fear. But freedom of speech and of worship had been left out because of British reluctance to apply them to its colonial possessions, especially India.

A member of the U.S. Navy plays "Goin' Home" on the accordian as Franklin D. Roosevelt's body is carried from the Warm Springs Foundation where he died suddenly on April 12, 1945.

The Four Freedoms speech and the Atlantic Charter had been primarily intended to highlight the differences between Anglo-American ideals and Nazism. Nonetheless, they had unanticipated consequences. As one of Roosevelt's speechwriters remarked, "when you state a moral principle, you are stuck with it, no matter how many fingers you have kept crossed at the moment." The language with which World War II was fought helped to lay the foundation for postwar ideals of human rights that extend to all mankind.

During the war, Mahatma Gandhi, the Indian nationalist leader, wrote to Roosevelt that the idea "that the Allies are fighting to make the world safe for freedom of the individual and for democracy seems hollow, so long as India, and for that matter, Africa, are exploited by Great Britain, and America has the Negro problem in her own home." Allied victory saved mankind from a living nightmare—a worldwide system of dictatorial rule and slave labor in which peoples deemed inferior suffered the fate of European Jews and the victims of Japanese outrages in Asia. But disputes over the freedom of colonial peoples overseas and non-whites in the United States foretold wars and social upheavals to come.

SUGGESTED READING

BOOKS

- Ambrose, Stephen E. *Citizen Soldiers* (1997). Discusses the experience of American soldiers fighting in Europe from D-Day to the end of the war.

- Anderson, Karen. *Wartime Women: Sex Roles, Family Relations, and the Status of Women during World War II* (1981). Explores how the experience of World War II opened new opportunities for women and challenged existing gender conventions.

- Blum, John M. *V Was for Victory: Politics and American Culture during World War II* (1976). A comprehensive account of the home front during World War II.

- Borgwardt, Elizabeth. *A New Deal for the World: America's Vision for Human Rights* (2005). The emergence during the war of the idea of human rights as an international entitlement.

- Brinkley, Alan. *The End of Reform: New Deal Liberalism in Recession and War* (1995). Describes how liberals' ideas and policies moved away, during the late New Deal and the war, from combating inequalities of economic power.

- Daniels, Rogers. *Prisoners without Trial: Japanese Americans in World War II* (1993). A brief history of the internment of Japanese-Americans during the war.

- Dower, John W. *War without Mercy: Race and Power in the Pacific War* (1986). Explores how racial fears and antagonisms motivated both sides in the Pacific theater.

- Escobedo, Elizabeth R. *From Coveralls to Zoot Suits: The Lives of Mexican American Women on the World War II Home Front* (2013). Examines how the rise of racial liberalism during World War II and the opening of new jobs affected Mexican-American women.

- Frydl, Kathleen. *The G.I. Bill* (2009). How this important piece of legislation changed American society.

- Isserman, Maurice. *Which Side Were You On? The American Communist Party during World War II* (1982). Traces the Communist Party's changing political positions during World War II.

- Kennedy, David M. *Freedom from Fear: The American People in Depression and War, 1929–1945* (1999). A detailed and lively account of American history from the Great Depression through the end of World War II.

- Lichtenstein, Nelson. *Labor's War at Home: The CIO in World War II* (1982). Examines the war's impact on workers and the labor movement.

- Rhodes, Richard. *The Making of the Atomic Bomb* (1986). A dramatic account of how the atomic bomb was created.

- Von Eschen, Penny. *Race against Empire: Black Americans and Anticolonialism, 1937–1957* (1997). Examines how black Americans responded to the rise of movements for colonial independence overseas during and after World War II.

- Zelizer, Julian E. *Arsenal of Democracy: The Politics of National Security—From World War II to the War on Terrorism* (2009). Traces the origins of the national security state from Roosevelt's "arsenal of democracy" speech of 1940 to the present, stressing the tension between the two elements, arsenal and democracy.

WEBSITES

- A More Perfect Union: Japanese Americans and the U.S. Constitution: http://amhistory.si.edu/perfectunion/experience/

- A People at War: www.archives.gov/exhibits/a_people_at_war/a_people_at_war.html

- Bittersweet Harvest: The Bracero Program 1942–1964: http://americanhistory.si.edu/exhibitions/bittersweet-harvest-bracero-program-1942-1964

- Remembering Nagasaki: www.exploratorium.edu/nagasaki/

CHAPTER REVIEW AND ONLINE RESOURCES

REVIEW QUESTIONS

1. Why did most Americans support isolationism in the 1930s?

2. What factors after 1939 led to U.S. involvement in World War II?

3. How did government, business, and labor work together to promote wartime production, and how did the war affect each group?

4. How did different groups understand or experience the Four Freedoms differently?

5. Explain how conservatives in Congress and business used the war effort to attack the goals and legacy of the New Deal.

6. How did the war alter the lives of women on the home front, and what did different groups think would happen to the status of women after the war?

7. How did a war fought to bring "essential human freedoms" to the world fail to protect the home-front liberties of blacks, Indians, Japanese-Americans, and Mexican-Americans?

8. Explain how World War II promoted an awareness of the links between racism in the United States and colonialism around the world.

9. What was the impact of the GI Bill of Rights on American society, including minorities?

10. Describe how the decisions made at the Bretton Woods conference in 1944 created the framework for postwar U.S. economic and foreign policy.

KEY TERMS

Four Freedoms (p. 847)

Good Neighbor Policy (p. 848)

isolationism (p. 850)

Neutrality Acts (p. 850)

Lend-Lease Act (p. 852)

Axis powers (p. 853)

D-Day (p. 856)

Holocaust (p. 858)

GI Bill of Rights (p. 868)

bracero program (p. 871)

zoot suit riots (p. 874)

Japanese-American internment (p. 875)

Korematsu v. United States (p. 876)

second Great Migration (p. 877)

double-V (p. 879)

V-E Day (p. 882)

Manhattan Project (p. 883)

Potsdam conference (p. 885)

Yalta conference (p. 885)

Bretton Woods conference (p. 885)

United Nations (p. 886)

Atlantic Charter (p. 887)

Go to 🐰 INQUIZITIVE

To see what you know—and learn what you've missed—with personalized feedback along the way.

Visit the *Give Me Liberty!* Student Site for primary source documents and images, interactive maps, author videos featuring Eric Foner, and more.

CHAPTER 23

THE UNITED STATES AND THE COLD WAR

★

1945–1953

On September 16, 1947, the 160th anniversary of the signing of the Constitution, the Freedom Train opened to the public in Philadelphia. A traveling exhibition of 133 historical documents, the train, bedecked in red, white, and blue, soon embarked on a sixteen-month tour that took it to more than 300 American cities. Never before or since have so many cherished pieces of Americana—among them the Mayflower Compact, the Declaration of Independence, and the Gettysburg Address—been assembled in one place. After leaving the train, visitors were encouraged to rededicate themselves to American values by taking the Freedom Pledge and adding their names to a Freedom Scroll.

The idea for the Freedom Train, perhaps the most elaborate peacetime patriotic campaign in American history, originated in 1946 with the Department of Justice. President Harry S. Truman endorsed it as a way of contrasting American freedom with "the destruction of liberty by the Hitler tyranny." Since direct government funding raised fears of propaganda, however, the administration turned the project over to a nonprofit group, the American Heritage Foundation, headed by Winthrop W. Aldrich, chairman of Chase Manhattan Bank.

By any measure, the Freedom Train was an enormous success. It attracted more than 3.5 million visitors, and millions more took part in the civic activities that accompanied its journey, including labor-management forums, educational programs, and patriotic parades. The powerful grassroots response to the train, wrote *The New Republic*, revealed a popular hunger for "tangible evidence of American freedom." Behind the scenes, however, the Freedom Train demonstrated that the meaning of freedom remained as controversial as ever.

The liberal staff members at the National Archives who proposed the initial list of documents had included the Wagner Act of 1935, which guaranteed workers the right to form unions, as well as President Roosevelt's Four Freedoms speech of 1941, with its promise to fight "freedom from want." The more conservative American Heritage Foundation removed these documents. They also deleted from the original list the Fourteenth and Fifteenth Amendments, which had established the principle of equal civil and political rights regardless of race after the Civil War, and FDR's 1941 order establishing the Fair Employment Practices Commission, which Congress had recently allowed to expire. In the end, nothing on the train referred to organized labor or any twentieth-century social legislation. The only documents relating to blacks were the Emancipation Proclamation, the Thirteenth Amendment, and a 1776 letter by South Carolina patriot Henry Laurens criticizing slavery.

Many black Americans initially voiced doubts regarding the exhibit. On the eve of the train's unveiling, the poet Langston Hughes wondered whether there would be "Jim Crow on the Freedom Train." "When it stops in Mississippi," Hughes asked, "will it be made plain / Everybody's got a right to board the Freedom Train?" In fact, with the Truman administration about to make civil rights a major priority, the train's organizers announced that they would not permit segregated viewing. In an unprecedented move, the American Heritage Foundation canceled visits to Memphis, Tennessee, and

FOCUS QUESTIONS

What series of events and ideological conflicts prompted the Cold War? –p. 892

How did the Cold War reshape ideas of American freedom? –p. 902

What major domestic policy initiatives did Truman undertake? –p. 907

What effects did the anticommunism of the Cold War have on American politics and culture? –p. 912

The Cold War led to widespread fears of a communist takeover in the United States (a task far beyond the capacity of the minuscule American Communist Party or the Soviet Union). This image is from the first page of *This Godless Communism*, an issue of a comic book series called *Treasure Chest* published from 1946 to 1972. The issue warned of the danger that communists might overthrow the government, and detailed the horrors of life in a communist America, including the arrest and jailing of priests and ministers. It was circulated to parochial schools by the Roman Catholic Church and contained an introduction by J. Edgar Hoover, head of the Federal Bureau of Investigation.

Birmingham, Alabama, when local authorities insisted on separating visitors by race. The Freedom Train visited forty-seven other southern cities without incident and was hailed in the black press for breaching, if only temporarily, the walls of segregation.

Even as the Freedom Train reflected a new sense of national unease about expressions of racial inequality, its journey also revealed the growing impact of the **Cold War**. Originally intended to contrast American freedom with Nazi tyranny, the train quickly became caught up in the emerging struggle with communism. In the spring of 1947, a few months before the train was dedicated, President Truman committed the United States to the worldwide **containment** of Soviet power and inaugurated a program to root out "disloyal" persons from government employment. Soon, Attorney General Tom C. Clark was praising the Freedom Train as a means of preventing "foreign ideologies" from infiltrating the United States and of "aiding the country in its internal war against subversive elements." The Federal Bureau of Investigation began compiling reports on those who found the train objectionable. The Freedom Train revealed how the Cold War helped to reshape freedom's meaning, identifying it ever more closely with anticommunism, "free enterprise," and the defense of the social and economic status quo.

ORIGINS OF THE COLD WAR

The Two Powers

The United States emerged from World War II as by far the world's greatest power. Although most of the army was quickly demobilized, the country boasted the world's most powerful navy and air force. The United States accounted for half the world's manufacturing capacity. It alone possessed the atomic bomb. As discussed in the previous chapter, the Roosevelt administration was determined to avoid a retreat to isolationism like the one that followed World War I. It believed that the United States could lead the rest of the world to a future of international cooperation, expanding democracy, and ever-increasing living standards. New institutions like the United Nations and World Bank had been created to promote these goals. American leaders also believed that the nation's security depended on the security of Europe and Asia, and that American prosperity required global economic reconstruction.

The only power that in any way could rival the United States was the Soviet Union, whose armies now occupied most of eastern Europe, including the eastern part of Germany. Its crucial role in defeating Hitler and its claim that communism had wrested a vast backward nation into modernity gave the Soviet Union considerable prestige in Europe and among colonial peoples struggling for independence. Like the United States, the Soviets looked forward to a world order modeled on their own society and values. Having lost more than 20 million dead and suffered vast devastation during the war, however, Stalin's government was in no position to embark on new military adventures. "Unless they were completely out of their minds," said American undersecretary of state Dean Acheson, the Russians were hardly likely to go to war with the far more powerful United States. But having done the largest amount of fighting in the defeat of Hitler, the Soviet government remained determined to establish a sphere of influence in eastern Europe, through which Germany had twice invaded Russia in the past thirty years.

The Roots of Containment

FDR seems to have believed that the United States could maintain friendly relations with the Soviet Union once World War II ended. In retrospect, however, it seems all but inevitable that the two major powers to emerge from the war would come into conflict. Born of a common foe rather than common long-term interests, values, or history, their wartime alliance began to unravel almost from the day that peace was declared.

The first confrontation of the Cold War took place in the Middle East. At the end of World War II, Soviet troops had occupied parts of northern Iran, hoping to pressure that country to grant it access to its rich oil fields. Under British and American pressure, however, Stalin quickly withdrew Soviet forces. At the same time, the Soviets installed procommunist governments in Poland, Romania, and Bulgaria, a step they claimed was no different from American domination of Latin America or Britain's determination to maintain its own empire. But many Americans became convinced that Stalin was violating the promise of free elections in Poland that had been agreed to at the Yalta conference of 1945.

Early in 1946, in his famous **Long Telegram** from Moscow, American diplomat George Kennan advised the Truman administration that the Soviets could not be dealt with as a normal government. Communist ideology drove them to try to expand their power throughout the world, he claimed, and only the United States had the ability to stop them. While Kennan believed that the Russians could not be dislodged from control of eastern Europe, his telegram laid the foundation for what became known as the policy of "containment," according to which the United States committed itself to preventing any further expansion of Soviet power.

The Iron Curtain

Shortly afterward, in a speech at Fulton, Missouri, Britain's former wartime prime minister Winston Churchill declared that an **iron curtain** had descended across Europe, partitioning the free West from the communist East. Churchill's speech helped to popularize the idea of an impending long-term struggle between the United States and the Soviets. But not until March 1947, in a speech announcing what came to be known as the **Truman Doctrine**, did the president officially embrace the Cold War as the foundation of American foreign policy and describe it as a worldwide struggle over the future of freedom.

The Truman Doctrine

Harry S. Truman never expected to become president. Until Democratic party leaders chose him to replace Henry Wallace as Roosevelt's running mate in 1944, he was an undistinguished senator from Missouri who had risen in politics

The cover of a comic book promoting the Freedom Train in 1948. The image links the train to Paul Revere's ride and, more broadly, the revolutionary era.

Kennan's Long Telegram

Churchill's speech

President Harry S. Truman delivering his Truman Doctrine speech before Congress on March 12, 1947.

A page from a Dutch pamphlet promoting the Marshall Plan.

through his connection with the boss of the Kansas City political machine, Tom Pendergast. When he assumed the presidency after Roosevelt's death in April 1945, Truman found himself forced to decide foreign policy debates in which he had previously played virtually no role.

Convinced that Stalin could not be trusted and that the United States had a responsibility to provide leadership to a world that he tended to view in stark, black-and-white terms, Truman soon determined to put the policy of containment into effect. The immediate occasion for this epochal decision came early in 1947 when Britain informed the United States that because its economy had been shattered by the war, it could no longer afford its traditional international role. Britain had no choice but to end military and financial aid to two crucial governments—Greece, a monarchy threatened by a communist-led rebellion, and Turkey, from which the Soviets were demanding joint control of the straits linking the Black Sea and the Mediterranean. Britain asked the United States to fill the vacuum.

The Soviet Union had little to do with the internal problems of Greece and Turkey, where opposition to corrupt, undemocratic regimes was largely homegrown. Neither had held truly free elections. But they occupied strategically important sites at the gateway to southeastern Europe and the oil-rich Middle East. Truman had been told by Senate leader Arthur Vandenberg that the only way a reluctant public and Congress would support aid to these governments was for the president to "scare hell" out of the American people. To rally popular backing, Truman rolled out the heaviest weapon in his rhetorical arsenal—the defense of freedom. As the leader of the "free world," the United States must now shoulder the responsibility of supporting "freedom-loving peoples" wherever communism threatened them. Twenty-four times in the eighteen-minute speech, Truman used the words "free" and "freedom."

Building on the wartime division of the globe into free and enslaved worlds, and invoking a far older vision of an American mission to defend liberty against the forces of darkness, the Truman Doctrine created the language through which most Americans came to understand the postwar world. More than any other statement, a prominent senator would write, this speech established "the guiding spirit of American foreign policy." Truman succeeded in persuading both Republicans and Democrats in Congress to support his policy, beginning a long period of bipartisan support for the containment of communism. As Truman's speech to Congress suggested, the Cold War was, in part, an ideological conflict. Both sides claimed to be promoting freedom and social justice while defending their own security, and each offered its social system as a model the rest of the world should follow.

While his request to Congress was limited to $400 million in military aid to two governments (aid that enabled both Greece and Turkey to defeat their domestic foes), Truman's rhetoric suggested that the United States had assumed a permanent global responsibility. The speech set a precedent for American assistance to anti-communist regimes throughout the world, no matter how undemocratic, and for the creation of a set of global military alliances directed against the Soviet Union.

There soon followed the creation of new national security bodies immune from democratic oversight, such as the Atomic Energy Commission, National Security Council, and Central Intelligence Agency (CIA), the last established in 1947 to gather intelligence and conduct secret military operations abroad.

National security programs

The Marshall Plan

The language of the Truman Doctrine and the future it sketched of open-ended worldwide responsibilities for the United States alarmed many Americans. "Are we to shoulder the mantle of nineteenth-century British imperialism?" asked the *San Francisco Chronicle.* "Are we asking for a third world war?" But the threat of American military action overseas formed only one pillar of containment. Secretary of State George C. Marshall spelled out the other in a speech at Harvard University in June 1947. Marshall pledged the United States to contribute billions of dollars to finance the economic recovery of Europe. Two years after the end of the war, much of the continent still lay in ruins. Food shortages were widespread, and inflation rampant. The economic chaos, exacerbated by the unusually severe winter of 1946–1947, had strengthened the communist parties of France and Italy. American policymakers feared that these countries might fall into the Soviet orbit.

Marshall's speech

The **Marshall Plan** offered a positive vision to go along with containment. It aimed to combat the idea, widespread since the Great Depression, that capitalism was in decline and communism the wave of the future. It defined the threat to American security not so much as Soviet military power but as economic and political instability, which could be breeding grounds for communism. Avoiding Truman's language of a world divided between free and unfree blocs, Marshall insisted, "Our policy is directed not against any country or doctrine, but against hunger, poverty, desperation, and chaos." Freedom meant more than simply anticommunism—it required the emergence of the "political and social conditions in which free institutions can exist." In effect, the Marshall Plan envisioned a New Deal for Europe, an extension to that continent of Roosevelt's wartime Four Freedoms. As a booklet explaining the idea to Europeans put it, the aim was "a higher standard of living for the entire nation; maximum employment for workers and farmers; greater production." Or, in the words of a slogan used to popularize the Marshall Plan, "Prosperity Makes You Free."

Bales of American cotton in a warehouse at the French port of Le Havre, 1949. Part of the Marshall Plan aid program, the shipment helped to revive the French cotton industry.

The Marshall Plan proved to be one of the most successful foreign aid programs in history. By 1950, western European production exceeded prewar levels and the region was poised to follow the United States down the road to a mass-consumption society. Since the Soviet Union refused to participate, fearing American control over the economies of eastern Europe, the Marshall Plan further solidified the division of the continent. At the same time, the United

COLD WAR EUROPE, 1956

Occupation Zones
- American
- British
- French
- Soviet

Berlin Wall, 1961
West Berlin
East Berlin

ICELAND

NORWAY   SWEDEN   FINLAND

North Sea

Baltic Sea

IRELAND

GREAT BRITAIN   DENMARK

London   NETHERLANDS   Berlin   POLAND   SOVIET UNION

Atlantic Ocean

BELGIUM   Bonn   EAST GERMANY   Warsaw

WEST GERMANY   Prague

Paris   LUXEMBOURG   CZECHOSLOVAKIA

FRANCE   SWITZERLAND   AUSTRIA   Budapest

HUNGARY   ROMANIA

Bucharest

YUGOSLAVIA   *Black Sea*

PORTUGAL   SPAIN   ITALY   Sofia

Lisbon   *Corsica*   BULGARIA

Tirane

ALBANIA

Sardinia   GREECE   Ankara   TURKEY

Athens

MOROCCO   SYRIA   IRAQ

Mediterranean Sea   Crete   CYPRUS   LEBANON

TUNISIA   (Great Britain)

ISRAEL   JORDAN

ALGERIA (France)

SAUDI ARABIA

NATO countries   LIBYA   EGYPT   *Red Sea*
Warsaw Pact countries

0   250   500 miles
0   250   500 kilometers

The division of Europe between communist and noncommunist nations, solidified by the early 1950s, would last for nearly forty years.

Chinese communists carrying portraits of Mao Zedong, who took control of the country's government in 1949 after a long civil war.

Korea had been divided in 1945 into Soviet and American zones. These soon evolved into two governments: communist North Korea, and anticommunist South Korea, undemocratic but aligned with the United States. In June 1950, the North Korean army invaded the south, hoping to reunify the country under communist control. North Korean soldiers soon occupied most of the peninsula. Viewing Korea as a clear test of the policy of containment, the Truman administration persuaded the United Nations Security Council to authorize the use of force to repel the invasion. (The Soviets, who could have vetoed the resolution, were boycotting Security Council meetings to protest the refusal to seat communist China.)

North Korean invasion

American troops did the bulk of the fighting on this first battlefield of the Cold War. In September 1950, General Douglas MacArthur launched a daring counterattack at Inchon, behind North Korean lines. The invading forces retreated northward, and MacArthur's army soon occupied most of North Korea. Truman now hoped to unite Korea under a pro-American government. But in October 1950, when UN forces neared the Chinese border, hundreds of thousands of Chinese troops intervened, driving them back in bloody fighting. MacArthur demanded the right to push north again and possibly even invade China and use nuclear weapons against it. But Truman, fearing an all-out war on the Asian mainland, refused. MacArthur did not fully accept the principle of civilian control of the military. When he went public with criticism of the president, Truman removed him from command. The war then settled into a stalemate around the thirty-eighth parallel, the original boundary between the two Koreas. Not until 1953 was an armistice agreed to, essentially restoring the prewar status quo. There has never been a formal peace treaty ending the **Korean War**.

Inchon

Chinese intervention

More than 33,000 Americans died in Korea. The Asian death toll reached an estimated 1 million Korean soldiers and 2 million civilians (many of them victims

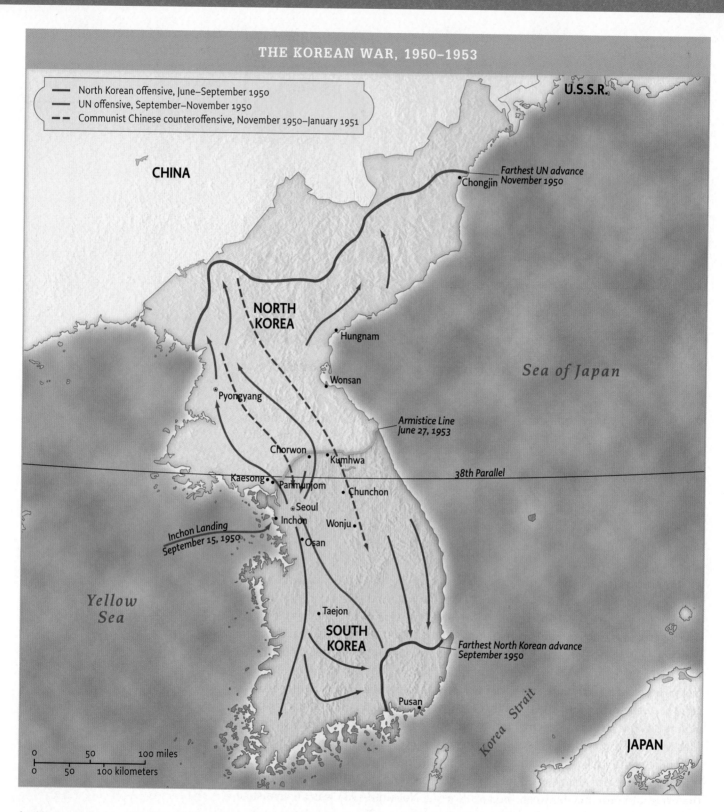

THE KOREAN WAR, 1950–1953

--- North Korean offensive, June–September 1950
--- UN offensive, September–November 1950
--- Communist Chinese counteroffensive, November 1950–January 1951

U.S.S.R.

CHINA

Chongjin • — Farthest UN advance November 1950

NORTH KOREA

Hungnam •

Sea of Japan

Wonsan •

⊛ Pyongyang

Armistice Line June 27, 1953

Chorwon • • Kumhwa
Kaesong • Panmunjom
• Chunchon
⊛ Seoul
Inchon • • Wonju
Inchon Landing September 15, 1950
• Osan

38th Parallel

Yellow Sea

• Taejon

SOUTH KOREA

Farthest North Korean advance September 1950

Pusan •

Korea Strait

JAPAN

0   50   100 miles
0   50   100 kilometers

As this map indicates, when General Douglas MacArthur launched his surprise landing at Inchon, North Korean forces controlled nearly the entire Korean peninsula.

A photograph of a street battle in Seoul, South Korea, during the Korean War illustrates the ferocity of the fighting.

of starvation after American bombing destroyed irrigation systems essential to rice cultivation), along with hundreds of thousands of Chinese troops. Korea made it clear that the Cold War, which began in Europe, had become a global conflict.

Taken together, the events of 1947–1953 showed that the world had moved very far from the hopes for global harmony symbolized by the founding of the United Nations in 1945. No longer did the United States speak of One World (the title of Wendell Willkie's influential wartime book). Instead, the world had been divided in two. The United States now stood as the undisputed leader of what was increasingly known as the West (although it included Japan, where permanent American military bases were established), or the Free World. NATO was soon followed by SEATO in Southeast Asia and CENTO in the Middle East, forming a web of military alliances that ringed the Soviet Union and China.

> *A divided world*

Cold War Critics

In the Soviet Union, Stalin had consolidated a brutal dictatorship that jailed or murdered millions of Soviet citizens. With its one-party rule, stringent state control of the arts and intellectual life, and government-controlled economy, the Soviet Union presented a stark opposite of democracy and "free enterprise." As a number of contemporary critics, few of them sympathetic to Soviet communism, pointed out, however, casting the Cold War in terms of a worldwide battle between freedom and slavery had unfortunate consequences. George Kennan, whose Long Telegram had inspired the policy of containment, observed that such language made it impossible to view international crises on a case-by-case basis, or to determine which genuinely involved either freedom or American interests.

> *Stalin's brutal dictatorship*

In a penetrating critique of Truman's policies, Walter Lippmann, one of the nation's most prominent journalists, objected to turning foreign policy into an "ideological crusade." To view every challenge to the status quo as part of a contest with the Soviet Union, Lippmann correctly predicted, would require the United

> *Walter Lippmann*

A poster for *The Red Menace*, one of numerous anticommunist films produced by Hollywood during the 1950s.

States to recruit and subsidize an "array of satellites, clients, dependents and puppets." It would have to intervene continuously in the affairs of nations whose political problems did not arise from Moscow and could not be easily understood in terms of the battle between freedom and slavery. World War II, he went on, had shaken the foundations of European empires. In the tide of revolutionary nationalism now sweeping the world, communists were certain to play an important role. It would be a serious mistake, Lippmann warned, for the United States to align itself against the movement for colonial independence in the name of anticommunism.

Imperialism and Decolonization

World War II had increased awareness in the United States of the problem of imperialism and had led many African-Americans to identify their own struggle for equality with the strivings of non-white colonial peoples overseas. Many movements for colonial independence borrowed the language of the American Declaration of Independence in demanding the right to self-government. Liberal Democrats and black leaders urged the Truman administration to take the lead in promoting worldwide **decolonization**, insisting that a Free World worthy of the name should not include colonies and empires. In 1946, the United States granted independence to the Philippines, a move hailed by nationalist movements in other colonies. But as the Cold War developed, the United States backed away from pressuring its European allies to move toward granting self-government to colonies like French Indochina, the Dutch East Indies, and British possessions like the Gold Coast and Nigeria in Africa and Malaya in Asia. Even after granting independence to India and Pakistan in 1947, Britain was determined to retain much of its empire.

In practice, geopolitical and economic interests shaped American foreign policy as powerfully as the idea of freedom. But American policymakers used the language of a crusade for freedom to justify actions around the world that had little to do with freedom by almost any definition. No matter how repressive to its own people, if a nation joined the worldwide anticommunist alliance led by the United States, it was counted as a member of the Free World. The Republic of South Africa, for example, was considered a part of the Free World even though its white minority had deprived the black population of nearly all their rights. Was there not some way, one critic asked, that the United States could accept "the aid of tyrants" on practical grounds "without corrupting our speeches by identifying tyranny with freedom"?

THE COLD WAR AND THE IDEA OF FREEDOM

Among other things, the Cold War was an ideological struggle, a battle, in a popular phrase of the 1950s, for the "hearts and minds" of people throughout the world. Like other wars, it required popular mobilization, in which the idea of freedom played a central role. During the 1950s, freedom became an inescapable theme of academic research, popular journalism, mass culture, and official pronouncements. Henry Luce, who had popularized the idea of an American Century, explained that "freedom" was the "one word out of the whole human vocabulary" through which *Time* magazine could best explain America to the rest of the world. In many ways, the Cold War established the framework for the discussion of freedom.

The Cultural Cold War

One of the more unusual Cold War battlefields involved American history and culture. Many scholars read the American Creed of pluralism, tolerance, and equality back into the past as a timeless definition of Americanism, ignoring the powerful ethnic and racial strains with which it had always coexisted. Under the code name "Militant Liberty," national security agencies encouraged Hollywood to produce anticommunist movies, such as *The Red Menace* (1949) and *I Married a Communist* (1950), and urged that film scripts be changed to remove references to less-than-praiseworthy aspects of American history, such as Indian removal and racial discrimination.

Anticommunism in Hollywood

The Central Intelligence Agency and Defense Department emerged as unlikely patrons of the arts. As noted in Chapter 21, the federal government had openly financed all sorts of artistic works during the 1930s. But Cold War funding for the arts remained top-secret—in part because Congress proved reluctant to spend money for this purpose, in part because Americans charged communist governments with imposing artistic conformity. In an effort to influence public opinion abroad, the Soviet Union sponsored tours of its world-famous ballet companies, folk dance troupes, and symphony orchestras. To counteract the widespread European view of the United States as a cultural backwater, the CIA secretly funded an array of overseas publications, conferences, publishing houses, concerts, and art exhibits. And to try to improve the international image of American race relations, the government sent jazz musicians and other black performers abroad, especially to Africa and Asia.

Secret sponsorship of the arts

Works produced by artists who considered themselves thoroughly nonpolitical became weapons in the cultural Cold War. The CIA promoted the so-called New York school of painters, led by Jackson Pollock. For Pollock, the essence of art lay in the process of creation, not the final product. His "action" paintings, made by spontaneously dripping and pouring paint over large canvases, produced works

Visitors to the Museum of Modern Art in New York City contemplate a work by Jackson Pollock, whose paintings exemplified the artistic school of abstract expressionism, promoted during the Cold War as a reflection of American freedom. The paintings had no recognizable subject other than reminding the viewer of how Pollock had created them, by flinging paint at the canvas. "I want to express my feelings, rather than illustrate them," Pollock declared.

Another painter whose works seemed to exemplify American artists' freedom from the constraints of European traditions was Mark Rothko. The painting has no subject other than color itself, with the different shades of red meant to evoke what Rothko called "the basic human emotions—tragedy, ecstasy, and doom."

of vivid color and energy but without any recognizable subject matter. Many members of Congress much preferred Norman Rockwell's readily understandable illustrations of small-town life to Pollock's "abstract expressionism." Some called Pollock's works un-American and wondered aloud if they were part of a communist plot. In 1946, for example, the State Department assembled a stylistically diverse exhibition of contemporary American paintings that it displayed in Europe and Latin America to demonstrate "the freedom of expression enjoyed by artists in America." But criticism emerged in Congress. Representative Fred Busbey of Illinois said the exhibit gave the impression that "the American people are despondent, broke down or of hideous shape." The State Department abandoned the project and sold the works at auction. In 2013, for the first time in half a century, they were exhibited, at Indiana University, with the overall title *Art Interrupted*.

The CIA, however, funded the Museum of Modern Art in New York, which championed the New York school, and helped arrange for exhibitions overseas. It hoped to persuade Europeans not only that these paintings demonstrated that the United States represented artistic leadership as well as military power, but that such art embodied the free, individual expression denied to artists in communist countries. Pollock's paintings, John Cage's musical compositions, which incorporated chance sounds rather than a fixed score, and the "graceful freedom" of George Balanchine's ballet choreography were all described as artistic reflections of the essence of American life.

Freedom and Totalitarianism

Along with freedom, the Cold War's other great mobilizing concept was **totalitarianism**. The term originated in Europe between the world wars to describe fascist Italy and Nazi Germany—aggressive, ideologically driven states that sought to subdue all of civil society, including churches, unions, and other voluntary associations, to their control. Such states, according to the theory of totalitarianism, left no room for individual rights or alternative values and therefore could never change from within. By 1950, the year the McCarran Internal Security Act barred "totalitarians" from entering the United States, the term had become a shorthand way of describing those on the other side in the Cold War. As the eventual collapse of communist governments in eastern Europe and the Soviet Union would demonstrate, the idea of totalitarianism greatly exaggerated the totality of government control of private life and thought in these countries. But its widespread use reinforced the view that the greatest danger to freedom lay in an overly powerful government.

Just as the conflict over slavery redefined American freedom in the nineteenth century and the confrontation with the Nazis shaped understandings of freedom during World War II, the Cold War reshaped them once again. Russia had already conquered America, the poet Archibald MacLeish complained in 1949, since politics was conducted "under a kind of upside-down Russian veto." Whatever Moscow stood for was by definition the opposite of freedom, including

Redefining freedom

anything to which the word "socialized" could be attached. In the largest public relations campaign in American history, the American Medical Association raised the specter of "socialized medicine" to discredit and defeat Truman's proposal for national health insurance. The real-estate industry likewise mobilized against public housing, terming it "socialized housing," similar to policies undertaken by Moscow.

Campaign against "socialism"

The Rise of Human Rights

The Cold War also affected the emerging concept of human rights. The atrocities committed during World War II, as well as the global language of the Four Freedoms and the Atlantic Charter, forcefully raised the issue of human rights in the postwar world. After the war, the victorious Allies put numerous German officials on trial before special courts at Nuremberg for crimes against humanity. For the first time, individuals were held directly accountable to the international community for violations of human rights. The trials resulted in prison terms for many Nazi officials and the execution of ten leaders.

The United Nations Charter includes strong language prohibiting discrimination on the basis of race, sex, or religion. In 1948, the UN General Assembly approved a far more sweeping document, the Universal Declaration of Human Rights, drafted by a committee chaired by Eleanor Roosevelt. It identified a broad range of rights to be enjoyed by people everywhere, including freedom of speech, religious toleration, and protection against arbitrary government, as well as social and economic entitlements like the right to an adequate standard of living and access to housing, education, and medical care. The document had no enforcement mechanism. Some considered it an exercise in empty rhetoric. But the core principle—that a nation's treatment of its own citizens should be subject to outside evaluation—slowly became part of the language in which freedom was discussed.

Universal Declaration of Human Rights

Ambiguities of Human Rights

The American and French Revolutions of the late eighteenth century had introduced into international relations the idea of basic rights belonging to all persons simply because they are human. In a sense, this was the origin of the idea of "human rights"—principles so fundamental that no government has a right to violate them. The antislavery movement had turned this idea into a powerful weapon against the legitimacy of slavery. Yet the debates over the Universal Declaration of Human Rights revealed the tensions inherent in the idea, tensions that persist to the present day. To what extent do human rights supersede national sovereignty? Who has the authority to enforce human rights that a government is violating? The United Nations? Regional bodies like the Organization of American States and the European Union? A single country (as the United States would claim to be doing in the Iraq War that began in 2003)? The Covenant of the League of Nations—the predecessor of the United Nations created after World War I—had contained a clause allowing the league to intervene when a government violated the rights of its own citizens.

Debates over human rights

One reason for the lack of an enforcement mechanism in the Universal Declaration of Human Rights was that both the United States and the Soviet Union refused to accept outside interference in their internal affairs. John Foster Dulles, an American delegate to the conference that created the UN, opposed any statement affirming human rights out of fear that it would lead to an international investigation of "the Negro question in this country." In 1947, the NAACP did file a petition with the United Nations asking it to investigate racism in the United States as a violation of human rights. Conditions in states like Mississippi should be of concern to all mankind, it argued, because if democracy failed to function in "the leading democracy in the world," the prospects for democracy were weakened everywhere. But the UN decided that it lacked jurisdiction. Nonetheless, since the end of World War II, the enjoyment of human rights has increasingly taken its place in definitions of freedom across the globe, especially where such rights are flagrantly violated.

> *Human rights violations in America*

After the Cold War ended, the idea of human rights would play an increasingly prominent role in world affairs. But during the 1950s, Cold War imperatives shaped the concept. Neither the United States nor the Soviet Union could resist emphasizing certain provisions of the Universal Declaration while ignoring others. The Soviets claimed to provide all citizens with social and economic rights, but violated democratic rights and civil liberties. Many Americans condemned the nonpolitical rights as a step toward socialism.

Eleanor Roosevelt saw the Universal Declaration of Human Rights as an integrated body of principles, a combination of traditional civil and political liberties with the social conditions of freedom outlined in her husband's Economic Bill of Rights of 1944. But to make it easier for member states to ratify the document, the UN divided it into two "covenants"—Civil and Political Rights, and Economic, Social, and Cultural Rights. It took until 1992 for the U.S. Congress to ratify the first. It has never approved the second.

> *Two "covenants" of human rights*

Human Rights. This cartoon from 1947 depicts delegates to a meeting of the UN Human Rights Commission as unruly schoolchildren. Eleanor Roosevelt lectures delegates from various countries about human rights. "Now children," she says, "all together: 'The rights of the individual are above the rights of the state.'" At the lower left, John Foster Dulles, an American delegate, aims a slingshot at the Soviet ambassador to the UN, Andrey Y. Vyshinsky, who stands in the lower right corner wearing a dunce cap. Charles Malik of Lebanon offers the teacher an apple. Several delegates seem bored; others are attentive.

THE TRUMAN PRESIDENCY

The Fair Deal

With the end of World War II, President Truman's first domestic task was to preside over the transition from a wartime to a peacetime economy. More than 12 million men remained in uniform in August 1945. Most wanted nothing more than to return home to their families. Demobilization proceeded at a rapid pace. Within a year, the armed forces had been reduced to 3 million. Some returning soldiers found the adjustment to civilian life difficult. The divorce rate in 1945 rose to double its prewar level. Others took advantage of the GI Bill of Rights (discussed in the previous chapter) to obtain home mortgages, set up small businesses, and embark on college educations. The majority of returning soldiers entered the labor force—one reason why more than 2 million women workers lost their jobs. The government abolished wartime agencies that regulated industrial production and labor relations, and it dismantled wartime price controls, leading to a sharp rise in prices.

A few of the numerous World War II veterans who attended college after the war, thanks to the GI Bill.

In the immediate aftermath of World War II, President Truman, backed by party liberals and organized labor, moved to revive the stalled momentum of the New Deal. Truman's program, which he announced in September 1945 and would later call the **Fair Deal**, focused on improving the social safety net and raising the standard of living of ordinary Americans. He called on Congress to increase the minimum wage, enact a program of national health insurance, and expand public housing, Social Security, and aid to education. Truman, complained one Republican leader, was "out-New Dealing the New Deal."

Raising the standard of living

The Postwar Strike Wave

In 1946, a new wave of labor militancy swept the country. The AFL and CIO launched **Operation Dixie**, a campaign to bring unionization to the South and, by so doing, shatter the hold of anti-labor conservatives on the region's politics. More than 200 labor organizers entered the region, seeking support especially in the southern textile industry, the steel industry in the Birmingham region, and agriculture. With war production at an end, overtime work diminished even as inflation soared following the removal of price controls. The resulting drop in workers' real income sparked the largest strike wave in American history. Nearly 5 million workers—including those in the steel, auto, coal, and other key industries—walked off their jobs, demanding wage increases. The strike of 750,000 steelworkers represented the largest single walkout in American history to that date. Even Hollywood studios shut down because of a strike of actors and other employees of the movie industry that lasted for the better part of a year. One historian calls this period "the closest thing to a national general strike in industry in the twentieth century."

National strikes

Resolving the strikes

President Truman feared the strikes would seriously disrupt the economy. When railroad workers stopped work and set up picket lines, the infuriated president prepared a speech in which he threatened to draft them all into the army and "hang a few traitors"—language toned down by his advisers. The walkout soon ended, as did a coal strike after the Truman administration secured a court order requiring the miners to return to work. To resolve other strikes, Truman appointed federal "fact-finding boards," which generally recommended wage increases, although not enough to restore workers' purchasing power to wartime levels.

The Republican Resurgence

In the congressional elections of 1946, large numbers of middle-class voters, alarmed by the labor turmoil, voted Republican. Many workers, disappointed by Truman's policies, stayed at home. This was a lethal combination for the Democratic Party. For the first time since the 1920s, Republicans swept to control of both houses of Congress. Meanwhile, in the face of vigorous opposition from southern employers and public officials and the reluctance of many white workers to join interracial labor unions, Operation Dixie failed to unionize the South or dent the political control of conservative Democrats in the region. The election of 1946 ensured that a conservative coalition of Republicans and southern Democrats would continue to dominate Congress.

The Taft-Hartley Act of 1947

Congress turned aside Truman's Fair Deal program. It enacted tax cuts for wealthy Americans and, over the president's veto, in 1947 passed the **Taft-Hartley Act**, which sought to reverse some of the gains made by organized labor in the past decade. The measure authorized the president to suspend strikes by ordering an eighty-day "cooling-off period," and it banned sympathy strikes and secondary boycotts (labor actions directed not at an employer but at those who did business with him). It outlawed the closed shop, which required a worker to be a union member when taking up a job, and authorized states to pass "right-to-work" laws, prohibiting other forms of compulsory union membership. It also forced union officials to swear that they were not communists. While hardly a "slave-labor bill," as the AFL and CIO called it, the Taft-Hartley Act made it considerably more difficult to bring unorganized workers into unions. Over time, as population and capital investment shifted to states with "right-to-work" laws like Texas, Florida, and North Carolina, Taft-Hartley contributed to the decline of organized labor's share of the nation's workforce.

Postwar Civil Rights

During his first term, Truman reached out in unprecedented ways to the nation's black community. The war, as noted in the previous chapter, had inspired a new black militancy and led many whites to reject American racial practices as reminiscent of Hitler's theory of a master race. In the years immediately following World War II, the status of black Americans enjoyed a prominence in national affairs unmatched since Reconstruction.

The postwar status of black Americans

Between 1945 and 1951, eleven states from New York to New Mexico established fair employment practices commissions, and numerous cities passed laws against discrimination in access to jobs and public accommodations. (Some of these

An NAACP youth march against racial segregation in Houston, Texas, in 1947 illustrates the civil rights upsurge of the years immediately following the end of World War II.

measures addressed other racial groups besides blacks: for example, California in 1947 repealed its laws permitting local school districts to provide segregated education for children of Chinese descent and those barring aliens from owning land.) A broad civil rights coalition involving labor, religious groups, and black organizations supported these measures. The NAACP, its ranks swollen during the war, launched a voter registration campaign in the South. By 1952, 20 percent of black southerners were registered to vote, nearly a seven-fold increase since 1940. (Most of the gains took place in the Upper South—in Alabama and Mississippi, the heartland of white supremacy, the numbers barely budged.) Law enforcement agencies finally took the crime of lynching seriously. In 1952, for the first time since record keeping began seventy years earlier, no lynchings took place in the United States. In 1946, the Superman radio show devoted several episodes to the man of steel fighting the Ku Klux Klan, a sign of changing race relations in the wake of World War II.

Jackie Robinson sliding into third base, 1949.

In another indication that race relations were in flux, the Brooklyn Dodgers in 1947 challenged the long-standing exclusion of black players from major league baseball by adding Jackie Robinson to their team. Robinson, who possessed both remarkable athletic ability and a passion for equality, had been tried and acquitted for insubordination in 1944 when he refused to move to the back of a bus at Fort Hood, Texas, while serving in the army. But he promised Dodger owner Branch Rickey that he would not retaliate when subjected to

Part of a series of giant murals painted for the lobby of the Rincon Center (formerly a post office, now a shopping mall in San Francisco), this work by the artist Anton Refregier links the Four Freedoms of World War II to a multicultural vision of American society. (In Norman Rockwell's celebrated paintings, shown in Chapter 22, nearly all the figures depicted are white.)

Desegregating the armed forces

Progressive Democratic platform

The 1948 Democratic national convention

racist taunts by opposing fans and players. His dignity in the face of constant verbal abuse won Robinson nationwide respect, and his baseball prowess earned him the Rookie of the Year award. His success opened the door to the integration of baseball and led to the demise of the Negro Leagues, to which black players had previously been confined.

To Secure These Rights

In October 1947, a Commission on Civil Rights appointed by the president issued *To Secure These Rights*, one of the most devastating indictments ever published of racial inequality in America. It called on the federal government to assume the responsibility for abolishing segregation and ensuring equal treatment in housing, employment, education, and the criminal justice system. Truman hailed the report as "an American charter of human freedom." The impact of America's race system on the nation's ability to conduct the Cold War was not far from his mind. Truman noted that if the United States were to offer the "peoples of the world" a "choice of freedom or enslavement," it must "correct the remaining imperfections in our practice of democracy."

In February 1948, Truman presented an ambitious civil rights program to Congress, calling for a permanent federal civil rights commission, national laws against lynching and the poll tax, and action to ensure equal access to jobs and education. Congress, as Truman anticipated, approved none of his proposals. But in July 1948, just as the presidential campaign was getting under way, Truman issued an executive order desegregating the armed forces. The armed services became the first large institution in American life to promote racial integration actively and to attempt to root out long-standing racist practices. The Korean War would be the first American conflict fought by an integrated army since the War of Independence.

Truman genuinely despised racial discrimination. But his focus on civil rights also formed part of a strategy to win reelection by reinvigorating and expanding the political coalition Roosevelt had created. With calls for federal health insurance, the repeal of the Taft-Hartley Act, and aid to public education, the Democratic platform of 1948 was the most progressive in the party's history. Led by Hubert Humphrey, the young mayor of Minneapolis, party liberals overcame southern resistance and added a strong civil rights plank to the platform.

The Dixiecrat and Wallace Revolts

"I say the time has come," Humphrey told the Democratic national convention, "to walk out of the shadow of states' rights and into the sunlight of human rights." Whereupon numerous southern delegates—dubbed **Dixiecrats** by the press—walked out of the gathering. They soon formed the States' Rights Democratic Party and nominated for president Governor Strom Thurmond of South Carolina. Although his platform called for the "complete segregation of the races" and his campaign drew most of its support from those alarmed by Truman's civil rights initiatives, Thurmond denied charges of racism. The real issue of the election, Thurmond insisted, was freedom—the States' Rights Democratic Party, he declared, stood for "individual liberty and freedom, the right of people to govern themselves." Truman's plans for extending federal power into the South to enforce civil rights, Thurmond charged, would "convert America into a Hitler state."

Also in 1948, a group of left-wing critics of Truman's foreign policy formed the Progressive Party and nominated former vice president Henry A. Wallace for president. Wallace advocated an expansion of social welfare programs at home and denounced racial segregation even more vigorously than Truman. When he campaigned in the South, angry white crowds attacked him. But his real difference with the president concerned the Cold War. Wallace called for international control of nuclear weapons and a renewed effort to develop a relationship with the Soviet Union based on economic cooperation rather than military confrontation. He announced his willingness to accept support from all Americans who agreed with him, including socialists and communists. The influence of the now much-reduced Communist Party in Wallace's campaign led to an exodus of New Deal liberals and severe attacks on his candidacy. A vote for Wallace, Truman declared, was in effect a vote for Stalin.

Henry A. Wallace

The 1948 Campaign

Wallace threatened to draw votes from Truman on the left, and Thurmond to undermine the president's support in the South, where whites had voted solidly for the Democrats throughout the twentieth century. But Truman's main opponent, fortunately for the president, was the colorless Republican Thomas A. Dewey. Certain of victory and an ineffective speaker and campaigner, Dewey seemed unwilling to commit himself on controversial issues. His speeches, wrote one hostile newspaper, amounted to nothing more than clichés: "Agriculture is important. Our rivers are full of fish. You cannot have freedom without liberty. Our future lies ahead." Truman, by contrast, ran an aggressive campaign. He crisscrossed the country by train, delivering fiery attacks on the Republican-controlled "do-nothing Congress." Truman revived New Deal rhetoric denouncing Wall Street and charged his opponent with threatening to undermine Social Security and other New Deal benefits. "Don't let them take it away," he repeated over and over.

The four-way 1948 campaign was the last before television put a premium on brief political advertisements and entertaining slogans rather than substantive debate, and the last in which a full spectrum of ideologies was presented to the American public. Virtually every public-opinion poll and newspaper report predicted a Dewey victory. Truman's success—by 303 to 189 electoral votes—represented one of the greatest upsets in American political history. For the first time since 1868, blacks (in the North, where they enjoyed the right to vote) played a decisive role in the outcome.

Thomas A. Dewey

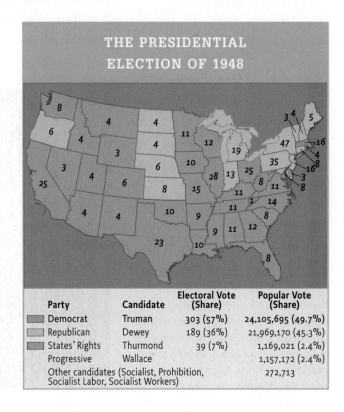

THE PRESIDENTIAL ELECTION OF 1948

Party	Candidate	Electoral Vote (Share)	Popular Vote (Share)
Democrat	Truman	303 (57%)	24,105,695 (49.7%)
Republican	Dewey	189 (36%)	21,969,170 (45.3%)
States' Rights	Thurmond	39 (7%)	1,169,021 (2.4%)
Progressive	Wallace		1,157,172 (2.4%)
Other candidates (Socialist, Prohibition, Socialist Labor, Socialist Workers)			272,713

Thurmond carried four Deep South states, demonstrating that the race issue, couched in terms of individual freedom, had the potential of leading traditionally Democratic white voters to desert their party. In retrospect, the States' Rights campaign offered a preview of the political transformation that by the end of the twentieth century would leave every southern state in the Republican column. As for Wallace, he suffered the humiliation of polling fewer popular votes (1.16 million) than Thurmond (1.17 million). His crushing defeat inaugurated an era in which public criticism of the foundations of American foreign policy became all but impossible.

THE ANTICOMMUNIST CRUSADE

For nearly half a century, the Cold War profoundly affected American life. There would be no return to "normalcy" as after World War I. The military-industrial establishment created during World War II would be permanent, not temporary. The United States retained a large and active federal government and poured money into weapons development and overseas bases. National security became the stated reason for a host of government projects, including aid to higher education and the building of a new national highway system (justified by the need to speed the evacuation of major cities in the event of nuclear war). The Cold War encouraged a culture of secrecy and dishonesty. Not until decades later was it revealed that during the 1950s and 1960s both the Soviet and American governments conducted experiments in which unwitting soldiers were exposed to chemical, biological, and nuclear weapons. American nuclear tests, conducted on Pacific islands and in Nevada, exposed thousands of civilians to radiation that caused cancer and birth defects.

A postcard promoting tourism to Las Vegas highlights as one attraction the city's proximity to a nuclear test site. Witnessing nearby atomic explosions became a popular pastime in the city. The government failed to issue warnings of the dangers of nuclear fallout, and only years later did it admit that many onlookers had contracted diseases from radiation.

Movie stars, led by actors Humphrey Bogart and Lauren Bacall, on their way to attend the 1947 hearings of the House Un-American Activities Committee, in a demonstration of support for those called to testify about alleged communist influence in Hollywood.

Cold War military spending helped to fuel economic growth and support scientific research that not only perfected weaponry but also led to improved aircraft, computers, medicines, and other products with a large impact on civilian life. Since much of this research took place at universities, the Cold War promoted the rapid expansion of American higher education. The Cold War reshaped immigration policy, with refugees from communism being allowed to enter the United States regardless of national-origin quotas. The international embarrassment caused by American racial policies contributed to the dismantling of segregation. And like other wars, the Cold War encouraged the drawing of a sharp line between patriotic Americans and those accused of being disloyal. Containment—not only of communism but of unorthodox opinions of all kinds—took place at home as well as abroad. At precisely the moment when the United States celebrated freedom as the foundation of American life, the right to dissent came under attack.

Scientific innovation and social changes

Loyalty and Disloyalty

Dividing the world between liberty and slavery automatically made those who could be linked to communism enemies of freedom. Although the assault on civil liberties came to be known as **McCarthyism**, it began before Senator Joseph R. McCarthy of Wisconsin burst onto the national scene in 1950. In 1947, less than two weeks after announcing the Truman Doctrine, the president established a loyalty review system that required government employees to demonstrate their patriotism without being allowed to confront accusers or, in some cases, knowing the charges against them. Along with persons suspected of disloyalty, the new national security system also targeted homosexuals who worked for the

Loyalty review system

government. They were deemed particularly susceptible to blackmail by Soviet agents as well as supposedly lacking in the manly qualities needed to maintain the country's resolve in the fight against communism. Ironically, the government conducted an anti-gay campaign at the very time that gay men enjoyed a powerful presence in realms of culture and commercial life being promoted as expressions of American freedom—modern art and ballet, fashion, and advertising. The loyalty program failed to uncover any cases of espionage. But the federal government dismissed several hundred persons from their jobs, and thousands resigned rather than submit to investigation.

Anti-gay campaign

Also in 1947, the House Un-American Activities Committee (HUAC) launched a series of hearings about communist influence in Hollywood. Calling well-known screenwriters, directors, and actors to appear before the committee ensured itself a wave of national publicity, which its members relished. Celebrities like producer Walt Disney and actors Gary Cooper and Ronald Reagan testified that the movie industry harbored numerous communists. But ten "unfriendly witnesses" refused to answer the committee's questions about their political beliefs or to "name names" (identify individual communists) on the grounds that the hearings violated the First Amendment's guarantees of freedom of speech and political association. The committee charged the **Hollywood Ten**, who included the prominent screenwriters Ring Lardner Jr. and Dalton Trumbo, with contempt of Congress, and they served jail terms of six months to a year. Hollywood studios blacklisted them (denied them employment), along with more than 200 others who were accused of communist sympathies or who refused to name names.

The HUAC hearings in Hollywood

The Spy Trials

A series of highly publicized legal cases followed, which fueled the growing anti-communist hysteria. Whittaker Chambers, an editor at *Time* magazine, testified before HUAC that during the 1930s, Alger Hiss, a high-ranking State Department official, had given him secret government documents to pass to agents of the Soviet Union. Hiss vehemently denied the charge, but a jury convicted him of perjury and he served five years in prison. A young congressman from California and a member of HUAC, Richard Nixon, achieved national prominence because of his dogged pursuit of Hiss. In another celebrated case, the Truman administration put the leaders of the Communist Party on trial for advocating the overthrow of the government. In 1951, eleven of them were sentenced to five years in prison.

The most sensational trial involved Julius and Ethel Rosenberg, a working-class Jewish communist couple from New York City (quite different from Hiss, a member of the eastern Protestant "establishment"). In 1951, a jury convicted the Rosenbergs of conspiracy to pass secrets concerning the atomic bomb to Soviet agents during World War II (when the Soviets were American allies). Their chief accuser was David Greenglass, Ethel Rosenberg's brother, who had worked at the Los Alamos nuclear research center.

The case against Julius Rosenberg rested on highly secret documents that could not be revealed in court. (When they were released many years later, the scientific information they contained seemed too crude to justify the government's charge that Julius had passed along the "secret of the atomic bomb," although he may have helped the Soviets speed up their atomic program.) The government had almost

Demonstrators at a 1953 rally in Washington, D.C., demanding the execution of Julius and Ethel Rosenberg.

no evidence against Ethel Rosenberg, and Greenglass later admitted that he had lied in some of his testimony about her. Indeed, prosecutors seem to have indicted her in the hope of pressuring Julius to confess and implicate others. But in the atmosphere of hysteria, their conviction was certain. Even though they had been convicted of conspiracy, a far weaker charge than spying or treason, Judge Irving Kaufman called their crime "worse than murder." They had helped, he declared, to "cause" the Korean War. Despite an international outcry, the death sentence was carried out in 1953. Controversy still surrounds the degree of guilt of both Hiss and the Rosenbergs, although almost no one today defends the Rosenbergs' execution. But these trials powerfully reinforced the idea that an army of Soviet spies was at work in the United States.

Senator Joseph R. McCarthy at the Army-McCarthy hearings of 1954. McCarthy points to a map detailing charges about the alleged extent of the communist menace, while the army's lawyer, Joseph Welch, listens in disgust.

McCarthy and McCarthyism

In this atmosphere, a little-known senator from Wisconsin suddenly emerged as the chief national pursuer of subversives and gave a new name to the anticommunist crusade. Joseph R. McCarthy had won election to the Senate in 1946, partly on the basis of a fictional war record (he falsely claimed to have flown combat missions in the Pacific). In a speech at Wheeling, West Virginia, in February 1950, McCarthy announced that he had a list of 205 communists working for the State Department. The charge was preposterous, the numbers constantly changed, and McCarthy never identified a single person guilty of genuine disloyalty. But with a genius for self-promotion, McCarthy used the Senate subcommittee he chaired to hold hearings and level wild charges against numerous individuals as well as the Defense Department, the Voice of America, and other government agencies. Although many Republicans initially supported his rampage as a weapon against the Truman administration, McCarthy became an embarrassment to the party after the election of Republican Dwight D. Eisenhower as president in 1952. But McCarthy did not halt his campaign. He even questioned Eisenhower's anticommunism.

McCarthy's allegations against the State Department

Few political figures had the courage to speak up against McCarthy's crusade. One who did was Margaret Chase Smith of Maine, the Senate's only woman member. On June 1, 1950, soon after McCarthy's Wheeling speech, Smith addressed the Senate with what she called a "declaration of conscience." She did not name McCarthy, but few could mistake the target of her condemnation of a "campaign of hate and character assassination." Most of her colleagues, however, remained silent.

Margaret Chase Smith

McCarthy's downfall came in 1954, when a Senate committee investigated his charges that the army had harbored and "coddled" communists. The nationally televised **Army-McCarthy hearings** revealed McCarthy as a bully who browbeat witnesses and made sweeping accusations with no basis in fact. The dramatic high point came when McCarthy attacked the loyalty of a young attorney in the firm of

"Fire!" Cartoonist Herbert Block, known as "Herblock," offered this comment in 1949 on the danger to American freedom posed by the anticommunist crusade.

State and local actions

Court inaction

Joseph Welch, the army's chief lawyer. "Let us not assassinate this lad further," Welch pleaded. "You have done enough. Have you no sense of decency, sir?" After the hearings ended, the Republican-controlled Senate voted to "condemn" McCarthy for his behavior. He died three years later. But the word "McCarthyism" had entered the political vocabulary, a shorthand for character assassination, guilt by association, and abuse of power in the name of anticommunism.

An Atmosphere of Fear

By the early 1950s, the anticommunist crusade had created a pervasive atmosphere of fear. One commentator described Washington, D.C., as a city rife with "spying, suspicion, [and] defamation by rumor," with "democratic freedoms" at risk as power slipped into the hands of those "whose values are the values of dictatorship and whose methods are the methods of the police state." But anticommunism was as much a local as a national phenomenon. States created their own committees, modeled on HUAC, that investigated suspected communists and other dissenters. States and localities required loyalty oaths of teachers, pharmacists, and members of other professions, and they banned communists from fishing, holding a driver's license, and, in Indiana, working as a professional wrestler.

Private organizations like the American Legion, National Association of Manufacturers, and Daughters of the American Revolution also persecuted individuals for their beliefs. The Better America League of southern California gathered the names of nearly 2 million alleged subversives in the region. Previous membership in organizations with communist influence or even participation in campaigns in which communists had taken part, such as the defense of the government of Spain during the Spanish Civil War of the 1930s, suddenly took on sinister implications. Throughout the country in the late 1940s and 1950s, those who failed to testify about their past and present political beliefs and to inform on possible communists frequently lost their jobs.

Local anticommunist groups forced public libraries to remove from their shelves "un-American" books like the tales of Robin Hood, who took from the rich to give to the poor. Universities refused to allow left-wing speakers to appear on campus and fired teachers who refused to sign loyalty oaths or to testify against others.

As during World War I, the courts did nothing to halt the political repression, demonstrating once again James Madison's warning that popular hysteria could override "parchment barriers" like the Bill of Rights that sought to prevent infringements on freedom. In 1951, in *Dennis v. United States*, the Supreme Court upheld the jailing of Communist Party leaders even though the charges concerned their beliefs, not any actions they had taken. Even many liberals retreated from the idea that freedom of expression was a birthright of all Americans. The American Civil Liberties Union condemned McCarthy's tactics but refused to defend the indicted Communist Party leaders.

The Uses of Anticommunism

There undoubtedly were Soviet spies in the United States. Yet the tiny Communist Party hardly posed a threat to American security. And the vast majority of those jailed or deprived of their livelihoods during the McCarthy era were guilty of nothing more than holding unpopular beliefs and engaging in lawful political activities.

Anticommunism had many faces and purposes. A popular mass movement, it grew especially strong among ethnic groups like Polish-Americans, with roots in eastern European countries now dominated by the Soviet Union, and among American Catholics in general, who resented and feared communists' hostility to religion. Government agencies like the Federal Bureau of Investigation (FBI) used anticommunism to expand their power. Under director J. Edgar Hoover, the FBI developed files on thousands of American citizens, including political dissenters, homosexuals, and others, most of whom had no connection to communism.

Anticommunist groups and goals

Anticommunism also served as a weapon wielded by individuals and groups in battles unrelated to defending the United States against subversion. McCarthy and his Republican followers often seemed to target not so much Stalin as the legacy of Roosevelt and the New Deal. For many Democrats, aggressive anticommunism became a form of self-defense against Republican charges of disloyalty and a weapon in a struggle for the party's future. The campaign against subversion redrew the boundaries of acceptable Democratic liberalism to exclude both communists and those willing to cooperate with them as in the days of the Popular Front. Indeed, "sympathetic association" with communists—past or present—became grounds for dismissal from one's job under the government's loyalty program.

As the historian Henry Steele Commager argued in a 1947 magazine article, the anticommunist crusade promoted a new definition of loyalty—conformity. Anything other than "uncritical and unquestioning acceptance of America as it is," wrote Commager, could now be labeled unpatriotic. For business, anticommunism became part of a campaign to identify government intervention in the economy with socialism. White supremacists employed anticommunism against black civil rights, business used it against unions, and upholders of sexual morality and traditional gender roles raised the cry of subversion against feminism and homosexuality, both supposedly responsible for eroding the country's fighting spirit.

Loyalty and conformity

Anticommunist Politics

At its height, from the late 1940s to around 1960, the anticommunist crusade powerfully structured American politics and culture. Especially after their unexpected defeat in 1948, Republicans in Congress used a drumbeat of charges of subversion to block Truman's political program. The most important actions of Congress were ones the president opposed. After launching the government's loyalty program in 1947, Truman had become increasingly alarmed at the excesses of the anticommunist crusade. He vetoed the McCarran Internal Security Bill of 1950, which required "subversive" groups to register with the government, allowed the denial of passports to their members, and authorized their deportation or detention on presidential order. But Congress quickly gave the measure the two-thirds majority necessary for it to become law.

The **McCarran-Walter Act** of 1952, the first major piece of immigration legislation since 1924, also passed over the president's veto. Truman had appointed a Commission on Immigration, whose report, *Whom Shall We Welcome?*, called for replacing the quotas based on national origins with a more flexible system taking into account family reunion, labor needs, and political asylum. But the McCarran-Walter Act kept the quotas in place. It also authorized the deportation of immigrants identified as communists, even if they had become citizens. But the renewed fear of aliens

The McCarran-Walter Act of 1952

VOICES OF FREEDOM

From JOSEPH R. MCCARTHY, SPEECH AT WHEELING (1950)

During the 1950s, the demagogic pursuit of supposed communists in government and other places of influence became known as McCarthyism, after Senator Joseph R. McCarthy, Republican of Wisconsin. In a speech in West Virginia in February 1950, McCarthy claimed to have a list of 205 communists working for the State Department. When he entered the speech into the Congressional Record a few days later, he reduced the number to fifty-seven. He never named any of them.

Today we are engaged in a final, all-out battle between communistic atheism and Christianity. The modern champions of communism have selected this as the time. And, ladies and gentlemen, the chips are down—they are truly down.

Six years ago, at the time of the first conference to map out peace . . . there was within the Soviet orbit 180 million people. Lined up on the antitotalitarian side there were in the world at that time roughly 1.625 billion people. Today, only six years later, there are 800 million people under the absolute domination of Soviet Russia—an increase of over 400 percent. On our side, the figure has shrunk to around 500 million. . . .

The reason why we find ourselves in a position of impotency is not because our only powerful, potential enemy has sent men to invade our shores, but rather because of the traitorous actions of those who have been treated so well by this nation. It has not been the less fortunate or members of minority groups who have been selling this nation out, but rather those who have had all the benefits that the wealthiest nation on earth has had to offer—the finest homes, the finest college education, and the finest jobs in government we can give.

This is glaringly true in the State Department. There the bright young men who are born with silver spoons in their mouths are the ones who have been worst. . . . In my opinion the State Department, which is one of the most important government departments, is thoroughly infested with communists.

I have in my hand 57 cases of individuals who would appear to be either card carrying members or certainly loyal to the Communist Party, but who nevertheless are still helping to shape our foreign policy. . . . One thing to remember in discussing the communists in our government is that we are not dealing with spies who get 30 pieces of silver to steal the blueprints of new weapons. We are dealing with a far more sinister type of activity because it permits the enemy to guide and shape our policy.

From MARGARET CHASE SMITH, SPEECH IN THE SENATE (1950)

Most of McCarthy's colleagues were cowed by his tactics. One who was not was Margaret Chase Smith of Maine, the Senate's only female member. On June 1, she delivered a brief speech, along with a Declaration of Conscience, signed by six other Republican senators.

―――――――――――――

The United States Senate has long enjoyed world-wide respect as the greatest deliberative body in the world. But recently that deliberative character has too often been debased to the level of a forum of hate and character assassination sheltered by the shield of congressional immunity. . . .

I think that it is high time for the United States Senate and its members to do some soul searching—for us to weigh our consciences—on the manner in which we are performing our duty to the people of America—on the manner in which we are using or abusing our individual powers and privileges. . . . I think that it is high time that we remembered; that the Constitution, as amended, speaks not only of the freedom of speech but also of trial by jury instead of trial by accusation.

Those of us who shout the loudest about Americanism in making character assassinations are all too frequently those who, by our own words and acts, ignore some of the basic principles of Americanism—

The right to criticize; The right to hold unpopular beliefs; The right to protest; The right of independent thought.

The exercise of these rights should not cost one single American citizen his reputation or his right to a livelihood nor should he be in danger of losing his reputation or livelihood merely because he happens to know someone who holds unpopular beliefs. Who of us doesn't? Otherwise none of us could call our souls our own. Otherwise thought control would have set in.

The American people are sick and tired of being afraid to speak their minds lest they be politically smeared as "Communists" or "Fascists" by their opponents. Freedom of speech is not what it used to be in America. It has been so abused by some that it is not exercised by others. The American people are sick and tired of seeing innocent people smeared and guilty people whitewashed.

The nation sorely needs a Republican victory. But I don't want to see the Republican Party ride to political victory on the Four Horsemen of Calumny—Fear, Ignorance, Bigotry and Smear. . . .

As a United States Senator, I am not proud of the way in which the Senate has been made a publicity platform for irresponsible sensationalism. . . . I don't like the way the Senate has been made a rendezvous for vilification, for selfish political gain at the sacrifice of individual reputations and national unity.

QUESTIONS

1. *What kind of social resentments are evident in McCarthy's speech?*

2. *What does Smith believe is the essence of freedom of speech?*

3. *What do these documents suggest about how the Cold War affected discussions of freedom in the early 1950s?*

sparked by the anticommunist crusade went far beyond communists. In 1954, the federal government launched Operation "Wetback," which employed the military to invade Mexican-American neighborhoods and round up and deport undocumented aliens. Within a year, some 1 million Mexicans had been deported. ("Wetback" is an insulting term sometimes directed at Mexican immigrants.)

Truman did secure passage of a 1950 law that added previously excluded self-employed and domestic workers to Social Security. Otherwise, however, the idea of expanding the New Deal welfare state faded. In its place, private welfare arrangements proliferated. The labor contracts of unionized workers established health insurance plans, automatic cost of living wage increases, paid vacations, and pension plans that supplemented Social Security. Western European governments provided these benefits to all citizens. In the United States, union members in major industries enjoyed them, but not the nonunionized majority of the population, a situation that created increasing inequality among laboring Americans.

The Cold War and Organized Labor

Every political and social organization had to cooperate with the anticommunist crusade or face destruction, a wrenching experience for movements like labor and civil rights, in which communists had been some of the most militant organizers. After the passage of the Taft-Hartley Act of 1947, which withdrew bargaining rights and legal protection from unions whose leaders failed to swear that they were not communists, the CIO expelled numerous left-wing officials and eleven communist-led unions, representing nearly 1 million workers. Organized labor emerged as a major supporter of the foreign policy of the Cold War. Internal battles over the role of communists and their allies led to the purging of some of the most militant union leaders, often the ones most committed to advancing equal rights to women and racial minorities in the workplace.

Cold War Civil Rights

The civil rights movement also underwent a transformation. At first, mainstream black organizations like the NAACP and Urban League protested the Truman administration's loyalty program. They wondered aloud why the program and congressional committees defined communism as "un-American," but not racism. Anticommunist investigators often cited attendance at interracial gatherings as evidence of disloyalty. But while a few prominent black leaders, notably the singer and actor Paul Robeson and the veteran crusader for equality W. E. B. Du Bois, became outspoken critics of the Cold War, most felt they had no choice but to go along. The NAACP purged communists from local branches. When the government deprived Robeson of his passport and indicted Du Bois for failing to register as an agent of the Soviet Union, few prominent Americans, white or black, protested. (The charge against Du Bois was so absurd that even at the height of McCarthyism, the judge dismissed it.)

The Cold War caused a shift in thinking and tactics among civil rights groups. Organizations like the Southern Conference for Human Welfare, in which communists and noncommunists had cooperated in linking racial equality with labor organizing and economic reform, had been crucial to the struggles of the 1930s and war years. Their demise left a gaping hole that the NAACP, with its narrowly legalistic strategy, could not fill. Black organizations embraced the language of the Cold War and used it for their own purposes. They insisted that by damaging the American image abroad, racial inequality played into the Russians' hands. Thus, they helped to cement Cold War ideology as the foundation of the political culture, while complicating the idea of American freedom.

President Truman, as noted above, had called for greater attention to civil rights in part to improve the American image abroad. All in all, however, the height of the Cold War was an unfavorable time to raise questions about the imperfections of American society. In 1947, two months after the Truman Doctrine speech, Under-secretary of State Dean Acheson delivered a major address defending the president's pledge to aid "free peoples" seeking to preserve their "democratic institutions." Acheson chose as his audience the Delta Council, an organization of Mississippi planters, bankers, and merchants. He seemed unaware that to make the case for the Cold War, he had ventured into what one historian has called the "American Siberia," a place of grinding poverty whose black population (70 percent of the total) enjoyed neither genuine freedom nor democracy. Most of the Delta's citizens were denied the very liberties supposedly endangered by communism.

After 1948, little came of the Truman administration's civil rights flurry. State and local laws banning discrimination in employment and housing remained largely unenforced. In 1952, the Democrats showed how quickly the issue had faded by nominating for president Adlai Stevenson of Illinois, a candidate with little interest in civil rights, with southern segregationist John Sparkman as his running mate. The following year, Hortense Gabel, director of the eminently respectable New York State Committee Against Discrimination in Housing, reported that the shadow of fear hung over the civil rights movement. Given the persecution of dissent and the widespread sentiment that equated any criticism of American society with disloyalty, "a great many people are shying away from all activity in the civil liberties and civil rights fronts."

Time would reveal that the waning of the civil rights impulse was only temporary. But it came at a crucial moment, the late 1940s and early 1950s, when the United States experienced the greatest economic boom in its history. The rise of an "affluent society" transformed American life, opening new opportunities for tens of millions of white Americans in rapidly expanding suburbs. But it left blacks trapped in the declining rural areas of the South and urban ghettos of the North. The contrast between new opportunities and widespread prosperity for whites and continued discrimination for blacks would soon inspire a civil rights revolution and, with it, yet another redefinition of American freedom.

Blacks, led by A. Philip Randolph (*left*), picketing at the 1948 Democratic national convention. The delegates' adoption of a strong civil rights plank led representatives of several southern states to withdraw and nominate their own candidate for president, Strom Thurmond.

The waning civil rights impulse

SUGGESTED READING

BOOKS

- Biondi, Martha. *To Stand and Fight: The Struggle for Civil Rights in Postwar New York City* (2003). A comprehensive account of the broad coalition that battled for racial justice in New York City, in areas such as jobs, education, and housing.

- Canaday, Margot. *The Straight State: Sexuality and Citizenship in Twentieth-Century America* (2009). Details the federal government's efforts to stigmatize and punish homosexuality.

- Cullather, Nick. *The Hungry World: America's Cold War Battle Against Poverty in Asia* (2010). Explores how divergent approaches to combating world poverty became a battleground in the Cold War.

- Donovan, Robert. *Conflict and Crisis: The Presidency of Harry S. Truman, 1945–1948* (1977). A careful account of Truman's first administration and his surprising election victory in 1948.

- Dudziak, Mary L. *Cold War Civil Rights: Race and the Image of American Democracy* (2000). Analyzes how the Cold War influenced and in some ways encouraged the civil rights movement at home.

- Gaddis, John. *Strategies of Containment: A Critical Analysis of Postwar American National Security* (1982). An influential analysis of the development of the containment policy central to American foreign policy during the Cold War.

- Glendon, Mary Ann. *A World Made New: Eleanor Roosevelt and the Universal Declaration of Human Rights* (2001). Relates the drafting of the Universal Declaration of Human Rights and the response of governments around the world, including the United States.

- Hogan, Michael. *The Marhsall Plan* (1987). A detailed look at a pillar of early Cold War policy.

- Hunt, Michael. *Ideology and U.S. Foreign Policy* (1987). Discusses how ideas, including the idea of freedom, have shaped America's interactions with the rest of the world.

- Leffler, Melvyn P. *A Preponderance of Power: National Security, the Truman Administration, and the Cold War* (1992). An influential account of the origins of the Cold War.

- Lipsitz, George. *Rainbow at Midnight: Labor and Culture in the 1940s* (1994). Examines the labor movement and its role in American life in the decade of perhaps its greatest influence.

- Saunders, Frances S. *The Cultural Cold War: The CIA and the World of Arts and Letters* (2000). Describes how the CIA and other government agencies secretly funded artists and writers as part of the larger Cold War.

- Schrecker, Ellen. *Many Are the Crimes: McCarthyism in America* (1998). A full account of the anticommunist crusade at home and its impact on American intellectual and social life.

- Stueck, William. *The Korean War: An International History* (1995). Studies the Korean War in its full global context.

- Sugrue, Thomas. *Origins of the Urban Crisis: Race and Inequality in Postwar Detroit* (1996). Explores race relations in a key industrial city after World War II and how they set the stage for the upheavals of the 1960s.

WEBSITES

- Cold War International History Project: www.wilsoncenter.org/program/cold-war-international-history-project

- The Korean War and its Origins, 1945–1953: www.trumanlibrary.org/korea/

CHAPTER REVIEW AND ONLINE RESOURCES

REVIEW QUESTIONS

1. What major ideological conflicts, security interests, and events brought about the Cold War?

2. President Truman referred to the Truman Doctrine and the Marshall Plan as "two halves of the same walnut." Explain the similarities and differences between these two aspects of containment.

3. How did the tendency of both the United States and the Soviet Union to see all international events through the lens of the Cold War lessen each country's ability to understand what was happening in other countries around the world?

4. Why did the United States not support movements for colonial independence around the world?

5. How did the government attempt to shape public opinion during the Cold War?

6. Explain the differences between the United States' and the Soviet Union's application of the UN Universal Declaration of Human Rights.

7. How did the anticommunist crusade affect organized labor in the postwar period?

8. What accounts for the Republican resurgence in these years?

9. What were the major components of Truman's Fair Deal? Which ones were implemented and which ones not?

10. How did the Cold War affect civil liberties in the United States?

KEY TERMS

Cold War (p. 892)

containment (p. 892)

Long Telegram (p. 893)

iron curtain (p. 893)

Truman Doctrine (p. 893)

Marshall Plan (p. 895)

North Atlantic Treaty Organization (p. 897)

NSC-68 (p. 897)

Korean War (p. 899)

decolonization (p. 902)

totalitarianism (p. 904)

Fair Deal (p. 907)

Operation Dixie (p. 907)

Taft-Hartley Act (p. 908)

Dixiecrats (p. 910)

McCarthyism (p. 913)

Hollywood Ten (p. 914)

Army-McCarthy hearings (p. 915)

McCarran-Walter Act (p. 917)

Go to 🐰 INQUIZITIVE

To see what you know—and learn what you've missed—with personalized feedback along the way.

Visit the *Give Me Liberty!* **Student Site** for primary source documents and images, interactive maps, author videos featuring Eric Foner, and more.

PART 6

WHAT KIND OF NATION?

1953-2015

In the last half of the twentieth century and the beginning of the twenty-first, the United States experienced profound changes both at home and in its role in the larger world. The Cold War produced increasing American involvement in the affairs of other nations across the globe. Sometimes indirectly, sometimes through direct military intervention, the United States sought to prevent the further spread of communism and to ensure the existence of governments friendly to American strategic and economic interests. The sudden and unexpected collapse of communism in the Soviet Union and eastern Europe between 1989 and 1991 left the United States by far the world's foremost military power. But the country still found it difficult to shape events in other parts of the world—nowhere more so than in the Middle East after the war in Iraq that began in 2003. At home, these years witnessed far-reaching changes in the nature of American society and a dramatic expansion in the rights of American citizens and their understandings of freedom. But the crisis that followed the collapse of the housing market in 2008 raised troubling questions about rapidly growing economic inequality.

On the surface, the decade of the 1950s seemed uneventful. It was a time of widespread affluence in the United States, the beginning of an unprecedented economic expansion that lasted until the early 1970s. Millions of Americans moved to the suburbs, where they enjoyed access to an astonishing array of consumer goods that poured out of American factories, including cars, television sets, and household appliances. The postwar "baby boom" dramatically increased the population. American understandings of freedom centered on the enjoyment of economic afflu-

ence and consumer choice within the context of traditional family life, with women finding fulfillment in suburban homes.

Even during this time of "consensus," when sharp political divisions and economic strife seemed to have vanished from American life, seeds of discontent sprouted. A few artists and social commentators began to criticize the stifling atmosphere of conformity. The Supreme Court's decision in 1954 outlawing racial segregation in public schools helped to inspire the revival of the struggle for racial justice. The Montgomery bus boycott of 1955 launched the southern phase of the civil rights movement, which forced the entire country to rethink whether the United States could genuinely call itself "the land of the free" if it confined millions of Americans to second-class citizenship.

These seeds of protest flowered in the 1960s, a decade of social conflict and of dramatic expansion of the boundaries of American freedom. The civil rights revolution reached its climax with demonstrations throughout the South and the passage in 1964 and 1965 of national laws protecting blacks' civil rights and restoring the right to vote in the South. Although the movement splintered thereafter and the nation failed to address adequately the economic plight of non-whites trapped in decaying urban ghettos, the 1960s ended with the structure of legal segregation having been dismantled. The black movement inspired other aggrieved groups—Latinos, Indians, homosexuals, and women—to claim their own "liberation." Their efforts further enlarged freedom's boundaries and helped to propel the idea of freedom into the most intimate areas of life. Under the leadership of Chief Justice Earl Warren, the Supreme Court gave constitutional recognition to the "rights revolution." By the end of the decade, both the meaning and the boundaries of freedom had expanded enormously.

At the same time, the country became more and more deeply involved in the Vietnam War. In this Cold War conflict, American policymakers viewed the nationalist movement in Vietnam, led by homegrown communists, as part of a worldwide conspiracy directed from Moscow. As the United States committed hundreds of thousands of soldiers to Vietnam in the mid-1960s, the foreign policy consensus disintegrated. For the first time in American history, college students took the lead in radical activism, organizing massive protests against the war. Political disaffection helped to spawn the counterculture, a youth rebellion against prevailing middle-class mores. Having brought twentieth-century liberalism to its high point with his Great Society programs that sought to uplift the poor, encourage the arts, and provide medical care to the aged and needy, President Lyndon B. Johnson saw his public support disintegrate.

Known as a time of radical protest, the 1960s also spawned a conservative backlash against the civil rights movement, the sexual revolution, public disorder, and the expansion of federal power. During the 1970s and 1980s, businessmen, antigovernment activists, a Christian Right that sought to restore what it considered to be traditional moral values, and Cold Warriors who desired a reinvigorated anticommunist crusade came together in an increasingly powerful conservative coalition. Their rise to power was hastened by the end of the postwar economic boom in 1973 and the inability of President Jimmy Carter to address the slump effectively. In 1980, conservative Ronald Reagan was elected president, ushering in the Reagan Revolution.

Reagan drastically increased military spending, cut funding for some social programs, reduced taxes, and attacked labor unions. Like Franklin D. Roosevelt, he consciously sought to redefine the meaning of freedom, associating it with anticommunism, free enterprise, and reduced government intervention in the economy. Although he put into effect conservative economic policies, Reagan failed to halt the rights revolution that had begun in the 1960s. Throughout the 1980s and 1990s, many conservatives lamented the fact that fewer and fewer women were embracing the traditional role of homemaker and that gays were gaining more and more recognition of their rights. Although

conservatives launched a furious campaign to overturn the Supreme Court's 1973 decision legalizing abortion, they failed to achieve success. Moreover, thanks to a 1965 law that ended the national-origins quotas for immigrants, newcomers from Asia and Latin America poured into the United States, setting off political battles over the country's increasingly visible racial and ethnic diversity.

The abrupt end of the Cold War between 1989 and 1991 left the United States as the world's lone superpower. During the 1990s, Americans became increasingly aware of the process of "globalization"—the international flow of people, investment, goods, and information across national boundaries. Some welcomed it as an expansion of economic freedom. Others worried that manufacturing jobs were leaving the United States for low-wage areas abroad and that crucial decisions affecting people's day-to-day lives were being made by institutions like the World Bank and World Trade Organization, over which no democratic control existed.

Events at the dawn of the twenty-first century revealed the extent and limitations of American power. The attacks of September 11, 2001, which killed some 3,000 persons, highlighted the nation's vulnerability at a time when terrorists, like goods and money, seemed able to cross national boundaries with ease. In response, President George W. Bush committed the United States to a "war on terrorism," a war without easily definable enemies, a predictable timetable, or a clear definition of victory. The federal government claimed the power to arrest persons suspected of involvement with terrorism, primarily individuals of Middle Eastern origin, without charge and to hold them indefinitely. It initiated a massive program of surveillance of Americans' phone calls and emails. The 2003 Iraq War, launched over the opposition of most members of the United Nations, suggested that in the post–Cold War world, America no longer needed to build alliances or concern itself with world opinion. Although the invasion successfully overthrew the Iraqi dictator Saddam Hussein, an anti-American insurgency soon developed, along with strife between Iraq's Shiite and Sunni Muslims. The nation's first African-American president, Barack Obama, was elected in 2008 in part because of his opposition to the war. He eventually withdrew American combat forces, but the Middle East remained aflame with conflict.

These events raised anew vital questions already debated many times in the country's history. What is the balance between civil liberties and security in times of crisis? What are the economic conditions of freedom? Should the country consider itself a democracy or an empire? Should certain groups have their rights diminished because of their racial or ethnic origins? The answers to these questions would go a long way toward defining the meaning and boundaries of American freedom in the twenty-first century.

CHAPTER 24

AN AFFLUENT SOCIETY

★

1953–1960

In 1958, during a "thaw" in the Cold War, the United States and the Soviet Union agreed to exchange national exhibitions in order to allow citizens of each "superpower" to become acquainted with life in the other. The Soviet Exhibition, unveiled in New York City in June 1959, featured factory machinery, scientific advances, and other illustrations of how communism had modernized a backward country. The following month, the American National Exhibition opened in Moscow. A showcase of consumer goods and leisure equipment, complete with stereo sets, a movie theater, home appliances, and twenty-two different cars, the exhibit, *Newsweek* observed, hoped to demonstrate the superiority of "modern capitalism with its ideology of political and economic freedom." Yet the exhibit's real message was not freedom but consumption—or, to be more precise, the equating of the two.

When Vice President Richard Nixon prepared for his trip to Moscow to launch the exhibition, a former ambassador to Russia urged him to emphasize American values: "We are idealists; they are materialists." But the events of the opening day seemed to reverse these roles. Nixon devoted his address, entitled "What Freedom Means to Us," not to freedom of expression or differing forms of government, but to the "extraordinarily high standard of living" in the United States, with its 56 million cars and 50 million television sets. The United States, he declared, had achieved what Soviets could only dream of—"prosperity for all in a classless society."

The Moscow exhibition became the site of a classic Cold War confrontation over the meaning of freedom—the "kitchen debate" between Nixon and Soviet premier Nikita Khrushchev. Twice during the first day Nixon and Khrushchev engaged in unscripted debate about the merits of capitalism and communism. The first took place in the kitchen of a model suburban ranch house, the second in a futuristic "miracle kitchen" complete with a mobile robot that swept the floors. Supposedly the home of an average steelworker, the ranch house was the exhibition's centerpiece. It represented, Nixon declared, the mass enjoyment of American freedom within a suburban setting—freedom of choice among products, colors, styles, and prices. It also implied a particular role for women. Throughout his exchanges with Khrushchev, Nixon used the words "women" and "housewives" interchangeably. Pointing to the automatic floor sweeper, the vice president remarked that in the United States "you don't need a wife."

Nixon's decision to make a stand for American values in the setting of a suburban kitchen was a brilliant stroke. Nixon recognized that "soft power"— the penetration across the globe of American goods and popular culture—was an even more potent form of influence than military might. Indeed, his stance reflected the triumph during the 1950s of a conception of freedom centered on economic abundance and consumer choice within the context of traditional family life—a vision that seemed to offer far more opportunities for the "pursuit of happiness" to men than women. In reply, Khrushchev ridiculed consumer culture and the American obsession with household gadgets. "Don't you have a machine," he quipped, "that puts food in the mouth and pushes it down?" Many of the items on display, he continued, served "no useful purpose." Yet, in a sense,

FOCUS QUESTIONS

What were the main characteristics of the affluent society of the 1950s? –*p. 930*

How were the 1950s a period of consensus in both domestic policies and foreign affairs? –*p. 944*

What were the major thrusts of the civil rights movement in this period? –*p. 954*

What was the significance of the presidential election of 1960? –*p. 964*

The Problem We All Live With. This 1964 painting by Norman Rockwell, which accompanied an article in *Look* magazine, depicts federal marshals escorting six-year-old Ruby Bridges to kindergarten in New Orleans in 1960 in accordance with a court order to integrate the city's schools. "There was a large crowd of people outside the school," she later recalled. "They were throwing things and shouting." But Rockwell, intent on focusing on the child, presents the mob only through their graffiti and tomatoes thrown against the wall, and does not show the faces of the marshals. Because of the decision to send her to the formerly white school, Bridges's father lost his job, and her grandparents, who worked as sharecroppers in Mississippi, were evicted from their land. In 2001, President Bill Clinton presented her with the Presidential Citizens Medal.

the Soviet leader conceded the debate when he predicted—quite incorrectly—that within seven years his country would surpass the United States in the production of consumer goods. For if material abundance was a battleground in the Cold War, American victory was certain.

THE GOLDEN AGE

The end of World War II was followed by what one scholar has called the "golden age" of capitalism, a period of economic expansion, stable prices, low unemployment, and rising standards of living that continued until 1973. Between 1946 and 1960, the American gross national product more than doubled and much of the benefit flowed to ordinary citizens in rising wages. In every measurable way—diet, housing, income, education, recreation—most Americans lived better than their parents and grandparents had. By 1960, an estimated 60 percent of Americans enjoyed what the government defined as a middle-class standard of living. The official poverty rate, 30 percent of all families in 1950, had declined to 22 percent a decade later (still, to be sure, representing more than one in five Americans).

Numerous innovations came into widespread use in these years, transforming Americans' daily lives. They included television, home air-conditioning, automatic dishwashers, inexpensive long-distance telephone calls, and jet air travel. Services like electricity, central heating, and indoor plumbing that within living memory had been enjoyed only by the rich and solidly middle class now became features of common life.

Between 1950 and 1973, the average real wages of manufacturing workers doubled. Wages rose faster for low-income than high-income Americans, lessening economic inequality. Significant numbers of blue-collar men were able to earn enough at an early age to marry and support a family. At the time, widespread affluence, the improving economic status of working-class men and women, and the narrowing gap between rich and poor seemed to have become a permanent feature of American society, a model for other countries to follow. History would show that this was, in fact, an exceptional moment, made possible by government policies, a strong union movement, and the country's global economic dominance in the wake of World War II. When the long postwar boom ended in 1973 it would be succeeded by an even longer period of stagnant incomes for most Americans and increasing inequality.

A Changing Economy

Despite the economic recovery of western Europe and Japan after World War II, the United States remained the world's predominant industrial power. Major industries like steel, automobiles, and aircraft dominated the domestic and world markets for their products. Like other wars, the Cold War fueled industrial production and promoted a redistribution of the nation's population and economic resources. The West, especially the Seattle area, southern California, and the Rocky Mountain states, benefited enormously from government contracts for aircraft, guided missiles, and radar systems. The South became the home of numerous military bases

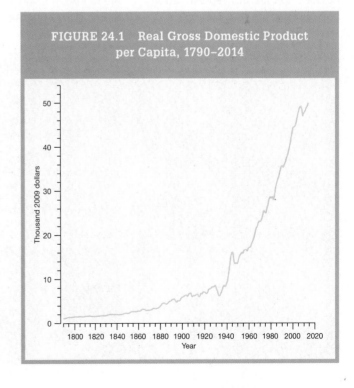

Vice President Richard Nixon, with hands folded, and Soviet premier Nikita Khrushchev during the "kitchen debate," a discussion, among other things, of the meaning of freedom, which took place in 1959 at the American National Exposition in Moscow. Khrushchev makes a point while a woman demonstrates a washing machine.

and government-funded shipyards. Growth in the construction of aircraft engines and submarines counterbalanced the decline of New England's old textile and machinery industries, many of which relocated in the South to take advantage of low-cost nonunion labor.

In retrospect, the 1950s appear as the last decade of the industrial age in the United States. Since then, the American economy has shifted rapidly toward services, education, information, finance, and entertainment, while employment in manufacturing has declined. Even during the 1950s, the number of factory laborers fell slightly while clerical workers grew by nearly 25 percent and salaried employees in large corporate enterprises rose by 60 percent. Unions' very success in raising wages inspired employers to mechanize more and more elements of manufacturing in order to reduce labor costs. In 1956, for the first time in American history, white-collar workers outnumbered blue-collar factory and manual laborers.

The long-term trend toward fewer and larger farms continued. During the 1950s, the farm population fell from 23 million to 15 million, yet agricultural production rose by 50 percent, thanks to more efficient machinery, the application of chemical fertilizers and insecticides, increased use of irrigation to open land to cultivation in the West, and the development of new crop strains. The decade witnessed an acceleration of the transformation of southern life that had begun during World War II. New tractors and harvesting machinery and a continuing shift from cotton production to less labor-intensive soybean and poultry raising reduced the need for farm workers. More than 3 million black and white

FIGURE 24.1   Real Gross Domestic Product per Capita, 1790–2014

Levittown, New York, perhaps the nation's most famous suburban community, photographed in 1954. Over time, home owners would make individualized changes to their houses, so today Levittown looks far less uniform than when it was built.

hired hands and sharecroppers migrated out of the region. The center of gravity of American farming shifted decisively to Texas, Arizona, and especially California. The large corporate farms of California, worked by Latino and Filipino migrant laborers, poured forth an endless supply of fruits and vegetables for the domestic and world markets. Items like oranges and orange juice, once luxuries, became an essential part of the American diet.

Corporate farms

A Suburban Nation

The main engines of economic growth during the 1950s, however, were residential construction and spending on consumer goods. The postwar baby boom (discussed later) and the shift of population from cities to suburbs created an enormous demand for housing, television sets, home appliances, and cars. By 1960, suburban residents of single-family homes outnumbered urban dwellers and those living in rural areas. (Today, they outnumber both combined.)

During the 1950s, the number of houses in the United States doubled, nearly all of them built in the suburbs that sprang up across the landscape. The dream of home ownership, the physical embodiment of hopes for a better life, came within reach of the majority of Americans. Developers pioneered inexpensive mass-building techniques, and government-backed low-interest loans to returning veterans allowed working-class men and women in large numbers to purchase homes. William and Alfred Levitt, who shortly after the war built the first **Levittown** on 1,200 acres of potato fields on Long Island near New York City, became the most famous suburban developers. Levittown's more than 10,000 houses were assembled quickly from prefabricated parts and priced well within the

This aerial view of Westchester, a community in Los Angeles, California, in 1949, illustrates how suburban "sprawl" spread over the landscape in the postwar era.

reach of most Americans. Levittown was soon home to 40,000 people. At the same time, suburbs required a new form of shopping center—the mall—to which people drove in their cars. In contrast to traditional mixed-use city centers crowded with pedestrians, malls existed solely for shopping and had virtually no public space.

Malls

The Growth of the West

The modern West emerged in the postwar years. Unlike the 1930s, when most migrants to the West came from the South and the Dust Bowl states, all parts of the country now contributed to the region's growth. Federal spending on dams, highways, and military installations helped to fuel the flow of people. So did the pleasant climate of many parts of the region, and the diffusion of air conditioning in warmer places such as Arizona and southern California. The rapid expansion of oil production (a result of the tremendous increase in automobile ownership) led to the explosive growth of urban centers connected to the oil industry such as Denver, Dallas, and Houston.

But it was California that became the most prominent symbol of the postwar suburban boom. Between World War II and 1975, more than 30 million Americans moved west of the Mississippi River. One-fifth of the population growth of the 1950s occurred in California alone. In 1963, it surpassed New York to become the nation's most populous state.

California's population growth

Most western growth took place in metropolitan areas, not on farms. But "centerless" western cities like Houston, Phoenix, and Los Angeles differed greatly from traditional urban centers in the East. Rather than consisting of downtown business districts linked to residential neighborhoods by public transportation, western cities were decentralized clusters of single-family homes and businesses

Ernst Haas's 1969 photograph of Albuquerque, New Mexico, could have been taken in any one of scores of American communities. As cities spread out, "strips," consisting of motels, gas stations, and nationally franchised businesses, became common. Meanwhile, older downtown business sections stagnated.

united by a web of highways. The Los Angeles basin, the largest western suburban region, had once had an extensive system of trains, trolleys, and buses. But local governments dismantled these lines after World War II, and the state and federal governments replaced them with freeways for cars and trucks. Suburban growth spilled into farm regions like the San Fernando and San Bernardino valleys. By one estimate, one-third of southern California's land area (presumably not including mountains and deserts) was paved over with roads and parking lots. Life centered around the car; people drove to and from work and did their shopping at malls reachable only by driving. In other sections of the country as well, shopping shifted to suburban centers, and old downtown business districts stagnated. The spread of suburban homes created millions of new lawns. Today, more land is cultivated in grass than any agricultural crop in the United States.

A Consumer Culture

"The consumer is the key to our economy," declared Jack Straus, chairman of the board of Macy's, New York City's leading department store. "Our ability to consume is endless. The luxuries of today are the necessities of tomorrow." The roots of the consumer culture of the 1950s date back to the 1920s and even earlier. But never before had affluence, or consumerism, been so widespread. In a consumer culture, the measure of freedom became the ability to gratify market desires. Modern society, wrote Clark Kerr, president of the University of California, may well have reduced freedom "in the workplace" by subjecting workers to stringent discipline on the job, but it offered a far greater range of "goods and services," and therefore "a greater scope of freedom" in Americans' "personal lives."

In this 1950 photograph, television sets move through an assembly line.

In a sense, the 1950s represented the culmination of the long-term trend in which consumerism replaced economic independence and democratic participation as central definitions of American freedom. Attitudes toward debt changed as well. Low interest rates and the spread of credit cards encouraged Americans to borrow money to purchase consumer goods. Americans became comfortable living in never-ending debt, once seen as a loss of economic freedom.

Consumer culture demonstrated the superiority of the American way of life to communism. From Coca-Cola to Levi's jeans, American consumer goods, once a status symbol for the rich in other countries, were now marketed to customers around the globe. The country's most powerful weapon in the Cold War, insisted a reporter for *House Beautiful* magazine, was "the freedom offered by washing machines and dishwashers, vacuum cleaners, automobiles, and refrigerators."

The TV World

Thanks to television, images of middle-class life and advertisements for consumer goods blanketed the country. By the end of the 1950s, nearly nine of ten American families owned a TV set. Television replaced newspapers as the most common source of information about public events, and TV watching became the nation's leading leisure activity. Television changed Americans' eating habits (the frozen TV dinner, heated and eaten while watching a program, went on sale in 1954).

With a few exceptions, like the Army-McCarthy hearings mentioned in the previous chapter, TV avoided controversy and projected a bland image of middle-class life. Popular shows of the early 1950s, such as *The Goldbergs* (with Jewish immigrants as the central characters) and *The Honeymooners* (in which Jackie Gleason played a bus driver), featured working-class families living in urban apartments. By the end of the decade, they had been replaced as the dominant programs by quiz shows, westerns, and comedies set in suburban homes like *Leave It to Beaver* and *The Adventures of Ozzie and Harriet.* Television also became the most effective advertising medium ever invented. To polish their image, large corporations sponsored popular programs—*The General Electric Theater* (hosted for several years by Ronald Reagan), *Alcoa Presents*, and others. TV ads, aimed primarily at middle-class suburban viewers, conveyed images of the good life based on endless consumption.

A New Ford

"The concept of freedom," wrote one commentator in 1959, "has become as familiar to us as an old hat or a new Ford." And a new Ford—or Chrysler or Chevrolet—now seemed essential to the enjoyment of freedom's benefits. Along with a home and television set, the car became part of what sociologists called "the standard consumer package" of the 1950s. By 1960, 80 percent of American families owned at least one car, and 14 percent had two or more, nearly all manufactured in the United States. Most were designed to go out of style within a year or two, promoting further purchases.

Auto manufacturers and oil companies vaulted to the top ranks of corporate America. Detroit and its environs were home to immense auto factories. The River Rouge complex had 62,000 employees, Willow Run 42,000. Since

Introduced in 1954, the frozen TV dinner was marketed in a package designed to look like a TV set. Within a year, Swanson had sold 25 million dinners.

TV advertising

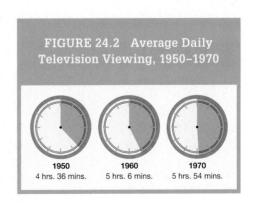

FIGURE 24.2 Average Daily Television Viewing, 1950–1970

1950	1960	1970
4 hrs. 36 mins.	5 hrs. 6 mins.	5 hrs. 54 mins.

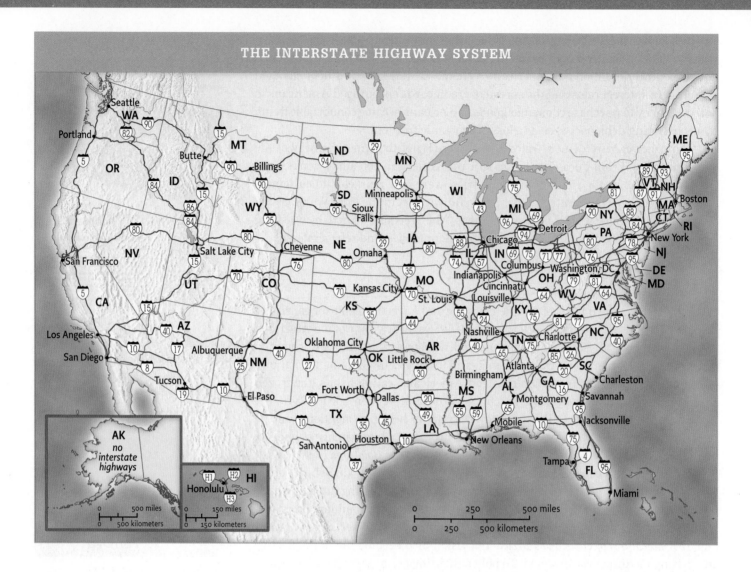

THE INTERSTATE HIGHWAY SYSTEM

Begun in 1956 and completed in 1993, the interstate highway system dramatically altered the American landscape and Americans' daily lives. It made possible more rapid travel by car and stimulated the growth of suburbs along its many routes.

Effects of the automobile

the military increasingly needed high-technology goods rather than the trucks and tanks that had rolled off assembly lines in World War II, the region around the Great Lakes lagged in defense contracts. In the long term, the continued funneling of federal dollars from the North and Midwest to the Sunbelt would prove devastating to the old industrial heartland. But during the 1950s, the booming automobile industry, with its demand for steel, rubber, and other products, assured the region's continued prosperity.

The automobile, the pivot on which suburban life turned, transformed the nation's daily life, just as the interstate highway system (discussed later) transformed Americans' travel habits, making possible long-distance vacationing by car and commuting to work from ever-increasing distances. The result was an altered American landscape, leading to the construction of motels, drive-in movie theaters, and roadside eating establishments. The first McDonald's fast food restaurant opened in Illinois in 1954. Within ten years, having been franchised by California businessman Ray Kroc, approximately 700 McDonald's stands had been built, which had sold over 400 million hamburgers. The car symbolized the identification of freedom with individual mobility and private choice. On the road,

Americans were constantly reminded in advertising, television shows, and popular songs, they truly enjoyed freedom. They could imagine themselves as modern versions of western pioneers, able to leave behind urban crowds and workplace pressures for the "open road."

Women at Work and at Home

The emergence of suburbia as a chief site of what was increasingly called the "American way of life" placed pressure on the family—and especially women—to live up to freedom's promise. After 1945, women lost most of the industrial jobs they had performed during the war. As during most of American history, women who worked outside the home remained concentrated in low-salary, nonunion jobs, such as clerical, sales, and service labor, rather than better-paying manufacturing positions. After a sharp postwar drop in female employment, the number of women at work soon began to rise. By 1955, it exceeded the level of World War II. But the nature and aims of women's work had changed. The modern woman, said *Look* magazine, worked part-time, to help support the family's middle-class lifestyle, not to help pull it out of poverty or to pursue personal fulfillment or an independent career. Working women in 1960 earned, on average, only 60 percent of the income of men.

Despite the increasing numbers of wage-earning women, the suburban family's breadwinner was assumed to be male, while the wife remained at home. Films, TV shows, and advertisements portrayed marriage as the most important goal of American women. And during the 1950s, men and women reaffirmed the virtues of family life. They married younger (at an average age of twenty-two for men and twenty for women), divorced less frequently than in the past, and had more children (3.2 per family). A **baby boom** that lasted into the mid-1960s followed the end of the war. At a time of low immigration, the American population rose by nearly 30 million (almost 20 percent) during the 1950s. The increase arose mostly from the large number of births, but it also reflected the fact that Americans now lived longer than in the past, thanks to the wide availability of "miracle drugs" like penicillin that had been developed during World War II to combat bacterial infections.

The family also became a weapon in the Cold War. The ability of women to remain at home, declared a government official, "separates us from the Communist world," where a high percentage of women worked. To be sure, the family life exalted during the 1950s differed from the patriarchal household of old. It was a modernized relationship, in which both partners reconciled family obligations with personal fulfillment through

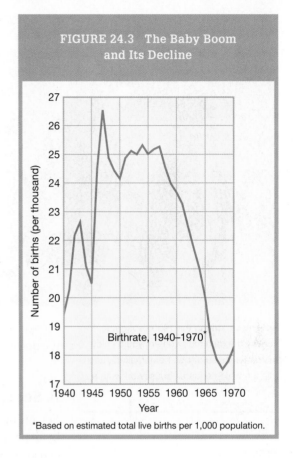

FIGURE 24.3 The Baby Boom and Its Decline

Birthrate, 1940–1970*

Number of births (per thousand)

Year

*Based on estimated total live births per 1,000 population.

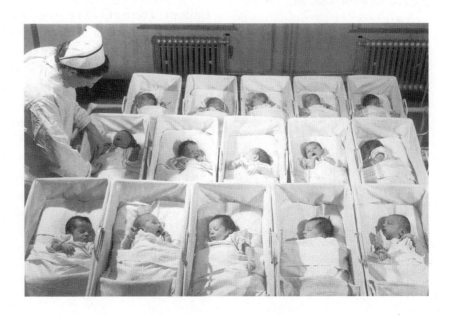

Jack Gould's 1946 photograph of a hospital maternity ward captures the first year of the postwar baby boom.

Advertisers during the 1950s sought to convey the idea that women would enjoy their roles as suburban homemakers, as in this ad, which equates housework with a game of golf.

Elliott Erwitt's photograph of a young mother in New Rochelle, a suburb of New York City, suggests that life for the suburban woman could be less idyllic than many advertisements implied.

shared consumption, leisure activities, and sexual pleasure. Thanks to modern conveniences, the personal freedom once associated with work could now be found at home. Frozen and prepared meals, exulted one writer in 1953, offered housewives "freedom from tedium, space, work, and their own inexperience"—quite a change from the Four Freedoms of World War II.

Like other forms of dissent, feminism seemed to have disappeared from American life or was widely dismissed as evidence of mental disorder. Prominent psychologists insisted that the unhappiness of individual women or even the desire to work for wages stemmed from a failure to accept the "maternal instinct." "The independent woman," declared the book *Modern Woman: The Lost Sex* (1947), "is a contradiction in terms." The idea of domestic life as a refuge and of full-time motherhood as a woman's "sphere" had a long history in the United States. But in the postwar suburbs, where family life was physically separated from work, relatives, and the web of social organizations typical of cities, it came close to realization.

A Segregated Landscape

For millions of city dwellers, the suburban utopia fulfilled the dream, postponed by depression and war, of home ownership and middle-class incomes. For beneficiaries of postwar prosperity, in the words of a Boston worker who made heroic sacrifices to move his family to the suburbs, the home became "the center of freedom." The move to the suburbs also promoted Americanization, cutting residents off from urban ethnic communities and bringing them fully into the world of mass consumption. But if the suburbs offered a new site for the enjoyment of American freedom, they retained at least one familiar characteristic—rigid racial boundaries.

Suburbia has never been as uniform as either its celebrants or its critics claimed. There are upper-class suburbs, working-class suburbs, industrial suburbs, and "suburban" neighborhoods within city limits. But if the class uniformity of suburbia has been exaggerated, its racial uniformity was all too real. As late as the 1990s, nearly 90 percent of suburban whites lived in communities with non-white populations of less than 1 percent—the legacy of decisions by government, real-estate developers, banks, and residents.

During the postwar suburban boom, federal agencies continued to insure mortgages that barred resale of houses to non-whites, thereby financing housing segregation. Even after the Supreme Court in 1948 declared such provisions legally unenforceable, banks and private developers barred non-whites from the suburbs and the government refused to subsidize their mortgages except in segregated enclaves. In 1960, blacks represented less than 3 percent of the population of Chicago's suburbs. The vast new communities built by William Levitt refused to allow blacks, including army veterans, to rent or purchase homes. "If we sell one house to a Negro family," Levitt explained, "then 90 or 95 percent of our white customers will not buy into the community." After a lawsuit, Levitt finally agreed during the

1960s to sell homes to non-whites, but at a pace that can only be described as glacial. In 1990, his Long Island community, with a population of 53,000, included 127 black residents.

Public Housing and Urban Renewal

A Housing Act passed by Congress in 1949 authorized the construction of more than 800,000 units of public housing in order to provide a "decent home for every American family." But the law set an extremely low ceiling on the income of residents—a rule demanded by private contractors seeking to avoid competition from the government in building homes for the middle class. This regulation limited housing projects to the very poor. Since white urban and suburban neighborhoods successfully opposed the construction of public housing, it was increasingly confined to segregated neighborhoods in inner cities, reinforcing the concentration of poverty in urban non-white neighborhoods. At the same time, under programs of **urban renewal**, cities demolished poor neighborhoods in city centers that occupied potentially valuable real estate. In their place, developers constructed retail centers and all-white middle-income housing complexes, and states built urban public universities like Wayne State in Detroit and the University of Illinois at Chicago. Los Angeles displaced a neighborhood of mixed ethnic groups in Chavez Ravine in order to build a stadium for the Dodgers, whose move in 1958 after sixty-eight years in Brooklyn seemed to symbolize the growing importance of California on the national scene. White residents displaced by urban renewal often moved to the suburbs. Non-whites, unable to do so, found housing in run-down city neighborhoods.

Segregated neighborhoods

The Divided Society

Suburbanization hardened the racial lines of division in American life. Between 1950 and 1970, about 7 million white Americans left cities for the suburbs. Meanwhile, nearly 3 million blacks moved from the South to the North, greatly increasing the size of existing urban ghettos and creating entirely new ones. And half a million Puerto Ricans, mostly small coffee and tobacco farmers and agricultural laborers forced off the land when American sugar companies expanded their landholdings on the island, moved to the mainland. Most ended up in New York City's East Harlem, until then an Italian-American community. Although set in a different part of New York, the popular Broadway musical *West Side Story* dramatized the tensions between Puerto Rican newcomers and longtime urban residents. By the late 1960s, more Puerto Ricans lived in New York City than San Juan, the island's capital.

The process of racial exclusion became self-reinforcing. Non-whites remained concentrated in manual and unskilled jobs, the result of employment discrimination and their virtual exclusion

An aerial photograph of Boulevard Houses, a low-income housing project in Brooklyn, illustrates how public housing concentrated poor Americans in structures separated from surrounding neighborhoods.

Students at an East Harlem elementary school in 1947. Most are recent migrants from Puerto Rico, although some are probably children of the area's older Italian-American community.

An image from a booklet issued by the American Economic Foundation illustrates the linkage of anticommunism and religious faith during the Cold War. The hairy hand in the bottom half of the drawing represents the communist threat, which endangers religious freedom in the United States.

from educational opportunities at public and private universities, including those outside the South. In 1950, only 12 percent of employed blacks held white-collar positions, compared with 45 percent of whites. As the white population and industrial jobs fled the old city centers for the suburbs, poorer blacks and Latinos remained trapped in urban ghettos, seen by many whites as places of crime, poverty, and welfare.

Suburbanites, for whom the home represented not only an emblem of freedom but the family's major investment, became increasingly fearful that any non-white presence would lower the quality of life and destroy property values. *Life* magazine quoted a white suburbanite discussing a prospective black neighbor: "He's probably a nice guy, but every time I see him, I see $2,000 drop off the value of my house." Residential segregation was reinforced by "blockbusting"—a tactic of real-estate brokers who circulated exaggerated warnings of an impending influx of non-whites, to persuade alarmed white residents to sell their homes hastily. Because of this practice, some all-white neighborhoods quickly became all-minority enclaves rather than places where members of different races lived side by side.

"Freedom is equal housing too" became a slogan in the campaign for residential integration. But suburban home ownership long remained a white entitlement, with the freedom of non-whites to rent or purchase a home where they desired overridden by the claims of private property and "freedom of association." Even as the old divisions between white ethnic Americans faded in the suburban melting pot, racial barriers in housing, and therefore in public education and jobs, were reinforced.

Cold War affluence coexisted with urban decay and racism, the seeds from which protest would soon flower. Yet to many observers in the 1950s it seemed that the ills of American society had been solved. Scholars celebrated the "end of ideology" and the triumph of a democratic, capitalist "consensus" in which all Americans except the maladjusted and fanatics shared the same liberal values of individualism, respect for private property, and belief in equal opportunity. If problems remained, their solutions required technical adjustments, not structural change or aggressive political intervention.

Religion and Anticommunism

Both Protestant and Roman Catholic religious leaders played crucial roles in the spread of anticommunism and Cold War culture. Official American values celebrated the nation's religiosity as opposed to "godless" communism. During the 1950s, a majority of Americans—the highest percentage in the nation's history—were affiliated with a church or synagogue. In 1954, to "strengthen our national resistance to communism," Congress added the words "under God" to the Pledge of Allegiance. In 1957, "**In God We Trust**" was included on paper money. Big-budget Hollywood films like *The Ten Commandments* and *Ben Hur* celebrated early Judaism and Christianity. As noted in the previous chapter, Soviet domination of strongly Catholic eastern Europe inspired powerful currents of anticommunism among Catholic ethnic groups in the United States. Leading clerics like Bishop Fulton J. Sheen of the Catholic Church and Protestant evangelist Billy Graham used radio and television to spread to millions a religious message heavily imbued with anticommunism. Communism, Graham declared, was not only an economic and political outlook but a religion—one "inspired, directed and motivated by the Devil himself."

As for religious differences, the source of persistent tension in American history, these were absorbed within a common "Judeo-Christian" heritage, a notion that became central to the cultural and political dialogue of the 1950s. This newly invented tradition sought to demonstrate that Catholics, Protestants, and Jews shared the same history and values and had all contributed to the evolution of American society. The idea of a unified Judeo-Christian tradition overlooked the long history of hostility among religious denominations. But it reflected the decline of anti-Semitism and anti-Catholicism in the wake of World War II, as well as the ongoing secularization of American life. As Will Herberg argued in his influential book *Protestant-Catholic-Jew* (1955), religion now had less to do with spiritual activities or sacred values than with personal identity, group assimilation, and the promotion of traditional morality. In an affluent suburban society, Herberg argued, the "common religion" was the American way of life, a marriage of democratic values and economic prosperity—in a phrase, "free enterprise."

> *Judeo-Christian tradition*

Selling Free Enterprise

The economic content of Cold War freedom increasingly came to focus on consumer capitalism, or, as it was now universally known, "free enterprise." More than political democracy or freedom of speech, which many allies of the United States outside western Europe lacked, an economic system resting on private ownership united the nations of the Free World. A week before his Truman Doctrine speech, in a major address on economic policy, the president reduced Roosevelt's Four Freedoms to three. Freedom of speech and worship remained, but freedom from want and fear had been replaced by freedom of enterprise, "part and parcel," said Truman, of the American way of life.

Even more than during World War II, what one historian calls the "selling of free enterprise" became a major industry, involving corporate advertising, school programs, newspaper editorials, and civic activities. Convinced that ads represented "a new weapon in the world-wide fight for freedom," the Advertising Council invoked cherished symbols like the Statue of Liberty and the Liberty Bell in the service of "competitive free enterprise." To be sure, the free enterprise campaigners did not agree on every issue. Some businessmen believed that defending free enterprise required rolling back much of the power that labor unions had gained in the past decade, dismantling New Deal regulations, and restricting the economic role of government. Representing what might be called business's more liberal wing, the Advertising Council, in its "American Economic System" ad campaign of 1949, reaffirmed labor's right to collective bargaining and the importance

This postage stamp depicts four chaplains who perished during the sinking of an American ship during World War II. Its original design listed their denominations: Catholic, Protestant, and Jewish. When the stamp was issued in 1948, these words were omitted, in keeping with the emphasis on the newly invented idea of a Judeo-Christian tradition shared by all Americans.

The reality of free enterprise

of government–business cooperation. Indeed, despite talk of the glories of the free market, government policies played a crucial role in the postwar boom. The rapid expansion of the suburban middle class owed much to federal tax subsidies, mortgage guarantees for home purchases, dam and highway construction, military contracts, and benefits under the GI Bill.

People's Capitalism

Free enterprise seemed an odd way of describing an economy in which a few large corporations dominated key sectors. Until well into the twentieth century, most ordinary Americans had been deeply suspicious of big business, associating it with images of robber barons who manipulated politics, suppressed economic competition, and treated their workers unfairly. Americans, wrote David Lilienthal, chairman of the Atomic Energy Commission, must abandon their traditional fear that concentrated economic power endangered "our very liberties." Large-scale production was not only necessary to fighting the Cold War, but it enhanced freedom by multiplying consumer goods. "By freedom," wrote Lilienthal, "I mean essentially *freedom to choose*. . . . It means a maximum range of choice for the consumer when he spends his dollar." By the end of the 1950s, public-opinion surveys revealed that more than 80 percent of Americans believed that "our freedom depends on the free enterprise system."

Changing views of big business

Investing in Wall Street

A sharp jump in the number of individuals investing in Wall Street inspired talk of a new "people's capitalism." In 1953, 4.5 million Americans—only slightly more than in 1928—owned shares of stock. By the mid-1960s, the number had grown to 25 million. In the face of widespread abundance, who could deny that the capitalist marketplace embodied individual freedom or that poverty would soon be a thing of the past? "It was American Freedom," proclaimed *Life* magazine, "by which and through which this amazing achievement of wealth and power was fashioned."

A portrait of affluence: In this photograph by Alex Henderson, Steve Czekalinski, an employee of the DuPont Corporation, poses with his family and the food they consumed in a single year, 1951. The family spent $1,300 (around $12,000 in today's money) on food, including 699 bottles of milk, 578 pounds of meat, and 131 dozen eggs. Nowhere else in the world was food so available and inexpensive.

The Libertarian Conservatives

During the 1950s, a group of thinkers began the task of reviving conservatism and reclaiming the idea of freedom from liberals. Although largely ignored outside their own immediate circle, they developed ideas that would define conservative thought for the next half-century. One was opposition to a strong national government, an outlook that had been given new political life in conservatives' bitter reaction against the New Deal. To these "libertarian" conservatives, freedom meant individual autonomy, limited government, and unregulated capitalism.

These ideas had great appeal to conservative entrepreneurs, especially in the rapidly growing South and West. Many businessmen who desired to pursue their economic fortunes free of government regulation, high taxes, and labor unions found intellectual reinforcement in the writings of the young economist Milton Friedman. In 1962, Friedman published *Capitalism and Freedom*, which identified the free market as the necessary foundation for individual liberty. This was not an uncommon idea during the Cold War, but Friedman pushed it to extreme conclusions. He called for turning over to the private sector virtually all government functions and the repeal of minimum wage laws, the graduated income tax, and the Social Security system. Friedman extended the idea of unrestricted free choice into virtually every realm of life. Government, he insisted, should seek to regulate neither the economy nor individual conduct.

TV became the most effective advertising medium in history. Here, an advertisement for Ford, one of the largest American corporations, is being filmed. The background evokes the idea of driving on the open road as a form of individual freedom.

The New Conservatism

Friedman was indirectly criticizing not only liberalism but also the "new conservatism," a second strand of thought that became increasingly prominent in the 1950s. Convinced that the Free World needed to arm itself morally and intellectually, not just militarily, for the battle against communism, "new conservatives" like writers Russell Kirk and Richard Weaver insisted that toleration of difference—a central belief of modern liberalism—offered no substitute for the search for absolute truth. Weaver's book, *Ideas Have Consequences* (1948), a rambling philosophical treatise that surprisingly became the most influential statement of this new traditionalism, warned that the West was suffering from moral decay and called for a return to a civilization based on values grounded in the Christian tradition and in timeless notions of good and evil.

> *Conservatives and the search for values*

The "new conservatives" understood freedom as first and foremost a moral condition. It required a decision by independent men and women to lead virtuous lives, or governmental action to force them to do so. Although they wanted government expelled from the economy, new conservatives trusted it to regulate personal behavior, to restore a Christian morality they saw as growing weaker and weaker in American society.

> *Moral condition*

Here lay the origins of a division in conservative ranks that would persist into the twenty-first century. Unrestrained individual choice and moral virtue are radically different starting points from which to discuss freedom. Was the purpose of conservatism, one writer wondered, to create the "free man" or the "good man"? Libertarian conservatives spoke the language of progress and personal autonomy; the "new conservatives" emphasized tradition, community, and moral commitment. The former believed that too many barriers existed to the pursuit of individual liberty. The latter condemned an excess of individualism and a breakdown of common values.

Division in conservatism

Fortunately for conservatives, political unity often depends less on intellectual coherence than on the existence of a common foe. And two powerful enemies became focal points for the conservative revival—the Soviet Union abroad and the federal government at home. Anticommunism, however, did not clearly distinguish conservatives from liberals, who also supported the Cold War. What made conservatism distinct was its antagonism to "big government" in America, at least so long as it was controlled by liberals who, conservatives believed, tolerated or encouraged immorality. Republican control of the presidency did not lessen conservatives' hostility to the federal government, partly because they did not consider President Eisenhower one of their own.

Anti-big government

THE EISENHOWER ERA

Ike and Nixon

Dwight D. Eisenhower, or "Ike," as he was affectionately called, emerged from World War II as the military leader with the greatest political appeal, partly because his public image of fatherly warmth set him apart from other successful generals like the arrogant Douglas MacArthur. Eisenhower's party affiliation was unknown. In 1948, he voted for Truman, and he accepted Truman's invitation to return to Europe as Supreme Commander of NATO forces. Both parties wanted him as their candidate in 1952. But Eisenhower became convinced that Senator Robert A. Taft of Ohio, a leading contender for the Republican nomination, would lead the United States back toward isolationism. Eisenhower entered the contest and won the Republican nomination.

As his running mate, Eisenhower chose Richard Nixon of California, a World War II veteran who had made a name for himself by vigorous anticommunism. In his first campaign for Congress, in 1946,

Dwight D. Eisenhower's popularity was evident at this appearance in Baltimore during the 1952 presidential campaign.

Nixon attacked his opponent as an advocate of "state socialism." He gained greater fame by his pursuit of Alger Hiss while a member of the House Un-American Activities Committee. Nixon won election to the U.S. Senate in 1950 in a campaign in which he suggested that the Democratic candidate, Congresswoman Helen Gahagan Douglas, had communist sympathies.

These tactics gave Nixon a lifelong reputation for opportunism and dishonesty. But Nixon was also a shrewd politician, who pioneered efforts to transform the Republican Party's image from defender of business to champion of the "forgotten man"—the hardworking citizen burdened by heavy taxation and unresponsive government bureaucracies. In using populist language to promote free market economics, Nixon helped to lay the foundation for the triumph of conservatism a generation later.

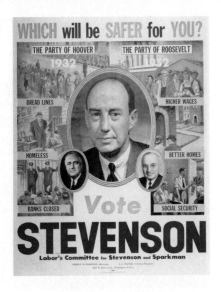

A poster for Adlai Stevenson, Democratic candidate for president in 1952. The party's main argument, it seems, was that Republican victory would usher in a return of the Great Depression. Stevenson was soundly defeated by Dwight D. Eisenhower.

The 1952 Campaign

Almost as soon as he won the vice-presidential nomination, Nixon ran into trouble over press reports that wealthy Californians had created a private fund for his family. Eisenhower considered dropping him from the ticket. But in an emotional nationally televised thirty-minute address in which he drew attention to his ordinary upbringing, war service, and close-knit family, Nixon denied the accusations. The "Checkers speech," named after the family dog—the one gift Nixon acknowledged receiving, but insisted he would not return—rescued his political career. It illustrated how television was beginning to transform politics by allowing candidates to bring a carefully crafted image directly into Americans' living rooms. The 1952 campaign became the first to make extensive use of TV ads. Parties, one observer complained, were "selling the president like toothpaste."

> *Television and politics*

More important to the election's outcome, however, was Eisenhower's popularity (invoked in the Republican campaign slogan "I Like Ike") and the public's weariness with the Korean War. Ike's pledge to "go to Korea" in search of peace signaled his intention to bring the conflict to an end. He won a resounding victory over the Democratic candidate, Adlai Stevenson. Four years later, Eisenhower again defeated Stevenson, by an even wider margin. His popularity, however, did not extend to his party. Republicans won a razor-thin majority in Congress in 1952, but Democrats regained control in 1954 and retained it for the rest of the decade. In 1956, Eisenhower became the first president to be elected without his party controlling either house of Congress.

In his two campaigns for president, the Texas-born Eisenhower made remarkable inroads in the Democratic South, a harbinger of the region's later political realignment. In 1952, he carried eight former slave states and won 48 percent of the votes cast in the states of the Confederacy. He ran strongly among moderate whites living in metropolitan and suburban areas of the upper South and border states. But his personal appeal did not translate into a "coattail" effect. For the time being, Democrats continued to control almost all southern state and local offices.

> *Democratic South*

During the 1950s, voters at home and abroad seemed to find reassurance in selecting familiar, elderly leaders to govern them. At age sixty-two, Eisenhower was one of the oldest men ever elected president. But he seemed positively youthful

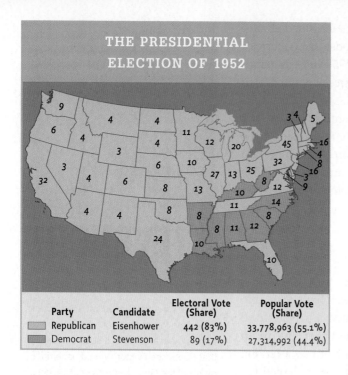

THE PRESIDENTIAL ELECTION OF 1952

Party	Candidate	Electoral Vote (Share)	Popular Vote (Share)
Republican	Eisenhower	442 (83%)	33,778,963 (55.1%)
Democrat	Stevenson	89 (17%)	27,314,992 (44.4%)

Accepting the New Deal

A mixed economy

Sputnik

compared with Winston Churchill, who returned to office as prime minister of Great Britain at age seventy-seven, Charles DeGaulle, who assumed the presidency of France at sixty-eight, and Konrad Adenauer, who served as chancellor of West Germany from age seventy-three until well into his eighties. In retrospect, Eisenhower's presidency seems almost uneventful, at least in domestic affairs—an interlude between the bitter party battles of the Truman administration and the social upheavals of the 1960s.

Modern Republicanism

With a Republican serving as president for the first time in twenty years, the tone in Washington changed. Wealthy businessmen dominated Eisenhower's cabinet. Defense Secretary Charles Wilson, the former president of General Motors, made the widely publicized statement: "What is good for the country is good for General Motors, and vice versa." A champion of the business community and a fiscal conservative, Ike worked to scale back government spending, including the military budget. But while right-wing Republicans saw his victory as an invitation to roll back the New Deal, Eisenhower realized that such a course would be disastrous. "Should any political party attempt to abolish Social Security, unemployment insurance, and eliminate labor laws and farm programs," he declared, "you would not hear of that party again in our political history."

Eisenhower called his domestic agenda Modern Republicanism. It aimed to sever his party's identification in the minds of many Americans with Herbert Hoover, the Great Depression, and indifference to the economic conditions of ordinary citizens. The core New Deal programs not only remained in place, but expanded. In 1955, millions of agricultural workers became eligible for the first time for Social Security. Nor did Ike reduce the size and scope of government. Despite the use of "free enterprise" as a weapon in the Cold War, the idea of a "mixed economy" in which the government played a major role in planning economic activity was widely accepted throughout the Western world. America's European allies like Britain and France expanded their welfare states and nationalized key industries like steel, shipbuilding, and transportation (that is, the government bought them from private owners and operated and subsidized them).

The United States had a more limited welfare state than western Europe and left the main pillars of the economy in private hands. But it too used government spending to promote productivity and boost employment. Eisenhower presided over the largest public-works enterprise in American history, the building of the 41,000-mile **interstate highway system**. As noted in the previous chapter, Cold War arguments—especially the need to provide rapid exit routes from cities in the event of nuclear war—justified this multibillion-dollar project. But automobile manufacturers, oil companies, suburban builders, and construction unions had very practical reasons for supporting highway construction regardless of any Soviet threat. When the Soviets launched **Sputnik**, the first artificial earth satellite, in 1957, the administration responded with the **National Defense Education Act**, which for the first time offered direct federal funding to higher education.

All in all, rather than dismantling the New Deal, Eisenhower's Modern Republicanism consolidated and legitimized it. By accepting its basic premises, he ensured that its continuation no longer depended on Democratic control of the presidency.

The Social Contract

The 1950s also witnessed an easing of the labor conflict of the two previous decades. The passage of the Taft-Hartley Act in 1947 (discussed in the previous chapter) had reduced labor militancy. In 1955, the AFL and CIO merged to form a single organization representing 35 percent of all nonagricultural workers. In leading industries, labor and management hammered out what has been called a new **social contract**. Unions signed long-term agreements that left decisions regarding capital investment, plant location, and output in management's hands, and agreed to try to prevent unauthorized "wildcat" strikes. Employers stopped trying to eliminate existing unions and granted wage increases and fringe benefits such as private pension plans, health insurance, and automatic adjustments to pay to reflect rises in the cost of living.

Unionized workers shared fully in 1950s prosperity. Although the social contract did not apply to the majority of workers, who did not belong to unions, it did bring benefits to those who labored in nonunion jobs. For example, trade unions in the 1950s and 1960s were able to use their political power to win a steady increase in the minimum wage, which was earned mostly by nonunion workers at the bottom of the employment pyramid. But these "spillover effects" were limited. The majority of workers did not enjoy anything close to the wages, benefits, and job security of unionized workers in such industries as automobiles and steel.

Indeed, nonunion employers continued to fight vehemently against labor organization, and groups like the National Association of Manufacturers still viewed unions as an unacceptable infringement on the power of employers. Some firms continued to shift jobs to the less-unionized suburbs and South. By the end of the 1950s, the social contract was weakening. In 1959, the steel industry sought to tighten work rules and limit wage increases in an attempt to boost profits battered by a recession that hit two years earlier. The plan sparked a strike of 500,000 steelworkers, which successfully beat back the proposed changes.

Massive Retaliation

Soon after he entered office, Eisenhower approved an armistice that ended fighting in Korea. But this failed to ease international tensions. Ike took office at a time when the Cold War had entered an extremely dangerous phase. In 1952, the United States exploded the first hydrogen bomb—a weapon far more powerful than those that had devastated Hiroshima and Nagasaki. The following year, the Soviets matched this achievement. Both sides feverishly developed long-range bombers capable of delivering weapons of mass destruction around the world.

"Do you call C-minus catching up with Russia?" Alan Dunn's cartoon for the *New Yorker* magazine comments on how Soviet success in launching an artificial earth satellite spurred a focus on improving scientific education in the United States.

Benefits for nonunion workers

The hydrogen bomb

A professional soldier, Ike hated war, which he viewed as a tragic waste. "Every gun that is made," he said in 1953, "every warship launched . . . signifies a theft from those who hunger and are not fed." But his secretary of state, John Foster Dulles, was a grim Cold Warrior. In 1954, Dulles announced an updated version of the doctrine of containment. **Massive retaliation**, as it was called, declared that any Soviet attack on an American ally would be countered by a nuclear assault on the Soviet Union itself. In some ways, this reliance on the nuclear threat was a way to enable the budget-conscious Eisenhower to reduce spending on conventional military forces. During his presidency, the size of the armed services fell by nearly half. But the number of American nuclear warheads rose from 1,000 in 1953 to 18,000 in 1960.

Massive retaliation

Massive retaliation ran the risk that any small conflict, or even a miscalculation, could escalate into a war that would destroy both the United States and the Soviet Union. Critics called the doctrine "brinksmanship," warning of the danger of Dulles's apparent willingness to bring the world to the brink of nuclear war. The reality that all-out war would result in "mutual assured destruction" (or MAD, in military shorthand) did succeed in making both great powers cautious in their direct dealings with one another. But it also inspired widespread fear of impending nuclear war. Government programs encouraging Americans to build bomb shelters in their backyards, and school drills that trained children to hide under their desks in the event of an atomic attack, aimed to convince Americans that nuclear war was survivable. But these measures only increased the atmosphere of fear.

"Brinksmanship"

Ike and the Russians

In his inaugural address, Eisenhower repeated the familiar Cold War formula: "Freedom is pitted against slavery; lightness against dark." But the end of the Korean War and the death of Stalin, both of which occurred in 1953, convinced him that rather than being blind zealots, the Soviets were reasonable and could be dealt with in conventional diplomatic terms. In 1955, Ike met in Geneva, Switzerland, with Nikita Khrushchev, the new Soviet leader, at the first "summit" conference since Potsdam a decade earlier. The following year, Khrushchev delivered a speech to the Communist Party Congress in Moscow that detailed Stalin's crimes, including purges of political opponents numbering in the millions. The revelations created a crisis of belief among communists throughout the world. In the United States, three-quarters of the remaining Communist Party members abandoned the organization, realizing that they had been blind to the nature of Stalin's rule.

Khrushchev's call in the same 1956 speech for "peaceful coexistence" with the United States raised the possibility of an easing of the Cold War. The "thaw" was abruptly shaken that fall, however, when Soviet troops put down an anticommunist uprising in Hungary. Many conservative Republicans had urged eastern Europeans to resist communist rule, and Secretary of State Dulles himself had declared "liberation,"

An advertisement for a government film explaining to children how to survive a nuclear attack by hiding under their desks. Thousands of schools instituted these "duck and cover" drills. They were meant to reduce Americans' fear of nuclear war.

rather than containment, to be the goal of American policy. But Eisenhower refused to extend aid to the Hungarian rebels, an indication that he believed it impossible to "roll back" Soviet domination of eastern Europe.

In 1958, the two superpowers agreed to a voluntary halt to the testing of nuclear weapons. The pause lasted until 1961. It had been demanded by the National Committee for a Sane Nuclear Policy, which publicized the danger to public health posed by radioactive fallout from nuclear tests. In 1959, Khrushchev toured the United States and had a friendly meeting with Eisenhower at Camp David. But the spirit of cooperation ended abruptly in 1960, when the Soviets shot down an American U-2 spy plane over their territory. Eisenhower first denied that the plane had been involved in espionage and refused to apologize even after the Russians produced the captured pilot. The incident torpedoed another planned summit meeting.

The Emergence of the Third World

Even as Europe, where the Cold War began, settled into what appeared to be a permanent division between a communist East and a capitalist West, an intense rivalry, which sometimes took a military form, persisted in what came to be called the Third World. The term was invented to describe developing countries aligned with neither of the two Cold War powers and desirous of finding their own model of development between Soviet centralized economic planning and free market capitalism. The Bandung Conference, which brought leaders of twenty-nine Asian and African nations together in Indonesia in 1955, seemed to announce the emergence of a new force in global affairs, representing a majority of the world's population. But none of these countries could avoid being strongly affected by the political, military, and economic contest of the Cold War.

The post–World War II era witnessed the crumbling of European empires. The "winds of change," said British prime minister Harold Macmillan, were sweeping Africa and Asia. Decolonization began when India and Pakistan (the latter carved out of India to give Muslims their own nation) achieved independence in 1947. Ten years later, Britain's Gold Coast colony in West Africa emerged as the independent nation of Ghana. Other new nations—including Indonesia, Malaysia, Nigeria, Kenya, and Tanzania—soon followed. In 1975, Portugal, which five centuries earlier had created the first modern overseas empire, granted independence to its African colonies of Mozambique and Angola.

Decolonization presented the United States with a complex set of choices. It created power vacuums in the former colonies into which, Americans feared, communists would move. The Soviet Union strongly supported the dissolution of Europe's overseas empires, and communists participated in movements for colonial independence. Many noncommunist leaders, like Jawaharlal Nehru of India and Kwame Nkrumah of Ghana, saw socialism of one sort or another as the best route to achieving economic independence and narrowing the social inequalities fostered by imperialism. Most of the new Third World nations resisted alignment with either major power bloc, hoping to remain neutral in the Cold War. On the other hand, many nationalists sincerely admired the United States and, indeed, saw the American struggle for independence as a model for their own struggles. Ho Chi Minh, the communist leader of the Vietnamese movement against rule by

A man helps his daughter into a backyard bomb shelter in Garden City, Long Island, New York, in a photograph from 1955. Manufacturers of such shelters assured purchasers that occupants could survive for five days after a nuclear attack.

Decolonization begins

Models of decolonization

France, modeled his 1945 proclamation of nationhood on the American Declaration of Independence. He even requested that President Truman establish a protectorate over Vietnam to guarantee its independence.

The Cold War in the Third World

By the end of the 1950s, the division of Europe appeared to be set in stone. Much of the focus of the Cold War shifted to the Third World. The policy of containment easily slid over into opposition to any government, whether communist or not, that seemed to threaten American strategic or economic interests. Jacobo Arbenz Guzmán in Guatemala and Mohammed Mossadegh in Iran were elected, homegrown nationalists, not agents of Moscow. But they were determined to reduce foreign corporations' control over their countries' economies. Arbenz embarked on a sweeping land-reform policy that threatened the domination of Guatemala's economy by the American-owned United Fruit Company. Mossadegh nationalized the Anglo-Iranian Oil Company, whose refinery in Iran was Britain's largest remaining overseas asset. Their foes quickly branded both as communists. In 1953 and 1954, the Central Intelligence Agency organized the ouster of both governments—a clear violation of the UN Charter, which barred a member state from taking military action against another except in self-defense.

In 1956, Israel, France, and Britain—without prior consultation with the United States—invaded Egypt after the country's nationalist leader, Gamal Abdel Nasser, nationalized the Suez Canal, jointly owned by Britain and France. A furious Eisenhower forced them to abandon the invasion. After the Suez fiasco, the United States moved to replace Britain as the major Western power in the Middle East, and American companies increasingly dominated the region's oil fields. In 1957, Eisenhower extended the principle of containment to the region, issuing the Eisenhower Doctrine, which pledged the United States to defend Middle Eastern governments threatened by communism or Arab nationalism. A year later, Ike dispatched 5,000 American troops to Lebanon to protect a government dominated by pro-Western Christians against Nasser's effort to bring all Arab states into a single regime under his rule.

Origins of the Vietnam War

In Vietnam, the expulsion of the Japanese in 1945 led not to independence but to a French military effort to preserve their Asian empire, which dated to the late nineteenth century, against Ho Chi Minh's nationalist forces. Anticommunism led the United States into deeper and deeper involvement. Following a policy initiated by Truman, the Eisenhower administration funneled billions of dollars

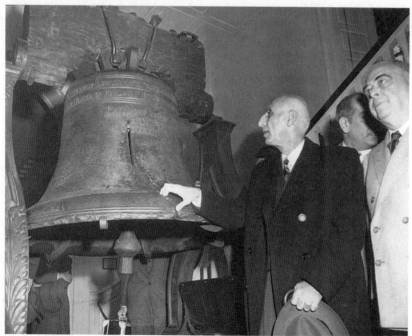

> Containment and the Third World

Mohammed Mossadegh, prime minister of Iran, views the Liberty Bell during his visit to the United States in 1951. The U.S.-sponsored coup that overthrew Mossadegh in 1953 created resentments that helped lead to Iran's Islamic Revolution twenty-five years later.

in aid to bolster French efforts. By the early 1950s, the United States was paying four-fifths of the cost of the war. Wary of becoming bogged down in another land war in Asia immediately after Korea, however, Ike declined to send in American troops when France requested them to avert defeat in 1954. He also rejected the National Security Council's advice to use nuclear weapons, leaving France no alternative but to agree to Vietnamese independence.

Issued from a peace conference in 1954, the **Geneva Accords** divided Vietnam temporarily into northern and southern districts, with elections scheduled for 1956 to unify the country. But the staunchly anticommunist southern leader Ngo Dinh Diem, urged on by the United States, refused to hold elections, which would almost certainly have resulted in a victory for Ho Chi Minh's communists. Diem's close ties to wealthy Catholic families—in predominantly Buddhist South Vietnam—and to landlords in a society dominated by small farmers who had been promised land by Ho alienated an increasing

The military junta installed in Guatemala by the CIA in 1954 enters Guatemala City in a Jeep driven by CIA agent Carlos Castillo Armas. Although hailed by the Eisenhower administration as a triumph for freedom, the new government suppressed democracy in Guatemala and embarked on a murderous campaign to stamp out opposition.

number of his subjects. American aid poured into South Vietnam in order to bolster the Diem regime. By the time Eisenhower left office in 1960, Diem nevertheless faced a full-scale guerrilla revolt by the communist-led National Liberation Front.

Events in Guatemala, Iran, and Vietnam, considered great successes at the time by American policymakers, cast a long shadow over American foreign relations. Little by little, the United States was becoming accustomed to intervention, both open and secret, in far-flung corners of the world. Despite the Cold War rhetoric of freedom, American leaders seemed more comfortable dealing with reliable military regimes than democratic governments. A series of military governments succeeded Arbenz. The shah of Iran replaced Mossadegh and agreed to give British and American oil companies 40 percent of his nation's oil revenues. He remained in office until 1979 as one of the world's most tyrannical rulers, until his overthrow in a revolution led by the fiercely anti-American radical Islamist Ayatollah Khomeini. In Vietnam, the American decision to prop up Diem's regime laid the groundwork for what would soon become the most disastrous military involvement in American history.

American intervention

Mass Society and Its Critics

The fatherly Eisenhower seemed the perfect leader for the placid society of the 1950s. Consensus was the dominant ideal in an era in which McCarthyism had defined criticism of the social and economic order as disloyalty and most

Americans located the enjoyment of freedom in private pleasures rather than the public sphere. With the mainstreams of both parties embracing the Cold War, political debate took place within extremely narrow limits. Even *Life* magazine commented that American freedom might be in greater danger from "disuse" than from communist subversion.

Dissenting voices could be heard. Some intellectuals wondered whether the celebration of affluence and the either-or mentality of the Cold War obscured the extent to which the United States itself fell short of the ideal of freedom. The sociologist C. Wright Mills challenged the self-satisfied vision of democratic pluralism that dominated mainstream social science in the 1950s. Mills wrote of a "power elite"—an interlocking directorate of corporate leaders, politicians, and military men whose domination of government and society had made political democracy obsolete. Freedom, Mills insisted, meant more than "the chance to do as one pleases." It rested on the ability "to formulate the available choices," and this most Americans were effectively denied.

Even as the government and media portrayed the United States as a beacon of liberty locked in a titanic struggle with its opposite, one strand of social analysis in the 1950s contended that Americans did not enjoy genuine freedom. These critics identified as the culprit not the unequal structure of power criticized by Mills, but the modern age itself, with its psychological and cultural discontents. Modern mass society, some writers worried, inevitably produced loneliness and anxiety, causing mankind to yearn for stability and authority, not freedom. In *The Lonely Crowd* (1950), the decade's most influential work of social analysis, the sociologist David Riesman described Americans as "other-directed" conformists who lacked the inner resources to lead truly independent lives. Other social critics charged that corporate bureaucracies had transformed employees into "organization men" incapable of independent thought.

Some commentators feared that the Russians had demonstrated a greater ability to sacrifice for common public goals than Americans. What kind of nation, the economist John Kenneth Galbraith asked in *The Affluent Society* (1958), neglected investment in schools, parks, and public services, while producing ever more goods to fulfill desires created by advertising? Was the spectacle of millions of educated middle-class women seeking happiness in suburban dream houses a reason for celebration or a waste of precious "woman power" at a time when the Soviets trumpeted the accomplishments of their female scientists, physicians, and engineers? Books like Galbraith's, along with William Whyte's *The Organization Man* (1956) and Vance Packard's *The Hidden Persuaders* (1957), which criticized the monotony of modern work, the emptiness of suburban life, and the pervasive influence of advertising, created the vocabulary for an assault on the nation's social values that lay just over the horizon. In the 1950s, however, while criticism of mass society became a minor industry among intellectuals, it failed to dent widespread complacency about the American way.

Commuters returning from work in downtown Chicago, leaving the railroad station at suburban Park Forest, Illinois, in 1953. Social critics of the 1950s claimed that Americans had become "organization men," too conformist to lead independent lives.

Rebels without a Cause

The social critics did not offer a political alternative or have any real impact on the parties or government. Nor did other stirrings of dissent. With teenagers a growing part of the population thanks to the baby boom, the emergence of a popular culture geared to the emerging youth market suggested that significant generational tensions lay beneath the bland surface of 1950s life. J. D. Salinger's 1951 novel *Catcher in the Rye* and the 1955 films *Blackboard Jungle* and *Rebel without a Cause* (the latter starring James Dean as an aimlessly rebellious youth) highlighted the alienation of at least some young people from the world of adult respectability. These works helped to spur a mid-1950s panic about "juvenile delinquency." *Time* magazine devoted a cover story to "Teenagers on the Rampage," and a Senate committee held hearings in 1954 on whether violent comic books caused criminal behavior among young people. (One witness even criticized Superman comics for arousing violent emotions among its readers.) To head off federal regulation, publishers—like movie producers earlier—adopted a code of conduct for their industry that strictly limited the portrayal of crime and violence in comic books.

Rebels without a cause. Teenagers, photographed at Coney Island, Brooklyn, in the late 1950s.

Cultural life during the 1950s seemed far more daring than politics. Indeed, many adults found the emergence of a mass-marketed teenage culture that rejected middle-class norms more alarming than the actual increase in juvenile arrests. Teenagers wore leather jackets and danced to rock-and-roll music that brought the hard-driving rhythms and sexually provocative movements of black musicians and dancers to enthusiastic young white audiences. They made Elvis Presley, a rock-and-roll singer with an openly sexual performance style, an immensely popular entertainment celebrity.

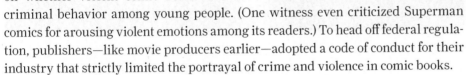

Rock-and-roll

Elvis Presley's gyrating hips appealed to teenagers but alarmed many adults during the 1950s.

Challenges of various kinds also arose to the family-centered image of personal fulfillment. *Playboy* magazine, which began publication in 1953, reached a circulation of more than 1 million copies per month by 1960. It extended the consumer culture into the most intimate realms of life, offering men a fantasy world of sexual gratification outside the family's confines. Although considered sick or deviant by the larger society and subject to constant police harassment, gay men and lesbians created their own subcultures in major cities.

The Beats

In New York City and San Francisco, as well as college towns like Madison, Wisconsin, and Ann Arbor, Michigan, **the Beats**, a small group of poets and writers, railed against mainstream culture. The novelist Jack Kerouac coined the term "beat"—a play on "beaten down" and "beatified" (or saintlike). His *On the Road*, written in the

A poetry meeting at a Beat coffeehouse in New York City, photographed in 1959, where poets, artists, and others who rejected 1950s mainstream culture gathered.

early 1950s but not published until 1957, recounted in a seemingly spontaneous rush of sights, sounds, and images its main character's aimless wanderings across the American landscape. The book became a bible for a generation of young people who rejected the era's middle-class culture but had little to put in its place.

"I saw the best minds of my generation destroyed by madness, starving hysterical naked," wrote the Beat poet Allen Ginsberg in *Howl* (1955), a brilliant protest against materialism and conformism written while the author was under the influence of hallucinogenic drugs. Ginsberg became nationally known when San Francisco police in 1956 confiscated his book and arrested bookstore owners for selling an obscene work. (A judge later overturned the ban on the grounds that *Howl* possessed redeeming social value.) Rejecting the work ethic, the "desperate materialism" of the suburban middle class, and the militarization of American life by the Cold War, the Beats celebrated impulsive action, immediate pleasure (often enhanced by drugs), and sexual experimentation. Despite Cold War slogans, they insisted, personal and political repression, not freedom, were the hallmarks of American society.

Allen Ginsberg

THE FREEDOM MOVEMENT

Not until the 1960s would young white rebels find their cause, as the seeds of dissent planted by the social critics and Beats flowered in an outpouring of political activism, new attitudes toward sexuality, and a full-fledged generational rebellion. A more immediate challenge to the complacency of the 1950s arose from the twentieth century's greatest citizens' movement—the black struggle for equality.

Origins of the Movement

Today, with the birthday of Martin Luther King Jr. a national holiday and the struggles of Montgomery, Little Rock, Birmingham, and Selma celebrated as heroic episodes in the history of freedom, it is easy to forget that at the time, the civil rights revolution came as a great surprise. Looking back, its causes seem clear: the destabilization of the racial system during World War II; the mass migration out of the segregated South that made black voters an increasingly important part of the Democratic Party coalition; and the Cold War and rise of independent states in the Third World, both of which made the gap between America's rhetoric and its racial reality an international embarrassment. Yet few predicted the emergence of the southern mass movement for civil rights.

Immediate causes

With blacks' traditional allies on the left decimated by McCarthyism, most union leaders unwilling to challenge racial inequalities within their own ranks, and the NAACP concentrating on court battles, new constituencies and new tactics were sorely needed. The movement found in the southern black church the organizing power for a militant, nonviolent assault on segregation.

The southern black church

The United States in the 1950s was still a segregated, unequal society. Half of the nation's black families lived in poverty. Because of labor contracts that linked promotions and firings to seniority, non-white workers, who had joined the industrial labor force later than whites, lost their jobs first in times of economic downturn. In the South, evidence of Jim Crow abounded—in separate public institutions and the signs "white" and "colored" at entrances to buildings, train carriages, drinking fountains, restrooms, and the like. In the North and West, the law did not require segregation, but custom barred blacks from many colleges, hotels, and restaurants, and from most suburban housing. Las Vegas, Nevada, for example, was as strictly segregated as any southern city. Hotels and casinos did not admit blacks except in the most menial jobs. Lena Horne, Sammy Davis Jr., Louis Armstrong, and other black entertainers played the hotel-casinos on the "strip" but could not stay as guests where they performed.

The persistence of Jim Crow

In 1950, seventeen southern and border states and Washington, D.C., had laws requiring the racial segregation of public schools, and several others permitted local districts to impose it. Around 40 percent of the nation's 28 million schoolchildren studied in legally segregated schools, and millions more attended classes in northern communities where housing patterns and school district lines created de facto segregation—separation in fact if not in law. Few white Americans felt any urgency about confronting racial inequality. "Segregation," the white writer John Egerton later recalled, "didn't restrict me in any way, so it was easy to accept things the way they were, to take my freedom for granted and not worry about anyone else's."

Segregation in schools

The Legal Assault on Segregation

With Truman's civil rights initiative having faded and the Eisenhower administration reluctant to address the issue, it fell to the courts to confront the problem of racial segregation. In the Southwest, the **League of United Latin American Citizens** (LULAC), the equivalent of the NAACP, challenged restrictive housing, employment discrimination, and the segregation of Latino students. It won an

VOICES OF FREEDOM

From MARTIN LUTHER KING JR.,
SPEECH AT MONTGOMERY, ALABAMA (DECEMBER 5, 1955)

On the evening of Rosa Parks's arrest for refusing to give up her seat on a Montgomery bus to a white passenger, a mass rally of local African-Americans decided to boycott city buses in protest. In his speech to the gathering, the young Baptist minister Martin Luther King Jr. invoked Christian and American ideals of justice and democracy—themes he would strike again and again during his career as the leading national symbol of the civil rights struggle.

We are here this evening . . . because first and foremost we are American citizens, and we are determined to apply our citizenship to the fullness of its means. We are here also because of our love for democracy. . . . Just the other day . . . one of the finest citizens in Montgomery—not one of the finest Negro citizens but one of the finest citizens in Montgomery—was taken from a bus and carried to jail and arrested because she refused to give her seat to a white person. . . .

Mrs. Rosa Parks is a fine person. And since it had to happen I'm happy that it happened to a person like Mrs. Parks, for nobody can doubt the boundless outreach of her integrity! Nobody can doubt the height of her character, nobody can doubt that depth of her Christian commitment and devotion to the teachings of Jesus. And I'm happy since it

had to happen, it happened to a person that nobody can call a disturbing factor in the community. Mrs. Parks is a fine Christian person, unassuming, and yet there is integrity and character there. And just because she refused to get up, she was arrested.

I want to say, that we are not here advocating violence. We have never done that. . . . We believe in the teachings of Jesus. The only weapon that we have in our hands this evening is the weapon of protest. . . . There will be no white persons pulled out of their homes and taken out to some distant road and lynched. . . .

We are not wrong in what we are doing. If we are wrong, then the Supreme Court of this nation is wrong. If we are wrong, the Constitution of the United States is wrong. If we are wrong, God Almighty is wrong. . . . If we are wrong, justice is a lie. . . .

We, the disinherited of this land, we who have been oppressed so long, are tired of going through the long night of captivity. And now we are reaching out for the daybreak of freedom and justice and equality. . . . Right here in Montgomery when the history books are written in the future, somebody will have to say, "There lived a race of people, a *black* people, . . . a people who had the moral courage to stand up for their rights. And thereby they injected a new meaning into the veins of history and of civilization."

From THE SOUTHERN MANIFESTO (1956)

Drawn up early in 1956 and signed by 96 southern members of the Senate and House of Representatives, the Southern Manifesto repudiated the Supreme Court decision in *Brown v. Board of Education* and offered support to the campaign of resistance in the South.

The unwarranted decision of the Supreme Court in the public school cases is now bearing the fruit always produced when men substitute naked power for established law. . . .

We regard the decisions of the Supreme Court in the school cases as a clear abuse of judicial power. It climaxes a trend in the Federal Judiciary undertaking to legislate, in derogation [violation] of the authority of Congress, and to encroach upon the reserved rights of the States and the people.

The original Constitution does not mention education. Neither does the 14th Amendment nor any other amendment. The debates preceding the submission of the 14th Amendment clearly show that there was no intent that it should affect the system of education maintained by the States.

In the case of *Plessy v. Ferguson* in 1896 the Supreme Court expressly declared that under the 14th Amendment no person was denied any of his rights if the States provided separate but equal facilities. This decision . . . restated time and again, became a part of the life of the people of many of the States and confirmed their habits, traditions, and way of life. It is founded on elemental humanity and commonsense, for parents should not be deprived by Government of the right to direct the lives and education of their own children.

Though there has been no constitutional amendment or act of Congress changing this established legal principle almost a century old, the Supreme Court of the United States, with no legal basis for such action, undertook to exercise their naked judicial power and substituted their personal political and social ideas for the established law of the land.

This unwarranted exercise of power by the Court, contrary to the Constitution, is creating chaos and confusion in the States principally affected. It is destroying the amicable relations between the white and Negro races that have been created through 90 years of patient effort by the good people of both races. It has planted hatred and suspicion where there has been heretofore friendship and understanding.

With the gravest concern for the explosive and dangerous condition created by this decision and inflamed by outside meddlers: . . . we commend the motives of those States which have declared the intention to resist forced integration by any lawful means. . . .

QUESTIONS

1. *How do religious convictions shape King's definition of freedom?*

2. *Why does the Southern Manifesto claim that the Supreme Court decision is a threat to constitutional government?*

3. *How do these documents illustrate contrasting understandings of freedom in the wake of the civil rights movement?*

A segregated school in West Memphis, Arkansas, photographed for *Life* magazine in 1949. Education in the South was separate but hardly equal.

LULAC and Mendez v. Westminster

important victory in 1946 in the case of *Mendez v. Westminster*, when a federal court ordered the schools of Orange County desegregated. In response, the state legislature repealed all school laws requiring racial segregation. The governor who signed the measure, Earl Warren, had presided over the internment of Japanese-Americans during World War II as the state's attorney general. After the war, he became convinced that racial inequality had no place in American life. When Chief Justice Fred Vinson died in 1953, Eisenhower appointed Earl Warren to replace him. Warren would play the key role in deciding **Brown v. Board of Education**, the momentous case that outlawed school segregation.

Thurgood Marshall and the NAACP

For years, the NAACP, under the leadership of attorneys Charles Hamilton Houston and Thurgood Marshall, had pressed legal challenges to the "separate but equal" doctrine laid down by the Court in 1896 in *Plessy v. Ferguson* (see Chapter 17). At first, the NAACP sought to gain admission to white institutions of higher learning for which no black equivalent existed. In 1938, the Supreme Court ordered the University of Missouri Law School to admit Lloyd Gaines, a black student, because the state had no such school for blacks. Missouri responded by setting up a segregated law school, satisfying the courts. But in 1950, the Supreme Court unanimously ordered Heman Sweatt admitted to the University of Texas Law School even though the state had established a "school" for him in a basement containing three classrooms and no library. There was no way, the Court declared, that this hastily constructed law school could be "equal" to the prestigious all-white institution.

The *Brown* Case

Marshall now launched a frontal assault on segregation itself. He brought the NAACP's support to local cases that had arisen when black parents challenged unfair school policies. For parents to do so required remarkable courage. In

Clarendon County, South Carolina, Levi Pearson, a black farmer who brought a lawsuit on behalf of his children, saw his house burned to the ground. The Clarendon case attacked not segregation itself but the unequal funding of schools. The local school board spent $179 per white child and $43 per black, and unlike white pupils, black children attended class in buildings with no running water or indoor toilets and were not provided with buses to transport them to classes. Five such cases from four states and the District of Columbia were combined in a single appeal that reached the Supreme Court late in 1952.

> *Unequal school funding*

When cases are united, they are listed alphabetically and the first case gives the entire decision its name. In this instance, the first case arose from a state outside the old Confederacy. Oliver Brown went to court because his daughter, a third grader, was forced to walk across dangerous railroad tracks each morning rather than being allowed to attend a nearby school restricted to whites. His lawsuit became *Brown v. Board of Education of Topeka, Kansas.*

Thurgood Marshall decided that the time had come to attack not the unfair applications of the "separate but equal" principle but the doctrine itself. Even with the same funding and facilities, he insisted, segregation was inherently unequal since it stigmatized one group of citizens as unfit to associate with others. Drawing on studies by New York psychologists Kenneth and Mamie Clark, Marshall argued that segregation did lifelong damage to black children, undermining their self-esteem. In its legal brief, the Eisenhower administration did not directly support Marshall's position, but it urged the justices to consider "the problem of racial discrimination . . . in the context of the present world struggle between freedom and tyranny." Other peoples, it noted, "cannot understand how such a practice can exist in a country which professes to be a staunch supporter of freedom, justice, and democracy."

The new chief justice, Earl Warren, managed to create unanimity on a divided Court, some of whose members disliked segregation but feared that a decision to outlaw it would spark widespread violence. On May 17, 1954, Warren himself read aloud the decision, only eleven pages long. Segregation in public education, he concluded, violated the equal protection of the laws guaranteed by the Fourteenth Amendment. "In the field of education, the doctrine of 'separate but equal' has no place. Separate educational facilities are inherently unequal."

The black press hailed the *Brown* decision as a "second Emancipation Proclamation." And like its predecessor it was in many ways a limited document. The decision did not address segregation in institutions other than public schools or ban all racial classifications in the law, such as statutes prohibiting interracial marriage. It did not address the de facto school segregation of the North, which rested on housing patterns rather than state law. It did not order immediate implementation but instead called for hearings as to how segregated schooling should be dismantled. But *Brown* marked the emergence of the "Warren Court" as an active agent of social change. And it inspired a wave of optimism

Linda Brown's parents sued the school board of Topeka, Kansas, demanding that it admit their daughter to a school near her home restricted to whites, rather than requiring her to walk across dangerous railroad tracks, each day, as in this photograph, to attend a black school. The result was the Supreme Court's landmark *Brown* decision outlawing school segregation.

that discrimination would soon disappear. "What a wonderful world of possibilities are unfolded for the children," wrote the black novelist Ralph Ellison.

The Montgomery Bus Boycott

Brown did not cause the modern civil rights movement, which, as noted in the previous two chapters, began during World War II and continued in cities like New York after the war. But the decision did ensure that when the movement resumed after waning in the early 1950s, it would have the backing of the federal courts. Mass action against Jim Crow soon reappeared. On December 1, 1955, Rosa Parks, a black tailor's assistant who had just completed her day's work in a Montgomery, Alabama, department store, refused to surrender her seat on a city bus to a white rider, as required by local law. Parks's arrest sparked a yearlong **Montgomery bus boycott**, the beginning of the mass phase of the civil rights movement in the South. Within a decade, the civil rights revolution had overturned the structure of legal segregation and regained the right to vote for black southerners. In 2000, *Time* magazine named Rosa Parks one of the 100 most significant persons of the twentieth century.

Parks is widely remembered today as a "seamstress with tired feet," a symbol of ordinary blacks' determination to resist the daily injustices and indignities of the Jim Crow South. In fact, her life makes clear that the civil rights revolution built on earlier struggles. Parks was a veteran of black politics. During the 1930s, she took part in meetings protesting the conviction of the Scottsboro Boys. She served for many years as secretary to E. D. Nixon, the local leader of the NAACP. In 1943, she tried to register to vote, only to be turned away because she supposedly failed a literacy test. After two more attempts, Parks succeeded in becoming one of the few blacks in Montgomery able to cast a ballot. In 1954, she attended a training session for political activists at the Highlander School in Tennessee, a meeting ground for labor and civil rights radicals.

For years, civil rights activists in Montgomery had been strategizing over how best to confront the city ordinance that required bus segregation. An earlier challenge had been abandoned because the person who refused to move was an unmarried pregnant teenager. The dignified, accomplished Parks was the ideal person to become a symbol of the fight. The date may have been chosen because an all-white jury in Mississippi had just acquitted the murderers of Emmett Till, a black teenager who had allegedly whistled at a white woman. Till's murder and the judicial outcome shocked the nation. When his body was returned to Chicago, his parents insisted that the casket remain open at the funeral, so people could see his severely bruised and disfigured body—dramatic witness to why the racial status quo desperately needed to change.

Jo Ann Robinson, a professor at the all-black Alabama State University, had been calling for a boycott of public transportation since 1954. When news of Parks's arrest spread, hundreds of blacks gathered in a local church and vowed to refuse to ride the buses until accorded equal treatment. For 381 days, despite legal harassment and occasional violence, black maids, janitors, teachers, and students walked to their destinations or rode an informal network of taxis. Finally, in November 1956, the Supreme Court ruled segregation in public transportation unconstitutional. The boycott ended in triumph.

Rosa Parks

The mug shot of Rosa Parks taken in December 1955 at a Montgomery, Alabama, police station after she was arrested for refusing to give up her seat on a city bus to a white passenger.

The Daybreak of Freedom

The Montgomery bus boycott marked a turning point in postwar American history. It launched the movement for racial justice as a nonviolent crusade based in the black churches of the South. It gained the support of northern liberals and focused unprecedented and unwelcome international attention on the country's racial policies. And it marked the emergence of twenty-six-year-old Martin Luther King Jr., who had recently arrived in Montgomery to become pastor of a Baptist church, as the movement's national symbol. On the night of the first protest meeting, King's call to action electrified the audience: "We, the disinherited of this land, we who have been oppressed so long, are tired of going through the long night of captivity. And now we are reaching out for the daybreak of freedom and justice and equality."

From the beginning, the language of freedom pervaded the black movement. It resonated in the speeches of civil rights leaders and in the hand-lettered placards of the struggle's foot soldiers. On the day of Rosa Parks's court appearance in December 1955, even before the bus boycott had officially been announced, a torn piece of cardboard appeared on a bus shelter in Montgomery's Court Square, advising passengers: "Don't ride the buses today. Don't ride it for freedom." During the summer of 1964, when civil rights activists established "freedom schools" for black children across Mississippi, lessons began with students being asked to define the word. Some gave specific answers ("going to public libraries"), some more abstract ("standing up for your rights"). Some insisted that freedom meant legal equality, others saw it as liberation from years of deference to and fear of whites. "Freedom of the mind," wrote one, was the greatest freedom of all.

For adults as well, freedom had many meanings. It meant enjoying the political rights and economic opportunities taken for granted by whites. It required eradicating historic wrongs such as segregation, disenfranchisement, confinement to low-wage jobs, and the ever-present threat of violence. It meant the right to be served at lunch counters and downtown department stores, central locations in the consumer culture, and to be addressed as "Mr.," "Miss," and "Mrs.," rather than "boy" and "auntie."

Black residents of Montgomery, Alabama, walking to work during the bus boycott of 1955–1956.

Language and meaning of freedom

The Leadership of King

In King's soaring oratory, the protesters' understandings of freedom fused into a coherent whole. For the title of his first book, relating the boycott's history, King chose the title *Stride Toward Freedom*. His most celebrated oration, the "I Have a Dream" speech of 1963, began by invoking the unfulfilled promise of emancipation ("one hundred years later, the Negro still is not free") and closed with a cry borrowed from a black spiritual: "Free at last! Free at last! Thank God Almighty, we are free at last!"

"I Have a Dream"

A master at appealing to the deep sense of injustice among blacks and to the conscience of white America, King presented the case for black rights in a vocabulary that merged the black experience with that of the nation. Having studied the writings on peaceful civil disobedience of Henry David Thoreau and Mohandas (Mahatma) Gandhi, as well as the nonviolent protests the Congress of Racial Equality had organized in the 1940s, King outlined a philosophy of struggle in which evil must be met with good, hate with Christian love, and violence with peaceful demands for change. "There will be no white persons pulled out of their homes and taken out to some distant road and lynched," he declared in his speech at the launching of the Montgomery bus boycott.

Echoing Christian themes derived from his training in the black church, King's speeches resonated deeply in both black communities and the broader culture. He repeatedly invoked the Bible to preach justice and forgiveness. Like Frederick Douglass before him, King appealed to white America by stressing the protesters' love of country and devotion to national values. The "daybreak of freedom," King made clear, meant a new dawn for the whole of American society. And like W. E. B. Du Bois, he linked the American "color line" with the degradation of non-white peoples overseas. "The great struggle of the Twentieth Century," he declared in a 1956 sermon, "has been between the exploited masses questing for freedom and the colonial powers seeking to maintain their domination." If Africa was gaining its freedom, he asked, why must black America lag behind?

Massive Resistance

Buoyed by success in Montgomery, King in 1956 took the lead in forming the **Southern Christian Leadership Conference**, a coalition of black ministers and civil rights activists, to press for desegregation. But despite the movement's success in popular mobilization, the fact that Montgomery's city fathers agreed to the boycott's demands only after a Supreme Court ruling indicated that without national backing, local action might not be enough to overturn Jim Crow. The white South's refusal to accept the *Brown* decision reinforced the conviction that black citizens could not gain their constitutional rights without Washington's intervention. This was not immediately forthcoming. When the Supreme Court finally issued its implementation ruling in 1955, the justices declared that desegregation should proceed "with all deliberate speed." This vague formulation unintentionally encouraged a campaign of "massive resistance" that paralyzed civil rights progress in much of the South.

In 1956, 96 of 106 southern congressmen—and every southern senator except Lyndon B. Johnson of Texas and Albert Gore and Estes Kefauver of Tennessee—signed a **Southern Manifesto**, denouncing the *Brown* decision as a "clear abuse of judicial power," and calling

A women's demonstration against racial integration in Poolesville, Maryland, 1956.

for resistance to "forced integration" by "any lawful means." State after state passed laws to block desegregation. Some made it illegal for the NAACP to operate within their borders. Virginia pioneered the strategy of closing any public schools ordered to desegregate and offering funds to enable white pupils, but not black, to attend private institutions. Prince Edward County, Virginia, shut its schools entirely in 1959; not until 1964 did the Supreme Court order them reopened. Many states adopted "freedom of choice" plans that allowed white students to opt out of integrated schools. As a symbol of defiance, Georgia's legislature incorporated the Confederate battle flag into its state flag in 1956, and Alabama and South Carolina soon began flying the battle flag over their state capitol buildings.

Blocking desegregation

Eisenhower and Civil Rights

The federal government tried to remain aloof from the black struggle. Thanks to the efforts of Senate majority leader Lyndon B. Johnson, who hoped to win liberal support for a run for president in 1960, Congress in 1957 passed the first national civil rights law since Reconstruction. It targeted the denial of black voting rights in the South, but with weak enforcement provisions it added few voters to the rolls. President Eisenhower failed to provide moral leadership. He called for Americans to abide by the law, but he made it clear that he found the whole civil rights issue distasteful. He privately told aides that he disagreed with the Supreme Court's reasoning. Ike failed to act in 1956 when a federal court ordered that Autherine Lucy be admitted to the University of Alabama; a mob prevented her from registering and the board of trustees expelled her. The university remained all white into the 1960s.

Weak enforcement of civil rights

In 1957, however, after Governor Orval Faubus of Arkansas used the National Guard to prevent the court-ordered integration of Little Rock's Central High School, Eisenhower dispatched federal troops to the city. In the face of a howling mob, soldiers of the 101st Airborne Division escorted nine black children into the school. Events in Little Rock showed that in the last instance, the federal government would not allow the flagrant violation of court orders. But because of massive resistance, the pace of the movement slowed in the final years of the 1950s. When Eisenhower left office, fewer than 2 percent of black students attended desegregated schools in the states of the old Confederacy.

A photograph by Gordon Parks shows a well-dressed black woman and her daughter at the "colored" entrance to a Mobile, Alabama, department store in 1956.

The World Views the United States

Ever since the beginning of the Cold War, American leaders had worried about the impact of segregation on the country's international reputation. President Truman had promoted his civil rights initiative, in part, by reminding Americans that they could not afford to "ignore what the world thinks of our record." The State Department filed a brief in the *Brown* case noting the damage segregation was doing to the country's image overseas.

Foreign nations and colonies paid close attention to the unfolding of the American civil rights movement. The global reaction to the *Brown* decision was overwhelmingly positive. "At Last! Whites and

Federal troops escort black children to Little Rock Central High School, enforcing a court order for integration in 1957.

International criticism

Blacks in the United States on the same school benches!" proclaimed a newspaper in Senegal, West Africa. But the slow pace of change led to criticism that embarrassed American diplomats seeking to win the loyalty of people in the non-white world. In a public forum in India, the American ambassador was peppered with questions about American race relations. Was it true that the Haitian ambassador to the United States had to live in a black ghetto in Washington? Why did no black person hold a high public office? Of course, the Soviet Union played up American race relations as part of the global "battle for hearts and minds of men" that was a key part of the Cold War.

THE ELECTION OF 1960

Kennedy and Nixon

JFK

The presidential campaign of 1960 turned out to be one of the closest in American history. Republicans chose Vice President Richard Nixon as their candidate to succeed Eisenhower. Democrats nominated John F. Kennedy, a senator from Massachusetts and a Roman Catholic, whose father, a millionaire Irish-American businessman, had served as ambassador to Great Britain during the 1930s. Kennedy's chief rivals for the nomination were Hubert Humphrey, leader of the party's liberal wing, and Lyndon B. Johnson of Texas, the Senate majority leader, who accepted Kennedy's offer to run for vice president.

The atmosphere of tolerance promoted by World War II had weakened traditional anti-Catholicism. But as recently as 1949, Paul Blanshard's *American Freedom*

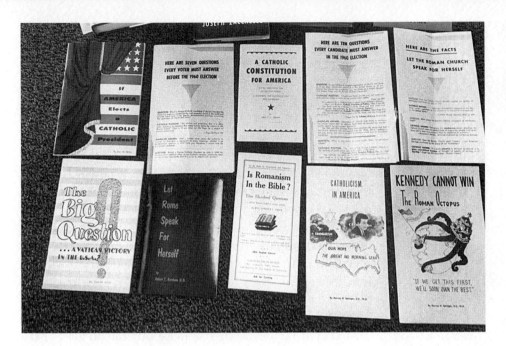

The 1960 presidential campaign produced a flood of anti-Catholic propaganda. Kennedy's victory, the first for an American Catholic, was a major step in the decline of this long-standing prejudice.

and Catholic Power, which accused the church of being antidemocratic, morally repressive, and essentially un-American, had become a national best-seller. Many Protestants remained reluctant to vote for a Catholic, fearing that Kennedy would be required to support church doctrine on controversial public issues or, in a more extreme version, take orders from the pope. Kennedy addressed the question directly. "I do not speak for my church on public matters," he insisted, and "the church does not speak for me." His defeat of Humphrey in the Democratic primary in overwhelmingly Protestant West Virginia put the issue of his religion to rest. At age forty-three, Kennedy became the youngest major-party nominee for president in the nation's history.

> *Religion and the election*

Both Kennedy and Nixon were ardent Cold Warriors. But Kennedy pointed to Soviet success in putting *Sputnik*, the first earth satellite, into orbit and subsequently testing the first intercontinental ballistic missile (ICBM) as evidence that the United States had lost the sense of national purpose necessary to fight the Cold War. He warned that Republicans had allowed a **missile gap** to develop in which the Soviets had achieved technological and military superiority over the United States. In fact, as both Kennedy and Nixon well knew, American economic and military capacity far exceeded that of the Soviets. But the charge persuaded many Americans that the time had come for new leadership. The stylishness of Kennedy's wife, Jacqueline, which stood in sharp contrast to the more dowdy public appearance of Mamie Eisenhower and Pat Nixon, reinforced the impression that Kennedy would conduct a more youthful, vigorous presidency.

A photograph of John F. Kennedy and his wife, Jacqueline, strolling along the pier at Hyannis Port, Massachusetts, illustrates their youthful appeal.

In the first televised debate between presidential candidates, judging by viewer response, the handsome Kennedy bested Nixon, who was suffering from a cold and appeared tired and nervous. Those who heard the encounter on the radio thought Nixon had won, but, on TV, image counted for more than substance. In November, Kennedy eked out a narrow victory, winning the popular vote by only 120,000

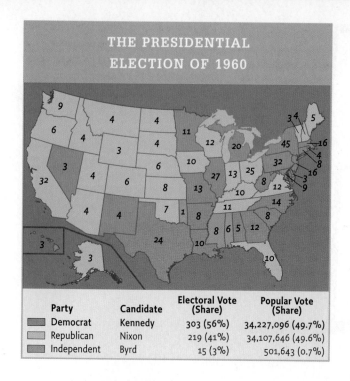

THE PRESIDENTIAL ELECTION OF 1960

Party	Candidate	Electoral Vote (Share)	Popular Vote (Share)
Democrat	Kennedy	303 (56%)	34,227,096 (49.7%)
Republican	Nixon	219 (41%)	34,107,646 (49.6%)
Independent	Byrd	15 (3%)	501,643 (0.7%)

out of 69 million votes cast (and, Republicans charged, benefiting from a fraudulent vote count by the notoriously corrupt Chicago Democratic machine).

The End of the 1950s

In January 1961, shortly before leaving office, Eisenhower delivered a televised Farewell Address, modeled to some extent on George Washington's address of 1796. Knowing that the missile gap was a myth, Ike warned against the drumbeat of calls for a new military buildup. He urged Americans to think about the dangerous power of what he called the **military-industrial complex**—the conjunction of "an immense military establishment" with a "permanent arms industry"—with an influence felt in "every office" in the land. "We must never let the weight of this combination," he advised his countrymen, "endanger our liberties or democratic processes." Few Americans shared Ike's concern—far more saw the alliance of the Defense Department and private industry as a source of jobs and national security rather than a threat to democracy. A few years later, however, with the United States locked in an increasingly unpopular war, Eisenhower's warning would come to seem prophetic.

By then, other underpinnings of 1950s life were also in disarray. The tens of millions of cars that made suburban life possible were spewing toxic lead, an additive to make gasoline more efficient, into the atmosphere. Penned in to the east by mountains that kept automobile emissions from being dispersed by the wind, Los Angeles had become synonymous with smog, a type of air pollution

Residents of Los Angeles don gas masks at a 1954 luncheon to protest the government's failure to combat the air pollution, or "smog," that hung over the city.

Wayne Thiebaud's painting *Pie Counter* both celebrates the abundance of the 1950s and suggests the uniformity and sterility of consumer culture.

produced by cars. Chlorofluorocarbons, used in air conditioners, deodorants, and aerosol hair sprays, were releasing chemicals into the atmosphere that trapped heat and damaged the ozone layer, producing global warming and an increase in skin cancer. (Both leaded gasoline and chlorofluorocarbons had been invented by General Motors research scientist Thomas Midgley. He "had more impact on the atmosphere," writes one historian, "than any other single organism" in the history of the world.) The chemical insecticides that enabled agricultural conglomerates to produce the country's remarkable abundance of food were poisoning farm workers, consumers, and the water supply. Housewives were rebelling against a life centered in suburban dream houses. Blacks were increasingly impatient with the slow progress of racial change. The United States, in other words, had entered that most turbulent of decades, the 1960s.

Pollution

SUGGESTED READING

BOOKS

- Branch, Taylor. *Parting the Waters: America in the King Years, 1954–1963* (1988). A comprehensive account of the civil rights movement from the *Brown* decision to the early 1960s.

- Cohen, Lizabeth. *A Consumer's Republic: The Politics of Mass Consumption in Postwar America* (2003). Considers how the glorification of consumer freedom shaped American public policy and the physical landscape.

- De Grazia, Victoria. *Irresistible Empire: America's Advance through Twentieth-Century Europe* (2005). An examination of American "soft power" and its triumphant penetration of twentieth-century Europe.

- Fones-Wolf, Elizabeth A. *Selling Free Enterprise: The Business Assault on Labor and Liberalism, 1945–1960* (1994). Examines the carefully developed campaign whereby business leaders associated capitalism and a union-free workplace with freedom.

- Freeman, Joshua B. *Working-Class New York: Life and Labor since World War II* (2000). An account of the lives of laborers in the nation's largest city, tracing the rise and decline of the labor movement.

- Inboden, William. *Religion and American Foreign Policy, 1945–1960: The Soul of Containment* (2008). How religious groups influenced American diplomacy at the height of the Cold War.

- Jackson, Kenneth T. *Crabgrass Frontier: The Suburbanization of America* (1985). The standard account of the development of American suburbia.

- Jacobs, Meg. *Pocketbook Politics: Economic Citizenship in Twentieth-Century America* (2005). Discusses how consumer freedom became central to Americans' national identity after World War II.

- Klarman, Michael J. *From Jim Crow to Civil Rights: The Supreme Court and the Struggle for Racial Equality* (2004). A full study of Supreme Court cases dealing with civil rights, and how they both reflected and helped to stimulate social change.

- Klein, Jennifer. *For All These Rights: Business, Labor, and the Shaping of America's Public-Private Welfare State* (2003). Examines the development of the "social contract" of the 1950s whereby many workers received social benefits from their employers rather than the government.

- May, Elaine T. *Homeward Bound: American Families in the Cold War Era* (1988). Studies the nuclear family as a bastion of American freedom during the Cold War, at least according to official propaganda.

- Nicolaides, Becky M. *My Blue Heaven: Life and Politics in the Working-Class Suburbs of Los Angeles, 1920–1965* (2002). Traces the transformation of Southgate, an industrial neighborhood of Los Angeles, into an all-white suburb, and the political results.

- Patterson, James T. *Grand Expectations: The United States, 1945–1974* (1996). A comprehensive account of American history over the three decades following World War II.

- Pells, Richard. *The Liberal Mind in a Conservative Age: American Intellectuals in the 1940s and 1950s* (1984). Examines how American writers and artists responded to the Cold War.

- Phillips-Fein, Kim. *Invisible Hands: The Making of the Conservative Movement from the New Deal to Reagan* (2009). Relates how a group of economic thinkers and businessmen worked to fashion a conservative movement in an attempt to reverse many of the policies of the New Deal.

- Wall, Wendy L. *Inventing the "American Way": The Politics of Consensus from the New Deal to the Civil Rights Movement* (2008). A careful examination of the political and ideological world of the Cold War era.

- Westad, Odd Arne. *The Global Cold War* (2005). A wide-ranging analysis of how the Cold War played out in the Third World.

WEBSITES

- Brown v. Board of Education: www.lib.umich.edu /brown-versus-board-education/

- Herblock's History: Political Cartoons from the Crash to the Millennium: www.loc.gov/rr/print/swann/herblock/

CHAPTER REVIEW AND ONLINE RESOURCES

REVIEW QUESTIONS

1. Explain the meaning of the "American standard of living" during the 1950s.

2. Describe how the automobile transformed American communities and culture in the 1950s.

3. Identify the prescribed roles and aspirations for women during the social conformity of the 1950s.

4. How did governmental policies, business practices, and individual choices contribute to racially segregated suburbs?

5. Explain the ideological rifts between conservatives in the 1950s. Why did many view President Eisenhower as "not one of them"?

6. What was the new "social contract" between labor and management, and how did it benefit both sides as well as the nation as a whole?

7. How did the United States and Soviet Union shift the focus of the Cold War to the Third World?

8. What were the most significant factors that contributed to the growing momentum of the civil rights movement in the 1950s?

9. How did many southern whites, led by their elected officials, resist desegregation and civil rights in the name of "freedom"?

10. How and why did the federal government's concern with U.S. relations overseas shape its involvement with the *Brown v. Board of Education* case?

KEY TERMS

Levittown (p. 932)

baby boom (p. 937)

urban renewal (p. 939)

"In God We Trust" (p. 940)

interstate highway system (p. 946)

Sputnik (p. 946)

National Defense Education Act (p. 947)

social contract (p. 947)

massive retaliation (p. 948)

Geneva Accords (p. 951)

the Beats (p. 953)

League of United Latin American Citizens (p. 955)

Brown v. Board of Education (p. 958)

Montgomery bus boycott (p. 960)

Southern Christian Leadership Conference (p. 962)

Southern Manifesto (p. 962)

missile gap (p. 965)

military-industrial complex (p. 966)

Go to   INQUIZITIVE

To see what you know—and learn what you've missed—with personalized feedback along the way.

Visit the *Give Me Liberty!* **Student Site** for primary source documents and images, interactive maps, author videos featuring Eric Foner, and more.

CHAPTER 25

THE SIXTIES

★

1960-1968

FREE YAWF LEADERS
JAILED FOR AIDING
ANTI-WAR G.I.s

On the afternoon of February 1, 1960, four students from North Carolina Agricultural and Technical State University, a black college in Greensboro, North Carolina, entered the local Woolworth's department store. After making a few purchases, they sat down at the lunch counter, an area reserved for whites. Told that they could not be served, they remained in their seats until the store closed. They returned the next morning and the next. As the protest continued, other students, including a few local whites, joined in. Demonstrations spread across the country. After resisting for five months, Woolworth's in July agreed to serve black customers at its lunch counters.

The **sit-in** reflected mounting frustration at the slow pace of racial change. White Greensboro prided itself on being free of prejudice. In 1954, the city had been the first in the South to declare its intention of complying with the *Brown* decision. But by 1960 only a handful of black students had been admitted to all-white schools, the economic gap between blacks and whites had not narrowed, and Greensboro was still segregated.

More than any other event, the Greensboro sit-in launched the 1960s: a decade of political activism and social change. Sit-ins had occurred before, but never had they sparked so massive a response. Similar demonstrations soon took place throughout the South, demanding the integration not only of lunch counters but of parks, pools, restaurants, bowling alleys, libraries, and other facilities as well. By the end of 1960, some 70,000 demonstrators had taken part in sit-ins. Angry whites often assaulted them. But having been trained in nonviolent resistance, the protesters did not strike back.

Even more than elevating blacks to full citizenship, declared the writer James Baldwin, the civil rights movement challenged the United States to rethink "what it really means by freedom"—including whether freedom applied to all Americans or only to part of the population. With their freedom rides, freedom schools, freedom marches, and the insistent cry "Freedom now," black Americans and their white allies made freedom once again the rallying cry of the dispossessed. Thousands of ordinary men and women—maids and laborers alongside students, teachers, businessmen, and ministers—risked physical and economic retribution to lay claim to freedom. Their courage inspired a host of other challenges to the status quo, including a student movement known as the New Left, the "second wave" of feminism, and activism among other minorities.

By the time the decade ended, these movements had challenged the 1950s' understanding of freedom linked to the Cold War abroad and consumer choice at home. They exposed the limitations of traditional New Deal liberalism. They forced a reconsideration of the nation's foreign policy and extended claims to freedom into the most intimate areas of life. They made American society confront the fact that certain groups, including students, women, members of racial minorities, and homosexuals, felt themselves excluded from full enjoyment of American freedom.

Reflecting back years later on the struggles of the 1960s, one black organizer in Memphis remarked, "All I wanted to do was to live in a free country." Of the movement's accomplishments, he added, "You had to fight for every inch of it. Nobody gave you anything. Nothing."

FOCUS QUESTIONS

What were the major events in the civil rights movement of the early 1960s? –*p. 972*

What were the major crises and policy initiatives of the Kennedy presidency? –*p. 975*

What were the purposes and strategies of Johnson's Great Society programs? –*p. 978*

How did the civil rights movement change in the mid-1960s? –*p. 985*

How did the Vietnam War transform American politics and culture? –*p. 988*

What were the sources and significance of the rights revolution of the late 1960s? –*p. 1000*

In what ways was 1968 a climactic year for the Sixties? –*p. 1008*

An antiwar demonstrator offers a flower to military police stationed outside the Pentagon at a 1967 rally against the Vietnam War. Some 100,000 protesters took part in this demonstration.

THE CIVIL RIGHTS REVOLUTION

The Rising Tide of Protest

With the sit-ins, college students for the first time stepped onto the stage of American history as the leading force for social change. In April 1960, Ella Baker, a longtime civil rights organizer, called a meeting of young activists in Raleigh, North Carolina. About 200 black students and a few whites attended. Out of the gathering came the **Student Nonviolent Coordinating Committee** (SNCC), dedicated to replacing the culture of segregation with a "beloved community" of racial justice and to empowering ordinary blacks to take control of the decisions that affected their lives. "We can't count on adults," declared SNCC organizer Robert Moses. "Very few . . . are not afraid of the tremendous pressure they will face. This leaves the young people to be the organizers, the agents of social and political change."

Other forms of direct action soon followed the sit-ins. Blacks in Biloxi and Gulfport, Mississippi, engaged in "wade-ins," demanding access to segregated public beaches. Scores were arrested and two black teenagers were killed. In 1961, the Congress of Racial Equality (CORE) launched the **Freedom Rides**. Integrated groups traveled by bus into the Deep South to test compliance with court orders banning segregation on interstate buses and trains and in terminal facilities. Violent mobs assaulted them. Near Anniston, Alabama, a firebomb was thrown into the vehicle and the passengers beaten as they escaped. In Birmingham, Klansmen attacked riders with bats and chains, while police refused to intervene. Many of the Freedom Riders were arrested. But their actions led the Interstate Commerce Commission to order buses and terminals desegregated.

As protests escalated, so did the resistance of local authorities. Late in 1961, SNCC and other groups launched a campaign of nonviolent protests against racial discrimination in Albany, Georgia. The protests lasted a year, but despite filling the jails with demonstrators—a tactic adopted by the movement to gain national sympathy—they failed to achieve their goals. In September 1962, a court ordered the University of Mississippi to admit James Meredith, a black student. The state police stood aside as a mob, encouraged by Governor Ross Barnett, rampaged through the streets of Oxford, where the university is located. Two bystanders lost their lives in the riot. President Kennedy was forced to dispatch the army to restore order.

Birmingham

The high point of protest came in the spring of 1963, when demonstrations took place in towns and cities across the South, dramatizing black discontent over inequality in education, employment, and housing. In one week in June, there were more than 15,000 arrests in 186 cities. The dramatic culmination came in Birmingham, Alabama, a citadel of segregation. Even for the Deep South, Birmingham was a violent city—there had been over fifty bombings of black homes and institutions since World War II. Local blacks had been demonstrating, with no result, for greater economic opportunities and an end to segregation by local businesses.

Participants in a sit-in in Raleigh, North Carolina, in 1960. The protesters, probably students from a local college, brought books and newspapers to emphasize the seriousness of their intentions and their commitment to nonviolence.

With the movement flagging, some of its leaders invited Martin Luther King Jr. to come to Birmingham. While serving a nine-day prison term in April 1963 for violating a ban on demonstrations, King composed one of his most eloquent pleas for racial justice, the "Letter from Birmingham Jail." Responding to local clergymen who counseled patience, King related the litany of abuses faced by black southerners, from police brutality to the daily humiliation of having to explain to their children why they could not enter amusement parks or public swimming pools. The "white moderate," King declared, must put aside fear of disorder and commit himself to racial justice.

"Letter from Birmingham Jail"

In May, King made the bold decision to send black schoolchildren into the streets of Birmingham. Police chief Eugene "Bull" Connor unleashed his forces against the thousands of young marchers. The images, broadcast on television, of children being assaulted with nightsticks, high-pressure fire hoses, and attack dogs produced a wave of revulsion throughout the world and turned the Birmingham campaign into a triumph for the civil rights movement. It led President Kennedy, as will be related later, to endorse the movement's goals. Leading businessmen, fearing that the city was becoming an international symbol of brutality, brokered an end to the demonstrations that desegregated downtown stores and restaurants and promised that black salespeople would be hired.

But more than these modest gains, the events in Birmingham forced white Americans to decide whether they had more in common with fellow citizens demanding their basic rights or with violent segregationists. The question became more insistent in the following weeks. In June 1963, a sniper killed Medgar Evers, field secretary of the NAACP in Mississippi. In September, a bomb exploded at a black Baptist church in Birmingham, killing four young girls. (Not until 2002 was the last of those who committed this act of domestic terrorism tried and convicted.)

Civil rights demonstrators in Orangeburg, South Carolina, in 1960.

THE CIVIL RIGHTS REVOLUTION | 973

A fireman assaulting young African-American demonstrators with a high-pressure hose during the climactic demonstrations in Birmingham. Broadcast on television, such pictures proved a serious problem for the United States in its battle for the "hearts and minds" of people around the world and forced the Kennedy administration to confront the contradiction between the rhetoric of freedom and the reality of racism.

The March on Washington

Black and white alliance

On August 28, 1963, two weeks before the Birmingham church bombing, 250,000 black and white Americans converged on the nation's capital for the **March on Washington**, often considered the high point of the nonviolent civil rights movement. Organized by a coalition of civil rights, labor, and church organizations led by A. Philip Randolph, the black unionist who had threatened a similar march in 1941, it was the largest public demonstration in the nation's history to that time. Calls for the passage of a civil rights bill pending before Congress took center stage. But the march's goals also included a public-works program to reduce unemployment, an increase in the minimum wage, and a law barring discrimination in employment. These demands, and the marchers' slogan, "Jobs and Freedom," revealed how the black movement had, for the moment, forged an alliance with white liberal groups. On the steps of the Lincoln Memorial, King delivered his most famous speech, including the words, "I have a dream that one day this nation will rise up and live out the true meaning of its creed: 'We hold these truths to be self-evident, that all men are created equal.'"

Tension within civil rights movement

The March on Washington reflected an unprecedented degree of black-white cooperation in support of racial and economic justice. But it also revealed some of the movement's limitations, and the tensions within it. Even though female activists like Jo Ann Robinson and Ella Baker had played crucial roles in civil rights organizing, every speaker at the Lincoln Memorial was male. The organizers ordered SNCC leader John Lewis (later a congressman from Georgia) to tone down his speech, the original text of which called on blacks to "free ourselves of the chains of political and economic slavery" and march "through the heart of Dixie the way Sherman did . . . and burn Jim Crow to the ground." Lewis's rhetoric forecast the more militant turn many in the movement would soon be taking.

"Seek the freedom in 1963 promised in 1863," read one banner at the March on Washington. And civil rights activists resurrected the Civil War–era vision of national authority as the custodian of American freedom. Despite the fact that the federal government had for many decades promoted segregation, blacks' historical experience suggested that they had more hope for justice from national power than from local governments or civic institutions—home owners' associations, businesses, private clubs—still riddled with racism. It remained unclear whether the federal government would take up this responsibility.

Three participants in the 1963 March on Washington stand in front of the White House with signs invoking freedom and the memory of slavery.

THE KENNEDY YEARS

John F. Kennedy served as president for less than three years and, in domestic affairs, had few tangible accomplishments. But his administration is widely viewed today as a moment of youthful glamour, soaring hopes, and dynamic leadership at home and abroad. Later revelations of the sexual liaisons Kennedy obsessively pursued while in the White House have not significantly damaged his reputation among the general public.

Kennedy's inaugural address of January 1961 announced a watershed in American politics: "The torch has been passed," he declared, "to a new generation of Americans" who would "pay any price, bear any burden," to "assure the survival and success of liberty." The speech seemed to urge Americans to move beyond the self-centered consumer culture of the 1950s: "Ask not what your country can do for you; ask what you can do for your country." But while the sit-ins were by now a year old, the speech said nothing about segregation or race. At the outset of his presidency, Kennedy regarded civil rights as a distraction from his main concern— vigorous conduct of the Cold War.

"The torch has been passed"

Kennedy and the World

Kennedy's agenda envisioned new initiatives aimed at countering communist influence in the world. One of his administration's first acts was to establish the Peace Corps, which sent young Americans abroad to aid in the economic and educational progress of developing countries and to improve the image of the United States there. By 1966, more than 15,000 young men and women were serving as Peace Corps volunteers. When the Soviets in April 1961 launched a satellite carrying the first man into orbit around the earth, Kennedy announced that the United States would mobilize its resources to land a man on the moon by the end of the decade. The goal seemed almost impossible when announced, but it was stunningly accomplished in 1969.

The Peace Corps

Kennedy also formulated a new policy toward Latin America, the Alliance for Progress. A kind of Marshall Plan for the Western Hemisphere, although involving far smaller sums of money, it aimed, Kennedy said, to promote both "political" and "material freedom." Begun in 1961 with much fanfare about alleviating poverty and counteracting the appeal of communism, the Alliance for Progress failed. Unlike the Marshall Plan, military regimes and local elites controlled Alliance for Progress aid. They enriched themselves while the poor saw little benefit.

Kennedy as Cold Warrior

Like his predecessors, Kennedy viewed the entire world through the lens of the Cold War. This outlook shaped his dealings with Fidel Castro, who had led a revolution that in 1959 ousted Cuban dictator Fulgencio Batista. Until Castro took power, Cuba was an economic dependency of the United States. When his government began nationalizing American landholdings and other investments and signed an agreement to sell sugar to the Soviet Union, the Eisenhower administration suspended trade and diplomatic relations with the island. The CIA began training anti-Castro exiles for an invasion of Cuba.

The Bay of Pigs disaster

In April 1961, Kennedy allowed the CIA to launch its invasion, at a site known as the Bay of Pigs. Military advisers predicted a popular uprising that would quickly topple the Castro government. But the **Bay of Pigs invasion** proved to be a total failure. Of 1,400 invaders, more than 100 were killed and 1,100 captured. Cuba became ever more closely tied to the Soviet Union. The Kennedy administration tried other methods, including assassination attempts, to get rid of Castro's government.

The Missile Crisis

Meanwhile, relations between the two "superpowers" deteriorated. In August 1961, in order to stem a growing tide of emigrants fleeing from East to West Berlin, the Soviets constructed a wall separating the two parts of the city. Until its demolition in 1989, the Berlin Wall would stand as a tangible symbol of the Cold War and the division of Europe.

The most dangerous crisis of the Kennedy administration, and in many ways of the entire Cold War, came in October 1962, when American spy planes discovered that the Soviet Union was installing missiles in Cuba capable of reaching the United States with nuclear weapons. Rejecting advice from military leaders that he authorize an attack on Cuba, which would almost certainly have triggered a Soviet response in Berlin and perhaps a nuclear war, Kennedy imposed a block-

The Cuba blockade

ade, or "quarantine," of the island and demanded the missiles' removal. After tense behind-the-scenes negotiations, Soviet premier Nikita Khrushchev agreed to withdraw the missiles; Kennedy pledged that the United States would not invade Cuba and secretly agreed to remove American Jupiter missiles from Turkey, from which they could reach the Soviet Union.

For thirteen days, the world teetered on the brink of all-out nuclear war. The **Cuban missile crisis** seems to have lessened Kennedy's passion for the Cold War. Indeed, he appears to have been shocked by the casual way military leaders spoke of "winning" a nuclear exchange in which tens of millions of Americans and Russians were certain to die. In 1963, Kennedy moved to reduce Cold War tensions. In a speech at American University, he called for greater cooperation with the

The test-ban treaty

Soviets. That summer, the two countries agreed to a treaty banning the testing of nuclear weapons in the atmosphere and in space. In announcing the agreement, Kennedy paid tribute to the small movement against nuclear weapons that had been urging such a ban for several years. He even sent word to Castro through a journalist that he desired a more constructive relationship with Cuba.

James Meredith, the first black student to attend the University of Mississippi, in a classroom where white classmates refused to sit near him.

Kennedy and Civil Rights

In his first two years in office, Kennedy was preoccupied with foreign policy. But in 1963, the crisis over civil rights eclipsed other concerns. Until then, Kennedy had been reluctant to take a forceful stand on black demands. He seemed to share FBI director J. Edgar Hoover's fear that the movement was inspired by communism. Attorney General Robert F. Kennedy, the president's brother, approved FBI wiretaps on King. Despite promising during the 1960 campaign to ban discrimination in federally assisted housing, Kennedy waited until the end of 1962 to issue the order. He used federal force when obstruction of the law became acute, as at the University of Mississippi. But he failed to protect civil rights workers from violence, insisting that law enforcement was a local matter.

Events in Birmingham in May 1963 forced Kennedy's hand. Kennedy realized that the United States simply could not declare itself the champion of freedom throughout the world while maintaining a system of racial inequality at home. In June, he went on national television to call for the passage of a law banning discrimination in all places of public accommodation, a major goal of the civil rights movement. The nation, he asserted, faced a moral crisis: "We preach freedom around the world, . . . but are we to say to the world, and much more importantly, to each other, that this is a land of the free except for Negroes?"

The impact of Birmingham

Kennedy did not live to see his civil rights bill enacted. On November 22, 1963, while riding in a motorcade through Dallas, Texas, he was shot and killed. Most likely, the assassin was Lee Harvey Oswald, a troubled former marine. Partly because Oswald was murdered two days later by a local nightclub owner while in police custody, speculation about a possible conspiracy continues to this day. In any event, Kennedy's death brought an abrupt and utterly unexpected end to his presidency. As with Pearl Harbor or September 11, 2001, an entire generation would always recall the moment when they first heard the news of Kennedy's death. It

Kennedy assassination

New York City train passengers reading the news of President Kennedy's assassination, November 22, 1963.

fell to his successor, Lyndon B. Johnson, to secure passage of the civil rights bill and to launch a program of domestic liberalism far more ambitious than anything Kennedy had envisioned.

LYNDON JOHNSON'S PRESIDENCY

Unlike John F. Kennedy, raised in a wealthy and powerful family, Lyndon Johnson grew up in one of the poorest parts of the United States, the central Texas hill country. Kennedy seemed to view success as his birthright; Johnson had to struggle ferociously to achieve wealth and power. By the 1950s, he had risen to become majority leader of the U.S. Senate. But Johnson never forgot the poor Mexican and white children he had taught in a Texas school in the early 1930s. Far more interested than Kennedy in domestic reform, he continued to hold the New Deal view that government had an obligation to assist less-fortunate members of society.

The Civil Rights Act of 1964

When he became president, nobody expected that Johnson would make the passage of civil rights legislation his first order of business or that he would come to identify himself with the black movement more passionately than any previous president. Just five days after Kennedy's assassination, however, Johnson called on Congress to enact the civil rights bill as the most fitting memorial to his slain predecessor. "We have talked long enough about equal rights in this country," he declared. "It is now time to write the next chapter and write it in the books of law."

In 1964, Congress passed the **Civil Rights Act**, which prohibited racial discrimination in employment, institutions like hospitals and schools, and privately owned public accommodations such as restaurants, hotels, and theaters. It also banned discrimination on the grounds of sex—a provision added by opponents of civil rights in an effort to derail the entire bill and embraced by liberal and female members of Congress as a way to broaden its scope. Johnson knew that many whites opposed the new law. After signing it, he turned to an aide and remarked, "I think we delivered the South to the Republican Party."

Lyndon B. Johnson being sworn in as president on the plane taking him to Washington from Dallas. On the left is Lady Bird Johnson, and on the right, Jacqueline Kennedy.

Freedom Summer

The 1964 law did not address a major concern of the civil rights movement—the right to vote in the South. That summer, a coalition of civil rights groups, including SNCC, CORE, and the NAACP, launched a voter registration drive in Mississippi.

Hundreds of white college students from the North traveled to the state to take part in Freedom Summer. An outpouring of violence greeted the campaign, including thirty-five bombings and numerous beatings of civil rights workers. In June, three young activists—Michael Schwerner and Andrew Goodman, white students from the North, and James Chaney, a local black youth—were kidnapped by a group headed by a deputy sheriff and murdered near Philadelphia, Mississippi. Between 1961 and 1965, an estimated twenty-five black civil rights workers paid with their lives. But the deaths of the two white students focused unprecedented attention on Mississippi and on the apparent inability of the federal government to protect citizens seeking to enjoy their constitutional rights. (In June 2005, forty-one years after Freedom Summer, a Mississippi jury convicted a member of the Ku Klux Klan of manslaughter in the deaths of the three civil rights workers.)

> *Violence against campaign*

Freedom Summer led directly to one of the most dramatic confrontations of the civil rights era—the campaign by the Mississippi Freedom Democratic Party (MFDP) to take the seats of the state's all-white official party at the 1964 Democratic national convention in Atlantic City, New Jersey. With blacks unable to participate in the activities of the Democratic Party or register to vote, the civil rights movement in Mississippi had created the MFDP, open to all residents of the state. At televised hearings before the credentials committee, Fannie Lou Hamer of the MFDP held a national audience spellbound with her account of growing up in poverty in the Yazoo-Mississippi Delta and of the savage beatings she had endured at the hands of police. Like many other black activists, Hamer was a deeply religious person who believed that Christianity rested on the idea of freedom and that the movement had been divinely inspired. "Is this America," she asked, "the land of the free and home of the brave, where . . . we [are] threatened daily because we want to live as decent human beings?" Johnson feared a southern walkout, as had happened at the 1948 party convention, if the MFDP were seated. Party liberals, including Johnson's

> *The MFDP*

> *Fannie Lou Hamer*

Two students at a Freedom School in Mississippi, photographed in 1964.

running mate, Hubert Humphrey, pressed for a compromise in which two black delegates would be granted seats. But the MFDP rejected the proposal.

The 1964 Election

The events at Atlantic City severely weakened black activists' faith in the responsiveness of the political system and forecast the impending breakup of the coalition between the civil rights movement and the liberal wing of the Democratic Party. For the moment, however, the movement rallied behind Johnson's campaign for reelection. Johnson's opponent, Senator Barry Goldwater of Arizona, had published *The Conscience of a Conservative* (1960), which sold more than 3 million copies. The book demanded a more aggressive conduct of the Cold War (he even suggested that nuclear war might be "the price of freedom"). But Goldwater directed most of his critique against "internal" dangers to freedom, especially the New Deal welfare state, which he believed stifled individual initiative and independence. He called for the substitution of private charity for public welfare programs and Social Security, and the abolition of the graduated income tax. Goldwater had voted against the Civil Rights Act of 1964. His acceptance speech at the Republican national convention contained the explosive statement, "Extremism in the defense of liberty is no vice."

Barry Goldwater's platform

Stigmatized by the Democrats as an extremist who would repeal Social Security and risk nuclear war, Goldwater went down to a disastrous defeat. Johnson received almost 43 million votes to Goldwater's 27 million. Democrats swept to two-to-one majorities in both houses of Congress. But although few realized it, the 1964 campaign marked a milestone in the resurgence of American conservatism. Goldwater's success in the Deep South, where he carried five states, coupled with the surprisingly strong showing of segregationist governor George Wallace of Alabama in Democratic primaries in Wisconsin, Indiana, and Maryland, suggested that politicians could strike electoral gold by appealing to white opposition to the civil rights movement.

Social conservatism in the South

One indication of problems for the Democrats came in California, with the passage by popular referendum of Proposition 14, which repealed a 1963 law banning racial discrimination in the sale of real estate. Backed by the state's realtors and developers, California conservatives made the "freedom" of home owners to control their property the rallying cry of the campaign against the fair housing law. Although Johnson carried California by more than 1 million votes, Proposition 14 received a considerable majority, winning three-fourths of the votes cast by whites.

The Conservative Sixties

The 1960s, today recalled as a decade of radicalism, clearly had a conservative side as well. With the founding in 1960 of Young Americans for Freedom (YAF), conservative students emerged as a force in politics. There were striking parallels between the Sharon Statement, issued by ninety young people

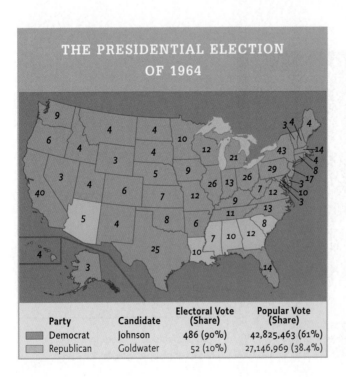

THE PRESIDENTIAL ELECTION OF 1964

Party	Candidate	Electoral Vote (Share)	Popular Vote (Share)
Democrat	Johnson	486 (90%)	42,825,463 (61%)
Republican	Goldwater	52 (10%)	27,146,969 (38.4%)

Ronald Reagan and his wife Nancy, at the center, along with popular singer Pat Boone, next to a replica of the Statue of Liberty, at an anticommunist "youth night" in Los Angeles in 1961. At this event, Boone made the widely circulated remark that he would rather have his four daughters shot than see them live under communism.

who gathered at the estate of conservative intellectual William F. Buckley in Sharon, Connecticut, to establish YAF, and the Port Huron Statement of SDS of 1962 (discussed later in this chapter). Both manifestos portrayed youth as the cutting edge of a new radicalism, and both claimed to offer a route to greater freedom. The Sharon Statement summarized beliefs that had circulated among conservatives during the past decade—the free market underpinned "personal freedom," government must be strictly limited, and "international communism," the gravest threat to liberty, must be destroyed.

> **The Sharon Statement**

YAF aimed initially to take control of the Republican Party from leaders who had made their peace with the New Deal and seemed willing to coexist with communism. YAF members became Barry Goldwater's shock troops in 1964. Despite his landslide defeat in the general election, Goldwater's nomination was a remarkable triumph for a movement widely viewed as composed of fanatics out to "repeal the twentieth century."

Goldwater also brought new constituencies to the conservative cause. His campaign aroused enthusiasm in the rapidly expanding suburbs of southern California and the Southwest. Orange County, California, many of whose residents had recently arrived from the East and Midwest and worked in defense-related industries, became a nationally known center of grassroots conservative activism. The funds that poured into the Goldwater campaign from the Sunbelt's oilmen and aerospace entrepreneurs established a new financial base for conservatism. And by carrying five states of the Deep South, Goldwater showed that the civil rights revolution had redrawn the nation's political map, opening the door to a "southern strategy" that would eventually lead the entire region into the Republican Party.

> **Conservative strength**

Well before the rise of Black Power, a reaction against civil rights gains offered conservatives new opportunities and threatened the stability of the Democratic coalition. During the 1950s, many conservatives had responded favorably to southern whites'

A white resident of Selma offers her support to civil rights demonstrators. The woman is Martha Jackson Ross, a native of Selma then living with her husband and six children in Maryland, who traveled alone to support the march.

condemnation of the *Brown v. Board of Education* desegregation decision as an invasion of states' rights. The *National Review,* an influential conservative magazine, referred to whites as "the advanced race" and defended black disenfranchisement on the grounds that "the claims of civilization supersede those of universal suffrage." In 1962, YAF bestowed its Freedom Award on Senator Strom Thurmond of South Carolina, one of the country's most prominent segregationists. During the 1960s, most conservatives abandoned talk of racial superiority and inferiority. But conservative appeals to law and order, "freedom of association," and the evils of welfare often had strong racial overtones. Racial divisions would prove to be a political gold mine for conservatives.

The Voting Rights Act

One last legislative triumph, however, lay ahead for the civil rights movement. In January 1965, King launched a voting rights campaign in Selma, Alabama, a city where only 355 of 15,000 black residents had been allowed to register to vote. In March, defying a ban by Governor Wallace, King attempted to lead a march from Selma to the state capital, Montgomery. When the marchers reached the bridge leading out of the city, state police assaulted them with cattle prods, whips, and tear gas.

Once again, violence against nonviolent demonstrators flashed across television screens throughout the world, compelling the federal government to take action. Calling Selma a milestone in "man's unending search for freedom," Johnson asked Congress to enact a law securing the right to vote. He closed his speech by quoting the demonstrators' song, "We Shall Overcome." Never before had the movement received so powerful an endorsement from the federal government. Congress quickly passed the **Voting Rights Act** of 1965, which allowed federal officials to register voters. Black southerners finally regained the suffrage that had been stripped from them at the turn of the twentieth century. In addition, the Twenty-fourth Amendment to the Constitution outlawed the poll tax, which had long prevented poor blacks (and some whites) from voting in the South.

A sharecropper's shack alongside Jefferson Davis Highway, the route followed from Selma to Montgomery, Alabama, in 1965, by marchers demanding voting rights. The photograph, by James "Spider" Martin, who chronicled the march, suggests the deep-seated inequalities that persisted a century after the end of the Civil War.

Immigration Reform

By 1965, the civil rights movement had succeeded in eradicating the legal bases of second-class citizenship. The belief that racism should no longer serve as a foundation of public policy spilled over into other realms. In 1965, the **Hart-Celler Act** abandoned the national-origins quota system of immigration, which had excluded Asians and severely restricted southern and eastern Europeans. The law established new, racially neutral criteria for immigration, notably family reunification and possession of skills in demand in the United States. On the other hand, because of growing hostility in the Southwest to Mexican immigration, the law established the first limit, 120,000, on newcomers from the Western Hemisphere. This created, for the first time, the category of "illegal aliens" from the Americas. Indeed, since the act set a maximum annual immigration quota of 20,000 persons for every country in the world, it guaranteed that a large part of Mexican immigration would be unauthorized, since labor demand for Mexican immigrants in the United States far exceeded that number. Establishing the same quota for Mexico and, say, Belgium or New Zealand made no sense. The act set the quota for the rest of the world at 170,000. However, because of special provisions for refugees from communist countries, immigration soon exceeded these caps.

The new law had many unexpected results. At the time, immigrants represented only 5 percent of the American population—the lowest proportion since the 1830s. No one anticipated that the new quotas not only would lead to an explosive rise in immigration but also would spark a dramatic shift in which newcomers from Latin America, the Caribbean, and Asia came to outnumber those from Europe. Taken together, the civil rights revolution and immigration reform marked the triumph of a pluralist conception of Americanism. By 1976, 85 percent of respondents to a public-opinion survey agreed with the statement, "The United States was meant to be . . . a country made up of many races, religions, and nationalities."

> *New wave of immigration*

The Great Society

After his landslide victory of 1964, Johnson outlined the most sweeping proposal for governmental action to promote the general welfare since the New Deal. Johnson's initiatives of 1965–1967, known collectively as the **Great Society**, provided health services to the poor and elderly in the new Medicaid and Medicare programs and poured federal funds into education and urban development. New cabinet offices—the Departments of Transportation and of Housing and Urban Development—and new agencies, such as the Equal Employment Opportunity Commission, the National Endowments for the Humanities and for the Arts, and a national public broadcasting network, were created. These measures greatly expanded the powers of the federal government, and they completed and extended the social agenda (with the exception of national health insurance) that had been stalled in Congress since 1938.

> *Medicaid and Medicare*

Unlike the New Deal, however, the Great Society was a response to prosperity, not depression. The mid-1960s was a time of rapid economic expansion, fueled by increased government spending and a tax cut on individuals and businesses initially proposed by Kennedy and enacted in 1964. Johnson and Democratic liberals believed that economic growth made it possible to fund ambitious new government programs and to improve the quality of life.

The War on Poverty

The centerpiece of the Great Society, however, was the crusade to eradicate poverty, launched by Johnson early in 1964. After the talk of universal affluence during the 1950s, economic deprivation had been rediscovered by political leaders, thanks in part to Michael Harrington's 1962 book *The Other America*. Harrington revealed that 40 to 50 million Americans lived in poverty, often in isolated rural areas or urban slums "invisible" to the middle class. The civil rights movement heightened the urgency of the issue, even though, as Harrington made clear, whites made up a majority of the nation's poor.

During the 1930s, Democrats had attributed poverty to an imbalance of economic power and flawed economic institutions. In the 1960s, the administration

As part of his War on Poverty, President Lyndon Johnson visited Appalachia, one of the poorest places in the United States.

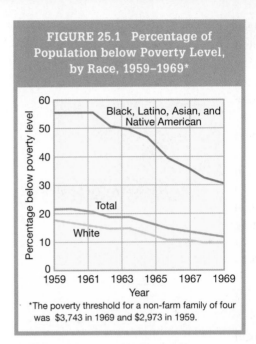

Percentage below poverty level

Black, Latino, Asian, and Native American

Total

White

Year

*The poverty threshold for a non-farm family of four was $3,743 in 1969 and $2,973 in 1959.

During the 1960s, an expanding economy and government programs assisting the poor produced a steady decrease in the percentage of Americans living in poverty.

Johnson's vision

attributed it to an absence of skills and a lack of proper attitudes and work habits. Thus, the **War on Poverty** did not consider the most direct ways of eliminating poverty—guaranteeing an annual income for all Americans, creating jobs for the unemployed, promoting the spread of unionization, or making it more difficult for businesses to shift production to the low-wage South or overseas. Nor did it address the economic changes that were reducing the number of well-paid manufacturing jobs and leaving poor families in rural areas like Appalachia and decaying urban ghettos with little hope of economic advancement.

One of the Great Society's most popular and successful components, food stamps, offered direct aid to the poor. But, in general, the War on Poverty concentrated on equipping the poor with skills and rebuilding their spirit and motivation. The new Office of Economic Opportunity oversaw a series of initiatives designed to lift the poor into the social and economic mainstream. It provided Head Start (an early childhood education program), job training, legal services, and scholarships for poor college students. It also created VISTA, a domestic version of the Peace Corps for the inner cities. In an echo of SNCC's philosophy of empowering ordinary individuals to take control of their lives, the War on Poverty required that poor people play a leading part in the design and implementation of local policies, a recipe for continuing conflict with local political leaders accustomed to controlling the flow of federal dollars.

Freedom and Equality

Johnson defended the Great Society in a vocabulary of freedom derived from the New Deal, when his own political career began, and reinforced by the civil rights movement. Soon after assuming office in 1963, he resurrected the phrase "freedom from want," all but forgotten during the 1950s. Echoing FDR, Johnson told the 1964 Democratic convention, "The man who is hungry, who cannot find work or educate his children, who is bowed by want, that man is not fully free." Recognizing that black poverty was fundamentally different from white, since its roots lay in "past injustice and present prejudice," Johnson sought to redefine the relationship between freedom and equality. Economic liberty, he insisted, meant more than equal opportunity: "You do not wipe away the scars of centuries by saying: Now you are free to go where you want, do as you desire, and choose the leaders you please. . . . We seek . . . not just equality as a right and a theory, but equality as a fact and as a result."

Johnson's Great Society may not have achieved equality "as a fact." But it represented the most expansive effort in the nation's history to mobilize the powers of the national government to address the needs of the least-advantaged Americans, especially those, like blacks, largely excluded from the original New Deal entitlements such as Social Security.

Coupled with the decade's high rate of economic growth, the War on Poverty succeeded in reducing the incidence of poverty from 22 percent to 13 percent of American families during the 1960s. It has fluctuated around the latter figure ever since. The sum spent, however, was too low to end poverty altogether or to transform conditions of life in poor urban neighborhoods. Today, thanks to the civil rights movement and the Great Society, the historic gap between whites and blacks in education, income, and access to skilled employment has narrowed considerably. But with deindustrialization and urban decay affecting numerous families, the median wealth of white households remains ten times greater than that of blacks, and nearly a quarter of all black children still lives in poverty.

THE CHANGING BLACK MOVEMENT

Even at its moment of triumph, the civil rights movement confronted a crisis as it sought to move from access to schools, public accommodations, and the voting booth to the economic divide separating blacks from other Americans. In the mid-1960s, economic issues rose to the forefront of the civil rights agenda. Violent outbreaks in black ghettos outside the South drew attention to the national scope of racial injustice and to inequalities in jobs, education, and housing that the dismantling of legal segregation left intact. Much of the animosity that came to characterize race relations arose from the belief of many whites that the legislation of 1964 and 1965 had fulfilled the nation's obligation to assure blacks equality before the law, while blacks pushed for more government action, sparking charges of "reverse discrimination."

"Reverse discrimination"

The Ghetto Uprisings

The first riots—really, battles between angry blacks and the predominantly white police (widely seen by many ghetto residents as an occupying army)—erupted in Harlem in 1964. Far larger was the Watts uprising of 1965, which took place in the black ghetto of Los Angeles only days after Johnson signed the Voting Rights Act. An estimated 50,000 persons took part in this "rebellion," attacking police

A semblance of normal life resumes amid the rubble of the Watts uprising of August 1965.

Betye Saar's 1972 installation, *The Liberation of Aunt Jemima*, illustrates modes of thought associated with Black Power. Quaker Oats Company has long used an image of a black woman reminiscent of the stereotypical slave "mammy" as a symbol for its brand of pancake mix. Saar gives Aunt Jemima a rifle to go along with her broom. In front of her is another Aunt Jemima, holding a light-skinned baby, a symbol, according to the artist, of the sexual exploitation of black women by white men. Images in the background reveal how Quaker Oats had already modified its advertising image, giving her a smaller kerchief and an Afro hairdo. By the end of the twentieth century, the kerchief had disappeared entirely, and Aunt Jemima had become slimmer and younger and was not smiling quite so broadly.

a change in language and fashion. They reflected a new sense of racial pride and a rejection of white norms.

Inspired by the idea of black self-determination, SNCC and CORE repudiated their previous interracialism, and new militant groups sprang into existence. Most prominent of the new groups, in terms of publicity, if not numbers, was the Black Panther Party. Founded in Oakland, California, in 1966, it became notorious for advocating armed self-defense in response to police brutality. It demanded the release of black prisoners because of racism in the criminal justice system. The party's youthful members alarmed whites by wearing military garb, although they also ran health clinics, schools, and children's breakfast programs. But internal disputes and a campaign against the Black Panthers by police and the FBI, which left several leaders dead in shootouts, destroyed the organization.

By 1967, with the escalation of U.S. military involvement in Vietnam, the War on Poverty ground to a halt. By then, with ghetto uprisings punctuating the urban landscape, the antiwar movement assuming massive proportions, and millions of young people ostentatiously rejecting mainstream values, American society faced its greatest crisis since the Depression.

VIETNAM AND THE NEW LEFT

Old and New Lefts

To most Americans, the rise of a protest movement among white youth came as a complete surprise. For most of the century, colleges had been conservative institutions that drew their students from a privileged segment of the population. During the 1950s, young people had been called a "silent generation." If blacks' grievances appeared self-evident, those of white college students were difficult to understand. What persuaded large numbers of children of affluence to reject the values and institutions of their society? In part, the answer lay in a redefinition of the meaning of freedom by what came to be called the **New Left**.

What made the New Left new was its rejection of the intellectual and political categories that had shaped radicalism and liberalism for most of the twentieth century. It challenged not only mainstream America but also what it dismissively called the Old Left. Unlike the Communist Party, it did not take the Soviet Union as a model or see the working class as the main agent of social change. Instead of economic equality and social citizenship, the language of New Deal liberals, the New Left spoke of loneliness, isolation, and alienation, of powerlessness in the face of bureaucratic institutions and a hunger for authenticity that affluence could not provide. These discontents galvanized a mass movement among what was rapidly becoming a major sector of the American population. By 1968, thanks to the coming of age of the baby-boom generation and the growing number of jobs that required post–high school skills, more than 7 million students attended college, more than the number of farmers or steelworkers.

The New Left was not as new as it claimed. Its call for a democracy of citizen participation harked back to the American Revolution, and its critique of the contrast between American values and American reality, to the abolitionists. Its

Members of Students for a Democratic Society (SDS) in a University of Delaware yearbook photo. Despite their raised fists, they appear eminently respectable compared to radicals who emerged later in the decade. The group is entirely white.

emphasis on authenticity in the face of conformity recalled the bohemians of the years before World War I, and its critique of consumer culture drew inspiration from 1950s writers on mass society. But the New Left's greatest inspiration was the black freedom movement. More than any other event, the sit-ins catalyzed white student activism.

Here was the unlikely combination that created the upheaval known as the Sixties—the convergence of society's most excluded members demanding full access to all its benefits, with the children of the middle class rejecting the social mainstream. The black movement and white New Left shared basic assumptions—that the evils to be corrected were deeply embedded in social institutions and that only direct confrontation could persuade Americans of the urgency of far-reaching change.

An unlikely coalition

The Fading Consensus

The years 1962 and 1963 witnessed the appearance of several pathbreaking books that challenged one or another aspect of the 1950s consensus. James Baldwin's *The Fire Next Time* gave angry voice to the black revolution. Rachel Carson's *Silent Spring* exposed the environmental costs of economic growth. Michael Harrington's *The Other America* revealed the persistence of poverty amid plenty. *The Death and Life of Great American Cities*, by Jane Jacobs, criticized urban renewal, the removal of the poor from city centers, and the destruction of neighborhoods to build highways, accommodating cities to the needs of drivers rather than pedestrians. What made cities alive, she insisted, was density and diversity, the social interaction of people of different backgrounds encountering each other on urban streets.

Pivotal books

Secretary of Defense Robert McNamara, on the left, and his deputy, Cyrus Vance, at a May 1965 meeting at the White House where the war in Vietnam was discussed. A bust of President Kennedy stands in the background. McNamara later wrote in his memoirs that his misgivings only grew as the war progressed.

Gulf of Tonkin resolution

Intervention in the Dominican Republic

a military coup that led to Diem's death. When Kennedy was assassinated the following month, there were 17,000 American military advisers in South Vietnam. Shortly before his death, according to the notes of a White House meeting, Kennedy questioned "the wisdom of involvement in Vietnam." But he took no action to end the American presence.

Lyndon Johnson's War

Lyndon B. Johnson came to the presidency with little experience in foreign relations. Johnson had misgivings about sending American troops to Vietnam. But he was an adept politician and knew that Republicans had used the "loss" of China as a weapon against Truman. "I am not going to be the president," he vowed, "who saw Southeast Asia go the way China went."

In August 1964, North Vietnamese vessels encountered an American ship on a spy mission off its coast. When North Vietnamese patrol boats fired on the American vessel, Johnson proclaimed that the United States was a victim of "aggression." In response, Congress passed the **Gulf of Tonkin resolution**, authorizing the president to take "all necessary measures to repel armed attack" in Vietnam. Only two members—Senators Ernest Gruening of Alaska and Wayne Morse of Oregon—voted against giving Johnson this blank check. The nearest the United States ever came to a formal declaration of war, the resolution passed without any discussion of American goals and strategy in Vietnam.

During the 1964 campaign, Johnson insisted that he had no intention of sending American troops to Vietnam. But immediately after Johnson's reelection, the National Security Council recommended that the United States begin air strikes against North Vietnam and introduce American ground troops in the south. When the Viet Cong in February 1965 attacked an American air base in South Vietnam, Johnson put the plan into effect. At almost the same time, he intervened in the Dominican Republic. Here, military leaders in 1963 had overthrown the left-wing but noncommunist Juan Bosch, the country's first elected president since 1924. In April 1965, another group of military men attempted to restore Bosch to power but were defeated by the ruling junta. Fearing the unrest would lead to "another Cuba," Johnson dispatched 22,000 American troops. The intervention outraged many Latin Americans. But the operation's success seemed to bolster Johnson's determination in Vietnam.

By 1968, the number of American troops in Vietnam exceeded half a million, and the conduct of the war had become more and more brutal. The North Vietnamese mistreated American prisoners of war held in a camp known sardonically by the inmates as the Hanoi Hilton. (One prisoner of war, John McCain, who

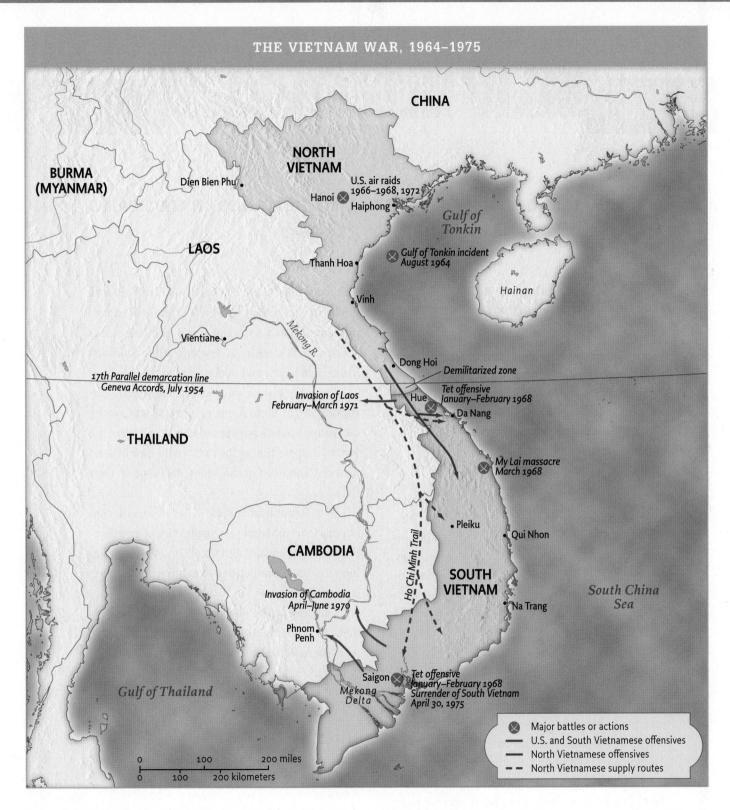

THE VIETNAM WAR, 1964–1975

CHINA

NORTH VIETNAM

BURMA (MYANMAR)

Dien Bien Phu

U.S. air raids 1966–1968, 1972

Hanoi Haiphong

Gulf of Tonkin

LAOS

Thanh Hoa

Gulf of Tonkin incident August 1964

Hainan

Vinh

Mekong R.

Vientiane

Dong Hoi

Demilitarized zone

17th Parallel demarcation line Geneva Accords, July 1954

Tet offensive January–February 1968

Invasion of Laos February–March 1971

Hue

Da Nang

THAILAND

My Lai massacre March 1968

Pleiku

Qui Nhon

CAMBODIA

Ho Chi Minh Trail

SOUTH VIETNAM

South China Sea

Invasion of Cambodia April–June 1970

Na Trang

Phnom Penh

Saigon

Tet offensive January–February 1968 Surrender of South Vietnam April 30, 1975

Gulf of Thailand

Mekong Delta

⊗	Major battles or actions
—	U.S. and South Vietnamese offensives
—	North Vietnamese offensives
- - -	North Vietnamese supply routes

0   100   200 miles
0   100   200 kilometers

A war of aerial bombing and small guerrilla skirmishes rather than fixed land battles, at the time it was fought, Vietnam was among the longest wars in American history and the only one the United States has lost.

VOICES OF FREEDOM

From BARRY GOLDWATER, SPEECH AT REPUBLICAN NATIONAL CONVENTION (1964)

In his speech accepting the Republican nomination for president in 1964, Senator Barry Goldwater of Arizona outlined a political vision rooted in the conservatism of the Southwest and California. Charged with being an extremist, Goldwater responded, "Extremism in the defense of liberty is no vice," an explosive statement that enabled President Lyndon Johnson to portray him as a dangerous radical.

My fellow Americans, the tide has been running against freedom. Our people have followed false prophets. We must, and we shall, return to proven ways—not because they are old, but because they are true. We must, and we shall, set the tide running again in the cause of freedom. And this party, with its every action, every word, every breath, and every heartbeat, has but a single resolve, and that is freedom—freedom made orderly for this Nation by our constitutional government; freedom under a government limited by laws of nature and of nature's God; freedom—balanced so that liberty lacking order will not become the slavery of the prison cell; balanced so that liberty lacking order will not become the license of the mob and of the jungle.

Now, we Americans understand freedom. We have earned it, we have lived for it, and we have died for it. This Nation and its people are freedom's model in a searching world. We can be freedom's missionaries in a doubting world. But, ladies and gentlemen, first we must renew freedom's mission in our own hearts and in our own homes. . . .

Tonight there is violence in our streets, corruption in our highest offices, aimlessness among our youth, anxiety among our elders and there is a virtual despair among the many who look beyond material success for the inner meaning of their lives. . . .

We Republicans seek a government that attends to its inherent responsibilities of maintaining a stable monetary and fiscal climate, encouraging a free and a competitive economy and enforcing law and order. . . .

Our towns and our cities, then our counties, then our states, then our regional contacts and only then, the national government. That, let me remind you, is the ladder of liberty, built by decentralized power. On it also we must have balance between the branches of government at every level. . . .

I would remind you that extremism in the defense of liberty is no vice. And let me remind you also that moderation in the pursuit of justice is no virtue.

From STATEMENT OF PURPOSE, NATIONAL ORGANIZATION FOR WOMEN (1966)

Founded in 1966, the National Organization for Women gave voice to the movement for equality for women known as the "second wave" of feminism. Written by Betty Friedan, and adopted at the group's organizing meeting in Washington, D.C., the statement of purpose outlined a wide range of areas, public and private, where women continued to be denied full freedom.

The time has come for a new movement toward true equality for all women in America, and toward a fully equal partnership of the sexes, as part of the worldwide revolution of human rights now taking place within and beyond our national borders.

The purpose of NOW is to take action to bring women into full participation in the mainstream of American society now, exercising all the privileges and responsibilities thereof in truly equal partnership with men. . . .

We organize to initiate or support action, nationally, or in any part of this nation, by individuals or organizations, to break through the silken curtain of prejudice and discrimination against women in government, industry, and professions, the churches, the political parties, the judiciary, the labor unions, in education, science, medicine, law, religion and every other field of importance in American society. . . .

The actual position of women in the United States has declined, and is declining, to an alarming degree throughout the 1950's and '60s. . . . Working women are becoming increasingly—not less—concentrated on the bottom of the job ladder. . . . Today, women earn only one in three of the B.A.'s and M.A.'s granted, and one in ten of the Ph.D.'s.

In all the professions considered of importance to society, and in the executive ranks of industry and government, women are losing ground. Where they are present it is only a token handful. Women comprise less than 1% of federal judges; less than 4% of all lawyers; 7% of doctors. . . .

We do not accept the traditional assumption that a woman has to choose between marriage and motherhood, on the one hand, and serious participation in industry or the professions on the other. . . . True equality of opportunity and freedom of choice for women requires such practical, and possible innovations as a nationwide network of child-care centers which will make it unnecessary for women to retire completely from society until their children are grown. . . .

We believe that a true partnership between the sexes demands a different concept of marriage and equitable sharing of the responsibilities of home and children and of the economic burdens of their support. We believe that proper recognition should be given to the economic and social value of homemaking and childcare. . . .

QUESTIONS

1. *Why does Goldwater stress the interconnection of order and liberty?*

2. *What social changes does NOW believe necessary to enable women to enjoy equality and freedom?*

3. *How do the two documents differ in assessing the dangers to American freedom?*

American soldiers in South Vietnam carrying wounded men to safety after a 1966 battle.

spent six years there, courageously refused to be exchanged unless his companions were freed with him. McCain later became a senator from Arizona and the Republican candidate for president in 2008.) American planes dropped more tons of bombs on the small countries of North and South Vietnam than both sides used in all of World War II. They spread chemicals that destroyed forests to deprive the Viet Cong of hiding places and dropped incendiary bombs filled with napalm, a gelatinous form of gasoline that clings to the skin of anyone exposed to it as it burns. The army pursued Viet Cong and North Vietnamese forces in "search and destroy" missions that often did not distinguish between combatants and civilians. Weekly reports of enemy losses or "body counts" became a fixation of the administration. But the United States could not break its opponents' ability to fight or make the South Vietnamese government any more able to survive on its own.

The Antiwar Movement

As casualties mounted and American bombs poured down on North and South Vietnam, the Cold War foreign policy consensus began to unravel. By 1968, the war had sidetracked much of the Great Society and had torn families, universities, and the Democratic Party apart. With the entire political leadership, liberal no less than conservative, committed to the war for most of the 1960s, young activists lost all confidence in "the system."

Political disillusionment

Opposition to the war became the organizing theme that united people with all kinds of doubts and discontents. "We recoil with horror," said a SNCC position paper, "at the inconsistency of a supposedly 'free' society where responsibility to freedom is equated with the responsibility to lend oneself to military aggression." With college students exempted from the draft, the burden of fighting fell on the working class and the poor. In 1967, Martin Luther King Jr. condemned the administration's Vietnam policy as an unconscionable use of violence and for draining resources from needs at home. At this point, King was the most prominent American to speak out against the war.

Widespread opposition

As for SDS, the war seemed the opposite of participatory democracy, since American involvement had come through secret commitments and decisions made by political elites, with no real public debate. In April 1965, SDS invited opponents of American policy in Vietnam to assemble in Washington, D.C. The turnout of 25,000 amazed the organizers, offering the first hint that the antiwar movement would soon enjoy a mass constituency. At the next antiwar rally, in November 1965, SDS leader Carl Ogelsby openly challenged the foundations of Cold War thinking.

He linked Vietnam to a critique of American interventions in Guatemala and Iran, support for South African apartheid, and Johnson's dispatch of troops to the Dominican Republic, all rooted in obsessive anticommunism. Some might feel, Ogelsby concluded, "that I sound mighty anti-American. To these, I say: 'Don't blame *me* for *that*! Blame those who mouthed my liberal values and broke my American heart.'" The speech, observed one reporter, marked a "declaration of independence" for the New Left.

> *SDS antiwar movement*

By 1967, young men were burning their draft cards or fleeing to Canada to avoid fighting in what they considered an unjust war. In October of that year, 100,000 antiwar protesters assembled at the Lincoln Memorial in Washington, D.C. Many marched across the Potomac River to the Pentagon, where photographers captured them placing flowers in the rifle barrels of soldiers guarding the nerve center of the American military.

The Counterculture

The New Left's definition of freedom initially centered on participatory democracy, a political concept. But as the 1960s progressed, young Americans' understanding of freedom increasingly expanded to include cultural freedom as well. Although many streams flowed into the generational rebellion known as the **counterculture**, the youth revolt was inconceivable without the war's destruction of young Americans' belief in authority. By the late 1960s, millions of young people openly rejected the values and behavior of their elders. Their ranks included not only college students but also numerous young workers, even though most unions strongly opposed antiwar demonstrations and countercultural displays (a reaction

> *Cultural freedom and rejection of authority*

Timothy Leary, promoter of the hallucinogenic drug LSD, at the Human Be-In in San Francisco in 1967.

that further separated young radicals from former allies on the traditional left). For the first time in American history, the flamboyant rejection of respectable norms in clothing, language, sexual behavior, and drug use, previously confined to artists and bohemians, became the basis of a mass movement. Its rallying cry was "liberation."

Here was John Winthrop's nightmare of three centuries earlier come to pass—a massive redefinition of freedom as a rejection of all authority. "Your sons and your daughters are beyond your command," Bob Dylan's song "The Times They Are A-Changin'" bluntly informed mainstream America. To be sure, the counterculture in some ways represented not rebellion but the fulfillment of the consumer marketplace. It extended into every realm of life the definition of freedom as the right to individual choice. Given the purchasing power of students and young adults, countercultural emblems—colorful clothing, rock music, images of sexual freedom, even symbols of black revolution and Native American resistance—were soon being mass-marketed as fashions of the day. Self-indulgence and self-destructive behavior were built into the counterculture. To followers of Timothy Leary, the Harvard scientist turned prophet of mind-expansion, the psychedelic drug LSD embodied a new freedom—"the freedom to expand your own consciousness." In 1967, Leary organized a Human Be-In in San Francisco, where he urged a crowd of 20,000 to "turn on, tune in, drop out."

Personal Liberation and the Free Individual

But there was far more to the counterculture than new consumer styles or the famed trio of sex, drugs, and rock and roll. To young dissenters, personal liberation represented a spirit of creative experimentation, a search for a way of life in which friendship and pleasure eclipsed the single-minded pursuit of wealth. It meant a release from bureaucratized education and work, repressive rules of personal behavior, and, above all, a militarized state that, in the name of freedom, rained destruction on a faraway people. It also encouraged new forms of radical action. "Underground" newspapers pioneered a personal and politically committed style of journalism. The Youth International Party, or "yippies," introduced humor and theatricality as elements of protest. From the visitors' gallery of the New York Stock Exchange, yippie founder Abbie Hoffman showered dollar bills onto the floor, bringing trading to a halt as brokers scrambled to retrieve the money.

The counterculture emphasized the ideal of community, establishing quasi-independent neighborhoods in New York City's East Village and San Francisco's Haight-Ashbury district and, in an echo of nineteenth-century utopian communities like New Harmony, some 2,000 communes nationwide. Rock festivals, like Woodstock in upstate New York in 1969, brought together hundreds of thousands of young people to celebrate their alternative lifestyle and independence from adult authority. The opening song at Woodstock, performed by Richie Havens, began with eight repetitions of the single word "freedom."

Faith and the Counterculture

Religious conviction, as has been noted, helped to inspire the civil rights movement. A different religious development, the sweeping reforms initiated in Roman

Bob Dylan

A poster listing some of the performers who took part in the Woodstock festival in 1969. A dove of peace sits on the guitar, symbolizing the overlap between the antiwar movement and counterculture.

A gathering of "Jesus People," one of the religious groups that sprang up in the 1960s.

Religious activism

Catholic practice (such as the delivery of the Mass in local languages, not Latin) by the Second Vatican Council of 1962–1965, led many priests, nuns, and lay Catholics to become involved in social justice movements. This produced a growing split in the church between liberals and conservatives. "Liberation theology," a movement that swept across parts of Latin America in which priests helped to mobilize rural peasants to combat economic inequality, also reverberated among some Catholics in the United States. Many members of the New Left were motivated by a quest for a new sense of brotherhood and social responsibility, which often sprang from Christian roots. Like adherents of the Social Gospel of the late nineteenth century, many young people came to see a commitment to social change as a fulfillment of Christian values.

The quest for personal authenticity, a feature of the counterculture, led to a flowering of religious and spiritual creativity and experimentation. The Jesus People (called by their detractors Jesus Freaks) saw the hippy lifestyle, with its long hair, unconventional attire, and quest for universal love, as an authentic expression of the outlook of the early church. The Sixties also witnessed a burgeoning interest in eastern religions. The Beats of the 1950s had been attracted to Buddhism as a religion that rejected violence and materialism—the antithesis of what they saw as key features of American society. Now, practices derived from Hinduism like yoga and meditation became popular with members of the counterculture and even in the suburban mainstream as a way of promoting spiritual and physical well-being. Some Americans traveled to Tibet and India to seek spiritual guidance from "gurus" (religious teachers) there.

More sinister was the emergence of religious cults based on single-minded devotion to a charismatic leader. The one with the most tragic outcome was the People's Temple, founded by Jim Jones, whose religious outlook combined intense spiritual commitment with strong criticism of racism. He attracted a racially mixed community of devout followers, whom he led from Indianapolis to San Francisco and finally to Guyana. There, in 1978 over 900 men, women, and children perished in a mass suicide/murder ordered by Jones.

Among the religious developments of the 1960s was the spread of interest in eastern religions and religious practices. The cover of *Yoga Journal* illustrates how one practice entered the mainstream of American life.

THE NEW MOVEMENTS AND THE RIGHTS REVOLUTION

The civil rights revolution, soon followed by the rise of the New Left, inspired other Americans to voice their grievances and claim their rights. Many borrowed the confrontational tactics of the black movement and activist students, adopting their language of "power" and "liberation" and their rejection of traditional organizations and approaches. By the late 1960s, new social movements dotted the political landscape.

The counterculture's notion of liberation centered on the free individual. Nowhere was this more evident than in the place occupied by sexual freedom in the generational rebellion. Starting in 1960, the mass marketing of birth-control pills made possible what "free lovers" had long demanded—the separation of sex from procreation. By the late 1960s, sexual freedom had become as much an element of the youth rebellion as long hair and drugs. Rock music celebrated the free expression of sexuality. The musical *Hair*, which gave voice to the youth rebellion, flaunted nudity on Broadway. The sexual revolution was central to another mass movement that emerged in the 1960s—the "second wave" of feminism.

> *The sexual revolution*

The Feminine Mystique

The achievement of the vote had not seemed to affect women's lack of power and opportunity. When the 1960s began, only a handful of women held political office, newspapers divided job ads into "male" and "female" sections, with the latter limited to low-wage clerical positions, and major universities limited the number of female students they accepted. In many states, husbands still controlled their wives' earnings. As late as 1970, the Ohio Supreme Court held that a wife was "at most a superior servant to her husband," without "legally recognized feelings or rights."

> *The state of sexism*

During the 1950s, some commentators had worried that the country was wasting its "woman power," a potential weapon in the Cold War. But the public reawakening of feminist consciousness did not get its start until the publication in 1963 of Betty Friedan's ***The Feminine Mystique***. Friedan had written pioneering articles during the 1940s on pay discrimination against women workers and racism in the workplace for the newspaper of the United Electrical Workers' union. But, like other social critics, she now took as her themes the emptiness of consumer culture and the discontents of the middle class. Her opening chapter, "The Problem That Has No Name," painted a devastating picture of talented, educated women trapped in a world that viewed marriage and motherhood as their primary goals. Somehow, after more than a century of agitation for access to the public sphere, women's lives still centered on the home. In Moscow in 1959, Richard Nixon had made the suburban home an emblem of American freedom. For Friedan, invoking the era's most powerful symbol of evil, it was a "comfortable concentration camp."

> *Betty Friedan*

Few books have had the impact of *The Feminine Mystique*. Friedan was deluged by desperate letters from female readers relating how the suburban dream had become a nightmare. "Freedom," wrote an Atlanta woman, "was a word I had always taken for granted. [I now realized that] I had voluntarily enslaved myself." To be sure, a few of Friedan's correspondents insisted that for a woman to create "a comfortable, happy home for her family" was "what God intended." But the immediate result of *The Feminine Mystique* was to focus attention on yet another gap between American rhetoric and American reality.

The law slowly began to address feminist concerns. In 1963, Congress passed the Equal Pay Act, barring sex discrimination among holders of the same jobs. The Civil Rights Act of 1964, as noted earlier, prohibited inequalities based on sex as well as race. Deluged with complaints of discrimination by working women, the Equal Employment Opportunity Commission established by the law became a major force in breaking down barriers to female employment. The year 1966 saw the formation of the **National Organization for Women** (NOW), with Friedan as president. Modeled on civil rights organizations, it demanded equal opportunity in jobs, education, and political participation and attacked the "false image of women" spread by the mass media.

> *Anti-discrimination laws*

Women's Liberation

If NOW grew out of a resurgence of middle-class feminism, a different female revolt was brewing within the civil rights and student movements. As in the days of abolitionism, young women who had embraced an ideology of social equality and personal freedom and learned methods of political organizing encountered inequality and sexual exploitation. Women like Ella Baker and Fannie Lou Hamer had played major roles in grass-roots civil rights organizing. But many women in the movement found themselves relegated to typing, cooking, and cleaning for male coworkers. Some were pressured to engage in sexual liaisons. Echoing the words of Abby Kelley a century earlier, a group of female SNCC activists concluded in a 1965 memorandum that "there seem to be many parallels that can be drawn between the treatment of Negroes and the treatment of women in our society as a whole." What bothered them most was the status of women within the movement, where assumptions of male supremacy seemed as deeply rooted as in society at large.

The same complaints arose in SDS. "The Movement is supposed to be for human liberation," wrote one student leader. "How come the condition of women inside it is no

In 1967, in a celebrated incident arising from the new feminism, a race official tried to eject Kathrine Switzer from the Boston Marathon, only to be pushed aside by other runners. Considered too fragile for the marathon (whose course covers more than twenty-six miles), women were prohibited from running. Switzer completed the race, and today hundreds of thousands of women around the world compete in marathons each year.

A 1970 women's liberation demonstration at the Statue of Liberty.

better than outside?" The rapidly growing number of women in college provided a ready-made constituency for the new feminism. By 1967, women throughout the country were establishing "consciousness-raising" groups to discuss the sources of their discontent. The time, many concluded, had come to establish a movement of their own, more radical than NOW. The new feminism burst onto the national scene at the Miss America beauty pageant of 1968, when protesters filled a "freedom trash can" with objects of "oppression"—girdles, brassieres, high-heeled shoes, and copies of *Playboy* and *Cosmopolitan*. (Contrary to legend, they did not set the contents on fire, which would have been highly dangerous on the wooden boardwalk. But the media quickly invented a new label for radical women—"bra burners.") Inside the hall, demonstrators unfurled banners carrying the slogans "Freedom for Women" and "Women's Liberation."

Personal Freedom

The women's liberation movement inspired a major expansion of the idea of freedom by insisting that it should be applied to the most intimate realms of life. Introducing the terms "sexism" and "sexual politics" and the phrase "the personal is political" into public debate, it insisted that sexual relations, conditions of marriage, and standards of beauty were as much "political" questions as the war, civil rights, and the class tensions that had traditionally inspired the left to action. The idea that family life is not off-limits to considerations of power and justice repudiated the family-oriented public culture of the 1950s, and it permanently changed Americans' definition of freedom.

The abortion issue

Radical feminists' first public campaign demanded the repeal of state laws that underscored women's lack of self-determination by banning abortions or leaving it up to physicians to decide whether a pregnancy could be terminated. Without the right to control her own reproduction, wrote one activist, "woman's other 'freedoms' are tantalizing mockeries that cannot be exercised." In 1969, a group of feminists disrupted legislative hearings on New York's law banning abortions, where the experts scheduled to testify consisted of fourteen men and a Roman Catholic nun.

The call for legalized abortions merged the nineteenth-century demand that a woman control her own body with the Sixties emphasis on sexual freedom. But the concerns of women's liberation went far beyond sexuality. *Sisterhood Is Powerful*, an influential collection of essays, manifestos, and personal accounts published in 1970, touched on a remarkable array of issues, from violence against women to

Mainstream feminism

inequalities in the law, churches, workplaces, and family life. By this time, feminist ideas had entered the mainstream. In 1962, a poll showed that two-thirds of American women did not feel themselves to be victims of discrimination. By 1974, two-thirds did.

Gay Liberation

In a decade full of surprises, perhaps the greatest of all was the emergence of the movement for gay liberation. Efforts of one kind or another for greater rights for racial minorities and women had a long history. Homosexuals, wrote Harry Hay, who in 1951 founded the Mattachine Society, the first gay rights organization, were "the one group of disadvantaged people who didn't even think of themselves as a group." Gay men and lesbians had long been stigmatized as sinful or mentally disordered. Most states made homosexual acts illegal, and police regularly harassed the gay subcultures that existed in major cities like San Francisco and New York. McCarthyism, which viewed homosexuality as a source of national weakness, made the discrimination to which gays were subjected even worse. Although homosexuals had achieved considerable success in the arts and fashion, most kept their sexual orientation secret, or "in the closet."

The Mattachine Society had worked to persuade the public that apart from their sexual orientation, gays were average Americans who ought not to be persecuted. But as with other groups, the Sixties transformed the gay movement. If one moment marked the advent of "gay liberation," it was a 1969 police raid on the **Stonewall Inn** in New York's Greenwich Village, a gathering place for homosexuals. Rather than bowing to police harassment, as in the past, gays fought back. Five days of rioting followed, and a militant movement was born. Gay men and lesbians stepped out of the "closet" to insist that sexual orientation is a matter of rights, power, and identity. Prejudice against homosexuals persisted. But within a few years, "gay pride" marches were being held in numerous cities.

A 1970 poster urging male and female homosexuals to join the Gay Liberation Front, one of the numerous movements that sprang to life in the late 1960s.

Latino Activism

As in the case of blacks, a movement for legal rights had long flourished among Mexican-Americans. But the mid-1960s saw the flowering of a new militancy challenging the group's second-class economic status. Like Black Power advocates, the movement emphasized pride in both the Mexican past and the new Chicano culture that had arisen in the United States. Unlike the Black Power movement and SDS, it was closely linked to labor struggles. Beginning in 1965, César Chavez, the son of migrant farm workers and a disciple of King, led a series of nonviolent protests, including marches, fasts, and a national boycott of California grapes, to pressure growers to agree to labor contracts with the United Farm Workers union (UFW). The UFW was as much a mass movement for civil rights as a campaign for economic betterment. The boycott mobilized Latino communities throughout the Southwest and drew national attention to the pitifully low wages and oppressive working conditions of migrant laborers. In 1970, the major growers agreed to contracts with the UFW.

In New York City, the Young Lords Organization, modeled on the Black Panthers, staged street demonstrations to protest the high unemployment rate among the city's Puerto Ricans and the lack of city services in Latino neighborhoods. (In one protest,

A scene in Denver in the mid-1960s. Rodolfo Corky Gonzáles, center, a former professional boxer who headed the city's War on Poverty program, greets demonstrators whose sign juxtaposes Latino inequality with Mexican-American service in the army in Vietnam.

Women and Latino activism

they dumped garbage on city streets to draw attention to the city's failure to collect refuse in poor areas.) Like SNCC and SDS, the Latino movement gave rise to feminist dissent. Many Chicano and Puerto Rican men regarded feminist demands as incompatible with the Latino heritage of *machismo* (an exaggerated sense of manliness, including the right to dominate women). Young female activists, however, viewed the sexual double standard and the inequality of women as incompatible with freedom for all members of *la raza* (the race, or people).

Red Power

Indian activism

The 1960s also witnessed an upsurge of Indian militancy. The Truman and Eisenhower administrations had sought to dismantle the reservation system and integrate Indians into the American mainstream—a policy known as "termination," since it meant ending recognition of the remaining elements of Indian sovereignty. Many Indian leaders protested vigorously against this policy, and it was abandoned by President Kennedy. Johnson's War on Poverty channeled increased federal funds to reservations. But like other minority groups, Indian activists compared their own status to that of underdeveloped countries overseas. They demanded not simply economic aid but self-determination, like the emerging nations of the Third World. Using language typical of the late 1960s, Clyde Warrior, president of the National Indian Youth Council, declared, "We are not free in the most basic sense of the word. We are not allowed to make those basic human choices about our personal life and the destiny of our communities."

Founded in 1968, the **American Indian movement** staged protests demanding greater tribal self-government and the restoration of economic resources guaranteed in treaties. In 1969, a group calling itself "Indians of All Tribes" occupied (or from their point of view, re-occupied) Alcatraz Island in San Francisco Bay, claiming that it had been illegally seized from its original inhabitants. The protest, which lasted into 1971, launched the Red Power movement. In the years that followed, many Indian tribes would win greater control over education and economic development on the reservations. Indian activists would bring land claims suits, demanding and receiving monetary settlements for past dispossession. As a result of a rising sense of self-respect, the number of Americans identifying themselves as Indians doubled between 1970 and 1990.

The occupation of Alcatraz Island in San Francisco Bay in 1969 by "Indians of All Tribes" symbolized the emergence of a new militancy among Native Americans.

Silent Spring

Liberation movements among racial minorities, women, and gays challenged long-standing social inequalities. Another movement, environmentalism, called into question different pillars of American life—the equation of progress with endless increases in consumption and the faith that science, technology, and economic growth would advance the social welfare. Concern for preserving the natural environment dated back to the creation of national parks and other conservation efforts during the Progressive era. But in keeping with the spirit of the Sixties, the new environmentalism was more activist and youth-oriented, and it spoke the language of empowering citizens to participate in decisions that affected their lives. Its emergence reflected the very affluence celebrated by proponents of the American Way. As the "quality of life"—including physical fitness, health, and opportunities to enjoy leisure activities—occupied a greater role in the lives of middle-class Americans, the environmental consequences of economic growth received increased attention. When the 1960s began, complaints were already being heard about the bulldozing of forests for suburban development and the contamination produced by laundry detergents and chemical lawn fertilizers seeping into drinking supplies.

Environmental activism

The publication in 1962 of ***Silent Spring*** by the marine biologist Rachel Carson brought home to millions of readers the effects of DDT, an insecticide widely used by home owners and farmers against mosquitoes, gypsy moths, and other insects. In chilling detail, Carson related how DDT killed birds and animals and caused sickness among humans. Chemical and pesticide companies launched a campaign to discredit her—some critics called the book part of a communist plot. *Time* magazine even condemned Carson as "hysterical" and "emotional"—words typically used by men to discredit women.

Rachel Carson

The New Environmentalism

Carson's work launched the modern environmental movement. The Sierra Club, founded in the 1890s to preserve forests, saw its membership more than triple, and other groups sprang into existence to alert the country to the dangers of water contamination, air pollution, lead in paint, and the extinction of animal species. Nearly every state quickly banned the use of DDT. In 1969, television brought home to a national audience the death of birds and fish and the despoiling of beaches caused by a major oil spill off the coast of California, exposing the environmental dangers of oil transportation and ocean drilling for oil.

The postwar economic boom, with its seemingly limitless demand for resources like land, energy, and building materials, placed enormous stress on the natural environment. As highways and suburbs paved over the landscape, more and more Americans became committed to the survival of places of natural beauty.

Despite vigorous opposition from business groups that considered its proposals a violation of property rights, environmentalism attracted the broadest bipartisan support of any of the new social movements. Under Republican president Richard Nixon, Congress during the late 1960s and early 1970s passed a series of measures to protect the environment, including the Clean Air and Clean Water Acts and the Endangered Species Act. On April 22, 1970, the first Earth Day, some 20 million people, most of them under the age of thirty, participated in rallies, concerts, and teach-ins.

Environmental legislation

Closely related to environmentalism was the consumer movement, spearheaded by the lawyer Ralph Nader. His book *Unsafe at Any Speed* (1965) exposed how auto manufacturers produced highly dangerous vehicles. General Motors, whose Chevrolet Corvair Nader singled out for its tendency to roll over in certain driving situations, hired private investigators to discredit him. When their

Consumer activism

campaign was exposed, General Motors paid Nader a handsome settlement, which he used to fund investigations of other dangerous products and of misleading advertising.

Consumer protection laws

Nader's campaigns laid the groundwork for the numerous new consumer protection laws and regulations of the 1970s. Unlike 1960s movements that emphasized personal liberation, environmentalism and the consumer movement called for limiting some kinds of freedom—especially the right to use private property in any way the owner desired—in the name of a greater common good.

The Rights Revolution

It is one of the more striking ironies of the 1960s that although the "rights revolution" began in the streets, it achieved constitutional legitimacy through the Supreme Court, historically the most conservative branch of government. Under the guidance of Chief Justice Earl Warren, the Court vastly expanded the rights enjoyed by all Americans and placed them beyond the reach of legislative and local majorities.

Civil liberties and the Supreme Court

As noted in Chapter 21, the Court's emergence as a vigorous guardian of civil liberties had been foreshadowed in 1937, when it abandoned its commitment to freedom of contract while declaring that the right of free expression deserved added protection. The McCarthy era halted progress toward a broader conception of civil liberties. It resumed on June 17, 1957, known as "Red Monday" by conservatives, when the Court moved to rein in the anticommunist crusade. The justices overturned convictions of individuals for advocating the overthrow of the government, failing to answer questions before the House Un-American Activities Committee, and refusing to disclose their political beliefs to state officials. The government, Warren declared, could prosecute illegal actions, but not "unorthodoxy or dissent." By the time Warren retired in 1969, the Court had reaffirmed the right of even the most unpopular viewpoints to First Amendment protection and had dismantled the Cold War loyalty security system.

Civil liberties had gained strength in the 1930s because of association with the rights of labor; in the 1950s and 1960s, they became intertwined with civil rights. Beginning with *NAACP v. Alabama* in 1958, the Court struck down southern laws that sought to destroy civil rights organizations by forcing them to make public their membership lists. In addition, in the landmark ruling in *New York Times v. Sullivan* (1964), it overturned a libel judgment by an Alabama jury against the nation's leading newspaper for carrying an advertisement critical of how local officials treated civil rights demonstrators. The "central meaning of the First Amendment," the justices declared, lay in the right of citizens to criticize their government. For good measure, they declared the Sedition Act of 1798 unconstitutional over a century and a half after it had expired. Before the 1960s, few Supreme Court cases had dealt with newspaper publishing. *Sullivan* created the modern constitutional law of freedom of the press.

The Court in the 1960s continued the push toward racial equality, overturning numerous local Jim Crow laws. In *Loving v. Virginia* (1967), it declared unconstitutional the laws still on the books in sixteen states that prohibited interracial marriage. This aptly named case arose from the interracial marriage of Richard and Mildred Loving. Barred by Virginia law from marrying, they did so

Karl Hubenthal's December 8, 1976, cartoon for the *Los Angeles Herald-Examiner* celebrates the rights revolution as an expansion of American liberty.

in Washington, D.C., and later returned to their home state. Two weeks after their arrival, the local sheriff entered their home in the middle of the night, roused the couple from bed, and arrested them. The Lovings were sentenced to five years in prison, although the judge gave them the option of leaving Virginia instead. They departed for Washington, but five years later, wishing to return, they sued in federal court, claiming that their rights had been violated. In 1968, in *Jones v. Alfred H. Mayer Co.*, the Court forbade discrimination in the rental or sale of housing. Eliminating "badges of slavery," such as unequal access to housing, the ruling suggested, was essential to fulfilling at long last the promise of emancipation.

Richard and Mildred Loving with their children in a 1965 photograph by Grey Villet. Their desire to live in Virginia as man and wife led to a Supreme Court decision declaring unconstitutional state laws that barred interracial marriages.

Policing the States

The Court simultaneously pushed forward the process of imposing upon the states the obligation to respect the liberties outlined in the Bill of Rights. It required states to abide by protections against illegal search and seizure, the right of a defendant to a speedy trial, the prohibition against cruel and unusual punishment, and the right of poor persons accused of a crime to receive counsel from publicly supplied attorneys. Among the most important of these decisions was the 5-4 ruling in *Miranda v. Arizona* (1966). This held that an individual in police custody must be informed of the rights to remain silent and to confer with a lawyer before answering questions and must be told that any statements might be used in court. The decision made "Miranda warnings" standard police practice.

The Court also assumed the power to oversee the fairness of democratic procedures at the state and local levels. *Baker v. Carr* (1962) established the principle that districts electing members of state legislatures must be equal in population. This "one man, one vote" principle overturned apportionment systems in numerous states that had allowed individuals in sparsely inhabited rural areas to enjoy the same representation as residents of populous city districts.

The cartoonist Herbert Block's comment on critics of the Supreme Court's decision barring prayer in public schools.

The justices also moved to reinforce the "wall of separation" between church and state. In 1961, they unanimously declared unconstitutional a clause in Maryland's constitution requiring that public officials declare their belief "in the existence of God." In the following year, in *Engel v. Vitale*, they decreed that prayers and Bible readings in public schools also violated the First Amendment. President Kennedy pointed out that Americans remained perfectly free to pray at home or in church, but these rulings proved to be the most unpopular of all the Warren Court's decisions. Polls showed that 80 percent of Americans favored allowing prayer in public schools.

"WHAT DO THEY EXPECT US TO DO — LISTEN TO THE KIDS PRAY AT HOME?"

The Right to Privacy

The Warren Court not only expanded existing liberties but also outlined entirely new rights in response to the rapidly changing contours of American society. Most dramatic was its assertion of a constitutional right to privacy in ***Griswold v. Connecticut***

(1965), which overturned a state law prohibiting the use of contraceptives. Justice William O. Douglas, who wrote the decision, had once declared, "The right to be let alone is the beginning of all freedom." Apart from decisions of the 1920s that affirmed the right to marry and raise children without government interference, however, few legal precedents existed regarding privacy. The Constitution does not mention the word. Nonetheless, Douglas argued that a constitutionally protected "zone of privacy" within marriage could be inferred from the "penumbras" (shadows) of the Bill of Rights.

Griswold linked privacy to the sanctity of marriage. But the Court soon transformed it into a right of individuals. It extended access to birth control to unmarried adults and ultimately to minors—an admission by the Court that law could not reverse the sexual revolution. These decisions led directly to the most controversial decision that built on the rulings of the Warren Court (even though it occurred in 1973, four years after Warren's retirement). This was **Roe v. Wade**, which created a constitutional right to terminate a pregnancy. The Court declared access to abortion a fundamental freedom protected by the Constitution, a fulfillment of radical feminists' earliest demand. *Roe* provoked vigorous opposition, which has continued to this day. Only two states banned contraception when *Griswold* was decided; *Roe* invalidated the laws of no fewer than forty-six.

Griswold and *Roe* unleashed a flood of rulings and laws that seemed to accept the feminist view of the family as a collection of sovereign individuals rather than a unit with a single head. The legal rights of women within the domestic sphere expanded dramatically. Law enforcement authorities for the first time began to prosecute crimes like rape and assault by husbands against their wives. Today, some notion of privacy is central to most Americans' conception of freedom.

The rights revolution completed the transformation of American freedom from a set of entitlements enjoyed mainly by white men into an open-ended claim to equality, recognition, and self-determination. For the rest of the century, the government and legal system would be inundated by demands by aggrieved groups of all kinds, and the Supreme Court would devote much of its time to defining the rights of Americans.

1968

A Year of Turmoil

The Sixties reached their climax in 1968, a year when momentous events succeeded each other so rapidly that the foundations of society seemed to be dissolving. Late January 1968 saw the **Tet offensive**, in which Viet Cong and North Vietnamese troops launched well-organized uprisings in cities throughout South Vietnam, completely surprising American military leaders. The United States drove back the offensive and inflicted heavy losses. But the intensity of the fighting, brought into America's homes on television, shattered public confidence in the Johnson administration, which had repeatedly proclaimed victory to be "just around the corner." Leading members of the press and political establishment joined the chorus criticizing American involvement. Eugene McCarthy, an antiwar

> **Abortion and contraception rights**

A 1968 poster produced by the Student Nonviolent Coordinating Committee starkly captures the impatient spirit of the social movements of the Sixties.

senator from Minnesota, announced that he would seek the Democratic nomination for President. Aided by a small army of student volunteers, McCarthy received more than 40 percent of the vote in the New Hampshire primary. With public support dissolving, Johnson rejected the military's request to send 200,000 more troops to Vietnam. Johnson then stunned the nation by announcing that he had decided not to seek reelection. Peace talks soon opened in Paris.

Meanwhile, Martin Luther King Jr. was organizing a Poor People's March, hoping to bring thousands of demonstrators to Washington to demand increased anti-poverty efforts. On April 4, having traveled to Memphis to support a strike of the city's grossly underpaid black garbage collectors, King was killed by a white assassin. The greatest outbreak of urban violence in the nation's history followed in ghettos across the country. Washington, D.C., had to be occupied by soldiers before order was restored. As a gesture to King's memory, Congress passed its last major civil rights law, the Open Housing Act, which prohibited discrimination in the sale and rental of homes and apartments, although with weak enforcement mechanisms.

Striking sanitation workers in Memphis, Tennessee. As their signs suggest, they demanded respect as well as higher wages. Having traveled to Memphis to support the strikers, Martin Luther King Jr. was assassinated on April 4, 1968.

At the end of April, students protesting Columbia University's involvement in defense research and its plan to build a gymnasium in a public park occupied seven campus buildings. New York police removed them in an assault that left hundreds of protesters and bystanders injured and led to a strike that closed the campus. In June, a young Palestinian nationalist assassinated Robert F. Kennedy, who was seeking the Democratic nomination as an opponent of the war. In August, tens of thousands of antiwar activists descended on Chicago for protests at the Democratic national convention, where the delegates nominated Vice President Hubert Humphrey as their presidential candidate. The city's police, never known for restraint, assaulted the marchers with nightsticks, producing hundreds of injuries outside the convention hall and pandemonium inside it.

The 1968 Democratic national convention

A later investigation called the event a "police riot." Nonetheless, the government indicted eight political radicals for conspiring to incite the violence. They included Tom Hayden of SDS, yippie leader Abbie Hoffman, and Bobby Seale of the Black Panthers. Five were found guilty after a tumultuous trial. But an appeals court overturned the convictions because Judge Julius Hoffman (no relation to Abbie Hoffman) had been flagrantly biased against the defendants.

The Global 1968

Motivating international movements

Like 1848 and 1919, 1968 was a year of worldwide upheaval. In many countries, young radicals challenged existing power structures, often borrowing language and strategies from the decade's social movements in the United States and

A mural in Belfast, Northern Ireland, depicts the black American abolitionist Frederick Douglass, illustrating how the movement for Catholic civil rights associated itself with the struggle for racial justice in the United States. The text points out that Douglass lectured in Ireland in the 1840s on abolitionism, women's rights, and Irish independence.

adapting them to their own circumstances. Television carried events in one country instantaneously across the globe.

Massive antiwar demonstrations took place in London, Rome, Paris, Munich, and Tokyo, leading to clashes with police and scores of injuries. In Italy, students occupied university buildings, bringing education to a halt. In Paris, a nationwide student uprising began in May 1968 that echoed American demands for educational reform and personal liberation. Unlike in the United States, millions of French workers soon joined the protest, adding their own demands for higher wages and greater democracy in the workplace. The result was a general strike that paralyzed the country and nearly led to the collapse of the government before it ended. In communist Czechoslovakia, leaders bent on reform came to power by promising to institute "socialism with a human face," only to be ousted by a Soviet invasion. Soldiers fired on students demonstrating for greater democracy on the eve of the opening of the Olympic Games in Mexico City, leading to more than 500 deaths. In Northern Ireland, which remained part of Great Britain after the rest of Ireland achieved independence, the police attacked a peaceful march of Catholics demanding an end to religious discrimination who were inspired by the American civil rights movement. This event marked the beginning of The Troubles, a period of both peaceful protest and violent conflict in the region that did not end until the turn of the twenty-first century.

And throughout the world, the second wave of American feminism found echoes among women who resented being relegated to unequal citizenship. As in the United States, personal liberation, including a woman's right to control her own body, became a rallying cry. In Catholic European countries like France and Italy, women's movements won significant legal changes, making it easier to obtain divorces and decriminalizing abortion. *Our Bodies, Ourselves*, a book originally published in 1973 by a group of Boston women, dealt frankly with widely misunderstood aspects of women's health, including pregnancy and childbirth, menopause, birth control, and sexually transmitted diseases. It was quickly translated into twenty languages.

Nixon's Comeback

In the United States, instead of radical change, the year's events opened the door for a conservative reaction. Turmoil in the streets produced a demand for public order. Black militancy produced white "backlash," which played an increasing role in politics. The fact that the unelected Supreme Court was inventing and protecting "rights" fed the argument that faraway bureaucrats rode roughshod over local traditions.

THE PRESIDENTIAL ELECTION OF 1968

Party	Candidate	Electoral Vote (Share)	Popular Vote (Share)
Republican	Nixon	301 (56%)	31,710,470 (43.2%)
Democrat	Humphrey	191 (36%)	30,898,055 (42.6%)
American Independent	Wallace	46 (8%)	9,906,473 (12.9%)

In August, Richard Nixon capped a remarkable political comeback by winning the Republican nomination. He campaigned as the champion of the "silent majority"—ordinary Americans who believed that change had gone too far—and called for a renewed commitment to "law and order." Humphrey could not overcome the deep divide in his party. With 43 percent of the vote, Nixon had only a razor-thin margin over his Democratic rival. But George Wallace, running as an independent and appealing to resentments against blacks' gains, Great Society programs, and the Warren Court, received an additional 13 percent. Taken together, the Nixon and Wallace totals, which included a considerable number of former Democratic voters, indicated that four years after Johnson's landslide election ushered in the Great Society, liberalism was on the defensive.

The year 1968 did not mark the end of the 1960s. The Great Society would achieve an unlikely culmination during the Nixon administration. The second wave of feminism achieved its largest following during the 1970s. Nixon's election did, however, inaugurate a period of growing conservatism in American politics. The conservative ascendancy would usher in yet another chapter in the story of American freedom.

The Legacy of the Sixties

The 1960s transformed American life in ways unimaginable when the decade began. It produced new rights and new understandings of freedom. It made possible the entrance of numerous members of racial minorities into the mainstream of American life, while leaving unsolved the problem of urban poverty. It set in motion a transformation of the status of women. It changed what Americans expected from government—from clean air and water to medical coverage in old age. At the same time, it undermined public confidence in national leaders. Relations between young and old, men and women, and white and non-white, along with every institution in society, changed as a result.

Just as the Civil War and New Deal established the framework for future political debates, so, it seemed, Americans were condemned to refight the battles of the 1960s long after the decade ended. Race relations, feminism, social policy, the nation's proper role in world affairs—these issues hardly originated in the 1960s. But the events of those years made them more pressing and more divisive. As the country became more conservative, the Sixties would be blamed for every imaginable social ill, from crime and drug abuse to a decline of respect for authority. Yet during the 1960s, the United States became a more open, more tolerant—in a word, a freer—country.

Signs, a 1970 painting by Robert Rauschenberg, presents a collage of images from the turbulent 1960s, including (clockwise from the upper-left corner) troops putting down urban rioting, Robert F. Kennedy, singer Janis Joplin, peace demonstrators, John F. Kennedy, Martin Luther King Jr. after his assassination, and an astronaut on the moon. Art © Robert Rauschenberg Foundation/Licensed by VAGA, New York, NY.

SUGGESTED READING

BOOKS

- Anderson, John A., III. *The Other Side of the Sixties: Young Americans for Freedom and the Rise of Conservative Politics* (1997). Considers conservative students of the 1960s and how they laid the groundwork for the later growth of their movement.

- Appy, Christian G. *Working-Class War: American Combat Soldiers and Vietnam* (1993). A careful account of how the draft operated to place the burden of fighting on working-class Americans.

- Brick, Howard. *Age of Contradiction: American Thought and Culture in the 1960s* (1998). A careful examination of the complex currents of thought that circulated during the decade.

- Carson, Clayborne. *In Struggle: SNCC and the Black Awakening of the 1960s* (1981). A study of the Student Nonviolent Coordinating Committee and its impact on the 1960s.

- D'Emilio, John. *Sexual Politics, Sexual Communities: The Making of a Homosexual Minority in the United States, 1940–1970* (1983). Explores the status of gay men and lesbians in mid-twentieth-century America and the rise of the gay movement.

- Dierenfield, Bruce. *The Battle over School Prayer: How* Engel v. Vitale *Changed America* (2007). One controversial Supreme Court decision of the 1960s and its long-term consequences.

- Dittmer, John. *Local People: The Struggle for Civil Rights in Mississippi* (1994). Traces the civil rights movement in one state, looked at from the experience of grassroots activists.

- Horwitz, Morton J. *The Warren Court and the Pursuit of Justice* (1998). Analyzes how the Supreme Court redefined the rights of Americans under Chief Justice Earl Warren.

- Isserman, Maurice, and Michael Kazin. *America Divided: The Civil War of the 1960s* (2000). A comprehensive account of the social movements and political debates of the 1960s.

- Joseph, Peniel E. *Waiting 'Til the Midnight Hour: A Narrative History of Black Power in America* (2007). Demonstrates how the rise of Black Power reconfigured both African-American identity and race relations in the late 1960s.

- Logevall, Frederik. *Embers of War: The Fall of an Empire and the Making of America's Vietnam* (2102). An international account of the origins of American military intervention in Vietnam.

- McCartin, James P. *Prayers of the Faithful: The Shifting Spiritual Life of American Catholics* (2010). Examines the impact of the 1960s on the Catholic Church.

- Rosen, Ruth. *The World Split Open: How the Modern Women's Movement Changed America* (2000). Considers how the "second wave" of feminism transformed the lives of American women and men.

- Sale, Kirkpatrick. *The Green Revolution: The American Environmental Movement, 1962–1992* (1993). A brief history of one of the most significant movements to emerge from the 1960s.

- Skretny, John. *The Minority Rights Revolution* (2002). An account of the rights revolution and how it affected American society and its understanding of the rights of citizens.

WEBSITES

- A Visual Journey: Photographs by Lisa Law, 1965–1971: http://americanhistory.si.edu/lisalaw/1.htm

- Free Speech Movement Digital Archive: http://bancroft.berkeley.edu/FSM/

- Freedom Now!: http://cds.library.brown.edu/projects/FreedomNow

CHAPTER REVIEW AND ONLINE RESOURCES

REVIEW QUESTIONS

1. How did the idea of a "zone of privacy" build on or change earlier notions of rights and freedom?

2. In what ways were President Kennedy's foreign policy decisions shaped by Cold War ideology?

3. How did immigration policies change in these years, and what were the consequences for the composition of the population in the United States?

4. Explain why many blacks, especially in the North, did not believe that the civil rights legislation went far enough in promoting black freedom.

5. What were the effects of President Johnson's Great Society and War on Poverty programs?

6. In what ways was the New Left not as new as it claimed?

7. How did the goals and actions of the United States in Vietnam cause controversy at home and abroad?

8. Discuss the impact of the Civil Rights movement on other movements for social change in the 1960s.

9. Identify the origins, goals, and composition of the feminist, or women's liberation, movement.

10. Describe how the social movements of the 1960s in the United States became part of global movements for change by 1968. How did those connections affect the United States' position in the world?

11. How did the counterculture expand the meaning of freedom in these years?

KEY TERMS

sit-ins (p. 971)

Student Nonviolent Coordinating Committee (p. 972)

Freedom Rides (p. 972)

March on Washington (p. 974)

Bay of Pigs invasion (p. 976)

Cuban missile crisis (p. 976)

Civil Rights Act (p. 978)

Voting Rights Act (p. 982)

Hart-Celler Act (p. 982)

Great Society (p. 983)

War on Poverty (p. 984)

Black Power (p. 987)

New Left (p. 988)

Students for a Democratic Society (p. 990)

Port Huron Statement (p. 990)

Gulf of Tonkin resolution (p. 992)

counterculture (p. 997)

The Feminine Mystique (p. 1000)

National Organization for Women (p. 1001)

Stonewall Inn (p. 1003)

American Indian movement (p. 1004)

Silent Spring (p. 1005)

Griswold v. Connecticut (p. 1007)

Roe v. Wade (p. 1008)

Tet offensive (p. 1008)

Go to INQUIZITIVE

To see what you know—and learn what you've missed—with personalized feedback along the way.

Visit the *Give Me Liberty!* **Student Site** for primary source documents and images, interactive maps, author videos featuring Eric Foner, and more.

CHAPTER 26

THE TRIUMPH OF CONSERVATISM

★

1969–1988

Beginning with the dramatic 1960 contest between John F. Kennedy and Richard M. Nixon, the journalist Theodore White published best-selling accounts of four successive races for the presidency. Covering the 1964 election, White attended civil rights demonstrations and rallies for Barry Goldwater, the Republican nominee. White noticed something that struck him as odd: "The dominant word of these two groups, which loathe each other, is 'freedom.' Both demand either Freedom Now or Freedom for All. The word has such emotive power behind it that . . . a reporter is instantly denounced for questioning what they mean by the word 'freedom.'" The United States, White concluded, sorely needed "a commonly agreed-on concept of freedom."

White had observed firsthand the struggle over the meaning of freedom that emerged in the 1960s, as well as the revival of conservatism in the midst of an era known for radicalism. Goldwater's campaign helped to crystallize and popularize ideas that would remain the bedrock of conservatism for years to come. To intense anticommunism, Goldwater added a critique of the welfare state for destroying "the dignity of the individual." He demanded a reduction in taxes and governmental regulations. Goldwater showed that with liberals in control in Washington, conservatives could claim for themselves the tradition of antigovernment populism, thus broadening their electoral base and countering their image as upper-crust elitists.

The second half of the 1960s and the 1970s witnessed pivotal developments that reshaped American politics—the breakup of the political coalition forged by Franklin D. Roosevelt; an economic crisis that traditional liberal remedies seemed unable to solve; a shift of population and economic resources to conservative strongholds in the Sunbelt of the South and West; the growth of an activist, conservative Christianity increasingly aligned with the Republican Party; and a series of setbacks for the United States overseas. Together, they led to growing popularity for conservatives' ideas, including their understanding of freedom.

PRESIDENT NIXON

From the vantage point of the early twenty-first century, it is difficult to recall how marginal conservatism seemed at the end of World War II. Associated in many minds with conspiracy theories, anti-Semitism, and preference for social hierarchy over democracy and equality, conservatism seemed a relic of a discredited past. When conservative ideas did begin to spread, liberals explained them as a rejection of the modern world by the alienated or psychologically disturbed.

Nonetheless, as noted in the previous two chapters, the 1950s and 1960s witnessed a conservative rebirth. And in 1968, a "backlash" among formerly Democratic voters against both black assertiveness and antiwar demonstrations helped to propel Richard Nixon into the White House. But conservatives found Nixon no more to their liking than his predecessors. Nixon echoed conservative language, especially in his condemnation of student protesters and his calls for

FOCUS QUESTIONS

What were the major policies of the Nixon administration on social and economic issues? –p. 1015

How did Vietnam and the Watergate scandal affect popular trust in the government? –p. 1022

In what ways did the opportunities of most Americans diminish in the 1970s? –p. 1026

What were the roots of the rise of conservatism in the 1970s? –p. 1034

How did the Reagan presidency affect American aims at home and abroad? –p. 1039

Ronald Reagan addressing the Republican national convention of 1984, which nominated him for president. His election that fall brought modern conservatism to the White House and launched the Reagan Revolution.

law and order, but in office he expanded the welfare state and moved to improve American relations with the Soviet Union and China. During his presidency, the social changes set in motion by the 1960s—seen by conservatives as forces of moral decay—continued apace.

Nixon's Domestic Policies

Having won the presidency by a very narrow margin, Nixon moved toward the political center on many issues. A shrewd politician, he worked to solidify his support among Republicans while reaching out to disaffected elements of the Democratic coalition. It is difficult to characterize Nixon's domestic agenda according to the traditional categories of liberal and conservative. Mostly interested in foreign policy, he had no desire to battle Congress, still under Democratic control, on domestic issues. Just as Eisenhower had helped to institutionalize the New Deal, Nixon accepted and even expanded many elements of the Great Society.

Conservatives applauded Nixon's New Federalism, which offered federal "block grants" to the states to spend as they saw fit, rather than for specific purposes dictated by Washington. On the other hand, the Nixon administration created a host of new federal agencies. The Environmental Protection Agency oversaw programs to combat water and air pollution, cleaned up hazardous wastes, and required "environmental impact" statements from any project that received federal funding. The Occupational Safety and Health Administration sent inspectors into the nation's workplaces. The National Transportation Safety Board instructed automobile makers on how to make their cars safer.

Nixon spent lavishly on social services and environmental initiatives. He abolished the Office of Economic Opportunity, which had coordinated Johnson's War on Poverty. But he signed congressional measures that expanded the food stamp program and indexed Social Security benefits to inflation—meaning that they would rise automatically as the cost of living increased. The Endangered Species Act prohibited spending federal funds on any project that might extinguish an animal species. The Clean Air Act set air quality standards for carbon monoxide and other chemicals released by cars and factories and led to a dramatic decline in air pollution.

Nixon and Welfare

Perhaps Nixon's most startling initiative was his proposal for a Family Assistance Plan, or "negative income tax," that would replace Aid to Families with Dependent Children (AFDC) by having the federal government guarantee a minimum income for all Americans. Universally known as "welfare," AFDC provided assistance, often quite limited, to poor families who met local eligibility requirements. Originally a New Deal program that mainly served the white poor, welfare had come to be associated with blacks, who by 1970 accounted for nearly half the recipients. The AFDC rolls expanded rapidly during the 1960s, partly because the federal government relaxed eligibility standards. This arose from an increase in births to unmarried women, which produced a sharp rise in the number of poor female-headed households, and from an aggressive campaign by welfare rights groups to encourage people to apply for benefits. Conservative politicians now attacked

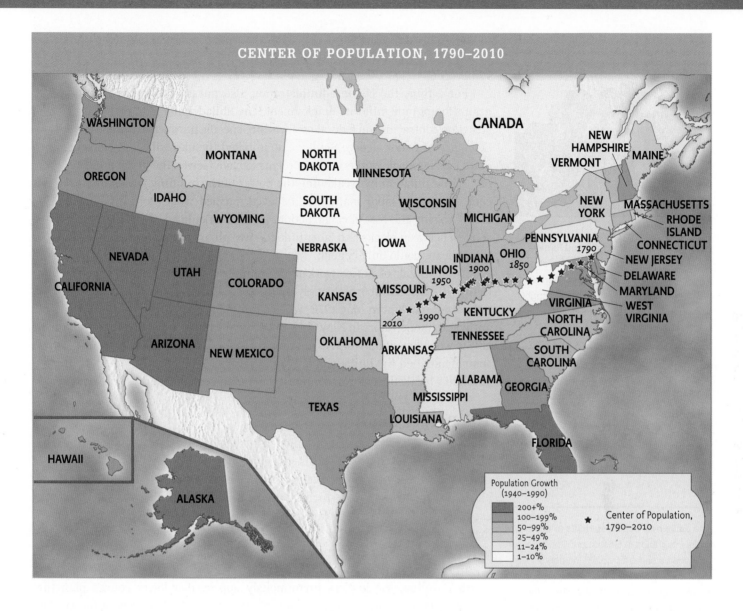

CENTER OF POPULATION, 1790–2010

Population Growth (1940–1990)

200+%	
100–199%	
50–99%	★ Center of Population, 1790–2010
25–49%	
11–24%	
1–10%	

recipients of welfare as people who preferred to live at the expense of honest taxpayers rather than by working.

A striking example of Nixon's willingness to break the political mold, his plan to replace welfare with a guaranteed annual income failed to win approval by Congress. It proved too radical for conservatives, who saw it as a reward for laziness, while liberals denounced the proposed level of $1,600 per year for a needy family of four as inadequate.

> *Guaranteed annual income plan*

Nixon and Race

Nixon's racial policies offer a similarly mixed picture. To consolidate support in the white South, he nominated to the Supreme Court Clement Haynsworth and G. Harrold Carswell, conservative southern jurists with records of support for segregation. Both were rejected by the Senate. On the other hand, because the courts finally lost patience with southern delaying tactics, extensive racial integration at last came

Richard Nixon (on the right) and former Alabama governor George Wallace at an "Honor America" celebration in February 1974. Nixon's "southern strategy" sought to woo Wallace's supporters into the Republican Party.

The battle over busing students to achieve racial integration in Boston public schools produced a series of violent incidents, this one in April 1976. The photographer, Stanley Forman, won a Pulitzer Prize for this image, to which he gave the title *The Soiling of Old Glory*.

to public schools in the South. In Nixon's first three years in office, the proportion of southern black students attending integrated schools rose from 32 percent to 77 percent.

For a time, the Nixon administration also pursued **affirmative action** programs to upgrade minority employment. The Philadelphia Plan required that construction contractors on federal projects hire specific numbers of minority workers. Secretary of Labor George Shultz, who initiated the idea, sincerely hoped to open more jobs for black workers. Nixon seems to have viewed the plan mainly as a way of fighting inflation by weakening the power of the building trades unions. Their control over the labor market, he believed, pushed wages to unreasonably high levels, raising the cost of construction. And, he calculated, if the plan caused dissension between blacks and labor unions—two pillars of the Democratic coalition—Republicans could only benefit.

Trade unions of skilled workers like plumbers and electricians, which had virtually no black members, strongly opposed the Philadelphia Plan. After a widely publicized incident in May 1970, when a group of construction workers assaulted antiwar demonstrators in New York City, Nixon suddenly decided that he might be able to woo blue-collar workers in preparation for his 1972 reelection campaign. He soon abandoned the Philadelphia Plan in favor of an ineffective one that stressed voluntary local efforts toward minority hiring instead of federal requirements.

The Burger Court

When Earl Warren retired as chief justice in 1969, Nixon appointed Warren Burger, a federal court-of-appeals judge, to succeed him. An outspoken critic of the "judicial activism" of the Warren Court—its willingness to expand old rights and create new ones by overturning acts of Congress and the states—Burger was expected to lead the justices in a conservative direction. But like Nixon, he surprised many of his supporters. While the pace of change slowed, the Burger Court, at least initially, consolidated and expanded many of the judicial innovations of the 1960s.

In 1971, in *Swann v. Charlotte-Mecklenburg Board of Education*, which arose from North Carolina, the justices unanimously approved a lower court's plan that required the extensive transportation of students to achieve school integration. The decision led to hundreds of cases in which judges throughout the country ordered the use of **busing** as a tool to achieve integration. With many white parents determined to keep their children in neighborhood schools and others willing to move to the suburbs or enroll them in private academies to avoid integration, busing became a lightning rod for protests. One of the most bitter fights took place in Boston in the mid-1970s. Residents of the tightly knit Irish-American community of South Boston demonstrated vociferously and sometimes violently against a busing plan decreed by a local judge.

The Supreme Court soon abandoned the idea of overturning local control of schools, or moving students great distances to achieve integration. In 1973, it rebuffed a group of Texas Latinos who sued to overturn the use of property taxes to finance public education. Because of the great disparity in wealth between districts, spending on predominantly Mexican-American schools stood far below that for white ones. But in *San Antonio Independent School District v. Rodriguez*, a 5-4 Court majority ruled that the Constitution did not require equality of school funding. In the following year, in *Milliken v. Bradley* (1974), the justices overturned a lower court order that required Detroit's predominantly white suburbs to enter into a regional desegregation plan with the city's heavily minority school system. By absolving suburban districts of responsibility for assisting in integrating urban schools, the decision guaranteed that housing segregation would be mirrored in public education. Indeed, by the 1990s, public schools in the North were considerably more segregated than those in the South.

> Milliken v. Bradley

The Court and Affirmative Action

Efforts to promote greater employment opportunities for minorities also spawned politically divisive legal issues. Many whites came to view affirmative action programs as a form of **reverse discrimination**. Even as such programs quickly spread from blacks to encompass women, Latinos, Asian-Americans, and Native Americans, conservatives demanded that the Supreme Court invalidate them all. The justices refused, but they found it difficult to devise a consistent approach to this politically charged issue.

> *Opposition to affirmative action*

In *Griggs v. Duke Power Company* (1971), the Court ruled that even racially neutral job requirements such as a written examination were illegal if they operated to exclude a disproportionate number of non-white applicants and were not directly related to job performance. Later in the decade, in *United Steelworkers of America v. Weber* (1979), it upheld a program devised by the Kaiser Aluminum & Chemical Corporation and its union that set quotas for training and hiring non-white workers in skilled jobs. Since this private, voluntary agreement did not involve government action, the Court ruled, it did not violate the Fourteenth Amendment's ban on state policies that discriminated among citizens.

One result of the sexual revolution was a sharp rise in the age at which Americans chose to marry, and an increase in the number of divorces.

The justices, however, proved increasingly hostile to governmental affirmative action policies. In *Regents of the University of California v. Bakke* (1978), the Court overturned an admissions program of the University of California at Davis, a public university, which set aside 16 of 100 places in the entering medical school class for minority students. Justice Lewis F. Powell, a Nixon appointee who cast the deciding vote in the 5-4 decision, rejected the idea of fixed affirmative action quotas. He added, however, that race could be used as one factor among many in admissions decisions, so affirmative action continued at most colleges and universities. *Bakke* continues to be the standard by which affirmative action programs are judged today.

The Continuing Sexual Revolution

As noted in the previous chapter, the social activism associated with the 1960s continued in the following decade. Both right and left took part in grassroots movements, ranging from campaigns against nuclear weapons and nuclear power plants and struggles to aid migrant workers to battles to stop the court-ordered busing of public school children and movements against abortion rights. But the most profound changes in American life arose from the continuing sexual revolution.

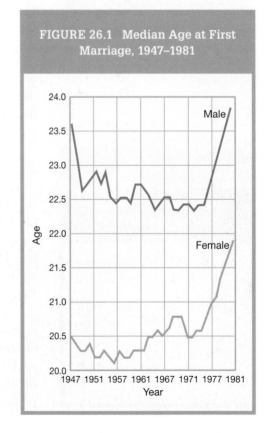

FIGURE 26.1 Median Age at First Marriage, 1947–1981

To the alarm of conservatives, during the 1970s the sexual revolution passed from the counterculture into the social mainstream. The number of Americans who told public-opinion polls that premarital sex was wrong plummeted. The number of divorces soared, reaching more than 1 million in 1975, double the number ten years earlier. The age at which both men and women married rose dramatically. The figure for divorces in 1975 exceeded the number of first-time marriages. A popular 1978 film, *An Unmarried Woman*, portrayed the dissolution of a marriage as a triumph for the wife, who discovered her potential for individual growth only after being abandoned by her husband. As a result of women's changing aspirations and the availability of birth control and legal abortions, the American birthrate declined dramatically. By 1976, the average woman was bearing 1.7 children during her lifetime, less than half the figure of 1957 and below the level at which a population reproduces itself. A 1971 survey of the last five graduating classes at Bryn Mawr, an elite women's college, reported the birth of more than seventy children. A similar survey covering the classes of 1971 through 1975 found that only three had been born. (Of course, many of these women eventually did marry and have children. But unlike their mothers of the "baby-boom" generation, they postponed these decisions to pursue careers.)

During the Nixon years, women made inroads into areas from which they had long been excluded. In 1972, Congress approved **Title IX**, which banned gender discrimination in higher education, and the Equal Credit Opportunity Act, which required that married women be given access to credit in their own name. The giant corporation American Telephone and Telegraph (AT&T) entered into a landmark agreement in which it agreed to pay millions of dollars to workers who had suffered gender discrimination and to upgrade employment opportunities for women. The number of women at work continued its upward climb. In 1960, only 20 percent of women with young children had been in the workforce. The figure reached 40 percent in 1980, and 55 percent in 1990. Working women were motivated by varied aims. Some sought careers in professions and skilled jobs previously open only to men. Others, spurred by the need to bolster family income as the economy faltered, flooded into the traditional, low-wage, "pink-collar" sector, working as cashiers, secretaries, and telephone operators.

In addition, the gay and lesbian movement, born at the end of the 1960s, expanded greatly during the 1970s and became a major concern of the right. In 1969, there had been about fifty local gay rights groups in the United States; ten years later, their numbers reached into the thousands. They began to elect local officials, persuaded many states to decriminalize homosexual relations, and succeeded in convincing cities with large gay populations to pass antidiscrimination laws. They actively encouraged gay men and lesbians to "come out of the closet"—that is, to reveal their sexual orientation. During the 1970s, the American Psychiatric Association removed homosexuality from its list of mental diseases.

As pre–World War I bohemians saw many of their ideas absorbed into the mass culture of the 1920s, values and styles of the 1960s became part of 1970s America, dubbed by the writer Tom Wolfe the "Me Decade." The demand of student protesters that individuals be empowered to determine their own "lifestyle" emerged in depoliticized form in Americans' obsession with self-improvement through fitness programs, health food diets, and new forms of psychological therapy.

TABLE 26.1 Rate of Divorce: Divorces of Existing Marriages per 1,000 New Marriages, 1950–1980

YEAR	DIVORCES
1950	385
1955	377
1960	393
1965	479
1970	708
1975	1,036
1980	1,189

Nixon and Détente

Just as domestic policies and social trends under Nixon disappointed conservatives, they viewed his foreign policy as dangerously "soft" on communism. To be sure, in the Third World, Nixon and Henry Kissinger, his national security adviser and secretary of state, continued their predecessors' policy of attempting to undermine governments deemed dangerous to American strategic or economic interests. Nixon funneled arms to dictatorial pro-American regimes in Iran, the Philippines, and South Africa. After Chile in 1970 elected socialist Salvador Allende as president, the CIA worked with his domestic opponents to destabilize the regime. On September 11, 1973, Allende was overthrown and killed in a military coup, which installed a bloody dictatorship under General Augusto Pinochet. Thousands of Allende backers, including a few Americans then in Chile, were tortured and murdered, and many others fled the country. The Nixon administration knew of the coup plans in advance but failed to warn Allende, and it continued to back Pinochet despite his brutal policies. Democracy did not return to Chile until the end of the 1980s.

The Allende affair

In his relations with the major communist powers, however, Nixon fundamentally altered Cold War policies. Nixon had launched his political career as a fierce and, critics charged, unscrupulous anticommunist. But in the language of foreign relations, he and Kissinger were "realists." They had more interest in power than ideology and preferred international stability to relentless conflict. Nixon also hoped that if relations with the Soviet Union improved, the Russians would influence North Vietnam to agree to an end to the Vietnam War on terms acceptable to the United States.

Nixon and Kissinger's "realist" foreign policy

Nixon realized that far from being part of a unified communist bloc, China had its own interests, different from those of the Soviet Union, and was destined to play a major role on the world stage. The policy of refusing to recognize China's communist government had reached a dead end. In 1971, Kissinger flew secretly to China, paving the way for Nixon's own astonishing public visit of February 1972. The trip led to the Beijing government's taking up China's seat at the United Nations, previously occupied by the exiled regime on Taiwan. Full diplomatic relations between the United States and the People's Republic of China were not established until 1979. But Nixon's visit sparked a dramatic increase in trade between the two countries.

Richard Nixon at a banquet celebrating his visit to China in February 1972. To his right is Premier Zhou Enlai.

Three months after his trip to Beijing, Nixon became the first Cold War American president to visit the Soviet Union, where he engaged in intense negotiations with his Soviet counterpart, Leonid Brezhnev. Out of this "summit" meeting came agreements for increased trade and two landmark arms-control treaties. SALT (named for the **Strategic Arms Limitation Talks** under way since 1969) froze each country's arsenal of intercontinental missiles capable of carrying nuclear warheads. The Anti–Ballistic Missile Treaty banned the development of systems designed to intercept incoming missiles, so

"Peaceful coexistence"

that neither side would be tempted to attack the other without fearing devastating retaliation. Nixon and Brezhnev proclaimed a new era of "peaceful coexistence," in which **détente** (cooperation) would replace the hostility of the Cold War.

VIETNAM AND WATERGATE

Nixon and Vietnam

Despite Nixon's foreign policy triumphs, one issue would not go away—Vietnam. Nixon ran for president in 1968 declaring that he had a "secret plan" to end the war. On taking office, he announced a new policy, Vietnamization. Under this plan, American troops would gradually be withdrawn while South Vietnamese soldiers, backed by continued American bombing, did more and more of the fighting. But Vietnamization neither limited the war nor ended the antiwar movement. Hoping to cut North Vietnamese supply lines, Nixon in 1970 ordered American troops into neutral Cambodia. The invasion did not achieve its military goals, but it destabilized the Cambodian government and set in motion a chain of events that eventually brought to power the Khmer Rouge. Before being ousted by a Vietnamese invasion in 1979, this local communist movement attempted to force virtually all Cambodians into rural communes and committed widespread massacres in that unfortunate country.

The invasion of Cambodia and its consequences

As the war escalated, protests again spread on college campuses, partly because the policy of exempting students from the draft had ended. In the wake of the killing of four antiwar protesters at Kent State University by the Ohio National Guard and two by police at Jackson State University in Mississippi, the student movement reached its high-water mark. In the spring of 1970, more than 350 colleges and universities experienced strikes, and troops occupied 21 campuses. The protests at Kent State, a public university with a largely working-class student body, and Jackson State, a black institution, demonstrated how antiwar sentiment had spread far beyond elite campuses like Berkeley and Columbia.

Tear gas envelops the campus as members of the Ohio National Guard prepare to fire on student demonstrators at Kent State University. Shortly after this photo was taken, four students lay dead.

At the same time, troop morale in Vietnam plummeted. For most of the war, college students had received exemptions. As a result, the army was predominantly composed of working-class whites and members of racial minorities. Of the 2.5 million Americans who served in the military during the war, around 80 percent came from poor and working-class families. African-Americans accounted for one-eighth of American casualties in Vietnam.

The same social changes sweeping the home front were evident among troops in Vietnam. Soldiers experimented with drugs, openly wore peace and black-power symbols, refused orders, and even assaulted unpopular officers. In 1971, thousands deserted the army, while at home Vietnam veterans held antiwar demonstrations. The decline of discipline within the army convinced increasing numbers of high-ranking officers that the United States must extricate itself from Vietnam.

Public support for the war was rapidly waning. In 1969, the *New York Times* published details of the **My Lai massacre** of 1968, in which a company of American troops killed some 350 South Vietnamese civilians. After a military investigation, one soldier, Lieutenant William Calley, was found guilty of directing the atrocity. (The courts released him from prison in 1974.) While hardly typical of the behavior of most servicemen, My Lai further undermined public support for the war.

In 1971, the *Times* began publishing the **Pentagon Papers**, a classified report prepared by the Defense Department that traced American involvement in Vietnam back to World War II and revealed how successive presidents had misled the American people about it. In a landmark freedom-of-the-press decision, the Supreme Court rejected Nixon's request for an injunction to halt publication. In 1973, Congress passed the **War Powers Act**. The most vigorous assertion of congressional control over foreign policy in the nation's history, it required the president to seek congressional approval for the commitment of American troops overseas.

In 1971, in one of the most dramatic demonstrations of the entire era, hundreds of veterans deposited on the steps of the Capitol medals they had received while fighting in Vietnam.

The End of the Vietnam War

Early in 1973, Nixon achieved what had eluded his predecessors—a negotiated settlement in Vietnam. The Paris peace agreement, the result of five years of talks, made possible the final withdrawal of American troops. The compromise left in place the government of South Vietnam, but it also left North Vietnamese and Viet Cong soldiers in control of parts of the South. American bombing ceased, and the military draft came to an end. Henceforth, volunteers would make up the armed forces. But the agreement did not solve the basic issue of the war—whether Vietnam would be one country or two. That question was answered in the spring of 1975, when the North Vietnamese launched a final military offensive. The government of South Vietnam collapsed; the United States did not intervene except to evacuate the American embassy, and Vietnam was reunified under communist rule.

> *Reunification*

The only war the United States has ever lost, Vietnam was a military, political, and social disaster. By the time it ended, 58,000 Americans had been killed, along with 3 million to 4 million Vietnamese. The war cost the United States many hundreds of millions of dollars and diverted funds from needs at home. But the nonmonetary price was far higher. Vietnam undermined Americans' confidence in their own institutions and challenged long-standing beliefs about the country and its purposes. The divisions caused by the war continued in debates over its legacy that persisted for many years. The war's supporters blamed critics at home for undermining a successful and winnable military effort. Others took the lesson

> *The consequences of the war*

VIETNAM AND WATERGATE | 1023

A campaign poster from the 1972 election does not even name Richard Nixon, referring to him only as "the president." It includes images of some of his accomplishments, including pursuing détente with China (bottom) and the Soviet Union (above and to the left).

The Watergate hearings

that the United States should be extremely reluctant to commit its armed forces overseas—an outlook sometimes called the **Vietnam Syndrome**.

Two decades after the war ended, former secretary of defense Robert McNamara published a memoir in which he admitted that the policy he had helped to shape had been "terribly wrong." Ignorance of the history and culture of Vietnam and a misguided belief that every communist movement in the world was a puppet of Moscow, he wrote, had led the country into a war that he now profoundly regretted. The *New York Times* rejected McNamara's apology. The "ghosts of those unlived lives," the young men sent to their death "for no purpose," it declared, could not so easily be wished away. But the *Times* itself, like the rest of the political establishment, had supported the war for most of its duration. For far too long, they had accepted its basic premise—that the United States had the right to decide the fate of a faraway people about whom it knew almost nothing.

Watergate

By the time the war ended, Richard Nixon was no longer president. His domestic policies and foreign policy successes had contributed greatly to his reelection in 1972. He won a landslide victory over liberal Democrat George McGovern, receiving 60 percent of the popular vote. Nixon made deep inroads into former Democratic strongholds in the South and among working-class white northerners. He carried every state but Massachusetts. But his triumph soon turned into disaster.

Nixon was obsessed with secrecy and could not accept honest difference of opinion. He viewed every critic as a threat to national security and developed an "enemies list" that included reporters, politicians, and celebrities unfriendly to the administration. When the Pentagon Papers were published, Nixon created a special investigative unit known as the "plumbers" to gather information about Daniel Ellsberg, the former government official who had leaked them to the press. The plumbers raided the office of Ellsberg's psychiatrist in search of incriminating records. In June 1972, five former employees of Nixon's reelection committee took part in a break-in at Democratic Party headquarters in the **Watergate** apartment complex in Washington, D.C. A security guard called police, who arrested the intruders.

No one knows precisely what the Watergate burglars were looking for (perhaps they intended to install listening devices), and the botched robbery played little role in the 1972 presidential campaign. But in 1973, Judge John J. Sirica, before whom the burglars were tried, determined to find out who had sponsored the break-in. A pair of *Washington Post* journalists began publishing investigative stories that made it clear that persons close to the president had ordered the burglary and then tried to "cover up" White House involvement. Congressional hearings followed that revealed a wider pattern of wiretapping, break-ins, and attempts to sabotage political opposition. When it became known that Nixon had made tape recordings of conversations in his office, Archibald Cox, a special prosecutor the president had reluctantly appointed to investigate the Watergate affair, demanded copies. In October 1973, Nixon proposed to allow Senator John C. Stennis of Mississippi to review the tapes, rather than release them. When Cox refused, Nixon fired him, whereupon Attorney General Elliot Richardson resigned in protest. These events, known as the Saturday Night Massacre, further undermined Nixon's standing. The Supreme Court unanimously ordered Nixon to provide the tapes—a decision that reaffirmed the principle that the president is not above the law.

> *Saturday Night Massacre*

Nixon's Fall

Week after week, revelations about the scandal unfolded. By mid-1974, it had become clear that whether or not Nixon knew in advance of the Watergate break-in, he had become involved immediately afterward in authorizing payments to the burglars to remain silent or commit perjury, and he had ordered the FBI to halt its investigation of the crime. In August 1974, the House Judiciary Committee voted to recommend that Nixon be impeached for conspiracy to obstruct justice. His political support having evaporated, Nixon became the only president in history to resign.

> *Nixon's resignation*

Nixon's presidency remains a classic example of the abuse of political power. In 1973, his vice president, Spiro T. Agnew, resigned after revelations that he had accepted bribes from construction firms while serving as governor of Maryland. Nixon's attorney general, John Mitchell, and White House aides H. R. Haldeman and John Ehrlichman, were convicted of obstruction of justice in the Watergate affair and went to jail. As for the president, he insisted that he had done nothing wrong—or at any rate, that previous presidents had also been guilty of lying and illegality.

Although it hardly excused his behavior, Nixon had a point. His departure from office was followed by Senate hearings headed by Frank Church of Idaho that laid bare a history of abusive actions that involved every administration since the beginning of the Cold War. In violation of the law, the FBI had spied on millions of Americans and had tried to disrupt the civil rights movement. The CIA had conducted secret operations to overthrow foreign governments and had tried to assassinate foreign leaders. It had even recruited a secret army to fight in Laos, a neighbor of Vietnam. Abuses of power, in other words, went far beyond the misdeeds of a single president.

Along with Watergate, the Pentagon Papers, and the Vietnam War itself, the Church Committee revelations seriously undermined Americans' confidence in their own government. They led Congress to enact new restrictions on the power of the FBI and CIA to spy on American citizens or conduct operations abroad without the knowledge of lawmakers. Congress also strengthened the Freedom of Information Act (FOIA), initially enacted in 1966. Since 1974, the FOIA has allowed scholars, journalists, and ordinary citizens to gain access to millions of pages of records of federal agencies.

Liberals, who had despised Nixon throughout his career, celebrated his downfall. They did not realize that the revulsion against Watergate undermined the foundations of liberalism itself, already weakened by the divisions of the 1960s. For liberalism rests, in part, on belief in the ability of government, especially the federal government, to solve social problems and promote both the public good and individual freedom. Nixon's fall and the revelations of years of governmental misconduct helped to convince many Americans that conservatives were correct

Herbert Block's 1973 cartoon depicts Americans' disbelief as revelations related to the Watergate scandal unfolded in Washington.

The World Trade Center under construction in New York City in the 1970s.

Because of economic dislocations and deindustrialization, Americans' real wages (wages adjusted to take account of inflation) peaked in the early 1970s and then began a sharp, prolonged decline.

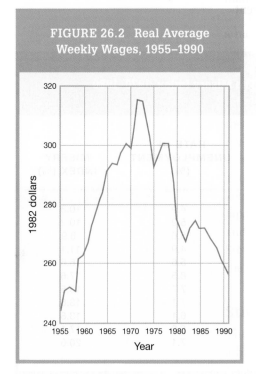

FIGURE 26.2 Real Average Weekly Wages, 1955–1990

competition, corporations stepped up the trend, already under way before 1970, toward eliminating well-paid manufacturing jobs through automation and shifting production to low-wage areas of the United States and overseas. The effects on older industrial cities were devastating. By 1980, Detroit and Chicago had lost more than half the manufacturing jobs that had existed three decades earlier.

Smaller industrial cities suffered even sharper declines. As their tax bases shriveled, many found themselves unable to maintain public services. In Paterson, New Jersey, where great silk factories had arisen in the early twentieth century, **deindustrialization** left a landscape of abandoned manufacturing plants. The poverty rate reached 20 percent, the city sold off public library buildings to raise cash, and the schools became so run down and overcrowded that the state government took control. The accelerating flow of jobs, investment, and population to the nonunion, low-wage states of the **Sunbelt** increased the political influence of this conservative region. Of population growth in metropolitan areas, during the 1970s, 96 percent occurred in the South and West. San Jose and Phoenix, with populations around 100,000 in 1950, neared 1 million by 1990.

In some manufacturing centers, political and economic leaders welcomed the opportunity to remake their cities as finance, information, and entertainment hubs. In New York, the construction of the World Trade Center, completed in 1977, symbolized this shift in the economy. Until destroyed by terrorists twenty-four years later, the 110-story "twin towers" stood as a symbol of New York's grandeur. But to make way for the World Trade Center, the city displaced hundreds of small electronics, printing, and other firms, causing the loss of thousands of manufacturing jobs.

Labor on the Defensive

Always a junior partner in the Democratic coalition, the labor movement found itself forced onto the defensive. It has remained there ever since. One example of the weakening of unions' power came in 1975 with the New York City fiscal crisis. Deeply in debt and unable to market its bonds, the city faced the prospect of bankruptcy. The solution to the crisis required a reduction of the city's workforce, severe cuts in the budgets of schools, parks, and the subway system, and an end to the century-old policy of free tuition at the City University. Even in this center of unionism, working-class New Yorkers had no choice but to absorb job losses and a drastic decline in public services.

The weakening of unions and the continuation of the economy's long-term shift from manufacturing to service employment had an adverse impact on ordinary Americans. Between 1953 and 1973, median family income had doubled. But in 1973, real wages began to fall. The popular song "The River," by Bruce Springsteen, captured the woes of blue-collar workers: "Is a dream a lie if it don't come true / Or is it something worse?"

Ford as President

Economic problems dogged the presidencies of Nixon's successors. Gerald Ford, who had been appointed to replace Vice President Agnew, succeeded to the White House when Nixon resigned. Ford named Nelson Rockefeller of New York as his own vice president. Thus, for the only time in American history, both offices were occupied by persons for whom no one had actually voted. Among his first acts as president, Ford pardoned Nixon, shielding him from prosecution for obstruction of justice. Ford claimed that he wanted the country to put the Watergate scandal behind it. But the pardon proved to be widely unpopular.

In domestic policy, Ford's presidency lacked significant accomplishment. Ford and his chief economic adviser, Alan Greenspan, believed that Americans spent too much on consumption and saved too little, leaving business with insufficient money for investment. They called for cutting taxes on business and lessening government regulation of the economy. But the Democratic majority in Congress was in no mood to accept these traditional Republican policies. To combat inflation, Ford urged Americans to shop wisely, reduce expenditures, and wear WIN buttons (for "Whip Inflation Now"). Although inflation fell, joblessness continued to rise. During the steep recession of 1974–1975 unemployment exceeded 9 percent, the highest level since the Depression.

In the international arena, 1975 witnessed the major achievement of Ford's presidency. In a continuation of Nixon's policy of détente, the United States and Soviet Union signed an agreement at Helsinki, Finland, that recognized the permanence of Europe's post–World War II boundaries (including the division of Germany). In addition, both superpowers agreed to respect the basic liberties of their citizens. Secretary of State Kissinger and his Soviet counterpart, Andrey Gromyko, assumed that this latter pledge would have little practical effect. But over time, the **Helsinki Accords** inspired movements for greater freedom within the communist countries of eastern Europe.

The Carter Administration

In the presidential election of 1976, Jimmy Carter, a former governor of Georgia, narrowly defeated Ford. A graduate of the U.S. Naval Academy who later became a peanut farmer, Carter was virtually unknown outside his state when he launched his campaign for the Democratic nomination. But realizing that Watergate and Vietnam had produced a crisis in confidence in the federal government, he turned his obscurity into an advantage. Carter ran for president as an "outsider," making a virtue of the fact that he had never held federal office. A devout "born-again" Baptist, he spoke openly of his religious convictions. His promise, "I'll never lie to you," resonated with an electorate tired of official dishonesty.

Carter had much in common with Progressives of the early twentieth century. His passions were making government more efficient, protecting the environment, and raising the moral tone of politics. Unlike the Progressives, however,

President Gerald Ford tried to enlist Americans in his "Whip Inflation Now" program. It did not succeed.

International agreement

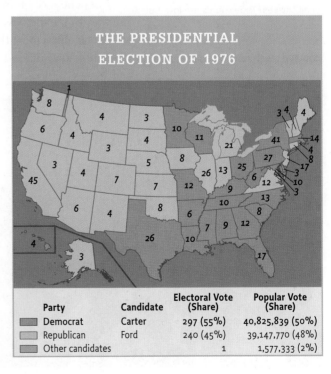

THE PRESIDENTIAL ELECTION OF 1976

Party	Candidate	Electoral Vote (Share)	Popular Vote (Share)
Democrat	Carter	297 (55%)	40,825,839 (50%)
Republican	Ford	240 (45%)	39,147,770 (48%)
Other candidates		1	1,577,333 (2%)

Carter and race

he embraced the aspirations of black Americans. As president, Carter appointed an unprecedented number of blacks to important positions, including Andrew Young, a former lieutenant of Martin Luther King Jr., as ambassador to the United Nations.

Carter and the Economic Crisis

The New Democrats

The Democratic Party found itself ill-equipped to deal with the economic crisis. The social upheavals of the 1960s had led to the emergence of politicians known as the New Democrats. Representing affluent urban and suburban districts, they viewed issues like race relations, gender equality, the environment, and improving the political process as more central than traditional economic matters. Although his party controlled both houses, Carter often found himself at odds with Congress. He viewed inflation, not unemployment, as the country's main economic problem, and to combat it he promoted cuts in spending on domestic programs. In the hope that increased competition would reduce prices, his administration enacted **deregulation** in the trucking and airline industries. Anticipating what would come to be called the supply-side economics of the Reagan administration, Carter in 1978 inaugurated tax cuts for wealthier Americans in the hope that this would stimulate investment and encourage economic growth. In 1980, with Carter's approval, Congress repealed usury laws—laws that limit how much interest lenders can charge—allowing credit card companies to push their interest rates up to 20 percent or even higher. Carter supported the Federal Reserve Bank's decision to raise interest rates to curtail economic activity until both wages and prices fell, traditionally a Republican policy. But oil prices kept rising, thanks to the overthrow of the shah of Iran, discussed later, and inflation did not decline.

Carter's economic plan

Carter also believed that expanded use of nuclear energy could help reduce dependence on imported oil. For years, proponents of nuclear power had hailed it as an inexpensive way of meeting the country's energy needs. By the time Carter took office, more than 200 nuclear plants were operating or on order. But in 1979 the industry suffered a near-fatal blow when an accident at the **Three Mile Island** plant in Pennsylvania released a large amount of radioactive steam into the atmosphere. The rise of the environmental movement had promoted public skepticism about scientific experts who touted the miraculous promise of technological innovations without concern for their social consequences. The Three Mile Island mishap reinforced fears about the environmental hazards associated with nuclear energy and put a halt to the industry's expansion.

The deregulation of the airline industry produced lower fares but also a drastic decline in service. Before deregulation, with prices fixed, airlines sought to attract customers by providing good service in all classes. Today, fares are low, but passengers are jammed in like sardines and have to pay for checked baggage, onboard meals, and other amenities.

Since the New Deal, Democrats had presented themselves as the party of affluence and economic growth. But Carter seemed to be presiding over a period of national decline. It did not help his popularity when, in a speech in 1979, he spoke of a national "crisis of confidence" and seemed to blame it on the American people themselves and their "mistaken idea of freedom" as "self-indulgence and consumption."

The 1979 accident at the Three Mile Island nuclear plant in Pennsylvania brought a halt to the industry's expansion.

The Emergence of Human Rights Politics

Under Carter, a commitment to promoting human rights became a centerpiece of American foreign policy for the first time. He was influenced by the proliferation of information about global denials of human rights spread by nongovernmental agencies like Amnesty International and the International League for Human Rights. The American membership of Amnesty International, a London-based organization, grew from 6,000 to 35,000 between 1970 and 1976. Its reports marked a significant break with dominant ideas about international affairs since World War II, which had viewed the basic division in the world as between communist and noncommunist countries. Such reports, along with congressional hearings, fact-finding missions, and academic studies of human rights, exposed misdeeds not only by communist countries but also by American allies, especially the death squads of Latin American dictatorships. Amnesty International pressured the United States to try to do something to promote human rights abroad. In 1977, Amnesty International received the Nobel Peace Prize, an indication of the rapid emergence of human rights as an international issue.

Amnesty International

In 1978, Carter cut off aid to the brutal military dictatorship governing Argentina, which in the name of anticommunism had launched a "dirty war" against its own citizens, kidnapping off the streets and secretly murdering an estimated 10,000 to 30,000 persons. Carter's action was a dramatic gesture, as Argentina was one of the most important powers in Latin America and previous American administrations had turned a blind eye to human rights abuses by Cold War allies. By the end of his presidency, the phrase "human rights" had acquired political potency. Its very vagueness was both a weakness and a strength. It was difficult to define exactly what rights should and should not be considered universally applicable, but various groups could and did unite under the umbrella of global human rights.

Carter's human rights foreign policy

President Jimmy Carter (*center*), Egyptian president Anwar Sadat (*left*), and Israeli prime minister Menachem Begin (*right*) celebrating the signing of the 1979 peace treaty between Israel and Egypt.

Carter's effectiveness

Human rights issues

Carter believed that in the post-Vietnam era, American foreign policy should de-emphasize Cold War thinking. Combating poverty in the Third World, preventing the spread of nuclear weapons, and promoting human rights should take priority over what he called "the inordinate fear of communism that once led us to embrace any dictator who joined us in that fear." In one of his first acts as president, he offered an unconditional pardon to Vietnam-era draft resisters.

Carter's emphasis on pursuing peaceful solutions to international problems and his willingness to think outside the Cold War framework yielded important results. In 1979, he brought the leaders of Egypt and Israel to the presidential retreat at Camp David and brokered a historic peace agreement, the **Camp David Accords**, between the two countries. He improved American relations with Latin America by agreeing to a treaty, ratified by the Senate in 1978, that provided for the transfer of the Panama Canal to local control by the year 2000. In 1979, he resisted calls for intervention when a popular revolution led by the left-wing Sandinista movement overthrew Nicaraguan dictator Anastasio Somoza, a longtime ally of the United States. Carter attempted to curb the murderous violence of death squads allied to the right-wing government of El Salvador, and in 1980 he suspended military aid after the murder of four American nuns by members of the country's army. He signed the SALT II agreement with the Soviets, which reduced the number of missiles, bombers, and nuclear warheads.

Both conservative Cold Warriors and foreign policy "realists" severely criticized Carter's emphasis on human rights. He himself found it impossible to translate rhetoric into action. He criticized American arms sales to the rest of the world. But with thousands of jobs and billions of dollars in corporate profits at stake, he did nothing to curtail them. The United States continued its support of allies with records of serious human rights violations such as the governments of Guatemala, the Philippines, South Korea, and Iran. Indeed, the American connection with the shah of Iran, whose secret police regularly jailed and tortured political opponents, proved to be Carter's undoing.

The Iran Crisis and Afghanistan

Occupying a strategic location on the southern border of the Soviet Union, Iran was a major supplier of oil and an importer of American military equipment. At the end of 1977, Carter traveled there to help celebrate the shah's rule, causing the internal opposition to become more and more anti-American. Early in 1979, a popular revolution inspired by the exiled Muslim cleric Ayatollah Khomeini overthrew the shah and declared Iran an Islamic republic.

The Iranian revolution marked an ideological shift in opposition movements in the Middle East from socialism and Arab nationalism to religious fundamentalism. This would have important long-term consequences for the United States. More immediately, when Carter in November 1979 allowed the deposed shah to seek medical treatment in the United States, Khomeini's followers invaded the American embassy in Tehran and seized sixty-six hostages. Fourteen people (women, African-American men, and a white man in ill health) were soon released, leaving fifty-two captives. They did not regain their freedom until January 1981, on the day Carter's term as president ended. Events in Iran made Carter seem helpless and inept and led to a rapid fall in his popularity.

Another crisis that began in 1979 undermined American relations with Moscow. At the end of that year, the Soviet Union sent thousands of troops into Afghanistan to support a friendly government threatened by an Islamic rebellion. In the long run, Afghanistan became the Soviet Vietnam, an unwinnable conflict whose mounting casualties seriously weakened the government at home. Initially, however, it seemed another example of declining American power.

Declaring the invasion the greatest crisis since World War II (a considerable exaggeration), the president announced the Carter Doctrine, declaring that the United States would use military force, if necessary, to protect its interests in the Persian Gulf. He placed an embargo on grain exports to the Soviet Union and organized a Western boycott of the 1980 Olympics, which took place in Moscow. He withdrew the SALT II treaty from consideration by the Senate and dramatically increased American military spending. In a reversion to the Cold War principle that any opponent of the Soviet Union deserved American support, the United States funneled aid to fundamentalist Muslims in Afghanistan who fought a decade-long guerrilla war against the Soviets. The alliance had unforeseen consequences. A faction of Islamic fundamentalists known as the Taliban eventually came to power in Afghanistan. Tragically, they would prove as hostile to the United States as to Moscow.

In an unsuccessful attempt to bring down inflation, Carter had abandoned the Keynesian economic policy of increased government spending to combat recession in favor of high interest rates. He had cut back on social spending and the federal government's economic regulations, while projecting a major increase in the military budget. By 1980, détente had been eclipsed and the Cold War reinvigorated. Thus, many of the conservative policies associated with his successor, Ronald Reagan, were already in place when Carter's presidency ended.

Iran hostage crisis

Soviet Vietnam

American hostages being paraded by their Iranian captors on the first day of the occupation of the American embassy in Tehran in 1979. Television gave extensive coverage to the plight of the hostages, leading many Americans to view the Carter administration as weak and inept.

THE RISING TIDE OF CONSERVATISM

The combination of domestic and international dislocations during the 1970s created a widespread sense of anxiety among Americans and offered conservatives new political opportunities. Economic problems heightened the appeal of lower taxes, reduced government regulation, and cuts in social spending to spur business investment. Fears about a decline of American power in the world led to calls for a renewal of the Cold War. The civil rights and sexual revolutions produced resentments that undermined the Democratic coalition. Rising urban crime rates reinforced demands for law and order and attacks on courts considered too lenient toward criminals. These issues brought new converts to the conservative cause.

Issues for conservatives

As the 1970s went on, conservatives abandoned overt opposition to the black struggle for racial justice. The fiery rhetoric and direct confrontation tactics of Bull Connor, George Wallace, and other proponents of massive resistance were succeeded by appeals to freedom of association, local control, and resistance to the power of the federal government. This language of individual freedom resonated throughout the country, appealing especially to the growing, predominantly white, suburban population that was fleeing the cities and their urban problems. The suburbs would become one of the bastions of modern conservatism.

Conservatives and freedom

Like predecessors as diverse as the civil rights and labor movements, conservatives organized at the grass roots. In order to spread conservative doctrines, they ran candidates for office even when they had little chance of winning, and worked to change the policies of local institutions like school boards, town councils, and planning commissions.

One set of recruits was the **neoconservatives**, a group of intellectuals who charged that the 1960s had produced a decline in moral standards and respect for authority. Once supporters of liberalism, they had come to believe that even well-intentioned government social programs did more harm than good. Welfare, for example, not only failed to alleviate poverty but also encouraged single motherhood and undermined the work ethic. High taxes and expensive government regulations drained resources from productive enterprises, stifling economic growth. Neoconservatives repudiated the attempts by Nixon, Ford, and Carter to reorient foreign policy away from the Cold War. Carter's focus on human rights and alleged blindness to the Soviet threat, they argued, endangered the "survival of freedom." Conservative "think tanks" created during the 1970s, like the Heritage Foundation and the American Enterprise Institute, refined and spread these ideas.

Neoconservatives

The Religious Right

Religious fundamentalism

The rise of religious fundamentalism during the 1970s expanded conservatism's popular base. Challenged by the secular and material concerns of American society, some denominations tried to bring religion into harmony with these interests; others reasserted more traditional religious values. The latter approach seemed to appeal to growing numbers of Americans. Even as membership in mainstream denominations like Episcopalianism and Presbyterianism declined, evangelical Protestantism flourished. Some observers spoke of a Third Great Awakening (like those of the 1740s and early nineteenth century). The election of Carter, the first "born-again" Christian to become president, highlighted the growing influence of evangelical religion. But unlike Carter, most fundamentalists who entered politics did so as conservatives.

Of course, there was nothing new about the involvement of churches in political life. There is a long tradition in American history of moral stewardship—devout Christians taking on responsibility for social reform and using political means to combat what they perceive as individual or collective sins. During the 1960s, many members of the burgeoning evangelical churches of the suburbs, South, and West had become more and more alienated from a culture that seemed to them to trivialize religion and promote immorality. Evangelicals of different denominations increasingly came to feel that they had more in common with each other than with more liberal coreligionists. They demanded the reversal of Supreme Court decisions banning prayer in public schools, protecting pornography as free speech, and legalizing abortion. Although it spoke of restoring traditional values, the Religious Right proved remarkably adept at using modern technology, including mass mailings and televised religious programming, to raise funds for their crusade and spread their message. In 1979, Jerry Falwell, a Virginia minister, created the self-styled Moral Majority, devoted to waging a "war against sin" and electing "pro-life, pro-family, pro-America" candidates to office. Falwell identified supporters of abortion rights, easy divorce, and "military unpreparedness" as the forces of Satan.

Christian conservatives seemed most agitated by the ongoing sexual revolution, which they saw as undermining the traditional family and promoting immorality. As a result of the 1960s, they believed, American freedom was out of control. The growing assertiveness of the new gay movement spurred an especially fierce reaction. In 1977, after a campaign led by the popular singer Anita Bryant, a familiar fixture in televised orange juice commercials, Dade County, Florida, passed an anti-gay ordinance under the banner "Save Our Children."

The Battle over the Equal Rights Amendment

During the 1970s, "family values" moved to the center of conservative politics, nowhere more so than in the battle over the Equal Rights Amendment (ERA). Originally proposed during the 1920s by Alice Paul and the Woman's Party, the ERA had been revived by second-wave feminists. In the wake of the rights revolution, the amendment's affirmation that "equality of rights under the law" could not be abridged "on account of sex" hardly seemed controversial. In 1972, with broad bipartisan support, Congress approved the ERA and sent it to the states for ratification. Designed to eliminate obstacles to the full participation of women in public life, it aroused unexpected protest from those who claimed it would discredit the role of wife and homemaker.

> Church and state

Phyllis Schlafly Campaigning against the Equal Rights Amendment. The activist Phyllis Schlafly, pictured here leading a rally at the Illinois State Capitol in 1978, was instrumental in grassroots organization of conservative men and women in opposition to the proposed Equal Rights Amendment to the Constitution, which would have barred all legal inequalities based on sex. She claimed that the amendment would take away "the right to be a housewife." The amendment's defeat was a major victory for the conservative movement.

A women's liberation march in Detroit in 1970 highlights the issue of equal pay for equal work. At the time, women earned less than men in virtually every category of employment.

Women divided

The ERA debate reflected a division among women as much as a battle of the sexes. To its supporters, the amendment offered a guarantee of women's freedom in the public sphere. To its foes, freedom for women still resided in the divinely appointed roles of wife and mother. Phyllis Schlafly, who helped to organize opposition to the ERA, insisted that the "free enterprise system" was the "real liberator of women," since labor-saving home appliances offered more genuine freedom than "whining about past injustices" or seeking fulfillment outside the home. Opponents claimed that the ERA would let men "off the hook" by denying their responsibility to provide for their wives and children. Polls consistently showed that a majority of Americans, male and female, favored the ERA. But thanks to the mobilization of conservative women, the amendment failed to achieve ratification by the required thirty-eight states.

The Abortion Controversy

Religious pro-life movement

An even more acrimonious battle emerged in the 1970s over abortion rights, another example, to conservatives, of how liberals in office promoted sexual immorality at the expense of moral values. The movement to reverse the 1973 *Roe v. Wade* decision began among Roman Catholics, whose church condemned abortion under any circumstances. But it soon enlisted evangelical Protestants and social conservatives more generally. Life, the movement insisted, begins at conception, and abortion is nothing less than murder. Between this position and the feminist insistence that a woman's right to control her body includes the right to a safe, legal abortion, compromise was impossible. Ironically, both sides showed how the rights revolution had reshaped the language of politics. Defenders of abortion exalted "the right to choose" as the essence of freedom. Opponents called

A 1979 anti-abortion rally in Washington, D.C., on the sixth anniversary of the Supreme Court's decision in *Roe v. Wade*, which barred states from limiting a woman's right to terminate a pregnancy.

themselves the "right to life" movement and claimed to represent the rights of the "unborn child."

The abortion issue drew a bitter, sometimes violent line through American politics. It affected battles over nominees to judicial positions and led to demonstrations at family-planning and abortion clinics. The anti-abortion movement won its first victory in 1976 when Congress, over President Ford's veto, ended federal funding for abortions for poor women through the Medicaid program. By the 1990s, a few fringe anti-abortion activists were placing bombs at medical clinics and murdering doctors who terminated pregnancies. Today, most women continue to have the legal right of access to abortion. But in many areas the procedure became more and more difficult to obtain as hospitals and doctors stopped providing it.

The Tax Revolt

With liberals unable to devise an effective policy to counteract deindustrialization and declining real wages, economic anxieties also created a growing constituency for conservative economics. Unlike during the Great Depression, economic distress inspired a critique of government rather than of business. New environmental regulations led to calls for less government intervention in the economy. The descent from affluence to stagflation increased the appeal of the conservative argument that government regulation raised business costs and eliminated jobs.

Economic decline also broadened the constituency receptive to demands for lower taxes. To conservatives, tax reductions served the dual purpose of enhancing business profits and reducing the resources available to government, thus making new social programs financially impossible.

Demonstrators at a rally supporting abortion rights.

Conservatism in the West

The West has always both reflected and contributed to national political trends. In the 1970s and 1980s it offered fertile soil for various strands of conservatism. The population movements of previous decades stimulated this development. Many southerners had left their homes for southern California, bringing with them their distinctive form of evangelical Christianity. Increasingly alienated from a Democratic Party that embraced the rights revolution and with it, evangelicals felt, the decline of traditional values, they gravitated to the California Republican Party, from which emerged national Republican leaders such as Richard Nixon and Ronald Reagan. California conservatives also embraced the new anti-tax mood.

California conservatives

In 1978, conservatives sponsored and California voters approved Proposition 13, a ban on further increases in property taxes. The vote demonstrated that the level of taxation could be a powerful political issue. Proposition 13 proved to be a windfall for businesses and home owners, while reducing funds available for schools, libraries, and other public services. Many voters, however, proved willing to accept this result of lower taxes. As anti-tax sentiment flourished throughout the country, many states followed California's lead.

California's Proposition 13

There have always been voices in the West insisting that the region has a colonial relationship with the rest of the country. They point to federal ownership of large swaths of western land, and the dependence of western development on investment from the East. In the late nineteenth century, this view helped give rise to western Populism, when the targets of protest were eastern banks and railroad companies, as well as a national economic policy that favored these corporations. Nearly a century later it became associated with a conservative upsurge known as the Sagebrush Rebellion (the name given to a bill passed by the Nevada legislature in 1979) directed at the federal government. The roots of this "rebellion" lie as far back as the 1920s, when the U.S. Forest Service announced plans to increase grazing fees and mineral rights in national forests and other public lands. Nevada's ranchers went to court to block these fees but were rebuffed by the Supreme Court. In the 1970s, new environmental regulations won fresh recruits to the movement. The Clean Air Act alarmed western coal operators. Westerners who believed the environmental policies of the Carter administration were closing the public domain to exploitation eagerly supported Ronald Reagan's presidential candidacy.

Sagebrush Rebellion

Using the language of freedom from government tyranny, leaders in western states insisted that the states themselves be given decision-making power over issues like grazing rights, mining development, and whether public lands should be closed to fishing and hunting. With the federal government reluctant to give up control over public lands in the West, the Sagebrush Rebellion had few concrete accomplishments, but it underscored the rising tide of antigovernment sentiment.

Growing anti-government sentiment

The Election of 1980

By 1980, Carter's approval rating had fallen to 21 percent—lower than Nixon's at the time of his resignation. A conservative tide seemed to be rising throughout the Western world. In 1979, Margaret Thatcher became prime minister of Great Britain. She promised to restore economic competitiveness by curtailing the power of unions, reducing taxes, selling state-owned industries to private owners, and cutting back the welfare state. In the United States, Ronald Reagan's 1980 campaign for the presidency brought together the many strands of 1970s conservatism. He pledged to end stagflation and restore the country's dominant role in the world and its confidence in itself. "Let's make America great again," he proclaimed. "The era of self-doubt is over."

Reagan also appealed skillfully to "white backlash." He kicked off his campaign in Philadelphia, Mississippi, where three civil rights workers had been murdered in 1964, with a speech emphasizing his belief in states' rights. Many white southerners understood this doctrine as including opposition to federal intervention on behalf of civil rights. During the campaign, Reagan repeatedly condemned welfare "cheats," school busing, and affirmative action. The Republican platform reversed the party's long-standing support for the Equal Rights Amendment and condemned moral permissiveness. Although not personally religious and the first divorced man to run for president, Reagan won the support of the Religious Right and conservative upholders of "family values."

Riding a wave of dissatisfaction with the country's condition, Reagan swept into the White House. He carried such Democratic strongholds as Illinois, Texas, and New York. Because moderate Republican John Anderson, running for president as an independent, received about 7 percent of the popular vote, Reagan won only a bare majority, although he commanded an overwhelming margin in the electoral college. Carter received 41 percent, a humiliating defeat for a sitting president.

Jimmy Carter's reputation improved after he left the White House. He went to work for Habitat for Humanity, an organization that constructs homes for poor families. In the 1990s, he negotiated a cease-fire between warring Muslim and Serb forces in Bosnia and arranged a peaceful transfer of power from the military to an elected government in Haiti. In 2002, Carter was awarded the Nobel Peace Prize. His presidency, however, is almost universally considered a failure. And his defeat in 1980 launched the **Reagan Revolution**, which completed the transformation of freedom from the rallying cry of the left to a possession of the right.

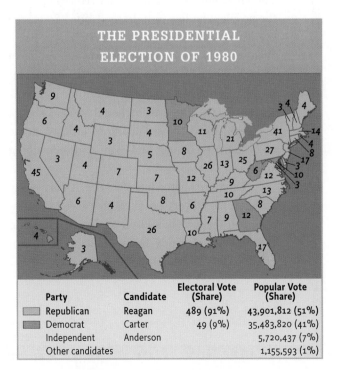

A delegate to the Republican national convention of 1980 wears a hat festooned with the flags of the United States and Texas, and a button with a picture of her hero, Ronald Reagan.

THE REAGAN REVOLUTION

Ronald Reagan followed a most unusual path to the presidency. Originally a New Deal Democrat and head of the Screen Actors Guild (the only union leader ever to reach the White House), he emerged in the 1950s as a spokesman for the General Electric Corporation, preaching the virtues of unregulated capitalism. His nominating speech for Barry Goldwater at the 1964 Republican convention brought Reagan to national attention. Two years later, California voters elected Reagan as governor. In 1976, he challenged President Ford for the Republican nomination and came close to winning it. His victory in 1980 brought to power a diverse coalition of old and new conservatives: Sunbelt suburbanites and urban working-class ethnics; antigovernment crusaders and advocates of a more aggressive foreign policy;

THE PRESIDENTIAL ELECTION OF 1980

Party	Candidate	Electoral Vote (Share)	Popular Vote (Share)
Republican	Reagan	489 (91%)	43,901,812 (51%)
Democrat	Carter	49 (9%)	35,483,820 (41%)
Independent	Anderson		5,720,437 (7%)
Other candidates			1,155,593 (1%)

VOICES OF FREEDOM

From BARRY COMMONER, *THE CLOSING CIRCLE* (1971)

Environmentalism, a movement born in the 1960s, expanded rapidly in the following decade. In *The Closing Circle*, Barry Commoner, a biologist later called the Paul Revere of the movement, warned that technological development and the pursuit of economic growth regardless of consequences were creating an environmental crisis. He called on Americans to alter their lifestyles to bring them into harmony with the "ecosphere"—the natural environment within which people live.

The environment has just been rediscovered by the people who live in it. In the United States the event was celebrated in April 1970, during Earth Week. It was a sudden, noisy awakening. School children cleaned up rubbish; college students organized new demonstrations; determined citizens recaptured the streets from the automobile, at least for a day. Everyone seemed to be aroused to the environmental danger and eager to do something about it.

They were offered lots of advice. Almost every writer, almost every speaker, on the college campuses, in the streets and on television and radio broadcasts, was ready to fix the blame and pronounce a cure for the environmental crisis.

Some blamed pollution on the rising population. . . . Some blamed man's innate aggressiveness. . . . Having spent some years in the effort simply to detect and describe the growing list of environmental problems—radioactive fallout, air and water pollution, the deterioration of the soil—and in tracing some of their links to social and political processes, the identification of a single cause and cure seemed a rather bold step. . . .

Any living thing that hopes to live on the earth must fit into the ecosphere or perish. The environmental crisis is a sign that the finely sculpted fit between life and its surroundings has begun to corrode. As the links between one living thing and another, and between all of them and their surroundings, begin to break down, the dynamic interactions that sustain the whole have begun to falter and, in some places, stop. . . .

We have broken out of the circle of life, converting its endless cycles into man-made, linear events; oil is taken from the ground, distilled into fuel, burned in an engine, converted thereby into noxious fumes, which are emitted into the air. At the end of the line is smog. Other man-made breaks in the ecosphere's cycle spew out toxic chemicals, sewage, heaps of rubbish—the testimony to our power to tear the ecological fabric that has, for millions of years, sustained the planet's life.

From RICHARD E. BLAKEMORE, REPORT ON THE SAGEBRUSH REBELLION (1979)

The rapid growth of the environmentalist movement sparked a conservative reaction, especially in the western states. What came to be called the Sagebrush Rebellion denounced federal control of large areas of western land as well as new environmental regulations that, the "rebels" claimed, threatened energy production and long-standing grazing rights. Richard E. Blakemore, a member of the Nevada state senate, offered this explanation of the outlook of many westerners.

The "sagebrush rebellion" is a catchy but somewhat misleading term used to describe the western states' demands for a greater role in determining the future of the west. Unlike the dictionary definition, in this rebellion there is no armed or unlawful resistance to government. Neither is western land desolate or worthless as the term "sagebrush" connoted. Moreover, if much of the land in the west ever was considered of little worth, the need for energy has changed that.

Statistics show that much of the west is controlled by the federal government.... On average, the federal government controls 52.6 percent of the land in the 12 western states.... For many years, the public domain was open to ranching, mining, and outdoor recreation. But a number of federal acts, passed to protect and conserve the environment, have closed great parts of the public domain to traditional uses....

The west today is at the confluence of two major movements—that for protection of the environment and that for production of energy. To a great extent, the success of the attempt for U.S. energy independence depends on resources of the west. In addition, the west is looked to for increased agricultural production and for its reserves of minerals necessary to modern industry. The environmental movement prompted the passage of federal legislation aimed at protecting the environment and maintaining great portions of the country in a natural state. Among the major environmental acts of the past 15 years are the Wilderness Act, the National Environmental Protection Act, the Federal Land Policy Management Act, the Wild and Scenic Rivers Act, and the National Forest Management Act.

The genesis of the sagebrush rebellion can be found in the conflict between the desires to protect and preserve the environment and the demands for food, minerals, and energy from the west....

While the particular issues on which the sagebrush rebellion are based are more common in the west, the principles behind the movement are national in scope....

Because of the federal omnipresence in the west, westerners have reached the crisis first. But reversing the trend towards centralization that threatens the economy, our lands, and our freedoms is of concern to all Americans.

QUESTIONS:

1. *How and why does Commoner ask Americans to rethink their definition of freedom?*

2. *What elements of environmental policy does Blakemore see as a threat to "our freedoms"?*

3. *How do the two writers differ in their visions of the future of American society?*

Before entering politics, Ronald Reagan was a prominent actor and a spokesperson for General Electric. In this 1958 photograph he demonstrates the use of a GE oven.

libertarians who believed in freeing the individual from restraint and the Christian Right, which sought to restore what they considered traditional moral values to American life.

Reagan and American Freedom

Reagan's opponents often underestimated him. By the time he left office at the age of seventy-seven, he had become the oldest man ever to serve as president. He "rose at the crack of noon," as one reporter put it, and relied on his wife to arrange his official schedule. Unlike most modern presidents, he was content to outline broad policy themes and leave their implementation to others.

Reagan, however, was hardly a political novice, having governed California during the turbulent 1960s. He was an excellent public speaker, and his optimism and affability appealed to large numbers of Americans. Reagan made conservatism seem progressive, rather than an attempt to turn back the tide of progress. He frequently quoted Thomas Paine: "We have it in our power to begin the world over again." Reagan repeatedly invoked the idea that America has a divinely appointed mission as a "beacon of liberty and freedom." Freedom, indeed, became the watchword of the Reagan Revolution. In his public appearances and state papers, Reagan used the word more often than any president before him.

Reagan reshaped the nation's agenda and political language more effectively than any president since Franklin D. Roosevelt. Like FDR, he seized on the vocabulary of his opponents and gave it new meaning. Reagan promised to free government from control by "special interests," but these were racial minorities, unionists, and others hoping to use Washington's power to attack social inequalities, not businessmen seeking political favors, the traditional target of liberals. His Justice Department made the principle that the Constitution must be "color-blind"—a remark hurled at the Supreme Court majority by Justice John Marshall Harlan in 1896 to challenge a system of legal segregation—a justification for gutting civil rights enforcement.

Overall, Reagan proved remarkably successful at seizing control of the terms of public debate. On issues ranging from taxes to government spending, national security, crime, welfare, and "traditional values," he put Democrats on the defensive. But he also proved to be a pragmatist, recognizing when to compromise so as not to fragment his diverse coalition of supporters.

Reagan's Economic Policies

Like Roosevelt and Johnson before him, Reagan spoke of "economic freedom" and proposed an "economic Bill of Rights." But in contrast to his predecessors, who used these phrases to support combating poverty and strengthening economic security, economic freedom for Reagan meant curtailing the power of unions, dismantling regulations, and radically reducing taxes. Taxation, he declared, violated the principle that "the right to earn your own keep and keep what you earn" was "what it means to be free."

In 1981, Reagan persuaded Congress to reduce the top tax rate from 70 percent to 50 percent and to index tax brackets to take inflation into account. Five years later, the Tax Reform Act reduced the rate on the wealthiest Americans to 28 percent. These measures marked a sharp retreat from the principle of progressivity (the idea that the wealthy should pay a higher percentage of their income in taxes

Reagan as leader

Tax reform

than other citizens), one of the ways twentieth-century societies tried to address the unequal distribution of wealth. Reagan also appointed conservative heads of regulatory agencies, who cut back on environmental protection and workplace safety rules about which business had complained for years.

Since the New Deal, liberals had tried to promote economic growth by using the power of the government to bolster ordinary Americans' purchasing power. Reagan's economic program, known as "supply-side economics" by proponents and "trickle-down economics" by critics, relied on high interest rates to curb inflation and lower tax rates, especially for businesses and high-income Americans, to stimulate private investment. The policy assumed that cutting taxes would inspire Americans at all income levels to work harder, since they would keep more of the money they earned. Everyone would benefit from increased business profits, and because of a growing economy, government receipts would rise despite lower tax rates.

Supply-side economics

Reagan and Labor

Reagan inaugurated an era of hostility between the federal government and organized labor. In August 1981, when 13,000 members of PATCO, the union of air traffic controllers, began a strike in violation of federal law, Reagan fired them all. He used the military to oversee the nation's air traffic system until new controllers could be trained. Reagan's action inspired many private employers to launch anti-union offensives. The hiring of workers to replace permanently those who had gone on strike, a rare occurrence before 1980, became widespread. Manufacturing employment, where union membership was concentrated, meanwhile continued its long-term decline. By the mid-1990s, the steel industry employed only

The air traffic controllers' strike

This photograph of the remains of the Bethlehem Steel plant in Lackawanna, New York, which closed in 1982, depicts the aftermath of deindustrialization. Today, the site is a wind farm, with eight windmills helping to provide electricity for the city.

A homeless St. Louis mother and her children, forced to live in their car, photographed in 1987.

The wealthiest American families benefited the most from economic expansion during the 1980s, while the poorest 40 percent of the population saw their real incomes decline. (Real income indicates income adjusted to take account of inflation.)

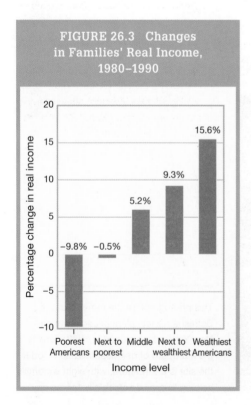

FIGURE 26.3 Changes in Families' Real Income, 1980–1990

170,000 persons—down from 600,000 in 1973. When Reagan left office, both the service and retail sectors employed more Americans than manufacturing, and only 11 percent of workers with non-government jobs were union members.

Reaganomics, as critics dubbed the administration's policies, initially produced the most severe recession since the 1930s. A long period of economic expansion, however, followed the downturn of 1981–1982. As companies "downsized" their workforces, shifted production overseas, and took advantage of new technologies such as satellite communications, they became more profitable. At the same time, the rate of inflation, 13.5 percent at the beginning of 1981, declined to 3.5 percent in 1988, partly because a period of expanded oil production that drove down prices succeeded the shortages of the 1970s. By the end of Reagan's presidency in 1989, the real gross domestic product had risen by 25 percent and unemployment was down to 5.5 percent. These were significant accomplishments.

The Problem of Inequality

Together, Reagan's policies, rising stock prices, and deindustrialization resulted in a considerable rise in economic inequality. By the mid-1990s, the richest 1 percent of Americans owned 40 percent of the nation's wealth, twice their share twenty years earlier. Most spent their income not on productive investments and charity as supply-side economists had promised, but on luxury goods, real-estate speculation, and corporate buyouts that often led to plant closings as operations were consolidated. The income of middle-class families, especially those with a wife who did not work outside the home, stagnated while that of the poorest one-fifth of the population declined. Because of falling investment in public housing, the release of mental patients from state hospitals, and cuts in welfare, homeless persons became a visible fixture on the streets of cities from New York to Los Angeles.

Deindustrialization and the decline of the labor movement had a particularly devastating impact on minority workers, who had only recently gained a foothold in better-paying manufacturing jobs. Thanks to the opening of colleges and professional schools to minority students as a result of the civil rights movement and affirmative action programs, the black middle class expanded considerably. But black workers, traditionally the last hired and first fired, were hard hit by economic changes.

During the 1970s, Jim Crow had finally ended in many workplaces and unions. But just as decades of painful efforts to obtain better jobs bore fruit, hundreds of thousands of black workers lost their jobs when factories closed their doors. In South Gate, a working-class suburb of Los Angeles, for example, the giant Firestone tire factory shut down in 1980, only a few years after black and Latino workers made their first breakthroughs in employment. When the national unemployment rate reached 8.9 percent at the end of 1981, the figure for blacks exceeded 20 percent. Nor did black workers share fully in the recovery that followed. Few had the education to take advantage of job openings in growing "knowledge-based" industries like technology and information services. Overall, during the 1980s black males fell farther than any other group in the population in terms of wages and jobs.

The Second Gilded Age

In retrospect, the 1980s, like the 1890s, would be widely remembered as a decade of misplaced values. Buying out companies generated more profits than running them; making deals, not making products, became the way to get rich. The merger of Nabisco and R. J. Reynolds Tobacco Company in 1988 produced close to $1 billion in fees for lawyers, economic advisers, and stockbrokers. "Greed is healthy," declared Wall Street financier Ivan Boesky (who ended up in prison for insider stock trading). "Yuppie"—the young urban professional who earned a high income working in a bank or stock brokerage firm and spent lavishly on designer clothing and other trappings of the good life—became a household word.

Taxpayers footed the bill for some of the consequences. The deregulation of savings and loan associations—banks that had generally confined themselves to financing home mortgages—allowed these institutions to invest in unsound real-estate ventures and corporate mergers. Losses piled up, and the Federal Savings and Loan Insurance Corporation, which insured depositors' accounts, faced bankruptcy. After Reagan left office, the federal government bailed out the savings and loan institutions, at a cost to taxpayers estimated at $250 billion.

Supply-side advocates insisted that lowering taxes would enlarge government revenue by stimulating economic activity. But spurred by large increases in funds for the military, federal spending far outstripped income, producing large budget deficits, despite assurances by supply-siders that this would not happen. During Reagan's presidency, the national debt tripled to $2.7 trillion. Nonetheless, Reagan remained immensely popular. He took credit for economic expansion while blaming congressional leaders for the ballooning federal deficit. He won a triumphant reelection in 1984. His opponent, Walter Mondale (best remembered for choosing Congresswoman Geraldine Ferraro of New York as his running mate, the first woman candidate on a major-party presidential ticket), carried only his home state of Minnesota and the District of Columbia.

Conservatives and Reagan

While he implemented their economic policies, Reagan in some ways disappointed ardent conservatives. The administration sharply reduced funding for Great Society antipoverty programs such as food stamps, school lunches, and federal financing of low-income housing. But it left intact core elements of the welfare state, such as Social Security, Medicare, and Medicaid, which many conservatives wished to curtail significantly or repeal. The Reagan era did little to advance the social agenda of the Christian Right. Abortion remained legal, women continued to enter the labor force in unprecedented numbers, and Reagan even appointed the first female member of the Supreme Court, Sandra Day O'Connor. In 1986, in *Bowers v. Hardwick*, in a rare victory for cultural conservatives, the Supreme Court did uphold the constitutionality of state laws outlawing homosexual acts. (In 2003, the justices would reverse the *Bowers* decision, declaring laws that criminalized homosexuality unconstitutional.)

LIBERTY LEADING THE PEOPLE — 1984

Loosely modeled on the French artist Eugène Delacroix's famous 1830 painting *Liberty Leading the People* (reproduced at the lower left), this campaign poster from 1984 depicts Geraldine Ferraro, the first woman nominated for vice president by a major party, as a modern-day rebel. She overshadows the Democratic presidential candidate, Walter Mondale, shown carrying a rifle emblazoned with "ERA," for the Equal Rights Amendment.

Reagan's social policies

First lady Nancy Reagan promoting her "Just Say No" campaign against the use of drugs, in a photo from 1986.

Reasserting America as a military power ▸

Troops overseas ▸

Foreign policy ▸

Reagan gave verbal support to a proposed constitutional amendment restoring prayer in public schools but did little to promote its passage. The administration launched a "Just Say No" campaign against illegal drug use. But this failed to halt the spread in urban areas of crack, a potent, inexpensive form of cocaine that produced an upsurge of street crime and family breakdown. Reagan's Justice Department cut back on civil rights enforcement and worked to curtail affirmative action programs. But to the end of Reagan's presidency, the Supreme Court continued to approve plans by private employers and city and state governments to upgrade minority employment.

Reagan and the Cold War

In foreign policy, Reagan breathed new life into the rhetorical division of the world into a free West and unfree East. He resumed vigorous denunciation of the Soviet Union—calling it an "evil empire"—and sponsored the largest military buildup in American history, including new long-range bombers and missiles. In 1983, he proposed an entirely new strategy, the Strategic Defense Initiative, based on developing a space-based system to intercept and destroy enemy missiles. The idea was not remotely feasible technologically, and, if deployed, it would violate the Anti-Ballistic Missile Treaty of 1972. But it appealed to Reagan's desire to reassert America's worldwide power. He persuaded NATO, over much opposition, to introduce short-range nuclear weapons into Europe to counter Soviet forces. But the renewed arms race and Reagan's casual talk of winning a nuclear war caused widespread alarm at home and abroad. In the early 1980s, a movement for a nuclear freeze—a halt to the development of nuclear weapons—attracted millions of supporters in the United States and Europe. In 1983, half of the American population watched *The Day After*, a television program that unflinchingly depicted the devastation that would be caused by a nuclear war.

Reagan came into office determined to overturn the "Vietnam syndrome"—as widespread public reluctance to commit American forces overseas was called. He sent American troops to the Caribbean island of Grenada to oust a pro-Cuban government. In 1982, Reagan dispatched marines as a peacekeeping force to Lebanon, where a civil war raged between the Christian government, supported by Israeli forces, and Muslim insurgents. But he quickly withdrew them after a bomb exploded at their barracks, killing 241 Americans. The public, Reagan realized, would support minor operations like Grenada but remained unwilling to sustain heavy casualties abroad.

Reagan generally relied on military aid rather than American troops to pursue his foreign policy objectives. Abandoning the Carter administration's emphasis on human rights, Reagan embraced the idea, advanced in 1979 by neoconservative writer Jeane Kirkpatrick, that the United States should oppose "totalitarian" communists but assist "authoritarian" noncommunist regimes. Kirkpatrick became the

Hollywood joined enthusiastically in the revived Cold War. The 1984 film *Red Dawn* depicted a Soviet invasion of the United States.

American ambassador to the United Nations, and the United States stepped up its alliances with Third World anticommunist dictatorships like the governments of Chile and South Africa. The administration poured in funds to combat insurgencies against the governments of El Salvador and Guatemala, whose armies and associated death squads committed flagrant abuses against their own citizens. When El Salvador's army massacred hundreds of civilians in the town of El Mozote in 1981, the State Department denied that the event, widely reported in the press, had taken place.

Latin America

The Iran-Contra Affair

American involvement in Central America produced the greatest scandal of Reagan's presidency, the **Iran-Contra affair**. In 1984, Congress banned military aid to the Contras (derived from the Spanish word for "against") fighting the Sandinista government of Nicaragua, which, as noted earlier, had ousted the American-backed dictator Anastasio Somoza in 1979. In 1985, Reagan secretly authorized the sale of arms to Iran—now involved in a war with its neighbor, Iraq—in order to secure the release of a number of American hostages held by Islamic groups in the Middle East. CIA director William Casey and Lieutenant Colonel Oliver North of the National Security Council set up a system that diverted some of the proceeds to buy military supplies for the Contras in defiance of the congressional ban. The scheme continued for nearly two years.

Arms for hostages

In 1987, after a Middle Eastern newspaper leaked the story, Congress held televised hearings that revealed a pattern of official duplicity and violation of the law reminiscent of the Nixon era. Eleven members of the administration eventually were convicted of perjury or destroying documents, or pleaded guilty before being tried. Reagan denied knowledge of the illegal proceedings, but the Iran-Contra affair undermined confidence that he controlled his own administration.

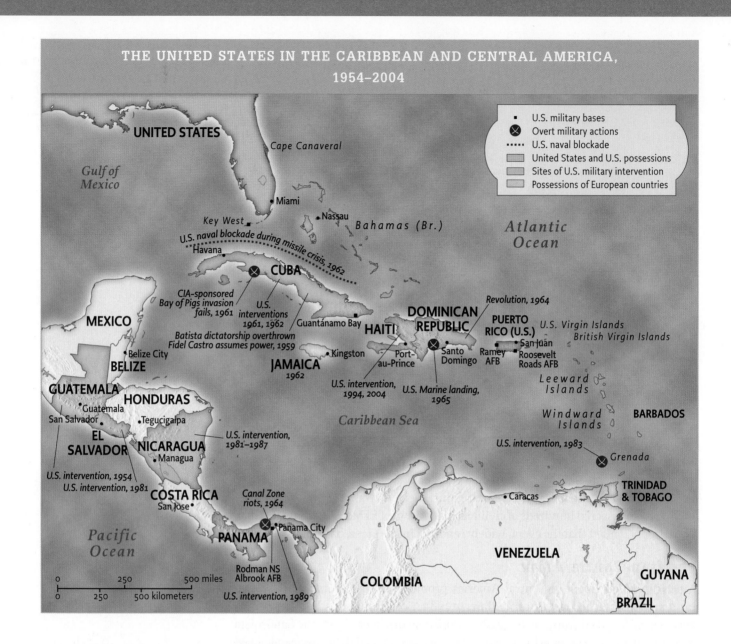

THE UNITED STATES IN THE CARIBBEAN AND CENTRAL AMERICA, 1954–2004

Legend:
- U.S. military bases
- Overt military actions
- U.S. naval blockade
- United States and U.S. possessions
- Sites of U.S. military intervention
- Possessions of European countries

As in the first part of the twentieth century, the United States intervened frequently in Caribbean and Central American countries during and immediately after the Cold War.

Reagan and Gorbachev

In his second term, to the surprise of both his foes and supporters, Reagan softened his anticommunist rhetoric and established good relations with Soviet premier Mikhail Gorbachev. Gorbachev had come to power in 1985, bent on reforming the Soviet Union's repressive political system and reinvigorating its economy. The country had fallen further and further behind the United States in the production and distribution of consumer goods, and it relied increasingly on agricultural imports to feed itself. Gorbachev inaugurated policies known as *glasnost* (political openness) and *perestroika* (economic reform).

Arms control agreements

Gorbachev realized that significant change would be impossible without reducing his country's military budget. Reagan was ready to negotiate. A series of talks between 1985 and 1987 yielded more progress on arms control than in the entire postwar period to that point, including an agreement to eliminate intermediate- and short-range nuclear missiles in Europe. In 1988, Gorbachev began pulling Soviet troops out of Afghanistan. Having entered office as an ardent Cold Warrior, Reagan left with hostilities between the superpowers much diminished. He even repudiated his earlier comment that the Soviet Union was an "evil empire," saying that it referred to "another era."

Reagan's Legacy

Reagan's presidency revealed the contradictions at the heart of modern conservatism. In some ways, the Reagan Revolution undermined the very values and institutions conservatives held dear. Intended to discourage reliance on government handouts by rewarding honest work and business initiative, Reagan's policies inspired a speculative frenzy that enriched architects of corporate takeovers and investors in the stock market while leaving in their wake plant closings, job losses, and devastated communities. Nothing proved more threatening to local traditions or family stability than deindustrialization, insecurity about employment, and the relentless downward pressure on wages. Nothing did more to undermine a sense of common national purpose than the widening gap between rich and poor.

Social and economic repercussions

Because of the Iran-Contra scandal and the enormous deficits the government had accumulated, Reagan left the presidency with his reputation somewhat tarnished. Nonetheless, few figures have so successfully changed the landscape and language of politics. Reagan's vice president, George H. W. Bush, defeated Michael Dukakis, the governor of Massachusetts, in the 1988 election partly because Dukakis could not respond effectively to the charge that he was a "liberal"—now a term of political abuse. Conservative assumptions about the virtues of the free market and the evils of "big government" dominated the mass media and political debates. Those receiving public assistance had come to be seen not as citizens entitled to help in coping with economic misfortune, but as a drain on taxes. During the 1990s, these and other conservative ideas would be embraced almost as fully by President Bill Clinton, a Democrat, as by Reagan and the Republicans.

Lasting conservative ideology

The Election of 1988

The 1988 election seemed to show politics sinking to new lows. Television advertisements and media exposés now dominated political campaigns. The race for the Democratic nomination had hardly begun before the front-runner, Senator Gary Hart of Colorado, withdrew after a newspaper reported that he had spent the night at his Washington town house with a woman other than his wife. Both parties ran negative campaigns. Democrats ridiculed the Republican vice-presidential nominee, Senator Dan Quayle of Indiana, for factual and linguistic mistakes. Republicans spread unfounded rumors that Michael Dukakis's wife had burned an American flag during the 1960s. The low point of the campaign came in a Republican television ad depicting the threatening image of Willie Horton, a black murderer and rapist who had been furloughed from prison during Dukakis's term as governor of Massachusetts. Rarely in the modern era had a major party appealed so blatantly to racial fears.

Although he did not match Reagan's landslide victory of 1984, Bush achieved a substantial majority, winning 54 percent of the popular vote. Democratic success in retaining control of Congress suggested that an electoral base existed for a comeback. But this would occur only if the party fashioned a new appeal to replace traditional liberalism, which had been eclipsed by the triumph of conservatism.

President Reagan visited Moscow in 1988, cementing his close relationship with Soviet leader Mikhail Gorbachev. They were photographed in Red Square.

SUGGESTED READING

BOOKS

- Adler, William M. *Mollie's Job: A Story of Life and Work on the Global Assembly Line* (2000). Tracks how a manufacturing job moved from the North to the South and eventually out of the country, and what happened to the workers who held it.

- Allitt, Patrick. *Religion in America since 1945* (2003). A survey of the main trends of religious development since World War II.

- Anderson, Terry H. *The Pursuit of Fairness: A History of Affirmative Action* (2004). A careful study of the origins and development of affirmative action policies.

- Busch, Andrew E. *Ronald Reagan and the Politics of Freedom* (2001). Discusses how Ronald Reagan interpreted the idea of freedom and how it influenced his presidency.

- Foley, Michael S. *Front Porch Politics: The Forgotten Heyday of American Activism in the 1970s and 1980s* (2013). A lively account of the grassroots movements, of both left and right, that followed the 1960s.

- Greenberg, David. *Nixon's Shadow: The History of an Image* (2003). Explores how Nixon's supporters and enemies thought about him during his long political career.

- Kruse, Kevin. *White Flight: Atlanta and the Making of Modern Conservatism* (2005). Explores how conservative politics took root in the predominantly white suburbs of Atlanta, with implications for similar communities across the country.

- Kutler, Stanley I. *The Wars of Watergate: The Last Crisis of Richard Nixon* (1990). The most thorough analysis of the Watergate scandal that brought down President Nixon.

- Luker, Kristin. *Abortion and the Politics of Motherhood* (1984). Describes how the abortion issue affected American politics and the ideas about gender relations that lay behind the debate.

- Mathews, Donald G., and Jane S. De Hart. *Sex, Gender, and the Politics of ERA* (1990). An in-depth examination of the debate over the Equal Rights Amendment and why its opponents were successful.

- McGirr, Lisa. *Suburban Warriors: The Origins of the New American Right* (2001). An influential study of the rise of conservatism in Orange County, California, once one of its more powerful centers.

- Moreton, Bethany. *To Serve God and Wal-Mart: The Making of Christian Free Enterprise* (2009). Explores how the nation's largest employer drew on evangelical Christianity to justify its often-criticized labor policies.

- Moyn, Samuel. *The Last Utopia: Human Rights in History* (2010). Traces the development of human rights consciousness, with special emphasis on the 1970s.

- Schulman, Bruce J. *The Seventies: The Great Shift in American Culture, Society, and Politics* (2001). A survey of the numerous political, social, and economic changes that took place during the 1970s.

- Self, Robert. *All in the Family: The Realignment of American Democracy Since the 1960s* (2013). Identifies changes in the role of women and the structure of the family as key issues in the rise of modern conservative politics.

- Stein, Judith. *Pivotal Decade: How the United States Traded Factories for Finance in the Seventies* (2010). A careful analysis of the economic transformations of the 1970s.

- Wilentz, Sean. *The Age of Reagan: A History, 1974–2008* (2008). Explores how Ronald Reagan set the terms of public debate during and after his presidency.

WEBSITES

- National Security Archive: http://nsarchive.gwu.edu

- Watergate: http://watergate.info/

CHAPTER REVIEW AND ONLINE RESOURCES

REVIEW QUESTIONS

1. Why were social issues associated with the sexual revolution so contested by all sides?

2. What were continuing challenges to the cohesiveness of the Democratic (New Deal) coalition? What were the consequences of those divisions?

3. What were the main features of Nixon's policy of "realism" in dealing with China and the Soviet Union?

4. Describe the basic events and the larger significance of the Watergate scandal.

5. What were the major causes for the decline of the U.S. economy in the 1970s?

6. What were the causes and consequences of the public's disillusionment with the federal government in the 1970s and 1980s?

7. Identify the groups and their agendas that combined to create the new conservative base in the 1970s and 1980s.

8. What impact did Ronald Reagan have on the American political scene?

9. Why was there growth in economic inequality in the 1980s?

10. How did various groups see the relationship between women's rights and freedom differently?

KEY TERMS

affirmative action (p. 1018)

busing (p. 1018)

reverse discrimination (p. 1019)

Title IX (p. 1020)

Strategic Arms Limitation Talks (p. 1021)

détente (p. 1022)

My Lai massacre (p. 1022)

Pentagon Papers (p. 1023)

War Powers Act (p. 1023)

Vietnam Syndrome (p. 1024)

Watergate (p. 1024)

oil embargo (p. 1027)

stagflation (p. 1027)

deindustrialization (p. 1028)

Sunbelt (p. 1028)

Helsinki Accords (p. 1029)

deregulation (p. 1030)

Three Mile Island (p. 1030)

Camp David Accords (p. 1032)

neoconservatives (p. 1034)

Reagan Revolution (p. 1039)

Reaganomics (p. 1044)

Iran-Contra affair (p. 1047)

Go to 🐰 INQUIZITIVE

To see what you know—and learn what you've missed—with personalized feedback along the way.

Visit the *Give Me Liberty!* Student Site for primary source documents and images, interactive maps, author videos featuring Eric Foner, and more.

CHAPTER 27

FROM TRIUMPH TO TRAGEDY

★

1989–2001

The year 1989 was one of the most momentous of the twentieth century. In April, tens of thousands of student demonstrators occupied Tiananmen Square in the heart of Beijing, demanding greater democracy in China. Workers, teachers, and even some government officials joined them, until their numbers swelled to nearly 1 million. Both the reforms Mikhail Gorbachev had introduced in the Soviet Union and the example of American institutions inspired the protesters. The students erected a figure reminiscent of the Statue of Liberty, calling it "The Goddess of Democracy and Freedom." In June, Chinese troops crushed the protest, killing an unknown number of people, possibly thousands.

In the fall of 1989, pro-democracy demonstrations spread across eastern Europe. Gorbachev made it clear that unlike in the past, the Soviet Union would not intervene. The climactic event took place on November 9 when crowds breached the Berlin Wall, which since 1961 had stood as the Cold War's most prominent symbol. One by one, the region's communist governments agreed to give up power. In 1990, a reunified German nation absorbed East Germany. The remarkably swift and almost entirely peaceful collapse of communism in eastern Europe became known as the "velvet revolution."

Meanwhile, the Soviet Union itself slipped deeper and deeper into crisis. Gorbachev's attempts at economic reform produced only chaos, and his policy of political openness allowed long-suppressed national and ethnic tensions to rise to the surface. In August 1991, a group of military leaders attempted to seize power to overturn the government's plan to give greater autonomy to the various parts of the Soviet Union. Russian president Boris Yeltsin mobilized crowds in Moscow that restored Gorbachev to office. Gorbachev then resigned from the Communist Party, ending its eighty-four-year rule. One after another, the republics of the Soviet Union declared themselves sovereign states. At the end of 1991, the Soviet Union ceased to exist; in its place were fifteen new independent nations.

The sudden and unexpected collapse of communism marked the end of the Cold War and a stunning triumph for the United States and its allies. For the first time since 1917, there existed a truly worldwide capitalist system. Even China, while remaining under Communist Party rule, had already embarked on market reforms and rushed to attract foreign investment. Other events suggested that the 1990s would also be a "decade of democracy." In 1990, South Africa released Nelson Mandela, head of the African National Congress, from prison. Four years later, as a result of the first democratic elections in the country's history, Mandela became president, ending the system of state-sponsored racial inequality, known as "apartheid," and white minority government. Throughout Latin America and Africa, civilian governments replaced military rule.

The sudden shift from a bipolar world to one of unquestioned American predominance promised to redefine the country's global role. President George H. W. Bush spoke of the coming of a **new world order**. But no one knew what its characteristics would be and what new challenges to American power might arise.

FOCUS QUESTIONS

What were the major international initiatives of the Clinton administration in the aftermath of the Cold War? –p. 1054

What forces drove the economic resurgence of the 1990s? –p. 1060

What cultural conflicts emerged in the 1990s? –p. 1067

How did a divisive political partisanship affect the election of 2000? –p. 1083

Why did Al Qaeda attack the United States on September 11, 2001? –p. 1085

Protesters dressed as sea turtles, an endangered species, at the demonstrations against the World Trade Organization in Seattle, December 1999.

THE POST–COLD WAR WORLD

A New World Order?

Bush's first major foreign policy action was a throwback to the days of American interventionism in the Western Hemisphere. At the end of 1989, he dispatched troops to Panama to overthrow the government of General Manuel Antonio Noriega, a former ally of the United States who had become involved in the international drug trade. The United States installed a new government and flew Noriega to Florida, where he was tried and convicted on drug charges.

The Gulf War

A far more serious crisis arose in 1990 when Iraq invaded and annexed Kuwait, an oil-rich sheikdom on the Persian Gulf. Fearing that Iraqi dictator Saddam Hussein might next attack Saudi Arabia, a longtime ally that supplied more oil to the United States than any other country, Bush rushed troops to defend Kuwait and warned Iraq to withdraw from the country or face war. His policy aroused intense debate in the United States. But the Iraqi invasion so flagrantly violated international law that Bush succeeded in building a forty-nation coalition committed to restoring Kuwait's independence, secured the support of the United Nations, and sent half a million American troops along with a naval armada to the region.

In February 1991, the United States launched Operation Desert Storm, which quickly drove the Iraqi army from Kuwait. Tens of thousands of Iraqis and 184 Americans died in the conflict. The United Nations ordered Iraq to disarm and imposed economic sanctions that produced widespread civilian suffering for the rest of the decade. But Hussein remained in place. So did a large American military establishment in Saudi Arabia, to the outrage of Islamic fundamentalists who deemed its presence an affront to their faith.

The **Gulf War** was the first post–Cold War international crisis. Relying on high-tech weaponry like cruise missiles that reached Iraq from bases and aircraft carriers hundreds of miles away, the United States was able to prevail quickly and avoid the prolonged involvement and high casualties of Vietnam. The Soviet Union, in the process of disintegration, remained on the sidelines. In the war's immediate aftermath, Bush's public approval rating rose to an unprecedented 89 percent.

Visions of America's Role

In a speech to Congress, President Bush identified the Gulf War as the first step in the struggle to create a world rooted in democracy and global free trade. But it remained unclear how this broad vision would be translated into policy. Soon after the end of the war, General Colin Powell, chairman of the Joint Chiefs of Staff, and Dick Cheney, the secretary of defense, outlined different visions of the future. Powell predicted that the post–Cold War world would be a dangerous environment with conflicts popping up in unexpected places. To avoid being drawn into an unending role as global policeman, he insisted, the United States should not

Demonstrators dancing atop the Berlin Wall on November 10, 1989. The next day, crowds began dismantling it, in the most dramatic moment of the collapse of communist rule in eastern Europe.

commit its troops abroad without clear objectives and a timetable for withdrawal. Cheney argued that with the demise of the Soviet Union, the United States possessed the power to reshape the world and prevent hostile states from achieving regional power. It must be willing to use force, independently if necessary, to maintain its strategic dominance. For the rest of the 1990s, it was not certain which definition of the American role in the post–Cold War world would predominate.

The Goddess of Democracy and Freedom, a statue reminiscent of the Statue of Liberty, was displayed by pro-democracy advocates during the 1989 demonstrations in Beijing's Tiananmen Square. After allowing it to continue for two months, the Chinese government sent troops to crush the peaceful occupation of the square.

The Election of Clinton

Had a presidential election been held in 1991, Bush would undoubtedly have been victorious. But in that year the economy slipped into recession. Despite victory in the Cold War and the Gulf, more and more Americans believed the country was on the wrong track. No one seized more effectively on the widespread sense of unease than Bill Clinton, a former governor of Arkansas. In 1992, Clinton won the Democratic nomination by combining social liberalism (he supported abortion rights, gay rights, and affirmative action for racial minorities) with elements of conservatism (he pledged to reduce government bureaucracy and, borrowing a page from Republicans, promised to "end welfare as we know it"). A charismatic campaigner, Clinton conveyed sincere concern for voters' economic anxieties.

Bush, by contrast, seemed out of touch with the day-to-day lives of ordinary Americans. On the wall of Democratic headquarters, Clinton's campaign director posted the slogan, "It's the Economy, Stupid"—a reminder that the economic downturn was the Democrats' strongest card. Bush was further weakened when conservative leader Pat Buchanan delivered a fiery televised speech at the Republican national convention that declared cultural war against gays, feminists, and supporters of abortion rights. This seemed to confirm the Democratic portrait of Republicans as intolerant and divisive.

EASTERN EUROPE AFTER THE COLD WAR

The end of the Cold War and breakup of the Soviet Union, Czechoslovakia, and Yugoslavia redrew the map of eastern Europe (compare this map with the map of Cold War Europe in Chapter 23). Two additional nations that emerged from the Soviet Union lie to the east and are not indicated here: Kyrgyzstan and Tajikistan.

Social changes

A third candidate, the eccentric Texas billionaire Ross Perot, also entered the fray. He attacked Bush and Clinton as lacking the economic know-how to deal with the recession and the ever-increasing national debt. That millions of Americans considered Perot a credible candidate—at one point, polls showed him leading both Clinton and Bush—testified to widespread dissatisfaction with the major parties. Perot's support faded as election day approached, but he still received 19 percent of the popular vote, the best result for a third-party candidate since Theodore Roosevelt in 1912. Clinton won by a substantial margin, a humiliating outcome for Bush, given his earlier popularity.

Clinton in Office

In his first two years in office, Clinton turned away from some of the social and economic policies of the Reagan and Bush years. He appointed several blacks and women to his cabinet, including Janet Reno, the first female attorney general, and named two supporters of abortion rights, Ruth Bader Ginsburg and Stephen Breyer, to the Supreme Court. He modified the military's strict ban on gay soldiers, instituting a "**Don't ask, don't tell**" policy by which officers would not seek out gays for dismissal from the armed forces. His first budget raised taxes on the wealthy and significantly expanded the Earned Income Tax Credit (EITC)—a cash payment for low-income workers begun during the Ford administration. The most effective antipoverty policy since the Great Society, the EITC raised more than 4 million Americans, half of them children, above the poverty line during Clinton's presidency.

Clinton shared his predecessor's passion for free trade. Despite strong opposition from unions and environmentalists, he obtained congressional approval in 1993 of the **North American Free Trade Agreement** (NAFTA), a treaty negotiated by Bush that created a free-trade zone consisting of Canada, Mexico, and the United States.

The major policy initiative of Clinton's first term was a plan devised by a panel headed by his wife, Hillary, a lawyer who had pursued an independent career after their marriage, to address the rising cost of health care and the increasing number of Americans who lacked health insurance. In Canada and western Europe, governments provided universal medical coverage. The United States had the world's most advanced medical technology and a woefully incomplete system of health insurance. The Great Society had provided coverage for the elderly and poor through the Medicare and Medicaid programs. Many employers offered health insurance to their workers. But tens of millions of Americans lacked any coverage at all.

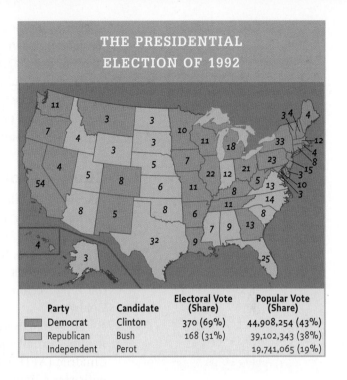

THE PRESIDENTIAL ELECTION OF 1992

Party	Candidate	Electoral Vote (Share)	Popular Vote (Share)
Democrat	Clinton	370 (69%)	44,908,254 (43%)
Republican	Bush	168 (31%)	39,102,343 (38%)
Independent	Perot		19,741,065 (19%)

Announced with great fanfare by Hillary Rodham Clinton at congressional hearings in 1993, Clinton's plan would have provided universal coverage through large groupings of medical care businesses. Doctors and health insurance and drug companies attacked it vehemently, fearing government regulations that would limit reimbursement for medical procedures and the price of drugs. Too complex to be easily understood by most voters, and vulnerable to criticism for further expanding the unpopular federal bureaucracy, the plan died in 1994.

Clinton's universal health insurance plan

The "Freedom Revolution"

With the economy recovering slowly from the recession and Clinton's first two years in office seemingly lacking in significant accomplishments, voters in 1994 turned against the administration. For the first time since the 1950s, Republicans won control of both houses of Congress. They proclaimed their triumph the "Freedom Revolution." Newt Gingrich, a conservative congressman from Georgia who became the new Speaker of the House, masterminded their campaign. Gingrich had devised a platform called the **Contract with America**, which promised to curtail the scope of government, cut back on taxes and economic and environmental regulations, overhaul the welfare system, and end affirmative action.

Republican control

Viewing their electoral triumph as an endorsement of the contract, Republicans moved swiftly to implement its provisions. The House approved deep cuts in social, educational, and environmental programs, including the popular Medicare system. With the president and Congress unable to reach agreement on a budget, the government in December 1995 shut down all nonessential operations, including Washington, D.C., museums and national parks.

Gingrich had assumed that the public shared his intense ideological convictions. He discovered that in 1994 they had voted against Clinton, not for the full implementation of the Contract with America. Most Americans blamed Congress for the impasse, and Congress soon retreated.

Clinton's Political Strategy

Like Truman after the Republican sweep of 1946, Clinton rebuilt his popularity by campaigning against a radical Congress. He opposed the most extreme parts of his opponents' program, while adopting others. In his state of the union address of January 1996, he announced that "the era of big government is over," in effect turning his back on the tradition of Democratic Party liberalism and embracing the antigovernment outlook associated with Republicans since the days of Barry Goldwater.

Ending AFDC

In 1996, ignoring the protests of most Democrats, Clinton signed into law a Republican bill that abolished the program of Aid to Families with Dependent Children (AFDC), commonly known as "welfare." Grants of money to the states, with strict limits on how long recipients could receive payments, replaced it. At the time of its abolition, AFDC assisted 14 million individuals, 9 million of them children. Thanks to stringent new eligibility requirements imposed by the states and the economic boom of the late 1990s, welfare rolls plummeted. But the number of children living in poverty remained essentially unchanged. Nonetheless, Clinton had succeeded in one of his primary goals: by the late 1990s, welfare, a hotly contested issue for twenty years or more, had disappeared from political debate.

"Triangulation"

Commentators called Clinton's political strategy "triangulation." This meant embracing the most popular Republican policies, like welfare reform, while leaving his opponents with extreme positions unpopular among middle-class voters, such as hostility to abortion rights and environmental protection. Clinton's strategy enabled him to neutralize Republican claims that Democrats were the party of high taxes and lavish spending on persons who preferred dependency to honest labor. Clinton's passion for free trade alienated many working-class Democrats but convinced much of the middle class that the party was not beholden to the unions.

Clinton easily defeated Republican Bob Dole in the presidential contest of 1996, becoming the first Democrat elected to two terms since FDR. Clinton had accomplished for Reaganism what Eisenhower had done for the New Deal, and Nixon for the Great Society—consolidating a basic shift in American politics by accepting many of the premises of his opponents.

Clinton and World Affairs

Like Jimmy Carter before him, Clinton's primary political interests concerned domestic, not international, affairs. But with the United States now indisputably the world's dominant power, Clinton, like Carter, took steps to encourage the settlement of long-standing international conflicts and tried to elevate support for human rights to a central place in international relations. He achieved only mixed success.

Clinton strongly supported a 1993 agreement, negotiated at Oslo, Norway, in which Israel for the first time recognized the legitimacy of the Palestine Liberation Organization. The **Oslo Accords** seemed to outline a road to Mideast peace. But neither side proved willing to implement them fully. Israeli governments continued to build Jewish settlements on Palestinian land in the West Bank—a part of Jordan that Israel had occupied during the 1967 Six-Day War. The new Palestinian Authority, which shared in governing parts of the West Bank as a stepping-stone to full statehood, proved to be corrupt, powerless, and unable to curb the growth of groups bent on violence against Israel. At the end of his presidency, Clinton brought Israeli and Palestinian leaders to Camp David to try to work out a final peace treaty. But the meeting failed, and violence soon resumed.

Like Carter, Clinton found it difficult to balance concern for human rights with strategic and economic interests and to formulate clear guidelines for humanitarian interventions overseas. For example, the United States did nothing in 1994 when tribal massacres racked Rwanda, in central Africa. More than 800,000 people were slaughtered in the **Rwandan genocide**, and 2 million refugees fled the country.

A twenty-acre tire pile in Smithfield, Rhode Island, shown here in 1999, exemplifies the threat posed by industrial waste to the natural environment. It sits less than ten miles from the state's main water supply.

The Balkan Crisis

The most complex foreign policy crisis of the Clinton years arose from the disintegration of Yugoslavia, a multiethnic state in southeastern Europe that had been carved from the old Austro-Hungarian empire after World War I. As in the rest of eastern Europe, the communist government that had ruled Yugoslavia since the 1940s collapsed in 1989. Within a few years, the country's six provinces dissolved into five new states. Ethnic conflict plagued several of these new nations. **Ethnic cleansing**—a terrible new term meaning the forcible expulsion from an area of a particular ethnic group—now entered the international vocabulary. By the end of 1993, more than 100,000 Bosnians, nearly all of them civilians, had perished in the **Balkan crisis**.

Ethnic conflict

With the Cold War over, protection of human rights in the Balkans gave NATO a new purpose. After considerable indecision, NATO launched air strikes against Bosnian Serb forces, with American planes contributing. UN troops, including 20,000 Americans, arrived as peacekeepers. In 1998, ethnic cleansing again surfaced, this time by Yugoslavian troops and local Serbs against the Albanian population of Kosovo, a province of Serbia. More than 800,000 Albanians fled the region. To halt the bloodshed, NATO launched a two-month war in 1999 against Yugoslavia that led to the deployment of American and UN forces in Kosovo.

NATO and the protection of human rights

Serbian refugees fleeing a Croat offensive during the 1990s. By the fall of 1995, the wars that followed the breakup of Yugoslavia and accompanying "ethnic cleansing" had displaced over 3 million people.

Human Rights

During Clinton's presidency, human rights played an increasingly important role in international affairs. Hundreds of nongovernmental agencies throughout the world defined themselves as protectors of human rights. During the 1990s, the agenda of international human rights organizations expanded to include access to health care, women's rights, and the rights of indigenous peoples like the Aborigines of Australia and the descendants of the original inhabitants of the Americas. Human rights emerged as a justification for interventions in matters once considered to be the internal affairs of sovereign nations. The United States dispatched the military to distant parts of the world to assist in international missions to protect civilians.

An expanding agenda

New institutions emerged that sought to punish violations of human rights. The Rwandan genocide produced a UN-sponsored war crimes court that sentenced the country's former prime minister to life in prison. An international tribunal put Yugoslav president Slobodan Milošević on trial for sponsoring the massacre of civilians. It remained to be seen whether these initiatives would grow into an effective international system of protecting human rights across national boundaries. Despite adopting human rights as a slogan, many governments continued to violate them in practice.

Punishing violators of human rights

GLOBALIZATION AND ITS DISCONTENTS

In December 1999, delegates from around the world gathered in Seattle for a meeting of the World Trade Organization (WTO), a 135-nation group created five years earlier to reduce barriers to international commerce and settle trade disputes. To the astonishment of residents of the city, more than 30,000 persons gathered to protest the meeting. Their marches and rallies brought together factory workers, who claimed that global free trade encouraged corporations to shift production to low-wage centers overseas, and "tree-huggers," as some reporters called environmentalists, who complained about the impact on the earth's ecology of unregulated economic development.

Protests in Seattle

Some of the latter dressed in costumes representing endangered species—monarch butterflies whose habitats were disappearing because of the widespread destruction of forests by lumber companies, and sea turtles threatened by unrestricted ocean fishing. Protesters drew attention to the depletion of ozone in the atmosphere, which shields the earth from harmful solar radiation. The heightened use of aerosol sprays and refrigerants containing damaging chemicals had caused a large hole in the ozone layer. A handful of self-proclaimed anarchists embarked on a window-breaking spree at local stores. The police sealed off the downtown and made hundreds of arrests, and the WTO gathering disbanded.

Once a center of labor radicalism, the Seattle area in 1999 was best known as the home of Microsoft, developer of the Windows operating system used in most of the world's computers. The company's worldwide reach symbolized **globalization**, the process by which people, investment, goods, information, and culture increasingly flowed across national boundaries. Globalization has been called "*the* concept of the 1990s." During that decade, the media resounded with announcements that a new era in human history had opened, with a borderless economy and a "global civilization" that would soon replace traditional cultures.

Globalization

Globalization, of course, was hardly a new phenomenon. The internationalization of commerce and culture and the reshuffling of the world's peoples had been going on since the explorations of the fifteenth century. But the scale and scope of late-twentieth-century globalization was unprecedented. Thanks to satellites and the Internet, information and popular culture flowed instantaneously to every corner of the world. Manufacturers and financial institutions scoured the world for profitable investment opportunities.

Perhaps most important, the collapse of communism between 1989 and 1991 opened the entire world to the spread of market capitalism and to the idea that government should interfere as little as possible with economic activity. American politicians and social commentators increasingly criticized the regulation of wages and working conditions, assistance to the less fortunate, and environmental protections as burdens on international competitiveness. During the 1990s, presidents Bush, a Republican, and Clinton, a Democrat, both spoke of an American mission to create a single global free market as the path to rising living standards, the spread of democracy, and greater worldwide freedom.

Spread of market capitalism

The media called the loose coalition of groups who organized the Seattle protests the "antiglobalization" movement. In fact, they challenged not globalization itself but its social consequences. Globalization, the demonstrators claimed, accelerated the worldwide creation of wealth but widened gaps between rich and poor countries and between haves and have-nots within societies. Decisions affecting the day-to-day lives of millions of people were made by institutions—the World Trade Organization, International Monetary Fund, World Bank, and

Gap between the haves and have-nots

The first Starbucks store, which opened in Seattle in 1971. By 2015, Starbucks had more than 22,000 such establishments in 66 countries around the globe.

multinational corporations—that operated without any democratic input. Demonstrators demanded not an end to global trade and capital flows, but the establishment of international standards for wages, labor conditions, and the environment, and greater investment in health and education in poor countries. The Battle of Seattle placed on the national and international agendas a question that promises to be among the most pressing concerns of the twenty-first century—the relationship between globalization, economic justice, and freedom.

Economic growth

The economy's performance in the 1990s at first seemed to justify the claims of globalization's advocates. After recovery from the recession of 1990–1991, economic expansion continued for the rest of the decade. By 2000, unemployment stood below 4 percent, a figure not seen since the 1960s. The boom became the longest uninterrupted period of economic expansion in the nation's history. Because Reagan and Bush had left behind massive budget deficits, Clinton worked hard to balance the federal budget—a goal traditionally associated with fiscal conservatives. Since economic growth produced rising tax revenues, Clinton during his second term not only balanced the budget but actually produced budget surpluses.

The Computer Revolution

Many commentators spoke of the 1990s as the dawn of a "new economy," in which computers and the Internet would produce vast new efficiencies and the production and sale of information would occupy the central place once held by the manufacture of goods. Computers had first been developed during and after World War II to solve scientific problems and do calculations involving enormous amounts of data. The early ones were extremely large, expensive, and, by modern standards, slow. Research for the space program of the 1960s spurred the development of improved computer technology, notably the miniaturization of parts thanks to the development of the microchip on which circuits could be imprinted.

Origins of computers

Microchips made possible the development of entirely new consumer products. Videocassette recorders, handheld video games, cellular phones, and digital cameras were mass-produced at affordable prices during the 1990s, mostly in Asia and Latin America rather than the United States. But it was the computer that transformed American life. Beginning in the 1980s, companies like Apple and IBM marketed computers for business and home use. As computers became smaller, faster, and less expensive, they found a place in businesses of every kind. In occupations as diverse as clerical work, banking, architectural design, medical diagnosis, and even factory production, they transformed the American workplace. They also changed private life. By the year 2000, nearly half of all American households owned a personal computer, used for entertainment, shopping, and sending and receiving electronic mail. Centers of computer technology, such as Silicon Valley south of San Francisco, the Seattle and Austin metropolitan areas, and lower Manhattan, boomed during the 1990s.

Computers in daily life

The Internet, first developed as a high-speed military communications network, was simplified and opened to commercial and individual use through personal computers. The Internet expanded the flow of information and communications more radically than any invention since the printing press. At a time when the ownership of newspapers, television stations, and publishing houses

The Internet

Two architects of the computer revolution, Steve Jobs (on the left), the head of Apple Computer, and Bill Gates, founder of Microsoft, which makes the operating system used in most of the world's computers.

Young people seemed to adapt to the computer revolution more readily than their elders. Here nine-year-old Anna Walter teaches several adults how to use the Internet in Wichita, Kansas.

was becoming concentrated in the hands of a few giant media conglomerates, the fact that anyone with a computer could post his or her ideas for worldwide circulation led "netizens" ("citizens" of the Internet) to hail the advent of a new, democratic public sphere in cyberspace.

The Stock Market Boom and Bust

Economic growth and talk of a new economy sparked a frenzied boom in the stock market that was reminiscent of the 1920s. Investors, large and small, poured funds into stocks, spurred by the rise of discount and online firms that advertised aggressively and charged lower fees than traditional brokers. By 2000, a majority of American households owned stocks directly or through investment in mutual funds and pension and retirement accounts.

Dot-com bubble

Investors were especially attracted to the new "dot coms"—companies that conducted business via the Internet and seemed to symbolize the promise of the new economy. The NASDAQ, a stock exchange dominated by new technology companies, rose more than 500 percent from 1998 to 1999. Many of these "high-tech" companies never turned a profit. But economic journalists and stock brokers explained that the new economy had so revolutionized business that traditional methods of assessing a company's value no longer applied.

Inevitably, the bubble burst. On April 14, 2000, stocks suffered their largest one-day point drop in history. For the first time since the Depression, stock prices declined for three successive years (2000–2002), wiping out billions of dollars in Americans' net worth and pension funds. The value of NASDAQ stocks fell by nearly 80 percent between 2000 and 2002. By 2001, the American economy had fallen into a recession. Talk of a new economy, it appeared, had been premature.

The Enron Syndrome

Finance fraud

Only after the market dropped did it become apparent that the stock boom of the 1990s had been fueled in part by fraud. For a time in 2001 and 2002, Americans were treated almost daily to revelations of incredible greed and corruption on the part of respected brokerage firms, accountants, and company executives. During the late 1990s, accounting firms like Arthur Andersen, giant banks like JPMorgan Chase and Citigroup, and corporate lawyers pocketed extravagant fees for devising complex schemes to help push up companies' stock prices by hiding their true financial condition. Enron, a Houston-based energy company that epitomized the new economy—it bought and sold electricity rather than actually producing it—reported as profits billions of dollars in operating losses.

In the early twenty-first century, the bill came due for many corporate criminals. The founder of Adelphia Communications was convicted of misuse of company funds. A jury found the chairman of Tyco International guilty of looting the company of millions of dollars. A number of former chief executives faced long prison terms. Kenneth Lay and Jeffrey Skilling, chief officers of Enron, were convicted by a Texas jury of multiple counts of fraud.

Fruits of Deregulation

At the height of the 1990s boom, with globalization in full swing, stocks rising, and the economy expanding, the economic model of free trade and deregulation appeared unassailable. But the retreat from government economic regulation, a policy embraced by both the Republican Congress and President Clinton, left no one to represent the public interest.

The public interest

The sectors of the economy most affected by the scandals—energy, telecommunications, and stock trading—had all been subjects of deregulation. Enron could manipulate energy prices because Congress had granted it an exemption from laws regulating the price of natural gas and electricity.

Many stock frauds stemmed from the repeal in 1999 of the Glass-Steagall Act, a New Deal measure that separated commercial banks, which accept deposits and make loans, from investment banks, which invest in stocks and real estate and take larger risks. The repeal made possible the emergence of "superbanks" that combined these two functions. Phil Gramm, the Texas congressman who wrote the repeal bill, which Clinton signed, explained his thinking in this way: "Glass-Steagall came at a time when the thinking was that government was the answer. In this era of economic prosperity, we have decided that freedom is the answer."

"Superbanks"

But banks took their new freedom as an invitation to engage in all sorts of misdeeds, knowing that they had become so big that if anything happened, the federal government would have no choice but to rescue them. Banks poured money into risky mortgages. When the housing bubble collapsed in 2007–2008, the banks suffered losses that threatened to bring down the entire financial system. The Bush and Obama administrations felt they had no choice but to expend hundreds of billions of dollars of taxpayer money to save the banks from their own misconduct.

Cartoonist David Jacobson's comment on the Enron scandal.

"Let's say I was Enron, how would you do my taxes?"

Rising Inequality

The boom that began in 1995 benefited nearly all Americans. For the first time since the early 1970s, average real wages and family incomes began to grow significantly. Economic expansion at a time of low unemployment brought rapid increases in wages for families at all income levels. It aided low-skilled workers, especially non-whites, who had been left out of previous periods of growth. Yet, despite these gains, in the last two decades of the twentieth century, the poor and the middle class became worse off while the rich became significantly richer. The wealth of the richest Americans exploded during the 1990s. Sales of luxury goods like yachts and mansions boomed. Bill Gates, head of Microsoft and the country's richest person, owned as much wealth as the bottom 40 percent of the American population put together.

Dot-com millionaires and well-paid computer designers and programmers received much publicity. But companies continued to shift manufacturing jobs overseas. Thanks to NAFTA, a thriving industrial zone emerged just across the southern border of the United States, where American manufacturers built plants to take advantage of cheap labor and weak environmental and safety regulations. Business, moreover, increasingly relied for profits on financial operations rather than making things. The financial sector of the economy accounted for around 10 percent of total profits in 1950; by 2000 the figure was up to 40 percent. Companies like Ford and General Electric made more money from interest on loans to customers and other financial operations than from selling their products.

The outsourcing of jobs soon moved from manufacturing to other areas, including accounting, legal services, banking, and other skilled jobs where companies could employ workers overseas for a fraction of their cost in the United States. All this lowered prices for consumers, but also threw millions of American workers into competition with those around the globe, producing a relentless downward pressure on American wages.

Overall, between 1990 and 2008, companies that did business in global markets contributed almost nothing to job growth in the United States. Microsoft,

A cartoonist offered this view in 1993 of the results of the North American Free Trade Agreement, suggesting that the United States was exporting manufacturing factories and jobs, and receiving immigrant workers in exchange.

symbol of the new economy, employed only 30,000 people. Apple, another highly successful company, whose computers, iPads, and iPhones were among the most ubiquitous consumer products of the early twenty-first century, in 2010 employed some 43,000 persons in the United States (the large majority a low-wage sales force in the company's stores). Its contractors, who made these products, had more than 700,000 employees, almost all of them overseas. In 1970, General Motors had been the country's largest corporate employer. In the early twenty-first century, it had been replaced by Wal-Mart, a giant discount retail chain that paid most of its 1.6 million workers slightly more than the minimum wage. Wal-Mart aggressively opposed efforts at collective bargaining. Not a single one of its employees belonged to a union. Thanks to NAFTA, which enabled American companies to expand their business in Mexico, by 2010 Wal-Mart was also the largest employer in that country.

Barbie's Liberty, a satirical work by the artist Hans Haacke, recasts the Barbie doll, one of America's most successful toys, in the image of the Statue of Liberty to comment on the loss of manufacturing jobs to low-wage areas overseas. Art © Hans Haacke/Artists Rights Society (ARS), New York/VG Bild-Kunst, Bonn.

CULTURE WARS

The end of the Cold War ushered in hopes for a new era of global harmony. Instead, what one observer called a "rebellion of particularisms"—renewed emphasis on group identity and insistent demands for group recognition and power—has racked the international arena. In the nineteenth and twentieth centuries, socialism and nationalism had united people of different backgrounds in pursuit of common goals. Now, in Africa, Asia, the Middle East, and parts of Europe, the waning of movements based on socialism and the declining power of nation-states arising from globalization seemed to unleash long-simmering ethnic and religious antagonisms. Partly in reaction to the global spread of a secular culture based on consumption and mass entertainment, intense religious movements attracted increasing numbers of followers—Hindu nationalism in India, orthodox Judaism in Israel, Islamic fundamentalism in much of the Muslim world, and evangelical Christianity in the United States. Like other nations, although in a far less extreme way and with little accompanying violence, the United States has experienced divisions arising from the intensification of ethnic and racial identities and religious fundamentalism.

Religious fundamentalism

The Newest Immigrants

Because of shifts in immigration, cultural and racial diversity have become increasingly visible in the United States. Until the immigration law of 1965, the vast majority of twentieth-century newcomers hailed from Europe. That measure, as noted in Chapter 25, sparked a wholesale shift in immigrants' origins. Between 1965 and 2010, nearly 38 million immigrants entered the United States, a number larger than the 27 million during the peak period of immigration between 1880 and 1924. About 50 percent came from Latin America and the Caribbean, 35 percent from Asia, and smaller numbers from the Middle East and Africa. Only 10 percent arrived from Europe, mostly from the war-torn Balkans and the former Soviet Union.

Increasing diversity

VOICES OF FREEDOM

From BILL CLINTON,
SPEECH ON SIGNING OF NAFTA (1993)

The North American Free Trade Agreement was signed by President Bill Clinton early in his first term. It created a free-trade zone (an area where goods can travel freely without paying import duties) composed of Canada, the United States, and Mexico. Clinton asked Americans to accept economic globalization as an inevitable form of progress and the path to future prosperity. "There will be no job loss," he promised. Things did not entirely work out that way.

As President, it is my duty to speak frankly to the American people about the world in which we now live. Fifty years ago, at the end of World War II, an unchallenged America was protected by the oceans and by our technological superiority and, very frankly, by the economic devastation of the people who could otherwise have been our competitors. We chose then to try to help rebuild our former enemies and to create a world of free trade supported by institutions which would facilitate it. . . . As a result, jobs were created, and opportunity thrived all across the world. . . .

For the last 20 years, in all the wealthy countries of the world—because of changes in the global environment, because of the growth of technology, because of increasing competition—the middle class that was created and enlarged by the wise policies of expanding trade at the end of World War II has been under severe stress. Most Americans are working harder for less. They are vulnerable to the fear tactics and the averseness to change that are behind much of the opposition to NAFTA. But I want to say to my fellow Americans: When you live in a time of change, the only way to recover your security and to broaden your horizons is to adapt to the change—to embrace, to move forward. . . . The only way we can recover the fortunes of the middle class in this country so that people who work harder and smarter can, at least, prosper more, the only way we can pass on the American dream of the last 40 years to our children and their children for the next 40, is to adapt to the changes which are occurring.

In a fundamental sense, this debate about NAFTA is a debate about whether we will embrace these changes and create the jobs of tomorrow or try to resist these changes, hoping we can preserve the economic structures of yesterday. . . . I believe that NAFTA will create 1 million jobs in the first 5 years of its impact. . . . NAFTA will generate these jobs by fostering an export boom to Mexico by tearing down tariff walls. . . . There will be no job loss.

From GLOBAL EXCHANGE, SEATTLE, DECLARATION FOR GLOBAL DEMOCRACY (DECEMBER 1999)

The demonstrations that disrupted the December 1999 meeting of the World Trade Organization in Seattle brought to public attention a widespread dissatisfaction with the effects of economic "globalization." In this declaration, organizers of the protest offered their critique.

———————————————

As citizens of global society, recognizing that the World Trade Organization is unjustly dominated by corporate interests and run for the enrichment of the few at the expense of all others, we demand:

Representatives from all sectors of society must be included in all levels of trade policy formulations. All global citizens must be democratically represented in the formulation, implementation, and evaluation of all global social and economic policies.

Global trade and investment must not be ends in themselves, but rather the instruments for achieving equitable and sustainable development including protection for workers and the environment.

Global trade agreements must not undermine the ability of each nation-state or local community to meet its citizens' social, environmental, cultural or economic needs.

The World Trade Organization must be replaced by a democratic and transparent body accountable to citizens—not to corporations.

No globalization without representation!

QUESTIONS

1. *Why does Clinton feel that free trade is necessary to American prosperity?*

2. *Why do the Seattle protesters feel that the World Trade Organization is a threat to democracy?*

3. *How do these documents reflect contradictory arguments about the impact of globalization in the United States?*

Erected on U.S. 5, an interstate highway running from the Mexican to Canadian borders along the Pacific Coast, this sign warns motorists to be on the lookout for people (i.e., undocumented immigrant families) crossing the road on foot. The sign's placement north of San Diego, about thirty miles north of Mexico, illustrates how the "border" had become an entire region, not simply a geographical boundary.

Diversity of backgrounds

In 2010, the number of foreign-born persons living in the United States stood at more than 40 million, or 13 percent of the population. Although less than the peak proportion of 14 percent in 1910, in absolute numbers this represented the largest immigrant total in the nation's history. The immigrant influx changed the country's religious and racial map. By 2010, more than 4 million Muslims resided in the United States, and the combined population of Buddhists and Hindus exceeded 1 million.

As in the past, many immigrants became urban residents, with New York City, Los Angeles, Chicago, and Miami the most common destinations. New ethnic communities emerged, with homes, shops, restaurants, foreign-language newspapers, radio and television stations, and ethnic professionals like businessmen and lawyers. Unlike in the past, rather than being concentrated in one or two parts of city centers, immigrants quickly moved into outlying neighborhoods and older suburbs. The immigrant influx revitalized neighborhoods like New York City's Washington Heights (a Dominican enclave) and Flushing (a center for Asian newcomers). By the turn of the century, more than half of all Latinos lived in suburbs. Orange County, California, which had been a stronghold of suburban conservatism between 1960 and 1990, elected a Latina Democrat to Congress in the late 1990s. While most immigrants settled on the East and West Coasts, some moved to other parts of the country. They brought cultural and racial diversity to once-homogeneous communities in the American heartland.

Post-1965 immigration formed part of the worldwide uprooting of labor arising from globalization. Those who migrated to the United States came from a wide variety of backgrounds. They included poor, illiterate refugees from places of economic and political crisis—Central Americans escaping the region's civil wars and poverty, Haitians and Cambodians fleeing repressive governments. But many immigrants were well-educated professionals from countries like India and South Korea, where the availability of skilled jobs had not kept pace with the spread of higher education. In the year 2000, more than 40 percent of all immigrants to the United States had a college education.

For the first time in American history, women made up the majority of newcomers, reflecting the decline of manufacturing jobs that had previously absorbed immigrant men, as well as the spread of employment opportunities in traditionally

TABLE 27.1 Immigration to the United States, 1961–2010

DECADE	TOTAL	EUROPE	ASIA	WESTERN HEMISPHERE	OTHER AREAS
1961–1970	3,321,584	1,123,492	427,642	1,716,374	54,076
1971–1980	4,493,302	800,368	1,588,178	1,982,735	122,021
1981–1990	7,336,940	761,550	2,738,157	3,615,225	222,008
1991–2000	9,042,999	1,359,737	2,795,672	4,486,806	400,784
2001–2010	14,974,975	1,165,176	4,088,455	8,582,601	1,138,743

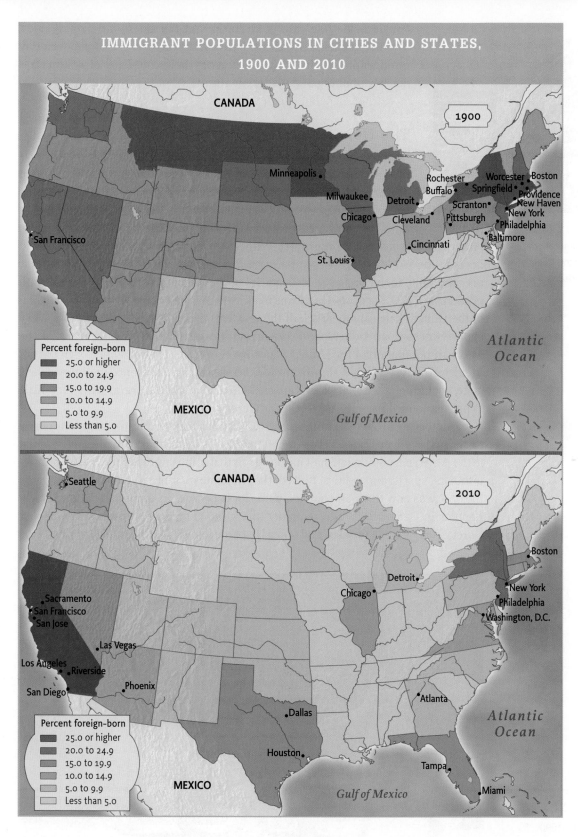

IMMIGRANT POPULATIONS IN CITIES AND STATES,
1900 AND 2010

Maps illustrating states' foreign-born populations and the twenty metropolitan areas with the most immigrants in 1900 and 2010. In 1900 nearly all went to the Northeast and Upper Midwest, the heartland of the industrial economy. In 2010 the largest number headed for cities in the South and West, especially California, although major cities of the Northeast also attracted many newcomers.

Recent immigrants at a naturalization ceremony held at Fenway Park, Boston, in 2008. Over 3,000 people became U.S. citizens at this event.

Latinos

female fields like care of children and the elderly and retail sales. Thanks to cheap global communications and jet travel, modern-day immigrants retain strong ties with their countries of origin, frequently phoning and visiting home.

The New Diversity

Latinos formed the largest single immigrant group. This term was invented in the United States and includes people from quite different origins—Mexicans, Central and South Americans, and migrants from Spanish-speaking Caribbean islands like Cuba, the Dominican Republic, and Puerto Rico (although the last group, of course, are American citizens, not immigrants). With 95 million people, Mexico in 2000 had become the world's largest Spanish-speaking nation. Its poverty, high birthrate, and proximity to the United States made it a source of massive legal and illegal immigration. In 2000, Mexican-Americans made up a majority of the Hispanic population of the United States and nearly half the residents of Los Angeles. But almost every state witnessed an influx of Mexican immigrants. In 1930, 90 percent of the Mexican population of the United States lived in states that had once been part of Mexico. Today, there is a significant Mexican-American presence in almost every state, including such places as Kansas, Minnesota, and Georgia, with very little experience, until recently, with ethnic diversity.

Numbering around 50 million in 2010, Latinos had become the largest minority group in the United States. Between 1990 and 2010, 30 million Hispanics were added to the American population, half its total growth. Latinos were highly visible in entertainment, sports, and politics. Indeed, the Hispanic presence transformed American life. José was now the most common name for baby boys in Texas and the third most popular in California. Smith remained the most common American surname, but Garcia, Rodriguez, Gonzales, and other Hispanic names were all in the top fifty.

Latina nannies pushing baby carriages in Beverly Hills, California. In the 1990s, for the first time in American history, female immigrants outnumbered male immigrants.

Latino communities remained far poorer than the rest of the country. A flourishing middle class developed in Los Angeles, Miami, and other cities with large Spanish-speaking populations. But most immigrants from Mexico and Central America competed at the lowest levels of the job market. The influx of legal and undocumented immigrants swelled the ranks of low-wage urban workers and agricultural laborers. Latinos lagged far behind other Americans in education. In 2010, their poverty rate stood at nearly double the national figure of 15 percent. Living and working conditions among predominantly Latino farm workers in the West fell back to levels as dire as when César Chavez established the United Farm Workers union in the 1960s.

Poverty in Latino communities

Asian-Americans also became increasingly visible. There had long been a small population of Asian ancestry in California and New York City, but only after 1965 did immigration from Asia assume large proportions. Like Latinos, Asian-Americans were a highly diverse population, including well-educated Koreans, Indians, and Japanese, as well as poor refugees from Cambodia, Vietnam, and China. Growing up in tight-knit communities that placed great emphasis on education, young Asian-Americans poured into American colleges and universities. Once subjected to harsh discrimination, Asian-Americans now achieved remarkable success. White Americans hailed them as a "model minority." By 2007, the median family income of Asian-Americans, $66,000, surpassed that of whites. But more than any other group, Asian-Americans clustered at opposite ends of the income spectrum. Large numbers earned either more than $75,000 per year (doctors, engineers, and entrepreneurs) or under $5,000 (unskilled laborers in sweatshops and restaurants).

Asian-Americans

The United States, of course, had long been a multiracial society. But for centuries race relations had been shaped by the black-white divide and the experience of slavery and segregation. The growing visibility of Latinos and Asians suggested that a two-race system no longer adequately described American life. Multiracial imagery filled television, films, and advertising. Interracial marriage, at one time

A multiracial society

The U.S. Border Patrol apprehending Mexicans who had entered the country in violation of immigration laws, near San Diego, California. In 1990, more than 1 million immigrants were arrested and deported after crossing the border illegally.

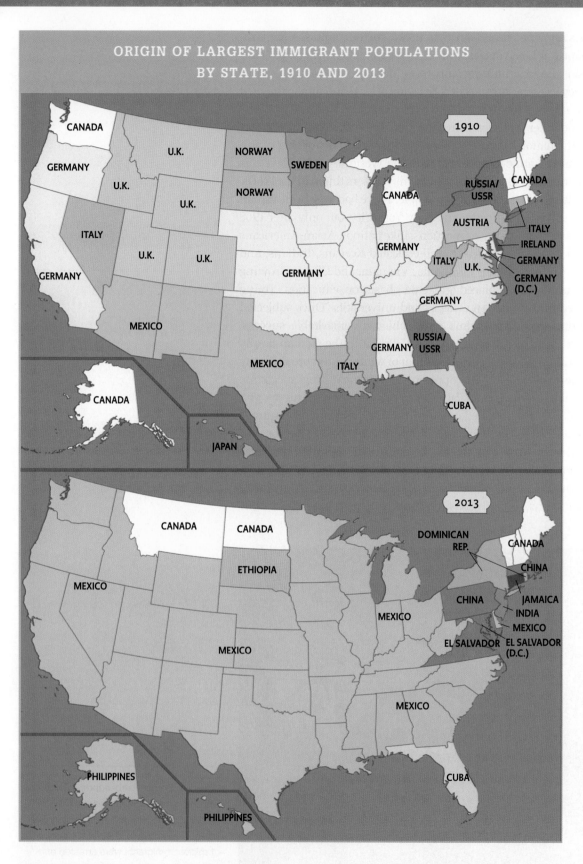

ORIGIN OF LARGEST IMMIGRANT POPULATIONS BY STATE, 1910 AND 2013

1910

CANADA
GERMANY
U.K.
U.K.
U.K.
NORWAY
SWEDEN
NORWAY
ITALY
U.K.
U.K.
GERMANY
MEXICO
GERMANY
MEXICO
ITALY
GERMANY
GERMANY
RUSSIA/USSR
AUSTRIA
GERMANY
ITALY
U.K.
CANADA
RUSSIA/USSR
CANADA
ITALY
IRELAND
GERMANY
GERMANY (D.C.)
CUBA
CANADA
JAPAN

2013

CANADA
CANADA
ETHIOPIA
MEXICO
MEXICO
MEXICO
MEXICO
MEXICO
DOMINICAN REP.
CHINA
CANADA
CHINA
JAMAICA
INDIA
MEXICO
EL SALVADOR
EL SALVADOR (D.C.)
CUBA
PHILIPPINES
PHILIPPINES

Maps depicting the birthplace of each state's largest immigrant population in 1910 and 2013. A century ago, most immigrants hailed from Europe, and the leading country of origin varied among the states. Today, in almost every state outside the Northeast, those born in Mexico constitute the largest number of immigrants.

banned in forty-two states, became more common and acceptable. Among Asian-Americans, half of all marriages involved a non-Asian partner. The figure for Latinos was 30 percent. Some commentators spoke of the "end of racism" and the emergence of a truly color-blind society. Others argued that while Asians and some Latinos were being absorbed into an expanded category of "white" Americans, the black-white divide remained almost as impenetrable as ever.

Interracial marriage

One thing, however, seemed clear at the dawn of the twenty-first century: diversity was here to stay. Because the birthrate of racial minorities is higher than that of whites, the Census Bureau projected that by 2050, less than 50 percent of the American population would be white.

The Changing Face of Black America

Compared with the situation in 1900 or 1950, the most dramatic change in American life at the turn of the century was the absence of legal segregation and the presence of blacks in areas of American life from which they had once been almost entirely excluded. Thanks to the decline in overt discrimination and the effectiveness of many affirmative action programs, blacks now worked in unprecedented numbers alongside whites in corporate board rooms, offices, and factories. The number of black policemen, for example, rose from 24,000 to 65,000 between 1970 and 2000, and in the latter year, 37 percent of the black population reported having attended college. The economic boom of the late 1990s aided black Americans enormously; the average income of black families rose more rapidly than that of whites.

One major change in black life was the growing visibility of Africans among the nation's immigrants. Between 1970 and 2010, more than twice as many Africans immigrated to the United States as had entered during the entire period of the Atlantic slave trade. For the first time, all the elements of the African diaspora—natives of Africa, Caribbeans, Central and South Americans of African descent, Europeans with African roots—could be found in the United States alongside the descendants of American slaves.

The African diaspora

Korean girls rehearsing a dance at the Veterans Administration Medical Center in Columbia, South Carolina, an illustration of the growing diversity of American society.

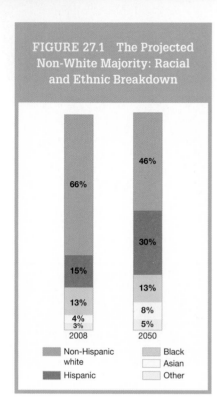

FIGURE 27.1 The Projected Non-White Majority: Racial and Ethnic Breakdown

66% | 46%
15% | 30%
13% | 13%
4% | 8%
3% | 5%
2008 | 2050

■ Non-Hispanic white   ■ Black
■ Hispanic   □ Asian
   ■ Other

Housing patterns and school segregation

Despite the ups and downs of unemployment, the rate for non-whites remains persistently higher than that for whites.

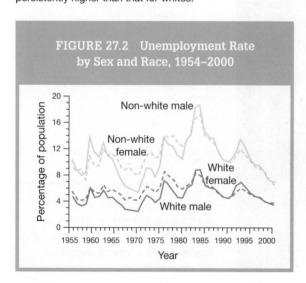

FIGURE 27.2 Unemployment Rate by Sex and Race, 1954–2000

Non-white male
Non-white female
White female
White male

Percentage of population
20
16
12
8
4
0
1955 1960 1965 1970 1975 1980 1985 1990 1995 2000
Year

Nigeria, Ghana, and Ethiopia provided the largest number of African immigrants, and they settled overwhelmingly in urban areas, primarily in New York, California, Texas, and the District of Columbia. Some were impoverished refugees fleeing civil wars in Somalia, Sudan, and Ethiopia, but many more were professionals—more than half the African newcomers had college educations, the highest percentage for any immigrant group. Indeed, some African countries complained of a "brain drain" as physicians, teachers, and other highly skilled persons sought opportunities in the United States that did not exist in their own underdeveloped countries. While some prospered, others found it difficult to transfer their credentials to the United States and found jobs driving taxis and selling African crafts at street fairs.

Most African-Americans, nonetheless, remained in a more precarious situation than whites or many recent immigrants. In the early twenty-first century, the black unemployment rate remained double that of whites. Half of all black children lived in poverty, two-thirds were born out of wedlock, and in every index of social well-being from health to quality of housing, blacks continued to lag. Despite the continued expansion of the black middle class, a far lower percentage of blacks than whites owned their homes or held professional and managerial jobs. Housing segregation remained pervasive. In 2010, more than one-third of the black population lived in suburbs, but mostly in predominantly black communities.

Despite the nation's growing racial diversity, school segregation—now resulting from housing patterns and the divide between urban and suburban school districts rather than laws requiring racial separation—was on the rise. Most city public school systems consisted overwhelmingly of minority students, large numbers of whom failed to receive an adequate education. The courts released more and more districts from desegregation orders. By 2000, the nation's black and Latino students were more isolated from white pupils than in 1970. Nearly 80 percent of white students attended schools where they encountered few if any pupils of another race. Since school funding rested on property taxes, poor communities continued to have less to spend on education than wealthy ones.

The Spread of Imprisonment

During the 1960s, the nation's prison population declined. But in the 1970s, with urban crime rates rising, politicians of both parties sought to convey the image of being "tough on crime." They insisted that the judicial system should focus on locking up criminals for long periods rather than rehabilitating them. They treated drug addiction as a violation of the law rather than as a disease. State governments greatly increased the penalties for crime and reduced the possibility of parole. Successive presidents launched "wars" on the use of illegal drugs. As a result, the number of Americans in prison rose dramatically, most of them incarcerated for nonviolent drug offenses.

During the 1990s, thanks to the waning of the crack epidemic and more effective urban police tactics, crime rates dropped dramatically across the country. But because of the sentencing laws of the previous two decades, this did nothing to stem the increase of the prison population. In 2011, it reached 2.3 million, ten times the figure of 1970. Several million more individuals were on parole, on probation, or under some other kind of criminal supervision. These figures dwarfed those of every other Western society.

As the prison population grew, a "prison-industrial complex" emerged. Struggling communities battered by deindustrialization saw prisons as a source of jobs and income. Between 1990 and 1995, the federal government and the states constructed more than 200 new prisons. In 2008, five states spent more money on their prison systems than on higher education. Convict labor, a practice the labor movement had managed to curtail in the late nineteenth century, revived in the late twentieth. Private companies in Oregon "leased" prisoners for three dollars per day. A call to Trans World Airlines for a flight reservation was likely to be answered by a California inmate.

TABLE 27.2 Home Ownership Rates by Group, 1970–2000				
	1970	**1980**	**1990**	**2000**
Whites	65.0%	67.8%	68.2%	73.8%
Blacks	41.6	44.4	43.4	47.2
Latinos	43.7	43.4	42.4	46.3
All families	62.9	64.4	64.2	67.4

The Burden of Imprisonment

Members of racial minorities experienced most strongly the paradox of growing islands of unfreedom in a nation that prided itself on liberty. In 1950, whites accounted for 70 percent of the nation's prison population and non-whites 30 percent. By 2010, these figures had been reversed. One reason was that severe penalties faced those convicted of using or selling crack, a particularly potent form of cocaine concentrated among the urban poor, while the use of powder cocaine, the drug of choice in suburban America, led to far lighter sentences.

The percentage of the black population in prison stood five times higher than the proportion for white Americans. More than one-quarter of all black men could expect to serve time in prison at some time during their lives. A criminal record made it very difficult for ex-prisoners to find jobs. Partly because so many young men were in prison, blacks had a significantly lower rate of marriage than other Americans. Their children became "prison orphans," forced to live with relatives or in foster homes.

Racial minorities and incarceration

A private, for-profit, maximum-security prison under construction in 1999 in California City, in the Mohave Desert, illustrates the expansion of the "prison-industrial complex."

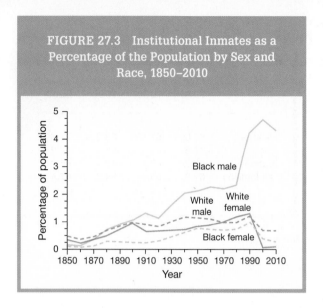

FIGURE 27.3 Institutional Inmates as a Percentage of the Population by Sex and Race, 1850–2010

Blacks convicted of crimes were also more likely than whites to receive the death penalty. In 1972, the Supreme Court had temporarily suspended states' use of this punishment. But the Court soon allowed it to resume, despite evidence of racial disparities in its application. Even as western Europe and other countries abolished the death penalty, the United States executed over 1,400 persons between 1977 and 2015. In the 1830s, Alexis de Tocqueville had described executions as common in Europe but rare in America. By the early twenty-first century, the United States ranked with China, Iran, and Saudi Arabia as the nations that most often executed their citizens. The 2.2 million Americans in prison in 2015 represented one-fifth of the entire world's inmates and far exceeded the number in any other country.

The continuing frustration of urban blacks exploded in 1992 when an all-white suburban jury found four Los Angeles police officers not guilty in the beating of black motorist Rodney King, even though an onlooker had captured their assault on videotape. The deadliest urban uprising since the New York draft riots of 1863 followed. Some fifty-two people died, and property damage approached $1 billion. Many Latino youths, who shared blacks' resentment over mistreatment by the police, joined in the violence. The uprising suggested that despite the civil rights revolution, the nation had failed to address the plight of the urban poor.

The Continuing Rights Revolution

The AIDS quilt, each square of which represents a person who died of AIDS, on display in Washington, D.C. The quilt was exhibited throughout the country, heightening public awareness of the AIDS epidemic.

Reflecting the continued power of the rights revolution, in 1990, newly organized disabled Americans won passage of the **Americans with Disabilities Act**. This far-reaching measure prohibited discrimination in hiring and promotion against persons with disabilities and required that entrances to public buildings be redesigned so as to ensure access for the disabled.

Some movements that were descended from the late 1960s achieved great visibility in the 1990s. Prominent among these was the campaign for gay rights, which in the last two decades of the century increasingly turned its attention to combating acquired immunodeficiency syndrome (AIDS), a fatal disease spread by sexual contact, drug use, and transfusions of contaminated blood. AIDS first emerged in the early 1980s. It quickly became epidemic among homosexual men. The gay movement mobilized to promote "safe sex," prevent discrimination against people suffering from AIDS, and press the federal government to devote greater resources to fighting the disease. The Gay Men's Health Crisis organized educational programs and assistance to those affected by the disease, and demanded that drug companies put AZT, a drug with some success in treating AIDS, on the market. A more radical group, ACT UP, disrupted a mass at New York's St. Patrick's Cathedral to protest what it called the Catholic Church's prejudices against gays. By 2000, even though more than 400,000 Americans had died of AIDS, its spread among gays had been sharply curtailed. But in other parts of the world, such as Africa, the AIDS epidemic remained out of control.

Gay groups also played an increasing role in politics. In cities with large gay populations, such as New York and San Francisco, politicians vied to attract their votes. Overall, the growth of public tolerance of homosexuality was among the most striking changes in American social attitudes in the last two decades of the century. In the second decade of the twenty-first century, this would lead to the remarkably rapid acceptance of the right of gay Americans to form legal marriages.

Gay rights

Native Americans in the New Century

Another social movement spawned by the 1960s that continued to flourish was the American Indian movement. The Indian population reached over 5 million (including people choosing more than one race) in the 2010 census, a sign not only of population growth but also of a renewed sense of pride that led many Indians for the first time to identify themselves as such to census enumerators. Meanwhile, with the assistance of the Native American Rights Fund, established in 1971, some tribes embarked on a campaign for restitution for past injustices. In 2001, for example, a New York court awarded the Cayuga Nation $248 million for illegal land seizures two centuries earlier.

American Indian movement

The legal position of Indians as American citizens who enjoy a kind of quasi-sovereignty still survives in some cases. Notable examples are the lucrative Indian casinos now operating in states that otherwise prohibit gambling. In 2011, Indian casinos took in over $27 billion, making some tribes very rich. One such group is the Pequot tribe of Connecticut. In 1637, as the result of a brief, bloody war, Puritan New Englanders exterminated or sold into slavery most of the tribe's members. The treaty that restored peace decreed that the tribe's name should be wiped from the historical record. Today, the few hundred members of the Pequot tribe operate Foxwoods, reputedly the world's largest casino. However, because of the recession that began in 2007, Foxwoods' receipts plummeted and its survival remains uncertain.

This work by the contemporary Eastern Band Cherokee artist Shan Goshorn, entitled *Unintended Legacy*, reproduces historical documents that are woven into a basket (a traditional Native American craft) such as the names and images of Indian children and adults at a typical boarding school. That history, she suggests, still affects Indian life today.

Half of today's Indians live in five western states (California, Oklahoma, Arizona, New Mexico, and Washington). Although some tribes have reinvested casino profits in improved housing and health care and college scholarships for Native American students, most Indian casinos are marginal operations whose low-wage jobs as cashiers, waitresses, and the like have done little to relieve Indian poverty. Native Americans continue to occupy the lowest rung on the economic ladder. At least half of those living on reservations have incomes below the poverty line.

Multiculturalism

The new face of American society went hand in hand with one of the most striking developments of the 1990s—the celebration of group difference and demands for group recognition. **Multiculturalism** became the term for a new awareness of the diversity of American society, past and present, and for vocal demands that jobs, education, and politics reflect that diversity. As the numbers of minority and female students at the nation's colleges and universities rose, these institutions moved aggressively to diversify their faculties and revise the traditional curriculum.

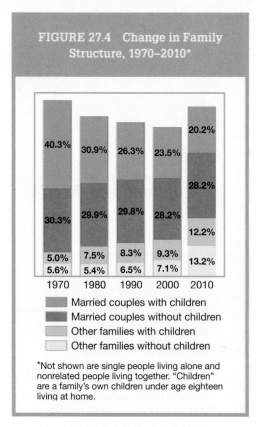

FIGURE 27.4   Change in Family Structure, 1970–2010*

1970	1980	1990	2000	2010
40.3%	30.9%	26.3%	23.5%	20.2%
30.3%	29.9%	29.8%	28.2%	28.2%
5.0%	7.5%	8.3%	9.3%	12.2%
5.6%	5.4%	6.5%	7.1%	13.2%

■ Married couples with children
■ Married couples without children
■ Other families with children
□ Other families without children

*Not shown are single people living alone and nonrelated people living together. "Children" are a family's own children under age eighteen living at home.

At the beginning of the twenty-first century, less than one-quarter of American households consisted of a "traditional" family—a married couple living with their children.

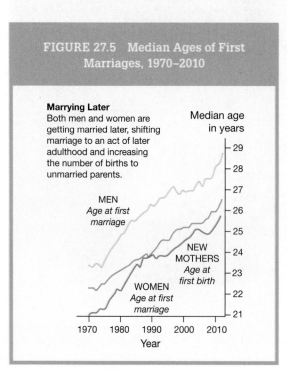

FIGURE 27.5   Median Ages of First Marriages, 1970–2010

Marrying Later
Both men and women are getting married later, shifting marriage to an act of later adulthood and increasing the number of births to unmarried parents.

Median age in years

MEN
Age at first marriage

NEW MOTHERS
Age at first birth

WOMEN
Age at first marriage

Year

One sign of multiculturalism could be seen in the spread of academic programs dealing with the experience of specific groups—Black Studies, Latino Studies, Women's Studies, and the like. Literature departments added the writings of female and minority authors to those of white men. Numerous scholars now taught and wrote history in ways that stressed the experiences of diverse groups of Americans, rather than a common national narrative.

The Identity Debate

Among some Americans, the heightened visibility of immigrants, racial minorities, and inheritors of the sexual revolution inspired not celebration of pluralism but alarm over perceived cultural fragmentation. Conservatives, and some traditional liberals as well, decried "identity politics" and multiculturalism for undermining a common sense of nationhood.

Increased cultural diversity and changes in educational policy inspired harsh debates over whether immigrant children should be required to learn English and whether further immigration should be discouraged. These issues entered politics most dramatically in California, whose voters in 1994 approved Proposition 187, which denied undocumented immigrants and their children access to welfare, education, and most health services. A federal judge soon barred implementation of the measure on the grounds that control over immigration policy rests with the federal government. By 2000, twenty-three states had passed laws establishing English as their official language (similar to measures enacted in the aftermath of World War I). The 1996 law that abolished welfare also barred most immigrants who had not become citizens from receiving food stamps.

But efforts to appeal to prejudice for political gain often backfired. In California, Republicans' anti-immigrant campaigns inspired minorities to mobilize politically and offended many white Americans. In 2000, Republican presidential candidate George W. Bush emphasized that his brand of conservatism was multicultural, not exclusionary.

Cultural Conservatism

Immigration occupied only one front in what came to be called the **Culture Wars**—battles over moral values that raged throughout the 1990s. The Christian Coalition, founded by evangelical minister Pat Robertson, became a major force in Republican politics. It launched crusades against gay rights, abortion, secularism in public schools, and government aid to the arts. Pat Buchanan's Republican convention speech of 1992 calling for a "religious war for the soul of America," mentioned earlier, alarmed many voters. But cultural conservatives hailed it as their new rallying cry.

It sometimes appeared during the 1990s that the country was refighting old battles between traditional religion and modern secular culture. In an echo of the 1920s, a number of localities required the teaching of creationism, a religious alternative to Darwin's theory of evolution. The battles of the 1960s seemed to be forever unresolved. Many conservatives railed against the erosion of the nuclear family, the changing racial landscape produced by immigration, and what they considered a general decline of traditional values. Cultural conservatives were not satisfied with a few victories over what they considered immorality, such as the **Defense of Marriage Act** of 1996, which barred gay couples from spousal benefits provided by federal law. (The Supreme Court would declare the law unconstitutional in 2013.)

Family Values in Retreat

The censuses of 2000 and 2010 showed **family values** increasingly in disarray. Half of all marriages ended in divorce (70 percent on the West Coast). In 2010, more than 40 percent of births were to unmarried women, not only sexually active teenagers, but growing numbers of professional women in their thirties and forties as well. For the first time, fewer than half of all households consisted of married couples, and only one-fifth were "traditional" families—a wife, husband, and their children. More than half of all adults were single or divorced. Two-thirds of married women worked outside the home. The pay gap between men and women, although narrowing, persisted. In 2010, the weekly earnings of women with full-time jobs stood at 82 percent of those of men—up from 63 percent in 1980. In only two occupational categories did women earn more than men—postal service clerks and special education teachers.

Although dominated by conservatives, the Supreme Court, in *Casey v. Planned Parenthood of Pennsylvania* (1992), reaffirmed a woman's right to terminate a pregnancy. The decision allowed states to enact mandatory waiting periods and anti-abortion counseling, but it overturned a requirement that the husband be given notification before the procedure was undertaken. "At the heart of liberty," said the Court, "is the right to . . . make the most intimate and personal choices" without outside interference. In effect, *Casey* repudiated the centuries-old doctrine that a husband has a legal claim to control the body of his wife.

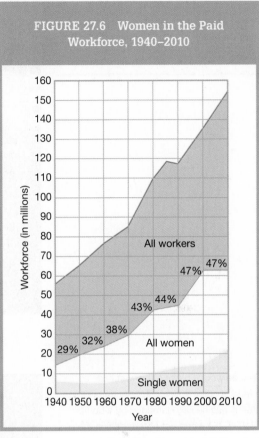

FIGURE 27.6   Women in the Paid Workforce, 1940–2010

By 2000, women represented nearly half of the American workforce, and unlike in the nineteenth century, a majority of women working outside the home were married.

The Antigovernment Extreme

At the radical fringe of conservatism, the belief that the federal government posed a threat to American freedom led to the creation of private militias who armed themselves to fend off oppressive authority. Groups like Aryan Nation, Posse Comitatus, and other self-proclaimed "Christian patriots" spread a mixture of racist, anti-Semitic, and antigovernment ideas. Private armies, like the Militia of Montana, vowed to resist enforcement of federal gun control laws. For millions of Americans, owning a gun became a prime symbol of liberty. "We're here because we love freedom," declared a participant in a 1995 Washington rally against proposed legislation banning semiautomatic assault weapons.

Many militia groups employed the symbolism and language of the American Revolution, sprinkling their appeals with warnings about the dangers of government tyranny drawn from the writings of Thomas Jefferson, Patrick Henry, and Thomas Paine. They warned that leaders of both major parties formed part of a

Private militias

A supporter of the National Rifle Association distributes literature linking gun ownership with freedom at a Texas gun convention in 1996.

Rescue workers sifting the wreckage of a federal office building in Oklahoma City after it was heavily damaged by a bomb in 1995, the worst act of terrorism in the United States during the twentieth century.

conspiracy to surrender American sovereignty to the United Nations, or to some shadowy international conspiracy. Although such organizations had been growing for years, they burst into the national spotlight in 1995 when Timothy McVeigh, a member of the militant antigovernment movement, exploded a bomb at a federal office building in Oklahoma City. The blast killed 168 persons, including numerous children at a day-care center. McVeigh was captured, convicted, and executed. The bombing alerted the nation to the danger of violent antigovernment right-wing groups.

IMPEACHMENT AND THE ELECTION OF 2000

The unusually intense partisanship of the 1990s seemed ironic, given Clinton's move toward the political center. Republicans' intense dislike of Clinton could only be explained by the fact that he seemed to symbolize everything conservatives hated about the 1960s. As a college student, the president had smoked marijuana and participated in antiwar demonstrations. He had married a feminist, made a point of leading a multicultural administration, and supported gay rights. Clinton's popularity puzzled and frustrated conservatives, reinforcing their conviction that something was deeply amiss in American life. From the very outset of his administration, Clinton's political opponents and scandal-hungry media stood ready to pounce. Clinton himself provided the ammunition.

The Impeachment of Clinton

Sexual misconduct by public officials had a long history. But in the 1980s and 1990s, scrutiny of politicians' private lives became far more intense than in the past. Gary Hart, as noted in the previous chapter, had been driven from the 1988 campaign because of an extramarital liaison. In 1991, Senate hearings on the nomination to the Supreme Court of Clarence Thomas, a black conservative, became embroiled in dramatic charges of sexual harassment leveled against Thomas by law professor Anita Hill. To the outrage of feminists, the Senate narrowly confirmed him. Nonetheless, because of her testimony, Americans became more aware of the problem of sexual harassment in and out of the workplace, and complaints shot up across the country.

From the day Clinton took office, charges of misconduct bedeviled him. In 1998, it became known that Clinton had carried on an affair with Monica Lewinsky, a White House intern. Kenneth Starr, the special counsel who had been appointed to investigate a previous scandal, shifted his focus to Lewinsky. He issued a lengthy report containing almost pornographic details of Clinton's sexual acts with the young woman and accused the president of lying when he denied the affair under oath. In December 1998, the Republican-controlled House of Representatives voted to impeach Clinton for perjury and obstruction of justice. He became the second president to be tried before the Senate. Early in 1999, the vote took place. Neither charge mustered a simple majority, much less than the two-thirds required to remove Clinton from office.

Karl Marx once wrote that historical events occur twice—first as tragedy, the second time as farce. The impeachment of Andrew Johnson in 1868 had revolved around some of the most momentous questions in American history—the Reconstruction of the South, the rights of the former slaves, relations between the federal government and the states. Clinton's impeachment had to do with what many

Herbert Block's 1998 cartoon comments humorously on Clinton's talent for political survival.

Political scrutiny

Monica Lewinsky

A member of a Florida election board trying to determine a voter's intent during the recount of presidential ballots in November 2000. The U.S. Supreme Court eventually ordered the recount halted.

Florida ballots

considered to be a juvenile escapade. Polls suggested that the obsession of Kenneth Starr and members of Congress with Clinton's sexual acts appalled Americans far more than the president's irresponsible behavior. Clinton's continuing popularity throughout the impeachment controversy demonstrated how profoundly traditional attitudes toward sexual morality had changed.

The Disputed Election

Had Clinton been eligible to run for reelection in 2000, he would probably have won. But after the death of FDR, the Constitution had been amended to limit presidents to two terms in office. Democrats nominated Vice President Al Gore to succeed Clinton (pairing him with Senator Joseph Lieberman of Connecticut, the first Jewish vice-presidential nominee). Republicans chose George W. Bush, the governor of Texas and son of Clinton's predecessor, as their candidate, with former secretary of defense Dick Cheney as his running mate.

The election proved to be one of the closest in the nation's history. The outcome remained uncertain until a month after the ballots had been cast. Gore won the popular vote by a tiny margin—540,000 of 100 million cast, or one-half of 1 percent. Victory in the electoral college hinged on which candidate had carried Florida. There, amid widespread confusion at the polls and claims of irregularities in counting the ballots, Bush claimed a margin of a few hundred votes. In the days after the election, Democrats demanded a hand recount of the Florida ballots for which machines could not determine a voter's intent. The Florida Supreme Court ordered the recount to proceed.

As in the disputed election that ended Reconstruction (a contest in which Florida had also played a crucial role), it fell to Supreme Court justices to decide the outcome. On December 12, 2000, by a 5-4 vote, the Court ordered a halt to the recounting of Florida ballots, allowing the state's governor Jeb Bush (George W. Bush's brother) to certify that the Republican candidate had carried the state and had therefore won the presidency.

The decision in ***Bush v. Gore*** was one of the oddest in Supreme Court history. In the late 1990s, the Court had reasserted the powers of the states within the federal system. Now, however, it overturned a decision of the Florida Supreme Court interpreting the state's election laws. The majority justified their decision by insisting that the "equal protection" clause of the Fourteenth Amendment required that all ballots within a state be counted in accordance with a single standard, something impossible given the wide variety of machines and paper ballots used in Florida. Perhaps recognizing that this new constitutional principle threatened to throw into question results throughout the country—since many states had voting systems as complex as Florida's—the Court added that it applied only in this single case.

The most remarkable thing about the election of 2000 was not so much its controversial ending as the even division of the

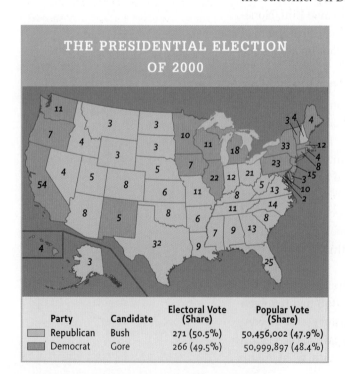

THE PRESIDENTIAL ELECTION OF 2000

Party	Candidate	Electoral Vote (Share)	Popular Vote (Share)
Republican	Bush	271 (50.5%)	50,456,002 (47.9%)
Democrat	Gore	266 (49.5%)	50,999,897 (48.4%)

country it revealed. Bush and Gore each received essentially half of the popular vote. The final count in the electoral college stood at 271-266, the narrowest margin since 1876. The Senate ended up divided 50-50 between the two parties. But these figures concealed deep political and social fissures. Bush carried the entire South and nearly all the states of the trans-Mississippi farm belt and Rockies. Gore won almost all the states of the Northeast, Old Northwest, and West Coast. Residents of urban areas voted overwhelmingly for Gore. Rural areas went just as solidly for Bush. Members of racial minorities gave Gore large majorities, while white voters preferred Bush. The results also revealed a significant "gender gap." Until the 1960s, women had tended to vote disproportionately Republican. In 2000, women favored Gore by 11 percent, while men preferred Bush by the same margin.

A Challenged Democracy

Coming at the end of the "decade of democracy," the 2000 election revealed troubling features of the American political system at the close of the twentieth century. The electoral college, devised by the founders to enable the country's prominent men rather than ordinary voters to choose the president, gave the White House to a candidate who did not receive the most votes—an odd result in a political democracy. A country that prided itself on modern technology had a voting system in which citizens' choices could not be reliably determined. Counting both congressional and presidential races, the campaign cost more than $1.5 billion, mostly raised from wealthy individuals and corporate donors. This reinforced the widespread belief that money dominated the political system. The implications for democracy of the ever-closer connection between power in the economic marketplace and power in the marketplace of politics and ideas would be widely debated in the early twenty-first century.

Evidence abounded of a broad disengagement from public life. As governments at all levels competed to turn their activities over to private contractors, and millions of Americans walled themselves off from their fellow citizens by taking up residence in socially homogeneous gated communities, the very idea of a shared public sphere seemed to dissolve. Nearly half the eligible voters did not bother to go to the polls, and in state and local elections, turnouts typically ranged between only 20 and 30 percent. More people watched the televised Nixon-Kennedy debates of 1960 than the Bush-Gore debates of 2000, even though the population had risen by 100 million. Both candidates sought to occupy the political center and relied on public-opinion polls and media consultants to shape their messages. Major issues like health care, race relations, and economic inequality went virtually unmentioned during the campaign. And no one discussed the issue that would soon come to dominate Bush's presidency—the threat of international terrorism.

THE ATTACKS OF SEPTEMBER 11

September 11, 2001, a beautiful late-summer morning, began with the sun rising over the East Coast of the United States in a crystal-clear sky. But September 11 soon became one of the most tragic dates in American history.

"IT'S STILL A REPRESENTATIVE FORM OF GOVERNMENT—THEY REPRESENT US"

Another cartoon by Herbert Block, from 2000, suggests that democracy has been corrupted by the influence of "big money interests" on government.

The twin towers of the World Trade Center after being struck by hijacked airplanes on September 11, 2001. Shortly after this photograph was taken, the towers collapsed.

Around 8 AM, hijackers seized control of four jet airliners filled with passengers. They crashed two into the World Trade Center in New York City, igniting infernos that soon caused these buildings, which dominated the lower Manhattan skyline, to collapse. A third plane hit a wing of the Pentagon, the country's military headquarters, in Washington, D.C. On the fourth aircraft, passengers who had learned of these events via their cell phones overpowered the hijackers. The plane crashed in a field near Pittsburgh, killing all aboard. Counting the nineteen hijackers, more than 200 passengers, pilots, and flight attendants, and victims on the ground, around 3,000 people died on September 11. The victims included nearly 400 police and firefighters who had rushed to the World Trade Center in a rescue effort and perished when the "twin towers" collapsed. Relatives and friends desperately seeking information about the fate of those lost in the attacks printed thousands of "missing" posters. These remained in public places in New York and Washington for weeks, grim reminders of the lives extinguished on September 11.

The Bush administration quickly blamed Al Qaeda, a shadowy terrorist organization headed by Osama bin Laden, for the attacks. A wealthy Islamic fundamentalist from Saudi Arabia, bin Laden had joined the fight against the Soviet occupation of Afghanistan in the 1980s. He had developed a relationship with the Central Intelligence Agency and received American funds to help build his mountain bases. But after the Gulf War of 1991, his anger increasingly turned against the United States. Bin Laden was especially outraged by the presence of American military bases in Saudi Arabia and by American support for Israel in its ongoing conflict with the Palestinians. More generally, bin Laden and his followers saw the United States, with its religious pluralism, consumer culture, and open sexual mores, as the antithesis of the rigid values in which they believed. He feared that American influence was corrupting Saudi Arabia, Islam's spiritual home, and

Osama bin Laden

helping to keep the Saudi royal family, which failed to oppose this development, in power.

In the last three decades of the twentieth century, terrorist groups who held the United States and other Western countries responsible for the plight of the Palestinians had engaged in hijackings and murders. After the Gulf War, Osama bin Laden declared "war" on the United States. Terrorists associated with Al Qaeda exploded a truck-bomb at the World Trade Center in 1993, killing six persons, and set off blasts in 1998 at American embassies in Kenya and Tanzania, in which more than 200 persons, mostly African embassy workers, died. Thus, a rising terrorist threat was visible before September 11. Nonetheless, the attack came as a complete surprise. With the end of the Cold War in 1991, most Americans felt more secure, especially within their own borders, than they had for decades.

> *Growing threat of terrorism*

The attacks of September 11, 2001, gave new prominence to ideas deeply embedded in the American past—that freedom was the central quality of American life, and that the United States had a mission to spread freedom throughout the world and to fight those it saw as freedom's enemies. The attacks and events that followed also lent new urgency to questions that had recurred many times in American history: Should the United States act in the world as a republic or an empire? What is the proper balance between liberty and security? Who deserves the full enjoyment of American freedom? None had an easy answer.

SUGGESTED READING

BOOKS

- Ash, Timothy Garton. *History of the Present: Essays, Sketches, and Dispatches from Europe in the 1990s* (2009). An account of the decade by a perceptive European commentator.

- Brands, H. W. *The Strange Death of American Liberalism* (2001). Explores how liberals' discrediting of the federal government through their criticisms of the Vietnam War and Watergate paved the way for the triumph of antigovernment conservatism.

- Cassidy, John. *Dot.con* (2002). Describes the rise and fall of the "new economy."

- Christianson, Scott. *With Liberty for Some: 500 Years of Imprisonment in America* (1998). A full-scale study of the history of imprisonment in the United States and its recent dramatic expansion.

- Foner, Nancy. *From Ellis Island to JFK: New York's Two Great Waves of Immigration* (2000). Studies the new immigration of the 1980s and 1990s and considers how it does and does not differ from earlier waves of newcomers.

- Friedman, Thomas L. *The Lexus and the Olive Tree* (1999). An influential account of globalization and its economic promise.

- Hodgson, Godfrey. *More Equal than Others: America from Nixon to the New Century* (2004). A survey of recent American history that identifies growing inequality as a major trend of these years.

- Johnson, Haynes. *The Best of Times: America in the Clinton Years* (2001). A sympathetic account of Clinton's presidency.

- Katz, Michael B. *The Price of Citizenship: Redefining the American Welfare State* (2001). Presents the history of welfare policy, with attention to the origins and impact of Clinton's welfare reform.

- Levitas, Daniel. *The Terrorist Next Door: The Militia Movement and the Radical Right* (2003). A careful study of right-wing extremism of the 1990s.

- Lichtenstein, Nelson. *The Retail Revolution: How Wal-Mart Created a Brave New World of Business* (2009). How Wal-Mart became the largest employer in the United States and one of the most profitable.

- Phillips, Kevin. *Wealth and Democracy* (2002). A critique of the influence of money on American politics.

- Power, Samantha. *A Problem from Hell: America and the Age of Genocide* (2002). Discusses genocides of the 1990s and the problem of the appropriate American response.

- Roberts, Sam. *Who We Are Now: The Changing Face of America in the Twenty-First Century* (2004). A social portrait of the American people based on the 2000 Census.

- Smelser, Neil J., and Jeffrey C. Alexander. *Diversity and Its Discontents: Cultural Conflict and Common Ground in Contemporary American Society* (1999). Describes the new social diversity of the 1990s and the cultural and political tensions arising from it.

- Spence, Michael. *The Next Convergence: The Future of Economic Growth in a Multispeed World* (2011). A Nobel Prize–winning economist examines the impact of globalization on jobs and incomes in the United States.

WEBSITES

- The Aids Crisis: http://americanhistory.si.edu/exhibitions/hiv-and-aids-thirty-years-ago

- September 11: http://americanhistory.si.edu/exhibitons/september-11-remembrance-and-reflection

- Global Exchange: www.globalexchange.org

- Making the Macintosh: Technology and Culture in Silicon Valley: http://library.stanford.edu/mac/

CHAPTER REVIEW AND ONLINE RESOURCES

REVIEW QUESTIONS

1. Why was the year 1989 one of the most momentous in the twentieth century?

2. Describe the different visions of the U.S. role in the post–Cold War world as identified by President George H. W. Bush and President Clinton.

3. Explain Clinton's political strategy of combining social liberalism with conservative economic ideas.

4. What are the causes and consequences of the growing "prison-industrial complex"?

5. Identify the factors that, in the midst of 1990s prosperity, increased the levels of inequality in the United States.

6. What are the similarities and differences between immigration patterns of the 1990s and earlier?

7. What main issues gave rise to the Culture Wars of the 1990s?

8. Assess the role of the Supreme Court in the presidential election of 2000.

9. What is globalization, and how did it affect the United States in the 1990s?

KEY TERMS

new world order (p. 1053)

Gulf War (p. 1054)

"Don't ask, don't tell"(p. 1056)

North American Free Trade Agreement (p. 1057)

Contract with America (p. 1057)

Oslo Accords (p. 1059)

Rwandan genocide (p. 1059)

ethnic cleansing (p. 1059)

Balkan crisis (p. 1059)

globalization (p. 1061)

Americans with Disabilities Act (p. 1078)

multiculturalism (p. 1079)

Culture Wars (p. 1080)

Defense of Marriage Act (p. 1081)

family values (p. 1081)

Bush v. Gore (p. 1084)

A NEW CENTURY
AND NEW CRISES

★

FREEDOM

The presidential election of 2008 produced not only a great political surprise but a historic moment in American history. Whatever one's opinion of Barack Obama's policies, there is no question that in view of the nation's racial history, the election of the first African-American president was an enormously important symbolic turning point.

A little-known forty-seven-year-old senator from Illinois when the campaign began in 2007, Obama owed his success both to his own exceptional skills as a speaker and campaigner and to the evolution of American politics and society.

Obama's life story exemplified the enormous changes the United States had undergone since 1960. Without the civil rights movement, his election would have been inconceivable. He was the product of an interracial marriage, which ended in divorce when he was two years old, between a Kenyan immigrant and a white American woman. When Obama was born in 1961, their marriage was still illegal in many states. He attended Harvard Law School, and worked in Chicago as a community organizer before going into politics. He also wrote two best-selling books about his upbringing in Indonesia (where his mother worked as an anthropologist) and Hawaii (where his maternal grandparents helped to raise him) and his search for a sense of identity given his complex background. Obama was elected to the U.S. Senate in 2004 and first gained national attention with an eloquent speech at the Democratic national convention that year. His early opposition to the Iraq War won the support of the Democratic Party's large antiwar element; his race galvanized the support of black voters; and his youth and promise of change appealed to the young.

Obama recognized how the Internet had changed politics. He established an email list containing the names of millions of voters with whom he could communicate instantaneously, and used web-based networks to raise enormous sums of money in small donations. His campaign put out videos on popular Internet sites. With its widespread use of modern technology and massive mobilization of new voters, Obama's was the first political campaign of the twenty-first century. But his election also rested on the deep unpopularity of his predecessor, George W. Bush, because of the seemingly endless war he launched in Iraq and the collapse of the American economy in 2008.

THE WAR ON TERROR

Bush before September 11

Before becoming president, George W. Bush had been an executive in the oil industry and had served as governor of Texas. He had worked to dissociate the Republican Party from the harsh anti-immigrant rhetoric of the mid-1990s and had proven himself an effective proponent of what he called "compassionate conservatism." Nonetheless, from the outset Bush pursued a strongly conservative agenda. In 2001, he persuaded Congress to enact the largest tax cut in American history. With the economy slowing, he promoted the plan

FOCUS QUESTIONS

What were the major policy elements of the war on terror in the wake of September 11, 2001? *–p. 1091*

How did the war in Iraq unfold in the wake of 9/11? *–p. 1094*

How did the war on terror affect the economy and American liberties? *–p. 1097*

What events eroded support for President Bush's policies during his second term? *–p. 1101*

What kinds of change did voters hope for when they elected Barack Obama? *–p. 1116*

What were the major challenges of Obama's first term? *–p. 1119*

What were the prevailing ideas of American freedom at the beginning of the 21st century? *–p. 1128*

Freedom: Certain Restrictions Apply. This work by the artist George Mill includes language that parodies the small print in advertisements and consumer warranties. This was part of a 2008 exhibit in which artists produced works on the theme "Thoughts on Freedom." Many suggested that the policies adopted after the attacks of September 11, 2001, had made Americans' freedom more precarious in the name of national security.

as a way of stimulating renewed growth. In keeping with the "supply-side" economic outlook embraced twenty years earlier by Ronald Reagan, most of the tax cuts were directed toward the wealthiest Americans, on the assumption that they would invest the money they saved in taxes in economically productive activities.

In foreign policy, Bush emphasized American freedom of action, unrestrained by international treaties and institutions. To great controversy, the Bush administration announced that it would not abide by the **Kyoto Protocol** of 1997, which sought to combat global warming—a slow rise in the earth's temperature that scientists warned could have disastrous effects on the world's climate. Global warming is caused when gases released by burning fossil fuels such as coal and oil remain in the upper atmosphere, trapping heat reflected from the earth. Evidence of this development first surfaced in the 1990s, when scientists studying layers of ice in Greenland concluded that the earth's temperature had risen significantly during the past century.

Today, most scientists consider global warming a serious situation. Climate change threatens to disrupt long-established patterns of agriculture, and the melting of glaciers and the polar ice caps because of rising temperatures may raise ocean levels and flood coastal cities. Since, at the time, the United States burned far more fossil fuel than any other nation, Bush's repudiation of the treaty, on the grounds that it would weaken the American economy, infuriated much of the world, as well as environmentalists at home.

"They Hate Freedom"

September 11 transformed the international situation, the domestic political environment, and the Bush presidency. An outpouring of popular patriotism followed the attacks, all the more impressive because it was spontaneous, not orchestrated by the government or private organizations. Throughout the country, people demonstrated their sense of resolve and their sympathy for the victims by displaying the American flag. Public trust in government rose dramatically, and public servants like firemen and policemen became national heroes. After two decades in which the dominant language of American politics centered on deregulation and individualism, the country experienced a renewed feeling of common social purpose.

The Bush administration benefited from this patriotism and identification with government. The president's popularity soared. Bush seized the opportunity to give his administration a new direction and purpose. Like presidents before him, he made freedom the rallying cry for a nation at war.

On September 20, 2001, Bush addressed a joint session of Congress and a national television audience. His speech echoed the words of FDR, Truman, and Reagan: "Freedom and fear are at war. The advance of human freedom . . . now depends on us." The country's antagonists, Bush went on, "hate our freedoms, our freedom of religion, our freedom of speech, our freedom to assemble and disagree with each other." In later speeches, he repeated this theme. Why did terrorists attack the United States? the president repeatedly asked. His answer: "Because we love freedom, that's why. And they hate freedom."

The Bush Doctrine

Bush's speech announced a new foreign policy principle, which quickly became known as the **Bush Doctrine**. The United States would launch a **war on terrorism**. Unlike previous wars, this one had a vaguely defined enemy—terrorist groups around the world that might threaten the United States or its allies—and no predictable timetable for victory. The American administration would recognize no middle ground in the new war: "Either you are with us, or you are with the terrorists." Bush demanded that Afghanistan, ruled by a group of Islamic fundamentalists called the Taliban, surrender Osama bin Laden, the architect of the 9/11 attacks, who had established a base in the country. When the Taliban refused, the United States on October 7, 2001, launched air strikes against its strongholds.

Bush gave the **war in Afghanistan** the name "Enduring Freedom." By the end of the year, the combination of American bombing and ground combat by the Northern Alliance (Afghans who had been fighting the Taliban for years) had driven the regime from power. A new government, friendly to and dependent on the United States, took its place. It repealed Taliban laws denying women the right to attend school and banning movies, music, and other expressions of Western culture but found it difficult to establish full control over the country. U.S. forces would remain in Afghanistan at least into 2017, making the war the longest in American history.

"Is This the End?" by the artist Owen Freeman, offers a warning about global warming, one of whose consequences in coming decades will be a rise in sea levels, flooding many low-lying coastal communities.

The "Axis of Evil"

Like the surprise attack on Pearl Harbor in 1941, September 11 not only plunged the United States into war but also transformed American foreign policy, inspiring a determination to reshape the world in terms of American ideals and interests. To facilitate further military action in the Middle East, the United States established military bases in Central Asia, including former republics of the Soviet Union like Kyrgyzstan, Uzbekistan, and Tajikistan. Such an action would have been inconceivable before the end of the Cold War.

Supporters of the Bush administration who turned out in Washington, D.C., late in 2001 to confront demonstrators opposed to the war in Afghanistan.

The toppling of the Taliban, Bush repeatedly insisted, marked only the beginning of the war on terrorism. In his State of the Union address of January 2002, the president accused Iraq, Iran, and North Korea of harboring terrorists and developing "weapons of mass destruction"—nuclear, chemical, and biological—that posed a potential threat to the United States. He called the three countries an "axis of evil," even though no evidence connected them with the attacks of September 11 and they had never cooperated with one another (Iraq and Iran, in fact, had fought a long and bloody war in the 1980s).

AN AMERICAN EMPIRE?

The "axis of evil" speech and National Security Strategy sent shock waves around the world. In the immediate aftermath of September 11, a wave of sympathy for the United States had swept across the globe. Most of the world supported the war in Afghanistan as a legitimate response to the terrorist attacks. By late 2002, however, many persons overseas feared that the United States was claiming the right to act as a world policeman in violation of international law.

The global response

Critics, including leaders of close American allies, wondered whether dividing the world into friends and enemies of freedom ran the danger of repeating some of the mistakes of the Cold War. Anti-Americanism in the Middle East, they argued, reached far beyond bin Laden's organization and stemmed not simply from dislike of American freedom but, rightly or wrongly, from opposition to specific American policies—toward Israel, the Palestinians, and the region's corrupt and undemocratic regimes.

A global empire

Charges quickly arose that the United States was bent on establishing itself as a new global empire. Indeed, September 11 and its aftermath highlighted not only the vulnerability of the United States but also its overwhelming strength. In every index of power—military, economic, cultural—the United States far outpaced the rest of the world. Its defense budget exceeded that of the next twenty powers combined. The United States was the only country that maintained military bases throughout the world and deployed its navy on every ocean. It was not surprising that in such circumstances many American policymakers felt that the country had a responsibility to impose order in a dangerous world, even if this meant establishing its own rules of international conduct.

Confronting Iraq

These tensions became starkly evident in the Bush administration's next initiative. The Iraqi dictatorship of Saddam Hussein had survived its defeat in the Gulf War of 1991. Hussein's opponents charged that he had flouted United Nations resolutions barring the regime from developing new weapons.

From the outset of the Bush administration, a group of conservative policymakers including Vice President Dick Cheney, Secretary of Defense Donald Rumsfeld, and Deputy Defense Secretary Paul D. Wolfowitz were determined to oust Hussein from power. They insisted that the oppressed Iraqi people would welcome an American army as liberators and quickly establish a democratic government, allowing for the early departure of American soldiers. This group seized on the opportunity presented by the attacks of September 11 to press their case, and President Bush adopted their outlook. Secretary of State Colin Powell, who believed the conquest and stabilization of Iraq would require hundreds of thousands of American soldiers and should not be undertaken without the support of America's allies, found himself marginalized in the administration.

Even though Hussein was not an Islamic fundamentalist, and no known evidence linked him to the terrorist attacks of September 11, the Bush administration in 2002 announced a goal of "regime change" in Iraq. Hussein, administration spokesmen insisted, must be ousted from power because he had developed an arsenal of chemical and bacterial "weapons of mass destruction" and was seeking

Steve Benson's 2003 cartoon, which alters a renowned World War II photograph of soldiers raising an American flag, illustrates widespread skepticism about American motivations in the Iraq War.

to acquire nuclear arms. American newspaper and television journalists repeated these claims with almost no independent investigation. Early in 2003, despite his original misgivings, Secretary of State Powell delivered a speech before the UN outlining the administration's case. He claimed that Hussein possessed a mobile chemical weapons laboratory, had hidden weapons of mass destruction in his many palaces, and was seeking to acquire uranium in Africa to build nuclear weapons. (Every one of these assertions later turned out to be false.)

The Iraq War

Foreign policy "realists," including members of previous Republican administrations like Brent Scowcroft, the national security adviser under the first President Bush, warned that the administration's preoccupation with Iraq deflected attention from its real foe, Al Qaeda, which remained capable of launching terrorist attacks. They insisted that the United States could not unilaterally transform the Middle East into a bastion of democracy, as the administration claimed was its long-term aim.

The decision to begin the **Iraq War** split the Western alliance and inspired a massive antiwar movement throughout the world. In February 2003, between 10 million and 15 million people across the globe demonstrated against the impending war. There were large-scale protests in the United States, which brought together veterans of the antiwar movement during the Vietnam era and a diverse group of young activists united in the belief that launching a war against a nation because it might pose a security threat in the future violated international law and the UN Charter.

Both traditional foes of the United States like Russia and China and traditional allies like Germany and France refused to support a "preemptive" strike against Iraq. Unable to obtain approval from the United Nations for attacking Iraq, the United States went to war anyway in March 2003, with Great Britain as its sole significant ally. President Bush called the war "Operation Iraqi Freedom." Its purpose, he declared, was to "defend our freedom" and "bring freedom to others." The Hussein regime proved no match for the American armed forces, with their precision bombing, satellite-guided missiles, and well-trained soldiers. Within a month, American troops occupied Baghdad. After hiding out for several months, Hussein was captured by American forces and subsequently put on trial before an Iraqi court. Late in 2006, he was found guilty of ordering the killing of many Iraqis during his reign, and was sentenced to death and executed.

Another Vietnam?

Soon after the fall of Baghdad, a triumphant President Bush appeared on the deck of an aircraft carrier beneath a banner reading "Mission Accomplished." But after the fall of Hussein, everything seemed to go wrong. Rather than parades welcoming American liberators, looting and chaos followed the fall of the Iraqi regime. An insurgency quickly developed that targeted American soldiers and Iraqis cooperating with them. Sectarian violence soon swept throughout Iraq, with militias of Shiite and Sunni Muslims fighting each other. (Under Hussein, Sunnis, a minority

Part of the massive crowd that gathered in New York City on February 15, 2003, a day of worldwide demonstrations against the impending war against Iraq.

"Operation Iraqi Freedom"

Sectarian conflict

Heavily armed police confront a resident of Ferguson, Missouri, during demonstrations there.

Protests and social media

Police with an armored vehicle in Ferguson. The response to demonstrations there illustrated how policing had become increasingly militarized in recent years.

used excessive force be held accountable. It gave public voice to the countless African-Americans who had experienced disrespect, harassment, or violence at the hands of police. The movement used social media and current technology to organize protests and disseminate videos of encounters between black persons and the police. The impact of these images had precedents, notably in the role of television in bringing the war in Vietnam and violent reactions to civil rights demonstrators to national awareness in the 1960s. But the creation of such images was now democratized—most of the videos that spurred outrage were taken by bystanders with cell phones. The Black Lives Matter movement was less an articulation of specific policy demands than a broad claim to black humanity. In this sense, it had historical precedents in abolitionism, with its slogan "Am I Not a Man and a Brother?" and in "I Am a Man," the defiant claim of Memphis sanitation workers during their 1968 strike, where Martin Luther King Jr. was assassinated.

In Ferguson, Missouri, Brown's death inspired weeks of sometimes violent street demonstrations. These led to the deployment of state police and National Guardsmen dressed in battle gear and armed with assault rifles and armored personnel carriers, as if equipped for a war zone overseas—a sign of how policing had become increasingly militarized since the 1960s. The death of Brown and the others, at the very least, suggested that half a century after the ghetto uprisings of the 1960s, many police departments still relied on excessive force in dealing with black men, and that the criminal justice system remained mired in racism. In Ferguson, investigations after the death of Michael Brown revealed that the almost entirely white police, city government, and local judiciary regularly preyed on black residents, seeing them not as citizens to be served and protected but as a source of revenue to balance the local budget. Blacks were hauled into court to pay fines for non-existent driving violations, jaywalking, even walking on the sidewalks too close to the street. Sometimes jail terms ensued for those unable to pay the fine. Over ninety percent of such arrests in Ferguson—which were entirely discretionary—were of black men and women. Nationally, public reaction to the Black Lives Matter movement revealed a sharp divide between white and black Americans. In public opinion polls, over eighty percent of blacks but just thirty percent of whites agreed with the statement that blacks are victims of discriminatory treatment by the police.

> *Racial divide*

Obama and the World

The most dramatic achievement of Obama's presidency in foreign affairs was fulfillment of his campaign promise to end American involvement in the Iraq War. At the end of 2011, the last American combat soldiers came home, although a few hundred advisers remained. Nearly 5,000 Americans and, according to the estimates of U.S. and Iraqi analysts, hundreds of thousands of Iraqis, most of them civilians, had died during this eight-year conflict. The war had cost the United States nearly $2 trillion, an almost unimaginable sum. Whether it would produce a stable, democratic Iraq remained to be seen.

> *Withdrawal from Iraq*

At the same time, Obama continued many of the policies of the Bush administration. Obama dramatically increased the American troop presence in Afghanistan, while pledging to withdraw American forces by the end of 2014 although he failed to meet this deadline. Here again, the long-term outcome remained uncertain, given the Taliban's resurgence and the unpopularity of the corruption-plagued American-backed Afghan government. Indeed, by 2012, polls showed that a large majority of Americans felt the war was a mistake and wanted it to end.

Like many of his predecessors, Obama found that criticizing presidential power from outside is one thing, dismantling it another. He reversed his previous promise to abolish the military tribunals Bush had established and to close the military prison at Guantánamo, Cuba. And in 2011 he signed a four-year extension of key provisions of the USA Patriot Act originally passed under Bush. In May 2011, to wide acclaim in the United States, Obama authorized an armed raid into Pakistan that resulted in the death of Osama bin Laden, who had been hiding there for years. More controversially, Obama claimed the right to order the assassination of American citizens in foreign countries if evidence indicated their connection with terrorism. And in 2011 he sent the air force to participate in a NATO campaign that assisted rebels who overthrew Libyan dictator Muammar Gadhafi. But an endless civil war followed, not the restoration of democracy. Obama did not seek congressional approval of the action, deeming it unnecessary. In fact, throughout Obama's presidency, American troops or planes were involved in combat as part of an expanded war

President Barack Obama, Vice President Joe Biden, Secretary of State Hillary Clinton, and other members of Obama's national security team receiving an update on the mission against Osama bin Laden at the White House on May 1, 2011.

on terror not only in Afghanistan but also in Yemen, Pakistan, and Somalia. American Special Forces were involved in efforts to suppress the drug trade in Honduras and Colombia.

International diplomacy

In 2014, Obama abandoned the half-century-old policy of isolating Cuba, and moved to resume diplomatic relations with the island nation. The policy of isolation had long outlived its Cold War origins and had made the United States seem petty and vindictive in the eyes of Latin Americans. In the following year, the administration, in conjunction with the European Union, Russia, and China, worked out an arrangement with Iran to ensure that that nation's nuclear energy program was confined to peaceful purposes and did not lead to the manufacture of nuclear weapons. This was a remarkable achievement in view of the decades of hostility between the United States and Iran dating back to the hostage crisis of 1979–1981. Also in 2015, the United States played a major role in the forging of an agreement committing every country in the world to reduce emissions (notably from the burning of coal and oil) that contributed to global warming. All told, Obama's conduct of foreign affairs proved to be considerably more bellicose than both his supporters and opponents had expected.

The Arab Spring

Events overseas presented new challenges and opportunities for the Obama administration. Beginning in 2011, to the surprise of almost everyone, popular revolts swept the Middle East. The uprisings brought millions of people into the streets, and toppled long-serving dictators in Tunisia, Egypt, and Libya. Freedom emerged as the rallying cry of those challenging autocratic governments. "I'm in Tahrir Square," one demonstrator yelled into his cellphone while standing at the epicenter of the Egyptian revolution. "In freedom, in freedom, in freedom." Once again, the tension between the ideals of freedom and democracy and American strategic interests posed a difficult challenge for policymakers. After some hesitation, the United States sided with those seeking the ouster of Hosni Mubarak, Egypt's long-serving dictator and a staunch American ally. It then stood on the sidelines throughout 2011 and 2012 as Egypt lurched from popular uprising to military rule, to electoral victory by the Muslim Brotherhood, a previously illegal Islamic group, with the final outcome of the revolution always in doubt. When a military coup in 2014 ousted the elected president and instituted a regime even more repressive than Mubarak's, the Obama administration suspended shipments of military equipment to Egypt, but soon resumed them. In general, like his predecessors during the Cold War, Obama used "human rights" as a political weapon, condemning abuses by adversaries like China while remaining largely silent in the face of serious abuses by allies in the "war on terror" such as Pakistan, Ethiopia, and Saudi Arabia.

The Rise of ISIS

Acts of terrorism

In his second term, Obama faced a new crisis when the self-proclaimed Islamic State took control of parts of Iraq, Syria, and Libya. **ISIS**, as it was called, conducted campaigns of exceptional brutality, beheading prisoners of war and driving religious minorities out of territory it conquered. The videos of these acts posted by ISIS on social media horrified most of the world but also attracted recruits to the organization. ISIS also sponsored terror attacks outside the Middle East. In 2015 over 100 persons were killed in a series of coordinated attacks in Paris. A few weeks later, two followers of ISIS in the United States killed fourteen people in San Bernardino, California. As 2015 ended, fear of terrorism in the United States reached a point not seen since the attacks of September 11, 2001. It remained to be seen whether the rampages of ISIS would draw the United States into further combat in the Middle East.

Another area in which Obama continued the policies initiated during the Bush administration's war on terror was governmental surveillance, both domestic and overseas. The extent of such activity became known in 2013 when **Edward Snowden**, a former employee of the National Security Agency, released documents online that detailed NSA programs that monitored virtually all telephone, instant messaging, and email traffic in the United States, tracked the location of numerous American cellphones, and spied on the private communications of world leaders, including close allies of the United States such as Chancellor Angela Merkel of Germany and French president François Hollande. The government also secretly worked with major Internet and communications companies like AT&T and Verizon to gain access to the private data of their users. Of course, the overwhelming majority of the people subject to government surveillance had no connection to terrorism or to any crime at all. The Obama administration responded by charging Snowden with violating the Espionage Act of 1917—a law passed during the height of World War I hysteria over security. To avoid prosecution, Snowden took up residence in Russia. But his revelations rekindled the age-old debate over the balance between national security and Americans' civil liberties and offered another example of how, whichever party is in power, the balance always seems to shift in favor of the former. In 2015, Congress approved a measure curtailing the government's sweeping surveillance of phone records. But much of the government's prying into Americans' communications continued.

"Get me everything on everybody."

A cartoon in the magazine *The New Yorker* inspired by revelations that the National Security Agency has been spying on the phone conversations and emails of millions of Americans.

The Republican Resurgence

In nearly all midterm elections in American history, the party in power has lost seats in Congress. But Democrats faced more serious difficulties than usual in the midterm elections of 2010. Grassroots Republicans were energized by hostility to Obama's sweeping legislative enactments. The **Tea Party**, named for the Boston Tea Party of the 1770s and inspired by its opposition to taxation by a far-away government, mobilized grassroots opposition to the administration. The Tea Party appealed to a long-established American fear of overbearing federal power, as well as to more recent anxieties, especially about immigration. Some supporters advocated repealing the provision of the Fourteenth Amendment granting automatic citizenship to all persons born in the United States. For a time, some activists denied that Obama was legally president at all, claiming that he had been born in Africa, not in the United States. (In fact, he was born in Hawaii.) With their opponents energized and their own supporters demoralized by the slow pace of economic recovery, Democrats suffered a severe reversal. Republicans swept to control of the House of Representatives and substantially reduced the

Grassroots Republicans

In the spring of 2009, Republicans and independents opposed to President Obama's "stimulus" plan held "tea parties" around the country, seeking to invoke the tradition of the Boston Tea Party and its opposition to taxation. In this demonstration in Austin, Texas, some participants wore hats reminiscent of the revolutionary era. One participant carries a sign urging the state to secede from the Union.

Mitt Romney

Democratic majority in the Senate. The outcome at the national level was political gridlock that lasted for the remainder of Obama's presidency. Obama could no longer get significant legislation through Congress.

Tea Party–inspired conservative gains at the state level in 2010 unleashed a rash of new legislation. Several states moved to curtail abortion rights. In Wisconsin, the legislature and Governor Scott Walker rescinded most of the bargaining rights of unions representing public employees. Workers and their supporters responded by occupying the state Capitol building for weeks, and then gathering petitions to force a recall election for Governor Walker in 2012, in which he succeeded in winning reelection. In Ohio, however, a similar anti-union law was repealed in a popular referendum.

New conservative legislatures also took aim at undocumented immigrants. Alabama, which has no land border with a foreign country and a small population of immigrants compared with other states, enacted the harshest measure, making it a crime for undocumented immigrants to apply for a job, and for anyone to transport them, even to a church or hospital. During the contest for the Republican presidential nomination in early 2012, candidates vied with each other to demonstrate their determination to drive undocumented immigrants from the country. Oddly, all this took place at a time when illegal immigration from Mexico, the largest source of undocumented workers, had ceased almost completely because of stricter controls at the border and the drying up of available jobs because of the recession. Despite the fact that the Obama administration had deported far more undocumented immigrants than its predecessor, these measures associated the Republican Party with intense nativism in the minds of many Hispanic voters.

The 2012 Campaign

Despite the continuing economic crisis, sociocultural issues played a major role in the campaign for the Republican presidential nomination in 2012, as candidates vied to win the support of the evangelical Christians who formed a major part of the party's base. The front-runner was Mitt Romney, the former governor of Massachusetts. Romney had made a fortune directing Bain Capital, a firm that specialized in buying up other companies and then reselling them at a profit after restructuring them, which often involved firing large numbers of employees. But the party's powerful conservative wing disliked Romney because of his moderate record (as governor he had instituted a state health-care plan remarkably similar to Obama's 2011 legislation) and a distrust of his Mormon faith among many evangelical Christians.

Romney spent the primary season attempting to demonstrate his conservative views and reaffirming his adherence to Christian beliefs. Issues long thought settled such as women's access to birth control suddenly roiled American politics. Eventually, using his personal fortune to outspend his rivals by an enormous amount, Romney emerged as the Republican candidate, the first Mormon to win a major party's nomination—a significant moment in the history of religious toleration in the United States. He chose as his running mate Congressman Paul D. Ryan of Wisconsin, a favorite of the Tea Party and a Roman Catholic. For the first time in its history, the Republican Party's ticket did not contain a traditional Protestant.

President Obama began the 2012 campaign with numerous liabilities. The enthusiasm that greeted his election had long since faded as the worst economic slump since the Great Depression dragged on, and voters became fed up with both the president and Congress because of the intensity of partisanship and legislative gridlock in Washington. The war in Afghanistan was increasingly unpopular and Obama's signature health-care law under ferocious assault by Republicans.

Weakening public support

Nonetheless, after a heated campaign, Obama emerged victorious, winning 332 electoral votes to Romney's 206, and 51 percent of the popular vote to his opponent's 47 percent. At the same time, while Democrats gained a few seats in the House and Senate, the balance of power in Washington remained unchanged. This set the stage for continued partisan infighting and political gridlock during Obama's second term.

Continued party tensions

Obama's victory stemmed from many causes, including an extremely efficient "get out the vote" organization on election day, and Romney's weaknesses as a campaigner. Romney never managed to shed the image of a millionaire who used loopholes to avoid paying taxes (his federal tax rate of 14 percent was lower than that of most working-class Americans) and who held ordinary people in contempt (an off-the-cuff remark that 47 percent of the people would not vote for him because they were "victims" dependent on government payments like Medicare and Social Security severely weakened his campaign). But more important, as in 2008, the result reflected the new diversity of the American population in the twenty-first century. Romney won 60 percent of the white vote, which in previous elections would have guaranteed victory. But Obama carried over 90 percent of the black vote and over 70 percent of Asians and Hispanics. Nonetheless, as frequently happens in midterm elections, the party that did not hold the White House, in this case the Republicans, made significant gains, strengthening its hold on the House in 2014 and taking control of the Senate.

The 2012 election reflected the new diversity in other ways as well. Hawaii elected Tulsi Gabbard, the first Hindu to serve in Congress, and the first Buddhist, Mazie K. Hirono, to the Senate. And for the first time, popular referendums in Maine and Maryland registered approval of gay marriage, bringing to nine the number of states where such marriages were now lawful.

But perhaps the most striking feature of the 2012 election was the unprecedented amount of money spent on the campaign. In

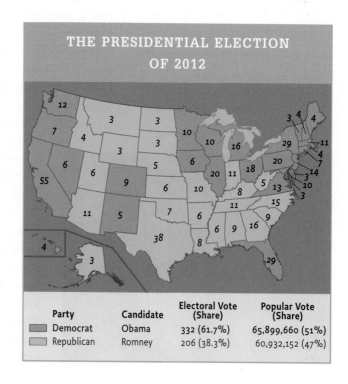

THE PRESIDENTIAL ELECTION OF 2012

Party	Candidate	Electoral Vote (Share)	Popular Vote (Share)
Democrat	Obama	332 (61.7%)	65,899,660 (51%)
Republican	Romney	206 (38.3%)	60,932,152 (47%)

Campaign finance

2010, in *Citizens United v. Federal Elections Commission*, the conservative majority on the Supreme Court had overturned federal restrictions on political contributions by corporations. At the same time, "political action committees" were allowed to spend as much money as they wished supporting or denigrating candidates for office so long as they did not coordinate their activities with the candidates' campaigns. Meanwhile, the Romney and Obama campaigns themselves raised and spent hundreds of millions of dollars from individual donors. All this resulted in an election that cost, for presidential and congressional races combined, some $6 billion.

FREEDOM IN THE TWENTY-FIRST CENTURY

International development and tragedy

The century that ended in 2000 witnessed vast human progress and unimaginable human tragedy. It saw the decolonization of Asia and Africa, the emergence of women into full citizenship in most parts of the world, and amazing advances in science, medicine, and technology. Thanks to the spread of new products, available at ever-cheaper prices, it brought more improvement in the daily conditions of life to more human beings than any other century in history. Worldwide life expectancy in the twentieth century rose from forty to sixty-seven years, and the literacy rate increased from 25 percent to 80 percent. This was the first century in which the primary economic activity for most of mankind moved beyond the acquisition of basic food, clothing, and shelter. But the twentieth century also witnessed the death of uncounted millions in wars and genocides and the widespread degradation of the natural environment, the underside of progress.

Exceptional America

In the early twenty-first century, people in the United States lived longer and healthier lives compared with previous generations, and they enjoyed a level of material comfort unimagined a century before. In 1900, the average annual income was $3,000 in today's dollars. The typical American had no indoor plumbing, had no telephone or car, and had not graduated from high school. As late as 1940, one-third of American households did not have running water. In 2013, health conditions had improved so much that the average life expectancy for men had risen to seventy-six and for women to eighty-one (from forty-six and forty-eight in 1900). More than 21 million Americans attended college in 2014, more than three times the figure for 1960.

In 2010, more than one American in seven was older than sixty-five. Certain to continue rising in the twenty-first century, this figure sparked worries about the future cost of health care and the economic stability of the Social Security system. But it also suggested that people would enjoy far longer and more productive periods of retirement than in the past. On the other hand, poverty, income inequality, and infant mortality in the United States considerably exceeded that of other economically advanced countries, and fewer than 10 percent of workers in private firms belonged to unions, a figure not seen since the nineteenth century.

A lock-down drill in Belle Plaine, Minnesota, trains an eighth-grade class how to respond in the event of a school shooting.

Many of the changes affecting American life, such as the transformed role of women, the better health and longer lifespan of the population, the spread of suburbanization, and the decline of industrial employment, have taken place in all economically advanced societies. In other ways, however, the United States at the dawn of the twenty-first century differed sharply from other developed countries. Prevailing ideas of freedom in the United States seemed more attuned to individual advancement than to broad social welfare. In 2003, when asked whether it was more important for the government to guarantee freedom from want or freedom to pursue individual goals, only 35 percent of Americans selected freedom from want, as opposed to 58 percent in Germany, 62 percent in France and Great Britain, and 65 percent in Italy. The United States was a far more religious country. Sixty percent of Americans agreed with the statement, "Religion plays a very important part in my life," while the comparable figure was 32 percent in Britain, 26 percent in Italy, and only 11 percent in France. One in three Americans said he or she believed in the literal truth of the Bible, and half that the United States enjoys "special protection from God." Religion and nationalism reinforced one another far more powerfully in the United States than in the more secular nations of western Europe.

The social fabric

Religion in America

Other forms of **American exceptionalism** had a darker side. Among advanced countries, the United States has by far the highest rate of murder using guns. In 2012, the last year for which comparative statistics are available, there were 9,146 murders with guns in the United States, as opposed to 158 in Germany, 173 in Canada, and 11 in Japan.

Indeed, in the last years of the twentieth century and the beginning of the twenty-first, the United States was the scene of a horrifying number of mass murders, often committed at schools. In 1999, two students killed twelve students and a teacher at Columbine High School in Colorado. In 2007, a student at Virginia Tech University shot and killed thirty-two people. Five years later, a lone gunman killed twenty children aged five and six, and seven adults at Sandy Hook Elementary School in Newtown, Connecticut. In the 1950s, schools across the country had conducted drills to enable students to survive a nuclear attack. Now they trained pupils in seeking shelter if a gunman entered the building. There were also mass killings at a movie theater in Aurora, Colorado, and at the Washington Navy Yard. In 2015, a gunman influenced by racist Internet sites murdered nine black participants in a Bible study group, including the minister, at Emanuel African Methodist Episcopal Church in Charleston. Other countries also experienced instances of mass violence, but not with the frequency of the United States. While each of these events led to calls for stricter regulations on the purchase of firearms, the strong commitment of many Americans to the Second Amendment's guarantee of the right to bear arms, coupled with the remarkable power of the National Rifle Association, one of the country's most influential lobbies, ensured that no new regulations were enacted.

The United States continued to lag behind other countries in providing social rights to its citizens. In Europe, workers are guaranteed by law a paid vacation each year and a number of paid sick days. American employers are not required to offer either to their workers. Only four countries in the world have no national provision for paid maternity leave after a woman gives birth to a child: Liberia, Papua New

American writers and artists continue to reflect on the history and symbolism of freedom. In a work entitled *Chillin' with Liberty*, the artist Renée Cox poses herself atop the Statue of Liberty, audaciously staking her own claim to American freedom.

Seeking the lessons of history: a young visitor at the Civil Rights Memorial in Montgomery, Alabama.

...UNTIL JUSTICE ROLLS DOWN LIKE WATERS AND RIGHTEOUSNESS LIKE A MIGHTY STREAM

MARTIN LUTHER KING JR

Guinea, Suriname, and the United States. And as noted in the previous chapter, the United States has by far the world's highest rate of imprisonment.

Varieties of Freedom

In the early twenty-first century, Americans were increasingly tolerant of divergent personal lifestyles, cultural backgrounds, and religious persuasions. They enjoyed a degree of freedom of expression unmatched in virtually any country in the world. Thanks to the rights revolution and the political ascendancy of antigovernment conservatives, the dominant definition of freedom stressed the capacity of individuals to realize their desires and fulfill their potential unrestricted by authority. Other American traditions—freedom as economic security, freedom as active participation in democratic government, freedom as social justice for those long disadvantaged—seemed to be in eclipse. Americans sought freedom within themselves, not through social institutions or public engagement.

Personal freedom

It was an irony of early twenty-first-century life that Americans enjoyed more personal freedom than ever before but less of what earlier generations called "industrial freedom." Globalization—which treated workers at home and abroad as interchangeable factors of production, capable of being uprooted or dismissed without warning—seemed to render individual and even national sovereignty all but meaningless. Since economic liberty has long been associated with economic security, and rights have historically been linked to democratic participation and membership in a nation-state, these processes had ominous implications for traditional understandings of freedom. It remained to be seen whether a conception of freedom grounded in access to the consumer marketplace and the glorification of individual self-fulfillment unrestrained by government, social citizenship, or a common public culture could provide an adequate way of comprehending the world of the twenty-first century.

Industrial freedom

Learning from History

"The owl of Minerva takes flight at dusk." Minerva was the Roman goddess of wisdom, and this saying suggests that the meaning of events only becomes clear once they are over. It is still far too soon to assess the full impact of September 11 on American life and the long-term consequences of the changes at home and abroad it inspired.

As of the end of 2015, the world seemed far more unstable than anyone could have predicted when the Cold War ended. An end to the war on terror seemed as remote as ever. The future of Iraq, Afghanistan, and, indeed, the entire Middle East, remained uncertain, and Pakistan, traditionally the closest ally of the United States in that volatile region, experienced serious political instability. No settlement of the long-standing conflict between Israel and its Arab neighbors seemed in sight. Other regions of the world also presented daunting problems for American policymakers. North Korea had acquired nuclear weapons and refused international pressure to give them up. China's rapidly growing economic power posed a challenge to American predominance. Relations with Russia, which was supporting a separatist movement in eastern Ukraine, were at their lowest point since the end of the Cold War.

An unstable world

No one could predict how any of these crises, or others yet unimagined, would be resolved. But the United States, it seemed clear, would remain involved in the affairs of every region of the world. The country had more than 1,000 military bases of one kind or another around the globe, with at least some American soldiers stationed in 175 countries. A study by American intelligence agencies predicted that by 2025 the United States would remain the world's most powerful nation, but that its economic and military predominance would have declined significantly. A "multipolar world," with countries like China and India emerging as major powers, would succeed the era of unquestioned American dominance. The consequences of these changes remain to be seen.

"Multipolar world"

What *is* clear is that as in the past, freedom remains central to Americans' sense of themselves as individuals and as a nation. Americans continue to debate contemporary issues in a political landscape shaped by ideas of freedom. Indeed, freedom remains, as it has always been, an evolving concept, its definition open to disagreement, its boundaries never fixed or final. Freedom is neither self-enforcing nor self-correcting. It cannot be taken for granted, and its preservation requires eternal vigilance, especially in times of crisis.

An evolving concept of freedom

More than half a century ago, the African-American poet Langston Hughes urged Americans both to celebrate the freedoms they enjoy and to remember that freedom has always been incomplete:

There are words like *Freedom*
Sweet and wonderful to say.
On my heartstrings freedom sings
All day everyday.

There are words like *Liberty*
That almost make me cry.
If you had known what I know
You would know why.

SUGGESTED READING

BOOKS

- Bacevich, Andrew. *American Empire: The Realities and Consequences of U.S. Diplomacy* (2003). Examines how the idea of an American empire reemerged after September 11, and some of the results.

- Brinkley, Douglas. *The Great Deluge: Hurricane Katrina, New Orleans, and the Mississippi Gulf Coast* (2006). A scathing account of how government at all levels failed the people of New Orleans.

- Cherlin, Andrew J. *Labor's Love Lost: The Rise and Fall of the Working-Class Family in America* (2015). Studies how class differences affect family life and opportunities for social mobility in today's America.

- Cole, David. *Terrorism and the Constitution* (rev. ed., 2006). Explores the constitutional issues raised by the war on terrorism.

- Fraser, Steve. *The Age of Acquiescence* (2015). A comparison of the late nineteenth century with the current era, exploring why protest against inequality was stronger in the former.

- Gardner, Lloyd C. *The Long Road to Baghdad: A History of U.S. Foreign Policy from the 1970s to the Present* (2008). A careful study of recent American foreign policy and the origins of the Iraq War.

- Krugman, Paul. *The Return of Depression Economics and the Crisis of 2008* (2009). A leading economist explains the origins of the Great Recession.

- Lakoff, George. *Whose Freedom? The Battle over America's Most Important Idea* (2006). Describes how conservatives and liberals continue to interpret freedom in very different ways.

- Lansley, Stewart. *Divided We Stand: Why Inequality Keeps Rising* (2011). A prominent economist explains the reasons for rising economic inequality.

- Levitas, Mitchell, ed. *A Nation Challenged: A Visual History of 9/11 and Its Aftermath* (2002). Presents striking photographs of the terrorist attacks and the days that followed.

- Little, Douglas. *American Orientalism: The United States and the Middle East since 1945* (2003). A careful study of American relations with a volatile region since World War II.

- Nye, Joseph S., Jr. *The Paradox of American Power* (2002). An argument that despite its overwhelming power, the United States cannot do as it pleases in international affairs.

- Zakaria, Fareed. *The Future of Freedom: Illiberal Democracy at Home and Abroad* (2003). A foreign policy analyst discusses how the United States should respond to threats to freedom in the world.

WEBSITES

- September 11 Digital Archive: http://911digitalarchive.org

- The White House: www.whitehouse.gov

CHAPTER REVIEW AND ONLINE RESOURCES

REVIEW QUESTIONS

1. How did the foreign policy initiatives of the George W. Bush administration depart from the policies of other presidents since World War II?

2. How did the September 11 attacks transform Americans' understanding of their security? How did the response compare with that after Pearl Harbor?

3. What are the similarities and differences between America's involvement in Afghanistan and Iraq since 2001?

4. In what ways did American leaders and citizens draw lessons from Vietnam when considering U.S. involvement in Iraq?

5. What does the war on terrorism suggest about the tension between freedom and security as priorities of the United States?

6. What were the goals and impact of the Bush Administration's economic policies?

7. How did Supreme Court decisions since 2001 indicate that the rights revolution was here to stay?

8. What were the political and social effects of Hurricane Katrina? Which were lasting?

9. In what ways did the Obama Administration diverge from the policies of other recent administrations? In what ways was it similar?

10. How did the 2012 election reveal changes in American political and social practices? How did it represent continuities?

11. What is meant by "American exceptionalism"? In what ways is the United States different from the rest of the world and how is it similar?

KEY TERMS

Kyoto Protocol (p. 1092)

Bush Doctrine (p. 1093)

war on terrorism (p. 1093)

war in Afghanistan (p. 1093)

Iraq War (p. 1095)

USA Patriot Act (p. 1097)

Guantánamo Bay (p. 1097)

Hurricane Katrina (p. 1102)

Obergefell v. Hodges (p. 1106)

Great Recession (p. 1111)

Sonia Sotomayor (p. 1116)

Gulf oil spill (p. 1116)

Occupy Wall Street (p. 1119)

Black Lives Matter (p. 1121)

ISIS (p. 1124)

Edward Snowden (p. 1125)

Tea Party (p. 1125)

American exceptionalism (p. 1129)

Go to INQUIZITIVE

To see what you know—and learn what you've missed—with personalized feedback along the way.

Visit the *Give Me Liberty!* Student Site for primary source documents and images, interactive maps, author videos featuring Eric Foner, and more.

APPENDIX

THE DECLARATION OF INDEPENDENCE (1776)

When in the course of human events, it becomes necessary for one people to dissolve the political bands which have connected them with another, and to assume among the Powers of the earth, the separate and equal station to which the Laws of Nature and of Nature's God entitle them, a decent respect to the opinions of mankind requires that they should declare the causes which impel them to the separation.

We hold these truths to be self-evident, that all men are created equal, that they are endowed by their Creator with certain unalienable rights, that among these are Life, Liberty, and the pursuit of Happiness. That to secure these rights, Governments are instituted among Men, deriving their just powers from the consent of the governed. That whenever any Form of Government becomes destructive of these ends, it is the Right of the People to alter or to abolish it, and to institute new Government, laying its foundation on such principles and organizing its powers in such form, as to them shall seem most likely to effect their Safety and Happiness. Prudence, indeed, will dictate that Governments long established should not be changed for light and transient causes; and accordingly all experience hath shown, that mankind are more disposed to suffer, while evils are sufferable, than to right themselves by abolishing the forms to which they are accustomed. But when a long train of abuses and usurpations, pursuing invariably the same Object evinces a design to reduce them under absolute Despotism, it is their right, it is their duty, to throw off such Government, and to provide new Guards for their future security.—Such has been the patient sufferance of these Colonies; and such is now the necessity which constrains them to alter their former Systems of Government. The history of the present King of Great Britain is a history of repeated injuries and usurpations, all having in direct object the establishment of an absolute Tyranny over these States. To prove this, let Facts be submitted to a candid world.

He has refused his Assent to Laws, the most wholesome and necessary for the public good.

He has forbidden his Governors to pass Laws of immediate and pressing importance, unless suspended in their operation till his Assent should be obtained; and when so suspended, he has utterly neglected to attend to them.

He has refused to pass other Laws for the accommodation of large districts of people, unless those people would relinquish the right of Representation in the Legislature, a right inestimable to them and formidable to tyrants only.

He has called together legislative bodies at places unusual, uncomfortable, and distant from the depository of their public Records, for the sole purpose of fatiguing them into compliance with his measures.

He has dissolved Representative Houses repeatedly, for opposing with manly firmness his invasions on the rights of the people.

He has refused for a long time, after such dissolutions, to cause others to be elected; whereby the Legislative powers, incapable of Annihilation, have returned to the People at large for their exercise; the State remaining in the mean time exposed to all dangers of invasion from without, and convulsions within.

He has endeavoured to prevent the population of these States; for that purpose obstructing the Laws of Naturalization of Foreigners; refusing to pass others to encourage their migrations hither, and raising the conditions of new Appropriations of Lands.

He has obstructed the Administration of Justice, by refusing his Assent to Laws for establishing Judiciary powers.

He has made Judges dependent on his Will alone, for the tenure of their offices, and the amount and payment of their salaries.

He has erected a multitude of New Offices, and sent hither swarms of Officers to harass our People, and eat out their substance.

He has kept among us, in times of peace, Standing Armies without the Consent of our legislatures.

He has affected to render the Military independent of and superior to the Civil Power.

He has combined with others to subject us to a jurisdiction foreign to our constitution, and unacknowledged by our laws; giving his Assent to their Acts of pretended Legislation:

For quartering large bodies of armed troops among us:

For protecting them, by a mock Trial, from Punishment for any Murders which they should commit on the Inhabitants of these States:

For cutting off our Trade with all parts of the world:

For imposing taxes on us without our Consent:

For depriving us of many cases, of the benefits of Trial by jury:

For transporting us beyond Seas to be tried for pretended offences:

For abolishing the free System of English Laws in a neighbouring Province, establishing therein an Arbitrary government, and enlarging its Boundaries so as to render it at once an example and fit instrument for introducing the same absolute rule into these Colonies:

For taking away our Charters, abolishing our most valuable Laws, and altering fundamentally the Forms of our Governments:

For suspending our own Legislatures, and declaring themselves invested with Power to legislate for us in all cases whatsoever.

He has abdicated Government here, by declaring us out of his Protection and waging War against us.

He has plundered our seas, ravaged our Coasts, burnt our towns, and destroyed the lives of our people.

He is at this time transporting large armies of foreign mercenaries to compleat the works of death, desolation, and tyranny, already begun with circumstances of Cruelty & perfidy scarcely paralleled in the most barbarous ages, and totally unworthy the Head of a civilized nation.

He has constrained our fellow Citizens taken Captive on the high Seas to bear Arms against their Country, to become the executioners of their friends and Brethren, or to fall themselves by their Hands.

He has excited domestic insurrections amongst us, and has endeavoured to bring on the inhabitants of our frontiers, the merciless Indian Savages, whose known rule of warfare, is an undistinguished destruction of all ages, sexes, and conditions.

In every stage of these Oppressions We have Petitioned for Redress in the most humble terms: Our repeated Petitions have been answered only by repeated injury. A Prince, whose character is thus marked by every act which may define a Tyrant, is unfit to be the ruler of a free people.

Nor have We been wanting in attention to our British brethren. We have warned them from time to time of attempts by their legislature to extend an unwarrantable jurisdiction over us. We have reminded them of the circumstances of our emigration and settlement here. We have appealed to their native justice and magnanimity, and we have conjured them by the ties of our common kindred to disavow these usurpations, which, would inevitably interrupt our connections and correspondence. They too must have been deaf to the voice of justice and of consanguinity. We must, therefore, acquiesce in the necessity, which denounces our Separation, and hold them, as we hold the rest of mankind, Enemies in War, in Peace Friends.

WE, THEREFORE, the Representatives of the UNITED STATES OF AMERICA, in General Congress, Assembled, appealing to the Supreme Judge of the world for the rectitude of our intentions, do, in the Name, and by Authority of the good People of these Colonies, solemnly publish and declare, That these United Colonies are, and of Right ought to be FREE AND INDEPENDENT STATES; that they are Absolved from all Allegiance to the British Crown, and that all political connection between them and the State of Great Britain, is and ought to be totally dissolved; and that as Free and Independent States, they have full Power to levy War, conclude Peace, contract Alliances, establish Commerce, and to do all other Acts and Things which Independent States may of right do. And for the support of this Declaration, with a firm reliance on the Protection of Divine Providence, we mutually pledge to each other our Lives, our Fortunes, and our sacred Honor.

The foregoing Declaration was, by order of Congress, engrossed, and signed by the following members:

John Hancock

NEW HAMPSHIRE	NEW YORK	DELAWARE	NORTH CAROLINA
Josiah Bartlett	*William Floyd*	*Caesar Rodney*	*William Hooper*
William Whipple	*Philip Livingston*	*George Read*	*Joseph Hewes*
Matthew Thornton	*Francis Lewis*	*Thomas M'Kean*	*John Penn*
	Lewis Morris		

MASSACHUSETTS BAY

Samuel Adams

John Adams

Robert Treat Paine

Elbridge Gerry

NEW JERSEY

Richard Stockton

John Witherspoon

Francis Hopkinson

John Hart

Abraham Clark

MARYLAND

Samuel Chase

William Paca

Thomas Stone

Charles Carroll, of Carrollton

SOUTH CAROLINA

Edward Rutledge

Thomas Heyward, Jr.

Thomas Lynch, Jr.

Arthur Middleton

RHODE ISLAND

Stephen Hopkins

William Ellery

VIRGINIA

George Wythe

Richard Henry Lee

Thomas Jefferson

Benjamin Harrison

Thomas Nelson, Jr.

Francis Lightfoot Lee

Carter Braxton

GEORGIA

Button Gwinnett

Lyman Hall

George Walton

PENNSYLVANIA

Robert Morris

Benjamin Rush

Benjamin Franklin

John Morton

George Clymer

James Smith

George Taylor

James Wilson

George Ross

CONNECTICUT

Roger Sherman

Samuel Huntington

William Williams

Oliver Wolcott

Resolved, That copies of the Declaration be sent to the several assemblies, conventions, and committees, or councils of safety, and to the several commanding officers of the continental troops; that it be proclaimed in each of the United States, at the head of the army.

THE CONSTITUTION OF THE UNITED STATES (1787)

We the People of the United States, in order to form a more perfect Union, establish Justice, insure domestic Tranquility, provide for the common defence, promote the general Welfare, and secure the Blessings of Liberty to ourselves and our Posterity, do ordain and establish this Constitution for the United States of America.

ARTICLE. I.

Section. 1. All legislative Powers herein granted shall be vested in a Congress of the United States, which shall consist of a Senate and House of Representatives.

Section. 2. The House of Representatives shall be composed of Members chosen every second Year by the People of the several States, and the Electors in each State shall have the Qualifications requisite for Electors of the most numerous Branch of the State Legislature.

No Person shall be a Representative who shall not have attained to the Age of twenty five Years, and been seven Years a Citizen of the United States, and who shall not, when elected, be an Inhabitant of that State in which he shall be chosen.

Representatives and direct Taxes shall be apportioned among the several States which may be included within this Union, according to their respective Numbers, which shall be determined by adding to the whole Number of free Persons, including those bound to Service for a Term of Years, and excluding Indians not taxed, three fifths of all other Persons. The actual Enumeration shall be made within three Years after the first Meeting of the Congress of the United States, and within every subsequent Term of ten Years, in such Manner as they shall by Law direct. The Number of Representatives shall not exceed one for every thirty Thousand, but each State shall have at Least one Representative; and until such enumeration shall be made, the State of New Hampshire shall be entitled to chuse three, Massachusetts eight, Rhode-Island and Providence Plantations one, Connecticut five, New York six, New Jersey four, Pennsylvania eight, Delaware one, Maryland six, Virginia ten, North Carolina five, South Carolina five, and Georgia three.

When vacancies happen in the Representation from any state, the Executive Authority thereof shall issue Writs of Election to fill such Vacancies.

The House of Representatives shall chuse their Speaker and other Officers; and shall have the sole Power of Impeachment.

Section. 3. The Senate of the United States shall be composed of two Senators from each State, chosen by the legislature thereof, for six Years; and each Senator shall have one Vote.

Immediately after they shall be assembled in Consequence of the first Election, they shall be divided as equally as may be into three Classes. The Seats of the Senators of the first Class shall be vacated at the Expiration of the second Year, of the second Class at the Expiration of the fourth Year, and of the third Class at the Expiration of the sixth Year, so that one third may be chosen every second Year; and if Vacancies happen by Resignation, or otherwise, during the Recess of the Legislature of any State, the Executive thereof may make temporary Appointments until the next Meeting of the Legislature, which shall then fill such Vacancies.

No Person shall be a Senator who shall not have attained to the Age of thirty Years, and been nine Years a Citizen of the United States, and who shall not, when elected, be an Inhabitant of that State for which he shall be chosen.

The Vice President of the United States shall be President of the Senate, but shall have no Vote, unless they be equally divided.

The Senate shall chuse their other Officers, and also a President pro tempore, in the Absence of the Vice President, or when he shall exercise the Office of President of the United States.

The Senate shall have the sole Power to try all Impeachments. When sitting for that Purpose, they shall be on Oath or Affirmation. When the President of the United States is tried, the Chief Justice shall preside: And no Person shall be convicted without the Concurrence of two thirds of the Members present.

Judgment in Cases of Impeachment shall not extend further than to removal from Office, and disqualification to hold and enjoy any Office of honor, Trust or Profit under the United States: but the Party convicted shall nevertheless be liable and subject to Indictment, Trial, Judgment and Punishment, according to Law.

Section. 4. The Times, Places and Manner of holding Elections for Senators and Representatives, shall be prescribed in each State by the Legislature thereof; but the Congress may at any time by Law make or alter such Regulations, except as to the Places of chusing Senators.

The Congress shall assemble at least once in every Year, and such Meeting shall be on the first Monday in December, unless they shall by Law appoint a different Day.

Section. 5. Each House shall be the Judge of the Elections, Returns and Qualifications of its own Members, and a Majority of each shall constitute a Quorum to do Business; but a smaller Number may adjourn from day to day, and may be authorized to compel the Attendance of absent Members, in such Manner, and under such Penalties as each House may provide.

Each House may determine the Rules of its Proceedings, punish its Members for disorderly Behaviour, and, with the Concurrence of two thirds, expel a Member.

Each House shall keep a Journal of its Proceedings, and from time to time publish the same, excepting such Parts as may in their Judgment require Secrecy; and the Yeas and Nays of the Members of either House on any question shall, at the Desire of one fifth of those Present, be entered on the Journal.

Neither House, during the Session of Congress, shall, without the Consent of the other, adjourn for more than three days, not to any other Place than that in which the two Houses shall be sitting.

Section. 6. The Senators and Representatives shall receive a Compensation for their Services, to be ascertained by Law, and paid out of the Treasury of the United States. They shall in all Cases, except Treason, Felony and Breach of the Peace, be privileged from Arrest during their Attendance at the Session of their respective Houses, and in going to and returning from the same; and for any Speech or Debate in either House, they shall not be questioned in any other Place.

No Senator or Representative shall, during the Time for which he was elected, be appointed to any civil Office under the Authority of the United States, which shall have been created, or the Emoluments whereof shall have been encreased during such time; and no Person holding any Office under the United States, shall be a Member of either House during his Continuance in Office.

Section. 7. All Bills for raising Revenue shall originate in the House of Representatives; but the Senate may propose or concur with Amendments as on other Bills.

Every Bill which shall have passed the House of Representatives and the Senate shall, before it become a Law, be presented to the President of the United States; If he approve he shall sign it, but if not he shall return it, with his Objections to that House in which it shall have originated, who shall enter the Objections at large on their Journal, and proceed to reconsider it. If after such Reconsideration two thirds of that House shall agree to pass the Bill, it shall be sent, together with the Objections, to the other House, by which it shall likewise be reconsidered, and if approved by two thirds of that House, it shall become a Law. But in all such Cases the Votes of both Houses shall be determined by Yeas and Nays, and the Names of the Persons voting for and against the Bill shall be entered on the Journal of each House respectively. If any Bill shall not be returned by the President within ten Days (Sundays excepted) after it shall have been presented to him, the Same shall be a Law, in like Manner as if he had signed it, unless the Congress by their Adjournment prevent its Return, in which Case it shall not be a Law.

Every Order, Resolution, or Vote to which the Concurrence of the Senate and House of Representatives may be necessary (except on a question of Adjournment) shall be presented to the President of the United States; and before the Same shall take Effect, shall be approved by him, or being disapproved by him, shall be repassed by two thirds of the Senate and House of Representatives, according to the Rules and Limitations prescribed in the Case of a Bill.

Section. 8. The Congress shall have Power To lay and collect Taxes, Duties, Imposts and Excises, to pay the Debts and provide for the common Defence and general Welfare of the United States; but all Duties, Imposts and Excises shall be uniform throughout the United States;

To borrow Money on the credit of the United States;

To regulate Commerce with foreign Nations, and among the several States, and with the Indian Tribes;

To establish an uniform Rule of Naturalization, and uniform Laws on the subject of Bankruptcies throughout the United States;

To coin Money, regulate the Value thereof, and of foreign Coin, and fix the Standard of Weights and Measures;

To provide for the Punishment of counterfeiting the Securities and current Coin of the United States;

To establish Post Offices and Post Roads;

To promote the Progress of Science and useful Arts, by securing for limited Times to Authors and Inventors the exclusive Right to their respective Writings and Discoveries;

To constitute Tribunals inferior to the supreme Court;

To define and punish Piracies and Felonies committed on the high Seas, and Offences against the Law of Nations;

To declare War, grant Letters of Marque and Reprisal, and make Rules concerning Captures on Land and Water;

To raise and support Armies, but no Appropriation of Money to that Use shall be for a longer Term than two Years;

To provide and maintain a Navy;

To make Rules for the Government and Regulation of the land and naval Forces;

To provide for calling forth the Militia to execute the Laws of the Union, suppress Insurrections and repel Invasions;

To provide for organizing, arming, and disciplining, the Militia, and for governing such Part of them as may be employed in the Service of the United States, reserving to the States respectively, the Appointment of the Officers, and the Authority of training the Militia according to the discipline prescribed by Congress;

To exercise exclusive Legislation in all Cases whatsoever, over such District (not exceeding ten Miles square) as may, by Cession of Particular States, and the Acceptance of Congress, become the Seat of the Government of the United States, and to exercise like Authority over all Places purchased by the Consent of the Legislature of the State in which the Same shall be, for the Erection of Forts, Magazines, Arsenals, dock-Yards, and other needful Buildings;—And

To make all Laws which shall be necessary and proper for carrying into Execution the foregoing Powers, and all other Powers vested by this Constitution in the Government of the United States, or in any Department or Officer thereof.

Section. 9. The Migration or Importation of such Persons as any of the States now existing shall think proper to admit, shall not be prohibited by the Congress prior to the Year one thousand eight hundred and eight, but a Tax or duty may be imposed on such Importation, not exceeding ten dollars for each Person.

The Privilege of the Writ of Habeas Corpus shall not be suspended, unless when in Cases of Rebellion or Invasion the public Safety may require it.

No Bill of Attainder or ex post facto Law shall be passed.

No Capitation, or other direct, Tax shall be laid, unless in Proportion to the Census or Enumeration herein before directed to be taken.

No Tax or Duty shall be laid on Articles exported from any State.

No Preference shall be given by any Regulation of Commerce or Revenue to the Ports of one State over those of another: nor shall Vessels bound to, or from, one State, be obliged to enter, clear, or pay Duties in another.

No Money shall be drawn from the Treasury, but in Consequence of Appropriations made by Law; and a regular Statement and Account of the Receipts and Expenditures of all public Money shall be published from time to time.

No Title of Nobility shall be granted by the United States: And no Person holding any Office of Profit or Trust under them, shall, without the Consent of the Congress, accept of any present, Emolument, Office, or Title, of any kind whatever, from any King, Prince, or foreign State.

Section. 10. No State shall enter into any Treaty, Alliance, or Confederation; grant Letters of Marque and Reprisal; coin Money; emit Bills of Credit; make any Thing but gold and silver Coin a Tender in Payment of Debts; pass any Bill of Attainder, ex post facto Law, or Law impairing the Obligation of Contracts, or grant any Title of Nobility.

No State shall, without the Consent of the Congress, lay any Imposts or Duties on Imports or Exports, except what may be absolutely necessary for executing its inspection Laws: and the net Produce of all Duties and Imposts, laid by any State on Imports or Exports, shall be for the Use of the Treasury of the United States; and all such Laws shall be subject to the Revision and Controul of the Congress.

No State shall, without the Consent of Congress, lay any Duty of Tonnage, keep Troops, or Ships of War in time of Peace, enter into any Agreement or Compact with another State, or with a foreign Power, or engage in War, unless actually invaded, or in such imminent Danger as will not admit of delay.

ARTICLE. II.

Section. 1. The executive Power shall be vested in a President of the United States of America. He shall hold his Office during the term of four Years, and, together with the Vice President, chosen for the same Term, be elected, as follows:

Each State shall appoint, in such Manner as the Legislature thereof may direct, a Number of Electors, equal to the whole Number of Senators and Representatives to which the State may be entitled in the Congress: but no Senator or Representative, or Person holding an Office of Trust or Profit under the United States, shall be appointed an Elector.

The Electors shall meet in their respective States, and vote by Ballot for two Persons, of whom one at least shall not be an Inhabitant of the same State with themselves. And they shall make a List of all the Persons voted for, and of the Number of Votes for each; which List they shall sign and certify, and transmit sealed to the Seat of the Government of the United States, directed to the President of the Senate. The President of the Senate shall, in the Presence of the Senate and House of Representatives, open all the Certificates, and the Votes shall then be counted. The Person having the greatest Number of Votes shall be the President, if such Number be a Majority of the whole Number of Electors appointed; and if there be more than one who have such Majority, and have an equal Number of Votes, then the House of Representatives shall immediately chuse by Ballot one of them for President; and if no Person have a Majority, then from the five highest on the List the said House shall in like Manner chuse the President. But in chusing the President, the Votes shall be taken by States, the Representation from each State having one Vote; A quorum for this Purpose shall consist of a Member or Members from two thirds of the States, and a Majority of all the States shall be necessary to a Choice. In every Case, after the Choice of the President, the Person having the greatest Number of Votes of the Electors shall be the Vice President. But if there should remain two or more who have equal Votes, the Senate shall chuse from them by Ballot the Vice President.

The Congress may determine the Time of chusing the Electors, and the Day on which they shall give their Votes; which Day shall be the same throughout the United States.

No Person except a natural born Citizen, or a Citizen of the United States, at the time of the Adoption of this Constitution, shall be eligible to the Office of President; neither shall any Person be eligible to that Office who shall not have attained to the Age of thirty five Years, and been fourteen Years a Resident within the United States.

In Case of the Removal of the President from Office, or of his Death, Resignation, or Inability to discharge the Powers and Duties of the said Office, the Same shall devolve on the Vice President, and the Congress may by Law provide for the Case of Removal, Death, Resignation or Inability, both of the President and Vice President, declaring what Officer shall then act as President, and such Officer shall act accordingly, until the Disability be removed, or a President shall be elected.

The President shall, at stated Times, receive for his Services, a Compensation, which shall neither be encreased or diminished during the Period for which he shall have been elected, and he shall not receive within that Period any other Emolument from the United States, or any of them.

Before he enters on the Execution of his Office, he shall take the following Oath or Affirmation:—"I do solemnly swear (or affirm) that I will faithfully execute the Office of President of the United States, and will to the best of my Ability, preserve, protect and defend the Constitution of the United States."

Section. 2. The President shall be Commander in Chief of the Army and Navy of the United States, and of the Militia of the several States, when called into the actual Service of the United States; he may require the Opinion, in writing, of the principal Officer in each of the executive Departments, upon any Subject relating to the Duties of their respective Offices, and he shall have Power to grant Reprieves and Pardons for Offences against the United States, except in Cases of Impeachment.

He shall have Power, by and with the Advice and Consent of the Senate, to make Treaties, provided two thirds of the Senators present concur; and he shall nominate, and by and with the Advice and Consent of the Senate, shall appoint Ambassadors, other public Ministers and Consuls, Judges of the supreme Court, and all other Officers of the United States, whose Appointments are not herein otherwise provided for, and which shall be established by Law; but the Congress may by Law vest the Appointment of such inferior Officers, as they think proper, in the President alone, in the Courts of Law, or in the Heads of Departments.

The President shall have Power to fill up all Vacancies that may happen during the Recess of the Senate, by granting Commissions which shall expire at the End of their next Session.

Section. 3. He shall from time to time give to the Congress Information of the State of the Union, and recommend to their Consideration such Measures as he shall judge necessary and expedient; he may, on extraordinary Occasions, convene both Houses, or either of them, and in Case of Disagreement between them, with Respect to the Time of Adjournment, he may adjourn them to such Time as he shall think proper; he shall receive Ambassadors and other public Ministers; he shall take Care that the Laws be faithfully executed, and shall Commission all the Officers of the United States.

Section. 4. The President, Vice President and all civil Officers of the United States, shall be removed from Office on Impeachment for, and Conviction of, Treason, Bribery, or other high Crimes and Misdemeanors.

ARTICLE. III.

Section. 1. The judicial Power of the United States, shall be vested in one supreme Court, and in such inferior Courts as the Congress may from time to time ordain and establish. The Judges, both of the supreme and inferior Courts, shall hold their Offices during good Behavior, and shall, at stated Times, receive for their Services, a Compensation, which shall not be diminished during their Continuance in Office.

Section. 2. The judicial Power shall extend to all Cases, in Law and Equity, arising under this Constitution, the Laws of the United States, and Treaties made, or which shall be made, under their Authority;—to all Cases affecting Ambassadors, other public Ministers and Consuls;—to all Cases of admiralty and maritime Jurisdiction;—the Controversies to which the United States shall be a Party;—to Controversies between two or more States;—between a State and Citizens of another State;—between Citizens of different States;—between Citizens of the same State claiming Lands under Grants of different States, and between a State, or the Citizens thereof, and foreign States, Citizens or Subjects.

In all cases affecting Ambassadors, other public Ministers and Consuls, and those in which a State shall be Party, the supreme Court shall have original Jurisdiction. In all the other Cases before mentioned, the supreme Court shall have appellate Jurisdiction, both as to Law and Fact, with such Exceptions, and under such Regulations as the Congress shall make.

The Trial of all Crimes, except in Cases of Impeachment, shall be by Jury; and such Trial shall be held in the State where the said Crimes shall have been committed; but when not committed within any State, the Trial shall be at such Place or Places as the Congress may by Law have directed.

Section. 3. Treason against the United States, shall consist only in levying War against them, or in adhering to their Enemies, giving them Aid and Comfort. No Person shall be convicted of Treason unless on the Testimony of two Witnesses to the same overt Act, or on Confession in open Court.

The Congress shall have Power to declare the Punishment of Treason, but no Attainder of Treason shall work Corruption of Blood, or Forfeiture except during the Life of the Person attainted.

ARTICLE. IV.

Section. 1. Full Faith and Credit shall be given in each State to the public Acts, Records, and judicial Proceedings of every other State. And the Congress may by general Laws prescribe the Manner in which such Acts, Records and Proceedings shall be proved, and the Effect thereof.

Section. 2. The Citizens of each State shall be entitled to all Privileges and Immunities of Citizens in the several States.

A Person charged in any State with Treason, Felony, or other Crime, who shall flee from Justice, and be found in another State, shall on Demand of the executive Authority of the State from which he fled, be delivered up, to be removed to the State having Jurisdiction of the Crime.

No Person held to Service or Labour in one State, under the Laws thereof, escaping into another, shall, in Consequence of any Law or Regulation therein, be discharged from such Service or Labour, but shall be delivered up on Claim of the Party to whom such Service or Labour may be due.

Section. 3. New States may be admitted by the Congress into this Union; but no new State shall be formed or erected within the Jurisdiction of any other State; nor any State be formed by the Junction of two or more States, or Parts of States, without the consent of the Legislatures of the States concerned as well as of the Congress.

The Congress shall have Power to dispose of and make all needful Rules and Regulations respecting the Territory or other Property belonging to the United States; and nothing in this Constitution shall be so construed as to Prejudice any Claims of the United States, or of any particular States.

Section. 4. The United States shall guarantee to every State in this Union a Republican Form of Government, and shall protect each of them against Invasion; and on Application of the Legislature, or of the Executive (when the Legislature cannot be convened) against domestic Violence.

within seven years from the date of its submission. [February 6, 1933]

AMENDMENT XXI.

Section 1. The eighteenth article of amendment to the Constitution of the United States is hereby repealed.

Section 2. The transportation or importation into any State, Territory or possession of the United States for delivery or use therein of intoxicating liquors, in violation of the laws thereof, is hereby prohibited.

Section 3. This article shall be inoperative unless it shall have been ratified as an amendment to the Constitution by convention in the several States, as provided in the Constitution, within seven years from the date of the submission thereof to the States by the Congress. [December 5, 1933]

AMENDMENT XXII.

Section 1. No person shall be elected to the office of the President more than twice, and no person who has held the office of President, or acted as President, for more than two years of a term to which some other person was elected President shall be elected to the office of the President more than once. But this Article shall not apply to any person holding the office of President when this Article was proposed by the Congress, and shall not prevent any person who may be holding the office of President, or acting as President, during the term within which this Article becomes operative from holding the office of President or acting as President during the remainder of such term.

Section 2. This article shall be inoperative unless it shall have been ratified as an amendment to the Constitution by the legislatures of three-fourths of the several States within seven years from the date of its submission to the States by the Congress. [February 27, 1951]

AMENDMENT XXIII.

Section 1. The District constituting the seat of government of the United States shall appoint in such manner as the Congress may direct:

A number of electors of President and Vice-President equal to the whole number of Senators and Representatives in Congress to which the District would be entitled if it were a State, but in no event more than the least populous State; they shall be in addition to those appointed by the States, but they shall be considered, for the purposes of the election of President and Vice-President, to be electors appointed by a State; and they shall meet in the District and perform such duties as provided by the twelfth article of amendment.

Section 2. The Congress shall have the power to enforce this article by appropriate legislation. [March 29, 1961]

AMENDMENT XXIV.

Section 1. The right of citizens of the United States to vote in any primary or other election for President or Vice President, for electors for President or Vice President, or for Senator or Representative in Congress, shall not be denied or abridged by the United States or any State by reason of failure to pay any poll tax or other tax.

Section 2. The Congress shall have power to enforce this article by appropriate legislation. [January 23, 1964]

AMENDMENT XXV.

Section 1. In case of the removal of the President from office or of his death or resignation, the Vice President shall become President.

Section 2. Whenever there is a vacancy in the office of Vice President, the President shall nominate a Vice President who shall take office upon confirmation by a majority vote of both Houses of Congress.

Section 3. Whenever the President transmits to the President pro tempore of the Senate and the Speaker of the House of Representatives his written declaration that he is unable to discharge the powers and duties of his office, and until he transmits to them a written declaration to the contrary, such powers and duties shall be discharged by the Vice President as Acting President.

Section 4. Whenever the Vice President and a majority of either the principal officers of the executive departments or of such other body as Congress may by law provide, transmit to the President pro tempore of the Senate and the Speaker of the House of Representatives their written declaration that the President is unable to discharge the powers and duties of his office, the Vice President shall immediately assume the powers and duties of the office as Acting President.

Thereafter, when the President transmits to the President pro tempore of the Senate and the Speaker of the House of Representatives his written declaration that no inability exists, he shall resume the powers and duties of his office unless the Vice President and a majority of either the principal officers of the executive departments or of such other body as Congress may by law provide, transmit within four days to the President pro tempore of the Senate and the Speaker of the House of Representatives their written declaration that the President is unable to discharge the powers and duties of his office. Thereupon Congress shall decide the issue, assembling within forty-eight hours for that purpose if not in session. If the Congress, within twenty-one days after receipt of the latter written declaration, or, if Congress is not in session, within twenty-one days after Congress is required to assemble, determines by two-thirds vote of both Houses that the President is unable to discharge the powers and duties of his office, the Vice-President shall continue to discharge the same as Acting President; otherwise, the President shall resume the powers and duties of his office. [February 10, 1967]

AMENDMENT XXVI.

Section 1. The right of citizens of the United States, who are eighteen years of age or older, to vote shall not be denied or abridged by the United States or by any State on account of age.

Section 2. The Congress shall have power to enforce this article by appropriate legislation. [June 30, 1971]

AMENDMENT XXVII.

No law, varying the compensation for the services of the Senators and Representatives shall take effect, until an election of Representatives shall have intervened. [May 8, 1992]

FROM GEORGE WASHINGTON'S FAREWELL ADDRESS (1796)

Friends and Citizens:

The period for a new election of a citizen to administer the executive government of the United States being not far distant, and the time actually arrived when your thoughts must be employed in designating the person who is to be clothed with that important trust, it appears to me proper, especially as it may conduce to a more distinct expression of the public voice, that I should now apprise you of the resolution I have formed, to decline being considered among the number of those out of whom a choice is to be made.

★ ★ ★

In looking forward to the moment which is intended to terminate the career of my public life, my feelings do not permit me to suspend the deep acknowledgment of that debt of gratitude which I owe to my beloved country for the many honors it has conferred upon me; still more for the steadfast confidence with which it has supported me; and for the opportunities I have thence enjoyed of manifesting my inviolable attachment, by services faithful and persevering, though in usefulness unequal to my zeal. If benefits have resulted to our country from these services, let it always be remembered to your praise, and as an instructive example in our annals, that under circumstances in which the passions, agitated in every direction, were liable to mislead, amidst appearances sometimes dubious, vicissitudes of fortune often discouraging, in situations in which not unfrequently want of success has countenanced the spirit of criticism, the constancy of your support was the essential prop of the efforts, and a guarantee of the plans by which they were effected. Profoundly penetrated with this idea, I shall carry it with me to my grave, as a strong incitement to unceasing vows that heaven may continue to you the choicest tokens of its beneficence; that your union and brotherly affection may be perpetual; that the free Constitution, which is the work of your hands, may be sacredly maintained; that its administration in every department may be stamped with wisdom and virtue; that, in fine, the happiness of the people of these States, under the auspices of liberty, may be made complete by so careful a preservation and so prudent a use of this blessing as will acquire to them the glory of recommending it to the applause, the affection, and adoption of every nation which is yet a stranger to it.

Here, perhaps, I ought to stop. But a solicitude for your welfare, which cannot end but with my life, and the apprehension of danger, natural to that solicitude, urge me, on an occasion like the present, to offer to your solemn contemplation, and to recommend to your frequent review, some sentiments which are the result of much reflection, of no inconsiderable observation, and which appear to me all-important to the permanency of your felicity as a people. These will be offered to you with the more freedom, as you can only see in them the disinterested warnings of a parting friend, who can possibly have no personal motive to bias his counsel. Nor can I forget, as an encouragement to it, your indulgent reception of my sentiments on a former and not dissimilar occasion.

Interwoven as is the love of liberty with every ligament of your hearts, no recommendation of mine is necessary to fortify or confirm the attachment.

The unity of government which constitutes you one people is also now dear to you. It is justly so, for it is a main pillar in the edifice of your real independence, the support of your tranquility at home, your peace abroad; of your safety; of your prosperity; of that very liberty which you so highly prize. But as it is easy to foresee that, from different causes and from different quarters, much pains will be taken, many artifices employed to weaken in your minds the conviction of this truth; as this is the point in your political fortress against which the batteries of internal and external enemies will be most constantly and actively (though often covertly and insidiously) directed, it is of infinite moment that you should properly estimate the immense value of your national union to your collective and individual happiness; that you should cherish a cordial, habitual, and immovable attachment to it; accustoming yourselves to think and speak of it as of the palladium of your political safety and prosperity; watching for its preservation with jealous anxiety; discountenancing whatever may suggest even a suspicion that it can in any event be abandoned; and indignantly frowning upon the first dawning of every attempt to alienate any portion of our country from the rest, or to enfeeble the sacred ties which now link together the various parts.

For this you have every inducement of sympathy and interest. Citizens, by birth or choice, of a common country, that country has a right to concentrate your affections. The name of American, which belongs to you in your national capacity, must always exalt the just pride of patriotism more than any appellation derived from local discriminations. With slight shades of difference, you have the same religion, manners, habits, and political principles. You have in a common cause fought and triumphed together; the independence and liberty you possess are the work of joint counsels, and joint efforts of common dangers, sufferings, and successes.

But these considerations, however powerfully they address themselves to your sensibility, are greatly outweighed by those which apply more immediately to your interest. Here every portion of our country finds the most commanding motives for carefully guarding and preserving the union of the whole.

The North, in an unrestrained intercourse with the South, protected by the equal laws of a common government, finds in the productions of the latter great additional resources of maritime and commercial enterprise and precious materials of manufacturing industry. The South, in the same intercourse, benefiting by the agency of the North, sees its agriculture grow and its commerce expand. Turning partly into its own channels the seamen of the North, it finds its particular navigation invigorated; and, while it contributes, in different ways, to nourish and increase the general mass of the national navigation, it looks forward to the protection of a maritime strength, to which itself is unequally adapted. The East, in a like intercourse with the West, already finds, and in the progressive improvement of interior communications by land and water, will more and more find a valuable vent for the commodities which it brings from abroad, or manufactures at home. The West derives from the East supplies requisite to its growth and comfort, and, what is perhaps of still greater consequence, it must of necessity owe the secure enjoyment of indispensable outlets for its own productions to the weight, influence, and the future maritime strength of the Atlantic side of the Union, directed by an indissoluble community of interest as one nation. Any other tenure by which the West can hold this essential advantage, whether derived from its own separate strength, or from an apostate and unnatural connection with any foreign power, must be intrinsically precarious.

While, then, every part of our country thus feels an immediate and particular interest in union, all the parts combined cannot fail to find in the united mass of means and efforts greater strength, greater resource, proportionably greater security from external danger, a less frequent interruption of their peace by foreign nations; and, what is of inestimable value, they must derive from union an exemption from those broils and wars between themselves, which so frequently afflict neighboring countries not tied together by the same governments, which their own rival ships alone would be sufficient to produce, but which opposite foreign alliances, attachments, and intrigues would stimulate and embitter. Hence, likewise, they will avoid the necessity of those overgrown military establishments which, under any form of government, are inauspicious to liberty, and which are to be regarded as particularly hostile to republican liberty. In this sense it is that your union ought to be considered as a main prop of your liberty, and that the love of the one ought to endear to you the preservation of the other.

These considerations speak a persuasive language to every reflecting and virtuous mind, and exhibit the continuance of the Union as a primary object of patriotic desire. Is there a doubt whether a common government can embrace so large a sphere? Let experience solve it. To listen to mere speculation in such a case were criminal. We are authorized to hope that a proper organization of the whole with the auxiliary agency of governments for the respective subdivisions, will afford a happy issue to the experiment. It is well worth a fair and full experiment. With such powerful and obvious motives to union, affecting all parts of our country, while experience shall not have demonstrated its impracticability, there will always be reason to distrust the patriotism of those who in any quarter may endeavor to weaken its bands.

★ ★ ★

To the efficacy and permanency of your Union, a government for the whole is indispensable. No alliance, however strict, between the parts can be an adequate substitute; they must inevitably experience the infractions and interruptions which all alliances in all times have experienced. Sensible of this momentous truth, you have improved upon your first essay, by the adoption of a constitution of government better calculated than your former for an intimate union, and for the efficacious management of your common concerns. This government, the offspring of our own choice, uninfluenced and unawed, adopted upon full investigation and mature deliberation, completely free in its principles, in the distribution of its powers, uniting security with energy, and containing within itself a provision for its own amendment, has a just claim to your confidence and your support. Respect for its authority, compliance with its laws, acquiescence in its measures, are duties enjoined by the fundamental maxims of true liberty. The basis of our political systems is the right of the people to make and to alter their constitutions of government. But the Constitution which at any time exists, till changed by an explicit and authentic act of the whole people, is sacredly obligatory upon all. The very idea of the power and the right of the people to establish government presupposes the duty of every individual to obey the established government.

★ ★ ★

I have already intimated to you the danger of parties in the State, with particular reference to the founding of them on geographical discriminations. Let me now take a more comprehensive view, and warn you in the most solemn manner against the baneful effects of the spirit of party generally.

This spirit, unfortunately, is inseparable from our nature, having its root in the strongest passions of the human mind. It exists under different shapes in all governments, more or less stifled, controlled, or repressed; but, in those of the popular form, it is seen in its greatest rankness, and is truly their worst enemy.

The alternate domination of one faction over another, sharpened by the spirit of revenge, natural to party dissension, which in different ages and countries has perpetrated the most horrid enormities, is itself a frightful despotism. But this leads at length to a more formal and permanent despotism. The disorders and miseries which result gradually incline the minds of men to seek security and repose in the absolute power of an individual; and sooner or later the chief of some prevailing faction, more able or more fortunate than his competitors, turns this disposition to the purposes of his own elevation, on the ruins of public liberty.

Without looking forward to an extremity of this kind (which nevertheless ought not to be entirely out of sight), the common and continual mischiefs of the spirit of party are sufficient to make it the interest and duty of a wise people to discourage and restrain it.

It serves always to distract the public councils and enfeeble the public administration. It agitates the community with ill-founded jealousies and false alarms, kindles the animosity of one part against another, foments occasionally riot and insurrection. It opens the door to foreign influence and corruption, which finds a facilitated access to the government itself through the channels of party passions. Thus the policy and the will of one country are subjected to the policy and will of another.

There is an opinion that parties in free countries are useful checks upon the administration of the government and serve to keep alive the spirit of liberty. This within certain limits is probably true; and in governments of a monarchical cast, patriotism may look with indulgence, if not with favor, upon the spirit of party. But in those of the popular character, in governments purely elective, it is a spirit not to be encouraged. From their natural tendency, it is certain there will always be enough of that spirit for every salutary purpose. And there being constant danger of excess, the effort ought to be by force of public opinion, to mitigate and assuage it. A fire not to be quenched, it demands a uniform vigilance to prevent its bursting into a flame, lest, instead of warming, it should consume.

It is important, likewise, that the habits of thinking in a free country should inspire caution in those entrusted with its administration, to confine themselves within their respective constitutional spheres, avoiding in the exercise of the powers of one department to encroach upon another. The spirit of encroachment tends to consolidate the powers of all the departments in one, and thus to create, whatever the form of government, a real despotism. A just estimate of that love of power, and proneness to abuse it, which predominates in the human heart, is sufficient to satisfy us of the truth of this position. The necessity of reciprocal checks in the exercise of political power, by dividing and distributing it into different depositaries, and constituting each the guardian of the public weal against invasions by the others, has been evinced by experiments ancient and modern; some of them in our country and under our own eyes. To preserve them must be as necessary as to institute them. If, in the opinion of the people, the distribution or modification of the constitutional powers be in any particular wrong, let it be corrected by an amendment in the way which the Constitution designates. But let there be no change by usurpation; for though this, in one instance, may be the instrument of good, it is the customary weapon by which free governments are destroyed. The precedent must always greatly overbalance in permanent evil any partial or transient benefit, which the use can at any time yield.

★ ★ ★

Observe good faith and justice towards all nations; cultivate peace and harmony with all. Religion and morality enjoin this conduct; and can it be, that good policy does not equally enjoin it? It will be worthy of a free, enlightened, and at no distant period, a great nation, to give to mankind the magnanimous and too novel example of a people always guided by an exalted justice and benevolence. Who can doubt that, in the course of time and things, the fruits of such a plan would richly repay any temporary advantages which might be lost by a steady adherence to it? Can it be that Providence has not connected the permanent felicity of a nation with its virtue? The experiment, at least, is recommended by every sentiment which ennobles human nature. Alas! is it rendered impossible by its vices?

In the execution of such a plan, nothing is more essential than that permanent, inveterate antipathies against particular nations, and passionate attachments for others, should be excluded; and that, in place of them, just and amicable feelings towards all should be cultivated. The nation which indulges towards another a habitual hatred or a habitual fondness is in some degree a slave. It is a slave to its animosity or to its affection, either of which is sufficient to lead it astray from its duty and its interest. Antipathy in one nation against another disposes each more readily to offer insult and injury, to lay hold of slight causes of umbrage, and to be haughty and intractable, when accidental or trifling occasions of dispute occur. Hence, frequent collisions, obstinate, envenomed, and bloody contests. The nation, prompted by ill-will and resentment, sometimes impels to war the government, contrary to the best calculations of policy. The government sometimes participates in the national propensity, and adopts through passion what reason would reject; at other times it makes the animosity of the nation subservient to projects of hostility instigated by pride, ambition, and other sinister and pernicious motives. The peace often, sometimes perhaps the liberty, of nations, has been the victim.

★ ★ ★

The great rule of conduct for us in regard to foreign nations is in extending our commercial relations, to have with them as little political connection as possible. So far as we have already formed engagements, let them be fulfilled with perfect good faith. Here let us stop. Europe has a set of primary interests which to us have none; or a very remote relation. Hence she must be engaged in frequent controversies, the causes of which are essentially foreign to our concerns. Hence, therefore, it must be unwise in us to implicate ourselves by artificial ties in the ordinary vicissitudes of her politics, or the ordinary combinations and collisions of her friendships or enmities.

Our detached and distant situation invites and enables us to pursue a different course. If we remain one people under an efficient government, the period is not far off when we may defy material injury from external annoyance; when we may take such an attitude as will

cause the neutrality we may at any time resolve upon to be scrupulously respected; when belligerent nations, under the impossibility of making acquisitions upon us, will not lightly hazard the giving us provocation; when we may choose peace or war, as our interest, guided by justice, shall counsel.

Why forego the advantages of so peculiar a situation? Why quit our own to stand upon foreign ground? Why, by interweaving our destiny with that of any part of Europe, entangle our peace and prosperity in the toils of European ambition, rivalship, interest, humor or caprice?

It is our true policy to steer clear of permanent alliances with any portion of the foreign world; so far, I mean, as we are now at liberty to do it; for let me not be understood as capable of patronizing infidelity to existing engagements. I hold the maxim no less applicable to public than to private affairs, that honesty is always the best policy. I repeat it, therefore, let those engagements be observed in their genuine sense. But, in my opinion, it is unnecessary and would be unwise to extend them.

Taking care always to keep ourselves by suitable establishments on a respectable defensive posture, we may safely trust to temporary alliances for extraordinary emergencies.

Harmony, liberal intercourse with all nations, are recommended by policy, humanity, and interest. But even our commercial policy should hold an equal and impartial hand; neither seeking nor granting exclusive favors or preferences; consulting the natural course of things; diffusing and diversifying by gentle means the streams of commerce, but forcing nothing; establishing (with powers so disposed, in order to give trade a stable course, to define the rights of our merchants, and to enable the government to support them) conventional rules of intercourse, the best that present circumstances and mutual opinion will permit, but temporary, and liable to be from time to time abandoned or varied, as experience and circumstances shall dictate; constantly keeping in view that it is folly in one nation to look for disinterested favors from another; that it must pay with a portion of its independence for whatever it may accept under that character; that, by such acceptance, it may place itself in the condition of having given equivalents for nominal favors, and yet of being reproached with ingratitude for not giving more.

★ ★ ★

Relying on its kindness in this as in other things, and actuated by that fervent love towards it, which is so natural to a man who views in it the native soil of himself and his progenitors for several generations, I anticipate with pleasing expectation that retreat in which I promise myself to realize, without alloy, the sweet enjoyment of partaking, in the midst of my fellow-citizens, the benign influence of good laws under a free government, the ever-favorite object of my heart, and the happy reward, as I trust, of our mutual cares, labors, and dangers.

Geo. Washington

THE SENECA FALLS DECLARATION OF SENTIMENTS AND RESOLUTIONS (1848)

1. DECLARATION OF SENTIMENTS

When, in the course of human events, it becomes necessary for one portion of the family of man to assume among the people of the earth a position different from that which they have hitherto occupied, but one to which the laws of nature and of nature's God entitle them, a decent respect to the opinions of mankind requires that they should declare the causes that impel them to such a course.

We hold these truths to be self-evident: that all men and women are created equal; that they are endowed by their Creator with certain inalienable rights; that among these are life, liberty, and the pursuit of happiness; that to secure these rights governments are instituted, deriving their just powers from the consent of the governed. Whenever any form of government becomes destructive of these ends, it is the right of those who suffer from it to refuse allegiance to it, and to insist upon the institution of a new government, laying its foundation on such principles, and organizing its powers in such form, as to them shall seem most likely to effect their safety and happiness. Prudence, indeed, will dictate that governments long established should not be changed for light and transient causes; and accordingly all experience hath shown that mankind are more disposed to suffer, while evils are sufferable, than to right themselves by abolishing the forms to which they are accustomed. But when a long train of abuses and usurpations, pursuing invariably the same object, evinces a design to reduce them under absolute despotism, it is their duty to throw off such government, and to provide new guards for their future security. Such has been the patient sufferance of the women under this government, and such is now the necessity which constrains them to demand the equal station to which they are entitled. The history of mankind is a history of repeated injuries and usurpations on the part of man toward woman, having in direct object the establishment of an absolute tyranny over her. To prove this, let facts be submitted to a candid world.

He has never permitted her to exercise her inalienable right to the elective franchise.

He has compelled her to submit to laws, in the formation of which she had no voice.

He has withheld from her rights which are given to the most ignorant and degraded men—both natives and foreigners.

Having deprived her of this first right of a citizen, the elective franchise, thereby leaving her without representation in the halls of legislation, he has oppressed her on all sides.

He has made her, if married, in the eye of the law, civilly dead. He has taken from her all right in property, even to the wages she earns.

He has made her, morally, an irresponsible being, as she can commit many crimes with impunity, provided they be done in the presence of her husband.

In the covenant of marriage, she is compelled to promise obedience to her husband, he becoming, to all intents and purposes, her master—the law giving him power to deprive her of her liberty, and to administer chastisement.

He has so framed the laws of divorce, as to what shall be the proper causes, and in case of separation, to whom the guardianship of the children shall be given, as to be wholly regardless of the happiness of women—the law, in all cases, going upon a false supposition of the supremacy of man, and giving all power into his hands.

After depriving her of all rights as a married woman, if single, and the owner of property, he has taxed her to support a government which recognizes her only when her property can be made profitable to it.

He has monopolized nearly all the profitable employments, and from those she is permitted to follow, she receives but a scanty remuneration. He closes against her all the avenues to wealth and distinction which he considers most honorable to himself. As a teacher of theology, medicine, or law, she is not known.

He has denied her the facilities for obtaining a thorough education, all colleges being closed against her.

He allows her in Church, as well as State, but a subordinate position, claiming Apostolic authority for her exclusion from the ministry, and, with some exceptions, from any public participation in the affairs of the Church.

He has created a false public sentiment by giving to the world a different code of morals for men and women, by which moral delinquencies which exclude women from society, are not only tolerated, but deemed of little account in man.

He has usurped the prerogative of Jehovah himself, claiming it as his right to assign for her a sphere of action, when that belongs to her conscience and to her God.

He has endeavored, in every way that he could, to destroy her confidence in her own powers, to lessen her self-respect and to make her willing to lead a dependent and abject life.

Now, in view of this entire disfranchisement of one-half the people of this country, their social and religious degradation—in view of the unjust laws above mentioned, and because women do feel themselves aggrieved, oppressed, and fraudulently deprived of their most sacred rights, we insist that they have immediate admission to all the rights and privileges which belong to them as citizens of the United States.

In entering upon the great work before us, we anticipate no small amount of misconception, misrepresentation, and ridicule; but we shall use every instrumentality within our power to effect our object. We shall employ agents, circulate tracts, petition the State and National legislatures, and endeavor to enlist the pulpit and the press in our behalf. We hope this Convention will be followed by a series of Conventions embracing every part of the country.

2. RESOLUTIONS

WHEREAS, The great precept of nature is conceded to be, that "man shall pursue his own true and substantial happiness." Blackstone in his Commentaries remarks, that this law of Nature being coeval with mankind, and dictated by God himself, is of course superior in obligation to any other. It is binding over all the globe, in all countries and at all times; no human laws are of any validity if contrary to this, and such of them as are valid, derive all their force, and all their validity, and all their authority, mediately and immediately, from this original; therefore,

Resolved, That such laws as conflict, in any way, with the true and substantial happiness of woman, are contrary to the great precept of nature and of no validity, for this is "superior in obligation to any other."

Resolved, That all laws which prevent woman from occupying such a station in society as her conscience shall dictate, or which place her in a position inferior to that of man, are contrary to the great precept of nature, and therefore of no force or authority.

Resolved, That woman is man's equal—was intended to be so by the Creator, and the highest good of the race demands that she should be recognized as such.

Resolved, That the women of this country ought to be enlightened in regard to the laws under which they live, that they may no longer publish their degradation by declaring themselves satisfied with their present position, nor their ignorance, by asserting that they have all the rights they want.

Resolved, That inasmuch as man, while claiming for himself intellectual superiority, does accord to woman moral superiority, it is pre-eminently his duty to encourage her to speak and teach, as she has an opportunity, in all religious assemblies.

Resolved, That the same amount of virtue, delicacy, and refinement of behavior that is required of woman in the social state, should also be required of man, and the same transgressions should be visited with equal severity on both man and woman.

Resolved, That the objection of indelicacy and impropriety, which is so often brought against woman when she addresses a public audience, comes with a very ill-grace from those who encourage, by their attendance, her appearance on the stage, in the concert. Or in feats of the circus.

Resolved, That woman has too long rested satisfied in the circumscribed limits which corrupt customs and a perverted application of the Scriptures have marked out for her, and that it is time she should move in the enlarged sphere which her great Creator has assigned her.

Resolved, That it is the duty of the women of this country to secure to themselves their sacred right to the elective franchise.

Resolved, That the equality of human rights results necessarily from the fact of the identity of the race in capabilities and responsibilities.

Resolved, therefore, That, being invested by the Creator with the same capabilities, and the same consciousness of responsibility for their exercise, it is demonstrably the right and duty of woman, equally with man, to promote every righteous cause by every righteous means; and especially in regard to the great subjects of morals and religion, it is self-evidently her right to participate with her brother in teaching them, both in private and in public, by writing and by speaking, by any instrumentalities proper to be used, and in any assemblies proper to be held; and this being a self-evident truth growing out of the divinely implanted principles of human nature, any custom or authority adverse to it, whether modern or wearing the hoary sanction of antiquity, is to be regarded as a self-evident falsehood, and at war with mankind.

Resolved, That the speedy success of our cause depends upon the zealous and untiring efforts of both men and women, for the overthrow of the monopoly of the pulpit, and for the securing to women an equal participation with men in the various trades, professions, and commerce.

FROM FREDERICK DOUGLASS'S "WHAT, TO THE SLAVE, IS THE FOURTH OF JULY?" SPEECH (1852)

★ ★ ★

This, for the purpose of this celebration, is the Fourth of July. It is the birthday of your National Independence, and of your political freedom. This, to you, is what the Passover was to the emancipated people of God. It carries your minds back to the day, and to the act of your great deliverance; and to the signs and to the wonders associated with that act and that day. This celebration also marks the beginning of another year of your national life; and reminds you that the Republic of America is now seventy-six years old. I am glad, fellow citizens, that your nation is so young. Seventy-six years, though a good old age for a man, is but a mere speck in the life of a nation. Three score years and ten is the allotted time for individual men; but nations number their years by thousands. According to this fact, you are, even now, only in the beginning of your national career, still lingering in the period of childhood. I repeat, I am glad this is so. There is hope in the thought, and hope is much needed, under the dark clouds which lower above the horizon. The eye of the reformer is met with angry flashes, portending disastrous times; but his heart may well beat lighter at the thought that America is young, and that she is still in the impressible stage of her existence. May he not hope that high lessons of wisdom, of justice and of truth, will yet give direction to her destiny? Were the nation older, the patriot's heart might be sadder and the reformer's brow heavier. Its future might be shrouded in gloom and the hope of its prophets go out in sorrow. There is consolation in the thought that America is young. Great streams are not easily turned from channels worn deep in the course of ages. They may sometimes rise in quiet and stately majesty, and inundate the land, refreshing and fertilizing the earth with their mysterious properties. They may also rise in wrath and fury, and bear away on their angry waves the accumulated wealth of years of toil and hardship. They, however, gradually flow back to the same old channel and flow on as serenely as ever. But, while the river may not be turned aside, it may dry up and leave nothing behind but the withered branch and the unsightly rock, to howl in the abyss-sweeping wind, the sad tale of departed glory. As with rivers, so with nations.

Fellow citizens, I shall not presume to dwell at length on the associations that cluster about this day. The simple story of it is, that seventy-six years ago the people of this country were British subjects. The style and title of your "sovereign people" (in which you now glory) was not then born. You were under the British Crown. Your fathers esteemed the English government as the home government, and England as the fatherland. This home government, you know, although a considerable distance from your home, did, in the exercise of its parental prerogatives, impose upon its colonial children such restraints, burdens and limitations as, in its mature judgment, it deemed wise, right and proper.

★ ★ ★

Feeling themselves harshly and unjustly treated by the home government, your fathers, like men of honesty and men of spirit, earnestly sought redress. They petitioned and remonstrated; they did so in a decorous, respectful and loyal manner. Their conduct was wholly unexceptionable. This, however, did not answer the purpose. They saw themselves treated with sovereign indifference, coldness and scorn. Yet they persevered. They were not the men to look back.

★ ★ ★

Citizens, your fathers . . . succeeded; and today you reap the fruits of their success. The freedom gained is yours; and you, therefore, may properly celebrate this anniversary. The Fourth of July is the first great fact in your nation's history—the very ringbolt in the chain of your yet undeveloped destiny.

Pride and patriotism, not less than gratitude, prompt you to celebrate and to hold it in perpetual remembrance. I have said that the Declaration of Independence is the ringbolt to the chain of your nation's destiny; so, indeed, I regard it. The principles contained in that instrument are saving principles. Stand by those principles, be true to them on all occasions, in all places, against all foes, and at whatever cost.

★ ★ ★

[The fathers of this republic] were peace men, but they preferred revolution to peaceful submission to bondage. They were quiet men; but they did not shrink from agitating against oppression. They showed forbearance, but that they knew its limits. They believed in order, but not in the order of tyranny. With them, nothing was "settled" that was not right. With them, justice, liberty and humanity were "final," not slavery and oppression. You may well cherish the memory of such men. They were great in their day and generation. Their solid manhood stands out the more as we contrast it with these degenerate times.

★ ★ ★

Fellow citizens, pardon me, allow me to ask, why am I called upon to speak here today? What have I, or those I represent, to do with your national independence? Are the great principles of political freedom and of natural justice, embodied in that Declaration of Independence, extended to us? and am I, therefore, called upon to bring our humble offering to the national altar and to confess the benefits and express devout gratitude for the blessings resulting from your independence to us?

★ ★ ★

But such is not the state of the case. I say it with a sad sense of the disparity between us. I am not included within the pale of this glorious anniversary! Your high independence only reveals the immeasurable distance between us. The blessings in which you, this day, rejoice, are not enjoyed in common. The rich inheritance of justice, liberty, prosperity and independence, bequeathed by your fathers, is shared by you, not by me. The sunlight that brought light and healing to you, has brought stripes and death to me. This Fourth of July is *yours*, not *mine. You* may rejoice, *I* must mourn.

★ ★ ★

Fellow citizens, above your national, tumultuous joy I hear the mournful wail of millions! whose chains, heavy and grievous yesterday, are today rendered more intolerable by the jubilee shouts that reach them. If I do forget, if I do not faithfully remember those bleeding children of sorrow this day, "may my right hand forget her cunning, and may my tongue cleave to the roof of my mouth!" To forget them, to pass lightly over their wrongs and to chime in with the popular theme would be treason most scandalous and shocking and would make me a reproach before God and the world. My subject, then, fellow citizens, is American slavery. I shall see this day and its popular characteristics from the slave's point of view. Standing there identified with the American bondman, making his wrongs mine, I do not hesitate to declare, with all my soul, that the character and conduct of this nation never looked blacker to me than on this Fourth of July. Whether we turn to the declarations of the past or to the professions of the present, the conduct of the nation seems equally hideous and revolting. America is false to the past, false to the present, and solemnly binds herself to be false to the future.

★ ★ ★

For the present, it is enough to affirm the equal manhood of the Negro race. It is not astonishing that, while we are plowing, planting and reaping, using all kinds of mechanical tools, erecting houses, constructing bridges, building ships, working in metals of brass, iron, copper, silver and gold; that, while we are reading, writing and ciphering, acting as clerks, merchants and secretaries, having among us lawyers, doctors, ministers, poets, authors, editors, orators and teachers; that, while we are engaged in all manner of enterprises common to other men, digging gold in California, capturing the whale in the Pacific, feeding sheep and cattle on the hillside, living, moving, acting, thinking, planning, living in families as husbands, wives and children, and, above all, confessing and worshiping the Christian's God and looking hopefully for life and immortality beyond the grave, we are called upon to prove that we are men!

Would you have me argue that man is entitled to liberty? that he is the rightful owner of his own body? You have already declared it. Must I argue the wrongfulness of slavery? Is that a question for republicans? Is it to be settled by the rules of logic and argumentation, as a matter beset with great difficulty, involving a doubtful application of the principle of justice, hard to be understood? How should I look today, in the presence of Americans, dividing and subdividing a discourse, to show that men have a natural right to freedom, speaking of it relatively and positively, negatively and affirmatively? To do so would be to make myself ridiculous and to offer an insult to your understanding. There is not a man beneath the canopy of heaven that does not know that slavery is wrong *for him.*

★ ★ ★

What, to the American slave, is your Fourth of July? I answer: a day that reveals to him, more than all other days in the year, the gross injustice and cruelty to which he is the constant victim. To him, your celebration is a sham; your boasted liberty an unholy license; your national greatness swelling vanity; your sounds of rejoicing are empty and heartless; your denunciation of tyrants brass-fronted impudence; your shouts of liberty and equality hollow mockery; your prayers and hymns, your sermons and thanksgivings, with all your religious parade and solemnity, are to Him mere bombast, fraud, deception, impiety and hypocrisy—a thin veil to cover up crimes which would disgrace a nation of savages. There is not a nation on the earth guilty of practices more shocking and bloody than are the people of the United States at this very hour.

Go where you may, search where you will, roam through all the monarchies and despotisms of the Old World, travel through South America, search out every abuse, and when you have found the last, lay your facts by the side of the everyday practices of this nation, and you will say with me, that, for revolting barbarity and shameless hypocrisy, America reigns without a rival.

★ ★ ★

Americans! your republican politics, not less than your republican religion, are flagrantly inconsistent. You boast of your love of liberty, your superior civilization and your pure Christianity, while the whole political power of the nation (as embodied in the two great political parties) is solemnly pledged to support and perpetuate the enslavement of three millions of your countrymen. You hurl your anathemas at the crowned-headed tyrants of Russia and Austria and pride yourselves on your democratic institutions, while you yourselves consent to be the mere *tools* and *bodyguards* of the tyrants of Virginia and Carolina. You invite to your shores fugitives of oppression from abroad, honor them with banquets, greet them with ovations, cheer them, toast them, salute them, protect them, and pour out your money to them like water; but the fugitives from your own land you advertise, hunt, arrest, shoot and kill. You glory in your refinement and your universal education; yet you maintain a system as barbarous and dreadful as ever stained the character of a nation—a system begun in avarice, supported in pride, and perpetuated in cruelty. You shed tears over fallen Hungary, and make the sad story of her wrongs the theme of your poets, statesmen and orators, till your gallant sons are ready to fly to arms to vindicate her cause against the oppressor;* but, in regard to the ten thousand wrongs of the American slave, you would enforce the strictest silence and would hail him as an enemy of the nation who dares to make those wrongs the subject of public discourse! You are all on fire at the mention of liberty for France or for Ireland, but are as cold as an iceberg at the thought of liberty for the enslaved of America. You discourse eloquently on the dignity of labor; yet, you sustain a system which, in its very essence, casts a stigma upon labor. You can bare your bosom to the storm of British artillery to throw off a three-penny tax on tea, and yet wring the last hard-earned farthing from the grasp of the black laborers of your country. You profess to believe "that of one blood God made all nations of men to dwell on the face of all the earth"† and hath commanded all men, everywhere, to love one another; yet you notoriously hate (and glory in your hatred) all men whose skins are not colored like your own. You declare before the world, and are understood by the world to declare, that you "*hold these truths to be self-evident, that all men are created equal; and are endowed by their Creator with certain unalienable rights; and that among these are, life, liberty and the pursuit of happiness*"; and yet, you hold securely, in a bondage which, according to your own Thomas Jefferson, "*is worse than ages of that which your fathers rose in rebellion to oppose,*" *a seventh part* of the inhabitants of your country.

Fellow citizens, I will not enlarge further on your national inconsistencies. The existence of slavery in this country brands your republicanism as a sham, your humanity as a base pretense, and your Christianity as a lie. It destroys your moral power abroad; it corrupts your politicians at home. It saps the foundation of religion; it makes your name a hissing and a byword to a mocking earth. It is the antagonistic force in your government, the only thing that seriously disturbs and endangers your union. It fetters your progress; it is the enemy of improvement; the deadly foe of education; it fosters pride; it breeds insolence; it promotes vice; it shelters crime; it is a curse to the earth that supports it; and yet you cling to it as if it were the sheet anchor of all your hopes.

★ ★ ★

Allow me to say, in conclusion, notwithstanding the dark picture I have this day presented, of the state of the nation, I do not despair of this country. There are forces in operation which must inevitably work the downfall of slavery.

★ ★ ★

---

*The fledgling Hungarian republic was invaded by Austria and Russia in 1849.
†Acts 17:26.

THE GETTYSBURG ADDRESS (1863)

Four score and seven years ago our fathers brought forth on this continent, a new nation, conceived in Liberty, and dedicated to the proposition that all men are created equal.

Now we are engaged in a great civil war, testing whether that nation, or any nation so conceived and so dedicated, can long endure. We are met on a great battle field of that war. We have come to dedicate a portion of that field, as a final resting place for those who here gave their lives that that nation might live. It is altogether fitting and proper that we should do this.

But, in a larger sense, we can not dedicate—we can not consecrate—we can not hallow—this ground. The brave men, living and dead, who struggled here, have consecrated it, far above our poor power to add or detract. The world will little note, nor long remember what we say here, but it can never forget what they did here. It is for us the living, rather, to be dedicated here to the unfinished work which they who fought here have thus far so nobly advanced. It is rather for us to be here dedicated to the great task remaining before us—that from these honored dead we take increased devotion to that cause for which they gave the last full measure of devotion—that we here highly resolve that these dead shall not have died in vain—that this nation, under God, shall have a new birth of freedom—and that government of the people, by the people, for the people, shall not perish from the earth.

Abraham Lincoln
November 19, 1863

ABRAHAM LINCOLN'S SECOND INAUGURAL ADDRESS (1865)

Fellow Countrymen:

At this second appearing to take the oath of the presidential office, there is less occasion for an extended address than there was at the first. Then a statement, somewhat in detail, of a course to be pursued, seemed fitting and proper. Now, at the expiration of four years, during which public declarations have been constantly called forth on every point and phase of the great contest which still absorbs the attention, and engrosses the energies of the nation, little that is new could be presented. The progress of our arms, upon which all else chiefly depends, is as well known to the public as to myself; and it is, I trust, reasonably satisfactory and encouraging to all. With high hope for the future, no prediction in regard to it is ventured.

On the occasion corresponding to this four years ago, all thoughts were anxiously directed to an impending civil war. All dreaded it—all sought to avert it. While the inaugural address was being delivered from this place, devoted altogether to *saving* the Union without war, insurgent agents were in the city seeking to *destroy* it without war—seeking to dissolve the Union, and divide effects, by negotiation. Both parties deprecated war; but one of them would *make* war rather than let the nation survive; and the other would *accept* war rather than let it perish. And the war came.

One eighth of the whole population were colored slaves, not distributed generally over the Union, but localized in the southern part of it. These slaves constituted a peculiar and powerful interest. All knew that this interest was, somehow, the cause of the war. To strengthen, perpetuate, and extend this interest was the object for which the insurgents would rend the Union, even by war; while the government claimed no right to do more than to restrict the territorial enlargement of it. Neither party expected for the war, the magnitude, or the duration, which it has already attained. Neither anticipated that the *cause* of the conflict might cease with, or even before, the conflict itself should cease. Each looked for an easier triumph, and a result less fundamental and astounding. Both read the same Bible, and pray to the same God; and each invokes His aid against the other. It may seem strange that any men should dare to ask a just God's assistance in wringing their bread from the sweat of other men's faces; but let us judge not that we be not judged. The prayers of both could not be answered; that of neither has been answered fully. The Almighty has His own purposes. "Woe unto the world because of offences! for it must needs be that offences come; but woe to that man by whom the offence cometh." If we shall suppose that American slavery is one of those offences which, in the providence of God, must needs come, but which, having continued through His appointed time, He now wills to remove, and that He gives to both North and South, this terrible war, as the woe due to those by whom the offence came, shall we discern therein any departure from those divine attributes which the believers in a living God always ascribe to Him? Fondly do we hope, fervently do we pray—that this mighty scourge of war may speedily pass away. Yet, if God wills that it continue until all the wealth piled by the bondsman's two hundred and fifty years of unrequited toil shall be sunk, and until every drop of blood drawn with the lash shall be paid by another drawn with the sword, as was said three thousand years ago, so still it must be said "the judgments of the Lord are true and righteous altogether."

With malice toward none; with charity for all; with firmness in the right as God gives us to see the right, let us strive on to finish the work we are in; to bind up the nation's wounds; to care for him who shall have borne the battle and for his widow and his orphan, to do all which may achieve and cherish a just and a lasting peace, among ourselves and with all nations.

THE POPULIST PLATFORM OF 1892

Assembled upon the 116th anniversary of the Declaration of Independence, the People's Party of America, in their first national convention, invoking upon their action the blessing of Almighty God, puts forth in the name and on behalf of the people of this country, the following preamble and declaration of principles:

PREAMBLE

The conditions which surround us best justify our co-operation; we meet in the midst of a nation brought to the verge of moral, political, and material ruin. Corruption dominates the ballot-box, the Legislatures, the Congress, and touches even the ermine of the bench. The people are demoralized; most of the States have been compelled to isolate the voters at the polling places to prevent universal intimidation and bribery. The newspapers are largely subsidized or muzzled, public opinion silenced, business prostrated, homes covered with mortgages, labor impoverished, and the land concentrating in the hands of the capitalists. The urban workmen are denied the right to organize for self-protection, imported pauperized labor beats down their wages, a hireling standing army, unrecognized by our laws, is established to shoot them down, and they are rapidly degenerating into European conditions. The fruits of the toil of millions are boldly stolen to build up the fortunes for a few, unprecedented in the history of mankind; and the possessors of these, in turn, despise the Republic and endanger liberty. From the same prolific womb of governmental injustice we breed the two great classes—tramps and millionaires.

The national power to create money is appropriated to enrich bondholders; a vast public debt, payable in legal tender currency, has been funded into gold-bearing bonds, thereby adding millions to the burdens of the people. Silver, which has been accepted as coin since the dawn of history, has been demonetized to add to the purchasing power of gold by decreasing the value of all forms of property as well as human labor, and the supply of currency is purposely abridged to fatten usurers, bankrupt enterprise, and enslave industry. A vast conspiracy against mankind has been organized on two continents, and it is rapidly taking possession of the world. If not met and overthrown at once it forebodes terrible social convulsions, the destruction of civilization, or the establishment of an absolute despotism.

We have witnessed for more than a quarter of a century the struggles of the two great political parties for power and plunder, while grievous wrongs have been inflicted upon the suffering people. We charge that the controlling influences dominating both these parties have permitted the existing dreadful conditions to develop without serious effort to prevent or restrain them. Neither do they now promise us any substantial reform. They have agreed together to ignore in the coming campaign every issue but one. They propose to drown the outcries of a plundered people with the uproar of a sham battle over the tariff, so that capitalists, corporations, national banks, rings, trusts, watered stock, the demonetization of silver, and the oppressions of the usurers may all be lost sight of. They propose to sacrifice our homes, lives, and children on the altar of mammon; to destroy the multitude in order to secure corruption funds from the millionaires.

Assembled on the anniversary of the birthday of the nation, and filled with the spirit of the grand general and chief who established our independence, we seek to restore the government of the Republic to the hands of "the plain people," with which class it originated. We assert our purpose to be identical with the purposes of the National Constitution, "to form a more perfect union and establish justice, insure domestic tranquility, provide for the common defense, promote the general welfare, and secure the blessings of liberty for ourselves and our posterity." We declare that this Republic can only endure as a free government while built upon the love of the whole people for each other and for the nation; that it cannot be pinned together by bayonets; that the civil war is over, and that every passion and resentment which grew out of it must die with it; and that we must be in fact, as we are in name, one united brotherhood of free men.

Our country finds itself confronted by conditions for which there is no precedent in the history of the world; our annual agricultural productions amount to billions of dollars in value, which must, within a few weeks or months, be exchanged for billions of dollars of commodities consumed in their production; the existing currency supply is wholly inadequate to make this exchange; the results are falling prices, the formation of combines and rings, the impoverishment of the producing class. We pledge ourselves, if given power, we will labor to correct these evils by wise and reasonable legislation, in accordance with the terms of our platform. We believe that the power of government—in other words, of the people—should be expanded (as in the case of the postal service) as rapidly and as far as the good sense of an intelligent people and the teaching of experience shall justify, to the end that oppression, injustice, and poverty shall eventually cease in the land.

While our sympathies as a party of reform are naturally upon the side of every proposition which will tend to make men intelligent, virtuous, and temperate, we nevertheless regard these questions—important as they are—as secondary to the great issues now pressing for solution, and upon which not only our individual prosperity but the very existence of free institutions depend; and we ask all men to first help us to determine whether we are to have a republic to administer before we differ as to the conditions upon which it is to be administered, believing that the forces of reform this day organized will never cease to move forward until every wrong is remedied, and equal rights and equal privileges securely established for all the men and women of this country.

PLATFORM

We declare, therefore—

First.—That the union of the labor forces of the United States this day consummated shall be permanent and perpetual; may its spirit enter into all hearts for the salvation of the Republic and the uplifting of mankind!

Second.—Wealth belongs to him who creates it, and every dollar taken from industry without an equivalent is robbery. "If any will not work, neither shall he eat." The interests of rural and civic labor are the same; their enemies are identical.

Third.—We believe that the time has come when the railroad corporations will either own the people or the people must own the railroads; and, should the government enter upon the work of owning and managing all railroads, we should favor an amendment to the Constitution by which all persons engaged in the government service shall be placed under a civil-service regulation of the most rigid character, so as to prevent the increase of the power of the national administration by the use of such additional government employees.

FINANCE.—We demand a national currency, safe, sound, and flexible, issued by the general government only, a full legal tender for all debts, public and private, and that without the use of banking corporations, a just, equitable, and efficient means of distribution direct to the people, at a tax not to exceed two per cent per annum, to be provided as set forth in the sub-treasury plan of the Farmers' Alliance, or a better system; also by payments in discharge of its obligations for public improvements.

1. We demand free and unlimited coinage of silver and gold at the present legal ratio of 16 to 1.

2. We demand that the amount of circulating medium be speedily increased to not less than $50 per capita.

3. We demand a graduated income tax.

4. We believe that the money of the country should be kept as much as possible in the hands of the people, and hence we demand that all State and national revenues shall be limited to the necessary expenses of the government, economically and honestly administered.

5. We demand that postal savings banks be established by the government for the safe deposit of the earnings of the people and to facilitate exchange.

TRANSPORTATION.—Transportation being a means of exchange and a public necessity, the government should own and operate the railroads in the interest of the people. The telegraph and telephone, like the post-office system, being a necessity for the transmission of news, should be owned and operated by the government in the interest of the people.

LAND.—The land, including all the natural sources of wealth, is the heritage of the people, and should not be monopolized for speculative purposes, and alien ownership of land should be prohibited. All land now held by railroads and other corporations in excess of their actual needs, and all lands now owned by aliens should be reclaimed by the government and held for actual settlers only.

EXPRESSION OF SENTIMENTS

Your committee on Platform and Resolutions beg leave unanimously to report the following:

Whereas, Other questions have been presented for our consideration, we hereby submit the following, not as a part of the Platform of the People's Party, but as resolutions expressive of the sentiment of this Convention:

1. *Resolved*, That we demand a free ballot and a fair count in all elections, and pledge ourselves to secure it to every legal voter without federal intervention, through the adoption by the States of the unperverted Australian or secret ballot system.

2. *Resolved*, That the revenue derived from a graduated income tax should be applied to the reduction of the burden of taxation now levied upon the domestic industries of this country.

3. *Resolved*, That we pledge our support to fair and liberal pensions to ex-Union soldiers and sailors.

4. *Resolved*, That we condemn the fallacy of protecting American labor under the present system, which opens our ports to the pauper and criminal classes of the world, and crowds out our wage-earners; and we denounce the present ineffective laws against contract labor, and demand the further restriction of undesirable emigration.

5. *Resolved*, that we cordially sympathize with the efforts of organized workingmen to shorten the hours of labor, and demand a rigid enforcement of the existing eight-hour law on Government work, and ask that a penalty clause be added to the said law.

6. *Resolved*, That we regard the maintenance of a large standing army of mercenaries, known as the Pinkerton system, as a menace to our liberties, and we demand its abolition; and we condemn the recent invasion of the Territory of Wyoming by the hired assassins of plutocracy, assisted by federal officers.

7. *Resolved*, That we commend to the favorable consideration of the people and the reform press the legislative system known as the initiative and referendum.

8. *Resolved*, That we favor a constitutional provision limiting the office of President and Vice-President to one term, and providing for the election of Senators of the United States by a direct vote of the people.

9. *Resolved*, That we oppose any subsidy or national aid to any private corporation for any purpose.

10. *Resolved*, That this convention sympathizes with the Knights of Labor and their righteous contest with the tyrannical combine of clothing manufacturers of Rochester, and declare it to be the duty of all who hate tyranny and oppression to refuse to purchase the goods made by the said manufacturers, or to patronize any merchants who sell such goods.

FRANKLIN D. ROOSEVELT'S FIRST INAUGURAL ADDRESS (1933)

I am certain that my fellow Americans expect that on my induction into the Presidency I will address them with a candor and a decision which the present situation of our Nation impels. This is preeminently the time to speak the truth, the whole truth, frankly and boldly. Nor need we shrink from honestly facing conditions in our country today. This great Nation will endure as it has endured, will revive and will prosper. So, first of all, let me assert my firm belief that the only thing we have to fear is fear itself—nameless, unreasoning, unjustified terror which paralyzes needed efforts to convert retreat into advance. In every dark hour of our national life a leadership of frankness and vigor has met with that understanding and support of the people themselves which is essential to victory. I am convinced that you will again give that support to leadership in these critical days.

In such a spirit on my part and on yours we face our common difficulties. They concern, thank God, only material things. Values have shrunken to fantastic levels; taxes have risen; our ability to pay has fallen; government of all kinds is faced by serious curtailment of income; the means of exchange are frozen in the currents of trade; the withered leaves of industrial enterprise lie on every side; farmers find no markets for their produce; the savings of many years in thousands of families are gone.

More important, a host of unemployed citizens face the grim problem of existence, and an equally great number toil with little return. Only a foolish optimist can deny the dark realities of the moment.

Yet our distress comes from no failure of substance. We are stricken by no plague of locusts. Compared with the perils which our forefathers conquered because they believed and were not afraid, we have still much to be thankful for. Nature still offers her bounty and human efforts have multiplied it. Plenty is at our doorstep, but a generous use of it languishes in the very sight of the supply. Primarily this is because the rulers of the exchange of mankind's goods have failed, through their own stubbornness and their own incompetence, have admitted their failure, and abdicated. Practices of the unscrupulous money changers stand indicted in the court of public opinion, rejected by the hearts and minds of men.

True they have tried, but their efforts have been cast in the pattern of an outworn tradition. Faced by failure of credit they have proposed only the lending of more money. Stripped of the lure of profit by which to induce our people to follow their false leadership, they have resorted to exhortations, pleading tearfully for restored confidence. They know only the rules of a generation of self-seekers. They have no vision, and when there is no vision the people perish.

The money changers have fled from their high seats in the temple of our civilization. We may now restore that temple to the ancient truths. The measure of the restoration lies in the extent to which we apply social values more noble than mere monetary profit.

Happiness lies not in the mere possession of money; it lies in the joy of achievement, in the thrill of creative effort. The joy and moral stimulation of work no longer must be forgotten in the mad chase of evanescent profits. These dark days will be worth all they cost us if they teach us that our true destiny is not to be ministered unto but to minister to ourselves and to our fellow men.

Recognition of the falsity of material wealth as the standard of success goes hand in hand with the abandonment of the false belief that public office and high political position are to be valued only by the standards of pride of place and personal profit; and there must be an end to a conduct in banking and in business which too often has given to a sacred trust the likeness of callous and selfish wrongdoing. Small wonder that confidence languishes, for it thrives only on honesty, on honor, on the sacredness of obligations, on faithful protection, on unselfish performance; without them it cannot live.

Restoration calls, however, not for changes in ethics alone. This Nation asks for action, and action now.

Our greatest primary task is to put people to work. This is no unsolvable problem if we face it wisely and courageously. It can be accomplished in part by direct recruiting by the Government itself, treating the task as we would treat the emergency of a war, but at the same time, through this employment, accomplishing greatly needed projects to stimulate and reorganize the use of our natural resources.

Hand in hand with this we must frankly recognize the overbalance of population in our industrial centers and, by engaging on a national scale in a redistribution, endeavor to provide a better use of the land for those best fitted for the land. The task can be helped by definite efforts to raise the values of agricultural products and with this the power to purchase the output of our cities. It can be helped by preventing realistically the tragedy of the growing loss through foreclosure of our small homes and our farms. It can be helped by insistence that the Federal, State, and local governments act forthwith on the demand that their cost be drastically reduced. It can be helped by the unifying of relief activities which today are often scattered, uneconomical, and unequal. It can be helped by national planning for and supervision of all forms of transportation and of communications and other utilities which have a definitely public character. There are many ways in which it can be helped, but it can never be helped merely by talking about it. We must act and act quickly.

Finally, in our progress toward a resumption of work we require two safeguards against a return of the evils of the old order; there must be a strict supervision of all banking and credits and investments; there must be an end to speculation with other people's money, and there must be provision for an adequate but sound currency.

There are the lines of attack. I shall presently urge upon a new Congress, in special session, detailed measures for their fulfillment, and I shall seek the immediate assistance of the several States.

Through this program of action we address ourselves to putting our own national house in order and making income balance outgo. Our international trade relations, though vastly important, are in point of time and necessity secondary to the establishment of a sound national economy. I favor as a practical policy the putting of first things first. I shall spare no effort to restore world trade by international economic readjustment, but the emergency at home cannot wait on that accomplishment.

The basic thought that guides these specific means of national recovery is not narrowly nationalistic. It is the insistence, as a first consideration, upon the interdependence of the various elements in all parts of the United States—a recognition of the old and permanently important manifestation of the American spirit of the pioneer. It is the way to recovery. It is the immediate way. It is the strongest assurance that the recovery will endure.

In the field of world policy I would dedicate this Nation to the policy of the good neighbor—the neighbor who resolutely respects himself and, because he does so, respects the rights of others—the neighbor who respects his obligations and respects the sanctity of his agreements in and with a world of neighbors.

If I read the temper of our people correctly, we now realize as we have never realized before our interdependence on each other; that we cannot merely take but we must give as well; that if we are to go forward, we must move as a trained and loyal army willing to sacrifice for the good of a common discipline, because without such discipline no progress is made, no leadership becomes effective. We are, I know, ready and willing to submit our lives and property to such discipline, because it makes possible a leadership which aims at a larger good. This I propose to offer, pledging that the larger purposes will bind upon us all as a sacred obligation with a unity of duty hitherto evoked only in time of armed strife.

With this pledge taken, I assume unhesitatingly the leadership of this great army of our people dedicated to a disciplined attack upon our common problems.

Action in this image and to this end is feasible under the form of government which we have inherited from our ancestors. Our Constitution is so simple and practical that it is possible always to meet extraordinary needs by changes in emphasis and arrangement without loss of essential form. That is why our constitutional system has proved itself the most superbly enduring political mechanism the modern world has produced. It has met every stress of vast expansion of territory, of foreign wars, of bitter internal strife, of world relations.

It is to be hoped that the normal balance of executive and legislative authority may be wholly adequate to meet the unprecedented task before us. But it may be that an unprecedented demand and need for undelayed action may call for temporary departure from that normal balance of public procedure.

I am prepared under my constitutional duty to recommend the measures that a stricken nation in the midst of a stricken world may require. These measures, or such other measures as the Congress may build out of its experience and wisdom, I shall seek, within my constitutional authority, to bring to speedy adoption.

But in the event that the Congress shall fail to take one of these two courses, and in the event that the national emergency is still critical, I shall not evade the clear course of duty that will then confront me. I shall ask the Congress for the one remaining instrument to meet the crisis—broad Executive power to wage a war against the emergency, as great as the power that would be given to me if we were in fact invaded by a foreign foe.

For the trust reposed in me I will return the courage and the devotion that befit the time. I can do no less.

We face the arduous days that lie before us in the warm courage of national unity; with the clear consciousness of seeking old and precious moral values; with the clean satisfaction that comes from the stern performance of duty by old and young alike. We aim at the assurance of a rounded and permanent national life.

We do not distrust the future of essential democracy. The people of the United States have not failed. In their need they have registered a mandate that they want direct, vigorous action. They have asked for discipline and direction under leadership. They have made me the present instrument of their wishes. In the spirit of the gift I take it.

In this dedication of a Nation we humbly ask the blessing of God. May He protect each and every one of us. May He guide me in the days to come.

FROM THE PROGRAM FOR THE MARCH ON WASHINGTON FOR JOBS AND FREEDOM (1963)

WHAT WE DEMAND*

1. Comprehensive and effective *civil rights legislation* from the present Congress—without compromise or filibuster—to guarantee all Americans

> access to all public accommodations
> decent housing
> adequate and integrated education
> the right to vote

2. Withholding of Federal funds from all programs in which discrimination exists.

3. *Desegregation of all school districts in 1963.*

4. Enforcement of the *Fourteenth Amendment*—reducing Congressional representation of states where citizens are disfranchised.

5. A new *Executive Order* banning discrimination in all housing supported by federal funds.

6. Authority for the Attorney General to institute *injunctive suits* when any constitutional right is violated.

7. A massive federal program to train and place all unemployed workers—Negro and white—on meaningful and dignified jobs at decent wages.

8. A national *minimum wage* act that will give all Americans a decent standard of living. (Government surveys show that anything less than $2.00 an hour fails to do this.)

9. A broadened *Fair Labor Standards Act* to include all areas of employment which are presently excluded.

10. A federal *Fair Employment Practices Act* barring discrimination by federal, state, and municipal governments, and by employers, contractors, employment agencies, and trade unions.

*Support of the March does not necessarily indicate endorsement of every demand listed. Some organizations have not had an opportunity to take an official position on all of the demands advocated here.

Senator Hatfield, Mr. Chief Justice, Mr. President, Vice President Bush, Vice President Mondale, Senator Baker, Speaker O'Neill, Reverend Moomaw, and my fellow citizens:

To a few of us here today this is a solemn and most momentous occasion, and yet in the history of our nation it is a commonplace occurrence. The orderly transfer of authority as called for in the Constitution routinely takes place, as it has for almost two centuries, and few of us stop to think how unique we really are. In the eyes of many in the world, this every-four-year ceremony we accept as normal is nothing less than a miracle.

Mr. President, I want our fellow citizens to know how much you did to carry on this tradition. By your gracious cooperation in the transition process, you have shown a watching world that we are a united people pledged to maintaining a political system which guarantees individual liberty to a greater degree than any other, and I thank you and your people for all your help in maintaining the continuity which is the bulwark of our republic. The business of our nation goes forward. These United States are confronted with an economic affliction of great proportions. We suffer from the longest and one of the worst sustained inflations in our national history. It distorts our economic decisions, penalizes thrift, and crushes the struggling young and the fixed-income elderly alike. It threatens to shatter the lives of millions of our people.

Idle industries have cast workers into unemployment, human misery, and personal indignity. Those who do work are denied a fair return for their labor by a tax system which penalizes successful achievement and keeps us from maintaining full productivity. But great as our tax burden is, it has not kept pace with public spending. For decades we have piled deficit upon deficit, mortgaging our future and our children's future for the temporary convenience of the present. To continue this long trend is to guarantee tremendous social, cultural, political, and economic upheavals.

You and I, as individuals, can, by borrowing, live beyond our means, but for only a limited period of time. Why, then, should we think that collectively, as a nation, we're not bound by that same limitation? We must act today in order to preserve tomorrow. And let there be no misunderstanding: We are going to begin to act, beginning today. The economic ills we suffer have come upon us over several decades. They will not go away in days, weeks, or months, but they will go away. They will go away because we as Americans have the capacity now, as we've had in the past, to do whatever needs to be done to preserve this last and greatest bastion of freedom.

In this present crisis, government is not the solution to our problem; government is the problem. From time to time we've been tempted to believe that society has become too complex to be managed by self-rule, that government by an elite group is superior to government for, by, and of the people. Well, if no one among us is capable of governing himself, then who among us has the capacity to govern someone else? All of us together, in and out of government, must bear the burden. The solutions we seek must be equitable, with no one group singled out to pay a higher price.

We hear much of special interest groups. Well, our concern must be for a special interest group that has been too long neglected. It knows no sectional boundaries or ethnic and racial divisions, and it crosses political party lines. It is made up of men and women who raise our food, patrol our streets, man our mines and factories, teach our children, keep our homes, and heal us when we're sick—professionals, industrialists, shopkeepers, clerks, cabbies, and truck drivers. They are, in short, "we the people," this breed called Americans.

Well, this administration's objective will be a healthy, vigorous, growing economy that provides equal opportunities for all Americans, with no barriers born of bigotry or discrimination. Putting America back to work means putting all Americans back to work. Ending inflation means freeing all Americans from the terror of runaway living costs. All must share in the productive work of this "new beginning," and all must share in the bounty of a revived economy. With the idealism and fair play which are the core of our system and our strength, we can have a strong and prosperous America, at peace with itself and the world.

So, as we begin, let us take inventory. We are a nation that has a government—not the other way around. And this makes us special among the nations of the Earth. Our government has no power except that granted it by the people. It is time to check and reverse the growth of government, which shows signs of having grown beyond the consent of the governed.

It is my intention to curb the size and influence of the federal establishment and to demand recognition of the distinction between the powers granted to the federal government and those reserved to the states or to the people. All of us need to be reminded that the federal government did not create the states; the states created the federal government.

Now, so there will be no misunderstanding, it's not my intention to do away with government. It is rather to make it work—work with us, not over us; to stand by our side, not ride on our back. Government can and must provide opportunity, not smother it; foster productivity, not stifle it.

If we look to the answer as to why for so many years we achieved so much, prospered as no other people on earth, it was because here in this land we unleashed the energy and individual genius of man to a greater extent than has ever been done before. Freedom and the dignity of the individual have been more available and assured here than in any other place on earth. The price for this freedom at times has been high, but we have never been unwilling to pay the price.

It is no coincidence that our present troubles parallel and are proportionate to the intervention and intrusion in our lives that result from unnecessary and excessive growth of government. It is time for us to realize that we're too great a nation to limit ourselves to small dreams. We're not, as some would have us believe, doomed to an inevitable decline. I do not believe in a fate that will fall on us no matter what we do. I do believe in a fate that will fall on us if we do nothing. So, with all the creative energy at our command, let us begin an era of national renewal. Let us renew our determination, our courage, and our strength. And let us renew our faith and our hope.

We have every right to dream heroic dreams. Those who say that we're in a time when there are no heroes, they just don't know where to look. You can see heroes every day going in and out of factory gates. Others, a handful in number, produce enough food to feed all of us and then the world beyond. You meet heroes across a counter, and they're on both sides of that counter. There are entrepreneurs with faith in themselves and faith in an idea who create new jobs, new wealth and opportunity. They're individuals and families whose taxes support the

government and whose voluntary gifts support church, charity, culture, art, and education. Their patriotism is quiet, but deep. Their values sustain our national life.

Now, I have used the words "they" and "their" in speaking of these heroes. I could say "you" and "your," because I'm addressing the heroes of whom I speak—you, the citizens of this blessed land. Your dreams, your hopes, your goals are going to be the dreams, the hopes, and the goals of this administration, so help me God.

We shall reflect the compassion that is so much a part of your makeup. How can we love our country and not love our countrymen; and loving them, reach out a hand when they fall, heal them when they're sick, and provide opportunity to make them self-sufficient so they will be equal in fact and not just in theory?

Can we solve the problems confronting us? Well, the answer is an unequivocal and emphatic "yes." To paraphrase Winston Churchill, I did not take the oath I've just taken with the intention of presiding over the dissolution of the world's strongest economy.

In the days ahead I will propose removing the roadblocks that have slowed our economy and reduced productivity. Steps will be taken aimed at restoring the balance between the various levels of government. Progress may be slow, measured in inches and feet, not miles, but we will progress. It is time to reawaken this industrial giant, to get government back within its means, and to lighten our punitive tax burden. And these will be our first priorities, and on these principles there will be no compromise.

On the eve of our struggle for independence a man who might have been one of the greatest among the Founding Fathers, Dr. Joseph Warren, president of the Massachusetts Congress, said to his fellow Americans, "Our country is in danger, but not to be despaired of . . . . On you depend the fortunes of America. You are to decide the important questions upon which rests the happiness and the liberty of millions yet unborn. Act worthy of yourselves." Well, I believe we, the Americans of today, are ready to act worthy of ourselves, ready to do what must be done to ensure happiness and liberty for ourselves, our children, and our children's children. And as we renew ourselves here in our own land, we will be seen as having greater strength throughout the world. We will again be the exemplar of freedom and a beacon of hope for those who do not now have freedom.

To those neighbors and allies who share our freedom, we will strengthen our historic ties and assure them of our support and firm commitment. We will match loyalty with loyalty. We will strive for mutually beneficial relations. We will not use our friendship to impose on their sovereignty, for our own sovereignty is not for sale. As for the enemies of freedom, those who are potential adversaries, they will be reminded that peace is the highest aspiration of the American people. We will negotiate for it, sacrifice for it; we will not surrender for it, now or ever.

Our forbearance should never be misunderstood. Our reluctance for conflict should not be misjudged as a failure of will. When action is required to preserve our national security, we will act. We will maintain sufficient strength to prevail if need be, knowing that if we do so we have the best chance of never having to use that strength. Above all, we must realize that no arsenal or no weapon in the arsenals of the world is so formidable as the will and moral courage of free men and women. It is a weapon our adversaries in today's world do not have. It is a weapon that we as Americans do have. Let that be understood by those who practice terrorism and prey upon their neighbors. I'm told that tens of thousands of prayer meetings are being held on this day, and for that I'm deeply grateful. We are a nation under God, and I believe God intended for us to be free. It would be fitting and good, I think, if on each Inaugural Day in future years it should be declared a day of prayer.

This is the first time in our history that this ceremony has been held, as you've been told, on the West Front of the Capitol. Standing here, one faces a magnificent vista, opening up on the city's special beauty and history. At the end of this open mall are those shrines to the giants on whose shoulders we stand.

Directly in front of me, the monument to a monumental man, George Washington, father of our country. A man of humility who came to greatness reluctantly. He led Americans out of revolutionary victory into infant nationhood. Off to one side, the stately memorial to Thomas Jefferson. The Declaration of Independence flames with his eloquence. And then, beyond the Reflecting Pool, the dignified columns of the Lincoln Memorial. Whoever would understand in his heart the meaning of America will find it in the life of Abraham Lincoln.

Beyond those monuments to heroism is the Potomac River, and on the far shore the sloping hills of Arlington National Cemetery, with its row upon row of simple white markers bearing crosses and Stars of David. They add up to only a tiny fraction of the price that has been paid for our freedom. Each one of those markers is a monument to the kind of hero I spoke of earlier. Their lives ended in places called Belleau Wood, the Argonne, Omaha Beach, Salerno, and halfway around the world on Guadalcanal, Tarawa, Pork Chop Hill, the Chosin Reservoir, and in a hundred rice paddies and jungles of a place called Vietnam.

Under one such marker lies a young man, Martin Treptow, who left his job in a small town barbershop in 1917 to go to France with the famed Rainbow Division. There, on the western front, he was killed trying to carry a message between battalions under heavy artillery fire.

We're told that on his body was found a diary. On the flyleaf under the heading "My Pledge," he had written these words: "America must win this war. Therefore I will work, I will save, I will sacrifice, I will endure, I will fight cheerfully and do my utmost, as if the issue of the whole struggle depended on me alone."

The crisis we are facing today does not require of us the kind of sacrifice that Martin Treptow and so many thousands of others were called upon to make. It does require, however, our best effort and our willingness to believe in ourselves and to believe in our capacity to perform great deeds, to believe that together with God's help we can and will resolve the problems which now confront us.

And after all, why shouldn't we believe that? We are Americans.

God bless you, and thank you.

BARACK OBAMA'S FIRST INAUGURAL ADDRESS (2009)

My fellow citizens: I stand here today humbled by the task before us, grateful for the trust you've bestowed, mindful of the sacrifices borne by our ancestors.

I thank President Bush for his service to our nation—(*applause*)—as well as the generosity and cooperation he has shown throughout this transition.

Forty-four Americans have now taken the presidential oath. The words have been spoken during rising tides of prosperity and the still waters of peace. Yet, every so often, the oath is taken amidst gathering clouds and raging storms. At these moments, America has carried on not simply because of the skill or vision of those in high office, but because we, the people, have remained faithful to the ideals of our forebears and true to our founding documents.

So it has been: so it must be with this generation of Americans.

That we are in the midst of crisis is now well understood. Our nation is at war against a far-reaching network of violence and hatred. Our economy is badly weakened, a consequence of greed and irresponsibility on the part of some, but also our collective failure to make hard choices and prepare the nation for a new age. Homes have been lost, jobs shed, businesses shuttered. Our health care is too costly, our schools fail too many—and each day brings further evidence that the ways we use energy strengthen our adversaries and threaten our planet.

These are the indicators of crisis, subject to data and statistics. Less measurable, but no less profound, is a sapping of confidence across our land; a nagging fear that America's decline is inevitable, that the next generation must lower its sights.

Today I say to you that the challenges we face are real. They are serious and they are many. They will not be met easily or in a short span of time. But know this America: They will be met. (*Applause*)

On this day, we gather because we have chosen hope over fear, unity of purpose over conflict and discord. On this day, we come to proclaim an end to the petty grievances and false promises, the recriminations and worn-out dogmas that for far too long have strangled our politics. We remain a young nation. But in the words of Scripture, the time has come to set aside childish things. The time has come to reaffirm our enduring spirit; to choose our better history; to carry forward that precious gift, that noble idea passed on from generation to generation; the God-given promise that all are equal, all are free, and all deserve a chance to pursue their full measure of happiness. (*Applause*)

In reaffirming the greatness of our nation we understand that greatness is never a given. It must be earned. Our journey has never been one of short-cuts or settling for less. It has not been the path for the faint-hearted, for those that prefer leisure over work, or seek only the pleasures of riches and fame. Rather, it has been the risk-takers, the doers, the makers of things—some celebrated, but more often men and women obscure in their labor—who have carried us up the long rugged path towards prosperity and freedom.

For us, they packed up their few worldly possessions and traveled across oceans in search of a new life. For us, they toiled in sweatshops, and settled the West, endured the lash of the whip, and plowed the hard earth. For us, they fought and died in places like Concord and Gettysburg, Normandy and Khe Sahn.

Time and again these men and women struggled and sacrificed and worked till their hands were raw so that we might live a better life. They saw America as bigger than the sum of our individual ambitions, greater than all the differences of birth or wealth or faction.

This is the journey we continue today. We remain the most prosperous, powerful nation on Earth. Our workers are no less productive than when this crisis began. Our minds are no less inventive, our goods and services no less needed than they were last week, or last month, or last year. Our capacity remains undiminished. But our time of standing pat, of protecting narrow interests and putting off unpleasant decisions—that time has surely passed. Starting today, we must pick ourselves up, dust ourselves off, and begin again the work of remaking America. (*Applause*)

For everywhere we look, there is work to be done. The state of our economy calls for action, bold and swift. And we will act, not only to create new jobs, but to lay a new foundation for growth. We will build the roads and bridges, the electric grids and digital lines that feed our commerce and bind us together. We'll restore science to its rightful place, and wield technology's wonders to raise health care's quality and lower its cost. We will harness the sun and the winds and the soil to fuel our cars and run our factories. And we will transform our schools and colleges and universities to meet the demands of a new age. All this we can do. All this we will do.

Now, there are some who question the scale of our ambitions, who suggest that our system cannot tolerate too many big plans. Their memories are short, for they have forgotten what this country has already done, what free men and women can achieve when imagination is joined to common purpose, and necessity to courage. What the cynics fail to understand is that the ground has shifted beneath them, that the stale political arguments that have consumed us for so long no longer apply.

The question we ask today is not whether our government is too big or too small, but whether it works—whether it helps families find jobs at a decent wage, care they can afford, a retirement that is dignified. Where the answer is yes, we intend to move forward. Where the answer is no, programs will end. And those of us who manage the public's dollars will be held to account, to spend wisely, reform bad habits, and do our business in the light of day, because only then can we restore the vital trust between a people and their government.

Nor is the question before us whether the market is a force for good or ill. Its power to generate wealth and expand freedom is unmatched. But this crisis has reminded us that without a watchful eye, the market can spin out of control. The nation cannot prosper long when it favors only the prosperous. The success of our economy has always depended not just on the size of our gross domestic product, but on the reach of our prosperity, on the ability to extend opportunity to every willing heart—not out of charity, but because it is the surest route to our common good. (*Applause*)

As for our common defense, we reject as false the choice between our safety and our ideals. Our Founding Fathers—(*applause*)—our Founding Fathers, faced with perils that we can scarcely imagine, drafted a charter to assure the rule of law and the rights of man—a charter expanded by the blood of generations. Those ideals still light the world, and we will not give them up for expedience sake. (*Applause*)

And so, to all the other peoples and governments who are watching today, from the grandest capitals to the small village where my father was born, know that America is a friend of each nation, and every man, woman and child who seeks a future of peace and dignity. And we are ready to lead once more. (*Applause*)

Recall that earlier generations faced down fascism and communism not just with missiles and tanks, but with the sturdy alliances and enduring convictions. They understood that our power alone cannot protect us, nor does it entitle us to do as we please. Instead they knew that our power grows through its prudent use; our security emanates from the justness of our cause, the force of our example, the tempering qualities of humility and restraint.

We are the keepers of this legacy. Guided by these principles once more we can meet those new threats that demand even greater effort, even greater cooperation and understanding between nations. We will begin to responsibly leave Iraq to its people and forge a hard-earned peace in Afghanistan. With old friends and former foes, we'll work tirelessly to lessen the nuclear threat, and roll back the specter of a warming planet.

We will not apologize for our way of life, nor will we waver in its defense. And for those who seek to advance their aims by inducing terror and slaughtering innocents, we say to you now that our spirit is stronger and cannot be broken—you cannot outlast us, and we will defeat you. (*Applause*)

For we know that our patchwork heritage is a strength, not a weakness. We are a nation of Christians and Muslims, Jews and Hindus, and non-believers. We are shaped by every language and culture, drawn from every end of this Earth: and because we have tasted the bitter swill of civil war and segregation, and emerged from that dark chapter stronger and more united, we cannot help but believe that the old hatreds shall someday pass; that the lines of tribe shall soon dissolve; that as the world grows smaller, our common humanity shall reveal itself; and that America must play its role in ushering in a new era of peace.

To the Muslim world, we seek a new way forward, based on mutual interest and mutual respect. To those leaders around the globe who seek to sow conflict, or blame their society's ills on the West, know that your people will judge you on what you can build, not what you destroy. (*Applause*)

To those who cling to power through corruption and deceit and the silencing of dissent, know that you are on the wrong side of history, but that we will extend a hand if you are willing to unclench your fist. (*Applause*)

To the people of poor nations, we pledge to work alongside you to make your farms flourish and let clean waters flow; to nourish starved bodies and feed hungry minds. And to those nations like ours that enjoy relative plenty, we say we can no longer afford indifference to the suffering outside our borders, nor can we consume the world's resources without regard to effect. For the world has changed, and we must change with it.

As we consider the role that unfolds before us, we remember with humble gratitude those brave Americans who at this very hour patrol far-off deserts and distant mountains. They have something to tell us, just as the fallen heroes who lie in Arlington whisper through the ages.

We honor them not only because they are the guardians of our liberty, but because they embody the spirit of service—a willingness to find meaning in something greater than themselves.

And yet at this moment, a moment that will define a generation, it is precisely this spirit that must inhabit us all. For as much as government can do, and must do, it is ultimately the faith and determination of the American people upon which this nation relies. It is the kindness to take in a stranger when the levees break, the selflessness of workers who would rather cut their hours than see a friend lose their job which sees us through our darkest hours. It is the firefighter's courage to storm a stairway filled with smoke, but also a parent's willingness to nurture a child that finally decides our fate.

Our challenges may be new. The instruments with which we meet them may be new. But those values upon which our success depends—honesty and hard work, courage and fair play, tolerance and curiosity, loyalty and patriotism—these things are old. These things are true. They have been the quiet force of progress throughout our history.

What is demanded, then, is a return to these truths. What is required of us now is a new era of responsibility—a recognition on the part of every American that we have duties to ourselves, our nation and the world; duties that we do not grudgingly accept, but rather seize gladly, firm in the knowledge that there is nothing so satisfying to the spirit, so defining of our character than giving our all to a difficult task.

This is the price and the promise of citizenship. This is the source of our confidence—the knowledge that God calls on us to shape an uncertain destiny. This is the meaning of our liberty and our creed, why men and women and children of every race and every faith can join in celebration across this magnificent mall; and why a man whose father less than 60 years ago might not have been served in a local restaurant can now stand before you to take a most sacred oath. (*Applause*)

So let us mark this day with remembrance of who we are and how far we have traveled. In the year of America's birth, in the coldest of months, a small band of patriots huddled by dying campfires on the shores of an icy river. The capital was abandoned. The enemy was advancing. The snow was stained with blood. At the moment when the outcome of our revolution was most in doubt, the father of our nation ordered these words to be read to the people:

"Let it be told to the future world . . . that in the depth of winter, when nothing but hope and virtue could survive . . . that the city and the country, alarmed at one common danger, came forth to meet [it]."

America: In the face of our common dangers, in this winter of our hardship, let us remember these timeless words. With hope and virtue, let us brave once more the icy currents, and endure what storms may come. Let it be said by our children's children that when we were tested we refused to let this journey end, that we did not turn back nor did we falter; and with eyes fixed on the horizon and God's grace upon us, we carried forth that great gift of freedom and delivered it safely to future generations.

Thank you. God bless you. And God bless the United States of America. (*Applause*)

PRESIDENTIAL ELECTIONS

Year	Number of States	Candidates	Parties	Popular Vote	% of Popular Vote	Electoral Vote	% Voter Participation
1789	11	**GEORGE WASHINGTON**	NO PARTY			69	
		John Adams	DESIGNATIONS			34	
		Other candidates				35	
1792	15	**GEORGE WASHINGTON**	NO PARTY			132	
		John Adams	DESIGNATIONS			77	
		George Clinton				50	
		Other candidates				5	
1796	16	**JOHN ADAMS**	FEDERALIST			71	
		Thomas Jefferson	Republican			68	
		Thomas Pinckney	Federalist			59	
		Aaron Burr	Republican			30	
		Other candidates				48	
1800	16	**THOMAS JEFFERSON**	REPUBLICAN			73	
		Aaron Burr	Republican			73	
		John Adams	Federalist			65	
		Charles C. Pinckney	Federalist			64	
		John Jay	Federalist			1	
1804	17	**THOMAS JEFFERSON**	REPUBLICAN			162	
		Charles C. Pinckney	Federalist			14	
1808	17	**JAMES MADISON**	REPUBLICAN			122	
		Charles C. Pinckney	Federalist			47	
		George Clinton	Republican			6	
1812	18	**JAMES MADISON**	REPUBLICAN			128	
		DeWitt Clinton	Federalist			89	

Year	Number of States	Candidates	Parties	Popular Vote	% of Popular Vote	Electoral Vote	% Voter Participation
1816	19	**JAMES MONROE** Rufus King	REPUBLICAN Federalist			183 34	
1820	24	**JAMES MONROE** John Quincy Adams	REPUBLICAN Independent			231 1	
1824	24	**JOHN QUINCY ADAMS** Andrew Jackson William H. Crawford Henry Clay	NO PARTY DESIGNATIONS	108,740 153,544 46,618 47,136	31.0 43.0 13.0 13.0	84 99 41 37	26.9
1828	24	**ANDREW JACKSON** John Quincy Adams	DEMOCRAT National Republican	647,286 508,064	56.0 44.0	178 83	57.6
1832	24	**ANDREW JACKSON** Henry Clay William Wirt John Floyd	DEMOCRAT National Republican Anti-Masonic Democrat	687,502 530,189 101,051	54.5 37.5 8.0	219 49 7 11	55.4
1836	26	**MARTIN VAN BUREN** William H. Harrison Hugh L. White Daniel Webster William P. Mangum	DEMOCRAT Whig Whig Whig Whig	765,483 739,795	51.0 49.0	170 73 26 14 11	57.8
1840	26	**WILLIAM H. HARRISON** Martin Van Buren	WHIG Democrat	1,274,624 1,127,781	53.0 47.0	234 60	80.2

Year	Number of States	Candidates	Parties	Popular Vote	% of Popular Vote	Electoral Vote	% Voter Participation
1844	26	**JAMES K. POLK**	DEMOCRAT	1,338,464	50.0	170	78.9
		Henry Clay	Whig	1,300,097	48.0	105	
		James G. Birney	Liberty	62,300	2.0		
1848	30	**ZACHARY TAYLOR**	WHIG	1,360,967	47.5	163	72.7
		Lewis Cass	Democrat	1,222,342	42.5	127	
		Martin Van Buren	Free Soil	291,263	10.0		
1852	31	**FRANKLIN PIERCE**	DEMOCRAT	1,601,117	51.0	254	69.6
		Winfield Scott	Whig	1,385,453	44.0	42	
		John P. Hale	Free Soil	155,825	5.0		
1856	31	**JAMES BUCHANAN**	DEMOCRAT	1,832,955	45.0	174	78.9
		John C. Frémont	Republican	1,339,932	33.0	114	
		Millard Fillmore	American	871,731	22.0	8	
1860	33	**ABRAHAM LINCOLN**	REPUBLICAN	1,865,593	40.0	180	81.2
		Stephen A. Douglas	Northern Democrat	1,382,713	29.0	12	
		John C. Breckinridge	Southern Democrat	848,356	18.0	72	
		John Bell	Constitutional Union	592,906	13.0	39	
1864	36	**ABRAHAM LINCOLN**	REPUBLICAN	2,206,938	55.0	212	73.8
		George B. McClellan	Democrat	1,803,787	45.0	21	
1868	37	**ULYSSES S. GRANT**	REPUBLICAN	3,013,421	53.0	214	78.1
		Horatio Seymour	Democrat	2,706,829	47.0	80	

Year	Number of States	Candidates	Parties	Popular Vote	% of Popular Vote	Electoral Vote	% Voter Participation
1872	37	**ULYSSES S. GRANT**	REPUBLICAN	3,596,745	55.6	286	71.3
		Horace Greeley	Democrat	2,843,446	43.9	66	
1876	38	**RUTHERFORD B. HAYES**	REPUBLICAN	4,036,572	48.0	185	81.8
		Samuel J. Tilden	Democrat	4,284,020	51.0	184	
1880	38	**JAMES A. GARFIELD**	REPUBLICAN	4,453,295	48.4	214	79.4
		Winfield S. Hancock	Democrat	4,414,082	48.3	155	
		James B. Weaver	Greenback-Labor	308,578	3.5		
1884	38	**GROVER CLEVELAND**	DEMOCRAT	4,879,507	48.5	219	77.5
		James G. Blaine	Republican	4,850,293	48.2	182	
		Benjamin F. Butler	Greenback-Labor	175,370	1.8		
		John P. St. John	Prohibition	150,369	1.5		
1888	38	**BENJAMIN HARRISON**	REPUBLICAN	5,447,129	47.9	233	79.3
		Grover Cleveland	Democrat	5,537,857	48.6	168	
		Clinton B. Fisk	Prohibition	249,506	2.2		
		Anson J. Streeter	Union Labor	146,935	1.3		
1892	44	**GROVER CLEVELAND**	DEMOCRAT	5,555,426	46.1	277	74.7
		Benjamin Harrison	Republican	5,182,690	43.0	145	
		James B. Weaver	People's	1,029,846	8.5	22	
		John Bidwell	Prohibition	264,133	2.2		
1896	45	**WILLIAM McKINLEY**	REPUBLICAN	7,102,246	51.0	271	79.3
		William J. Bryan	Democrat	6,492,559	47.0	176	

Year	Number of States	Candidates	Parties	Popular Vote	% of Popular Vote	Electoral Vote	% Voter Participation
1900	45	**WILLIAM McKINLEY**	REPUBLICAN	7,218,491	52.0	292	73.2
		William J. Bryan	Democrat; Populist	6,356,734	46.0	155	
		John C. Wooley	Prohibition	208,914	1.5		
1904	45	**THEODORE ROOSEVELT**	REPUBLICAN	7,628,461	56.4	336	65.2
		Alton B. Parker	Democrat	5,084,223	37.6	140	
		Eugene V. Debs	Socialist	402,283	3.0		
		Silas C. Swallow	Prohibition	258,536	1.9		
1908	46	**WILLIAM H. TAFT**	REPUBLICAN	7,675,320	52.0	321	65.4
		William J. Bryan	Democrat	6,412,294	43.4	162	
		Eugene V. Debs	Socialist	420,793	2.8		
		Eugene W. Chafin	Prohibition	253,840	1.7		
1912	48	**WOODROW WILSON**	DEMOCRAT	6,296,547	41.9	435	58.8
		Theodore Roosevelt	Progressive	4,118,571	27.4	88	
		William H. Taft	Republican	3,486,720	23.2	8	
		Eugene V. Debs	Socialist	900,672	6.0		
		Eugene W. Chafin	Prohibition	206,275	1.4		
1916	48	**WOODROW WILSON**	DEMOCRAT	9,127,695	49.4	277	61.6
		Charles E. Hughes	Republican	8,533,507	46.2	254	
		A. L. Benson	Socialist	585,113	3.2		
		J. Frank Hanly	Prohibition	220,506	1.2		
1920	48	**WARREN G. HARDING**	REPUBLICAN	16,153,115	60.6	404	49.2
		James M. Cox	Democrat	9,133,092	34.3	127	
		Eugene V. Debs	Socialist	915,490	3.4		
		P. P. Christensen	Farmer-Labor	265,229	1.0		
1924	48	**CALVIN COOLIDGE**	REPUBLICAN	15,719,921	54.0	382	48.9
		John W. Davis	Democrat	8,386,704	29.0	136	
		Robert M. La Follette	Progressive	4,832,532	16.5	13	

Year	Number of States	Candidates	Parties	Popular Vote	% of Popular Vote	Electoral Vote	% Voter Participation
1928	48	**HERBERT C. HOOVER**	REPUBLICAN	21,437,277	58.2	444	56.9
		Alfred E. Smith	Democrat	15,007,698	40.9	87	
1932	48	**FRANKLIN D. ROOSEVELT**	DEMOCRAT	22,829,501	57.7	472	56.9
		Herbert C. Hoover	Republican	15,760,684	39.8	59	
		Norman Thomas	Socialist	884,649	2.2		
1936	48	**FRANKLIN D. ROOSEVELT**	DEMOCRAT	27,757,333	60.8	523	61.0
		Alfred M. Landon	Republican	16,684,231	36.6	8	
		William Lemke	Union	892,267	2.0		
1940	48	**FRANKLIN D. ROOSEVELT**	DEMOCRAT	27,313,041	54.9	449	62.5
		Wendell L. Willkie	Republican	22,348,480	44.9	82	
1944	48	**FRANKLIN D. ROOSEVELT**	DEMOCRAT	25,612,610	53.5	432	55.9
		Thomas E. Dewey	Republican	22,017,617	46.0	99	
1948	48	**HARRY S. TRUMAN**	DEMOCRAT	24,179,345	49.7	303	53.0
		Thomas E. Dewey	Republican	21,991,291	45.3	189	
		J. Strom Thurmond	States' Rights	1,176,125	2.4	39	
		Henry A. Wallace	Progressive	1,157,326	2.4		
1952	48	**DWIGHT D. EISENHOWER**	REPUBLICAN	33,936,234	55.1	442	63.3
		Adlai E. Stevenson	Democrat	27,314,992	44.4	89	

Year	Number of States	Candidates	Parties	Popular Vote	% of Popular Vote	Electoral Vote	% Voter Participation
1956	48	**DWIGHT D. EISENHOWER** Adlai E. Stevenson	REPUBLICAN Democrat	35,590,472 26,022,752	57.6 42.1	457 73	60.6
1960	50	**JOHN F. KENNEDY** Richard M. Nixon	DEMOCRAT Republican	34,226,731 34,108,157	49.7 49.6	303 219	62.8
1964	50	**LYNDON B. JOHNSON** Barry M. Goldwater	DEMOCRAT Republican	43,129,566 27,178,188	61.0 38.4	486 52	61.9
1968	50	**RICHARD M. NIXON** Hubert H. Humphrey George C. Wallace	REPUBLICAN Democrat American Independent	31,785,480 31,275,166 9,906,473	43.2 42.6 12.9	301 191 46	60.9
1972	50	**RICHARD M. NIXON** George S. McGovern John G. Schmitz	REPUBLICAN Democrat American	47,169,911 29,170,383 1,099,482	60.7 37.5 1.4	520 17	55.2
1976	50	**JIMMY CARTER** Gerald R. Ford	DEMOCRAT Republican	40,830,763 39,147,793	50.0 48.0	297 240	53.5
1980	50	**RONALD REAGAN** Jimmy Carter John B. Anderson Ed Clark	REPUBLICAN Democrat Independent Libertarian	43,904,153 35,483,883 5,720,060 921,299	50.9 41.1 6.6 1.1	489 49	52.6

Year	Number of States	Candidates	Parties	Popular Vote	% of Popular Vote	Electoral Vote	% Voter Participation
1984	50	**RONALD REAGAN**	REPUBLICAN	54,455,075	58.8	525	53.1
		Walter F. Mondale	Democrat	37,577,185	40.5	13	
1988	50	**GEORGE H. BUSH**	REPUBLICAN	48,886,097	53.4	426	50.1
		Michael Dukakis	Democrat	41,809,074	45.6	111	
1992	50	**BILL CLINTON**	DEMOCRAT	44,909,326	42.9	370	55.0
		George H. Bush	Republican	39,103,882	37.4	168	
		H. Ross Perot	Independent	19,741,657	18.9		
1996	50	**BILL CLINTON**	DEMOCRAT	47,402,357	49.2	379	49.0
		Bob Dole	Republican	39,198,755	40.7	159	
		H. Ross Perot	Reform Party	8,085,402	8.4		
2000	50	**GEORGE W. BUSH**	REPUBLICAN	50,455,156	47.9	271	50.4
		Albert Gore	Democrat	50,992,335	48.4	266	
		Ralph Nader	Green Party	2,882,738	2.7		
2004	50	**GEORGE W. BUSH**	REPUBLICAN	62,040,610	50.7	286	56.2
		John F. Kerry	Democrat	59,028,111	48.3	251	
2008	50	**BARACK H. OBAMA**	DEMOCRAT	66,882,230	52.9	365	56.8
		John S. McCain	Republican	58,343,671	45.7	173	
2012	50	**BARACK H. OBAMA**	DEMOCRAT	62,611,250	57.1	332	53.6
		W. Mitt Romney	Republican	59,134,475	47.2	206	
2016	50	**DONALD J. TRUMP**	REPUBLICAN	62,379,366	46.5	306	54
		Hillary Clinton	Democrat	64,469,963	48.1	232	

Candidates receiving less than 1 percent of the popular vote have been omitted. Thus, the percentage of popular vote given for any election year may not total 100 percent.

Before the passage of the Twelfth Amendment in 1804, the electoral college voted for two presidential candidates; the runner-up became vice president.

ADMISSION OF STATES

Order of Admission	State	Date of Admission	Order of Admission	State	Date of Admission
1	Delaware	December 7, 1787	26	Michigan	January 26, 1837
2	Pennsylvania	December 12, 1787	27	Florida	March 3, 1845
3	New Jersey	December 18, 1787	28	Texas	December 29, 1845
4	Georgia	January 2, 1788	29	Iowa	December 28, 1846
5	Connecticut	January 9, 1788	30	Wisconsin	May 29, 1848
6	Massachusetts	February 7, 1788	31	California	September 9, 1850
7	Maryland	April 28, 1788	32	Minnesota	May 11, 1858
8	South Carolina	May 23, 1788	33	Oregon	February 14, 1859
9	New Hampshire	June 21, 1788	34	Kansas	January 29, 1861
10	Virginia	June 25, 1788	35	West Virginia	June 30, 1863
11	New York	July 26, 1788	36	Nevada	October 31, 1864
12	North Carolina	November 21, 1789	37	Nebraska	March 1, 1867
13	Rhode Island	May 29, 1790	38	Colorado	August 1, 1876
14	Vermont	March 4, 1791	39	North Dakota	November 2, 1889
15	Kentucky	June 1, 1792	40	South Dakota	November 2, 1889
16	Tennessee	June 1, 1796	41	Montana	November 8, 1889
17	Ohio	March 1, 1803	42	Washington	November 11, 1889
18	Louisiana	April 30, 1812	43	Idaho	July 3, 1890
19	Indiana	December 11, 1816	44	Wyoming	July 10, 1890
20	Mississippi	December 10, 1817	45	Utah	January 4, 1896
21	Illinois	December 3, 1818	46	Oklahoma	November 16, 1907
22	Alabama	December 14, 1819	47	New Mexico	January 6, 1912
23	Maine	March 15, 1820	48	Arizona	February 14, 1912
24	Missouri	August 10, 1821	49	Alaska	January 3, 1959
25	Arkansas	June 15, 1836	50	Hawaii	August 21, 1959

POPULATION OF THE UNITED STATES

Year	Number of States	Population	% Increase	Population per Square Mile
1790	13	3,929,214		4.5
1800	16	5,308,483	35.1	6.1
1810	17	7,239,881	36.4	4.3
1820	23	9,638,453	33.1	5.5
1830	24	12,866,020	33.5	7.4
1840	26	17,069,453	32.7	9.8
1850	31	23,191,876	35.9	7.9
1860	33	31,443,321	35.6	10.6
1870	37	39,818,449	26.6	13.4
1880	38	50,155,783	26.0	16.9
1890	44	62,947,714	25.5	21.1
1900	45	75,994,575	20.7	25.6
1910	46	91,972,266	21.0	31.0
1920	48	105,710,620	14.9	35.6
1930	48	122,775,046	16.1	41.2
1940	48	131,669,275	7.2	44.2
1950	48	150,697,361	14.5	50.7
1960	50	179,323,175	19.0	50.6
1970	50	203,235,298	13.3	57.5
1980	50	226,504,825	11.4	64.0
1985	50	237,839,000	5.0	67.2
1990	50	250,122,000	5.2	70.6
1995	50	263,411,707	5.3	74.4
2000	50	281,421,906	6.8	77.0
2005	50	296,410,404	5.3	81.7
2010	50	308,745,538	4.2	87.4
2015	50	321,418,820	4.1	91.0

HISTORICAL STATISTICS OF THE UNITED STATES

LABOR FORCE—SELECTED CHARACTERISTICS EXPRESSED AS A PERCENTAGE OF THE LABOR FORCE, 1800–2010

Year	Agriculture	Manufacturing	Domestic service	Clerical, sales, and service	Professions	Slave	Nonwhite	Foreign-born	Female
1800	74.4	—	2.4	—	—	30.2	32.6	—	21.4
1860	55.8	13.8	5.4	4.8[1]	3.0[1]	21.7	23.6	24.5[1]	19.6
1910	30.7	20.8	5.5	14.1	4.7	—	13.4	22.0	20.8
1950	12.0	26.4	2.5	27.3	8.9	—	10.0	8.7	27.9
2000	2.4	14.7	0.6	38.0[2]	15.6	—	16.5	10.3[2]	46.6
2010	1.6	10.1	1.6	40.2	22.2	—	18.7	15.8	46.7

[1]Values for 1870 are presented here because the available data for 1860 exclude slaves.
[2]1990.
Note: "Clerical, sales, and service" excludes domestic service.

IMMIGRATION, BY ORIGIN (in thousands)

Period	Europe	Americas	Asia
1820–30	106	12	—
1831–40	496	33	—
1841–50	1,597	62	—
1851–60	2,453	75	42
1861–70	2,065	167	65
1871–80	2,272	404	70
1881–90	4,735	427	70
1891–1900	3,555	39	75
1901–10	8,065	362	324
1911–20	4,322	1,144	247
1921–30	2,463	1,517	112
1931–40	348	160	16
1941–50	621	355	32
1951–60	1,326	997	150
1961–70	1,123	1,716	590
1971–80	800	1,983	1,588
1981–90	762	3,616	2,738
1991–2000	1,360	4,487	2,796
2001–10	1,318	4,478	3,621

UNEMPLOYMENT RATE, 1890–2015

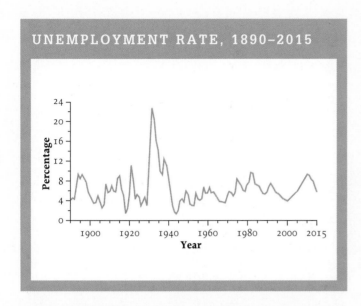

UNION MEMBERSHIP AS A PERCENTAGE OF NONAGRICULTURAL EMPLOYMENT, 1880–2015

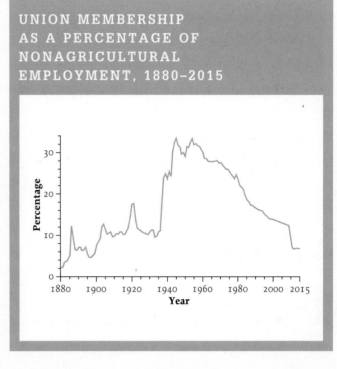

VOTER PARTICIPATION IN PRESIDENTIAL ELECTIONS, 1824–2016

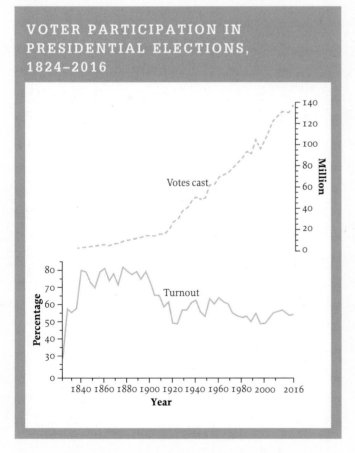

BIRTHRATE, 1820–2015

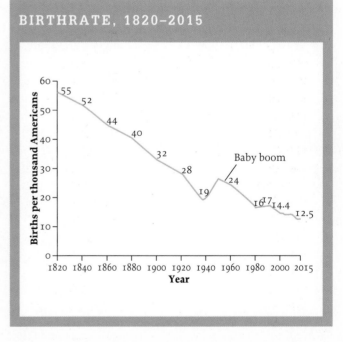

GLOSSARY

abolition Social movement of the pre–Civil War era that advocated the immediate emancipation of the slaves and their incorporation into American society as equal citizens.

Act Concerning Religion (or Maryland Toleration Act) 1649 law that granted free exercise of religion to all Christian denominations in colonial Maryland.

Adkins v. Children's Hospital 1923 Supreme Court case that reversed *Muller v. Oregon,* the 1908 case that permitted states to set maximum hours to protect working women. Justices ruled in *Adkins* that women no longer deserved special treatment because they could vote.

affirmative action Policy efforts to promote greater employment opportunities for minorities.

Agricultural Adjustment Act New Deal legislation passed in 1933 that established the Agricultural Adjustment Administration (AAA) to improve agricultural prices by limiting market supplies; declared unconstitutional in *United States v. Butler* (1936).

Albany Plan of Union A failed 1754 proposal by the seven northern colonies in anticipation of the French and Indian War, urging the unification of the colonies under one crown-appointed president.

Alien and Sedition Acts Four measures passed in 1798 during the undeclared war with France that limited the freedoms of speech and press and restricted the liberty of noncitizens.

American Anti-Slavery Society Founded in 1833, the organization that sought an immediate end to slavery and the establishment of equality for black Americans. It split in 1840 after disputes about the role of women within the organization and other issues.

American Civil Liberties Union Organization founded during World War I to protest the suppression of freedom of expression in wartime; played a major role in court cases that achieved judicial recognition of Americans' civil liberties.

American Colonization Society Organized in 1816 to encourage colonization of free blacks to Africa; West African nation of Liberia founded in 1822 to serve as a homeland for them.

American exceptionalism The belief that the United States has a special mission to serve as a refuge from tyranny, a symbol of freedom, and a model for the rest of the world.

American Federation of Labor A federation of trade unions founded in 1881, composed mostly of skilled, white, native-born workers; its long-term president was Samuel Gompers.

American Indian Movement (AIM) Movement founded in 1963 by Native Americans who were fed up with the poor conditions on Indian reservations and the federal government's unwillingness to help. In 1973, AIM led 200 Sioux in the occupation of Wounded Knee. After a ten-week standoff with the federal authorities, the government agreed to reexamine Indian treaty rights and the occupation ended.

"American standard of living" The Progressive-era idea that American workers were entitled to a wage high enough to allow them full participation in the nation's mass consumption economy.

American System Program of internal improvements and protective tariffs promoted by Speaker of the House Henry Clay in his presidential campaign of 1824; his proposals formed the core of Whig ideology in the 1830s and 1840s.

American system of manufactures A system of production that relied on the mass production of interchangeable parts that could be rapidly assembled into standardized finished products. First perfected in Connecticut by clockmaker Eli Terry and by small-arms producer Eli Whitney in the 1840s and 50s.

Americans with Disabilities Act 1990 law that prohibited the discrimination against persons with disabilities in both hiring and promotion. It also mandated accessible entrances for public buildings.

the *Amistad* Ship that transported slaves from one port in Cuba to another, seized by the slaves in 1839. They made their way northward to the United States, where the status of the slaves became the subject of a celebrated court case; eventually most were able to return to Africa.

Anglican Church The established state church of England, formed by Henry VII after the pope refused to annul his marriage to Catherine of Aragon.

annuity system System of yearly payments to Native American tribes by which the federal government justified and institutionalized its interference in Indian tribal affairs.

Antietam, Battle of One of the bloodiest battles of the Civil War, fought to a standoff on September 17, 1862, in western Maryland.

Anti-Federalists Opponents of the Constitution who saw it as a limitation on individual and states' rights; their demands led to the addition of a Bill of Rights to the document.

Anti-Imperialist League Coalition of anti-imperialist groups united in 1899 to protest American territorial expansion, especially in the Philippine Islands; its membership included prominent politicians, industrialists, labor leaders, and social reformers.

Appomattox Courthouse, Virginia Site of the surrender of Confederate general Robert E. Lee to Union general Ulysses S. Grant on April 9, 1865, marking the end of the Civil War.

Army-McCarthy hearings Televised U.S. Senate hearings in 1954 on Senator Joseph McCarthy's charges of disloyalty in the army; his tactics contributed to his censure by the Senate.

Arnold, Benedict A traitorous American commander who planned to sell out the American garrison at West Point to the British. His plot was discovered before it could be executed and he joined the British army.

Articles of Confederation First frame of government for the United States; in effect from 1781 to 1788, it provided for a weak central authority and was soon replaced by the Constitution.

Atlanta Compromise Speech to the Cotton States and International Exposition in 1895 by educator Booker T. Washington, the leading black spokesman of the day; black

scholar W. E. B. Du Bois gave the speech its derisive name and criticized Washington for encouraging blacks to accommodate segregation and disenfranchisement.

Atlantic Charter Agreement issued August 12, 1941, following meetings in Newfoundland between President Franklin D. Roosevelt and British Prime Minister Winston Churchill, that signaled the Allies' cooperation and stated their war aims.

Atlantic slave trade The systematic importation of African slaves from their native continent across the Atlantic Ocean to the New World, largely fueled by rising demand for sugar, rice, coffee, and tobacco.

Attucks, Crispus During the Boston Massacre, the individual who was supposedly at the head of the crowd of hecklers and who baited the British troops. He was killed when the British troops fired on the crowd.

Axis powers In World War II, the nations of Germany, Italy, and Japan.

Aztec Mesoamerican people who were conquered by the Spanish under Hernan Cortes, 1519–1528.

baby boom Markedly higher birthrate in the years following World War II; led to the biggest demographic "bubble" in American history.

backcountry In colonial America, the area stretching from central Pennsylvania southward through the Shenandoah Valley of Virginia and into upland North and South Carolina.

Bacon's Rebellion Unsuccessful 1676 revolt led by planter Nathaniel Bacon against Virginia governor William Berkeley's administration because of governmental corruption and because Berkeley had failed to protect settlers from Indian raids and did not allow them to occupy Indian lands.

Balkan crisis A series of ethnic and political crises that arose following the dissolution of Yugoslavia in the 1990s. Many atrocities were committed during the conflict, and NATO, the United Nations, and the United States intervened several times.

Bank of the United States Proposed by the first secretary of the treasury, Alexander Hamilton, the bank that opened in 1791 and operated until 1811 to issue a uniform currency, make business loans, and collect tax monies. The Second Bank of the United States was chartered in 1816 but President Andrew Jackson vetoed the recharter bill in 1832.

Bank War Political struggle in the early 1830s between President Jackson and financier Nicholas Biddle over the renewing of the Second Bank's charter.

Barbary Wars The first wars fought by the United States, and the nation's first encounter with the Islamic world. The wars were fought from 1801 to 1805 against plundering pirates off the Mediterranean coast of Africa after President Thomas Jefferson's refusal to pay them tribute to protect American ships.

Bargain of 1877 Deal made by a Republican and Democratic special congressional commission to resolve the disputed presidential election of 1876; Republican Rutherford B. Hayes, who had lost the popular vote, was declared the winner in exchange for the withdrawal of federal troops from involvement in politics in the South, marking the end of Reconstruction.

Bay of Pigs invasion U.S. mission in which the CIA, hoping to inspire a revolt against Fidel Castro, sent 1,500 Cuban exiles to invade their homeland on April 17, 1961; the mission was a spectacular failure.

the Beats A term coined by Jack Kerouac for a small group of poets and writers who railed against 1950s mainstream culture.

Bill for Establishing Religious Freedom A Virginia law, drafted by Thomas Jefferson in 1777 and enacted in 1786, that guarantees freedom of, and from, religion.

Bill of Rights First ten amendments to the U.S. Constitution, adopted in 1791 to guarantee individual rights against infringement by the federal government.

birth control movement An offshoot of the early twentieth-century feminist movement that saw access to birth control and "voluntary motherhood" as essential to women's freedom. The birth-control movement was led by Margaret Sanger.

Black Codes Laws passed from 1865 to 1866 in southern states to restrict the rights of former slaves; to nullify the codes, Congress passed the Civil Rights Act of 1866 and the Fourteenth Amendment.

Black Legend Idea that the Spanish New World empire was more oppressive toward the Indians than other European empires; was used as a justification for English imperial expansion.

Black Lives Matter Civil rights movement sparked by a series of incidents of police brutality and lethal force against people of color.

Black Power Post-1966 rallying cry of a more militant civil rights movement.

"Bleeding Kansas" Violence between pro- and antislavery settlers in the Kansas Territory, 1856.

bonanza farms Large farms that covered thousands of acres and employed hundreds of wage laborers in the West in the late nineteenth century.

borderland A place between or near recognized borders where no group of people has complete political control or cultural dominance.

Boston Massacre Clash between British soldiers and a Boston mob, March 5, 1770, in which five colonists were killed.

Boston Tea Party The incident on December 16, 1773, in which the Sons of Liberty, dressed as Indians, dumped hundreds of chests of tea into Boston Harbor to protest the Tea Act of 1773. Under the Tea Act, the British exported to the colonies millions of pounds of cheap—but still taxed—tea, thereby undercutting the price of smuggled tea and forcing payment of the tea duty.

***bracero* program** System agreed to by Mexican and American governments in 1942 under which tens of thousands of Mexicans entered the United States to work temporarily in agricultural jobs in the Southwest; lasted until 1964 and inhibited labor organization among farm workers since *braceros* could be deported at any time.

Brant, Joseph The Mohawk leader who led the Iroquois against the Americans in the Revolutionary War.

Bretton Woods conference International meeting held in the town of Bretton Woods, New Hampshire, in 1944 in which participants agreed that the American dollar would replace the British pound as the most important international currency. The conference also created the World Bank and International Monetary Fund to promote rebuilding after

World War II and to ensure that countries did not devalue their currencies.

Brook Farm Transcendentalist commune in West Roxbury, Massachusetts, populated from 1841 to 1847 principally by writers (Nathaniel Hawthorne, for one) and other intellectuals.

Brown v. Board of Education 1954 U.S. Supreme Court decision that struck down racial segregation in public education and declared "separate but equal" unconstitutional.

Bull Run, first Battle of The first land engagement of the Civil War which took place on July 21, 1861, at Manassas Junction, Virginia, and at which Union troops quickly retreated.

Bull Run, second Battle of Civil War engagement that took place one year after the first Battle of Bull Run, on August 29–30, during which Confederates captured the federal supply depot at Manassas Junction, Virginia, and forced Union troops back to Washington.

Bunker Hill, Battle of First major battle of the Revolutionary War; it actually took place at nearby Breed's Hill, Massachusetts, on June 17, 1775.

the Bush Doctrine President George W. Bush's foreign policy principle wherein the United States would launch a war on terrorism.

Bush v. Gore U.S. Supreme Court case that determined the winner of the disputed 2000 presidential election.

busing The means of transporting students via buses to achieve school integration in the 1970s.

Camp David Accords Peace agreement between the leaders of Israel and Egypt, brokered by President Jimmy Carter in 1978.

captivity narratives Accounts written by colonists after their time in Indian captivity, often stressing the captive's religious convictions.

caravel A fifteenth-century European ship capable of long-distance travel.

carpetbaggers Derisive term for northern emigrants who participated in the Republican governments of the Reconstruction South.

checks and balances A systematic balance to prevent any one branch of the national government from dominating the other two.

Chinese Exclusion Act 1882 law that halted Chinese immigration to the United States.

Church of Jesus Christ of Latter-Day Saints Religious sect founded in 1830 by Joseph Smith; it was a product of the intense revivalism of the "burned-over district" of New York. Smith's successor Brigham Young led 15,000 followers to Utah in 1847 to escape persecution.

Civil Rights Act (1964) Law that outlawed discrimination in public accommodations and employment.

Civil Rights Act of 1875 The last piece of Reconstruction legislation, which outlawed racial discrimination in places of public accommodation such as hotels and theaters. Many parts of it were ruled unconstitutional by the Supreme Court in 1883.

Civil Rights Bill of 1866 Along with the Fourteenth Amendment, legislation that guaranteed the rights of citizenship to former slaves.

Civil Service Act of 1883 Law that established the Civil Service Commission and marked the end of the spoils system.

Civilian Conservation Corps (CCC) 1933 New Deal public work relief program that provided outdoor manual work for unemployed men, rebuilding infrastructure and implementing conservation programs. The program cut the unemployment rate, particularly among young men.

Cold War Term for tensions, 1945–1989, between the Soviet Union and the United States, the two major world powers after World War II.

collective bargaining The process of negotiations between an employer and a group of employees to regulate working conditions.

Columbian Exchange The transatlantic flow of goods and people that began with Columbus's voyages in 1492.

Committee of Correspondence Group organized by Samuel Adams in retaliation for the *Gaspée* incident to address American grievances, assert American rights, and form a network of rebellion.

common school Tax-supported state schools of the early nineteenth century open to all children.

Common Sense A pamphlet anonymously written by Thomas Paine in January 1776 that attacked the English principles of hereditary rule and monarchical government.

Commonwealth v. Hunt Landmark 1842 ruling of the Massachusetts Supreme Court establishing the legality of labor unions.

communitarianism Social reform movement of the nineteenth century driven by the belief that by establishing small communities based on common ownership of property, a less competitive and individualistic society could be developed.

Compromise of 1850 Complex compromise devised by Senator Henry Clay that admitted California as a free state, included a stronger fugitive slave law, and delayed determination of the slave status of the New Mexico and Utah territories.

Congress of Industrial Organizations Umbrella organization of semiskilled industrial unions, formed in 1935 as the Committee for Industrial Organization and renamed in 1938.

conquistadores Spanish term for "conquerors," applied to Spanish and Portuguese soldiers who conquered lands held by indigenous peoples in central and southern America as well as the current states of Texas, New Mexico, Arizona, and California.

conservation movement A progressive reform movement focused on the preservation and sustainable management of the nation's natural resources.

Constitutional Convention Meeting in Philadelphia, May 25–September 17, 1787, of representatives from twelve colonies—excepting Rhode Island—to revise the existing Articles of Confederation; the convention soon resolved to produce an entirely new constitution.

containment General U.S. strategy in the Cold War that called for containing Soviet expansion; originally devised by U.S. diplomat George F. Kennan.

Continental army Army authorized by the Continental Congress in 1775 to fight the British; commanded by General George Washington.

Continental Congress First meeting of representatives of the colonies, held in Philadelphia in 1774 to formulate actions against British policies; in the Second Continental Congress (1775–1789), the colonial representatives conducted the war and adopted the Declaration of Independence and the Articles of Confederation.

"the contrabands" Slaves who sought refuge in Union military camps or who lived in areas of the Confederacy under Union control.

Contract with America A list of conservatives' promises in response to the supposed liberalism of the Clinton administration, that was drafted by Speaker of the House Newt Gingrich and other congressional Republicans as the GOP platform for the 1994 midterm elections. It was more a campaign tactic than a practical program; few of its proposed items ever became law.

cotton gin Invented by Eli Whitney in 1793, the machine that separated cotton seed from cotton fiber, speeding cotton processing and making profitable the cultivation of the more hardy, but difficult to clean, short-staple cotton; led directly to the dramatic nineteenth-century expansion of slavery in the South.

"Cotton Is King" Phrase from Senator James Henry Hammond's speech extolling the virtues of cotton, and, implicitly, the slave system of production that led to its bounty for the South. "King Cotton" became a shorthand for Southern political and economic power.

Cotton Kingdom Cotton-producing region, relying predominantly on slave labor, that spanned from North Carolina west to Louisiana and reached as far north as southern Illinois.

counterculture "Hippie" youth culture of the 1960s, which rejected the values of the dominant culture in favor of illicit drugs, communes, free sex, and rock music.

Court packing President Franklin D. Roosevelt's failed 1937 attempt to increase the number of U.S. Supreme Court justices from nine to fifteen in order to save his Second New Deal programs from constitutional challenges.

Covenant Chain Alliance formed in the 1670s between the English and the Iroquois nations.

coverture Principle in English and American law that a married woman lost her legal identity, which became "covered" by that of her husband, who therefore controlled her person and the family's economic resources.

Coxey's Army A march on Washington organized by Jacob Coxey, an Ohio member of the People's Party. Coxey believed in abandoning the gold standard and printing enough legal tender to reinvigorate the economy. The marchers demanded that Congress create jobs and pay workers in paper currency not backed by gold.

creoles Persons born in the New World of European ancestry.

crop lien Credit extended by merchants to tenants based on their future crops; under this system, high interest rates and the uncertainties of farming often led to inescapable debts.

Cuban missile crisis Tense confrontation caused when the United States discovered Soviet offensive missile sites in Cuba in October 1962; the U.S.-Soviet confrontation was the Cold War's closest brush with nuclear war.

cult of domesticity The nineteenth-century ideology of "virtue" and "modesty" as the qualities that were essential to proper womanhood.

Culture Wars Battles over moral values that occurred throughout the 1990s. The Culture Wars touched many areas of American life—from popular culture to academia. Flashpoints included the future of the nuclear family and the teaching of evolution.

Dartmouth College v. Woodward 1819 U.S. Supreme Court case in which the Court upheld the original charter of the college against New Hampshire's attempt to alter the board of trustees; set the precedent of support of contracts against state interference.

Dawes Act Law passed in 1887 meant to encourage adoption of white norms among Indians; broke up tribal holdings into small farms for Indian families, with the remainder sold to white purchasers.

D-Day June 6, 1944, when an Allied amphibious assault landed on the Normandy coast and established a foothold in Europe, leading to the liberation of France from German occupation.

Declaration of Independence Document adopted on July 4, 1776, that made the break with Britain official; drafted by a committee of the Second Continental Congress, including principal writer Thomas Jefferson.

decolonization The process by which African and Asian colonies of European empires became independent in the years following World War II.

Defense of Marriage Act 1996 law that barred gay couples from receiving federal benefits. Ruled unconstitutional in 2013.

deindustrialization Term describing decline of manufacturing in old industrial areas in the late twentieth century as companies shifted production to low-wage centers in the South and West or in other countries.

Deism Enlightenment thought applied to religion; emphasized reason, morality, and natural law.

Democracy in America Two works, published in 1835 and 1840, by the French thinker Alexis de Tocqueville on the subject of American democracy. Tocqueville stressed the cultural nature of American democracy, and the importance and prevalence of equality in American life.

Democratic-Republican societies Organizations created in the mid-1790s by opponents of the policies of the Washington administration and supporters of the French Revolution.

Denmark Vesey's conspiracy An 1822 failed slave uprising in Charleston, South Carolina, purported to have been led by Denmark Vesey, a free black man.

deregulation Reagan-Clinton era legislation that removed regulations on many industries, including finance and air travel.

détente Period of improving relations between the United States and Communist nations, particularly China and the Soviet Union, during the Nixon administration.

disenfranchisement To deprive of the right to vote; in the United States, exclusionary policies were used to deny groups, especially African-Americans and women, their voting rights.

Dissenters Protestants who belonged to denominations outside of the established Anglican Church.

division of powers The division of political power between the state and federal governments under the U.S. Constitution (also known as federalism).

Dix, Dorothea An important figure in increasing the public's awareness of the plight of the mentally ill. After a two-year investigation of the treatment of the mentally ill in Massachusetts, she presented her findings and won the support of leading reformers. She eventually convinced twenty states to reform their treatment of the mentally ill.

Dixiecrats Deep South delegates who walked out of the 1948 Democratic National Convention in protest of the party's support for civil rights legislation and later formed the States' Rights Democratic (Dixiecrat) Party, which nominated Strom Thurmond of South Carolina for president.

Dollar Diplomacy A foreign policy initiative under President William Howard Taft that promoted the spread of American influence through loans and economic investments from American banks.

Dominion of New England Consolidation into a single colony of the New England colonies—and later New York and New Jersey—by royal governor Edmund Andros in 1686; dominion reverted to individual colonial governments three years later.

"Don't ask, don't tell" President Clinton's compromise measure that allowed gay people to serve in the military incognito, as officers could no longer seek them out for dismissal but they could not openly express their identity. "Don't ask, don't tell" was ended under the Obama administration, when gay military service was allowed.

the Dorr War A movement in Rhode Island against property qualifications for voting. The movement formed an extralegal constitutional convention for the state and elected Thomas Dorr as a governor, but was quashed by federal troops dispatched by President John Tyler.

double-V Led by *The Pittsburgh Courier*, the movement that pressed for victory over fascism abroad and over racism at home. It argued that since African-Americans were risking their lives abroad, they should receive full civil rights at home.

dower rights In colonial America, the right of a widowed woman to inherit one-third of her deceased husband's property.

Dred Scott v. Sandford 1857 U.S. Supreme Court decision in which Chief Justice Roger B. Taney ruled that Congress could not prohibit slavery in the territories, on the grounds that such a prohibition would violate the Fifth Amendment rights of slaveholders, and that no black person could be a citizen of the United States.

Dust Bowl Great Plains counties where millions of tons of topsoil were blown away from parched farmland in the 1930s; massive migration of farm families followed.

Eighteenth Amendment Prohibition amendment passed in 1919 that made illegal the manufacture, sale, or transportation of alcoholic beverages; repealed in 1933.

Ellis Island Reception center in New York Harbor through which most European immigrants to America were processed from 1892 to 1954.

Emancipation Proclamation Declaration issued by President Abraham Lincoln; the preliminary proclamation on September 22, 1862, freed the slaves in areas under Confederate control as of January 1, 1863, the date of the final proclamation, which also authorized the enrollment of black soldiers into the Union army.

Embargo Act Attempt in 1807 to exert economic pressure by prohibiting all exports from the United States, instead of waging war in reaction to continued British impressment of American sailors; smugglers easily circumvented the embargo, and it was repealed two years later.

Emergency Banking Act Passed in 1933, the First New Deal measure that provided for reopening the banks under strict conditions and took the United States off the gold standard.

empire of liberty The idea, expressed by Jefferson, that the United States would not rule its new territories as colonies, but rather would eventually admit them as full member states.

enclosure movement A legal process that divided large farm fields in England that were previously collectively owned by groups of peasants into smaller, individually owned plots. The enclosure movement took place over several centuries, and resulted in eviction for many peasants.

Enforcement Acts Three laws passed in 1870 and 1871 that tried to eliminate the Ku Klux Klan by outlawing it and other such terrorist societies; the laws allowed the president to deploy the army for that purpose.

English Bill of Rights A series of laws enacted in 1689 that inscribed the rights of Englishmen into law and enumerated parliamentary powers such as taxation.

English liberty The idea that English people were entitled to certain liberties, including trial by jury, habeas corpus, and the right to face one's accuser in court. These rights meant that even the English king was subject to the rule of law.

English Toleration Act A 1690 act of Parliament that allowed all English Protestants to worship freely.

Enlightenment Revolution in thought in the eighteenth century that emphasized reason and science over the authority of traditional religion.

Equal Rights Amendment Amendment to guarantee equal rights for women, introduced in 1923 but not passed by Congress until 1972; it failed to be ratified by the states.

Era of Good Feelings Contemporary characterization of the administration of popular Republican president James Monroe, 1817–1825.

Erie Canal Most important and profitable of the canals of the 1820s and 1830s; stretched from Buffalo to Albany, New York, connecting the Great Lakes to the East Coast and making New York City the nation's largest port.

Espionage Act 1917 law that prohibited spying and interfering with the draft as well as making "false statements" that hurt the war effort.

ethnic cleansing The systematic removal of an ethnic group from a territory through violence or intimidation in order to create a homogeneous society; the term was popularized by the Yugoslav policy brutally targeting Albanian Muslims in Kosovo.

Ex parte Milligan 1866 Supreme Court case that declared it unconstitutional to bring accused persons before military tribunals where civil courts were operating.

Exposition and Protest Document written in 1828 by Vice President John C. Calhoun of South Carolina to protest the so-called Tariff of Abominations, which seemed to favor northern industry; introduced the concept of state interposition and became the basis for South Carolina's Nullification Doctrine of 1833.

Fair Deal Domestic reform proposals of the Truman administration; included civil rights legislation, national health insurance, and repeal of the Taft-Hartley Act, but only extensions of some New Deal programs were enacted.

family values Set of beliefs usually associated with conservatism that stressed the superiority of nuclear family, heterosexual marriage, and traditional gender roles.

family wage Idea that male workers should earn a wage sufficient to enable them to support their entire family without their wives' having to work outside the home.

Federal Housing Administration (FHA) A government agency created during the New Deal to guarantee mortgages, allowing lenders to offer long-term (usually thirty-year) loans with low down payments (usually 10 percent of the asking price). The FHA seldom underwrote loans in racially mixed or minority neighborhoods.

Federal Trade Commission (FTC) Independent agency created by the Wilson administration that replaced the Bureau of Corporations as an even more powerful tool to combat unfair trade practices and monopolies.

federalism A system of government in which power is divided between the central government and the states.

The Federalist Collection of eighty-five essays that appeared in the New York press in 1787–1788 in support of the Constitution; written by Alexander Hamilton, James Madison, and John Jay and published under the pseudonym "Publius."

Federalists and Republicans The two increasingly coherent political parties that appeared in Congress by the mid-1790s. The Federalists, led by George Washington, John Adams, and Alexander Hamilton, favored a strong central government. The Republicans, first identified during the early nineteenth century, supported a strict interpretation of the Constitution, which they believed would safeguard individual freedoms and states' rights from the threats posed by a strong central government.

The Feminine Mystique The book widely credited with sparking second-wave feminism in the United States. Author Betty Friedan focused on college-educated women, arguing that they would find fulfillment by engaging in paid labor outside the home.

feminism Term that entered the lexicon in the early twentieth century to describe the movement for full equality for women, in political, social, and personal life.

Fifteenth Amendment Constitutional amendment ratified in 1870, which prohibited states from discriminating in voting privileges on the basis of race.

flappers Young women of the 1920s whose rebellion against prewar standards of femininity included wearing shorter dresses, bobbing their hair, dancing to jazz music, driving cars, smoking cigarettes, and indulging in illegal drinking and gambling.

Force Act 1833 legislation, sparked by the nullification crisis in South Carolina, that authorized the president's use of the army to compel states to comply with federal law.

Fordism Early twentieth-century term describing the economic system pioneered by Ford Motor Company based on high wages and mass consumption.

Fort McHenry Fort in Baltimore Harbor unsuccessfully bombarded by the British in September 1814; Francis Scott Key, a witness to the battle, was moved to write the words to "The Star-Spangled Banner."

Fort Sumter First battle of the Civil War, in which the federal fort in Charleston (South Carolina) Harbor was captured by the Confederates on April 14, 1861, after two days of shelling.

Four Freedoms Freedom of speech, freedom of worship, freedom from want, and freedom from fear, as described by President Franklin D. Roosevelt during his January 6, 1941, State of the Union Address.

Fourteen Points President Woodrow Wilson's 1918 plan for peace after World War I; at the Versailles peace conference, however, he failed to incorporate all of the points into the treaty.

Fourteenth Amendment 1868 constitutional amendment that guaranteed rights of citizenship to former slaves, in words similar to those of the Civil Rights Act of 1866.

franchise The right to vote.

free blacks African-American persons not held in slavery; immediately before the Civil War, there were nearly a half million in the United States, split almost evenly between North and South.

Free Soil Party Political organization formed in 1848 to oppose slavery in the territory acquired in the Mexican War; nominated Martin Van Buren for president in 1848. By 1854 most of the party's members had joined the Republican Party.

free trade The belief that economic development arises from the exchange of goods between different countries without governmental interference.

the Freedmen's Bureau Reconstruction agency established in 1865 to protect the legal rights of former slaves and to assist with their education, jobs, health care, and landowning.

freedom petitions Arguments for liberty presented to New England's courts and legislatures in the early 1770s by enslaved African-Americans.

Freedom Rides Bus journeys challenging racial segregation in the South in 1961.

French and Indian War The last—and most important—of four colonial wars fought between England and France for control of North America east of the Mississippi River.

Fugitive Slave Act 1850 law that gave the federal government authority in cases involving runaway slaves; aroused considerable opposition in the North.

fugitive slaves Slaves who escaped from their owners.

fundamentalism Anti-modernist Protestant movement started in the early twentieth century that proclaimed the literal truth of the Bible; the name came from *The Fundamentals*, published by conservative leaders.

Gabriel's Rebellion An 1800 uprising planned by Virginian slaves to gain their freedom. The plot was led by a blacksmith named Gabriel, but was discovered and quashed.

Gadsden Purchase Thirty thousand square miles in present-day Arizona and New Mexico bought by Congress from Mexico in 1853 primarily for the Southern Pacific Railroad's transcontinental route.

gag rule Rule adopted by House of Representatives in 1836 prohibiting consideration of abolitionist petitions;

opposition, led by former president John Quincy Adams, succeeded in having it repealed in 1844.

Garvey, Marcus The leading spokesman for Negro Nationalism, which exalted blackness, black cultural expression, and black exclusiveness. He called upon African-Americans to liberate themselves from the surrounding white culture and create their own businesses, cultural centers, and newspapers. He was also the founder of the Universal Negro Improvement Association.

Geneva Accords A 1954 document that had promised elections to unify Vietnam and established the Seventeenth Parallel demarcation line which divided North and South Vietnam.

"gentlemen of property and standing" Well-to-do merchants who often had commercial ties to the South and resisted abolitionism, occasionally inciting violence against its adherents.

Gettysburg, Battle of Battle fought in southern Pennsylvania, July 1–3, 1863; the Confederate defeat and the simultaneous loss at Vicksburg marked the military turning point of the Civil War.

Ghost Dance A spiritual and political movement among Native Americans whose followers performed a ceremonial "ghost dance" intended to connect the living with the dead and make the Indians bulletproof in battles intended to restore their homelands.

GI Bill of Rights The 1944 legislation that provided money for education and other benefits to military personnel returning from World War II.

Gibbons v. Ogden 1824 U.S. Supreme Court decision reinforcing the "commerce clause" (the federal government's right to regulate interstate commerce) of the Constitution; Chief Justice John Marshall ruled against the State of New York's granting of steamboat monopolies.

the Gilded Age The popular but derogatory name for the period from the end of the Civil War to the turn of the century, after the title of the 1873 novel by Mark Twain and Charles Dudley Warner.

globalization Term that became prominent in the 1990s to describe the rapid acceleration of international flows of commerce, financial resources, labor, and cultural products.

Glorious Revolution A coup in 1688 engineered by a small group of aristocrats that led to William of Orange taking the British throne in place of James II.

gold rush The massive migration of Americans into California territory in the late 1840s and 1850s in pursuit of gold, which was discovered there in 1848.

gold standard Policy at various points in American history by which the value of a dollar is set at a fixed price in terms of gold (in the post–World War II era, for example, $35 per ounce of gold).

Good Neighbor Policy Policy proclaimed by President Franklin D. Roosevelt in his first inaugural address in 1933 that sought improved diplomatic relations between the United States and its Latin American neighbors.

gradual emancipation A series of acts passed in state legislatures throughout the North in the years following the Revolution that freed slaves after they reached a certain age, following lengthy "apprenticeships."

grandfather clause Loophole created by southern disenfranchising legislatures of the 1890s for illiterate white males whose grandfathers had been eligible to vote before the Civil War.

Great Awakening Fervent religious revival movement in the 1720s through the 1740s that was spread throughout the colonies by ministers like New England Congregationalist Jonathan Edwards and English revivalist George Whitefield.

Great Depression Worst economic depression in American history; it was spurred by the stock market crash of 1929 and lasted until World War II.

Great League of Peace An alliance of the Iroquois tribes, originally formed sometime between 1450 and 1600, that used their combined strength to pressure Europeans to work with them in the fur trade and to wage war across what is today eastern North America.

Great Migration Large-scale migration of southern blacks during and after World War I to the North, where jobs had become available during the labor shortage of the war years.

Great Migration (1630s) The migration of approximately 21,000 English Puritans to the Massachusetts Bay Colony.

Great Railroad Strike A series of demonstrations, some violent, held nationwide in support of striking railroad workers in Martinsburg, West Virginia, who refused to work due to wage cuts.

Great Recession A period of major economic stagnation across the United States and western Europe, characterized by rising unemployment and inflation and a 37 percent decline in the stock market between March and December 1974.

Great Society Term coined by President Lyndon B. Johnson in his 1965 State of the Union address, in which he proposed legislation to address problems of voting rights, poverty, diseases, education, immigration, and the environment.

Griswold v. Connecticut Supreme Court decision that, in overturning Connecticut law prohibiting the use of contraceptives, established a constitutional right to privacy.

Guantánamo Bay A detention center at the American naval base at Guantánamo Bay, Cuba, where beginning in 2002 suspected terrorists and war prisoners were held indefinitely and tried by extrajudicial military tribunals. During his 2008 presidential campaign, Senator Barack Obama pledged to close the prison, but as of 2015 it remained open.

Gulf of Tonkin resolution Legislation passed by Congress in 1964 in reaction to supposedly unprovoked attacks on American warships off the coast of North Vietnam; it gave the president unlimited authority to defend U.S. forces and members of SEATO.

Gulf oil spill Environmental disaster that occurred in 2010 after an explosion on the *Deepwater Horizon* oil rig. Hundreds of millions of gallons of oil were spilled into the Gulf of Mexico, resulting in one of the largest environmental calamities in human history.

Gulf War Military action in 1991 in which an international coalition led by the United States drove Iraq from Kuwait, which it had occupied the previous year.

hacienda Large-scale farm in the Spanish New World empire worked by Indian laborers.

Haitian Revolution A slave uprising that led to the establishment of Haiti as an independent country in 1804.

Half-Way Covenant A 1662 religious compromise that allowed baptism and partial church membership to colonial New Englanders whose parents were not among the Puritan elect.

Harlem Renaissance African-American literary and artistic movement of the 1920s centered in New York City's Harlem neighborhood; writers Langston Hughes, Jean Toomer, Zora Neale Hurston, and Countee Cullen were among those active in the movement.

Harpers Ferry, Virginia Site of abolitionist John Brown's failed raid on the federal arsenal, October 16–17, 1859; Brown became a martyr to his cause after his capture and execution.

Hart-Celler Act 1965 law that eliminated the national origins quota system for immigration established by laws in 1921 and 1924; led to radical change in the origins of immigrants to the United States, with Asians and Latin Americans outnumbering Europeans.

Hartford Convention Meeting of New England Federalists on December 15, 1814, to protest the War of 1812; proposed seven constitutional amendments (limiting embargoes and changing requirements for officeholding, declaration of war, and admission of new states), but the war ended before Congress could respond.

Haymarket Affair Violence during an anarchist protest at Haymarket Square in Chicago on May 4, 1886; the deaths of eight, including seven policemen, led to the trial of eight anarchist leaders for conspiracy to commit murder.

Haynes, Lemuel A black member of the Massachusetts militia and celebrated minister who urged that Americans extend their conception of freedom to enslaved Africans during the Revolutionary Era.

headright system A land-grant policy that promised fifty acres to any colonist who could afford passage to Virginia, as well as fifty more for any accompanying servants. The headright policy was eventually expanded to include any colonists—and was also adopted in other colonies.

Helsinki Accords 1975 agreement between the USSR and the United States that recognized the post–World War II boundaries of Europe and guaranteed the basic liberties of each nation's citizens.

Hessians German soldiers, most from Hesse-Cassel principality (hence, the name), paid to fight for the British in the Revolutionary War.

Hollywood Ten A group called before the House Un-American Activities Committee who refused to speak about their political leanings or "name names"—that is, identify communists in Hollywood. Some were imprisoned as a result.

Holocaust Systematic racist attempt by the Nazis to exterminate the Jews of Europe, resulting in the murder of over 6 million Jews and more than a million other "undesirables."

Homestead Act 1862 law that authorized Congress to grant 160 acres of public land to a western settler, who had to live on the land for five years to establish title.

horizontal expansion The process by which a corporation acquires or merges with its competitors.

House of Burgesses The first elected assembly in colonial America, established in 1619 in Virginia. Only wealthy landowners could vote in its elections.

House Un-American Activities Committee (HUAC) Committee formed in 1938 to investigate subversives in the government and holders of radical ideas more generally; best-known investigations were of Hollywood notables and of former State Department official Alger Hiss, who was accused in 1948 of espionage and Communist Party membership. Abolished in 1975.

Hundred Days Extraordinarily productive first three months of President Franklin D. Roosevelt's administration in which a special session of Congress enacted fifteen of his New Deal proposals.

Hurricane Katrina 2005 hurricane that devastated much of the Gulf Coast, especially New Orleans. The Bush administration's response was widely criticized as inadequate.

illegal alien A new category established by the Immigration Act of 1924 that referred to immigrants crossing U.S. borders in excess of the new immigration quotas.

Immigration Restriction League A political organization founded in 1894 that called for reducing immigration to the United States by requiring a literacy test for immigrants.

impeachment Bringing charges against a public official; for example, the House of Representatives can impeach a president for "treason, bribery, or other high crimes and misdemeanors" by majority vote, and after the trial the Senate can remove the president by a vote of two-thirds. Two presidents, Andrew Johnson and Bill Clinton, have been impeached and tried before the Senate; neither was convicted.

impressment The British navy's practice of using press-gangs to kidnap men in British and colonial ports who were then forced to serve in the British navy.

"In God We Trust" Phrase placed on all new U.S. currency as of 1954.

indentured servants Settlers who signed on for a temporary period of servitude to a master in exchange for passage to the New World; Virginia and Pennsylvania were largely peopled in the seventeenth and eighteenth centuries by English and German indentured servants.

Indian New Deal Phrase that refers to the reforms implemented for Native Americans during the New Deal era. John Collier, the commissioner of the Bureau of Indian Affairs (BIA), increased the access Native Americans had to relief programs and employed more Native Americans at the BIA. He worked to pass the Indian Reorganization Act. However, the version of the act passed by Congress was a much diluted version of Collier's original proposal and did not greatly improve the lives of Native Americans.

Indian Removal Act 1830 law signed by President Andrew Jackson that permitted the negotiation of treaties to obtain the Indians' lands in exchange for their relocation to what would become Oklahoma.

individualism Term that entered the language in the 1820s to describe the increasing emphasis on the pursuit of personal advancement and private fulfillment free of outside interference.

Industrial Workers of the World Radical union organized in Chicago in 1905 and nicknamed the Wobblies; its opposition to World War I led to its destruction by the federal government under the Espionage Act.

inflation An economic condition in which prices rise continuously.

Insular Cases Series of cases between 1901 and 1904 in which the Supreme Court ruled that constitutional protection of individual rights did not fully apply to residents of "insular" territories acquired by the United States in the Spanish-American War, such as Puerto Rico and the Philippines.

Interstate Commerce Commission Organization established by Congress, in reaction to the U.S. Supreme Court's ruling in *Wabash Railroad v. Illinois* (1886), in order to curb abuses in the railroad industry by regulating rates.

interstate highway system National network of interstate superhighways; its construction began in the late 1950s for the purpose of commerce and defense. The interstate highways would enable the rapid movement of military convoys and the evacuation of cities after a nuclear attack.

Intolerable Acts Four parliamentary measures in reaction to the Boston Tea Party that forced payment for the tea, disallowed colonial trials of British soldiers, forced their quartering in private homes, and reduced the number of elected officials in Massachusetts.

Iran-Contra Affair Scandal of the second Reagan administration involving sales of arms to Iran in partial exchange for release of hostages in Lebanon and use of the arms money to aid the Contras in Nicaragua, which had been expressly forbidden by Congress.

Iraq War Military campaign in 2003 in which the United States, unable to gain approval by the United Nations, unilaterally occupied Iraq and removed dictator Saddam Hussein from power.

iron curtain Term coined by Winston Churchill to describe the Cold War divide between western Europe and the Soviet Union's eastern European satellites.

ISIS An insurgency that emerged from the sectarian civil wars that destabilized Syria and post–Saddam Hussein Iraq. Beginning in 2014, ISIS forces attacked towns and cities in Iraq, Syria, and Lybia, systematically murdering members of ethnic and religious minorities.

isolationism The desire to avoid foreign entanglements that dominated the U.S. Congress in the 1930s; beginning in 1935, lawmakers passed a series of Neutrality Acts that banned travel on belligerents' ships and the sale of arms to countries at war.

Japanese-American internment Policy adopted by the Roosevelt administration in 1942 under which 110,000 persons of Japanese descent, most of them American citizens, were removed from the West Coast and forced to spend most of World War II in internment camps; it was the largest violation of American civil liberties in the twentieth century.

Jay's Treaty Treaty with Britain negotiated in 1794 by Chief Justice John Jay; Britain agreed to vacate forts in the Northwest Territories, and festering disagreements (border with Canada, prewar debts, shipping claims) would be settled by commission.

Kansas Exodus A migration in 1879 and 1880 by some 40,000–60,000 blacks to Kansas to escape the oppressive environment of the New South.

Kansas-Nebraska Act 1854 law sponsored by Illinois senator Stephen A. Douglas to allow settlers in newly organized territories north of the Missouri border to decide the slavery issue for themselves; fury over the resulting repeal of the Missouri Compromise of 1820 led to violence in Kansas and to the formation of the Republican Party.

"King Cotton diplomacy" An attempt during the Civil War by the South to encourage British intervention by banning cotton exports.

King Philip's War A multiyear conflict that began in 1675 with an Indian uprising against white colonists. Its end result was broadened freedoms for white New Englanders and the dispossession of the region's Indians.

Knights of Labor Founded in 1869, the first national union; lasted, under the leadership of Terence V. Powderly, only into the 1890s; supplanted by the American Federation of Labor.

Know-Nothing Party Nativist, anti-Catholic third party organized in 1854 in reaction to large-scale German and Irish immigration; the party's only presidential candidate was Millard Fillmore in 1856.

Korean War Conflict touched off in 1950 when Communist North Korea invaded South Korea; fighting, largely by U.S. forces, continued until 1953.

Korematsu v. United States 1944 Supreme Court case that found Executive Order 9066 to be constitutional. Fred Korematsu, an American-born citizen of Japanese descent, defied the military order that banned all persons of Japanese ancestry from designated western coastal areas. The Court upheld Korematsu's arrest and internment.

Ku Klux Klan Group organized in Pulaski, Tennessee, in 1866 to terrorize former slaves who voted and held political offices during Reconstruction; a revived organization in the 1910s and 1920s that stressed white, Anglo-Saxon, fundamentalist Protestant supremacy; revived a third time to fight the civil rights movement of the 1950s and 1960s in the South.

Kyoto Protocol A 1997 international agreement that sought to combat global warming. To great controversy, the Bush administration announced in 2001 that it would not abide by the Kyoto Protocol.

Las Casas, Bartolomé de A Catholic missionary who renounced the Spanish practice of coercively converting Indians and advocated their better treatment. In 1552, he wrote *A Brief Relation of the Destruction of the Indies*, which described the Spanish's cruel treatment of the Indians.

League of Nations Organization of nations to mediate disputes and avoid war established after World War I as part of the Treaty of Versailles; President Woodrow Wilson's "Fourteen Points" speech to Congress in 1918 proposed the formation of the league, which the United States never joined.

League of United Latin American Citizens Often called LULAC, an organization that challenged restrictive housing, employment discrimination, and other inequalities faced by Latino Americans.

Lend-Lease Act 1941 law that permitted the United States to lend or lease arms and other supplies to the Allies, signifying increasing likelihood of American involvement in World War II.

Letters from an American Farmer 1782 book by Hector St. John de Crèvecoeur that popularized the notion that the United States was a "melting pot" while excluding people of color from the process of assimilation.

Levittown Low-cost, mass-produced developments of suburban tract housing built by William Levitt after World War II on Long Island and elsewhere.

Lewis and Clark expedition Led by Meriwether Lewis and William Clark, a mission to the Pacific coast commissioned for the purposes of scientific and geographical exploration.

Lexington and Concord, Battles of The first shots fired in the Revolutionary War, on April 19, 1775, near Boston; approximately 100 minutemen and 250 British soldiers were killed.

liberal internationalism Woodrow Wilson's foreign policy theory, which rested on the idea that economic and political freedom went hand in hand, and encouraged American intervention abroad in order to secure these freedoms globally.

liberalism Originally, political philosophy that emphasized the protection of liberty by limiting the power of government to interfere with the natural rights of citizens; in the twentieth century, belief in an activist government promoting greater social and economic equality.

liberty of contract A judicial concept of the late nineteenth and early twentieth centuries whereby the courts overturned laws regulating labor conditions as violations of the economic freedom of both employers and employees.

Liberty Party Abolitionist political party that nominated James G. Birney for president in 1840 and 1844; merged with the Free Soil Party in 1848.

Lincoln-Douglas debates Series of senatorial campaign debates in 1858 focusing on the issue of slavery in the territories; held in Illinois between Republican Abraham Lincoln, who made a national reputation for himself, and incumbent Democratic senator Stephen A. Douglas, who managed to hold on to his seat.

the Little Bighorn, Battle of Most famous battle of the Great Sioux War; took place in 1876 in the Montana Territory; combined Sioux and Cheyenne warriors massacred a vastly outnumbered U.S. Cavalry commanded by Lieutenant Colonel George Armstrong Custer.

Long Telegram A telegram by American diplomat George Kennan in 1946 outlining his views of the Soviet Union that eventually inspired the policy of containment.

Lord Dunmore's proclamation A proclamation issued in 1775 by the earl of Dunmore, the British governor of Virginia, that offered freedom to any slave who fought for the king against the rebelling colonists.

Lords of Trade An English regulatory board established to oversee colonial affairs in 1675.

the Lost Cause A romanticized view of slavery, the Old South, and the Confederacy that arose in the decades following the Civil War.

Louisiana Purchase President Thomas Jefferson's 1803 purchase from France of the important port of New Orleans and 828,000 square miles west of the Mississippi River to the Rocky Mountains; it more than doubled the territory of the United States at a cost of only $15 million.

Loyalists Colonists who remained loyal to Great Britain during the War of Independence.

Lusitania British passenger liner sunk by a German U-boat, May 7, 1915, creating a diplomatic crisis and public outrage at the loss of 128 Americans (roughly 10 percent of the total aboard); Germany agreed to pay reparations, and the United States waited two more years to enter World War I.

lynching Practice, particularly widespread in the South between 1890 and 1940, in which persons (usually black) accused of a crime were murdered by mobs before standing trial. Lynchings often took place before large crowds, with law enforcement authorities not intervening.

Manhattan Project Secret American program during World War II to develop an atomic bomb; J. Robert Oppenheimer led the team of physicists at Los Alamos, New Mexico.

manifest destiny Phrase first used in 1845 to urge annexation of Texas; used thereafter to encourage American settlement of European colonial and Indian lands in the Great Plains and the West and, more generally, as a justification for American empire.

Marbury v. Madison First U.S. Supreme Court decision to declare a federal law—the Judiciary Act of 1801—unconstitutional.

March on Washington Civil rights demonstration on August 28, 1963, where the Reverend Martin Luther King Jr. gave his "I Have a Dream" speech on the steps of the Lincoln Memorial.

Marshall Plan U.S. program for the reconstruction of post–World War II Europe through massive aid to former enemy nations as well as allies; proposed by General George C. Marshall in 1947.

massive retaliation Strategy that used the threat of nuclear warfare as a means of combating the global spread of communism.

maternalist reforms Progressive-era reforms that sought to encourage women's child-bearing and -rearing abilities and to promote their economic independence.

Mayflower Compact Document signed in 1620 aboard the *Mayflower* before the Pilgrims landed at Plymouth; the document committed the group to majority-rule government.

McCarran-Walter Act Immigration legislation passed in 1952 that allowed the government to deport immigrants who had been identified as communists, regardless of whether or not they were citizens.

McCarthyism Post–World War II Red Scare focused on the fear of Communists in U.S. government positions; peaked during the Korean War; most closely associated with Joseph McCarthy, a major instigator of the hysteria.

McCulloch v. Maryland 1819 U.S. Supreme Court decision in which Chief Justice John Marshall, holding that Maryland could not tax the Second Bank of the United States, supported the authority of the federal government versus the states.

McNary-Haugen bill Vetoed by President Calvin Coolidge in 1927 and 1928, the bill to aid farmers that would have artificially raised agricultural prices by selling surpluses overseas for low prices and selling the reduced supply in the United States for higher prices.

mercantilism Policy of Great Britain and other imperial powers of regulating the economies of colonies to benefit the mother country.

mestizos Spanish word for persons of mixed Native American and European ancestry.

Metacom The chief of the Wampanoags, whom the colonists called King Philip. He resented English efforts to convert Indians to Christianity and waged a war against the English colonists, one in which he was killed.

métis Children of marriages between Indian women and French traders and officials.

Mexican War Controversial war with Mexico for control of California and New Mexico, 1846–1848; the Treaty of Guadalupe

Hidalgo fixed the border at the Rio Grande and extended the United States to the Pacific coast, annexing more than a half-million square miles of Mexican territory.

middle ground A borderland between European empires and Indian sovereignty where various native peoples and Europeans lived side by side in relative harmony.

Middle Passage The hellish and often deadly middle leg of the transatlantic "Triangular Trade" in which European ships carried manufactured goods to Africa, then transported enslaved Africans to the Americas and the Caribbean, and finally conveyed American agricultural products back to Europe; from the late sixteenth to the early nineteenth centuries, some 12 million Africans were transported via the Middle Passage, unknown millions more dying en route.

military-industrial complex The concept of "an immense military establishment" combined with a "permanent arms industry," which President Eisenhower warned against in his 1961 Farewell Address.

mill girls Women who worked at textile mills during the Industrial Revolution who enjoyed new freedoms and independence not seen before.

missile gap The claim, raised by John F. Kennedy during his campaign for president in 1960, that the Soviet Union had developed a technological and military advantage during Eisenhower's presidency.

Missouri Compromise Deal proposed by Kentucky senator Henry Clay in 1820 to resolve the slave/free imbalance in Congress that would result from Missouri's admission as a slave state; Maine's admission as a free state offset Missouri, and slavery was prohibited in the remainder of the Louisiana Territory north of the southern border of Missouri.

Monroe Doctrine President James Monroe's declaration to Congress on December 2, 1823, that the American continents would be thenceforth closed to European colonization, and that the United States would not interfere in European affairs.

Montgomery bus boycott Sparked by Rosa Parks's arrest on December 1, 1955, for refusing to surrender her seat to a white passenger, a successful year-long boycott protesting segregation on city buses; led by the Reverend Martin Luther King Jr.

moral imperialism The Wilsonian belief that U.S. foreign policy should be guided by morality, and should teach other peoples about democracy. Wilson used this belief to both repudiate Dollar Diplomacy and justify frequent military interventions in Latin America.

moral suasion The abolitionist strategy that sought to end slavery by persuading both slaveowners and complicit northerners that the institution was evil.

muckraking Writing that exposed corruption and abuses in politics, business, meatpacking, child labor, and more, primarily in the first decade of the twentieth century; included popular books and magazine articles that spurred public interest in reform.

Muller v. Oregon 1908 Supreme Court decision that held that state interest in protecting women could override liberty of contract. Louis D. Brandeis, with help from his sister-in-law Josephine Goldmark of the National Consumers League, filed a brief in *Muller* that used statistics about women's health to argue for their protection.

multiculturalism Term that became prominent in the 1990s to describe a growing emphasis on group racial and ethnic identity and demands that jobs, education, and politics reflect the increasingly diverse nature of American society.

Murray, Judith Sargent A writer and early feminist thinker prominent in the years following the American Revolution.

My Lai massacre Massacre of 347 Vietnamese civilians in the village of My Lai by Lieutenant William Calley and troops under his command. U.S. army officers covered up the massacre for a year until an investigation uncovered the events. Eventually twenty-five army officers were charged with complicity in the massacre and its cover-up, but only Calley was convicted. He served little time for his crimes.

Nat Turner's Rebellion Most important slave uprising in nineteenth-century America, led by a slave preacher who, with his followers, killed about sixty white persons in Southampton County, Virginia, in 1831.

National Association for the Advancement of Colored People Founded in 1910, the civil rights organization that brought lawsuits against discriminatory practices and published *The Crisis*, a journal edited by African-American scholar W. E. B. Du Bois.

National Defense Education Act 1958 law passed in reaction to America's perceived inferiority in the space race; encouraged education in science and modern languages through student loans, university research grants, and aid to public schools.

National Industrial Recovery Act 1933 law passed on the last of the Hundred Days; it created public-works jobs through the Federal Emergency Relief Administration and established a system of self-regulation for industry through the National Recovery Administration, which was ruled unconstitutional in 1935.

National Organization for Women Organization founded in 1966 by writer Betty Friedan and other feminists; it pushed for abortion rights, nondiscrimination in the workplace, and other forms of equality for women.

National Recovery Administration (NRA) Controversial federal agency created in 1933 that brought together business and labor leaders to create "codes of fair competition" and "fair labor" policies, including a national minimum wage.

nativism Anti-immigrant and anti-Catholic feeling especially prominent in the 1830s through the 1850s; the largest group of its proponents was New York's Order of the Star-Spangled Banner, which expanded into the American (Know-Nothing) Party in 1854.

Navajo's Long Walk The forced removal of 8,000 Navajos from their lands by Union forces to a reservation in the 1860s.

Navigation Act Law passed by the English Parliament to control colonial trade and bolster the mercantile system, 1650–1775; enforcement of the act led to growing resentment by colonists.

neoconservatives The leaders of the conservative insurgency of the early 1980s. Their brand of conservatism was personified in Ronald Reagan, who believed in less government, supply-side economics, and "family values."

Neolin A Native American religious prophet who, by preaching pan-Indian unity and rejection of European technology and commerce, helped inspire Pontiac's Rebellion.

Neutrality Acts Series of laws passed between 1935 and 1939 to keep the United States from becoming involved in war by prohibiting American trade and travel to warring nations.

New Deal Franklin D. Roosevelt's campaign promise, in his speech to the Democratic National Convention of 1932, to combat the Great Depression with a "new deal for the American people"; the phrase became a catchword for his ambitious plan of economic programs.

new feminism A new aspect of the women's rights movement that arose in the early part of the twentieth century. New feminism added a focus on individual and sexual freedom to the movement, and introduced the word "feminism" into American life.

New Freedom Democrat Woodrow Wilson's political slogan in the presidential campaign of 1912; Wilson wanted to improve the banking system, lower tariffs, and, by breaking up monopolies, give small businesses freedom to compete.

New Harmony Community founded in Indiana by British industrialist Robert Owen in 1825; the short-lived New Harmony Community of Equality was one of the few nineteenth-century communal experiments not based on religious ideology.

new immigrants Wave of newcomers from southern and eastern Europe, including many Jews, who became a majority among immigrants to America after 1890.

New Jersey Plan New Jersey's delegation to the Constitutional Convention's plan for one legislative body with equal representation for each state.

New Left Radical youth protest movement of the 1960s, named by leader Tom Hayden to distinguish it from the Old (Marxist-Leninist) Left of the 1930s.

New Nationalism Platform of the Progressive Party and slogan of former president Theodore Roosevelt in the presidential campaign of 1912; stressed government activism, including regulation of trusts, conservation, and recall of state court decisions that had nullified progressive programs.

New Negro Term used in the 1920s, in reference to a slow and steady growth of black political influence that occurred in northern cities, where African-Americans were freer to speak and act. This political activity created a spirit of protest that expressed itself culturally in the Harlem Renaissance and politically in "new Negro" nationalism.

New Orleans, Battle of Last battle of the War of 1812, fought on January 8, 1815, weeks after the peace treaty was signed but prior to the news' reaching America; General Andrew Jackson led the victorious American troops.

New South *Atlanta Constitution* editor Henry W. Grady's 1886 term for the prosperous post–Civil War South he envisioned: democratic, industrial, urban, and free of nostalgia for the defeated plantation South.

new world order President George H. W. Bush's term for the post–Cold War world.

Ninety-Five Theses The list of moral grievances against the Catholic Church by Martin Luther, a German priest, in 1517.

"no taxation without representation" The rallying cry of opponents to the 1765 Stamp Act. The slogan decried the colonists' lack of representation in Parliament.

North American Free Trade Agreement (NAFTA) Approved in 1993, the agreement with Canada and Mexico that allowed goods to travel across their borders free of tariffs. Critics of the agreement argued that American workers would lose their jobs to cheaper Mexican labor.

North Atlantic Treaty Organization (NATO) Alliance founded in 1949 by ten western European nations, the United States, and Canada to deter Soviet expansion in Europe.

Northwest Ordinance of 1787 Law that created the Northwest Territory (area north of the Ohio River and west of Pennsylvania), established conditions for self-government and statehood, included a Bill of Rights, and permanently prohibited slavery.

Notes on the State of Virginia Thomas Jefferson's 1785 book that claimed, among other things, that black people were incapable of becoming citizens and living in harmony alongside white people due to the legacy of slavery and what Jefferson believed were the "real distinctions that nature has made" between races.

NSC-68 Top-secret policy paper approved by President Truman in 1950 that outlined a militaristic approach to combating the spread of global communism.

nullification crisis The 1832 attempt by the State of South Carolina to nullify, or invalidate within its borders, the 1832 federal tariff law. President Jackson responded with the Force Act of 1833.

Obergefell v. Hodges 2015 Supreme Court decision that allowed same-sex couples to marry throughout the United States.

Occupy Wall Street A grassroots movement in 2011 against growing economic inequality, declining opportunity, and the depredations of Wall Street banks.

oil embargo Prohibition on trade in oil declared by the Organization of Petroleum Exporting Countries, dominated by Middle Eastern producers, in October 1973 in response to U.S. and western European support for Israel in the 1973 Yom Kippur War. The rise in gas prices and fuel shortages resulted in a global economic recession and profoundly affected the American economy.

Oneida Utopian community founded in 1848; the Perfectionist religious group practiced "complex marriage" under leader John Humphrey Noyes.

Open Door Policy Demand in 1899 by Secretary of State John Hay, in hopes of protecting the Chinese market for U.S. exports, that Chinese trade be open to all nations.

open immigration American immigration laws under which nearly all white people could immigrate to the United States and become naturalized citizens.

Operation Dixie CIO's largely ineffective post–World War II campaign to unionize southern workers.

Ordinance of 1784 A law drafted by Thomas Jefferson that regulated land ownership and defined the terms by which western land would be marketed and settled; it established stages of self-government for the West. First Congress would govern a territory; then the territory would be admitted to the Union as a full state.

Ordinance of 1785 A law that regulated land sales in the Old Northwest. The land surveyed was divided into 640-acre plots and sold at $1 per acre.

Oslo Accords 1993 roadmap for peace between Israel and the newly created Palestinian Authority, negotiated under the Clinton administration.

Panama Canal Zone The small strip of land on either side of the Panama Canal. The Canal Zone was under U.S. control from 1903 to 1979 as a result of Theodore Roosevelt's assistance in engineering a coup in Colombia that established Panama's independence.

Panic of 1819 Financial collapse brought on by sharply falling cotton prices, declining demand for American exports, and reckless western land speculation.

Panic of 1837 Beginning of major economic depression lasting about six years; touched off by a British financial crisis and made worse by falling cotton prices, credit and currency problems, and speculation in land, canals, and railroads.

paternalism A moral position developed during the first half of the nineteenth century which claimed that slaves were deprived of liberty for their own "good." Such a rationalization was adopted by some slaveowners to justify slavery.

the "peculiar institution" A phrase used by whites in the antebellum South to refer to slavery without using the word "slavery."

Pentagon Papers Informal name for the Defense Department's secret history of the Vietnam conflict; leaked to the press by former official Daniel Ellsberg and published in the *New York Times* in 1971.

Pequot War An armed conflict in 1637 that led to the destruction of one of New England's most powerful Indian groups.

perfectionism The idea that social ills once considered incurable could in fact be eliminated, popularized by the religious revivalism of the nineteenth century.

Perry, Commodore Matthew U.S. naval officer who negotiated the Treaty of Kanagawa in 1854. That treaty was the first step in starting a political and commercial relationship between the United States and Japan.

pet banks Local banks that received deposits while the charter of the Bank of the United States was about to expire in 1836. The choice of these banks was influenced by political and personal connections.

Philippine War American military campaign that suppressed the movement for Philippine independence after the Spanish-American War; America's death toll was over 4,000 and the Philippines' was far higher.

Pilgrims Puritan separatists who broke completely with the Church of England and sailed to the New World aboard the *Mayflower*, founding Plymouth Colony on Cape Cod in 1620.

plantation An early word for a colony, a settlement "planted" from abroad among an alien population in Ireland or the New World. Later, a large agricultural enterprise that used unfree labor to produce a crop for the world market.

Platt Amendment 1901 amendment to the Cuban constitution that reserved the United States' right to intervene in Cuban affairs and forced newly independent Cuba to host American naval bases on the island.

Plessy v. Ferguson U.S. Supreme Court decision supporting the legality of Jim Crow laws that permitted or required "separate but equal" facilities for blacks and whites.

Pontiac's Rebellion An Indian attack on British forts and settlements after France ceded to the British its territory east of the Mississippi River, as part of the Treaty of Paris in 1763, without consulting France's Indian allies.

Popular Front A period during the mid-1930s when the Communist Party sought to ally itself with socialists and New Dealers in movements for social change, urging reform of the capitalist system rather than revolution.

popular sovereignty Program that allowed settlers in a disputed territory to decide the slavery issue for themselves; most closely associated with Senator Stephen A. Douglas of Illinois.

Populists Founded in 1892, a group that advocated a variety of reform issues, including free coinage of silver, income tax, postal savings, regulation of railroads, and direct election of U.S. senators.

Porkopolis Nickname of Cincinnati, coined in the mid-nineteenth century, after its numerous slaughter houses.

Port Huron Statement A manifesto by Students for a Democratic Society that criticized institutions ranging from political parties to corporations, unions, and the military-industrial complex, while offering a new vision of social change.

Potsdam conference Last meeting of the major Allied powers; the conference that took place outside Berlin from July 17 to August 2, 1945, at which U.S. president Harry Truman, Soviet dictator Joseph Stalin, and British prime minister Clement Attlee finalized plans begun at Yalta.

Proclamation of 1763 Royal directive issued after the French and Indian War prohibiting settlement, surveys, and land grants west of the Appalachian Mountains; caused considerable resentment among colonists hoping to move west.

Progressive Party Political party created when former president Theodore Roosevelt broke away from the Republican Party to run for president again in 1912; the party supported progressive reforms similar to those of the Democrats but stopped short of seeking to eliminate trusts. Also the name of the party backing Robert La Follette for president in 1924.

Progressivism Broad-based reform movement, 1900–1917, that sought governmental action in solving problems in many areas of American life, including education, public health, the economy, the environment, labor, transportation, and politics.

proslavery argument The series of arguments defending the institution of slavery in the South as a positive good, not a necessary evil. The arguments included the racist belief that black people were inherently inferior to white people, as well as the belief that slavery, in creating a permanent underclass of laborers, made freedom possible for whites. Other elements of the argument included biblical citations.

Public Works Administration A New Deal agency that contracted with private construction companies to build roads, bridges, schools, hospitals, and other public facilities.

Pueblo Revolt Uprising in 1680 in which Pueblo Indians temporarily drove Spanish colonists out of modern-day New Mexico.

Pure Food and Drug Act Passed in 1906, the first law to regulate manufacturing of food and medicines; prohibited dangerous additives and inaccurate labeling.

Puritans English religious group that sought to purify the Church of England; founded the Massachusetts Bay Colony under John Winthrop in 1630.

Radical Republicans Group within the Republican Party in the 1850s and 1860s that advocated strong resistance to the expansion of slavery, opposition to compromise with the South in the secession crisis of 1860–1861, emancipation and arming of black soldiers during the Civil War, and equal civil and political rights for blacks during Reconstruction.

Reagan Revolution The rightward turn of American politics following the 1980 election of Ronald Reagan. The Reagan Revolution made individual "freedom" a rallying cry for the right.

Reaganomics Popular name for President Ronald Reagan's philosophy of "supply side" economics, which combined tax cuts with an unregulated marketplace.

reconquista The "reconquest" of Spain from the Moors completed by King Ferdinand and Queen Isabella in 1492.

Reconstruction Act 1867 law that established temporary military governments in ten Confederate states—excepting Tennessee—and required that the states ratify the Fourteenth Amendment and permit freedmen to vote.

Reconstruction Finance Corporation Federal program established in 1932 under President Herbert Hoover to loan money to banks and other institutions to help them avert bankruptcy.

Red Scare of 1919–1920 Fear among many Americans after World War I of Communists in particular and noncitizens in general, a reaction to the Russian Revolution, mail bombs, strikes, and riots.

Redeemers Post–Civil War Democratic leaders who supposedly saved the South from Yankee domination and preserved the primarily rural economy.

redemptioners Indentured families or persons who received passage to the New World in exchange for a promise to work off their debt in America.

Regulators Groups of backcountry Carolina settlers who protested colonial policies.

repartimiento system Spanish labor system under which Indians were legally free and able to earn wages but were also required to perform a fixed amount of labor yearly. Replaced the *encomienda* system.

republic Representative political system in which citizens govern themselves by electing representatives, or legislators, to make key decisions on the citizens' behalf.

republican motherhood The ideology that emerged as a result of American independence where women played an indispensable role by training future citizens.

republicanism Political theory in eighteenth-century England and America that celebrated active participation in public life by economically independent citizens as central to freedom.

reverse discrimination Belief that affirmative action programs discriminate against white people.

Revolution of 1800 First time that an American political party surrendered power to the opposition party; Jefferson, a Republican, had defeated incumbent Adams, a Federalist, for president.

Roanoke colony English expedition of 117 settlers, including Virginia Dare, the first English child born in the New World; the colony disappeared from Roanoke Island in the Outer Banks sometime between 1587 and 1590.

robber barons Also known as "captains of industry"; Gilded-Age industrial figures who inspired both admiration, for their economic leadership and innovation, and hostility and fear, due to their unscrupulous business methods, repressive labor practices, and unprecedented economic control over entire industries.

Roe v. Wade 1973 U.S. Supreme Court decision requiring states to permit first-trimester abortions.

Roosevelt Corollary 1904 Announcement by President Theodore Roosevelt, essentially a corollary to the Monroe Doctrine, that the United States could intervene militarily to prevent interference from European powers in the Western Hemisphere.

Rwandan genocide 1994 Genocide conducted by the Hutu ethnic group upon the Tutsi minority in Rwanda.

Sacco-Vanzetti case A case held during the 1920s in which two Italian-American anarchists were found guilty and executed for a crime in which there was very little evidence linking them to the particular crime.

Salem witch trials A crisis of trials and executions in Salem, Massachusetts, in 1692 that resulted from anxiety over witchcraft.

salutary neglect Informal British policy during the first half of the eighteenth century that allowed the American colonies considerable freedom to pursue their economic and political interests in exchange for colonial obedience.

Sanitary Fairs Fund-raising bazaars led by women on behalf of Civil War soldiers. The fairs offered items such as uniforms and banners, as well as other emblems of war.

Santa Anna, Antonio López de The military leader who, in 1834, seized political power in Mexico and became a dictator. In 1835, Texans rebelled against him, and he led his army to Texas to crush their rebellion. He captured the missionary called the Alamo and killed all of its defenders, which inspired Texans to continue their resistance and Americans to volunteer to fight for Texas. The Texans captured Santa Anna during a surprise attack, and he bought his freedom by signing a treaty recognizing Texas's independence.

Saratoga, Battle of Major defeat of British general John Burgoyne and more than 5,000 British troops at Saratoga, New York, on October 17, 1777.

scalawags Southern white Republicans—some ·former Unionists—who supported Reconstruction governments.

Schenck v. United States 1919 U.S. Supreme Court decision upholding the wartime Espionage and Sedition Acts; in the opinion he wrote for the case, Justice Oliver Wendell Holmes set the now-familiar "clear and present danger" standard.

scientific management Management campaign to improve worker efficiency using measurements like "time and motion" studies to achieve greater productivity; introduced by Frederick Winslow Taylor in 1911.

Scopes trial 1925 trial of John Scopes, Tennessee teacher accused of violating state law prohibiting teaching of the theory of evolution; it became a nationally celebrated confrontation between religious fundamentalism and civil liberties.

Scottsboro case Case in which nine black youths were convicted of raping two white women; in overturning the verdicts of this case, the Court established precedents in *Powell v. Alabama* (1932) that adequate counsel must be appointed in capital cases, and in *Norris v. Alabama* (1935) that African-Americans cannot be excluded from juries.

Sea Islands experiment The 1861 pre-Reconstruction social experiment that involved converting slave plantations into places where former slaves could work for wages or own land. Former slaves also received education and access to improved shelter and food.

Second American Revolution The transformation of American government and society brought about by the Civil War.

Second Great Awakening Religious revival movement of the early decades of the nineteenth century, in reaction to the growth of secularism and rationalist religion; began the predominance of the Baptist and Methodist Churches.

second Great Migration The movement of black migrants from the rural South to the cities of the North and West, which occurred from 1941 through World War II, that dwarfed the Great Migration of World War I.

Second Middle Passage The massive trade of slaves from the upper South (Virginia and the Chesapeake) to the lower South (the Gulf states) that took place between 1820 and 1860.

Sedition Act 1918 law that made it a crime to make spoken or printed statements that criticized the U.S. government or encouraged interference with the war effort.

Selective Service Act Law passed in 1917 to quickly increase enlistment in the army for the United States' entry into World War I; required men to register with the draft.

"separate but equal" Principle underlying legal racial segregation, upheld in *Plessy v. Ferguson* (1896) and struck down in *Brown v. Board of Education* (1954).

separation of powers Feature of the U.S. Constitution, sometimes called "checks and balances," in which power is divided between executive, legislative, and judicial branches of the national government so that no one can dominate the other two and endanger citizens' liberties.

Serra, Father Junípero Missionary who began and directed the California mission system in the 1770s and 1780s. Serra presided over the conversion of many Indians to Christianity, but also engaged them in forced labor.

settlement house Late-nineteenth-century movement to offer a broad array of social services in urban immigrant neighborhoods; Chicago's Hull House was one of hundreds of settlement houses that operated by the early twentieth century.

Seven Years' War The last—and most important—of four colonial wars fought between England and France for control of North America east of the Mississippi River.

Seventeenth Amendment Progressive reform passed in 1913 that required U.S. senators to be elected directly by voters; previously, senators were chosen by state legislatures.

Shakers Religious sect founded by Mother Ann Lee in England. The United Society of Believers in Christ's Second Appearing settled in Watervliet, New York, in 1774, and subsequently established eighteen additional communes in the Northeast, Indiana, and Kentucky.

Share Our Wealth movement Program offered by Huey Long as an alternative to the New Deal. The program proposed to confiscate large personal fortunes, which would be used to guarantee every poor family a cash grant of $5,000 and every worker an annual income of $2,500. It also promised to provide pensions, reduce working hours, and pay veterans' bonuses and ensured a college education to every qualified student.

sharecropping Type of farm tenancy that developed after the Civil War in which landless workers—often former slaves— farmed land in exchange for farm supplies and a share of the crop.

Shays's Rebellion Attempt by Massachusetts farmer Daniel Shays and 1,200 compatriots, seeking debt relief through issuance of paper currency and lower taxes, to prevent courts from seizing property from indebted farmers.

Sherman Antitrust Act Passed in 1890, first law to restrict monopolistic trusts and business combinations; extended by the Clayton Antitrust Act of 1914.

Silent Spring A 1962 book by biologist Rachel Carson about the destructive impact of the widely used insecticide DDT that launched the modern environmentalist movement.

single tax Concept of taxing only landowners as a remedy for poverty, promulgated by Henry George in *Progress and Poverty* (1879).

sit-down strike Tactic adopted by labor unions in the mid- and late 1930s, whereby striking workers refused to leave factories, making production impossible; proved highly effective in the organizing drive of the Congress of Industrial Organizations.

sit-ins Tactic adopted by young civil rights activists, beginning in 1960, of demanding service at lunch counters or public accommodations and refusing to leave if denied access; marked the beginning of the most militant phase of the civil rights struggle.

Sixteenth Amendment Constitutional amendment passed in 1913 that legalized the federal income tax.

the Slave Power The Republican and abolitionist term for pro-slavery dominance of southern and national governments.

Smith, John A swashbuckling soldier of fortune with rare powers of leadership and self-promotion who was appointed to the resident council to manage Jamestown.

Smoot-Hawley Tariff 1930 act that raised tariffs to an unprecedented level and worsened the Great Depression by raising prices and discouraging foreign trade.

Snowden, Edward An NSA contractor turned whistleblower, who released classified information relating to the United States' intelligence gathering both at home and abroad.

social contract Agreement hammered out between labor and management in leading industries; called a new "social contract." Unions signed long-term agreements that left decisions regarding capital investment, plant location, and output in management's hands, and they agreed to try to prevent unauthorized "wildcat" strikes.

Social Darwinism Application of Charles Darwin's theory of natural selection to society; used the concept of the "survival of the fittest" to justify class distinctions and to explain poverty.

Social Gospel Ideals preached by liberal Protestant clergymen in the late nineteenth and early twentieth centuries; advocated the application of Christian principles to social problems generated by industrialization.

Social Security Act 1935 law that created the Social Security system with provisions for a retirement pension, unemployment insurance, disability insurance, and public assistance (welfare).

Socialist Party Political party demanding public ownership of major economic enterprises in the United States as well as reforms like recognition of labor unions and women's suffrage; reached peak of influence in 1912 when presidential candidate Eugene V. Debs received over 900,000 votes.

Society of American Indians Organization founded in 1911 that brought together Native American intellectuals of many tribal backgrounds to promote discussion of the plight of Indian peoples.

Society of Friends (Quakers) Religious group in England and America whose members believed all persons possessed the "inner light" or spirit of God; they were early proponents of abolition of slavery and equal rights for women.

soft money and hard money In the 1830s, "soft money" referred to paper currency issued by banks. "Hard money" referred to gold and silver currency—also called specie.

Sons of Liberty Organizations formed by Samuel Adams, John Hancock, and other radicals in response to the Stamp Act.

Sotomayor, Sonia First Supreme Court Justice of Hispanic descent. Justice Sotomayor was appointed by President Barack Obama in 2009.

Southern Christian Leadership Conference (SCLC) Civil rights organization founded in 1957 by the Reverend Martin Luther King Jr. and other civil rights leaders.

Southern Manifesto A document written in 1956 that repudiated the Supreme Court decision in *Brown v. Board of Education* and supported the campaign against racial integration in public places.

spoils system The term meaning the filling of federal government jobs with persons loyal to the party of the president; originated in Andrew Jackson's first term.

Sputnik First artificial satellite to orbit the earth; launched October 4, 1957, by the Soviet Union.

stagflation A combination of stagnant economic growth and high inflation present during the 1970s.

Stamp Act Parliament's 1765 requirement that revenue stamps be affixed to all colonial printed matter, documents, and playing cards; the Stamp Act Congress met to formulate a response, and the act was repealed the following year.

staple crops Important cash crops; for example, cotton or tobacco.

steamboats Paddlewheelers that could travel both up- and down-river in deep or shallow waters; they became commercially viable early in the nineteenth century and soon developed into America's first inland freight and passenger service network.

stock market crash Also known as Black Tuesday, a stock market panic in 1929 that resulted in the loss of more than $10 billion in market value (worth approximately ten times more today). One among many causes of the Great Depression.

Stonewall Inn A gathering place for New York's gay community, the site of the 1969 police raids and resulting riots that launched the modern gay rights movement.

Stono Rebellion A slave uprising in 1739 in South Carolina that led to a severe tightening of the slave code and the temporary imposition of a prohibitive tax on imported slaves.

Strategic Arms Limitation Talks 1972 talks between President Nixon and Secretary Brezhnev that resulted in the Strategic Arms Limitation Treaty (or SALT), which limited the quantity of nuclear warheads each nation could possess, and prohibited the development of missile defense systems.

Student Nonviolent Coordinating Committee (SNCC) Organization founded in 1960 to coordinate civil rights sit-ins and other forms of grassroots protest.

Students for a Democratic Society (SDS) Major organization of the New Left, founded at the University of Michigan in 1960 by Tom Hayden and Al Haber.

suffrage The right to vote.

Sugar Act 1764 decision by Parliament to tax refined sugar and many other colonial products.

Sunbelt The label for an arc that stretched from the Carolinas to California. During the postwar era, much of the urban population growth occurred in this area.

Taft-Hartley Act 1947 law passed over President Harry Truman's veto; the law contained a number of provisions to weaken labor unions, including the banning of closed shops.

tariff of abominations Tariff passed in 1828 by Parliament that taxed imported goods at a very high rate; aroused strong opposition in the South.

tariff of 1816 First true protective tariff, intended to protect certain American goods against foreign competition.

Tea Party A grassroots Republican movement that emerged in 2009 named for the Boston Tea Party of the 1770s. The Tea Party opposed the Obama administration's sweeping legislative enactments and advocated for a more stringent immigration policy.

Teapot Dome Harding administration scandal in which Secretary of the Interior Albert B. Fall profited from secret leasing to private oil companies of government oil reserves at Teapot Dome, Wyoming, and Elk Hills, California.

Tecumseh and Tenskwatawa Tecumseh—a leader of the Shawnee tribe who tried to unite all Indians into a confederation to resist white encroachment on their lands. His beliefs and leadership made him seem dangerous to the American government. He was killed at the Battle of the Thames. His brother, Tenskwatawa—a religious prophet who called for complete separation from whites, the revival of traditional Indian culture, and resistance to federal policies.

Tejanos Texas settlers of Spanish or Mexican descent.

temperance movement A widespread reform movement, led by militant Christians, focused on reducing the use of alcoholic beverages.

Tennessee Valley Authority Administrative body created in 1933 to control flooding in the Tennessee River valley, provide work for the region's unemployed, and produce inexpensive electric power for the region.

Tenochtitlán The capital city of the Aztec Empire. The city was built on marshy islands on the western side of Lake Tetzcoco, which is the site of present-day Mexico City.

Ten-Percent Plan of Reconstruction President Lincoln's proposal for reconstruction, issued in 1863, in which southern states would rejoin the Union if 10 percent of the 1860 electorate signed loyalty pledges, accepted emancipation, and had received presidential pardons.

Tenure of Office Act 1867 law that required the president to obtain Senate approval to remove any official whose appointment had also required Senate approval; President Andrew Johnson's violation of the law by firing Secretary of War Edwin Stanton led to Johnson's impeachment.

Tet offensive Surprise attack by the Viet Cong and North Vietnamese during the Vietnamese New Year of 1968; turned American public opinion strongly against the war in Vietnam.

the Texas Revolt The 1830s rebellion of residents of the territory of Texas—many of them Americans emigrants—against Mexican control of the region.

Thirteenth Amendment Constitutional amendment adopted in 1865 that irrevocably abolished slavery throughout the United States.

Three Mile Island Nuclear power plant near Harrisburg, Pennsylvania, site of 1979 accident that released radioactive steam into the air; public reaction ended the nuclear power industry's expansion.

three-fifths clause A provision signed into the Constitution in 1787 that three-fifths of the slave population would be counted in determining each state's representation in the House of Representatives and its electoral votes for president.

Title IX Part of the Educational Amendments Act of 1972 that banned gender discrimination in higher education.

totalitarianism The term that describes aggressive, ideologically driven states that seek to subdue all of civil society to their control, thus leaving no room for individual rights or alternative values.

Townshend Acts 1767 parliamentary measures (named for the chancellor of the Exchequer) that taxed tea and other commodities, and established a Board of Customs Commissioners and colonial vice-admiralty courts.

Trail of Tears Cherokees' own term for their forced removal, 1838–1839, from the Southeast to Indian lands (later Oklahoma); of 15,000 forced to march, 4,000 died on the way.

transcendentalists Philosophy of a small group of mid-nineteenth-century New England writers and thinkers, including Ralph Waldo Emerson, Henry David Thoreau, and Margaret Fuller; they stressed personal and intellectual self-reliance.

transcontinental railroad First line across the continent from Omaha, Nebraska, to Sacramento, California, established in 1869 with the linkage of the Union Pacific and Central Pacific railroads at Promontory, Utah.

Treaty of Greenville 1795 treaty under which twelve Indian tribes ceded most of Ohio and Indiana to the federal government, and which also established the "annuity" system.

Treaty of Paris Signed on September 3, 1783, the treaty that ended the Revolutionary War, recognized American independence from Britain, established the border between Canada and the United States, fixed the western border at the Mississippi River, and ceded Florida to Spain.

Truman Doctrine President Harry S. Truman's program announced in 1947 of aid to European countries—particularly Greece and Turkey—threatened by communism.

trusts Companies combined to limit competition.

Tubman, Harriet Abolitionist who was born a slave, escaped to the North, and then returned to the South nineteen times and guided 300 slaves to freedom.

Tulsa riot A race riot in 1921—the worst in American history—that occurred in Tulsa, Oklahoma, after a group of black veterans tried to prevent a lynching. Over 300 African-Americans were killed, and 10,000 lost their homes in fires set by white mobs.

Uncle Tom's Cabin Harriet Beecher Stowe's 1852 antislavery novel that popularized the abolitionist position.

Underground Railroad Operating in the decades before the Civil War, a clandestine system of routes and safehouses through which slaves were led to freedom in the North.

United Nations Organization of nations to maintain world peace, established in 1945 and headquartered in New York.

Uprising of 1622 Unsuccessful uprising of Virginia Native Americans that wiped out one-quarter of the settler population, but ultimately led to the settlers gaining supremacy.

urban renewal A series of policies supported by all levels of government that allowed local governments and housing authorities to demolish so-called blighted areas in urban centers to replace them with more valuable real estate usually reserved for white people.

USA Patriot Act A 2001 mammoth bill that conferred unprecedented powers on law-enforcement agencies charged with preventing domestic terrorism, including the power to wiretap, read private messages, and spy on citizens.

U.S.S. *Maine* Battleship that exploded in Havana Harbor on February 15, 1898, resulting in 266 deaths; the American public, assuming that the Spanish had mined the ship, clamored for war, and the Spanish-American War was declared two months later.

utopian communities Ideal communities that offered innovative social and economic relationships to those who were interested in achieving salvation.

V-E Day May 8, 1945, the day World War II officially ended in Europe.

Versailles Treaty The treaty signed at the Versailles peace conference after World War I which established President Woodrow Wilson's vision of an international regulating body, redrew parts of Europe and the Middle East, and assigned economically crippling war reparations to Germany, but failed to incorporate all of Wilson's Fourteen Points.

vertical integration Company's avoidance of middlemen by producing its own supplies and providing for distribution of its product.

Vicksburg, Battle of The fall of Vicksburg, Mississippi, to General Ulysses S. Grant's army on July 4, 1863, after two months of siege; a turning point in the war because it gave the Union control of the Mississippi River.

Vietnam Syndrome The belief that the United States should be extremely cautious in deploying its military forces overseas that emerged after the end of the Vietnam War.

Virginia and Kentucky resolutions Legislation passed in 1798 and 1799 by the Virginia and the Kentucky legislatures; written by James Madison and Thomas Jefferson in response to the Alien and Sedition Acts, the resolutions advanced the state-compact theory of the Constitution. Virginia's resolution called on the federal courts to protect free speech. Jefferson's draft for Kentucky stated that a state could nullify federal law, but this was deleted.

Virginia Company A joint-stock enterprise that King James I chartered in 1606. The company was to spread Christianity in the New World as well as find ways to make a profit in it.

Virginia Plan Virginia's delegation to the Constitutional Convention's plan for a strong central government and a two-house legislature apportioned by population.

virtual representation The idea that the American colonies, although they had no actual representative in Parliament, were "virtually" represented by all members of Parliament.

Voting Rights Act Law passed in the wake of Martin Luther King Jr.'s Selma-to-Montgomery March in 1965; it authorized federal protection of the right to vote and permitted federal enforcement of minority voting rights in individual counties, mostly in the South.

Wade-Davis Bill Radical Republicans' 1864 plan for reconstruction that required loyalty oaths, abolition of slavery, repudiation of war debts, and denial of political rights to high-ranking Confederate officials; President Lincoln refused to sign the bill.

Wagner Act (National Labor Relations Act of 1935) Law that established the National Labor Relations Board and facilitated unionization by regulating employment and bargaining practices.

Walking Purchase An infamous 1737 purchase of Indian land in which Pennsylvanian colonists tricked the Lenni Lanape Indians. The Lanape agreed to cede land equivalent to the distance a man could walk in thirty-six hours, but the colonists marked out an area using a team of runners.

war in Afghanistan War fought against the Taliban and Al-Qaeda in Afghanistan following the attacks of September 11, 2001. It remains the longest war in American history.

War Industries Board Board run by financier Bernard Baruch that planned production and allocation of war materiel, supervised purchasing, and fixed prices, 1917–1919.

War of 1812 War fought with Britain, 1812–1814, over issues that included impressment of American sailors, interference with shipping, and collusion with Northwest Territory Indians; settled by the Treaty of Ghent in 1814.

War on Poverty Plan announced by President Lyndon B. Johnson in his 1964 State of the Union address; under the Economic Opportunity Bill signed later that year, Head Start, VISTA, and the Jobs Corps were created, and programs were created for students, farmers, and businesses in efforts to eliminate poverty.

war on terrorism Global crusade to root out anti-American, anti-Western Islamist terrorist cells; launched by President George W. Bush as a response to the 9/11 attacks.

War Powers Act Law passed in 1973, reflecting growing opposition to American involvement in the Vietnam War; required congressional approval before the president sent troops abroad.

Watergate Washington office and apartment complex that lent its name to the 1972–1974 scandal of the Nixon administration; when his knowledge of the break-in at the Watergate and subsequent cover-up were revealed, Nixon resigned the presidency under threat of impeachment.

The Wealth of Nations The 1776 work by economist Adam Smith that argued that the "invisible hand" of the free market directed economic life more effectively and fairly than governmental intervention.

Webster-Hayne debate U.S. Senate debate of January 1830 between Daniel Webster of Massachusetts and Robert Hayne of South Carolina over nullification and states' rights.

welfare state A term that originated in Britain during World War II to refer to a system of income assistance, health coverage, and social services for all citizens.

Whiskey Rebellion Violent protest by western Pennsylvania farmers against the federal excise tax on whiskey, 1794.

Wilmot Proviso Proposal to prohibit slavery in any land acquired in the Mexican War; defeated by southern senators, led by John C. Calhoun of South Carolina, in 1846 and 1847.

Winthrop, John Puritan leader and governor of the Massachusetts Bay Colony who resolved to use the colony as a refuge for persecuted Puritans and as an instrument of building a "wilderness Zion" in America.

woman suffrage Movement to give women the right to vote through a constitutional amendment, spearheaded by Susan B. Anthony and Elizabeth Cady Stanton's National Woman Suffrage Association.

Worcester v. Georgia 1832 Supreme Court case that held that the Indian nations were distinct peoples who could not be dealt with by the states—instead, only the federal government could negotiate with them. President Jackson refused to enforce the ruling.

Works Progress Administration (WPA) Part of the Second New Deal; it provided jobs for millions of the unemployed on construction and arts projects.

Wounded Knee massacre Last incident of the Indian Wars; it took place in 1890 in the Dakota Territory, where the U.S. Cavalry killed over 200 Sioux men, women, and children.

writs of assistance One of the colonies' main complaints against Britain; the writs allowed unlimited search warrants without cause to look for evidence of smuggling.

XYZ affair Affair in which French foreign minister Talleyrand's three anonymous agents demanded payments to stop French plundering of American ships in 1797; refusal to pay the bribe was followed by two years of undeclared sea war with France (1798–1800).

Yalta conference Meeting of Franklin D. Roosevelt, Winston Churchill, and Joseph Stalin at a Crimean resort to discuss the postwar world on February 4–11, 1945; Joseph Stalin claimed large areas in eastern Europe for Soviet domination.

Yamasee uprising Revolt of Yamasee and Creek Indians, aggravated by rising debts and slave traders' raids, against

Carolina settlers. Resulted in the expulsion of many Indians to Florida.

yellow press Sensationalism in newspaper publishing that reached a peak in the circulation war between Joseph Pulitzer's *New York World* and William Randolph Hearst's *New York Journal* in the 1890s; the papers' accounts of events in Havana Harbor in 1898 led directly to the Spanish-American War.

yeoman farmers Small landowners (the majority of white families in the Old South) who farmed their own land and usually did not own slaves.

Yorktown, Battle of Last battle of the Revolutionary War; General Lord Charles Cornwallis along with over 7,000 British troops surrendered at Yorktown, Virginia, on October 17, 1781.

Zimmermann Telegram Telegram from the German foreign secretary to the German minister in Mexico, February 1917, instructing the minister to offer to recover Texas, New Mexico, and Arizona for Mexico if it would fight the United States to divert attention from Germany in the event that the United States joined the war.

zoot suit riots 1943 riots in which sailors on leave attacked Mexican-American youths.

CREDITS

PHOTOS

Title page: Library of Congress; **Frontispiece:** Granger Collection; **Author photo:** Flynn Larsen; **p. viii:** Digital Image © 2016 Museum Associates / LACMA. Licensed by Art Resource, NY; **p. ix:** Adoc-photos / Art Resource, NY; **p. x:** Roosevelt 560.51 1902–156, Houghton Library, Harvard University; **p. xi:** Library of Congress; **p. xii:** Granger Collection; **p. xiii:** Courtesy of The WASP Archive, The TWU Libraries Woman's Collection, Texas Woman's University, Denton, Texas; **p. xiv:** American Catholic History Research Center and University Archives, Catholic University of America; **p. xv:** Burt Glinn / Magnum Photos; **p. xvi:** AP Photo / Ira Schwartz; **p. xvii:** AP Photo / Steven Senne; **p. xviii:** Official White House Photo by Pete Souza; **p. xxi:** Granger Collection; **p. xxvi:** Whitney Curtis / The New York Times / Redux; **p. xxiv:** Bettmann / Getty Images; **p. 1:** Library of Congress. **Chapter 15: p. 550:** Chicago Historical Society; **p. 553 (top):** Library of Congress; **(bottom):** Photographic History Collection, Division of Information Technology and Communications, National Museum of American History, Smithsonian Institution; **p. 554 (top):** Library of Congress; **(bottom):** Granger Collection; **p. 556:** Smithsonian American Art Museum, Washington, DC / Art Resource, NY; **p. 557 (both):** Library of Congress; **p. 558 (top):** Digital Image © [year] Museum Associates / LACMA. Licensed by Art Resource, NY; **(bottom):** Cook Collection, Valentine Richmond History Center; **p. 560:** Library of Congress; **p. 564:** Kemper Leila Williams Foundation / The Historic New Orleans Collection; **p. 566 (both):** Library of Congress; **p. 567:** Ed Sullivan Collection, Special Collections, University of Hartford; **p. 568:** Library of Congress; **p. 569:** Library of Congress; **p. 570:** Manuscripts, Archives & Rare Books Division, Schomburg Center for Research in Black Culture, The New York Public Library, Astor, Lenox and Tilden Foundations / Art Resource, NY; **p. 571:** Library of Congress; **p. 573:** Library of Congress; **p. 574:** Library of Congress; **p. 575:** Library of Congress; **p. 567 (both):** Library of Congress; **p. 577:** Granger Collection; **p. 578 (top):** Library of Congress; **(bottom):** Clements Library Collection, University of Michigan; **p. 579:** Granger Collection; **p. 580:** Wikimedia, public domain; **p. 581 (top):** Niday Picture Library / Alamy; **(bottom):** © Fine Arts Museums of San Francisco, Gift of Joseph Martin, Jr., 1994.120.4; **p. 582 (both top):** Library of Congress; **(bottom):** National Archives; **p. 584:** Granger Collection; **p. 585:** Library of Congress. **Chapter 16: p. 588: (top)** Library of Congress; **(bottom):** Wikimedia Commons, public domain; **p. 589:** Library of Congress; **p. 590:** Private Collection / The Bridgeman Art Library; **p. 593:** © The Metropolitan Museum of Art. Image source: Art Resource, NY; **p. 595:** Library of Congress; **p. 596:** The Art Archive / Art Resource; **p. 597 (both):** Granger Collection; **p. 599 (both):** Library of Congress; **p. 600:** Library of Congress; **p. 601:** Jacob A. (Jacob August) Riis (1849-1914) / Museum of the City of New York. 90.13.4.111A; **p. 602:** Bettmann / Corbis; **p. 603 (top):** Bullock Texas State History Museum, Austin TX; **(bottom):** Solomon Butcher Collection. Nebraska State Historical Society; **p. 604:** Courtesy of the California History Room, California State Library, Sacramento, California; **p. 605:** Courtesy of the author; **p. 606:** Granger Collection; **p. 608:** Library of Congress; **p. 609:** Courtesy of the Braun Research Library Collection, Autry National Center, Los Angeles; Photo # P.13250; **p. 610:** Image copyright © The Metropolitan Museum of Art / Art Resource, NY; **p. 611 (top):** Image copyright © The Metropolitan Museum of Art. Image source: Art Resource, NY; **(bottom):** Bettmann / Corbis; **p. 614:** Adoc-photos / Art Resource, NY; **p. 615:** Missouri History Museum, St. Louis; **p. 617 (top):** Courtesy of the Museum of the South Dakota State Historical Society, Pierre SD; **(bottom both):** Smithsonian Institution, National Anthropological Archives; **p. 618 (both):** Library of Congress; **p. 619:** Library of Congress; **p. 620:** Library of Congress; **p. 623:** The Ohio State University Billy Ireland Cartoon Library & Museum; **p. 624:** Library of Congress; **p. 625:** Thomas Pollock Anshutz, *The Ironworker's Noontime*, 1880, oil on canvas 17 × 23 7/8 (43.2 × 60.6 cm), © Fine Arts Museum of San Francisco, Gift of Mr. And Mrs. John D. Rockefeller 3rd, 1979.7.4; **p. 628:** Image copyright © The Metropolitan Museum of Art / Art Resource, NY; **p. 629 (top):** bpk, Berlin / Art Resource, NY; **(bottom):** *Scribner's Magazine*, July 1895, public domain; **p. 630:** Library of Congress; **p. 631:** Bettmann / Corbis; **p. 632:** Bettmann / Corbis; **p. 634:** L1987-06_2, 19th and Early 20th Century Labor Prints, Southern Labor Archives. Special Collections and Archives, Georgia State University Library; **p. 635:** Wisconsin Historical Society, WHS-47662. **Chapter 17: p. 638:** High Museum of Art, Atlanta. Photo by James Schoomaker; **p. 641 (top):** Library of Congress; **(bottom):** Kansas State Historical Society; **p. 642 (top):** Ed Sullivan Collection, Special Collections, University of Hartford; **(bottom):** Park, Milton, editor. *The Southern Mercury.* (Dallas, Tex.), Vol. 10, No. 36, Ed. 1 Thursday, September 3, 1891, Newspaper, September 3, 1891; (http://texashistory.unt.edu/ark:/67531/metapth185428/ : accessed October 08, 2015), University of North Texas Library; **p. 644:** The Denver Public Library, Western History Collection, WH2129RMN; **p. 645 (top):** Library of Congress; **(bottom):** Corbis; **p. 646:** Library of Congress; **p. 647:** The Denver Public Library, Western History Collection, WH2129RMN; **p. 648:** Florida State Archives; **p. 649 (both):** Library of Congress; **p. 650 (both):** Library of Congress; **p. 653 (both):** Library of Congress; **p. 654:** Research Division of the Oklahoma Historical Society; **p. 655:** Courtesy of the Tennessee State Museum; **p. 656:** *Judge Magazine*, August 22, 1903; **p. 657:** The Denver Public Library, Western History Collection, X-21518; **p. 658 (top):** National Archives; **(bottom):** University of Washington Libraries, Special Collections, #UW1678; **p. 659:** Library of Congress; **p. 662:** Library of Congress; **p. 663:** Library of Congress; **p. 665:** Courtesy of the Bernice Pauahi Bishop Museum Archives; **p. 666:** Library of Congress; **p. 668:** Frederic Remington Art Museum; **p. 669:** Francisco Oller (Puerto Rican, 1833-1917). Hacienda La Fortuna, 1885. Oil on canvas, 26 × 40 in. (66 × 101.6 cm). Brooklyn Museum, Gift of Lilla Brown in memory of her husband, John W. Brown, by exchange, 2012.19; **p. 671:** Granger Collection; **p. 672 (top):** National Archives; **(bottom):** W.C. Brown Photograph Collection, U.S. Army Military History Institute; **p. 673:** Library of Congress; **p. 674 (top):** North Wind Picture Archives / Alamy; **(bottom):** Library of Congress; **p. 675:** National Portrait Gallery, Smithsonian Institution / Art Resource, NY. **Chapter 18: p. 678:** © 2013 Delaware Art Museum / Artists Rights Society (ARS), New York / The Philadelphia Museum of Art / Art Resource, NY; **p. 681 (top):** Library of Congress; **(bottom):** Byron Company (New York, N.Y.) / Museum of the City of New York. 93.1.1.10529; **p. 682 (top):** The J. Paul Getty Museum, Los Angeles, © 2013 Georgia O'Keeffe Museum / Artists Rights Society (ARS), New York; **(bottom):** Library of Congress; **p. 683:** Peter Roberts' The New Immigrants, 1921, public domain; **p. 685:** Library of Congress; **p. 686 (both):** Library of Congress; **p. 687:** Courtesy of the author; **p. 688:** The Art Archive at Art Resource, NY; **p. 689 (top):** John Sloan © 2013 Delaware Art Museum / Artists Rights Society (ARS), New York. Granger Collection; **(bottom):** Library of Congress; **p. 690:** Image Courtesy of The Advertising Archives; **p. 691:** Corbis; **p. 693:** Walter P. Reuther Library, Wayne State University; **p. 696 (top):** Brown Brothers; **(bottom):** From the Albert R. Stone Negative Collection, Rochester Museum & Science Center Rochester, N.Y.; **p. 697:** Library of Congress; **p. 698 (top):** Sam DeVincent Collection of Illustrated Sheet Music, Archives Center, National Museum of American History, Behring Center, Smithsonian Institution; **(bottom):** Library of Congress; **p. 699 (top):** Bettmann / Corbis; **(bottom):** Department of Special Collections, Davidson Library, University of California, Santa Barbara; **p. 700:** Reprinted with permission from Planned Parenthood ® Federation of America, Inc. © 2004 PPFA. All rights reserved; **p. 701:** Library of Congress; **p. 702:** Byron Company (New York, N.Y.) / Museum of the City of New York. 93.1.1.8018; **p. 704:** "Children in Hull-House Court," Hull-House Yearbook, 1913, page 50. University of Illinois at Chicago Library, Special Collections; **p. 705 (top):** Courtesy of the Visiting Nurse Service of New York; **(bottom):** Utah State Historical Society; **p. 706:** Minnesota Historical Society; **p. 707 (top):** archive.org. pd; **p. 708:** Courtesy of the Bancroft Library. University of California, Berkeley; **p. 709:** Roosevelt 560.51 1902-156, Houghton Library, Harvard University; **p. 710 (top):** provided courtesy

© HarpWeek LLC; **(bottom):** Purchase, Jim and Carol Kautz, class of 1955, in honor of Richard and Ronay Menschel / Francis Lehman Loeb Art Center, Vassar College; **p. 711:** Roosevelt 560.51 1903-115, Houghton Library, Harvard University; **p. 713:** Fotosearch / Getty Images. **Chapter 19: p. 718:** Imperial War Museum / The Art Archive at Art Resource, NY; **p. 723:** Library of Congress; **p. 725:** Arizona Historical Society; **p. 726:** Smithsonian Institution / National Air and Space Museum; **p. 727:** Private Collection / Chris Deakes / The Art Archive. Art Resource, NY; **p. 728 (top):** Bettmann / Corbis; **(bottom):** Albin Egger-Lienz, Nordfrankreich, 1917 / Photo by Ji-Elle. 2012 http://creativecommons.org/licenses/by-sa/3.0/deed.en; **p. 730:** The U.S. Army Military History Institute; **p. 731 (top):** Library of Congress; **(bottom):** © Imperial War Museum (Art.IWM PST 6921); **p. 732:** National Archives; **p. 733 (left):** National Archives; **(right):** Library of Congress; **p. 734 (top):** Library of Congress; **(bottom):** Cover of Union Signal, Jan 27, 1916, Frances E. Willard Memorial Library and Archives; **p. 736:** Granger Collection; **p. 737 (top):** Library of Congress; **(bottom):** Jerry L. Thompson / Art Resource, NY; **p. 738:** Arizona State Library, Archives and Public Records, History and Archives Division, Phoenix, #01-3116; **p. 739 (top):** Collection of Robert MacKay; **(bottom):** Wisconsin Historical Society, WHS-5348; **p. 742:** Library of Congress; **p. 743:** Wikimedia, public domain; **p. 744:** Paris Pierce / Alamy Stock Photo; **p. 745:** St. Louis Post-Dispatch, 17 April 1906; **p. 746:** Photographs and Prints Division, Schomburg Center for Research in Black Culture, The New York Public Library, Astor, Lenox, and Tilden Foundations. Art Resource, NY; **p. 747:** © 2016 The Jacob and Gwendolyn Knight Lawrence Foundation, Seattle / Artist Rights Society (ARS), New York. Digital Image © The Museum of Modern Art / Licensed by SCALA / Art Resource, NY; **p. 748:** Tulsa Historical Society; **p. 749:** Library of Congress; **p. 751 (top):** Courtesy of the author; **(bottom):** Bettmann / Corbis; **p. 752:** National Archives; **p. 756:** Bettmann / Corbis; **p. 757:** Granger Collection. **Chapter 20: p. 760 (top):** Honolulu Academy of Arts: Gift of Philip H. Roach, Jr., 2001; **(bottom):** Library of Congress; **p. 761 (top):** Library of Congress; **(bottom):** Cover to the propaganda comic book, Catechetical Guild "Is This Tomorrow" http://en.wikipedia.org/wiki/Public_domain; **p. 762:** The Metropolitan Museum of Art, Gift of AXA Equitable, 2012 (2012.478 a–j) © The Metropolitan Museum of Art Image copyright © The Metropolitan Museum of Art. Image source: Art Resource, NY; **p. 765 (top):** Library of Congress; **(bottom):** Underwood Archives / Getty Images; **p. 767 (top):** George Eastman House / Getty Images; **(bottom):** Minnesota Historical Society; **p. 768:** kansasmemory.org, Kansas State Historical Society, Copy and Reuse Restrictions Apply; **p. 769:** Charles Sheeler (1883-1965) River Rouge Plant 1932, oil on canvas, 20x24 1/8 in. (50.8x61.28 cm) Whitney Museum of American Art, New York; Purchase 32.43. Photography copyright © 1996 Whitney Museum; **p. 771 (top):** Honolulu Academy of Arts: Gift of Philip H. Roach, Jr., 2001; **p. 771:** Library of Congress; **p. 772 (both):** Granger Collection; **p. 773 (top):** The Art Archive / Culver Pictures. Art Resource, NY; **(bottom):** Library of Congress; **p. 774:** Library of Congress; **p. 775:** Granger Collection; **p. 778:** Courtesy of the Drew University Library; **p. 779:** Bettmann / Corbis; **p. 780:** Paul Avrich Anarchism Collection, Rare Book and Special Collections Division, Library of Congress; **p. 781:** San Diego Museum of Art Bridgeman Images; **p. 782:** The Denver Public Library, Western History Collection, Rh-1158; **p. 783 (top):** City of Vancouver Archives, Image AM54-S4-I-: CVA 20-2; **(bottom):** © San Diego History Center; **p. 784:** Smithsonian Institutions Archives; **p. 785:** Washington State Historical Society; **p. 787 (top):** Granger Collection; **(bottom):** Los Angeles Public Library Photo Collection; **p. 789:** Nebraska State Historical Society; **p. 790:** Photographs and Prints Division, Schomburg Center for Research in Black Culture, The New York Public Library, Astor, Lenox, and Tilden Foundations / Art Resource, NY; **p. 791 (top):** Library of Congress; **(bottom):** Scurlock Studio Records, Archives Center, National Museum of American History, Smithsonian Institution; **p. 792:** Collection of David J. And Janice L. Frent / Corbis; **p. 793:** Library of Congress; **p. 794 (top):** Courtesy of author; **(bottom):** Library of Congress; **p. 795 (both):** National Archives; **p. 796:** National Archives; **p. 797:** John Tresilian / NY Daily News Archive via Getty Images; **p. 798:** Granger Collection; **p. 799:** AP Photo. **Chapter 21: p. 802:** Jeff R. Bridgman American Antiques; **p. 806:** Smithsonian American Art Museum / Art Resource; **p. 807 (top):** Granger Collection; **(bottom):** Bettmann / Corbis; **p. 808:** Library of Congress; **p. 809:** National Archives; **p. 810:** David Rumsey Map Collection; **p. 812:** Kansas State Historical Society; **p. 813:** Library of Congress; **p. 814 (both):** Library of Congress; **p. 815:** Punch Limited; **p. 816 (top):** Underwood Archives / Getty Images; **(bottom):** Highlander Research and Education Center, Tennessee; **p. 817:** Bettmann / Corbis; **p. 818:** Library of Congress; **p. 819:** Billy Graham Center Archives, Wheaton College, Wheaton, IL; **p. 820:** Library of Congress; **p. 821:** National Archives; **p. 822:** Library of Congress; **p. 823:** Franklin D. Roosevelt Library; **p. 826:** Granger Collection; **p. 827:** Franklin D. Roosevelt Library; **p. 829:** Bettmann / Corbis; **p. 830:** Library of Congress; **p. 831:** Library of Congress; **p. 832:** Library of Congress; **p. 833:** Herald-Examiner Collection / Los Angeles Public Library; **p. 834:** Photograph © Morgan and Marvin Smith; **p. 835:** HOLC Residential Security Map, Federal Home Loan Bank Board, Records of the City Survey Program," RG 195, 450/68/03/02, National Archives II, College Park, MD; **p. 836:** Library of Congress; **p. 837 (top):** Special Collections, University of Hartford; **(bottom):** Franklin D. Roosevelt Presidential Library; **p. 838 (top):** Library of Congress; **(bottom):** Barbara and Willard Morgan Photographs and Papers, UCLA Library Special Collections; **p. 839:** Bettmann / Corbis / Getty Images; **p. 840:** © Harvard Art Museum / Art Resource, NY; **p. 842:** Isaac Soyer, 1907-1981 Employment Agency, (1937) Oil on canvas, 34 1/8 × 45 1/8in. (86.7 × 114.36 cm Whitney Museum of American Art, New York; Purchase 37.44 Digital image © Whitney Museum of American Art, NY. **Chapter 22: p. 846:** Published with the permission of The Wolfsonian - Florida International University (Miami, Florida); **p. 849:** Library of Congress; **p. 851:** Washington Star; **p. 852:** Andreas Feininger / George Eastman House / Getty Images; **p. 853:** National Archive; **p. 854 (top):** Bettmann / Corbis; **(bottom):** National Archives; **p. 856:** Bettmann / Corbis; **p. 858:** National Archives; **p. 859:** Mariners' Museum / Corbis; **p. 860:** PhotoQuest / Getty Images; **p. 862 (top):** Library of Congress; **(bottom):** Courtesy of the Bard Graduate Center for Studies in the Decorative Arts Design and Culture, New York, Photographer: Bruce White; **p. 863 (left):** Courtesy Herb Friedman, retired U.S. Army Sergeant Major / www.psywarrior.com; **(right):** Courtesy Northwestern University Library; **p. 864:** Library of Congress; **p. 865:** Library of Congress; **p. 866:** Courtesy of The WASP Archive, The TWU Libraries Woman's Collection, Texas Woman's University, Denton, Texas; **p. 867:** National Archives; **p. 868:** Art © Estate of Ben Shahn / Licensed by VAGA, New York, NY; Photo: Library of Congress; **p. 870:** National Archives; **p. 871:** Eileen Tweedy / The Art Archive at Art Resource, NY; **p. 874:** National Archives; **p. 875:** Library of Congress / Getty Images; **p. 877:** Library of Congress; **p. 878:** Library of Congress; **(bottom):** AP Photo; **p. 882:** National Archives; **p. 883:** Unidentified Photographer, (Interior damage to steel frame of Honkawa Grammar School Auditorium, Hiroshima), November 8, 1945 International Center Of Photography, Purchase, with funds provided by the ICP Acquisitions Committee, 2006; **p. 884:** Los Alamos Scientific Laboratory, Courtesy of Harry S. Truman Library; **p. 885:** Library of Congress; **p. 887:** Ed Clark / The LIFE Picture Collection / Getty Images. **Chapter 23: p. 890:** American Catholic History Research Center and University Archives, Catholic University of America; **p. 893:** The Lincoln Highway National Museum & Archives; **p. 894 (top):** Bettmann / Corbis; **(bottom):** Library of Congress; **p. 895:** Bettmann / Corbis; **p. 896:** AP Photo; **p. 897 (top):** Bettmann / Corbis; **(bottom):** PhotoQuest / Getty Images; **p. 899:** AP Photo; **p. 901:** AP Photo; **p. 902:** Michael Barson Collection; **p. 903:** Photopat / Alamy; **p. 904:** © 1998 Kate Rothko & Christopher Rothko / Artist Rights Society (ARS), New York Mark Rothko, 1903-1970 Four Darks in Red, (1958) Oil on canvas, 101 13/16 × 116 3/8in. (258.6 × 295.6 cm) Whitney Museum of American Art, New York; Purchase, with funds from the Friends of the Whitney Museum of American Art, Mr. and Mrs. Eugene M. Schwartz, Mrs. Samuel A. Seaver and Charles Simon 68.9 Digital image © Whitney Museum of American Art, N.Y. ; **p. 906:** Derso and Kelen Collection. Public Policy Papers Division, Department of Rare Books and Special Collections, Princeton University Library; **p. 907:** Bettmann / Corbis; **p. 909 (top):** Library of Congress; **(bottom):** The Hy Peskin Collection, www.HyPeskin.com; **p. 910:** The Jon B. Lovelace Collection of California Photographs in Carol M. Highsmith's America Project, Library of Congress; **p. 912:** Lake County Illinois Discovery Museum, Curt Teich Postcard Archives; **p. 913:** Bettmann / Corbis; **p. 914:** Elliott Erwitt / Magnum Photos; **p. 915:** Bettmann / Corbis; **p. 916:** A 1949 Herblock Cartoon, © The Herb Block Foundation; **p. 921:** Bettmann / Corbis. **Chapter 24: p. 924:** Bettmann / Corbis; **p. 925 (top):** National Archives; **(bottom):** Time Life Pictures / Getty Images; **p. 926:** © 2004 Bob Sacha; **p. 927:** Mario Tama / Getty Images; **p. 928:** Norman Rockwell Artwork courtesy of the Norman Rockwell Family Agency **p. 931:** Howard Sochurek / Time Life Pictures / Getty Images;

TEXT

in any language in whole or in part without written permission is prohibited. **LULAC News**: "Editorial on World War II and Mexican-Americans (1945)" from *LULAC News*, Volume 12, October 1945. Reprinted by permission of LULAC News. **National Organization for Women**: Excerpts from "The National Organization for Women's 1966 Statement of Purpose," by Betty Friedan. Reprinted with permission of National Organization for Women. This is a historical document and may not reflect the current language or priorities of the organization. **John Steinbeck**: Excerpt from *The Harvest Gypsies* by John Steinbeck. Copyright © 1936 by *The San Francisco News*. Reprinted by permission of Heyday Books, Berkeley, California.

TABLES AND FIGURES

Map 27.3: Map 1 from "Contemporary Immigrant Gateways in Historical Perspective," by Audrey Singer. *Daedalus*, Summer 2013, Vol. 142, No. 3: 76–91. Reprinted by permission of the author. **Map 27.4:** Map: Where Each State's Largest Immigrant Population Was Born, from "From Germany to Mexico: How America's source of immigrants has changed over a century," by Jens Manuel Krogstad and Michael Keegan. Pew Research Center, October 7, 2015. Reprinted by permission of Pew Research Center. **Figure 27.5:** Figure: Marrying Later, from "The Changing American Family," by Natalie Angier. *New York Times*, Nov. 25, 2013. Copyright © 2013 The New York Times.

All rights reserved. Used by permission and protected by the Copyright Laws of the United States. The printing, copying, redistribution, or retransmission of the Material without express written permission is prohibited. **Figure 28.3:** Figure: Income Inequality in the United States, 1910-2010, From *Capital in the Twenty-First Century* by Thomas Piketty. Reprinted by permission of the author.

INDEX

Page numbers in *italics* refer to illustrations.